From Talking Drums to the Internet:

An Encyclopedia of
Communications Technology

From Talking Drums to the Internet:

An Encyclopedia of Communications Technology

Robert Gardner
Dennis Shortelle

ABC-CLIO

Santa Barbara, California
Denver, Colorado
Oxford, England

Library of Congress Cataloging-in-Publication Data

Gardner, Robert, 1929–
    From talking drums to the Internet : an encyclopedia of
communications technology / Robert Gardner, Dennis Shortelle.
      p.   cm.
    Includes bibliographical references and index.
    1. Communication and technology—Dictionaries. I. Shortelle,
Dennis. II. Title.
P96.T42G374   1997
302.2'03—dc21   97-22415
                                    CIP

    ISBN 0-87436-832-4 (hc)
    ISBN 1-57607-034-4 (pbk)

03 02 01 00 99 98 97 10 9 8 7 6 5 4 3 2 1

ABC-CLIO, Inc.
130 Cremona Drive, P.O. Box 1911
Santa Barbara, California 93116-1911

This book is printed on acid-free paper ∞ ·

Manufactured in the United States of America

CONTENTS

Although there is fascinating evidence to support the notion that communication is not limited to humans, this text focuses primarily on communication as practiced by *Homo sapiens*. It is likely that early humans, or their predecessors, conveyed signals and meaning by body language, grunts, cries, moans, and whines. The question of whether the enlarged brain or primitive speech came first in human evolution remains unresolved, but certainly speech preceded written symbols, and as groups of humans became separated and isolated, a variety of different languages evolved.

The acquisition of speech provided the basis for human culture based on oral communication. Ideas, traditions, and stories could be transmitted through speech from one generation to the next. Of course, spoken words are often misinterpreted, and because their transmission to others depends on memory, the meaning they convey can change dramatically with time. Later, drawings were used to represent reality and to convey meaning to objects and activities in the past and future as well as the present. Gradually, drawings were reduced to the pictographs and symbols that are found in cuneiform and hieroglyphics—early forms of a written language.

Writing formed the basis for a more complex culture, for now records, ideas, and stories—often written literally in stone—could

be passed on from generation to generation. History was born! Through writing, ideas could be transmitted without distortion. Writing provided a means of communicating thoughts, feelings, and concepts without an actual presence. It made communication with faraway people possible, provided that a means of transporting the writing was available. Of course, the written messages could be appreciated only by the relatively few who could read.

The earliest known writing was done using a stylus to make marks on clay tablets that were then dried or baked. Soon after, writing was done on a paperlike material called papyrus, and later on parchment— dried sheep or goat skin—as well as other materials. Paper, our present writing surface, originated in China and eventually spread to Europe.

Gutenberg's invention of the printing press in the fifteenth century marked the beginning of a revolution in human communication. It became possible to make thousands of copies of the same document, copies that could be sent across the globe. New ideas could now spread relatively quickly to humans separated by what were then considered vast distances.

After Gutenberg's breakthrough, the rate of change in communication remained slow until the nineteenth century, when the metamorphosis of communication began to accelerate. Photography made it possible to record accurate images and retain them for indefinite periods. The invention of the telegraph allowed almost instantaneous long-distance communication of words to take place. Later in the nineteenth century, the invention of the telephone made long-distance communication by voice a reality, and the phonograph made it possible to retain and listen to words spoken, and music sung and played, long after the sounds had been made. During the same period, improved methods of printing, the production of paper from wood pulp, and the growth of universal education fostered a boom in journalism. Newspapers and magazines flourished, and books and textbooks designed for schools became an important and lucrative market for publishers.

By the end of the nineteenth century, the electromagnetic waves first generated by Heinrich Hertz were applied in a practical way by Guglielmo Marconi, who succeeded in transmitting telegraphic signals without wires. At the beginning of the twentieth century, wireless telegraphy through space was soon followed by radio, which in a sense is the wireless equivalent of the telephone. Widespread availability of home radios, however, did not occur until after World War I. In the 1920s, commercial radio stations spread across the United States, bringing with them public awareness of news events almost as soon as the events took place. The early twentieth century also marked the rise of motion pictures as a form of entertainment as well as a source of information through newsreels and documentaries. Although early films were silent, "talkies" were introduced in the late 1920s, and color film soon followed.

Only after World War II did television—which uses electromagnetic waves to transmit sounds and images through space—become commonplace. Nearly instantaneous global transmission of television signals awaited the beginning of the Space Age, which is generally associated with the launch of *Sputnik* in 1958. By the 1960s, satellites dedicated to communicating television and telephone signals were in stable orbits around the earth, making live television a global rather than a national happening.

In the Computer Age, information has become an industry as well as a source of knowledge. Today, the Internet allows not only personal communication on a worldwide basis, but also the exchange of documents, images, and various kinds of information. The rate of change in the way we communicate continues to accelerate as we anticipate the arrival of the Information Superhighway. This future form of communication will unite television, computers, and telephones, using fiber-optic cables to carry digital signals at a rate thousands of times faster than is now possible. The combination of computer, television, telephone, and printer, all under a single control, will allow users to shop, bank, pay bills, buy stocks or tickets to sports events from home, correspond by E-mail, watch current movies as well as a vast assortment of TV programs, play video games, talk on videophones, and obtain information about almost anything imaginable.

Because changes in communications occur almost daily, any book on the subject is immediately out of date. Nevertheless, the people who brought about the changes that led to our present state of communications, the devices and techniques they invented or devised, and the social changes these modes of communication fostered are now a matter of history, which will remain unchanged regardless of what the future brings.

Abacus

The abacus is a device that is used as an aid in counting and doing arithmetical computations. The primitive predecessor of the modern computer, it was first developed in the Western world in Babylonia about 5,000 years ago. Today, in the age of pocket calculators, it is sometimes used as an instructional aid to teach place value to students in schools.

Devices similar to the abacus were also invented in China and Japan, where they are known as *suan pans* and *sorobans*, respectively. The Romans, who were handicapped in mathematics because of their use of letters to represent numerals (Is, Vs, Xs, Ls, Cs, Ds, and Ms), found counting boards useful for counting and making calculations, especially where large numbers were involved. A counting board, or abacus, consists of beads that rest in parallel grooves cut in a board. The beads, which represent 1s, 5s, 10s, 50s, and so on, were called *calculi* (the plural of calculus)—a word that means pebbles. Obviously, the origin of our word *calculate* is from the Roman word for pebble—the beads used on their abacuses. The calculi used on Asian versions of the abacus usually have holes drilled through their diameters so they can be slid along metal rods.

Why did early merchants, tax collectors, and others who had to use numbers in their work use abacuses rather than paper and pencil? There are several reasons. Paper was not available in much of the world until the twelfth century, lead pencils didn't appear until the sixteenth century, and because most people were not educated, they did not know how to write numbers. They could, however, count and push beads along rods or grooves—the skills needed to use an abacus. Armed with an abacus, a person skilled in its use can add and subtract numbers as fast or faster than on a pocket calculator. Multiplication and division are more time consuming on an abacus because multiplication consists of a complex number of moves or adding a number the required number of times. Similarly, division proceeds in a complex manner or by subtracting a number re-

peatedly until nothing or a fraction remains. For example, to multiply 453 by 5, an abacus could be used to add 453 five times (453 + 453 + 453 + 453 + 453). Similarly, to divide 156 by 12, a person could use an abacus to find out how many times 12 can be subtracted from 156. (The answer is 13.)

In most abacuses, there are beads (calculi) to represent 5s and 1s. These beads are arranged in columns or rows that represent units, 10s, 100s, 1,000s, 10,000s, and so on. In the abacus shown in Figure 1*a*, there are seven beads in each column. The top two beads in each column represent 5s; the bottom five beads represent 1s. The column farthest to the right represents units (1–9), the second column from the right represents 10s (10–90), the third column represents 1,000s, and so on. The number 1,475 is shown on the abacus. To add 9,926 to the 1,475 using the abacus, begin by adding 6 to the 5 already shown on the abacus on the far right column. This is done by moving the second top bead (representing a 5) down to the divider and bringing one bead from the bottom of that column up to the divider. But the two 5s and a 1 make 11; consequently, the operator adds one bead to the 10s column (second from the right) by pushing another of the lower beads up to the divider and subtracting 10 from the column on the far right by pushing the top two beads in that column (each of which represents 5) back up away from the divider.

Next, 20 in 9,926 must be added to the 10s column. However, 10 has already been added to that column. Remember, it was "carried" from the 1s column. Adding 30 to the 70 that was there to start with in the 1,475 gives 100, so a bead is raised from the bottom

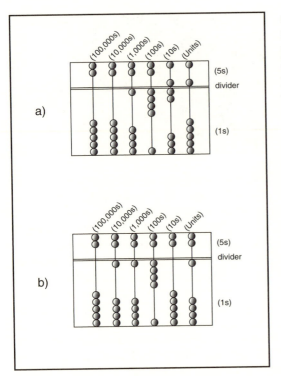

Figure 1. Abacus showing the number 1,475 (a) and after 9,926 has been added to 1,475 (b).

of the 100s column to the divider and all the beads in the 10s column are returned to their original positions since their total value (100) has been carried to the next column.

Now it is time to add the 900 in 9,926 to the 400 in 1,475. The 400 is now 500 because 100 was transferred from the 10s column. To add 900, push the two top beads (each of which represent 500) down to the divider and take away 100 by pushing one of the lower beads down to the bottom of the column, leaving four beads up near the divider. The total value shown at the divider in the third, or 100s column, is now 1,400. Consequently, 1,000 is transferred to the fourth, or 1,000s, column by moving one more bead from the bottom of that column up to the divider, and 1,000 is subtracted from the 100s column by moving the two top beads, each representing 500, up away from the divider.

Next, add the 9,000 in 9,926 to the 1,000 in 1,475. One thousand has already carried 1,000 to that column from the 100s column, as indi-

cated by the one additional bead that was raised to the divider. To add another 9,000, push the two top beads (representing 10,000) down to the divider and push one of the lower beads back down, away from the divider so that 9,000 has been added by first adding 10,000 and then subtracting 1,000. The two top beads (representing 10,000) and one of the lower beads (representing 1,000) are now at the divider, giving a total of 11,000. Finally, add 10,000 to the fifth column, where 10,000s are represented, by pushing the two top beads in the fourth (1,000s) column back up (away from the divider) and raising one of the lower beads in the fifth column up to the divider. The abacus now looks like the drawing in Figure 1b, which shows the number 11,401, the sum of 1,475 and 9,926.

Subtraction is carried out in a similar way on the abacus. Simply remember that moving one of the lower beads in one column and then adding that amount to the next column to the right on the abacus is the equivalent of "borrowing" in arithmetic.

The abacus works in a manner similar to that of a computer. The "carrying" process used by moving beads in adjacent columns is the same as that used by a full adder with binary numbers. The difference is that a computer uses electrical pulses instead of beads and operates on base 2 (0s and 1s) instead of base 10 (0, 1, 2, 3, 4, 5, 6, 7, 8, 9).

See also:
Computer.

References:
Gardner, Robert. *Communication.* New York: Twenty-First Century, 1994.
Macaulay, David. *The Way Things Work.* Boston: Houghton Mifflin, 1988.
Newman, James R., ed. *The World of Mathematics.* New York: Simon & Schuster, 1956.
Williams, Trevor I. *The History of Invention: From Stone Axes to Silicon Chips.* New York: Facts on File, 1987.

Abstract Symbols
See Number.

Airmail
See Postal Service.

Almanac

An almanac is usually an annual book or table containing a calendar of the days, weeks, and months of the year. Almanacs may contain information about the rising and setting times of the sun and moon, tidal tables, long-range weather predictions, astronomical data, seasonal suggestions for agriculturists, witty sayings, and facts about history, government, and geography. Many consider the inexpensive almanac the forerunner of the modern magazine and city directory.

Scholars believe that the development of the almanac coincided with the beginning of astrology and astronomy. Superstition, the desire to predict the future, and belief in the significance of planetary and celestial motion produced a ready market for the almanac. Some form of almanac was probably in use in ancient Egypt. The earliest examples of the modern almanac appeared in Europe during the period 1300–1400.

The first American almanac was the second publication of the colonial press in the New World. Stephen Daye's *Almanack for New England for the Year 1639* was printed at Cambridge, Massachusetts, under the auspices of Harvard College. Similar volumes soon appeared in the other colonies as Pennsylvania and New York followed Massachusetts, the recognized leader in the almanac trend. The initial ventures were modest efforts, single newspaper-like sheets folded to a 16-page format, although there were some larger versions. The almanac was intended as a practical guide, and its content was similar to that of its European relative. The calendar, with a page usually devoted to each month, was a compilation of various data, including the requisite astronomical information and weather predictions. The pamphletlike almanacs were usually local productions and were distributed regionally by the widely recognized Yankee peddler. In colonial America the almanac was second only to the Bible for household reading and was widely used by all Americans.

As the seventeenth century drew to a close, the almanac began to change, largely due to competition for a market beyond farmers and sailors. In such a scramble, an accurate calendar would not be enough to ensure survival. Nathaniel Ames of Dedham, Massachusetts, produced the era's dominant almanacs. His *Astronomical Diary and Almanack*, published between 1725 and 1775, provided a greater variety of information than its predecessors. Bits of history, scraps of wisdom, some literary notes, and observations on current events provided instruction as well as entertainment. James Franklin's popular *Rhode Island Almanac* continued the fashion of creating a more widely appealing small magazine format for the almanac. He peppered his almanac with the pithy sayings of his fictional character, Poor Robin.

In the public's mind, James Franklin's younger brother Benjamin came to embody the American almanac and its tradition. In fact, *Poor Richard's Almanac* was the basis of Benjamin Franklin's early popularity and reputation. Using the pseudonym Richard Saunders, Franklin first published his famous almanac in 1733, borrowing his brother's idea of dispensing advice in the form of catchy aphorisms. In creating his almanacs, which were best-sellers for 20 years, the younger Franklin included literary pieces and even lists of regional roads. *Poor Richard's* was a prime example of the many almanacs that circulated throughout the country. There were even foreign-language almanacs like those popularized by the Pennsylvania Germans.

The longest-lived almanac is the *Old Farmer's Almanac*, which was founded by Robert Bailey Thomas in 1793. Supposedly Abraham Lincoln, as a young Illinois lawyer, used the almanac to prove a lack of moonlight on the night of a murder. In so doing he discredited a witness and won an acquittal for his client. By the close of the eighteenth century, almanacs began to provide more information and were approaching the encyclopedic almanac of today.

The popularity and accessibility of the almanac made it an ideal advertising and propaganda vehicle. In the nineteenth century, it seemed that any group that wanted to be taken seriously had to publish an almanac of some sort. Fraternal groups, professional organizations, businesses, and even major religious denominations trumpeted their interests in almanac form. Even the opposing sides in the Civil War had almanacs like *Uncle Sam's Union Almanac* and *The Confederate Almanac and Register.*

The information in these nineteenth-century almanacs was decidedly different from that in their colonial ancestors. There was no escaping the calendar and astronomical features, which by this point were standard fare. However, more emphasis was placed on information that dealt with local matters and national affairs than previously. For example, there was a growing interest in current events and especially politics. No respectable almanac would be without "valuable receipts" for improving soil, curing livestock diseases, or aiding gout, headaches, toothaches, and other human ailments. Almanacs gave more than a passing nod to history. A reader could count on finding prominent historical documents like Washington's "Farewell Address" or Lincoln's "Gettysburg Address" in the almanac. To capture the public's imagination, there were also stories on topics like Indian captures or exotic animals like the giraffe or elephant. Almanacs also contained information about specific areas or cities. Listings of prominent institutions such as school or churches, descriptions of the political leadership, business advertising, and even a directory of families could all be contained in an almanac. As a result, almanacs have provided historians with an interesting source of information on American life and values at the time of publication.

Today's almanacs have evolved to cover a much wider range of material. Typical items in the modern almanac include sports records, a chronological review of the major events of the past year, population statistics, and lists of officials in world government. Consequently, the almanac has become the most popular desk reference in the world, supplying a myriad of statistics and facts on demand. Pure information is the main func-

tion of the modern almanac, and the agrarian basis of the publication is long forgotten. *The World Almanac,* founded in 1868, provides facts on history, industry, religion, education, and politics and is the most recognizable of these modern reference books. *The Information Please Almanac* was an immediate success when it was founded in 1947. *The Reader's Digest Almanac* first appeared in 1965.

References:
Dodge, Robert. "Access to Popular Culture: Early American Almanacs." *Kentucky Folklore Record,* January/June 1979.
Kittredge, George L. *The Old Farmers and His Almanack.* Ganesevoort, NY: Corner House, 1974.

AM
See Modulation.

America Online
See Online Services.

American Sign Language
American Sign Language (ASL) is the sign language most hearing-impaired and deaf people in the United States use when they are communicating among themselves.

ASL is a visual-spatial language; one *sees* ASL. Most languages are based on sounds. However, ASL is based on movements of various parts of the body. It has semantic rules that differ from those of spoken language. It is not a way of coding English but rather a language of its own with its own grammatical rules.

ASL consists not only of signs made with the hands, but also of facial expressions, head movements, and use of the space around the person signing. Signs have meanings just as words do, but these meanings can be changed by different facial expressions. The same sign will require different expressions at different times depending on the feeling the signer wishes to communicate. The furrowing of an eyebrow can mean that a question is being asked. To a deaf person, a face with no expression is the same as someone speaking in a monotone.

Body language is also an important component of ASL. Information can be communicated by movement of the head, shoulders, arms, torso, legs, and feet. For example, to indicate to a class to be quiet, a teacher could hold up her hand in the stop position and stamp her foot to get the students' attention. The head can tilt forward, backward, or to the sides while the hands are moving to help demonstrate what the signer is communicating. The use of the whole body in sign language is absolutely essential for clear communication.

American Sign Language developed from French Sign Language that was used by deaf individuals in the nineteenth century. It was brought to the United States by Thomas Gallaudet, whose neighbor in Hartford, Connecticut, was a young deaf girl named Alice Cogswell. Alice's father, a well-known doctor, was impressed by Gallaudet's efforts to teach his daughter to read and write, and he encouraged Gallaudet to begin a school for the deaf in America. Cogswell and others raised money to send Gallaudet to Europe to study methods for teaching the deaf.

Gallaudet first went to Great Britain, where the oral method of instruction was used. This method used speaking, reading, and writing, and its adherents were opposed to using signs. It was being used in the Braidwood Schools in Scotland and near London. These institutions refused to help Gallaudet or give him the information he wanted. However, while in London he met the director of a French school for the deaf who, with two of his students (who were also teachers), was demonstrating the French method of teaching deaf students through signs. The director agreed to teach Gallaudet the language.

A short time later, Gallaudet and one of the French teachers, Laurent Clerc, brought a modified French Sign Language to the United States. With money from the state of Connecticut, the U.S. Congress, and private groups, Gallaudet and Clerc in 1817 established the first school for the deaf in Hartford, Connecticut. Called the Institution for

Deaf-Mutes, it was later renamed the American Asylum at Hartford for the Education and Instruction of the Deaf and Dumb and now is known as the American School for the Deaf.

It seems likely that before the establishment of this school the approximately 2,000 deaf people in the United States were using different sign languages that they had brought from their native countries or had developed to communicate with others. Just such a case occurred on Martha's Vineyard, off the coast of Massachusetts, where a large number of deaf people lived from the late 1600s into the early 1900s. The whole population, both hearing and hearing impaired, could use sign language, which was taught to all the children and incorporated into their community. This fact helps confirm the theory that signed languages were used in America before Gallaudet and Clerc introduced their system. It is probable that deaf people combined signs from their own sign languages with the French signs taught at Gallaudet's school, ultimately developing the American Sign Language of today.

—Barbara Gardner Conklin

See also:
Communication among the Hearing Impaired; Communication among the Visually Impaired; Keller, Helen Adams; Sign Language.

References:
Baker, Charlotte, and Dennis Cokely. *American Sign Language: A Teacher's Resource Text on Grammar and Culture*. Silver Spring, MD: T. J. Publishers, 1980.
Baker, Charlotte, and Carol Padden. *American Sign Language: A Look at Its History, Structure, and Community*. Silver Spring, MD: T. J. Publishers, 1979.

American Telephone & Telegraph Company

Until recently, the growth of the telephone industry in the United states has been largely controlled by one company—the American Telephone & Telegraph Company (AT&T).

An early AT&T advertisement. Established as National Bell in 1879, the company reorganized as AT&T in the 1880s and went on to dominate the telephone industry for over 100 years.

In most other countries, telephones, like the postal system, were developed and controlled by the government.

Shortly after the telephone's invention, users rented a telephone and strung lines to those few nearby places with which they wished to communicate. Soon, exchanges were established in local areas. Lines leading from residences and businesses to a central exchange could be connected by an operator sitting in front of a switchboard. In the telephone's early years, Western Union and National Bell competed for customers following Western Union's decision not to buy National Bell for $100,000. National Bell, which later became Bell Telephone, had been formed in Boston in 1877 by the telephone's inventor, Alexander Graham Bell, and two financial backers. Western Union, which claimed that Elisha Gray was the true inventor of the telephone, established the subsidiary American Speaking Telephone Company to provide telephone service. They sold a telephone devised by Gray that had been modified by Thomas Edison, who used a carbon button variable resistor transmitter. The Gray-Edison telephone produced clearer sounds than Bell's magneto-induction transmitter and receiver and his acidified-water variable resistance system. Nevertheless, Bell had filed his patent a few hours before Gray filed his on 14 February 1876, and in a letter to Bell, Gray agreed that Bell's patent application had preceded his.

Late in 1879, Western Union, fearing that it would lose if it sued National Bell because of Bell's prior patent filing, and firmly convinced that the telephone could never compete with the telegraph for long-distance communication, agreed to relinquish all its patents, claims, and facilities to Bell. In return, Western Union was to receive 20 percent of Bell's telephone rental profits during the 17-year duration of the Bell patents and a promise that Bell would not engage in message-for-hire service. As a result, Bell obtained the 56,000 phones that Western Union had established in 55 cities and could now manufacture and lease the Gray-Edison telephone. The agreement gave National Bell a monopoly on telephones, and the value of its stock increased by a factor of 20.

During the 1880s, National Bell reorganized as AT&T, which specialized in long-distance telephone communication, with the Bell System as a subsidiary that concentrated on establishing local exchanges. AT&T bought Western Electric to manufacture the telephones and associated equipment that it needed, and by 1908 AT&T had interconnected local networks so that long-distance calls could be made throughout much of the country.

In the meantime, Bell's patents expired in 1894. The result was a rash of competition, which drove prices downward, and an increase in the number of telephones, which left Bell with only half the market. Because Bell and competing firms strung separate lines and built their own exchanges, it became necessary in many communities for patrons to have two phones—one connected to each company's exchange. However, these newly established companies could offer only local service and had to turn to AT&T for long-distance connections.

To maintain its dominance, AT&T assumed ownership of the entire Bell operation in 1899. By doing so, its subsidiary became a New York company and consequently was subject to less-restrictive laws governing corporations than had been the case in Massachusetts. Under less stringent control, AT&T proceeded to buy or form agreements with competing firms so that they could connect with AT&T's local and long-distance lines provided they conformed to the dominant company's equipment and operational standards. Independent companies that didn't go along were denied access to long-distance lines.

In 1909, Theodore N. Vail, chief executive officer at AT&T, engineered the purchase of 300,000 shares (30 percent) of Western Union stock, enough to give AT&T working control of the telegraph giant. A year later, after Vail became president of Western Union, one of his first acts was to allow telegrams to be delivered by telephone, negating the message-for-hire agreement made in 1879.

Early in the twentieth century, AT&T and smaller telephone companies began to be subject to governmental regulations. In 1913, under increasing threats of an antitrust suit

by the United States Justice Department, AT&T vice-president Nathan C. Kingsbury wrote a letter, which came to be known as the Kingsbury Commitment, to the attorney general. Kingsbury, in an effort to avoid a lengthy suit that the company might well lose, agreed to allow independent companies access to its lines, sell all its Western Union stock, and purchase no additional independent telephone companies without Interstate Commerce Commission approval.

In 1921, AT&T was enjoying wide public approval. During World War I, the federal government had taken over AT&T for a one-year period amid promises of lower rates. When rates continued to rise, people clamored for a return of telephone operations to the private sector. In response to public opinion, Congress passed the Graham Act, which was basically a legislative endorsement of the Kingsbury Commitment and a clause that exempted telephony from the Sherman Antitrust Act. With the law behind them, AT&T proceeded to buy up competing companies and reestablish its monopoly.

In 1925, Bell Laboratories, the research arm of the Bell System and one of the world's most celebrated research labs, was formally established as a corporation jointly owned by AT&T and Western Electric. However, it had existed since 1907 as a division of the engineering departments of AT&T and Western Electric.

In 1948, Bell Lab researchers William Shockley, Walter Brattain, and John Bardeen announced their discovery of the transistor—a discovery that led to their receiving a Noble Prize in 1956. Unable to see the full significance of their discovery, they reported in 1946 that the device would have several applications in radio. Today, of course, transistors—together with diodes, resistors, and capacitors—make up the integrated circuits found on silicon chips the size of match heads. It is these chips that have made desktop computers a reality. For AT&T, these same chips led to electronic switching that made it possible for a caller to dial anyone else in the world and greatly reduced the need for telephone operators.

The Great Depression of the 1930s had little effect on AT&T. People continued to need and use telephones. Consequently, the company, even though it laid off many workers, was able to pay its stockholders a traditional annual dividend of $9 per share.

During World War II, AT&T subsidiary Western Electric became a giant war plant with 100,000 employees fulfilling 1,600 government contracts. At the same time, Bell Laboratories designed radar, developed M-9 gun directors, and invented microgel, a rubber substitute.

Because of AT&T's size and dominance, threats of antitrust suits and legislation continued after World War II. However, prosecution was delayed after the corporate giant, following a special request from President Harry Truman, agreed to take over the management of the Sandia operation in New Mexico, where atomic bombs were being manufactured. Nevertheless, the Justice Department's antitrust division continued its investigation, and in 1956 an agreement was reached whereby AT&T was allowed to retain ownership of Western Electric provided that the subsidiary sought no additional markets. It was agreed, too, that Bell would restrict its business to common carrier communications and grant nonexclusive licenses and technical information to any applicant on fair terms.

As the Space Age dawned in December 1959, AT&T asked the National Aeronautics and Space Administration (NASA) for permission to develop an entire satellite communications system at its own expense in return for exclusive rights subject to regulation by NASA and the Federal Communications Commission (FCC). The request was turned down, in part because other companies strenuously objected to giving AT&T such a lead in satellite communications. Nine months later, NASA launched Echo I, a thin, plastic-skinned satellite with a diameter of 100 feet that was used to reflect radio and television signals. Early in 1961, AT&T was authorized to send Telstar into orbit. Unlike Echo, Telstar was an active satellite; that is, it was able to retransmit signals rather than simply reflect them. A year later, the Communication-Satellite Act established Comsat as a government-sponsored corporation with ownership split equally between private companies and investors. With its satellites already in orbit, AT&T became Comsat's primary customer.

The development of microwave technology led to the rise of competing companies, such as Microwave Communications Incorporated (MCI) and others, who sought to establish long-distance lines between large cities. In 1969, for example, the FCC approved MCI service between Chicago and Saint Louis. AT&T tried to discourage such competition by denying these companies access to its local lines. This led to lawsuits in which courts ruled that all carriers should be able to use local networks. After another lengthy antitrust suit against AT&T that began in 1974, a settlement was reached in 1982 that led to the restructuring of AT&T. The company was allowed to retain control of Western Electric as well as Bell Laboratories, but was required to relinquish its 22 Bell System companies, which became 7 regional holding companies. These regional Bell Companies remained as regulated local service providers whose lines were required to be open to all long-distance carriers. AT&T became a much smaller regulated long-distance firm that still controlled 90 percent of that market, but with the right to enter new areas such as computers. Anyone who watches television ads or answers his or her phone can attest to the fierce competition for long-distance service that has followed the breakup of AT&T.

In September 1995, AT&T chairman Robert Allen announced a voluntary move to break AT&T into three independent corporations. On 2 January 1996, the company reduced its workforce by 40,000 employees. During the nine months that followed, AT&T stock fell by 24 percent, representing a loss in value to stockholders of $25 billion, at a time when the stock market overall rose 11 percent.

The three companies became independent by the end of 1996. One company, with expected annual revenues of $49 billion, retained the AT&T name and continues to focus on the core business—communications services. These include long-distance telephone calls, cellular phones, business communications, and credit cards. With the deregulation of telecommunications, AT&T can once again offer local telephone service, which it plans to do in addition to providing Internet connections and digital satellite television services. By providing all these services as a package deal, AT&T can offer a considerable discount.

A second company, Lucent Technologies, with annual revenues of approximately $20 billion and growing at about 5 percent annually, turned a profit of approximately $630 million in 1995. This company, like the old Western Electric, manufactures communications equipment, including telephones, answering machines, switching equipment, and computer chips. It owns what is left of Bell Laboratories.

The third company is the NCR Corporation, which AT&T purchased in 1991 for $7.58 billion. It is a computer company that lost $4 billion between 1991 and 1996. However, its losses of $39 million during the first half of 1996 were only one-tenth as large as the losses it sustained during the same period in 1995.

As Lucent Technologies and NCR were spun off, AT&T stockholders received shares in each of the new companies based on a ratio of their shares in the original AT&T. In the case of Lucent Technologies, which was spun off in September 1996, the 525 million shares distributed to 3 million stockholders was the largest number of shares ever issued at one time. AT&T stockholders received one share of Lucent Technologies for approximately every three shares of AT&T that they owned. In December of the same year, the divestment of NCR was completed. AT&T stockholders received one share of NCR stock for every 16 shares of AT&T, and NCR once again became an independent corporation.

See also:
Answering Machine; Bell, Alexander Graham; Telephone; Telephone Switching.

References:
American Telephone & Telegraph Company. *AT&T: The World's Networking Leader.* Shareowners report for the quarter ended 30 September 1995.
Baida, Peter. "Breaking the Connection." *American Heritage*, June/July 1985.
Brooks, John. *Telephone: The First Hundred Years.* New York: Harper, 1976.
Church, George J. "Just Three Easy Pieces." *Time*, 2 October 1995.
Cohen, Sarah. "AT&T in Lucent Technologies Moves." *Electronic News*, 7 October 1996.
Haber, Carol. "Two Legends Cross Paths and Part." *Electronic News*, 6 January 1997.
International Encyclopedia of Communications. New York: Oxford University Press, 1989.
Kupfer, Andrew. "AT&T: Ready to Run, Nowhere to Hide." *Fortune*, 29 April 1996.
Landler, Mark. "AT&T to Split into Three Companies." *New York Times*, reprinted in *Cape Cod Times*, 21 September 1995.
Sloane, Alan. "The Howling Wolves: Wall Street Has AT&T on the Run." *Newsweek*, 7 October 1996.
Verity, John. "Is NCR Ready to Ring Up Some Cash?" *Business Week*, 14 October 1996.

Amniocentesis
See Sonography.

Amplifier
An amplifier is an electronic device that is designed to increase the strength of a signal without changing any of its other characteristics, such as frequency or modulation. Amplifiers are vital to communication; they are found in radios, television sets, tape recorders, microphones, loudspeakers, computers, radar, and most other electronic devices.

For 50 years following its invention in 1906, the vacuum tube triode was used to amplify signals. During the 1950s, however, semiconductor devices—diodes and transistors—began to replace vacuum tubes in electronic devices. This dramatic change in the electronics industry was based on the development of the transistor by William Shockley, John Bardeen, and Walter Brattain at Bell

Laboratories in 1948. Today, amplifiers are built around transistors, which operate far more efficiently and cheaply than vacuum tubes and require much less space.

The output of an amplifier exceeds the input. The ratio of output to input is called the gain (output/input = gain). The gain can be a gain in power (watts), voltage (volts), or current (amps), but in all cases, the output is controlled by the input.

Often, amplifiers are connected in series so that the output of the first becomes the input of the second and so on. Modern amplifiers on tiny silicon wafers no larger than 2 millimeters on a side can provide gains of 10,000 to 100,000.

There are many kinds of amplifiers. Audio amplifiers operate at 0 to 100,000 hertz, intermediate frequency (IF) amplifiers at 400 kilohertz to 5 megahertz, radio-frequency (RF) amplifiers at up to several hundred megahertz, and ultrahigh-frequency (UHF) amplifiers at frequencies exceeding 100 megahertz. The gain varies somewhat with frequency. At the high-frequency end of an amplifier's range, gain will diminish because it takes a finite period of time for the capacitor elements in the circuits to fully charge. If the period of the signal being amplified exceeds the time to fully charge the elements, the amplification will be less than for signals of lower frequency.

See also:
Computer; Diode; Microelectronics; Transistor.

References:
Haber-Schaim, Uri, et al. *PSSC Physics,* 7th ed. Dubuque, IA: Kendall/Hunt, 1991.
Macaulay, David. *The Way Things Work.* Boston: Houghton Mifflin, 1988.
Sears, Francis W., Mark W. Zemansky, and Hugh D. Young. *College Physics.* Reading, MA: Addison-Wesley, 1985.

Analog and Digital Signals

Analog signals lie along a continuous spectrum, whereas digital signals are made up of discrete units. For example, in an analog system used to convert sound to electrical energy, the shape of the electrical signals is analogous to the sound waves that gave rise to them. The hands on a clock provide an analog measurement of time because the hands move in continuous fashion around the clock's face. A digital clock, on the other hand, measures time in discrete numbers. The clock reads either 12 hours: 30 minutes: 14 seconds or 12 hours: 30 minutes: 15 seconds and registers nothing between those two values.

Analog signals can be used to record sound on magnetic tape. This analog system stores on tape a continuous magnetic pattern, which corresponds to the varying electric current generated by the sounds transmitted to the microphone. Sound waves entering a microphone generate electric currents that can vary over a continuous range of values. The changing currents pass through the coils of an electromagnet (the recording head), where they produce corresponding changes in its magnetic field. The chemically coated tape travels just beneath the magnetic field of the recording heads, which produce a magnetic pattern in the tiny crystals of iron or chromium oxide embedded in the tape. When the same tape passes through the playback head, it produces weak electric currents that are amplified and fed to a loudspeaker, where the original sound is reproduced.

When digital sound recordings are made, the electrical (analog) signal from the microphone is sampled as frequently as 50,000 times per second. The signal's frequency and intensity are converted to a binary code—a series of on-or-off (1s or 0s) electric pulses—that is recorded on tape as strong or weak magnetic fields.

A compact disc is recorded digitally. Along the very thin recording track of the disc, the 0s (offs) are recorded as pits, the 1s (ons) are recorded as the unchanged surface of the disc. As the disc turns on a playback device, the codes of 0s and 1s (pits and non-pits or offs and ons) are scanned by a laser beam and converted to electric currents. These signals, when amplified and used to drive loudspeakers, produce a sound that is superior in quality to those produced by an analog system.

Digital recordings are superior to analog because copies can be made with virtually no loss of data. Although the original master of an analog tape might be as good as a digital tape, the original tape is always copied and then edited to remove mistakes or certain frequencies that are not pleasing to the ear. Quality is lost during the copying of analog tapes; however, very little loss occurs in copying digital tapes. Furthermore, a digital recording provides a dynamic range—a range of loudness as measured in decibels—that is about 30 percent greater than the best analog recording.

By 1990, AT&T was using digitized signals for all its long-distance calls. The analog voice signal is converted to digital form by electronic circuitry that samples the incoming information in a manner similar to that described for sound recording. At the receiving end, the digital signal is converted to its analog form, and sounds are produced. Digitization reduces background noise and makes it possible to carry more calls on the same cable because digital signals are transmitted more rapidly than analog signals.

See also:
Computer; Telephone Switching.
References:
Macaulay, David. *The Way Things Work.* Boston: Houghton Mifflin, 1988.
The New Book of Popular Science. Danbury, CT: Grolier, 1992.

Animation

Animation is a technique that uses art and cinematography to produce the illusion of motion. Drawings, puppets, or sculpted figures, not live actors, constitute the main characters in animated films.

Most animated films use two-dimensional art, but three-dimensional puppets, sculptures, and other objects may be used as well. The animated film, like all sound films, is projected at 24 frames per second. Each frame is a separate photograph taken, typically, of a two-dimensional drawing resting on a table. In each succeeding frame the drawing is changed slightly. For example, one frame may show a figure with her right foot slightly behind her and flat on a floor, while her left foot is slightly in front of her body with the heel touching a floor and the toes elevated slightly above a floor. In the next frame the figure's left foot is flat on the floor and the right heel is raised slightly. In the same two frames the positions of the figure's arms and hands are also changed slightly. The artist makes similar small changes in position of limbs and body in succeeding frames so that when the frames are seen at 1/24-second intervals, the figure appears to be moving. Similar methods can be used with puppets or other three-dimensional figures by changing their positions ever so slightly between frames.

Animated films are both labor and time intensive. One minute of film, shot at 24 frames per second, requires 1,440 drawings; an hour-long movie requires 86,400 drawings.

Animation grew out of flip-page books and other devices that used persistence of vision to give the illusion of motion. The artwork used in the first animated film, *Humorous Phases of Funny Faces*, consisted of faces drawn in chalk on a blackboard by J. Stuart Blackton. The expression on a face would appear to change as successive frames were projected. A number of other animated films followed, and most were enthusiastically received by audiences.

In 1914, John Bray and Earl Hurd formed the Bray-Hurd Process Company and introduced the use of transparent celluloids, or "cels." By using these transparent sheets, artists could eliminate some repetitive work. They could, for example, draw a background on a bottom sheet, fix it to a table, and then place a second sheet showing an automobile above it. A third sheet with a drawing of a character (often a cartoon character) could be placed on top of the other two so that he or she appeared to be in the automobile. Then, in successive frames, the background drawing could remain unchanged. The position of the car relative to the background could be changed by simply moving the second sheet

Cartoon characters Bugs Bunny and Daffy Duck bicker in a 1950s cartoon. Following World War II, Warner Brothers and MGM studios produced such well-known animated cartoons as Road Runner, Tom and Jerry, and Wile E. Coyote.

slightly. If the character was to gesture, then the third or top sheet would be modified to give the illusion of body movement, but no change would be needed in the lower two drawings.

In 1919, Otto Messmer introduced Felix the Cat in a cartoon entitled *Feline Follies.* Messmer's successful cartoon films were followed in 1922 by Walt Disney's first in a series of "Laugh-O-Grams." It was Disney who in 1928 produced the first animated sound film, *Steamboat Willie*, featuring his soon to be famous Mickey Mouse. Many animated film cartoons followed. They were usually shown as a short subject before a feature film, but in 1937 Disney produced *Snow White and the Seven Dwarfs*, the first feature-length animated film. It was followed by a number of others, including *Pinocchio* and *Fantasia* (1940), *Cinderella* (1950), *Peter Pan* (1953), and

Sleeping Beauty (1959). These animated films were prepared by teams of artists who specialized in drawing a particular character.

During World War II, animation was used to make training and propaganda films. In those war years, former Disney artists David Hilberman, Zachary Schwartz, and Stephen Bosustow formed United Productions of America (UPA), a studio where they used stylized artwork inspired by such artists as Picasso and Matisse to produce their own brand of animated films, films that required fewer drawings because of their stylized nature. The movements in UPA films were less realistic, but the brilliant colors and zany characters, such as Mr. Magoo and Gerald McBoing-Boing, made them appealing to a wide audience.

Following World War II, Warner Brothers and MGM studios produced such well-known animated cartoons as Bugs Bunny, Road Runner, Tom and Jerry, and Wile E. Coyote. Many of the cartoons developed at these studios, as well as those produced by UPA and Disney, remain favorites among adults as well as children.

The computer has made an impact on animation. Today, an artist can draw figures on an electronic "easel," select "paints" for figures and backgrounds from an array of colors, and change the position of these same images by tiny increments of distance. Animation developed on the computer can be reproduced on a television monitor and stored on disc. Computerized animation is widely used in making television commercials, music videos, and special effects used in feature films.

See also:
Cartoon; Disney, Walter Elias; Motion Pictures; Special Effects.
References:
Bailey, Adrian. *Walt Disney's World of Fantasy.* New York: Gallery Books, 1987.
International Encyclopedia of Communications. New York: Oxford University Press, 1989.
Solomon, Charles. *The History of Animation: Enchanted Drawings.* Avenal, NJ: Random House Value, 1994.

Answering Machine

An answering machine is a device that automatically answers a telephone, plays a prerecorded answering message, and then records the caller's response on tape.

After a predetermined number of rings, an electrical signal connects the caller and activates a continuous-loop tape, which plays a prerecorded answering message that usually ends by inviting the caller to leave a message. After the call is terminated by the caller disconnecting the circuit, the tape advances to its starting position and is ready for the next call. A "beep" at the end of the first tape activates a second tape that records the caller's message. On some machines the recording tape is voice activated and runs only during the time the caller talks. Each call is recorded in sequence, and on most machines the calls are counted. At their convenience, users can

rewind the tape and listen to any recorded messages that were left by callers. The tape can be saved for replay or, because the recorder has an erase head, the messages can be erased so that the entire tape is available for future callers. Some machines have two answering tapes so that alternate messages can be prerecorded and a choice made as to which message callers will hear.

With most modern answering machines, it is possible to activate the recording tape from another phone. This allows the owners to call from outside the home and listen to the messages that have been recorded on their home answering machine. After dialing the home phone number and activating the machine, the owner enters a remote access code by touching the proper numbers. The machine will respond and allow the caller a number of different options such as playing all the recorded messages, playing only new messages, rewinding the tape, clearing messages, or recording memos.

See also:
Tape Recorder; Telephone.
References:
How It Works: The Illustrated Encyclopedia of Science and Technology, vol. 1. New York and London: Marshall Cavendish, 1978.
Science and Technology Illustrated, vol. 3. Chicago: Encyclopedia Britannica, 1984.

Antenna

An antenna is a conductor along which electric charges are accelerated in response to a changing electric field. As Maxwell theorized and Hertz demonstrated, electromagnetic waves are produced when electric charges are accelerated. The radiation is produced when an oscillating electric field forces electrons back and forth or up and down a conductor. Consequently, when electrons are forced to accelerate along a transmitting antenna, electromagnetic waves are released and travel through space at the speed of light (300,000 kilometers per second).

For an amplitude modulation (AM) radio transmitting antenna (which is essentially a straight wire with a length approximately one-quarter the wavelength of the radiation emitted), the electric field portion of the wave will be parallel to the antenna, and the magnetic field portion will be perpendicular to the antenna. Because AM antennas are vertically oriented, the wave's electric field will oscillate up and down, producing a vertically polarized signal, while the accompanying magnetic field will oscillate horizontally.

In most AM radios, the receiving antenna is in the form of a tuning coil wound around a ferrite rod. The rod concentrates the magnetic field portion of the radiation, which has been greatly weakened because of the distance from its source. The electrons in the receiving antenna, which are forced to oscillate in response to the changing magnetic field of the incoming modulated electromagnetic waves, produce an electrical signal that is amplified and converted to sound. Since the received signal will be at a maximum when the axis of the rod is parallel to the fluctuating magnetic field, reception can vary with the orientation of the radio.

The radiation from frequency modulation (FM) radio stations has a frequency roughly 100 times that of AM waves, and the electric field of these waves is usually horizontally polarized. Very high (VHF) and ultrahigh-frequency (UHF) television waves are transmitted from a parabolic reflector (dish antenna). The antenna is placed one focal length from the reflecting surface so that a beam of radiation is emitted, much like the light beam produced by a searchlight. Similar parabolic devices are used to transmit microwaves to and from communications satellites and to receive radiation from distant stars and galaxies.

See also:
Electromagnetic Waves; Hertz, Heinrich Rudolf; Marconi, Guglielmo; Maxwell, James Clerk; Modulation; Radio; Television.

References:
Haber-Schaim, Uri, et al. *PSSC Physics,* 7th ed. Dubuque, IA: Kendall/Hunt, 1991.
Sears, Francis W., Mark W. Zemansky, and Hugh D. Young. *College Physics.* Reading, MA: Addison-Wesley, 1985.

Architecture

Architecture does not communicate in the sense of messages or words. Nevertheless, buildings—like art and music—can move us emotionally in ways that words cannot, even though we may not fully comprehend the perceptions they inspire within us.

In ancient Greece, the Pythagoreans believed that numbers are the basis for all knowledge. They found that musical harmony depends on the frequency ratio of the notes played; some ratios are harmonious, others are not. In much the same way, good architecture may foster harmony. For Greek architects, the key to harmonious architecture was the golden section, a ratio of 1.618. The Parthenon at Athens is an example of a building in which the dimensions reflect the golden section, a number that was obtained by geometric constructions.

In addition to harmony, good architecture can provide a sense of stability, a bulwark against the vicissitudes of time. Who has not seen a house and felt that it would be a great place to live? Its proportions and setting create an image of the ideal home. In Western culture, the steeples that adorn many churches convey a religious sense or remind us of our mortality, skyscrapers against the horizon denote an urban setting, and, sadly, the dilapidated buildings and paper-strewn vacant lots associated with urban sprawl suggest a decaying society.

References:
Ching, Francis D. K. *Architecture: Form, Space, and Order.* New York: Van Nostrand, 1979.
International Encyclopedia of Communications. New York: Oxford University Press, 1989.
Peel, Lucy, Polly Powell, and Alexander Garrett. *An Introduction to Twentieth Century Architecture.* Secaucus, NJ: Chartwell Books, 1989.
Roth, Leland M. *A Concise History of American Architecture.* New York: Harper & Row, 1979.

Archives

Archives are the records of an institution or organization. The term also applies to the places where the records are kept. Archival material can be used to document past procedures, policies, functions, and actions of various institutions and organizations, including governments. Archives may hold the answers to such questions as, "Who was president of XYZ company in 1922?" or "What happened at the board meeting on 3 June 1913?" The minutes of that meeting should be found in the archives of the company in question.

The oldest archives go back five millennia to the clay tablets used by the Sumerians. For half of human history, archival records consist of clay tablets. All major civilizations, following the development of writing, recognized the value of keeping records and did so. However, it was not until 1543 that Spain established a national archive. France eventually followed suit, but not until the end of the eighteenth century, during their Revolution. Other countries established government record offices during the nineteenth and early twentieth centuries. The United States was the last major nation to do so, in 1934. The National Archives of the United States are housed at Pennsylvania Avenue and Seventh Street in Washington, D.C., under the control of the National Archives and Records Administration (NARA), an independent agency of the executive branch of government. In the NARA museum are the original Declaration of Independence, the U.S. Constitution, and the Bill of Rights.

Archives are a firsthand source of data for historians because they authoritatively document the activities, procedures, and functions of the agency, business, school, or other organization that has maintained the records through time. The French Revolution led to the principle of the public's right to view government records. However, because of national defense and security, access to some government archives is limited. As a result, there is an ongoing struggle between the right to know and the need of the government to protect and defend its citizens. Generally, archival access, if restricted, is restricted for a specified period after which the records become available. For example, many of the government records pertaining to the assassination of President John F.

Kennedy were recently made available, as were tapes of conversations made by President Richard Nixon prior to his resignation during the Watergate investigation.

Of course, the volume of records becomes so great that criteria for selecting which documents shall be saved and for how long, and which shall be discarded, must be made by government and most other organizations. There is also the question of the media best suited for preserving records. Interestingly, the clay tablets of ancient history provide the most durable records, but the convenience of papyrus, parchment, and, later, paper led to the demise of clay. However, paper undergoes gradual decay, requiring the development of various techniques to increase its longevity, particularly for those documents of great historical value. The use of microfilm has greatly reduced archival costs and volume for documents such as books and journals while enhancing the ease of academic and scholarly research. More recently, magnetic tapes and discs and electronic storage have changed the very nature of archives, but the durability of such archival materials is unknown.

One major use of archives is related to genealogy, which is often of personal interest as well as relevant to legal matters involving records and inheritances. The Church of Jesus Christ of Latter-day Saints maintains extensive genealogical records in Salt Lake City, Utah, but researchers don't have to travel to Utah to use them. Most major cities have a church library with access to genealogical databases in Utah.

There are many kinds of archives, including some that house musical and video recordings. For example, the archives of the former Soviet Union's broadcasting network contain nearly a half-million hours of recordings that include those made by some of the world's outstanding pianists, violinists, orchestras, and singers.

See also:
Computer; Library; Writing.
References:
Alger, Alexandra. "Bringing an Ancestor to Life." *Forbes*, 9 September 1996.

International Encyclopedia of Communications. New York: Oxford University Press, 1989. "National Treasure for Sale." *World Press Review*, February 1996.

Armstrong, Edwin

See Heterodyning; Radio; Sarnoff, David.

Artifact

An artifact is generally regarded as an object made or modified by human hands some time ago. They are the material remains of a culture that may or may not still exist. Tools, weapons, ornaments, utensils, clothes, art objects, religious objects, or other materials may be all that remain of a culture that once flourished. Just as the skeletal remains of early humans and prehumans provide evidence of their anatomy, how they walked, and how they were adapted for making and using tools and weapons, so artifacts can tell us much about the people who made up a society, how they lived, hunted, ate, worshipped, and fought.

Of course, some artifacts are ephemeral. The ice sculptures, flower arrangements, New Year's Day floats, banana splits, and similar aspects of our culture that we enjoy now will not remain for future generations to see or discover. The same is true of Navajo sand paintings and Pueblo prayer sticks, which are not made to be lasting.

Artifacts can bring an added dimension to history. Seeing a copy of the *Philadelphia Spelling Book*, which was displayed at the New York Public Library in 1996, is more convincing than reading about it as the first book to receive a copyright under the original 1790 federal copyright law. Examining the studio artifacts as well as the original paintings, printing plates, and prints of Frederick Remington, which were displayed at a number of museums during 1996 and 1997, provides insight into this Western artist's creativity and popularity. Similarly, an opportunity to see Abraham Lincoln memorabilia—his letters and documents, such as the Gettysburg Address, as well as personal possessions, photographs, campaign items, and other artifacts—provides a viewer with the kind of primary sources used by professional historians.

Biblical archeologists working in the Middle East have found artifacts that both confirm and deny biblical accounts. In one of the patriarch stories, Joseph, a son of Jacob, is sold into slavery for 20 shekels. Egyptologist Kenneth Kitchen points out that documents found in Syria dating to the eighteenth and nineteenth centuries B.C. contain prices for slaves that match closely with the price paid for Joseph. This is but one of many archeological finds that support biblical accounts of events in early history. On the other hand, there are numerous discoveries that apparently contradict passages from the Bible. For example, Kathleen Kenyon, a British archeologist who excavated the ancient city of Jericho, could find no wall to match the one that supposedly fell when Joshua's trumpets sounded sometime between 1300 and 1200 B.C.

Based on the artifacts gathered to date, there is evidence that the Bible is both fact and fiction. However, the search continues, and archeologists and historians now realize that the emphasis on tracing biblical accounts was a mistake because it tended to ignore or even destroy artifacts that were important in understanding the culture of the people who lived in the Middle East long before Christ. In an effort to learn as much as possible from archeological digs, experts in geology, climatology, zoology, anthropology, mathematics, and computers have joined forces with archeologists and historians. The result has been an increase in the number of questions raised that were never considered before. And as any good scholar knows, only by asking the right questions can we hope to find answers.

See also:
Cave Painting.
References:
"Art and Artifacts." *American History*, May/June 1996.
International Encyclopedia of Communications. New York: Oxford University Press, 1989.

"Mysteries of the Bible." *U.S. News & World Report*, 17 April 1995.
"NYPL Exhibit Draws Link between Cave Paintings and the Web." *School Library Journal*, May 1996.

Artificial Language

Artificial languages are deliberately invented, unlike regular languages that develop naturally and for the most part without conscious plan. Artificial languages were originally conceived to provide more precise and logical expression of ideas than natural language and to eliminate the misunderstanding and lack of communication inherent in a multilingual world.

Arguments in favor of a universal artificial language are simple. Such a language would increase international goodwill as well as lead to closer cultural and economic relations at a time when the "global village" is becoming a reality. Critics oppose the movement because they feel that such an innovation will inevitably favor one linguistic tradition over others. Furthermore, opponents believe that although natural languages are accessible and used by all people, artificial languages have traditionally been the preserve of educated classes.

The most famous and successful artificial language, and the one that has become synonymous with the movement, is Esperanto. Developed in 1887 by Ludwig Zamenhof of Poland, Esperanto is derived from root words in Indo-European languages. Its uncomplicated grammar consists of only 16 rules, and its 28-letter alphabet has only one sound for each letter. Advocates of Esperanto emphasize the easy acquisition of the language as well as its simplicity of use.

Esperanto is not the only artificial language, nor is it the first. In the seventeenth century, it was generally believed that the biblical account of the confusion of languages at the Tower of Babel was true and that at one time all mankind spoke a common tongue. By rediscovering the lost universal language, it was believed, man could be closer to his original pure state. To this end the French philosopher René Descartes and his contemporary John Comenius, a Bohemian bishop, independently suggested developing a universal language. Descartes contributed a language based on numbers. Wilhelm von Liebwitz proposed developing a system of universal symbolism. Other attempts to construct an auxiliary language included Sobersol, created in 1817 by Jean François Sudre, in which all words were formed by a combination of syllables designating notes on a scale. Sir Francis Bacon suggested a written system similar to Chinese ideographs. None of these attempts left any lasting legacy in the linguistic field.

The first major movement to gain much acceptance as an international language was Volapuk. The name of the language originated from two of its words meaning "world" and "speak." Johann Martin Schleyer, a German priest, invented the language in 1879. The vocabulary of Volapuk was based on English, but the words were so distorted in form and sound that the resemblance was minimal. Supposedly done to create a more natural appearance, words like *lol*, meaning "rose," *nim* for "animal," and *splan* for "explain" proved too difficult for nonlinguists. The publication of Esperanto in 1887 led to the demise of Volapuk, although a later, simplified form was presented in 1902 as Idiom Neutral. This was reworked to form a third language, Latino Sine Flexione, a derivative of classical Latin. Other proposals included Ido (a revised form of Esperanto), Interglossa, Novial, and Spelin. Rene Saussure of Switzerland created his Nov-Esperanto in 1934.

In 1924, the International Auxiliary Language Association was formed to professionally develop a universal language. For almost 30 years, teams of linguists considered essential characteristics such as neutrality, naturalness, and ease of acquisition. Their efforts culminated in 1951 with the publication of Alexander Gode's Interlingua-English Dictionary of 27,000 words. Using the principle of familiarity with natural languages as a base, the linguists established four control languages—English, French, Italian, and Spanish/Portuguese—

to determine truly international words. To be included in Interlingua, a word, or a reasonable variant, had to appear in three of the four languages. If a word was necessary to the new language but was found in only two of the control languages, its presence in German or Russian could justify its inclusion in the lexicon. Grammar was established in a similar manner. No grammatical construct was included that was not commonly shared by the control languages.

Interlingua has advanced beyond the theoretical stages. It has been used in the summaries of scientific monographs as well as at some international meetings. The innovative language's greatest success was in 1976 and 1977, when it was used in cooperation with the United States Department of Agriculture in publishing a two-volume *Compendium of Plant Diseases*. Interlingua is not limited to the scientific community, however. It has also been used in publishing poetry, plays, and short stories, and it has it own journal, *Panorama*.

James Cooke introduced another language, Loglan, in the *Scientific American* in June 1960. Loglan is a contraction of the term *logical language*. Cooke believed that language inhibited the development of human thought and that a more expressive, liberating tongue was necessary to improve thinking and human culture. Incorporating modern logical and mathematical principles, Cooke based the international vocabulary of Loglan on common root words found in the world's eight most widely used natural languages. He believed the vocabulary would be easy to learn due to association with the speaker's natural language. Phonetic spelling, a short list of speech sounds common to natural languages, and simplified grammar and syntax characterize the development of Loglan. A unique property of this artificial language is that it can be reduced to symbolic expression. In this form it appears to be particularly significant for communication between man and computer, although this is still in the research stage.

See also:
Esperanto.
References:
Cooke, James. "Loglan." *Scientific American*, June 1960.
Large, Andrew. *The Artificial Language Movement*. Cambridge, MA: Basil Blackwell, 1985.
Wallechinsky, David, and Irving Wallace. *The People's Almanac*. Garden City, NY: Doubleday, 1975.

AT&T

See American Telephone & Telegraph Company.

Babbage, Charles
(1792–1871)

An English mathematician and inventor, Charles Babbage devised two mechanical computation machines that anticipated many of the twentieth-century concepts that launched the modern computer age.

Babbage, the oldest son of a prominent banker, quickly established a reputation as a mathematical genius. He taught himself algebra and calculus prior to enrolling at Cambridge University in 1810. Babbage was disappointed by university education when he realized that he knew more math than most of his professors. In 1812, he and some like-minded classmates formed the Analytical Society to help revitalize the English math curriculum as well as to study continental European advances in the field. His experiences led to a lifelong belief that the sciences were neglected by the educational establishment as well as the government. In 1830, he published *Reflections on the Decline of Science* in England, in which he argued that it was the government's duty to support scientific activity and aid inventors. In the next year he became one of the founders of the British Society for the Advancement of Science.

The only paying position Babbage ever held was that of a mathematics professor at Cambridge. Ironically, this was a position from which Babbage might have furthered his coveted pedagogical reforms, but he was never sufficiently interested to apply his considerable talents to the job. Due to his family's financial status, Babbage lived a comfortable life that allowed him to pursue his varied interests from his home in London. After earning his master of arts degree in 1817, Babbage established a solid academic reputation for himself. He published papers on a wide range of mathematical topics, including applied mathematics, probability and statistics, geometry, and physics. Collateral topics, such as meteorology, lock picking, and lighthouses, also excited his attention. He was considered one of the leading cryptologists of his era as well. However, Babbage was obsessed with the idea of mechanical computation, and he devoted his life and fortune to it.

As early as 1812 or 1813, Babbage was appalled to discover the numerous errors and inaccuracies in the British trigonometric and logarithmic function tables generated by contemporary mathematicians. As a child of the Industrial Revolution, he envisioned a machine that could make accurate calculations as well as print out the results to avoid any errors in transcription. In designing the Difference Engine, the first mechanical calculator, Babbage's goal was a 20-decimal capacity plus the ability to print out results. His smaller prototype was well received, and by 1823 he began construction with financial aid from the English government.

A number of factors conspired to relegate the Difference Engine to obscurity. Work on the calculator was sporadic and plagued by financial concerns. Babbage knew what he wanted, but much of the technical work was beyond the capabilities of the machine shops of the day. Babbage's own efforts to help, by designing new machine tool techniques and improved drafting methods, did little to change matters. Babbage's insistence on incorporating improvements as he devised them, and the subsequent conflict with the construction engineers, further complicated the building process. The death of Babbage's wife in midproject was a shattering personal blow as well. However, the major reason the Difference Engine was never completed was Babbage's preoccupation with a new, more sophisticated, and more versatile scheme that he christened the Analytical Engine.

In 1834, Babbage was inspired by the work of Jacque-Marie Jacquard, a French silk weaver, who invented a loom that made automatic weaving practicable for the first time. Jacquard used punched cards with spring needles, which lifted only those threads corresponding to the punched patterns in cards, to weave complex designs. Babbage, foreshadowing the development of modern computers, saw the possibility of using similar principles in his Analytical Engine. He imagined two sets of cards feeding instructions to his calculator, one for the program or mathematical operation and the second for data on complex problems. He also included the printout feature as well. His dream—a machine capable of a 50-decimal capacity—turned into a haunting nightmare. The initial favorable professional response soon waned, and government support was withdrawn in 1842. The embittered genius, frustrated by the lack of recognition accorded his work and his failure to build the machine, carried on as best he could for the remainder of his life, but the Analytical Engine never advanced beyond the planning stage.

The validity of Babbage's ideas was vindicated on at least two occasions. In 1855, a Swedish engineer, George Schuetz, working from an account of the Englishman's efforts in the *Edinburgh Review*, built a less ambitious Difference Engine. The device was used successfully for a number of years at the Dudley Observatory in Albany, New York. After Babbage's death, his son, working with others, built a small-scale working model of the Analytical Engine, which is displayed at the Science Museum in London.

The principles that Babbage pioneered—punched cards, separate entry of data and program, memory, and printouts—have earned him recognition as one of the forefathers of the Computer Age.

See also:
Computer.

References:
Goldstine, Herman H. *The Computer from Pascal to von Neumann*. Princeton, NJ: Princeton University Press, 1972.
Hyman, Anthony. *Charles Babbage: Pioneer of the Modern Computer*. Princeton, NJ: Princeton University Press, 1982.
Moseley, Maboth. *Irascible Genius: A Life of Charles Babbage, Inventor*. London: Hutchinson, 1964.

Baird, John Logie (1888–1946)

A Scottish television pioneer, John Logie Baird achieved the first television transmission in his attic workshop on 25 October 1925. On 27 January 1926, Baird demonstrated his mechanical television system publicly to a meeting of the Royal Institution in London. By the early 1930s, Baird, using the British Broadcasting Company's (BBC's) equipment after the day's radio broadcasts ended, began regularly transmitting his video signals, constituting the world's first full-scale television service.

Once Guglielmo Marconi demonstrated that sound could be conveyed by radio waves, it was only a question of time before a similar system was developed to transmit images. Baird, born in Scotland and educated at Glasgow University, was convinced that the basis of successful image broadcasting lay in a scanning disc invented by Paul Nipkow, a German scientist, in 1884. Baird tried to convince others of this but was ignored. Left to his own devices, he spent two years experimenting in an attic lab while living in poverty. With no finances other than his own resources, Baird improvised, using easily acquired everyday objects. An old tea chest formed a base and held a motor. An empty tea box housed a projection lamp. The vital Nipkow discs were hand cut from cardboard hatboxes and mounted on scrap lumber and darning needles. Endless lengths of wire and string plus a bicycle headlight and sealing wax completed Baird's contraption.

The important discs contained a set of perforations in a spiral pattern. Light reflected from the object passed through the holes as the disc rotated and created what appeared to be a succession of lines. These points of light struck a device that produced electrical current that varied in intensity with the brightness of the light. The current then traveled to a receiver with a screen the size of a saucer. The receiver held a similar set of slides synchronized with those in Baird's "camera" and duplicated the light pattern sent from it. The points of light formed a series of 30 lines that flashed ten times per second, creating a terrible flicker on the screen. Nonetheless, the lines produced a recognizable though fuzzy image. In 1924, Baird felt he was progressing when he produced the image of a Maltese Cross at a distance of 10 feet.

Strapped for finances to continue his work, Baird accepted a job at a local retail store where he demonstrated the new curiosity. In 1925, he succeeded in transmitting the image of the head of a discarded ventriloquist's dummy. Though the picture was of dubious quality, these were the first television images. Baird became a national hero and, at last, had access to funds to aid his work.

Companies in the United States—American Telephone & Telegraph, the Radio Corporation of America, and Westinghouse— were busy developing an electrical television system and ignored Baird's accomplishments. A spirited rivalry developed between Baird and his well-financed competitors. In 1928, Baird appeared to surpass his American rivals by beaming the first transatlantic television signals to Hartsdale, New York. The *New York Times* ranked Baird with Marconi as an inventor and in September 1931 cited Baird's efforts in "The Outstanding Inventions of the Past 80 Years." In 1929, Baird's television system was adopted for use by the German Post Office and the BBC.

Baird's apparent success was short lived. Electronic television produced a better picture than Baird's mechanical system, and though Baird did improve his system's visual definition it was obvious he could not produce as steady and detailed a picture as the competition. The BBC dropped Baird's version in favor of Marconi's electrical system. Mechanical television lasted longer in Germany, but ultimately it was replaced there as well. Too late, Baird realized he had been passed by a new technology. His efforts were an important phase in the development of television that stimulated others to advance the medium in an alternate direction.

See also:
Sarnoff, David; Television; Television and Society; Zworykin, Vladimir Kosma.
References:
Feldman, Anthony, and Peter Ford. *Scientists and Inventors*. New York: Facts on File, 1979.
Flatlow, Ira. *They All Laughed*. New York: HarperCollins, 1992.

Bandwidth

Bandwidth is the range of frequencies occupied by a modulated electromagnetic wave signal. It is usually measured in hertz; that is, in waves per second, or as a percentage of the frequency transmitted. For example, a radio station broadcasting at 1 megahertz with a frequency range of 10,000 hertz (10 kilohertz) is said to have a bandwidth of 10 kilohertz, or 1 percent.

In the United States, the bandwidths of television channels are 6 megahertz wide. The video carrier frequency is placed 1.25 megahertz above the lower frequency, and the audio carrier has a frequency that is 0.25 megahertz below the highest frequency in the bandwidth. Thus, the bandwidth of a television channel is 600 times that of a channel used for broadcasting sound by radio (6 megahertz vs. 10 kilohertz).

In the case of telephone signals, the bandwidth is equal to the maximum frequency transmitted, namely, 3,300 hertz. The range of sounds transmitted by telephone, 0 to 3,300 hertz, easily covers the range of the human voice, which is 80 to 1,100 hertz. Most telephone signals are now converted from analog to digital. To convert signals from analog to digital, a fundamental theorem, known as the sampling theorem, states that the signal may be uniquely represented by discrete samples spaced no more than $1/2B$ apart, where B is the bandwidth. Thus, in the case of telephone signals where B is 3,300 hertz, the sampling should be done at intervals no farther apart than $1/6,600$ hertz, or every $1/6,600$ seconds, which means the signal should be sampled 6,600 times per second. In practice, digital telephone signals are produced by sampling the analog signal 8,000 times per second.

See also:
Analog and Digital Signals; Electromagnetic Waves; Radio; Telephone; Television; Television Network.

Bar Code
See Universal Product Code.

Bar Graph
See Histogram.

Battery

A battery is a device that converts chemical energy to electrical energy. Batteries are used extensively in communication. Tape recorders, hearing aids, pocket radios, laptop computers, pocket calculators, wrist watches, and a variety of other electronic devices are powered by batteries.

Technically, a battery consists of two or more electric cells; however, in common usage, we often refer to single electric cells as batteries. For example, we speak of flashlight batteries even though they are really electric cells. Two or more such cells placed end to end (positive to negative), as they often are in the casing of a flashlight, constitutes a battery.

An electric cell can be made from two different materials (usually metals or carbon) separated by an electrolyte—a nonmetallic material that will conduct charged atoms (ions). The two different metals form the electrodes or poles of the battery, and the electrolyte conducts the charge and undergoes chemical changes inside the cell when the electrodes are connected to a circuit.

Alesandro Volta made the world's first battery, known as a voltaic pile, in 1800. His electrodes, which were piled in alternate fashion on top of one another, were discs of zinc and copper. For an electrolyte, he used pieces of felt that had been soaked in salt water. The moist pieces of felt were used to separate the metal discs.

A simple electric cell can be made by sticking two different metals into a lemon. One metal, which will provide electrons, will serve as the negative electrode; the other metal, to which the electrons will flow, will be the positive electrode. The lemon is the electrolyte. A sensitive ammeter (an instrument that measures electric current) connected to the two electrodes will indicate a flow of charge. Electrons will move from the negative electrode through the meter to the positive electrode. Inside the cell, its electrolyte (lemon juice and pulp) allows ions to move. As a result, there is a continuous flow of charge from one electrode to the other and back through the electrolyte.

In the early days of telegraphy, electric cells originally designed by John Daniell in 1836 were enlarged and modified to provide the electrical energy needed to operate telegraphs. A large piece of zinc, called a crow's foot because of its shape, served as the negative electrode. It was held in place near the top of a large jar by a hook that fit over the jar's edge. At the bottom of the jar was a fan-shaped piece of copper, which was the cell's positive electrode. A blue solution of concentrated copper sulfate ($CuSO_4$) was used to surround and cover the copper. A less dense solution of zinc sulfate ($ZnSO_4$) floated on the blue liquid and surrounded the zinc crow's foot.

When a switch connecting the cell to a telegraph sender or receiver was closed, a current was drawn from the cell. Electrons flowed from the negative zinc electrode as the zinc released electrons, forming zinc ions (Zn^{++}) that dissolved in the surrounding solution. The electrons flowed from the zinc through the telegraph and back to the positive copper electrode, where they combined with copper ions (Cu^{++}) to form neutral copper atoms that were deposited on the copper electrode. Within the electrolyte (the zinc and copper sulfate solutions), there was a flow of positive ions toward the copper electrode, as shown in Figure 1.

The reaction at the negative (zinc) electrode can be summarized by the following equation in which Zn is the symbol for a zinc

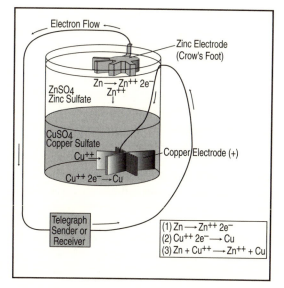

Figure 1. A Daniell cell like the one shown here was used to operate early telegraphs. Reaction 1 occurs at the negative (zinc) electrode. Reaction 2 occurs at the positive (copper) electrode. The overall reaction is shown by reaction 3.

atom, Zn^{++} is the symbol for a zinc ion that has lost two electrons, and e^- represents an electron, which carries a negative charge.

$$Zn \rightarrow Zn^{++} + 2e^-$$

The electrons lost by the zinc atoms are picked up by copper ions (Cu^{++}) at the other (positive) electrode. That reaction can be written as

$$Cu^{++} + 2e^- \rightarrow Cu.$$

The migration of positive copper and zinc ions within the electrolyte, as shown in the figure, is the equivalent of electrons moving in the opposite direction. After all, two positive charges moving one way have the same effect as two negative charges moving in the opposite direction. In effect, negative charge has moved all the way around the circuit, from zinc electrode to copper electrode and back through the electrolyte to the zinc.

The source of the energy that drives this cell is the spontaneous reaction between zinc and copper ions. If a piece of zinc is placed in copper sulfate, the zinc will dissolve as it forms ions by giving its electrons to positively charged copper ions (Cu^{++}). The reaction can be represented by the following equation:

$$Zn + Cu^{++} \rightarrow Zn^{++} + Cu.$$

This equation is the sum of the two equations written for the two electrodes. The sulfate ions ($SO_4^=$), which were associated with the zinc and copper ions in the electrolytes, are called spectator ions here. They simply "watch" the zinc atoms and copper ions react.

Separating the copper ions from the zinc causes the electrons released by zinc atoms to travel along wires to and from the telegraph in order to reach the copper ions. These are the electrons that activate the electromagnet in a telegraph sender or receiver. The same electrons can be used to light bulbs, turn motors, or make possible a variety of other actions in an electric circuit.

To prevent the copper ions from diffusing upward to the zinc, where they would react with it, telegraph operators allowed a small current to flow even when the telegraph was not in use. This trickle current would maintain a small but steady flow of positive ions toward the copper electrode and away from the zinc.

Ordinary flashlight (Leclanché) cells also use zinc as the negative electrode and, thus, the source of electrons. The zinc electrode surrounds the electrolyte and provides the casing that keeps the rest of the cell's contents in place. A carbon rod serves as the positive electrode, but it is not really engaged in the reaction that drives the cell. The electrons lost by the zinc are gained by manganese dioxide and ammonium ions, which are part of the electrolyte that surrounds the carbon rod. The electrolyte is a moist (water) mixture of manganese dioxide (MnO_2), ammonium chloride (NH_4Cl), zinc chloride ($ZnCl_2$), and a little starch to make the mixture pasty so that it is less likely to leak.

Daniell cells and flashlight "batteries" are called primary cells because they cannot be recharged. Secondary or storage cells can be recharged. The best known secondary cell is the lead storage battery, which is the battery found in automobiles. Storage batteries use sulfuric acid as an electrolyte; consequently, the cells are surrounded by leakproof containers made of hard rubber or plastic. Each cell provides 2 volts, that is, 2.0 joules of energy for every coulomb of charge that flows in the circuit. A coulomb is equivalent to 6.25×10^{19}, or 62.5 billion electrons. Since most automobiles carry 12-volt batteries, they contain six cells connected end to end (positive electrode to negative electrode). The electrons that emerge from the negative electrode of a storage cell are supplied by lead (Pb). The electrons are gained by lead peroxide (PbO_2) that coats a plate of lead. To recharge the battery, electrons are driven in the reverse direction; that is, from the lead dioxide electrode to the lead electrode. Normally, this is accomplished by a generator connected to the car engine's drive shaft.

References:

How It Works: The Illustrated Encyclopedia of Science and Technology, vol. 2. New York and London: Marshall Cavendish, 1978.
Macaulay, David. *The Way Things Work.* Boston: Houghton Mifflin, 1988.
Science and Technology Illustrated, vol. 3. Chicago: Encyclopedia Britannica, 1984.
Williams, Trevor I. *The History of Invention: From Stone Axes to Silicon Chips.* New York: Facts on File, 1987.

Beeper

See Pager.

Bell, Alexander Graham (1847–1922)

Inventor of the telephone and renowned authority on the education of the hearing impaired, Alexander Graham Bell always considered his true vocation to be a teacher of the deaf. Perhaps he realized that his invention of the telephone—what many consider the single most valuable patent ever issued—was an accident. Bell was not a scientist or an engineer, nor was he even a very

good mechanic, and he had to rely on others to bring his ideas to reality. The telephone originated from Bell's desire to improve the telegraph and make it more efficient. More than 30 years after the initial success of Samuel F. B. Morse's telegraph, the device remained very simple. A single wire carried a single message. There was a fortune to be made for anyone who could devise a system for sending several simultaneous messages over a single wire without interference. This was the challenge that initially spurred Bell's work.

Born in Edinburgh, Scotland, in 1847, the second of three brothers, Alexander Graham Bell appeared destined to follow in the illustrious footsteps of his father and grandfather. The senior Bells were highly respected in the fields of vocal physiology and elocution. There is some speculation that the older Bell served as the inspiration for George Bernard Shaw's character Henry Higgins in the play *Pygmalion*, on which the musical *My Fair Lady* was later based. The Bell family specialized not only in elocution but in correcting speech impediments and teaching the deaf to speak. To this end the father and son created Visible Speech, a system of written symbols indicating how to use the vocal chords to create sound. At age 15 Alexander was in London working with his grandfather, and by 18 he was a skilled practitioner of the family craft and teacher of the deaf. During this time Bell read the work of Herman von Helmholtz and began the preliminary experiments that provided the basis for the telephone.

Bell was inspired by Helmholtz's efforts, but he misinterpreted the results. Bell thought that Helmholtz actually transmitted sounds, when in fact he only created sounds electrically. Due to his experimentation with tuning forks and sound, Bell was familiar with the principle of sympathetic vibration. A tuning fork will vibrate when a similarly tuned fork is vibrating close by. Likewise, a chord on a piano will vibrate the same chord in another instrument if the striker is raised. Bell speculated that an electrically reproduced sound, transmitted over a wire, could be received by an array of specially tuned forks, each at its own frequency, at the end of the line. The number of messages sent over the line would be limited only by the receptors at the end of the line. Bell dubbed his conception the harmonic telegraph. Bell mentally filed his idea and continued with what he considered a more important innovation, the phonautograph, a device invented in France by Leon Scott that allowed deaf students to analyze speech through a visual record.

In 1870, the Bell family was struck by tragedy when a second son was felled by tuberculosis. Concerned about the health of their only surviving son, the Bells moved to Brantford, Ontario, Canada. Two years later, at age 25, Alexander moved to Boston to promote the visible speech system. Bell worked for the Boston School for Deaf Mutes and eventually established himself at Boston University as professor of vocal physiology and elocution. An 1872 report detailing Western Union's attempts to solve the problem of a multiple telegraph revived Bell's earlier scheme for the harmonic telegraph. Bell sought the advice of Joseph Henry, the dean of American physicists, to whom he lamented his lack of scientific and electrical training. Henry encouraged the aspiring inventor and urged him to get the skills necessary to forge ahead. The meeting was the turning point of Bell's inventive career.

The next year complemented the turn in Bell's creative fortunes. There was renewed interest in his works, the promise of financial support, and a more personal landmark. In 1873, Bell met his future wife, Mabel Hubbard, when her lawyer-financier father sought Bell's expertise in deaf education. The 16-year-old girl lost her hearing at age 4 due to disease and subsequently developed problems speaking. The student and teacher fell in love, but the disparity in their financial situations stalled any plans. When Gardiner Greene Hubbard learned of Bell's electrical experiments, and in particular the harmonic telegraph concept, he and Thomas Sanders, the father of another student, agreed to finance development of the device in return

for a share of the patent rights. Anxious to beat Western Union and reap the rewards of telegraphic improvement, Hubbard intimated to Bell: no telegraph, no wife.

The final piece of the telephone saga fell into place when Bell went to Charles Williams's workshop in Boston and met Thomas Watson. Bell lacked the mechanical skills to build his own projects, and the Williams works was one of many establishments that catered to amateur tinkerers by constructing models of their innovations. Watson, the son of a Salem, Massachusetts, stable hand, was a school dropout but an exceptional mechanic and was well versed in the new science of electricity. In 1875, the 21-year-old mechanic left his job to work full time with Bell.

By the spring of 1875, Bell, despite the protestations of his financiers, scrapped his telegraphy ideas to work on the more exciting and revolutionary concept of electronically reproducing the human voice. Bell reasoned that if sound could be transmitted over a wire, then so could a voice. To Bell, perfecting the tuned reeds of the harmonic telegraph appeared to provide the best chance for success. Time was of the essence since Bell was aware that others, particularly Elisha Gray of Chicago, were working toward the same end. So similar were Bell's and Gray's devices that there was a controversy over patent rights that was only settled out of court years later.

By July 1875, a set of receivers and transmitters built by Watson could produce and send sound, but not intelligible speech. A frustrated Bell attributed the lack of progress to a poorly conceived wire and magnet transmitter problem. On 9 March 1876, Bell worked out a new version of the transmitter using highly corrosive acid. Watson and Bell separated to distant rooms to begin the experiment. Bell shouted the now-famous words, "Mr. Watson, come here. I want you." An astounded Watson received the first telephone message and ran to Bell. The story most often remembered by students, that Bell spilled acid on himself and called for help, is probably apocryphal. Neither man recorded the incident in his notes of the day, and Bell biographer Robert V. Bruce believes that Watson, who recalled the occasion years later, might have confused it with another event. Nonetheless, the two collaborators worked for several more months to ensure that the invention was ready for the market. They never satisfactorily solved the transmitter problem, but Thomas Edison did patent a transmitter that became the standard.

Convinced that he was on the verge of a major communications revolution, Bell took his device to the Philadelphia Centennial Exposition of 1876. However, the public showed little enthusiasm for the telephone, which was considered merely a scientific curiosity. Prominent scientists in attendance, like Joseph Henry and Sir William Thomson (Lord Kelvin), were impressed with the scientific achievement but ambivalent about the practical value of the telephone.

On 9 July 1877, the principal partners formed the Bell Telephone Company. Bell, Watson, Hubbard, and Sanders held all the original stock in the company. Two days later Bell married Mabel Hubbard. Newly married and short of money during the formative days of the company, Bell offered to sell his patents to Western Union for $100,000. The telegraphic giant declined, saying they had no use for the fad.

Someone other than Bell and his associates must have realized the potential of the telephone. In 1877 began a series of protracted legal battles over the patent rights. In all, some 600 claims were filed against the Bell patent, the strongest of which came from Elisha Gray with the backing of Western Union. In 1893, the U.S. Supreme Court ruled in Bell's favor, and he was officially recognized as the father of the telephone. The first commercial telephone switchboard went into service in New Haven, Connecticut, and by 1880 the telephone was well established and accepted as a characteristic of a modern household.

Bell's major fame rests on the invention of the telephone. However, that success overshadowed other far-reaching interests and innovations that would have made Bell a giant of the age regardless of the telephone. By 1881, Bell freely admitted that the technological refinement of the telephone did not interest him. He was joined in this sentiment by Watson, and both men retired early from Bell Telephone. Watson went on to a variety of careers as a gentlemen farmer, geologist, and shipbuilder before setting on a profession in the theater. His father-in-law's management of the company allowed Bell to pursue his own scientific inquiry and enabled him to finance deserving scientists and their projects. Bell successfully developed a vacuum jacket respirator, also known as the iron lung, in 1892. His induction balance located metal objects in the body and was used unsuccessfully on President James Garfield in 1881 as he lay dying of an assassin's bullet. During the Spanish-American War, Bell worked on a speedboat that eventually established several records. He served as president of the National Geographic Society and chief financial supporter of the magazine *Science*, and he developed a system of construction based on tetrahedral frames. In the last 25 years of Bell's life, aviation occupied much of his time. His work with the hearing impaired remained of prime importance for him as well. Helen Keller dedicated her autobiography to Bell in recognition of his work in the field of deaf education.

Bell died in 1922 at his summer home on Cape Breton Island, Nova Scotia, Canada. People throughout North America were urged not to use their telephones on the day of his burial as a silent tribute to one of the most important inventors in history.

See also:
American Telephone & Telegraph Company; Communication among the Hearing Impaired; Henry, Joseph; Telephone.

References:
Barnett, Lincoln. "The Voice Heard Round the World." *American Heritage*, April 1965.
Bruce, Robert. *Alexander G. Bell and the Conquest of Solitude*. Boston: Little, Brown, 1973.
Bruce, Robert. "A Conquest of Solitude." *American Heritage*, April 1973.
Eastman, John. "Who Really Invented the Telephone?" in *People's Almanac #2*. New York: Bantam Books, 1978.

Bell, Chichester
See Edison, Thomas Alva; Phonograph.

Bell Labs
See American Telephone & Telegraph Company.

Body Language
See Nonverbal Communication.

Book
A book consists of closely related pages of text bound together as a volume for reading. Normally, a book contains text in the form of alphabetical or ideographic print together with illustrations such as drawings or photographs. Other than speech, no device has played a more important role in communication for so long a time as the book.

History
Before there were books there had to be writing. Evidence of written records extends back to more than three millennia B.C. Books are sometimes referred to as volumes, from the Latin *volumen*, which means roll, and the earliest books were long rolls of papyrus wound around sticks. Papyrus was made by weaving together fibers peeled from reeds. Because there were no pencils or pens, writing was done by scratching lines on the papyrus with a sharp stick, stone, or reed. Later papyruses were coated with gum (sized) to provide a smooth surface that could be written on with an inked brush. On each roll were many books written in succession. Some books in the library at Alexandria in Egypt were 9 meters (30 feet) long. By 300 B.C., these long volumes were being cut into tomes, or books.

The Ptolemies, who ruled Egypt from 323 to 30 B.C., forbade the export of papyrus in an effort to maintain the superiority of their library at Alexandria. Meanwhile, in Pergamum during the reign of King Eumenes II (ca. 150 B.C.), vellum (the skin of calves, lambs, and kids) and the somewhat coarser parchment (skin from sheep, pigs, and goats) were being used to produce bound volumes that were the antecedents of our present-day books.

The papyrus industry became well established under Roman rule, and considerable money and labor was tied up in its production. As a result, the use of vellum and parchment as media for writing was slow to develop. The change from rolls to codex (folded sheets of paper fastened together at the center with wooden covers on each side) followed the same conservative trend. The changeover from roll to codex extended from the first to the fifth century A.D., but the conversion began to accelerate during the fourth century, and by the fifth century most writings were in the codex format. Although papyrus was produced in Egypt until about the twelfth century, vellum and parchment became the predominant writing media for books much earlier. But vellum and parchment were replaced by paper, which was made from mulberry and bamboo bark in China as early as 105 B.C. according to Ts'ai Lun, who might have invented paper. The Chinese replaced the silk, bamboo, and wooden tablets that had been used to write on with paper made by mixing fibrous hemp and ramie plants with rattan and mulberry, which was then finely chopped before being boiled with wood ashes. After washing, the liquid pulp was poured onto porous screens, where it dried to form sheets of paper.

Papermaking spread slowly westward from Asia. The Moors brought paper to Europe at the end of the eleventh century, and it was manufactured in Spain a short time later. By the sixteenth century there were paper mills throughout Europe.

The change in book format from roll to codex was in part associated with the rise of Christianity. Perhaps in an effort to distinguish Christian writings from those of Jewish and pagan origin, early Christian manuscripts, including the Christian Bible, were written on papyrus codices. These codices, which consisted of folded leaves of papyrus or vellum held together at the center and encased in wood, were the ancestor of our

A worker in a Chinese factory watches from a platform as a paper-processing machine rolls paper on a cylinder. Beginning in the late nineteenth century, paper was produced from wood pulp, a cheaper and more abundant source than rags. The change contributed to making books more affordable.

modern book. They were illustrated and copied by hand, usually by monks who used a calligraphic style to copy manuscripts that were primarily religious in nature. Although the rise of Christianity might have played a part in the conversion from roll to codex, there were practical reasons for the change as well. Unlike rolled papyrus or parchment, codices were compact and portable. Furthermore, the ease of reference to page by index made codices far easier to use.

After Gutenberg's invention of the printing press around 1450, books changed very little in terms of production or style between the fifteenth and eighteenth centuries, but during the eighteenth century publishing became an industry as technological improvements reduced the cost of printed matter. Illustrated magazines became widespread, as did religious books and pamphlets. Text-

books and readers were written for schools, and children's books appeared for the first time. During the Victorian era, cloth bindings replaced the more expensive leather covers and further reduced the price of books.

At the end of the nineteenth century, books were being produced by mechanical means. Printing companies used power-driven, rotary printing presses and Linotype typesetting machines. Wood pulp rather than rags became the source for paper, making it cheaper and more abundant. The combination of cheaper paper and mechanized methods for printing led to the mass production of books. Thousands of copies of an edition could be printed quickly. During the twentieth century, computer-driven photographic offset printing led to books being printed in the tens of thousands of copies per edition.

The Cultural Impact of Books

Gutenberg's printing press, which helped foster the Renaissance, provided an increasing number of books and a growing rate of literacy. New ideas could be widely disseminated, criticized, and tested, errors corrected, and concepts expanded by others who would, in turn, write their own books to refute, support, enhance, or enlarge upon an author's treatise, or present totally new ideas. Numbered pages and alphabetized indices referring to those pages made it easy to find information. However, printed books also served to disseminate outdated knowledge, such as Aristotelian science. And while the availability of books improved, they were expensive and few could read them. Libraries where people could read books without buying them were rare, poorly stocked, and costly to maintain. Nevertheless, it may well be that the Renaissance persisted only because printed books prevented texts from being lost, as was frequently the case with handwritten manuscripts that were often left in some forgotten corner of a monastery.

Religious writings were the most frequent handwritten manuscripts because generally, unlike most segments of society before the nineteenth century, the clergy could read and write. And it was probably those religious books and their capacity for spreading information quickly and widely that led to the reformation. At the same time, printed matter hardened the position of the established church. Issues that earlier church authorities would have talked through, tolerated, or ignored were now firmly established in writing. The doctrinal differences between the established church and dissidents such as Martin Luther, John Calvin, and others were in print and available to all who could read.

Books and Science

Although the technology of printing was established through the work of craftsmen rather than through scientific research, the growth of science itself, because it is so dependent on the repetition of experiments by critics, could never have blossomed without printed books and journals. Books enabled scientists from all parts of the world to become familiar with new ideas established by experiment and careful reasoning. These readers could readily perform their own experiments to confirm or deny the discoveries of others. Printed tables of data—log and trig tables, standard distances, square roots, derivatives, for example—eliminated tedious repetitive computations and enabled competent minds to pursue fruitful avenues of inquiry.

Binding Books

The printed sheets or webs that emerge from a printing press are folded and cut to make sections of a book called signatures. Signatures, which contain 16, 24, or 32 pages, must be collated and bound before the separately prepared cover is attached. Binding involves sewing and gluing the signatures together. The pages are then trimmed before a lining is glued to the back and the cover is glued to the lining. Early books were bound by hand; today, the binding is done by machine.

In the case of paperbacks, the folds are often cut to form single leaves rather than signatures. The backs of the leaves are glued together and a heavy paper cover applied. Though less durable than hardcover books, paperbacks are so inexpensive that they have been a boon to book sales during the second half of the twentieth century.

See also:
Computer; Mergenthaler, Ottmar; Photography; Photojournalism; Printing; Writing; Xerography.

References:
International Encyclopedia of Communications. New York: Oxford University Press, 1989.
Macaulay, David. *The Way Things Work*. Boston: Houghton Mifflin, 1988.
Williams, Trevor I. *The History of Invention: From Stone Axes to Silicon Chips*. New York: Facts on File, 1987.

Braille

See Communication among the Visually Impaired.

Burglar Alarm

Burglar alarms are devices that produce a signal indicating that an unauthorized person has entered a perimeter or space protected by the device. Perimeter alarms detect intruders at points vulnerable to unauthorized entrance such as a window, door, or fence. Space alarms detect the motion of anyone who enters a restricted area such as a room, office, or vault.

Alarm Systems

All alarm systems have three components: a protective circuit, an output mechanism that provides an alarm signal, and a control panel where the circuit is monitored. A change in voltage produced in the protective circuit will cause the control panel to activate the alarm. The control panel also allows a user to turn off or reset the system.

Protective circuits installed in windows and doors will produce a response whenever a window or door is opened. A permanent magnet fixed to the movable portion of the window attracts a metal arm of a buzzerlike device attached to the frame of the window or door. When the window or door is opened, the magnet is moved away from the metal arm and no longer attracts it. A spring pulls the bar back, activating another circuit in the control panel that sounds an alarm in the home and, perhaps, at a central station that will notify police.

In tall buildings where entrance through windows poses no threat, the floors of office entrances are often covered with pressure mats that consist of two metal foils separated by a porous insulating foam. When someone steps on the pad, the foils are forced together, creating a conducting path (circuit) that changes the voltage at a control panel and activates an alarm.

Another common protective device is an invisible beam of infrared or ultraviolet light that is reflected back and forth across a room or other protected space by a system of mirrors. The beam terminates when it strikes a photoelectric cell. The photosensitive surface of the cell, when struck by the light beam, emits electrons that maintain a small but steady electric current. When the beam is interrupted, as it would be by a burglar crossing the room, the current is momentarily interrupted because no light reaches the photocell. The break in the current activates a relay that establishes a current through the alarm mechanism.

Other systems use ultrasonic or microwave beams that act much like the radar used by police to detect speeding vehicles. When the beam strikes a moving object, the frequency of the sound or microwaves is changed. The change in frequency is sensed by the system's receiver, which sends a signal to the control panel that activates an alarm.

There are also protective devices that will respond to sound, gases, structural vibrations, body heat (infrared radiation), changes in inertia, or changes in the infrared spectrum caused by fire. One of the most effective systems is television surveillance. Cameras mounted in key locations photograph and store on tape images of any persons who enter the space covered by the camera's lens. Most banks utilize television surveillance. If the bank is robbed, the video tape of the event may provide vital clues that will help police track down the perpetrators.

Advantages and Cost

The risk of burglary can be halved by a few commonsense precautions, such as properly secured doors and windows that include bolt locks on doors, lights that go on automatically when residents are away at night, and alert neighbors. The risk can be reduced still further by installing an alarm system. While such an installation may cost a homeowner between $1,000 and $3,000 depending on conditions, burglar and fire alarm systems may reduce the cost of insurance by as much as 20 percent.

See also:
Electromagnet; Radar; Relay.

References:
"Alarm Systems for Home Security." *Consumers' Research Magazine*, October 1994.
Macaulay, David. *The Way Things Work.* Boston: Houghton Mifflin, 1988.
Science and Technology Illustrated, vol. 15. Chicago: Encyclopedia Britannica, 1984.

Cable Television

See Television.

Calendar

A calendar is a timekeeping device. Usually, it divides a year—the time the earth takes to make one revolution about the sun—into months, weeks, and days. It was and is useful in communicating to its users general assumptions about weather, when crops should be planted, and when various holidays or days of rest should be observed or celebrated.

The year and the day (the time required for the earth to make one revolution) components of the calendar are natural units of time, but the week and month are of human origin, although the month in many early calendars was the time for the moon to pass through all its phases—a period of about 29.5 days. History reveals that in various cultures the week has been ten and nine days long as well as seven. As recently as 1929 and 1931, the Soviet Union experimented with five- and six-day weeks in an effort to stamp out religion.

One of the first calendars—one based on the moon's cycle—was developed by the Babylonians about 5,000 years ago. They realized that if the sun rose 29 times between one full moon and the next, it would rise 30 times before the moon was again full. Realizing that the moon's period was 29.5 days, their months were alternately 29 and 30 days. A bit of simple arithmetic reveals that 12 Babylonian months contained only 354 days. To compensate for a year that was about 11 days too short, they would occasionally add a few days to their calendar.

The Egyptian Calendar

The Egyptians, who were good astronomers, made use of the stars in developing a calendar. A tunnel in one of the pyramids was pointed toward a position on the eastern horizon where Sirius, the brightest star in the heavens, was known to rise. The Egyptians' year began on the day that Sirius rose with the sun. The date was vital to their civiliza-tion because it indicated that the Nile would soon flood, bringing fresh soil to the farmland along its banks.

The star-based Egyptian calendar also consisted of 12 months, but all were 30 days long. Although somewhat better than the Babylonian calendar, it was still necessary to add five or six "monthless" days to each year.

As centuries passed, priests, who were the astronomers in the Egyptian culture, realized that Sirius's rising position had shifted. Eventually, its rising could no longer be viewed through the tunnel. Although the priests could not explain their observations, present-day astronomers realize that it was the first evidence that the earth's axis precesses much like that of a spinning top. The period of earth's precession is nearly 26,000 years. As a result, 26,000 years from now the earth's north pole will again lie almost directly below Polaris (the present North Star). In the meantime, the stars will appear to shift very slightly relative to the earth each year. In about 12 millennia, Vega, a bright star in the constellation Lyra, will be our pole star.

The Julian Calendar

The ten-month calendar developed in ancient Rome and described in Table 1 was a disaster. Nevertheless, the names of its months reveal that it was a forerunner of our present calendar.

Although the Babylonian and Egyptian calendars were a few days shy of a year, the Roman calendar was missing two months. After the last day of December, 61 or 62 days would pass before the priests would announce the beginning of a new year on Martius 1.

Table 1. The Number of Days in the Months of the Ancient Roman Calendar			
Name of month	No. of days	Name of month	No. of days
Martius	31	Sextilis	30
Aprilis	30	September	30
Maius	31	October	31
Junius	30	November	30
Quintilus	31	December	30

Beginning in about 700 B.C., Roman rulers began tinkering with the calendar. Two months, Januarius and Februarius, were inserted between December and Martius. The Romans then tried to make the 12 months correspond to the moon's period by making the months alternate between 29 and 30 days. Of course, this resulted in a year that was 11 or 12 days short, so an abbreviated month (Mercedinus) consisting alternately of 22 and 23 days was added to the calendar every two years.

By 46 B.C., politically motivated adjustments to the calendar had taken their toll. The first day of spring, which traditionally was supposed to coincide with the vernal equinox (the point at which the sun lies directly over the equator), was arriving nearly three months late according to the calendar.

In an effort to bring calendar and tradition into agreement, Julius Caesar hired the astronomer Sosigenes to find a solution. The calendar Sosigenes developed, which became known as the Julian calendar, contained 12 months. Each month was 30 or 31 days long, except February, which had 28 days. The sum of the days in these 12 months provided a 365-day year. Sosigenes knew that it took 365.25 days for the sun to make a full cycle, so he added one day to the month of February every fourth year (leap year), which made the average year 365.25 days long. To move the vernal equinox back to its traditional date in late March, Caesar decreed that 80 days would be added to the year we now refer to as 46 B.C. The Romans called it the "year of confusion."

After Julius Caesar's death, Quintilus (the fifth month in the old Roman calendar) was renamed July in his honor. Later, Sextilis (originally the sixth month) was renamed August to honor Augustus Caesar, Julius's successor.

The Gregorian Calendar

Today, we use what is known as the Gregorian calendar. The Julian calendar worked well for 1,500 years. However, a year is 11 minutes and 14 seconds shorter than 365.25 days, and by 1582 this small difference in time was causing the vernal equinox to occur in early March instead of late March. Because Easter was and is traditionally celebrated by many Christians on the first Sunday following the first full moon after the vernal equinox, the small inaccuracy in the calendar caused Easter to be celebrated in March rather than April. This time Pope Gregory XIII, following a format established by Julius Caesar, decreed that the day following 4 October 1582 would be 15 October, not 5 October, thus moving the vernal equinox from 11 March to 21 March in 1583.

To prevent the problem from recurring, leap years were redefined. End-of-century years, even though divisible by 4, are leap years only if they are divisible by 400. Consequently, the years 1600 and 2000 were defined as leap years, but 1700, 1800, and 1900 were not.

Possible Future Calendars

There are efforts to reform the Gregorian calendar in order to provide months of equal length, ensure that holidays fall on the same day of the week each year, and establish equal numbers of weekdays each month.

One reform movement advocates 13 months of 28 days each year. Such a calendar would ensure that each month begins on a

Sunday and ends on a Saturday. To provide the extra day needed to make a year, a second Saturday would be added to the end of each year. Leap years could end with three Saturdays, or an additional Saturday holiday could be added to a particular month.

Another reform movement would establish a world calendar with 12 months and a year divided into four identical quarters. January, February, and March would be identical with April, May, and June, and so on. Each quarter would begin on a Sunday of a 31-day month. Second and third months would have 30 days, causing the quarter to end on a Saturday.

Worldsday, a new worldwide holiday, would follow Saturday, 30 December, preceding Sunday, 1 January. On leap years, there would be a second Worldsday following 30 June.

References:

Crumpley, Elsa. *It's about Time: All You Need to Know about the Origin of Time and Calendars.* Saratoga, CA: R & E Publishers, 1992.
Gardner, Robert. *Experimenting with Time.* New York: Watts, 1995.
Williams, Trevor I. *The History of Invention: From Stone Axes to Silicon Chips.* New York: Facts on File, 1987.

Camcorder

See Tape Recorder.

Camera

Cameras are used to take photographs—images produced by the action of light on sensitized materials. There are great similarities between the camera and the human eye, both of which can form images. Light enters the eye through an opening in the iris (the colored portion of the eye). The camera has an aperture in the diaphragm through which light enters when a shutter, which corresponds to the human eyelid, opens. Both camera and eye have a lens to focus light into images that fall on the camera's film or the eye's retina. In the eye, a light image forms as chemical changes take place. To record these

images in dim light, more sensitive film is used in a camera. In the eye, light falling on the retina gives rise to nerve impulses that travel to the brain, where we actually "see." Images on the film in a camera produce chemical changes in deposits of silver that remain on the film until it is developed. The eye is lined with a black choroid coat that prevents light from being reflected inside the eye. A flat black surface inside the camera serves the same purpose.

There are also significant differences between eye and camera. Light, in all but inexpensive cameras, is focused by moving the lens toward or away from the subject being photographed. In the eye, it is the shape of the lens that is used to change the points where light converges to form images. There are muscles that control tension in the suspensory ligament that surrounds and controls the shape of the lens. To view near objects, the lens is made more convex. To view distant objects clearly, light must be bent (refracted) less; consequently, the lens is made less convex by reducing tension in the suspensory ligament.

Exposure

Whether automatic or set by the photographer, a camera has f-stops, or diaphragm settings, that control the amount of light allowed to enter the lens. At first, the f-stop numbers may seem to be an arbitrary or strange series of numbers. The f-stop numbers usually consist of all or part of the following series: $f/2$, $f/2.8$, $f/4$, $f/5.6$, $f/8$, $f/11$, $f/16$, $f/22$, $f/32$. The lowest f-stop number on a camera indicates that the diaphragm will be wide open. Each succeeding number means the area of the opening is halved so that half as much light can enter. Thus, changing an f-stop setting from $f/2.8$ to $f/4$ halves the light entering the lens. Changing from $f/2.8$ to $f/5.6$ reduces the amount of light passing through the lens to one-fourth. The amount of light allowed through the diaphragm is actually proportional to the inverse of the f-stop number squared.

Only when the shutter control button is pushed does the shutter open and allow light to enter the camera. The amount of light passing through the lens or lenses is also affected by the shutter speed, which may be controlled automatically or manually. Setting the shutter speed at 1/25 means that the shutter will be open for 1/25 second. If the shutter speed is set for 1/50, the shutter will allow half as much light to pass as a setting of 1/25, but twice as much as a setting of 1/100.

Both f-stop and shutter speed control the light that passes through the lens system and reaches the film. An f/8 setting at 1/50 allows the same amount of light to enter the camera as an f/5.6 at 1/100. The change in f-stop doubled the size of the aperture through which light could pass, but halving the shutter speed reduced the time the shutter was open by one-half, so the two factors canceled one another in terms of total light admitted. If the camera is used to photograph moving objects, such as the players in an athletic contest, a fast shutter speed is required to avoid blurred images. On many cameras, a built-in light meter automatically sets shutter speed and f-stop to the proper setting for the amount of light available. However, increasing the size of the opening through the diaphragm reduces the depth of field; that is, the portion of the picture that is in focus and not blurry. A picture taken with a pinhole camera, which has no lens but simply a tiny hole through which light passes, will have an infinite depth of field. Every image will be clear; however, such pictures require a long exposure because the amount of light that passes through the pinhole is quite limited when compared to the light that comes through a lens even at a high f-stop setting.

The Single-Lens Reflex Camera

A single-lens reflex camera has a mirror set at a 45-degree angle in front of the film. This allows the operator to use the same lens system to view a subject and to converge light on the film. As the photographer views the subject, light that has passed through the lenses is reflected upward by the mirror to a refractive viewer that bends the light so the photographer can see the image that will later fall on film. When the shadelike shutter opens to expose the film to light, a hinged device flips the mirror upward so as not to interfere with the light's path to the film.

See also:
Motion Pictures; Photography; Photography, Amateur; Photography, Color.

References:
"A Camera-Ready Revolution?" *Consumers' Research Magazine*, October 1994.
Macaulay, David. *The Way Things Work.* Boston: Houghton Mifflin, 1988.
"Negative Vibes." *The Economist*, 26 August 1995.
Noldechen, Arno. "Brief Exposures." *World Press Review*, November 1993.
Williams, Trevor I. *The History of Invention: From Stone Axes to Silicon Chips.* New York: Facts on File, 1987.

Capacitor

A capacitor is a device for storing charge. It consists of two conductors separated by a dielectric (an insulator) such as air, glass, or mica. When equal charges of opposite sign are placed on the conductors, an electric field is established between them.

A capacitor usually consists of two parallel plates separated by a dielectric. The electric field and the potential difference (voltage) between the conductors is proportional to the charge on the plates.

The capacitance of a capacitor is a measure of its ability to store charge. To increase the capacitance of a pair of plates, the area of the plates may be increased, the plates may be moved closer together, or a better dielectric may be placed between them.

The unit of capacitance, C, is the *farad*, named in honor of Michael Faraday. Capacitance is defined as the charge (Q) stored per volt (V); thus,

$$C = Q/V.$$

A charge of 1 coulomb per volt is defined as 1 farad. Because a farad is a very large capacitance, a more practical unit, the microfarad, is more commonly used to measure capacitance. If one plate of a capacitor is grounded, charge placed on the other plate will induce charge of opposite sign to collect on the grounded plate.

Capacitors are widely used in electronic and microelectronic circuits. Together with inductor coils, they are used for tuning radios and for "smoothing" the voltage obtained from a rectifier.

See also:
Electric Field; Inductor; Microelectronics; Radio.

References:
Haber-Schaim, Uri, et al. *PSSC Physics,* 7th ed. Dubuque, IA: Kendall/Hunt, 1991.
Sears, Francis W., Mark W. Zemansky, and Hugh D. Young. *College Physics*. Reading, MA: Addison-Wesley, 1985.

Carbon Dating

Carbon, an element found in all living or once-living tissue, can be used to determine the age of artifacts. Knowing the approximate date of an artifact communicates to historians and archeologists valuable information about the age and stage of development of a culture.

The carbon dating method depends upon the fact that not all carbon atoms are the same. Nearly 99 percent of carbon atoms have nuclei that contain six protons and six neutrons. Protons (p) and neutrons (n) have virtually the same mass. Each is equivalent to one atomic mass unit (amu); consequently, these carbon atoms have a mass of 12 amu and are known as carbon-12 (C-12) atoms. Approximately 1 percent of carbon atoms have an extra neutron, giving them a mass of 13 amu. These are carbon-13 (C-13) atoms.

There are also trace amounts of carbon-14 (C-14) atoms, which have eight neutrons and, like all carbon atoms, six protons. Carbon-14 atoms are formed when cosmic rays, in this case neutrons, collide with nitrogen atoms in the atmosphere to form C-14 atoms and release a proton. The reaction is summarized by the equation

N-14 (7 p + 7 n) + n $\rightarrow$ C-14 (6 p + 8 n) + p.

The three different kinds of carbon atoms are called isotopes of carbon. All contain six protons and behave the same in chemical reactions. As a result, approximately 99 percent of the carbon in the chemical compounds found in living tissue are C-12 atoms, 1 percent are C-13 atoms, and trace amounts are carbon-14 atoms.

Carbon-14 is radioactive; that is, it releases radiation. In fact, it changes back to nitrogen by releasing a beta ray (electron) from its nucleus. The loss of the electron, in effect, changes a neutron into a proton, giving the atom an additional proton. Since the mass of an electron is only about 1/2,000 the mass of a proton, the mass of the atom remains very nearly the same. The equation below summarizes the process.

C-14 (6 p + 8 n) $\rightarrow$ N-14 (7 p + 7 n) + e$^-$

The half life of C-14 is 5,730 years. This means that if we start with X number of C-14 atoms, only half of them (X/2) will remain after 5,730 years. The other half will have changed to N-14 atoms. After another 5,730 years, only one-fourth (X/4) of the C-14 atoms will remain.

Because the concentration of C-14 atoms in the atmosphere is constant, the ratio of C-14 to C-12 in all living tissue is fixed because carbon enters the life cycle through the carbon dioxide in the atmosphere. This ratio is very small, but it can be determined with modern instruments. When a living organism dies, its tissue no longer takes in carbon, and so the ratio of C-14 to C-12 slowly decreases. Assuming that the concentration of C-14 in the atmosphere has been the same over the past 50,000 years, we can determine the age of artifacts that were once living tissue such as wood, bone, charcoal, and shells. If, for example, a piece of wood is found to have half as much C-14 as we find in living wood, we would place its age at 5,730 years. If it has one-fourth as much C-14 as living wood, we would estimate its age to be 11,460 years.

Of course, the technique is based on the assumption that the C-14 level in the atmosphere has remained constant through time.

The assumption has been confirmed to some extent by comparing the age of artifacts using C-14 dating and other dating methods. Carbon-14 dating has been used to establish the age of the Dead Sea Scrolls (1,950 years old), various cave paintings, and a great variety of other artifacts.

The technique is quite satisfactory for objects 50,000 years old or less. For older materials and for inorganic matter, other methods using the half-lives of different radioactive isotopes are used. Uranium dating, for example, can often be used on uranium-bearing rocks. It is based on the fact that U-235, a uranium isotope with a half-life of 700 million years, and U-238, an isotope with a half-life of 4.5 billion years, change to lead-207 and lead-206, respectively. By comparing the concentrations of the isotopes of uranium and lead in a rock that contains uranium, the age of the rock can be determined.

See also:
Artifact; Cave Painting.

Caricature

The word *caricature* comes from the Italian *caricatura,* meaning "to exaggerate" or "to overload." A caricature is a pictorial representation, ordinarily of a person and usually of the face, that grossly exaggerates individual physical features for comic effect. Caricatures most often are simple line drawings with a political orientation that not only reflects the artist's viewpoint and bias, but also comments on the character of the subject. Modern concepts of cartooning grew out of caricature, and political cartoons are the most visible form of caricature today.

The earliest use of caricature was in Renaissance Italy. The simplicity of the artwork and new techniques in wood carving, engraving, and etching made caricatures accessible to the masses and allowed large-scale reproduction of the drawings. The Renaissance philosophy of humanism lent itself to the new art form by emphasizing the uniqueness of each individual. The first important caricaturists were the Italian artists Agostino Carracci and Giovanni Bernini,

Carracci's successor. Even the greatest Renaissance artists, like Albrecht Dürer and Leonardo da Vinci, also dabbled in early caricature.

The invention of lithography in 1798 and the continued improvements in other artistic techniques provided inexpensive methods of reproduction that encouraged the development of caricature.

Political upheavals, characterized by the French Revolution and other social and economic agitation, supplied ample material and opportunity for popular recognition of the caricaturist's art and wit. The nineteenth century was the golden age of the genre, and the worldwide quantity and quality of the work was unequaled.

Thomas Rowlandson and James Gillray were largely responsible for the popularity of English caricature. Rowlandson, originally a watercolorist and portraitist, was known for his skillful satire of English manners. Gillray was politically insightful, and his special subjects were Napoleon Bonaparte and George III. Gillray's contemporaries, the father-and-son combination of Isaac and George Cruikshank, were also widely recognized for their work.

Frenchmen Charles Philipon and Honoré Daumier produced some of the nineteenth century's best-known caricatures, which are widely reproduced in textbooks today. The journalist Philipon developed the magazine *La Caricature* in 1830. More importantly, he produced the famous four-drawing series of Louis Philippe of France transforming into a pear. Philipon's associate was the greatest French caricaturist, Honoré Daumier. Daumier, a painter and lithographer, was particularly concerned with governmental corruption and the smugness of Parisian society. His famous caricature of Louis Philippe as Gargantua got him a prison sentence in 1832. In 1834, the hostile government closed down *La Caricature*. Philipon established a new journal, *Le Charwari*, which continued to lampoon Louis Philippe until he was overthrown. Philipon's success inspired the creation of a number of other publications devoted to humor and satire: *Judge* and *Puck* in

A caricature of a big-mouthed orator (undated woodcut).

Political caricature in Germany dates from the 1848 revolutionary era. Draftsman Wilhelm Busch was the country's most influential caricaturist. He created poems illustrated with caricature. His humorous depiction of people and situations in Germany ultimately earned him recognition as the first professional comic strip artist. Thomas Heine was noted for his caustic observations on the Prussian upper class. Caricature was not as strong in the United States. Thomas Nast, whose work appeared primarily in *Harper's Weekly*, combined personal caricature with his political cartoons. He became a national figure through his consistent and devastating critiques of the realities of New York City political life under William "Boss" Tweed and his Tammany Hall cronies. Charles Dana Gibson developed caricatures of Theodore Roosevelt and Woodrow Wilson.

By the turn of the century, personal political caricature was increasingly confined to editorial cartoons or to the sports and theatrical pages. During World War I the art was revived briefly for propaganda purposes. However, the end of World War I relegated caricature to the back pages, where it merged with cartoons. Modern American caricaturists are best represented by Al Hirschfeld, famous for his caricatures of theatrical people, and David Levine, of the *New York Review of Books*.

See also:
Cartoon; Printing.

References:
Applebaum, Stanley, ed. *Simplicissimus*. New York: Dover, 1975.
Panofsky, Erwin. *The Life and Art of Albrecht Dürer*. Princeton, NJ: Princeton University Press, 1971.

the United States, *Simplicissimus* in Germany, and *Punch* in England.

Henry Mayhew of England founded *Punch*, one of the world's most famous humor magazines, in 1840. Caricature was not a staple of the publication, but the social and literary satire of Max Beerbohm, the most highly regarded English caricaturist, certainly aided the magazine's reputation. In fact, *Punch* was part of a transitional phase in which caricature became increasingly identified with cartoons. *Punch* was proud of its full-page political cartoons, forerunners of modern editorial drawings. Sir John Tenniel's "Dropping the Pilot" was the most famous of the magazine's numerous contributions.

Carlson, Chester F. (1906–1968)

American physicist, patent lawyer, and inventor, Chester F. Carlson revolutionized business offices and communication with his invention of xerography. From the Greek, meaning "dry writing," xerography is the photoconductive duplicating process most commonly used today. Marshall McLuan observed, "Whereas Caxton and Gutenburg enabled all men to become readers, Xerox has enabled all men to become publishers." Today, the term *Xerox,* a registered trademark, is often used incorrectly as a generic name for photocopying.

Carlson grew up on the West Coast, and his family eventually settled in San Bernardino, California. His father's disabilities forced Carlson to take odd jobs to support the family while he attended school. He graduated from the California Institute of Technology as a physicist in 1930 and began his career with Bell Labs. The Depression cost Carlson his job, but in 1934 he accepted a position in the patent division of P. R. Mallory, a New York electronics firm. He attended law school at night and was admitted to the bar in 1940. Carlson stayed with the company until 1945, when he left as the head of the patent department.

Nearsighted and arthritic, the physicist-lawyer realized the need for a quick, clean, inexpensive duplicating method as a result of his patent work. The constant demand for patent blueprints, specifications, and documents was overwhelming. The standard methods of reproduction were restrictive and inefficient. Making carbon copies was a labor-intensive process in which only a few reproductions could be produced at a time, and the results were frequently blurred. The photographic/chemical process was expensive and required the use of messy chemicals as well as some expertise and training. The stencils and chemicals used in the mimeograph and ditto offered no better answer. In 1934, Carlson set up shop in his kitchen in Queens, New York, to try to arrive at some solution.

Carlson quickly determined that there had to be an alternative to the photographic systems that a number of companies were trying to improve and streamline. Carlson was impressed by the work of Paul Selenyi, who had success in sending pictures over the radio, and after corresponding with the Hungarian inventor, Carlson formulated his idea. He theorized he could produce an image on a photoconductive plate exposed to light. When light was projected through an image, the darkest elements (lines of type, for example) would retain the electrostatic charge, while in the areas exposed to the light the charge would disperse. The image would then be imprinted on the plate. Carlson believed that oppositely charged powder lightly sprinkled over the plate would attach itself to the latent image, making it visible. The powder image could then be brought into contact with paper, heated to fix the image, and the copy would be complete. In the fall of 1937, Carlson patented his electrophotography idea, which was still speculative and far from commercially viable.

In 1938, Carlson moved his laboratory to a room in the rear of a beauty salon in Astoria, New York, and hired Austrian physicist Otto Kornei as an assistant. Fighting money problems as well as neighbor's concerns about noxious fumes and fear of fire, the would-be inventor labored for seven months to test his hypothesis. The big breakthrough occurred on 22 October 1938, when Carlson electrostatically charged a zinc-coated plate by vigorously rubbing his handkerchief over it and pressed a glass slide inked with "10-22-38 Astoria" on the plate. He next exposed the plate to his light source, a common desk lamp. After a few minutes' exposure, he turned the lamp off and removed the slide. Using lycopodium powder, he raised the writing on the plate and pressed a piece of wax paper on the image. He gently heated the paper, blew away the excess powder, and produced the first photocopy.

Further research and development were all Carlson needed to fully realize his vision, but the necessary investment was beyond his means. Carlson could find no investors, although he looked for six years. The two associates even built a demonstration model but still could not stimulate any investment. More than 20 companies, including General Electric, the Radio Corporation of America, and IBM, rejected Carlson's proposal. The frustrated Kornei joined IBM while Carlson continued to search.

In 1944, the Battell Memorial Institute of

Columbus, Ohio, a nonprofit research organization, reached an agreement with Carlson. For a $3,000 research and development investment, the two parties agreed to a 60-40 split of any profits. Carlson's lesser share was a small price to pay to have his ideas validated and marketed. After three years and some improvements, Battell began to rethink its involvement, and once again Carlson had to be saved.

James Dessauer, the director of research for the Haloid Company, a small Rochester, New York, photo supply business, wanted to diversify his firm's holdings. He read an article by Carlson and negotiated with Battelle for the manufacturing and marketing rights to the dry copier. Successful in acquiring the rights, Haloid changed the name of the process from the cumbersome *electrostatic photography* to *xerography*. Carlson was never employed by Haloid, but he served as a consultant and ultimately held 42 patents pertaining to the copier.

On 22 October 1948, ten years to the day after the crucial Astoria experiment, Haloid demonstrated its copying machine at the annual meeting of the Optical Society of America in Detroit. The mildly enthusiastic reception convinced company executives that more work was necessary. By 1956, Haloid was convinced that the machine was finally ready for the general market. Their first effort, although successful, had only limited public appeal because of its huge size, large price tag, and complicated operating procedures. In 1958, Haloid recognized its niche in the business market and changed its name to Haloid-Xerox to reflect the success of its major product. In 1959, the company introduced the Xerox 914, the first copier to use ordinary paper, and only then began to realize the impact of Carlson's invention. In 1961, Haloid-Xerox dropped its original name and became Xerox.

Carlson's name seldom makes the list of great inventors studied in schools. Nonetheless, he became a multimillionaire from his Xerox royalties, and his machine may be second only to the computer in changing business practices across the world.

See also:
Xerography.
References:
"Chester F. Carlson Dead at 62; Invented Xerography Process." *New York Times*, 20 September 1968.
Feldman, Anthony, and Peter Ford. *Scientists and Inventors*. New York: Facts on File, 1979.
Flatrow, Ira. *They All Laughed*. New York: HarperCollins, 1992.

Cartography

Cartography is the art and technology of mapmaking.

Maps are most commonly used to communicate information about our position on the earth. However, they are also used to convey additional information associated with geography. Topographical maps, for example, use thin brown contour lines to represent points of equal elevation. The spacing between contour lines indicate the steepness of the land. Other symbols on these maps reveal the location of roads, trails, bridges, railroads, buildings, power lines, and quarries. Color and shading can be used to indicate lakes, streams, marshes or swamps, woods, and tundra.

Maps used by mariners convey information about coastlines, ocean depths or currents, prevailing winds, magnetic declination, hazards, buoys, and other features. Still other maps are used to reveal variation in vegetation, temperature, population, and other variables as a function of geography. In fact, any phenomenon related to geography, be it national boundaries, religious affiliation, trade, disease, or other data, can be mapped.

Maps are essentially models used to represent the surface geography of a region and whatever particular variables of interest pertain to that geography. The region may be the universe, the solar system, the earth, an ocean, a country, a state, a county, or someone's property. The most commonly used maps are road maps, which are two-dimensional, scaled models of the relative locations of roads and towns as seen from above.

All modern maps are views of the land as

seen from above. Since aerial photography began, photographs taken from airplanes have served as the basis for maps. An aerial photograph is projected onto a screen and matched with known points on the ground whose latitude and longitude are known with great accuracy. The images are adjusted to fit the known positions on the ground. From these images, the maps are drawn and the symbols added.

Today, photographs of the earth can be taken from satellites orbiting the earth. These photographs, used in televised weather reports, show the clouds covering parts of the earth from the perspective of an observer far above the earth's surface.

Scaling

Maps are drawn to scale so that the distances between points on a map can be easily determined. Scales commonly used are 1:24,000, 1:50,000, 1:62,500, and 1:250,000. A scale of 1:24,000, for example, means that 1 inch on the map equals 24,000 inches along the earth's horizontal surface.

Normally, the top of a map is north and the bottom is south. This means that west on the map will be to the viewer's left and east to the right. As a result, lines of latitude will be horizontal and lines of longitude vertical. On some maps, one arrow indicates true north and another arrow indicates magnetic north. Only along so-called agonic lines does a magnetic compass needle point in the direction of the north pole.

Coordinates and Mercator Projections

In 1406, Ptolemy's *Geography* was translated from Greek into Latin and became available to European scholars. By using geographical coordinates (latitudes and longitudes), Ptolemy was able to establish fixed points on the earth that could be measured relative to the stars. The distance between the points on Ptolemy's maps were based on distances estimated by marching Roman soldiers.

The maps of Europe, the Mediterranean, and the Middle East that were drawn after the rediscovery of Ptolemy's work were rea-

sonably accurate. However, mappings of the Far East were vague and the distances, which were based on sailors' dead reckonings, turned out to be greatly exaggerated. It was the supposed great distances to the Far East that led to the idea that a faster route might be found by sailing west across the Atlantic.

In 1568, the Flemish mapmaker Gerardus Mercator devised a system that allowed him to project the three-dimensional globe onto a two-dimensional map. The map of the world familiar to most people today is drawn according to the Mercator projection. Mercator's cartographic innovation was to project the earth's spherical surface onto a cylinder. To see what he did, imagine a hollow cylinder with a diameter that matches earth's diameter. The cylinder encircles the earth and extends above and below it. They touch only at the earth's equator. Now imagine a point of light at the earth's center that casts a permanent image of the earth's surface features on the surrounding cylinder. When the cylinder is unwrapped, it will be a map of the world made by Mercator projection.

The lines of longitude drawn on a Mercator projection map will be vertical and parallel, while the lines of latitude will be horizontal, parallel, and increasingly farther apart as they move north or south from the map's equator. Since lines of longitude on a globe grow closer together until they meet at the poles, east-west distances are greatly exaggerated on a map made by Mercator projection. Because lines of latitude on a globe are separated by equal distances, north-south distances on a map made by Mercator projection will also be inflated. As a result, on these maps the areas of places such as Antarctica and Greenland are grossly magnified. This can be observed quite clearly by comparing a globe to a map of the world made by Mercator projection.

It was Mercator who gave rise to the word *atlas* as the term used to describe a book of maps. In his later years, Mercator prepared a bound series of maps. On the cover of his book was a drawing of Atlas, a Titan condemned to support the heavens on his shoulders. Thereafter, a book of maps was referred to as an atlas.

Cassini's Map of the World

Truly accurate maps of countries and the world were not made until the end of the seventeenth century, when the astronomer Giovanni Domenico Cassini and his staff, with the support of King Louis XIV, prepared the first accurate map of France and of the world at the Observatoire de Paris.

Cassini had developed a means of determining virtually simultaneous moments in time anywhere on earth. He determined the periods of the moons of Jupiter and could predict the exact time when each would be eclipsed or emerge from behind the planet. From his observations, he prepared tables of the times that various events regarding the moons of Jupiter would take place. Because Jupiter is so far away, its moons appear the same regardless of your position on earth. Consequently, by using Cassini's tables, an astronomer anywhere in the world could determine the exact time in Paris when a particular moon entered or emerged from Jupiter's shadow. By knowing the local time based on the position of stars or the sun, the longitude of the astronomer's position could be established. Latitude could be easily determined from the altitude of the North Star or the sun.

Using Cassini's tables, benchmarks (markers that indicate the precise latitude, longitude, and altitude of that point) were established across all of France. Using these well-determined points of position, France was carefully mapped, and its coast was revealed to be about 50 miles east of where earlier surveys had placed it. King Louis XIV, upon learning of the new mapping, is reported to have said, "I paid my academicians well, and they have diminished my kingdom!"

Cassini next sent missions to various parts of the world to establish benchmarks. From these 40 or so positions, he mapped the world. The points on his map are within 50 miles of the more accurate mappings established today.

References:

Gardner, Robert. *Where on Earth Am I?* New York: Watts, 1996.

Harley, J. B., and David Woodward, eds. *The History of Cartography,* vol. I . Chicago: University of Chicago Press, 1987.

Harley, J. B., and David Woodward, eds. *The History of Cartography,* vol. II. Chicago: University of Chicago Press, 1993.

International Encyclopedia of Communications. New York: Oxford University Press, 1989.

Morrison, Philip, and Phylis Morrison. *The Ring of Truth: An Inquiry into How We Know What We Know.* New York: Random House, 1987.

Williams, Trevor I. *The History of Invention: From Stone Axes to Silicon Chips.* New York: Facts on File, 1987.

Cartoon

The word *cartoon* comes from the Italian *cartone,* meaning "cardboard" or "paper." The term refers to the preliminary working drawings of chalk, charcoal, or pen used by artists to transfer the outline of their works to other surfaces. The drawings were used in creating stained glass, mosaics, tapestries, and, especially, frescoes. Michelangelo used *cartones* in creating the ceiling of the Sistine Chapel. Often damaged in the transfer process, the *cartones* were casual drawings not intended for circulation, much less for artistic consideration.

In the eighteenth century, cartoon art established itself not only as a vehicle of political persuasion, but also as a means of social protest. English artists like William Hogarth, recognized as the first great cartoonist, moved away from personal caricature and focused on social satire. With the Industrial Revolution in full swing, Hogarth and his disciples sought to influence the moral and social affairs of the country. Thomas Rowlandson refined the political cartoon further, with assaults on the aristocracy, cabinet, and sometimes even the monarchy for the injustices of English society. Similarly, James Gillray assailed the English upper classes using a gallery of stereotypical spokespeople, from an old maid to the local parson to a barmaid.

The recurring nature of the characters made Gillray's work very popular.

The current meaning of the term *cartoon*—a drawing or painting used for amusement, education, or advertising purposes—derives from *Punch*, an English humor magazine. In 1843, the English government sponsored a competition to select mural designs for the new Parliament buildings. The *cartones* of the entries were put on exhibition. The satirical weekly decided to hold its own exhibition, parodying the overblown submissions. *Punch's* "Cartoons" appeared on 15 July 1843, and John Leech's "Cartoon No. 1" may be considered the first modern cartoon. The term quickly caught on with the public and was used to describe the full-page drawings regularly featured in the journal.

Cartoons soon spread outside of England. In Germany, David Chodorwiecki satirized contemporary society. Francisco de Goya published his "Capricho" etchings, which depicted the terrible state of human affairs in Spain. In France, Honoré Daumier became the continent's foremost cartoonist. In his drawings, Daumier portrayed all facets of French life, creating a portfolio that generations of historians have studied for the detail of everyday life. England even introduced the cartoon to China in the 1840s and to Japan in the 1860s. In America, eighteenth-century cartoonists devoted themselves to attacking the English Parliament and the privileges of the British. American cartoons were less artistic, simpler, and more concerned with making a point. The most famous early American artist was Benjamin Franklin, whose best-known work was the severed snake depicting the 13 colonies as segments of the snake with the legend, "Join or Die."

By the second half of the nineteenth century, editorial cartoons had become the mainstay of the profession worldwide. Photoengraving and improved printing techniques made reproduction of drawings more efficient and economical. Presses made the newspaper an important part of life, and the editorial cartoon drew readers to the inner sections of the paper. Thomas Nast was America's best-known editorial cartoonist. His biting criticism of New York City's "Boss" Tweed for *Harpers Weekly* earned him a national reputation.

By the 1890s, cartoons changed stylistically, adapting to a more literate population capable of grasping the subtle symbolism of simpler, less cluttered drawings. The simpler drawing was believed to have a more immediate impact on readers. The twentieth century saw continued development in the art form directed at increasingly more sophisticated consumers. The one-line caption and pictorial jokes without words are typified by the cartoons of *The New Yorker* magazine.

The gag, or humor, cartoon is a relatively new concept in cartooning. With the establishment and success of a number of humor magazines such as *Punch* and *Puck*, publishers realized that humor would attract readers more readily than political and social commentary. During the 1860s, cartoons were introduced that were less political or social in content but instead focused on local and ethnic satire. As usual, a technological change in mass communication—lithography—made these one-panel cartoons a national institution. The most significant American cartoonists in this field were Charles Dana Gibson and Hy Meyer.

See also:
Animation; Caricature; Printing.

References:
Horn, Maurice, ed. *The World Encyclopedia of Cartoons*. New York: Chelsea House, 1980.
St. Hell, Thomas Nast. "The Life and Death of Thomas Nast." *American Heritage*, October 1971.
White, David Manning, and Robert Abel. *The Funnies: An American Idiom*. New York: Free Press, 1963.

CAT Scan (Computerized Axial Tomography)
See Scanner.

CATV (Community Antenna Television)
See Television.

Cave Painting

Long before there were symbols to represent words, there were drawings, paintings, engravings, and carvings, both fixed and portable. Such art, some of it quite magnificent and some of it 30,000 years old, is probably the work of the Cro-Magnons from whom we descended. The prognathous Neanderthals, who disappeared about 35,000 years ago, left no such art, or at least none that has been discovered.

The first cave art was discovered in 1880 by Marcellino Sanz de Santuola and his daughter Maria in Altamira, Spain. Because no one at that time believed that such beautiful work could have been done by primitive people, another 20 years passed before the discovery was recognized as significant. In the meantime, additional discoveries of cave paintings were made in France, adding credence to the earlier discovery. The most concentrated areas of cave paintings discovered to date are in France and Spain, but findings have been made in other parts of Europe, South America, and Australia, and new caves filled with paleolithic art are now discovered frequently. Australian archeologist Rhys Jones has dating evidence to support his claim that humans were painting in Australia as early as 60,000 years ago, but doubling the age of the earliest human art makes Jones's claim a difficult one for most archeologists to accept, and many question his evidence.

Cave paintings usually depict animals, primarily horses, bison, wild cattle, deer, mammoth, bears, and cave lions. Often, dots or markings are found beneath or within the painting. Were these marks an indication of the number killed or needed?

The Paintings at Grotte Chauvet

A recent discovery of more than 300 cave paintings by Jean-Marie Chauvet, a government guard of prehistoric sites, and two others on 24 December 1994, near the French town of Vallon-Pont-d'Arc in the Rhone Alps, revealed seldom-seen paintings of panthers, hyenas, and an owl (which had never been seen on cave walls or ceilings be-fore), as well as running horses and rhinoceroses. The paintings at the site, now referred to as Grotte Chauvet, were regarded as forgeries by some archeologists and artists. Archeologists wondered why paintings of a panther, rhinoceros, and owl were found in this cave and not in others in the Mediterranean area. Alex Melamid, a Russian artist, claimed that the paintings were made by someone who had experienced photography because the positions of the legs of the running horses were so accurate. Prior to the "freezing" of motion photographer Eadweard Muybridge in the late nineteenth century, artists had great difficulty drawing running animals because they could not really see how the legs moved. In his opinion, the paintings might be a century old, but not a millennium.

Jean Clottes, the French archeologist who is now in charge of the research at Grotte Chauvet, originally estimated the paintings to be 17,000 to 20,000 years old. More recently, carbon dating involving eight pigment samples indicates that these paintings are about 30,000 years old, older and far superior in quality to the findings in the Cosquer cave near Marseilles, which are not as old. Confirmation of the age of the site leads archeologists to conclude that painting did not necessarily improve with time. Perhaps the painter or painters at Grotte Chauvet possessed a genius that was not repeated for thousands of years.

What Meaning Did Cave Paintings Have?

We will probably never know for certain what meaning the cave paintings had, but many believe the art was related to magical rituals associated with hunting. These Neolithic people may have believed that painting, engraving, or sculpting the animals would somehow improve their success as hunters of the animals they depicted.

On the other hand, the bones found in the cave, probably the remains of food eaten by the artists involved, are seldom from the animals painted on the walls, and the outlines of human hands frequently found on cave walls seem unrelated to the hunt. Reindeer, believed to be an important food source for these people, are rarely depicted in the caves.

In addition to hand prints and negative silhouettes of hands made from pigment brushed on or blown on through hollow bones, many caves reveal parallel finger tracings that sometimes loop and cross. Were they symbols for rivers or maps of food sources, or were they merely produced by people at play?

Regardless of their meaning, these paintings reveal that at least some of these people had exceptional artistic talent as well as superb powers of observation and memory. After extensive study of cave paintings, Annette Laming-Emperiare and André Leroi-Gourham found repeated patterns of horses and bison within the cave sites. Their findings suggest that the paintings were not done randomly but as a way of expressing an underlying theme or idea. The art must have been significant. It certainly required intense effort and planning. Scaffolds had to be built to reach the high walls and ceilings; colored pigments had to be sought and often prepared (many of the paints were not natural substances); animal fat had to be collected and placed on flat, concave stones, where it was burned to provide light; and people had to be freed from other duties, such as hunting, to produce these artistic gems. Whatever these early artists were trying to communicate through their work will likely remain a matter of speculation for centuries to come.

See also:
Carbon Dating, Forgery; Motion Photography.

References:
Caird, Rod. *Ape Man: The Story of Human Evolution*. New York: Macmillan, 1994.
Clottes, Jean. "Rhinos and Lions and Bears (Oh My!)." *Natural History*, May 1995.
Cockburn, Alexander. "'New Lacaux' a Forgery?" *The Nation*, 20 February 1995.
Johanson, Donald, Lenora Johanson, and Blake Edgar. *Ancestors: In Search of Human Origins*. New York: Villard, 1994.
Morell, Virginia. "The Earliest Art Becomes

Older—and More Common." *Science*, 31 March 1995.
———. "Stone Age Menagerie." *Audubon*, May/June 1995.
Putman, John J. "The Search for Modern Humans." *National Geographic*, October 1988.
Rigaud, Jean-Philippe. "Art Treasures from the Ice Age: Lascaux Cave." *National Geographic*, October 1988.

CD-ROM
See Compact Disc.

Cellular Telephone
See Telephone Switching.

Censorship
Censorship is the suppression of information of any kind. The term comes from the Latin word *censere*, meaning "to assess, estimate, or judge." It is generally divided into governmental censorship, which is widespread in authoritarian countries, and nongovernment censorship, which is widespread and often subtle in nature.

Government and Church Censorship
Governments often censor any political, military, artistic, scientific, or economic activity they regard as potentially subversive. In authoritarian nations the government often owns the newspapers, as well as radio and television stations, to ensure that the people see and hear only information that is favorable. If the means of communication are privately owned, censorship is maintained by terrorism or intimidation. But even democratic governments censor material, particularly in wartime, if it poses a threat to national security. During and after World War II, the United States censored all documents pertaining to the atomic and hydrogen bombs. The atomic bomb, which brought the war with Japan to a speedier end, was one of the best-kept secrets in American history.

The threat to authority that the printing press offered became evident shortly after its invention. Martin Luther and others made good use of printed matter during the Reformation, which began in 1517. Their actions led Pope Pius V to establish the Congregation of the Index in 1571 to decide which documents should be censored and placed on the Index—a list of manuscripts viewed as heretical by the Catholic Church. The index was first published in 1559 and persisted until the twentieth century.

In 1529, the English government published a list of books that were prohibited. Later, the government and the Church of England collaborated with printers to prevent the publication of any matter that might threaten established authorities. During the eighteenth and nineteenth centuries, the same government resorted to more subtle methods of censorship by taxing and licensing printers and prosecuting those who provided libelous material. However, during the nineteenth century, the effects of the Age of Enlightenment led writers such as John Stuart Mill to make telling cases against government censorship. Mill argued that censorship assumes the infallibility of the censor, an assumption that history had proven wrong. He further maintained that censorship stifles debate, creativity, and intellectual development, as well as the resulting increase in knowledge, and discourages the exposure of those who abuse their power.

In the United States, the founding fathers established a ban against censorship in the eighteenth century with the First Amendment to the Constitution, which guarantees freedom of speech and press. Despite this guarantee, the government does engage in censorship. Classification of documents is permitted to maintain national security, and public employees are not allowed to talk to the press. In fact, Central Intelligence Agency employees must agree never to publish any information acquired through their employment unless it is first reviewed by the agency.

Historically there has been cooperation between the government and the press through press conferences and press releases, and in other ways. The press has been generally cooperative in self-censoring infor-

mation that might place the nation's security at risk. During wartime, censorship has been extensive even in democratic countries, and citizens generally accept it as a way to reduce casualties and ensure victory. Judges often censor pretrial publicity that might jeopardize a fair trial, and police censor personal information that might invade an individual's right to privacy.

Nongovernment Censorship

Not all censorship is performed by governments. A considerable amount of censoring is the result of policies established by professional groups—publishers, radio and television stations, and virtually any organization that provides information to the public. A scientist who publishes must follow the conventions and standards related to the scientific method, and other professions and academic disciplines have similar guidelines. Editorial policies, broadcast standards, film production codes, and other policies govern what people will see, hear, and read. Censorship is often self-imposed for economic reasons. Newspapers are reluctant to publish stories that would place their best advertising customers in a bad light. Similarly, a magazine might decide not to publish an article that would offend a significant number of its readers for fear they might cancel their subscriptions. Writers often censor their own material in order to sell their books or articles.

Public schools and libraries also censor material. Teachers or administrators choose what students will read, or restrict what they assign, because of pressure from parent organizations or other groups. However, the courts have generally upheld the students' rights to circulate underground newspapers and other information free of adult censorship as long as it is not disruptive.

The state of Texas, through its Textbook Commission, in effect has the power to censor America's textbooks. All textbooks used in Texas public schools must be approved by the Textbook Commission, and because Texas has one of the nation's largest student populations, publishers censor material that they know will offend that commission in order to prevent a loss of sales.

School libraries as well as textbooks have come under the scrutiny of various pressure groups that find certain books objectionable and petition school boards to ban such books or teachings. They may object to biology texts that include the theory of evolution, particularly human evolution; to objectionable language; to unpatriotic ideas; or to material they regard as immoral. Although the Supreme Court has ruled that parents and students have the right to ask for court reviews of such decisions, the same court has ruled that school board decisions violate the First Amendment only if they suppress ideas "in a narrowly partisan or political manner."

In *Memoirs* v. *Attorney General of Massachusetts* (1966), the Supreme Court ruled that a work was pornographic and not protected by the First Amendment only if it was "utterly without redeeming social value." However, in *Miller* v. *California* (1973), the Supreme Court ruled that a work did not have to be "utterly without redeeming social value" to be pornographic. The Court's decision established stricter guidelines for determining whether material can be censored. The new tests were:

- Would the average person, in terms of contemporary community standards, find the work as a whole to appeal to the prurient interest?
- Does the work depict, in a patently offensive way, sexual conduct defined by state law?
- Does the work, taken as a whole, lack serious literary, artistic, political, or scientific value?

The result of this decision left local communities with greater control over pornography. Despite the Supreme Court's decision that laws prohibiting the dissemination of obscene material do not violate the First Amendment, adult bookstores and theaters that show X-rated movies continue to thrive because they rate books and films as inappropriate for children under certain ages. However, the Court's decisions have been protective of children, and it did uphold the Federal Communications Commission's (FCC's) decision requiring broadcasters to confine the airing of programs containing indecent language to times when children would not be expected to be watching or listening.

Censoring the Internet

How does one deal with obscenity on the Internet, an international network of computers? One approach was tried on 8 February 1996, when President Clinton signed the Communications Decency Act (CDA), which was passed by Congress in an effort to eliminate pornography from the Internet and keep such material from children.

The CDA imposed fines up to $100,000 and prison terms up to two years on anyone who knowingly exposed minors to indecency online. On the surface the bill looked good, and its passage made Congress and the president look good in an election year, but the Justice Department said that it had all the laws it needed to pursue child molesters who use the Internet. Unfortunately, the bill sought to criminalize online transmission of words and images that fell short of the tests established by the Supreme Court for determining when material is pornographic. Although the FCC can control the output of television stations by refusing to issue licenses, controlling individual computer users would seem to be an impossible task.

In June of the same year, a panel of federal judges pronounced the law in violation of the First Amendment. The judges noted that obscenity and child pornography are already illegal under existing statutes and that online materials that might be regarded as indecent are generally indicated as inappropriate for children. In the opinion of these judges, it is up to parents and teachers to determine what online materials may be viewed or downloaded by children. The Supreme Court in June 1997 agreed unanimously that the CDA was an infringement of the First Amendment. Justice John Paul Stevens wrote, "The interest in encouraging freedom of expression in a democratic society outweighs any theoretical but unproven benefit of censorship."

A better solution may lie in self-control. Internet users sending indecent or pornographic material can label material not appropriate for children, and many commercial and local providers, such as America Online, already allow parents to make some sites off-limits for their children. The role of access providers could be expanded to require them to deny entry to sites where pornographic material is available. Of course, the problem of foreign sites remains. Does an access provider have the right to forbid access to a foreign site on the Internet?

A number of software programs now available, such as Net Nanny and Cyber Patrol, make it possible to filter out most online pornography or sexually explicit material. However, these programs are not foolproof. It is likely that only parental vigilance can prevent children from accessing inappropriate material.

In February 1997, Thomas Menino, mayor of Boston, responded to angry cries from parents and city councilors who had discovered that children were viewing pornographic material available on the Internet at public libraries. He ordered that software filters be installed in all city computers to block out any sexually explicit material. Although Menino's response was supported by teachers and many librarians, Deborah Liebow, assistant director of the Office for Intellectual Freedom at the American Library Association, was quoted as saying, "Censoring the Internet at home is appropriate, but it is not appropriate at public institutions like libraries."

See also:
Defamation; Pornography.
References:
Caragata, Warren. "Crime in Cybercity." *Maclean's*, 22 May 1995.
Dibbell, Julian (reported by John F. Dickerson). "Muzzling the Internet." *Time*, 18 December 1995.
Geeta, Arand. "Library Internet Censoring Planned." *Boston Globe*, 13 February 1997.
Huber, Peter. "Electronic Smut." *Forbes*, 13 July 1995.
"Only Disconnect." *The Economist*, 1 July 1995.
Orr, Lisa, ed. *Censorship: Opposing Viewpoints*. San Diego, CA: Greenhaven Press, 1990.
Pornography: Women, Violence, and Civil Liberties. New York: Oxford University Press, 1992.
Quittner, Joshua, Viveca Novak, et al. "Free Speech for the Net." *Time*, 24 June 1996.

Census

A census is an official count or enumeration of people, houses, businesses, or any other items of interest. The term is most commonly used to describe a count of the population of a nation or some other political entity. A census is one of the most significant sources of information about a country. It provides data on the standard of living, demographic trends, employment, education, and any of a number of other categories. The count has become a necessity in planning policy at all governmental levels.

Census information of some sort has been collected since the ancient era. The early simple censuses did not account for all the people but were used almost entirely to establish a tax base and to determine who in the population was eligible for military service as well as for required labor. The Chinese might have conducted a census as early as 3000 B.C., and a number of counts are mentioned in the New Testament. The Greeks also had censuses, but the records are so fragmentary that it is difficult to determine a pattern or garner much information. The Romans carried out the most complete ancient censuses at 5-year intervals for over 400 years. Again, not much of the record survives, and most of what scholars know is from secondary historical references.

During the Middle Ages there were few noteworthy censuses. Most were local enumerations under the auspices of the church. One major exception was England's *Domesday Book*. Commissioned by William the Conqueror and begun at Christmas 1085, the census was completed in September 1087. Its purpose was to establish a more equitable basis for taxation. It listed landholders—even the king and his nobles—their lands, houses, tenants, and servants. Remarkable in its detail and precision, the *Domesday Book* set a census standard for several centuries. Nonetheless, provincial, municipal, parish, or county censuses continued to be the rule well into the sixteenth century. Spanish and Incan archives indicate that the civilization centered in Peru might have made the first known census in the New World. As early as 1576, colonial powers, concerned about the extent of their landholdings and population, conducted censuses in the New World.

The first modern, scientific census designed to obtain a statistical profile on the population for governmental and scientific use was conducted in 1666 in New France (now Canada). The French conducted regular censuses until they lost Canada to the English in 1763. In 1871, Canada inaugurated a regular decennial (ten-year) census. The first modern count in Europe might have been in Iceland in 1703, but generally the honor falls to Sweden's 1750 census. By the early nineteenth century, most European countries undertook censuses of some sort. Certainly, reliable enumerations were standard in most countries by the mid–nineteenth century, although they were not always taken on a regular basis. England established its census in 1801. At the same time, France instituted its count at five-year intervals. Russia joined the rest of Europe in 1897, and since Germany was not unified until 1871, its censuses are also fairly recent.

The U.S. Census

One observer noted that the United States is the only country in the world that has regularly counted its population since the nation's inception. The U.S. Census is unique because it is an integral part of the government. The Constitution mandated a decennial population census to determine the number of representatives from each state and for taxation purposes. The initial 1790 census took 18 months to complete at a cost of $45,000, a staggering sum for a country already burdened by a war debt. The population was rather crudely fixed at 3.9 million people. The census was concerned primarily with counting the population and asked only one extra question—the occupation of

each respondent. Censuses have become much more elaborate and detailed over time, establishing dozens of individual population characteristics.

The first 12 censuses, 1790 through 1900, were conducted without a permanent census organization. Congress passed decennial legislation appropriating the necessary funds and simultaneously began a search for a supervisor and a staff. For the first nine censuses, through 1870, the supervisors were U.S. marshals, and the field-workers were their deputies from the country's judicial districts. The poorly trained, poorly paid staff could never profit from experience the way permanent workers might have. In 1880, the census supervisor position was established in an overhaul of the system. Many consider the 1880 census the first modern enumeration, due to the professionalization of the count.

In 1902, Congress established the Census Bureau to plan and direct the collection of information on a number of different categories and to publish the results in government reports. The bureau, directly responsible to Congress, operates under the auspices of the Department of Commerce. Headquartered in Maryland, the Census Bureau has 12 field offices in major cities.

The administration and content of the census have grown considerably in scope since the 1790 effort, reflecting the nation's needs and interest. The country's involvement in the first Industrial Revolution was reflected in the questions on manufacturing in the 1810 census. Questions on mining, agriculture, and fisheries were added to the census in 1840. Originally part of the decennial count, government interest and planning required more frequent reports in the modern era, and the Census Bureau responded with reviews every five years. Census reviews on manufacturing, now done every two years, record such factors as the number of plants and workers, as well as the cost of equipment, material, and labor. The statistical account of mining, similar to manufacturing, described the cost of development, operation, and labor, and the value of mineral production. The agricultural inventory details the number and types of livestock, how land is used, and the amount of farm production. Faced with a nearly overwhelming influx of immigrants, the nation included statistics on nativity and immigration for the first time in 1850. The Census Bureau compiles data on housing, business, construction, foreign trade, and other topics according to governmental needs on weekly, monthly, quarterly, and annual schedules. The bureau also functions beyond these counts. It processes statistics for other government agencies and also serves as a consultant to foreign governments in their census work and statistical research.

As the demand for raw data has increased, the census has adjusted its collection techniques to fulfill its many purposes. Toward the end of the nineteenth century, Herman Hollerith, an employee of the Census Bureau, used punch cards to record data in code form. Hollerith's machines, ancestors of the modern computer, tabulated the results of the 1890 census, saving an estimated $5 million and two years of processing time. By 1940, it was obvious that the punch card system was too slow and labor intensive. Technology developed during World War II provided the basis for electronics in computing machines, and in 1950 the Census Bureau used the first computer, UNIVAC, in tabulating its newest results. The new machine worked nonstop for 14 months, seven days a week, to process census figures. UNIVAC was retired in 1963, but computers remain an integral part of the census system.

In 1940, the census employed sampling techniques for the first time in collecting data. Based upon mathematical probability, sampling used responses from a small, representative group to provide an accurate profile of the greater nation. Improvements in the accuracy of the count and quality of the data continued into the 1960s with Film Optical Sensing Device for Input to Computers (FOSDIC) and self-enumeration. FOSDIC was the transfer of census questionnaire data from microfilm to magnetic computer tapes. Self-enumeration was a shift away from face-to-face interviews to answering a questionnaire. Self-enumeration failed when originally tried in the 1930s, but in the 1960 and 1970 censuses it was remarkably successful. The forms, returned to the bureau, were reviewed with the aid of computers, and if there were problems or if a questionnaire was not returned, census agents called at the home to clarify any questions.

Census material is used in a variety of ways. It is most evident in government planning at all levels. Programs concerning immigration, housing, welfare, employment, and education are developed from the census. The bureau also publishes the *Statistical Abstract of the United States* (an annual summary of the social, political, and economic life of the United States) and a smaller *Pocket Data Book*.

See also:
Computer.

References:
Anderson, Margo J. *The American Census: A Social History.* New Haven, CT: Yale University Press, 1988.
Carson, Gerald L. "The Great Enumeration." *American Heritage,* December 1979.
Taeuber, Conrad. "Census," in *International Encyclopedia of Social Sciences.* New York: Macmillan and the Free Press, 1968.

CETI
See Communication with Extraterrestrial Intelligence.

Cipher
See Cryptology.

Citizens' Band (CB) Radio
See Radio and Society.

Clay Tablet
See Cuneiform; Hieroglyphics.

Clock
Clocks are devices designed to communicate time and to divide it into discrete units such

as hours, minutes, and seconds. Time-related communications based on clocks or similar timekeeping devices has become essential to our culture. Clocks tell us when to awaken, when to go to work or school, when to come home, and when to go to bed. We have become so structured by clock time that we ignore, whenever possible, natural sun-determined time. Not only our work but our entertainment, transportation, government, and community functions are regulated by time as communicated by clocks.

Before Clocks

Mechanical clocks were preceded by a number of other timekeeping devices such as sundials, water clocks, hourglasses, and various uniformly burning timers such as candles and oil lamps. Ancient Egyptians measured the passage of time during the day by the movement of a stick's shadow. Although the movement of the shadow through equal angles did provide hours of equal length, ancient Egyptians did not think that dividing a day into precisely equal intervals was particularly important. At night they used water clocks (clepsydras) to measure time. The volume of water flowing through a hole served to measure the passage of time.

In ancient Greece the sandglass was used, as it is today, to measure relatively short time intervals. Larger sandglasses, designed to measure longer units of time and more correctly referred to as hourglasses, appeared during the Middle Ages. The clergy and teachers used them to time their sermons or lectures.

A calibrated glass reservoir below the burning wick of an oil lamp was also used to measure time. Time was measured, too, by the length of a candle that remained after burning. At English auctions, for example, a pin was often stuck in the side of a lighted candle. When the pin fell, the person holding the bid at that moment was considered the buyer.

Mechanical Clocks

The exact origin of the mechanical clock is unknown, but by the fourteenth century several clocks driven by falling weights existed in Europe. The weights were attached to a horizontal shaft (foliot) that turned a gear one tooth at a time. The gear's turning was restricted by a vertical shaft (verge) with stops (pallets) that interrupted the weights' fall each time the pallet engaged one of the gear's teeth. This regulating device that causes the periodic interruption of the clock's movement is known as the escapement. It is characteristic of all mechanical clocks.

The earliest clocks had but one hand—the hour hand—to indicate time. They were reset according to a sundial, which at the time was a more accurate timekeeper than clocks. In fact, the direction that the hands of a clock turn has its origin in the way that the shadow moves across a sundial in the Northern Hemisphere.

Mechanical clocks improved with the replacement of the foliot by a swinging pendulum. As Galileo had discovered in the late sixteenth century, the period of a pendulum is constant as long as its length is constant and its amplitude small. From the late seventeenth century onward, there were dramatic improvements in clock making. Metalcutting machines were used to make escape wheels with identical teeth. Escapement mechanisms improved, and temperature-compensated pendulums were developed to avoid changes in length that occur when the temperature of metal rises or falls.

Spring-driven clocks appeared late in the fifteenth century and, because these clocks could be made much smaller than weight-driven timepieces, pocket watches were first made a century later. The first wristwatches appeared in 1790 but did not become popular until after World War I. In spring-driven timepieces, a spring drives the gears that turn the minute and hour hands. A balance wheel, which oscillates like a pendulum, controls the speed at which the gears turn.

By the early part of the twentieth century, most electric power in the United States was being transmitted as 60-cycle alternating current. Clocks with synchronous electric motors—motors turning at the same rate as the oscillating electric current—were replacing pendulum or spring clocks in American homes. By 1940, half the clocks sold in the United States were electric.

Clocks and Geography

Spring-driven clocks could be used on ships at sea where rolling waves would quickly disable a pendulum clock. In 1763, John Harrison built a very accurate spring-driven clock known as a Marine Chronometer. Harrison's timepiece lost less than two minutes in 147 days.

Harrison's invention allowed a ship's navigator to accurately determine his longitude. Latitude could be obtained quite easily by measuring the altitude of Polaris or the sun, but determining longitude, degrees east or west of the meridian through Greenwich, England, was a far more difficult task without good clocks. The sun was known to move 15 degrees per hour, and its midday position (the peak of its arc), or local noon, was easily determined, but unless the navigator knew the time along the Greenwich meridian, it was impossible to know the ship's exact longitude. A chronometer set for Greenwich time made it easy to determine longitude.

Navigators on modern ships establish both their latitude and longitude by using the NAVSTAR Global Positioning System (GPS). Satellites in orbits about the earth's poles transmit radio signals that can be picked up by a receiver on the ship. A computer is used to compare the time a signal was sent with the time it is received. Because the radio signal travels at the speed of light (300,000 kilometers per second), the distance to the satellite is readily calculated. Three such signals from different satellites will quickly determine the ship's position to an accuracy of a few meters.

Quartz and Atomic Clocks

Quartz clocks were first developed in 1929. These timepieces contain quartz crystals, which, when subjected to a varying electric potential, vibrate at a frequency that depends on their dimensions. By 1940, quartz clocks were being manufactured that were accurate to within 0.002 second per year. In 1969, following the development of microelectronics, quartz wristwatches appeared on the market.

Atomic clocks are the world's most accurate timepieces. They are the clocks found in NAVSTAR satellites. These clocks have no face, hands, or readout, but they serve as a world standard for time. Tracking time according to events that take place on the atomic level, these clocks are accurate to one second in 300,000 years.

In atomic clocks, the radiation emitted or absorbed by atoms serves the same purpose as did pendulums or quartz crystals in earlier clocks. Most atomic clocks use cesium atoms, which absorb microwaves with a frequency of 9,192,631,770 hertz as they "jump" from one energy level to another. This frequency, which is unchanging and characteristic of cesium atoms, became the standard for time in 1967. One second was redefined to be 9,192,631,770 periods or wavelengths of radiation emitted by the cesium-133 atom.

Today, International Atomic Time, which is based on the cesium clock, is periodically compared with mean solar time, our clock time, after it has been corrected for the effects of the precession of the earth's axis. Tidal friction is slowly reducing the earth's rate of rotation, causing mean solar time to fall behind atomic time. When the two times differ by more than 0.9 second, a "leap second" is added to clock time.

References:

Crumpley, Elsa. *It's about Time: All You Need to Know about the Origin of Time and Calendars.* Saratoga, CA: R & E Publishers, 1992.

Dale, Rodney. *Timekeeping.* New York: Oxford University Press, 1992.

Gardner, Robert. *Experimenting with Time.* New York: Watts, 1995.

Jones, Roger S. *Physics for the Rest of Us.* Chicago: Contemporary Books, 1992.

Morrison, Philip, and Phylis Morrison. *The Ring of Truth: An Inquiry into How We Know What We Know.* New York: Random House, 1987.

Williams, Trevor I. *The History of Invention: From Stone Axes to Silicon Chips.* New York: Facts on File, 1987.

Clothes

The items worn on the human body often convey information; clothes have a "language" of their own. Unlike ordinary language, clothes cannot be used to reason or describe objects not present, but clothes may well indicate a person's sex, relative age, status, profession, religion, and possibly much more. However, the message conveyed cannot be changed without changing the clothing. A candidate who goes to a job interview with lipstick stains on his collar and mustard on his sleeves shouldn't count on being hired.

The primary function of clothing is to help control body temperature and protect us from the environment, but clothing can tell us much more about the person who is wearing it. Clothing is frequently associated with status. The executive wears a pinstripe suit, a conservative necktie, dark socks and shoes, and a three-pointed handkerchief in the pocket of his jacket, while the mail clerk wears casual trousers or dungarees and a denim shirt.

We readily recognize that someone wearing white cotton shorts and T-shirt and a sun helmet is in a very different climate than someone dressed in an anorak or a space suit. A man wearing a tuxedo and accompanied by a woman in a long evening dress is attending a very different social event than a couple sporting shorts, sneakers, and baseball caps. From their attire, we can readily distinguish the participants at a wedding from those at a funeral, graduation, or bar mitzva.

Often we can tell a person's occupation by his or her clothing. This is certainly true of a police officer or a firefighter, but uniforms or clothes can also be used to distinguish a carpenter, a painter, a laboratory technician, or a nurse. We can identify the sport played by most athletes simply by looking at the clothes they wear. Even from century-old photographs we can identify baseball and football players.

Their attire can often identify the members of a culture or a social unit. We can readily distinguish a bedouin from a western European, a bohemian from a bourgeois, a Scotsman from a Bavarian when both are in folk dress, and a member of an urban youth gang from a preppie. Those associated with a particular culture or social group can tell much more about other members from their clothing than can outsiders. An American sees a kalbak as simply a brimless red hat, but to a Russian it indicates that the wearer is a doctor. To most of us, the mutz worn by an Amish male is simply a blue- or charcoal-colored jacket. But to members of the culture it identifies him as Amish, babtized, and less than 35 years of age if the mutz is blue and over 35 if the jacket is charcoal in color.

Culture also determines when and where certain clothing is appropriate. Americans would agree that it is proper to wear pajamas to bed but not to a dinner party. On the other hand, it is not inappropriate to let children dressed in pajamas say good-night to their parents and the dinner guests. Furthermore, in Western culture what is regarded as proper dress changes with time. What is in fashion changes from year to year, and those who can afford to be fashionable can be distinguished from those who can't or won't. And attire appropriate for different social functions changes with time as well. Several decades ago it would have been unthinkable for a man to attend church or eat at an expensive restaurant without a jacket and tie. Today, acceptable dress at these places covers a wide range of attire.

Often, clothing is worn to send a clear message. A sheriff's uniform at a crime scene makes it clear that someone with authority is present. The Halloween costumes of children tell homeowners that "trick-or-treaters" are approaching. The black horizontal striped pants and shirts worn by prisoners leaves no doubt about their present residence, and a prostitute's revealing street attire is readily recognized by potential customers. On the other hand, a plain-clothes detective, a thief in a mechanic's coveralls, an ensign in a captain's uniform, or a bachelor wearing a wedding ring all know that clothing can be used to hide one's true identity.

See also:
Language; Nonverbal Communication.
References:
Blair, Gwenda. "Dress Smart for Your Job."
Mademoiselle, October 1995.
Crawford, Michael. "The Language of Prom Dresses." *New Yorker*, 12 June 1995.
International Encyclopedia of Communications.
New York: Oxford University Press, 1989.

Code
See Cryptology.

Coherer

The coherer is a device designed to respond to electromagnetic radiation. It was invented by the English physicist Oliver Joseph Lodge in 1889 following D. E. Hughes's discovery that zinc and silver filings become more conductive when placed near an electric spark.

Heinrich Hertz, who was the first to generate electromagnetic waves and demonstrate their similarity to light, used an induction coil and spark gap to generate the waves and a single coil with a very narrow spark gap to detect the radiation. While Hertz's device worked over relatively short distances, it was not sufficiently sensitive to detect radiation at positions more than a few yards from the source. Lodge found that a more sensitive detecting device, which he later called a coherer, could be made if the spark gap were enclosed in an evacuated glass tube filled with loose metal filings (95 percent nickel and 5 percent silver) that was connected across a battery and a galvanometer. The resistance of the loose filings was enough to prevent significant current flow if connected to a single-celled battery, but even a weak oscillating electric field produced by a distant electrical spark caused the filings to compact (cohere), reducing the resistance and allowing a measurable current to flow—a current that could be detected by the galvanometer. In 1894, at a British Association meeting in Oxford, Lodge demonstrated a coherer that detected electromagnetic waves 150 yards from the source.

Unfortunately, after detecting a spark, the coherer would remain stuck in its conducting state and not respond to further signals. In the 1890s—still the mechanical age—the solution was a windup device called a tapper, which produced a series of rapid taps on the glass following the detection of an electromagnetic pulse. The tapping broke up the cohering filings so that they could respond to the next signal.

In their early experiments with wireless radio during the last decade of the nineteenth century, Marconi, in Italy, and Popov, in Russia, made use of coherers to detect signals. Without the device, their work could not have gone forward. Marconi used a tapper that was activated by the flow of current through the coherer so that the coherer was resensitized after every wave pulse. He also placed a bell in a secondary circuit so that the signal produced a sound as well as a deflection of the galvanometer needle.

While the coherer was an improvement over Hertz's spark gap, it was still relatively insensitive. It was the development of the vacuum tube diode by Fleming in 1904 and the triode by De Forest in 1906 that led to the ultimate success of radio as a form of voice as well as telegraphic communication.

See also:
Electromagnetic Waves; Marconi, Guglielmo; Radio.
References:
Asimov, Isaac. *Asimov's Encyclopedia of Science and Technology.* Garden City, NY: Doubleday, 1964.
Canby, Edward Tatnall. "More Marconi."
Audio, August 1995.
Davidovits, Paul. *Communication.* New York: Holt, 1972.

Color Printing
See Printing.

Communication among the Hearing Impaired

People who are hearing impaired are usually not able to effectively use the language common to most people. Factors affecting

Hearing-impaired and deaf students at the California School for the Deaf try out the radioear teaching set, a device designed to determine the degree of "latent hearing" in each student and amplify the voice of the teacher accordingly. The school, pictured here in 1930, followed the oral method, which emphasized lipreading and auditory training.

hearing-impaired persons' use of ordinary language include the degree and pattern of individual hearing loss and the way in which they are taught to communicate.

Since the sixteenth century, the oralism-manualism controversy has centered on how deaf people should communicate—the oral method versus the manual method. The oral method promotes the teaching of speech to the deaf, whereas the manual method advocates the use of manual communication such as sign language and fingerspelling.

Manualism was the predominant method until the mid–nineteenth century, when oralism began to gain popularity. Alexander Graham Bell, whose wife was deaf, was instrumental in popularizing the oral method. He was a strong supporter of oralism and donated a large part of his fortune to support schools and programs that used this approach. In 1890, the Alexander Graham Bell Association for the Deaf (AGB) was formed to support oral methods of teaching deaf stu-

dents. The association aids schools in efforts to teach speech, speechreading, and the use of residual hearing.

Oralism

Oralism uses speech, speechreading, auditory training, and hearing aids, where possible, to help deaf people communicate. This method advocates teaching deaf people to speak and to understand speech through speechreading.

Speechreading has been called lipreading, but it involves more than reading lips. The deaf person also watches for visual cues from facial expressions and the position of the jaw and tongue. Cued speech is a method of supplementing speechreading. The speaker uses hand shapes made near the chin to represent specific sounds while speaking, which helps the deaf person identify sounds that cannot be distinguished through speechreading. Cued speech is used in many educational programs for hearing-impaired students in Australia, but it is not widely used in the United States.

Auditory training is a program for teaching hearing-impaired individuals to use the minimal hearing they possess. Hearing aids, instruments that amplify sound, are an important part of auditory training. In auditory training, hearing-impaired individuals develop their individual ability to detect, discriminate, and identify different sounds, such as environmental sounds as compared to speech sounds. The hearing aid can be programmed to match the needs of each user. However, if a person's hearing loss is one that distorts sound, the hearing aid will only amplify the distortion. It cannot eliminate the distortion.

Manualism

Manualism is the method of communication that was brought to the United States by Thomas Gallaudet and Laurent Clerc in the early nineteenth century. Gallaudet had gone to Europe to learn about different methods used to teach the deaf. He returned with Clerc, a French instructor, and in 1817 founded the first school for the deaf in the United States, in Hartford, Connecticut.

In the manual approach, the deaf learn to communicate through some type of manual communication, such as American Sign Language (ASL). There is also the total communication approach, a blend of the oral and manual methods. In this method, deaf persons communicate using a combination of speechreading, sign language, and their own voices. The manual communication used most often in the total communication approach is one of the signing English systems, rather than ASL. ASL has its own word order and is a true language, whereas the signing English systems present signs using English word order and are systems developed for teaching deaf people to communicate rather than true languages. There is a great deal of controversy surrounding which type of manual communication should be taught to deaf children. Advocates of ASL, including the Deaf Culture, contend that ASL is the most natural and efficient way for deaf children to learn about the world and that signing English systems are awkward and slow. Advocates of the signing English systems contend that it is easier for children to learn English by using the signing English systems because one can sign and speak at the same time and with the standard English word order.

Devices to Aid the Hearing Impaired

Rapid technological advances in the late nineteenth and twentieth centuries have led to the development of many devices to help deaf individuals. Auditory training has been enhanced by advances in the development of better hearing aids and by computer-assisted instruction with devices such as speech production aids that help people who are deaf to monitor and improve their own speech.

Group-assistive listening devices help hearing-impaired people hear at school or at a lecture. A radio link is established between the teacher or lecturer and the hearing-impaired individuals. The speaker wears a small microphone-transmitter, and the listener wears a receiver, which can be either a personal hearing aid or a headphone. Using FM radio frequency, the device produces a level of sound that is comparable to having the speaker 6 inches away from the listeners' ears.

Telephone communication for the hearing-impaired or deaf person is done through teletypewriters, or TTY. With a TTY, a person can communicate by placing the telephone receiver into an acoustic coupler and typing a message, which is sent through the telephone lines to another TTY user, who sees the message on a visual display similar to a small computer screen.

Special flashing light systems that are attached to sound-sensitive apparatus let someone who cannot hear know that a telephone, doorbell, or alarm clock is ringing. There are also vibration signaling devices, such as smoke alarms or alarm clocks, that vibrate the bed or pillow when activated to awake the person. Hearing-ear dogs can be used in similar ways to point out the source of a sound, alerting their masters when a doorbell rings or a baby cries.

Closed captioning for television programs is available when a special device that makes captions visible on the screen is attached to a regular TV. Sign language interpreters are sometimes used on television shows. Interpreters often sign for the deaf at political speeches and at some theatrical performances. Real-time graphic display, a new type of technology, allows rapid captioning of live presentations such as public speeches.

A medical procedure involving cochlear implants has been developed. This controversial process utilizes an electromagnetic coil with an electrode, which runs into the cochlea of the inner ear, and an external coil. A microphone worn by the deaf person picks up sound, which is transmitted to the external coil and then to the internal electrode. It enables a person with profound sensorineural hearing loss to make use of residual hearing but is considered controversial since members of the Deaf Culture feel the procedure is too intrusive. They do not consider themselves handicapped, but rather a linguistic minority whose education should be a type of bilingual education consisting of ASL as the primary language and English as the secondary language.

— *Barbara Gardner Conklin*

See also:
American Sign Language; Communication among the Visually Impaired; Keller, Helen Adams; Sign Language.

References:
Giangreco, C. Joseph, and Marianne Ranson Giangreco. *The Education of the Haering Impaired*. Springfield, IL: C. C. Thomas, 1970.
Hallahan, Daniel P., and James M. Kauffman. *Exceptional Children*. Boston: Allyn & Bacon, 1994.
Heward, William L. *Exceptional Children*. Engelwood Cliffs, NJ: Prentice-Hall, 1995.
Watson, Thomas J. *The Education of Hearing Impaired Children*. Springfield, IL: C. C. Thomas, 1967.

Communication among the Visually Impaired

The blind and visually impaired depend on their listening skills and tactile sense to learn about their environment. Since speech is acquired through mostly auditory perception, visually impaired individuals are able to use spoken language effectively. However, the visually impaired miss such cues as facial expressions, hand gestures, or body movements, which are used to express feelings.

The areas of communication most difficult for the blind or visually impaired are reading and writing. Depending on the degree and type of disability, a visually impaired person will be able to use different methods of written communication for reading and writing. Some are able to read with the help of magnifying devices. Books are available in large print, print can be magnified with glasses or handheld lenses, and television cameras or computers can produce enlarged images of print on a monitor.

One method of reading and writing for the visually impaired was developed in France during the nineteenth century by Louis Braille. The Braille system, shown in Figure 1, is based on a rectangle made of six raised dot positions. By changing the number and position of the dots in the rectangle, all 26 letters, ten numerals, and punctuation can be represented. Braille print, which is read by feeling the raised dots that signify letters, uses many abbreviations (called contractions) to save space and allow faster reading. For example, words such as "the" and "for" have their own special contractions.

To write in Braille, a person can use the Perkins Brailler, which resembles a small typewriter. It has six keys to represent the positions of the six dots. Keys can be pressed down simultaneously to leave embossed print on paper.

Another way to write in Braille is with paper, slate, and stylus. Paper is held in a slate and the stylus is pressed through openings representing the six dot positions to make indentations in the paper. The indentations are made from right to left in reverse order so it can be turned over and read left to right.

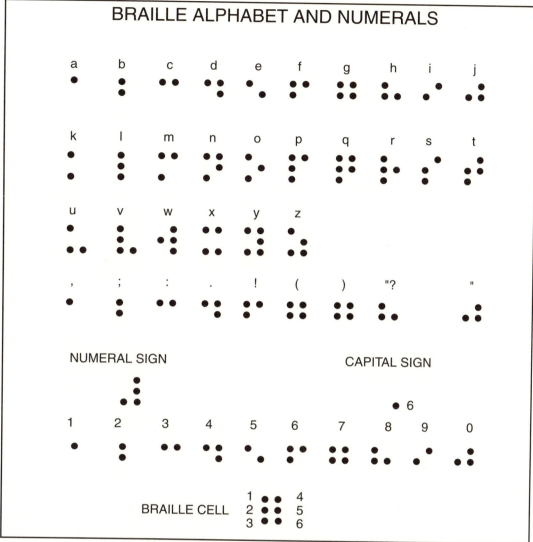

Figure 1. Braille alphabet and numerals. The six dots of the Braille cell are arranged in two columns of three, as shown. Dot 6 before a letter signifies that it is upper case. The numeral sign (dots 3, 4, 5, and 6) indicates the next symbol is a number. The first ten letters correspond to numbers 1 through 10.

Technology and the Visually Impaired

Techniques for communication by writing and reading among the visually impaired have been greatly aided by the technological advances of this century. Computers incorporated in such machines as the Kurzweil Reading Machine and the Kurzweil Personal Reader that are now available can convert print into speech. With these computers, called optical character recognition systems (OCRs), printed material is put on a scanner and the words are read at about the same speed as human speech by an electronic voice. Devices with electronic voice can help the visually impaired in other ways, too. There are alarm clocks, spelling aids, and calculators that can talk.

Another electronic device developed to help the visually impaired read is the Optacon. This method, which is slower than computers with synthesized speech, uses a camera to convert print to tactile letters that the reader feels with the index finger. With VersaBraille one can record Braille onto tape cassettes that can be played back on its reading board. A laptop computer, VersaBraille II, has a keyboard with six keys that correspond to the six dot positions in Braille, a numeric scale, and a joystick. The written material can be checked on a tactile display, and the text can be printed in Braille or regular print.

Television viewing for the visually impaired has been aided by the development of larger screens. The Descriptive Video Service, begun in Boston, adds an audio narrative of important visual features of a television program during dialogue lapses.

— Barbara Gardner Conklin

See also:
American Sign Language; Communication among the Hearing Impaired; Keller, Helen Adams; Sign Language.

References:
Hallahan, Daniel P., and James M. Kauffman. *Exceptional Children*. Boston: Allyn & Bacon, 1994.
Heward, William L. *Exceptional Children*. Englewood Cliffs, NJ: Prentice-Hall, 1995.

Communication with Extraterrestrial Intelligence (CETI)

The idea that communication with extraterrestrial intelligent beings (CETI) may be possible has existed ever since it became evident that we do not live in a geocentric universe. The emergence of space travel during the latter half of the twentieth century intensified speculation about extraterrestrial communication among scientists and science fiction writers.

Life and Space

Although some early scientists and writers speculated about life on other planets and moons within our solar system, the conditions necessary for life—proper temperatures, water, and an atmosphere—exist only on earth. There is evidence that water once existed on Mars, and its equatorial temperatures are appropriate; however, its atmosphere is carbon dioxide with a pressure only 0.6 percent that of earth's.

Fossil records indicate that life on earth began about 3.5 billion years ago, shortly after the earth had cooled. Since the earth itself is believed to be about 5 billion years old, the evidence suggests that life emerges quite quickly under the right conditions.

In 1953, Harold Urey and Stanley Miller at the University of Chicago carried out an experiment to discover what would happen in an environment similar to the conditions believed to exist in earth's early atmosphere. They placed water vapor, methane, ammonia, and hydrogen in a sealed flask through which they sent electrical sparks to simulate lightning. After a few weeks, they found a brown residue rich in organic molecules, including amino acids, the building blocks of protein. Their experiment suggested that the ingredients necessary for the origin of life were available in earth's primitive atmosphere. Furthermore, there is solid evidence that organic materials exist in outer space. The presence of radiation characteristically emitted by organic molecules has been discovered by radio astronomers.

Despite the early emergence of life on earth, what we call intelligent forms of life (meaning us) have probably existed for only a hundred millennia, although humanoids have existed for several million years. Clearly, the emergence of intelligent life on another planet—life that can communicate through speech, writing, and the many technological means of communication—is less likely than other forms of life. Nevertheless, the vastness of our galaxy, let alone the universe, suggest that the evolution of intelligent life is probably not limited to this tiny planet.

Attempts to Communicate or Listen

Human attempts to communicate with other intelligent life began with Project Ozma in 1960. Frank Drake, a radio astronomer at the National Radio Astronomy Observatory in Greenbank, West Virginia, sent signals toward the stars Tau Ceti and Epsilon Eridani. Since these stars are about 11 light years from earth, a reply might have been expected by now, but none has been detected.

Drake even developed an equation to estimate the number of civilizations in the Milky Way Galaxy that might be expected to try to communicate with other forms of intelligent life. His equation, shown below, contains eight variables.

$$N = Rf_g f_p \, nf_l f_i f_c \, L$$

N is the number of civilizations in the galaxy that can be expected to be attempting to communicate with other intelligent forms of life. That number depends on R, the rate of star formation; f_g, the fraction of the stars that might produce conditions essential to life; f_p, the fraction of the stars with planets; n, the percentage of earthlike planets; f_l, the fraction of habitable, earthlike planets that could be expected to give rise to living organisms; f_i, the probability of life emerging from such planets; f_c, the fraction of those planets where life exists that might develop intelligent civilizations who would attempt to communicate with other intelligent life; and L, the expected average lifespan of such an intelligent civilization.

The bases for making these estimates of the number of life-forms that might try to communicate with one another are so uncertain that the number ranges from one (earth) to more than a million. One thing on which everyone agrees is that any attempt to communicate would be through electromagnetic radiation, not space vehicles. To communicate directly by sending mass through space requires so much energy and time that any intelligent life-form would opt for radiation, which requires far less energy and travels at the maximum velocity—the speed of light.

Based on the unlikely assumption that they might encounter an alien intelligent civilization, the *Pioneer 10* and *11* spacecraft each bear an engraved plaque with a message from earth, and *Voyager 1* and *2* carry recorded messages of words and music. All four spacecraft are heading toward interstellar space.

In 1974, a three-minute message was directed toward M 13, a star cluster in Hercules. It was sent by means of the 305-meter radio telescope at the Arecibo Observatory in Puerto Rico. Since these stars are 24,000 light-years away, no immediate response is expected. Several other attempts to initiate communication with extraterrestrials have been made, but no answers have been received, at least none that have been detected.

A number of programs are in place to search for extraterrestrial intelligence (SETI). SETI differs from CETI in that a search does not imply that any communication will take place, only that signals from an intelligent life-form may be detected. A SETI program established by the National Aeronautics and Space Administration (NASA) in 1992 was canceled for lack of funding the following year, but the privately funded SETI Institute in Mountain View, California, under the direction of Frank Drake, established project Phoenix to continue some of the work begun by NASA. In addition, the Billion-channel Extra-Terrestrial Assay (BETA), sponsored by the Planetary Society, has established a two-hemisphere program. A huge 84-foot dish-like radio telescope near Harvard University scans the sky over the Northern Hemisphere, while a similar instrument at the Argentine Institute of Radio Astronomy surveys the southern sky. BETA sweeps the sky, capturing and analyzing radio waves with a frequency of 1,400 to 1,720 megahertz. If a signal is detected that meets the criteria for being unnatural, the telescope will return to that position in the sky. If a similar signal is detected, BETA computers will alert astronomers to the anomaly.

Of course, no one is certain what frequency an alien intelligence would use or for what frequency they might tune their antennas. That is why BETA searches many channels for signals that appear unique and possibly of alien origin. In 1959, Philip Morrison and Giuseppe Cocconi suggested a frequency of 1,420 megahertz (a wavelength of 21 centimeters) as appropriate for extraterrestrial communication. Their suggestion was based on the fact that 1,420 megahertz is the frequency emitted when an electron in an atom of hydrogen, the most abundant element in the universe, reverses its spin. Furthermore, stars are dim in this low-energy (microwave) region, absorption is minimal, and the galaxy is quiet at these frequencies except for the cosmic background left over from the Big Bang.

It is believed that the most detectable signals would be transmitted as pulses on a narrow bandwidth or as a constant tone. What information might we expect to find in an alien signal? Perhaps the simple repetition of a prime number, a language encoded and taught in successive lessons, or binary digits that, when arranged properly in rows and columns, would provide recognizable patterns or pictures.

A skeptical Congress has been reluctant to fund CETI or SETI projects designed to look for what some have called "little green fellows." Some scientists, however, oppose CETI projects not because they doubt the existence of extraterrestrial intelligent beings but because they fear that communication with aliens more intelligent than ourselves could lead to an invasion of earth that would destroy the human race. However, by early 1996, the discovery of clear evidence indicating the presence of at least three planets orbiting stars within our galaxy has stepped up the search for extraterrestrial life.

References:
"Bagging the Little Green Man." *Natural History,* February 1994: 60.
International Encyclopedia of Communications. New York: Oxford University Press, 1989.
Kaufmann, William J., III. *Universe.* New York: Freeman, 1985.
Lemonick, Michael D. "Searching for Other Worlds." *Time,* 5 February 1996.

Compact Disc

A compact disc has a thin plastic surface with a spiral track consisting of pits of varied lengths that encode information in digital form. The information can be read by scanning the disc with a laser beam.

The first compact discs (CDs) were marketed in 1983. Unlike phonograph records, compact discs are not grooved, and there is no needle to place in the groove. In fact, no contact takes place between the disc and the instrument used to transfer the data to the amplifier. The discs, like computers, use a digital system of 1s and 0s. A disc, which is about 12 centimeters (4.75 inches) in diameter, has a spiral pattern of pits and unpitted or smooth surfaces that is several kilometers long. The tiny pits, separated by about 1.5 micrometers, are about 1 to 3 micrometers long, 0.5 micrometer wide, and 0.1 micrometer deep. (A micrometer is 0.001 millimeter, or a millionth of a meter.) As the disc turns, a system of mirrors and lenses focuses a scanning laser beam onto the pattern of pits, which do not reflect light, and the smooth unpitted surfaces in between, which do reflect light. The pulses of reflected light enter a photodiode, where the light energy is converted to electrical pulses. Since the pits do not reflect light, they produce 0s (no current); the unpitted surface produces 1s (electric current). The on-and-off electrical pulses constitute a digital signal that is the same as the signal that was recorded on the disc. This digital signal is then converted to its original analog form, amplified, and sent to loudspeakers.

In addition to an audio signal, the pitted disc also conveys information about the stereo aspects of the sound and the speed at which the disc turns. Because the rate at which the laser beam scans the pitted pattern is constant, the disc must rotate faster when the beam is near the center of the disc than it does when the beam is near the outside edge.

Making a Compact Disc

Making a compact disc begins with the master disc, a flat piece of glass coated with a chemical that is resistant to hydrofluoric acid, which can etch (dissolve) glass. The master disc is placed on a turntable, where it rotates beneath a very thin, pulsating laser beam. The laser is controlled by a digital signal derived from the original analog signals that came from microphones. When the laser is on, it burns away the chemical that coats the master disc. As the disc turns, the laser moves along a radius from a point near the disc's center outward to its circumference. The result is a spiral set of holes in the disc's coating.

The master disc is then placed in a hydrofluoric acid bath, which etches the glass that was exposed when the chemical coating was burned away by the laser. The result is a spiral pattern of tiny holes etched in the glass. This glass master disc can then be used to make copies on aluminum-coated clear plastic. These are the copies that are sold to the public.

Laser discs can also store video signals, and since more information can be stored on a laser disc than on a videocassette, a video disc will provide a better, more detailed television picture. Unlike a videocassette, a videodisc, which looks like an enlarged compact disc, cannot be used to record new programs. However, it does provide users with random access; that is, any part of the disc can be played without passing forward or backward through other parts of the recorded material. Because the laser beam can be controlled, it is possible to freeze particular frames, watch action in slow motion, and read written material, such as a magazine article, at any rate desired.

Compact discs have virtually replaced grooved phonograph records, which were used to record primarily music for a century. The quality of the sound from compact discs is so good that the demand for phonograph records has dwindled to the vanishing point.

The price of table-model compact disc players ranges from about $100 to $175. Single-disc models are generally less expensive than multiple-disc changers. Portable models range in price from about $100 to $250, and many of them can be connected to a sound system or a car stereo with a CD jack or an adapter.

CD-ROMs

CD-ROM discs look like compact discs, but the content is different. Instead of music they contain computer programs. The read-only memory (ROM) is utilized by a computer to give the user access to data stored on the disc. The information stored on CD-ROMs can be an entire encyclopedia with pictures and diagrams, journal articles, telephone numbers for the entire country, stock market information, or virtually any other data. Many libraries have a large number of CD-ROMs, and the discs are becoming popular among personal computer users as well. Many home computers are now equipped with CD-ROM players. The price of CD-ROM discs varies from about $10 to hundreds of dollars, depending on the content.

See also:
Analog and Digital Signals; Computer; Loudspeaker; Microphone.

References:
"Consumer Reports 1995 Buying Guide." *Consumer Reports*, 15 December 1994.
Gardner, Robert. *Communication*. New York: Twenty-First Century, 1994.
Macaulay, David. *The Way Things Work*. Boston: Houghton Mifflin, 1988.
The New Book of Popular Science. Danbury, CT: Grolier, 1992.
Science and Technology Illustrated, vol. 15. Chicago: Encyclopedia Britannica, 1984.

CompuServe
See Online Services.

Computer
Computers are devices designed to receive, process, store, and display information. The first computers were analog computers, mechanical devices with gears and levers that performed mathematical operations and displayed results as continuously varying quantities that were a function of the input supplied to the machine. Analog computers, such as the speedometers found in every car and the electric meters on every line leading to a power company's customers, are still the most prevalent type of computer.

Despite the prevalence of analog computers, we normally associate the term *computer* with the personal computers found in homes and schools or the mainframes used by large corporations and government agencies. These computers use digital signals and represent variables with symbols. Although digital computers do not use electrical circuits that can produce a continuously variable quantity, they can provide excellent accuracy by simply using as many figures as are found in the measurements used as input. Unlike analog computers, which are generally designed for one function, digital computers are general-purpose machines that will perform many functions. They can carry out calculations and compare, select, and organize numbers very rapidly. Because almost any data can be translated into numbers, digital computers can be used for writing, keeping accounts, assigning seats on an airplane or at a sports stadium, playing games, or filing (storing) vast amounts of data in letter, number, or graphic form.

Digital Data

Computers use the binary (base 2) system because it has only two numbers, 0 and 1. A 1 can be represented by an electrical pulse and a 0 by no pulse. Each digit (0 or 1) is called a bit, and letters or numbers can be represented by a byte (8 digits). Since each bit is either a 1 or a 0, 8 bits can produce 256 (2^8) different bytes. In American standard code for information interchange (ASCII), which is used to exchange data between different programs, the capital letter A is represented by 10000001 and a lower-case a by 11000001, a B by 1000010, a C by 1000011, and a Z by 1011010. Numbers and other symbols can be represented in a similar manner.

Computer Hardware

A computer's hardware consists of all the physical parts of which it is made. The hardware that makes up a personal computer includes a monitor, a keyboard and mouse, a main unit containing the central processing unit (CPU) and memory, one or more disc drives, and usually a hard disc and a printer. The monitor is an output device similar to a television screen—basically a cathode-ray tube (CRT) or video display terminal (VDT).

Laptop computers use liquid crystal displays. The results of the calculations, writing, drawing, or whatever outcomes have resulted from data input are shown on the monitor. If a printer is connected to the computer, the materials displayed on the monitor can be printed on paper or other material (hard copy).

Input data is usually fed to the computer by means of a keyboard and mouse that allow a user to type, draw, or select information. In some computers a stylus—a penlike device—together with a graphics tablet allows a user to write or draw images that can be used as input. Input data can also come from a scanner, digital camera, or modem, and the same modem can be used to provide output through a telephone line to another computer.

The heart of a computer's hardware is a main unit that holds the microprocessor, where the computer's CPU and memory units are located. The CPU contains the arithmetic/logic unit where all numerical and logical operations on binary digits take place and the control unit where all the various input and output signals are coordinated and sent along the proper circuits. The control unit contains the central clock (oscillator) that produces a steady and very rapid rate of pulses to control the rhythm of all CPU processes. Clock rates, which are generally measured in megahertz, determine the speed at which a computer can work.

A personal computer's internal memory unit, which is part of the main unit, contains two types of memory—read-only memory (ROM) and random-access memory (RAM). It might, for example, hold 1 megabyte of ROM and 8 megabytes of RAM. ROM is permanent memory that contains the programs or data a computer needs to do its work. As the name implies, it cannot be accessed or changed and does not disappear when the computer is turned off.

RAM, also called "read and write" memory, is in a sense the user's computer work space, because information stored in RAM can be accessed and changed. In using a word-processing program, for example, the words that appear on the monitor are part of the computer's RAM. The contents can be changed or erased entirely, and the material will disappear when the computer is turned off. However, the material in RAM can be transferred and stored in an external memory device, such as a hard or floppy disc or a tape backup unit. That stored information can then be transferred back to the computer's main unit for additional processing at a later date.

Computer Memory

A memory chip in a computer is essentially a grid of circuits laid out in miniature like the streets of a well-planned city. At the intersections are storage cells (solid-state components) that store one bit of information. If the cells are arranged in groups of eight, each location (address) will hold one byte of data. In a RAM chip, capacitors can be used to store bits. A positive voltage across a capacitor can be used to represent a 1, while a negative voltage can represent a 0. One end of the capacitor is connected to a pair of diodes that maintain the capacitor's charge. The other end is connected to a grounded resistor. The stored bit is "read" by reducing the voltage across the diodes to zero so that the capacitor discharges, producing a positive or a negative voltage across the resistor that is amplified to produce a reading of 1 or 0. The memory can be restored by feeding back the amplified output to the resistor.

A ROM chip is also a grid of conductors, but it retains its memory cells even when it is disconnected from a power source. If the cell is the storage site for a 1 bit, the grid lines (address and data lines) are connected by a diode. If a 0 bit is stored, there is no diode connection.

Hard or floppy discs or tape use magnetism as a storage medium. A hard disc is a metal disc (or a stack of such discs) coated with a thin layer of a magnetizable material such as an alloy of nickel, iron, and cobalt. A floppy disc, which holds less data than a hard disc, is a flexible plastic disc coated in a similar way. Information is transferred to the disc and read in much the same way as it is

on a tape recorder. Electrical pulses in a head produce a magnetic pattern that is simply oriented as a north-seeking or a south-seeking field to indicate a 1 or a 0. Although data is written and read in much the same way as on a tape recorder, the data on a disc, unlike that on a tape, can be accessed at any point. The information need not be presented in a sequential manner.

Finally, data can be written and read by using an on-off laser beam to produce pitted and reflective regions on a plastic disc. Such discs, sold as CD-ROMs, are now an integral part of most personal computers because they can store vast amounts of information. The contents of an encyclopedia, graphics and all, can be stored on a single 4.8-inch (12-centimeter) disc.

Computer Software

Computer hardware is just plain dumb unless it is told what to do. It is software—the instructions the computer needs to operate—that enables the hardware to work in useful ways. There are two levels of software. The first is the operating system, which controls all the computer's actions. It consists of the instructions that enable the computer to read information from discs, interpret signals from the keyboard, schedule the various tasks the computer will be asked to perform, monitor these tasks, detect errors, and direct output to the proper channel. The second layer, the one that users are aware of, consists of applications that make it possible to do word processing, accounting, drawing or painting, establish a database, send E-mail, or connect to the Internet. The application programs must be written so that they can function within the parameters of the operating system.

Kinds of Computers

The most common computers are the personal computers (PCs) that can be purchased for a little more than $1,000 and are found in millions of homes, most schools, and many small businesses. A few years ago PCs had memories that were limited to a few thousand bytes and could carry out a limited number of tasks. However, with the rapid development of microelectronics and integrated circuits that allow thousands of resistors, capacitors, diodes, and transistors to be placed on a single tiny silicon chip, PCs now have RAM memories that are measured in megabytes, and hard discs that can store gigabytes of data. Personal computers can now operate programs that even the largest computers could not handle 15 years ago.

Mainframe computers are much larger than PCs, have considerably more memory, are faster, and can operate a number of different programs simultaneously. They are expensive and generally owned by large corporations or government agencies. People using a mainframe usually work at terminals that are connected by cable to the computer. Each of a thousand or more terminals may be using a different program, but the computer processes data so quickly that it can output information far faster than all the users can input it.

Supercomputers are very expensive, high-speed machines with vast amounts of memory. They are used in military and scientific research that require complex calculations. For example, meteorologists use them to develop models of world weather systems in which large amounts of data are required and the variables are numerous. Supercomputers have also made it possible to expand the Internet to tens of millions of users.

See also:
Analog and Digital Signals; Compact Disc; Computer Addition; Computer Programming; Computers and Society; Internet; Microprocessor; Modem; Number; Scanner; Tape Recorder.

References:
Haber-Schaim, Uri, et al. *PSSC Physics*, 7th ed. Dubuque, IA: Kendall/Hunt, 1991.
International Encyclopedia of Communications. New York: Oxford University Press, 1989.
Macaulay, David. *The Way Things Work.* Boston: Houghton Mifflin, 1988.

Computer Addition

The operations that take place inside a computer are numerous and complex, and only the basic principles of how a computer adds two numbers will be presented here.

Binary Addition

The concept of binary addition is essential to understanding how a computer adds numbers, a process that it can do repeatedly and very rapidly. Normally, we work in base 10, which requires 10 symbols—0, 1, 2, 3, 4, 5, 6, 7, 8, and 9. For large numbers, the location of the symbol that represents a particular digit determines the power of 10 by which it is multiplied. For example, $349 = 3 \times 10^2 + 4 \times 10^1 + 9 \times 10^0$; that is, 3 hundreds, 4 tens, and nine ones $(300 + 40 + 9)$.

Sometimes, as when we add two numbers such as 175 and 56, we have to "carry"; that is, we have to add a 1 to the next column on the left. Adding the 5 and 6 in 175 and 56 results in 11, so we write down a 1 and carry a 1 to the next column, as shown below. The 1 we carry represents the additional 10 we needed when we added 5 and 6. Now we add the left column of 1, 5, and 7 to get 13. We write down the 3 and carry the 1 to a new column, where it represents ten 10s, or 100, giving us a grand total of 231.

```
1 | 1 numbers carried
  175
   56
  231
```

Using base 2, there are only two symbols, 0 and 1. In base 2, a number like 7 is written as 111; 5 is written as 101:

$$7 = 1 \times 2^2 + 1 \times 2^1 + 1 \times 2^0;$$
$$5 = 1 \times 2^2 + 0 \times 2^1 + 1 \times 20.$$

Clearly, more digits are needed to express numbers in base 2 than in base 10. Furthermore, the "carry" operation will be more frequent in base 2 because even the addition of 1 and 1 moves us to the next power of 2 $(1 \times 2^0 + 1 \times 2^0 = 1 \times 2^1$. Consider, for example, adding 3 (11 in base 2) and 1 (which is 1 in any base) in base 2. The result is

```
1 | 1 numbers carried
  11
   1
 100.
```

Table 1. Addition in Base 2				
Addition needed	Addends A_1	A_2	Total Sum	Carry
0+0	0	0	0	0
0+1	0	1	1	0
1+0	1	0	1	0
1+1	1	1	0	1

Table 2. An AND Gate		
Inputs I_1	I_2	Output (0)
0	0	0
0	1	0
1	0	0
1	1	1

The number 100 in base 2 is equal to 4 in base 10.

An adding machine designed to work in base 2 must have the properties shown in Table 1. Such addition is one of the basic jobs of a computer. The rest of this entry will focus on how that is done.

Table 3. An OR Gate		
Inputs I_1	I_2	Output (0)
0	0	0
0	1	1
1	0	1
1	1	1

Computer Gates

Within a computer are devices called gates, which are designed to transmit or turn off the electrical pulses sent by the central processing unit's (CPU's) rhythmic clock (oscillator). These gates consist of many very tiny diodes, resistors, capacitors, transistors, and connecting conductors. One type of gate, known as an AND gate, is shown diagrammatically in Figure 1. Like all computer gates, the AND gate can accept only two types of input —a 1 (an electrical pulse) or a 0 (no pulse)—and its output likewise is either a 0 or a 1. The gate's name comes from the fact that its electronic components are so constructed that an electrical output of 1 (an electrical pulse) occurs only if both inputs I_1 AND I_2 in Table 2 are 1s; otherwise, the output is a 0. On the other hand, an OR gate

Table 4. A NOT Gate	
O	P
1	0
0	1

Table 5. A NAND Gate		
Inputs I_1	I_2	Output (P)
0	0	1
0	1	1
1	0	1
1	1	0

(Table 3), is so named because if either one OR the other of two inputs is a 1 (an electrical pulse), the output will be a 1. A NOT gate (Table 4) is simply a gate that reverses the output of another gate. It changes a 1 to a 0 or a 0 to a 1, a task easily accomplished by a transistor.

An AND gate followed immediately by a NOT gate is called a NAND gate. The output from a NAND gate is simply the reverse of

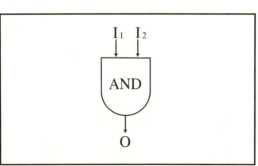

Figure 1. An AND gate, like an OR gate, accepts two inputs and produces one output.

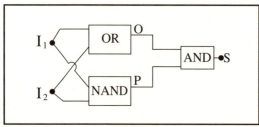

Figure 2. An Exclusive-OR gate contains an OR and a NAND gate in parallel, followed by an AND gate in series.

Table 6. An Exclusive-OR Gate

Inputs		Outputs		
I_1	I_2	O	P	S
0	0	0	1	0
0	1	1	1	1
1	0	1	1	1
1	1	1	0	0

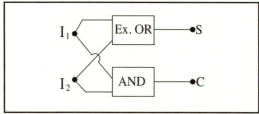

Figure 3. A half-adder consists of an Exclusive-OR gate and an AND gate in parallel. It accepts two inputs and produces two outputs.

Table 7. A Half-Adder

Inputs		Outputs	
I_1	I_2	S	C
0	0	0	0
0	1	1	0
1	0	1	0
1	1	0	1

the output from an AND gate, as shown in Table 5.

An OR gate connected in parallel with a NAND gate and followed by an AND gate in series, as shown in Figure 2, is called an Exclusive-OR gate (Ex. OR) because it produces an output of 1 if one or the other of two inputs, but not both, is a 1. (See Table 6.) If you follow the diagram in Figure 2 and the tables for the various gates, you will see that the outputs (O, P, and S) given in Table 6 are correct.

Half-Adders and Full-Adders

Connecting an Exclusive-OR gate and an AND gate in parallel produces a device known as a half-adder (HA), which will provide two outputs from two inputs as shown in Figure 3. The outputs from the inputs, as shown in Table 7, are just what is needed to add (output S) and carry (output C) binary digits (see Table 1).

Using three half-adders and an OR gate, as shown in Figure 4, the computer can add two numbers such as 3 (11) and 2 (10). The

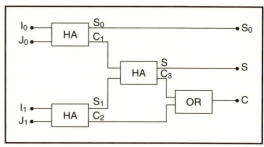

Figure 4. A full-adder, consisting of three half-adders and an OR gate, is used to add two two-digit binary numbers (I_1, I_0 and J_1, J_0), such as 11 (3) and 10 (2).

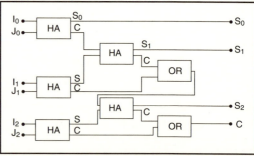

Figure 5. By extending the full-adder circuit shown in Figure 4, two three-digit binary numbers (I_2, I_1, I_0, and J_2, J_1, J_0) such as 101 (5) and 111 (7) can be added to obtain 1100 (12).

Table 8. Addition of Two Numbers Using a Full-Adder

J_0	I_0	J_1	I_1	S_0	C_1	S_1	C_2	S	C_3	C
0	1	1	1	1	0	0	1	0	0	1

digits in the number 10 are represented by inputs J_1 and J_0, respectively, as shown in Figure 4 and Table 8. The digits for the number 11 are represented by I_1 and I_0. Using Figure 4 and Tables 7 and 8, you can follow the operations carried out by the adder to obtain the three-digit result, 101, or 5 in base 10.

If the circuit shown in Figure 4 is extended as shown in Figure 5, it can be used to add two three-digit binary numbers. The output from the OR gate of the first full-adder is used as an input for the next full-adder. Of course, the circuit can be further extended to add binary numbers of any size.

See also:
Analog and Digital Signals; Capacitor; Computer; Computer Programming; Computers and Society; Diode; Internet; Microprocessor; Modem; Number; Transistor.
References:
Haber-Schaim, Uri, et al. *PSSC Physics*, 7th ed. Dubuque, IA: Kendall/Hunt, 1991.
Macaulay, David. *The Way Things Work*. Boston: Houghton Mifflin, 1988.

Computer Programming

Computer programming is the development of the sets of instructions that are needed to make computers carry out useful tasks. The work is done by computer programmers who prepare the flow sheets, write the programs, and install them in computer chips so that they will produce the results desired.

Computers are only dumb hardware until they are told what to do. The job of computer programmers is to prepare the instructions that will allow a user to tell a computer what to do. Using relatively few instructions, a computer can carry out very complex processes because it can repeat the same procedure again and again without becoming bored or tired. As a simple example, suppose you asked a computer to multiply 345 by 237. It would, in essence, accomplish the task by adding 345 to itself 236 times. It would take you a long time to do this, but a computer can do it in a fraction of a second because its circuits carry signals at very rapid speeds.

Programmers may write a computer program in what is called a high-level language, such as beginner's all-purpose symbolic instruction code (BASIC) or formula translation (FORTRAN) language, but at some point the program must be converted to a binary code. This code is called machine language because the computer can respond only to 1s and 0s—current on or current off. Thus, a simple program written in BASIC, such as the one on the left in Table 1, which asks the computer to add two numbers, must be converted to the machine language shown on the right before it can be transmitted to the computer.

The program written in BASIC is fairly easy to understand. It tells the computer to

Table 1. BASIC versus Machine Language

BASIC Program	Machine Language
10 READ A, B	1100 | 000000000001
20 LET C=A+B	1100 | 000000000010
30 PRINT C	1000 | 000000000001
40 DATA 2, 3	1001 | 000000000001
	1110 | 000000000011
	1101 | 000000000011

take two numbers, A and B, which in this case are the numbers 2 and 3 given in line 40, add them, and print the result.

On the other hand, the program written in machine language—a long string of 1s and 0s—is incomprehensible to most of us. The 16-digit number is divided into two parts as indicated by the vertical line (not part of the program) following the first four digits in each line. The first four digits are the operation code, which directs the CPU to make the correct connections needed to read two values, add them, store the sum, and print the sum. The last 12 digits tell the computer where these values are to be stored in computer memory.

Computer Languages
High-level languages, such as BASIC and Pascal, are based on a set vocabulary and grammatical rules. The language allows a programmer to use words to write a pro-

gram that tells the computer what to do. Usually a compiler is used to translate the words into machine language, which is the only language that can ultimately direct the computer.

There are many high-level languages. Ada, developed in 1979 by the military, was used in a variety of applications ranging from the operation of missile guidance systems to accounting. BASIC, considered the easiest language to learn, was developed at Dartmouth College in 1965 and was widely used in high school and college programming courses. Pascal, developed in 1971 and named for Blaise Pascal, a seventeenth-century scientist who built the first adding machine, has also been widely used to teach programming skills to high school and college students. Common business-oriented language (COBOL) was developed in 1959 for business purposes and is used by businesses throughout the world. FORTRAN— the oldest high-level language—was developed in 1956 at IBM for applications in science and mathematics.

Assembly languages, which use both words and numbers, lie between high-level languages and machine language. Assembly languages, too, must be converted to machine language—the only language that computers can "understand." Machine language consists entirely of binary digits, and each CPU must be addressed by a machine language based on its own specific hardware.

See also:
Analog and Digital Signals; Computer; Computer Addition; Computers and Society; Microprocessor; Number.

Computer Translation

Computer translations are translations of written material from one language to another that are carried out by a computer. Although computer translations can be performed quickly, their quality remains inferior to translations performed by competent humans familiar with the nuances of a foreign language.

A translator program recently has been developed that is quite successful in translating from German, French, and Spanish into English, and vice versa. Because word-for-word translations often miss grammatical structures such as idioms and word order, this program translates sentence by sentence. The program can be used with most popular word-processing programs and allows a viewer to see the original and translated languages side by side on the monitor. It also has an editing function that allows a user to make small corrections if necessary.

Another system, at the State University of New York at Buffalo, has great promise. It successfully converts Chinese ideograms into English words and phrases. Furthermore, as the program translates, it becomes better able to understand the text and so revises material it translated earlier. The program also has a memory and can answer questions about the text it has translated.

The program's capacity to revise and remember stems from Cassie, an artificial intelligence program that has been undergoing development at Buffalo for three decades. Such an approach is crucial in translating Chinese. Word order is much looser in Chinese than in English; consequently, it is necessary to understand the context in order to generate the appropriate translation.

Until computer translation programs are perfected, anyone preparing a document that will be translated, such as a business that reaches a worldwide market, should write as simply as possible. Avoid long, complex sentences or punctuation as well as parentheses, dashes, and quotations. Present computer translation programs produce the most accurate results when short, simple, declarative sentences are used.

A long-term approach, as suggested by George Jenner, might be to construct what he calls an "Interlingua"—a language that could act as an intermediary between any two languages. A computer would translate Japanese, for example, into Interlingua; Interlingua could then be translated into English, Russian, French, or any other language. Such an intermediary language would reduce the number of translations that a universal translating program would have to include. Jenner recognizes that the task might be impossible as well as costly. Many linguists do not believe Interlingua can exist; however, Jenner argues that if we can spend billions of dollars trying to find the nature of the universe or the sequence of the human genome, why not seek an Interlingua? At the very least it will improve translation programs, and a world that is growing increasingly interdependent would benefit immensely.

See also:
Computer; Computers and Society.
References:
Jenner, George. "Building a Babel Machine." *New Scientist*, 8 June 1996.
Sisco, Peter. "Power Translator Professional Speaks Your Language." *PC World*, March 1995.
"Translations: Computer Getting Better." *Business Week*, 11 December 1995.

Computers and Society

Computers have had a profound and continuing effect on all aspects of society, including the way we communicate.

History

As early as 1642, Blaise Pascal (for whom a computer programming language is named) devised a machine that would add and subtract numbers. Half a century later, Gottfried Leibniz developed a mechanical calculator that would carry out the four basic arithmetic functions. During the nineteenth century, Charles Babbage designed a computer that used binary numbers with punch-card input and output to generate tables of polynomials, but he lacked the engineering and technology needed to produce a practical machine. By the end of the nineteenth century, the required technology was available, and Herman Höllerith used a combination of electrical and mechanical sensing techniques to build a punch-card tabulating machine that was used in compiling the 1890 census. Höllerith's success led him, in 1896, to form the Tabulating Machine Company, which in turn merged with two other companies to become International Business Machines

Corporation (IBM) in 1924. IBM's punch-card systems became widely used for business accounting and for the extensive calculations required by some science researchers.

Military research during World War II gave rise to electronic calculators. John Mauchly and J. Presper Eckert, in 1946 at the University of Pennsylvania, developed the first functional electronic computer, ENIAC, in response to the military's need to rapidly compute accurate ballistic trajectories. ENIAC used vacuum-tube circuitry and required switches to be thrown by hand.

After John von Neumann joined the research effort, a new machine, EDVAC, was designed and finally built in 1951. EDVAC used punched cards to install instructions and data, and it could store a program for future use. During the same year, a similar computer, UNIVAC, was built by the Eckert-Mauchly Computer Corporation under a contract from Remington Rand. UNIVAC received wide public exposure because it was used to predict the election outcome in 1952. With just 7 percent of the returns available, the computer predicted the electoral vote to within 0.9 percent.

Although UNIVAC could make calculations rapidly and accurately, it was huge and very expensive to build and maintain. Because it contained 18,000 vacuum tubes, filled a large room, and drew nearly 150 kilowatts of power, heating filament burnouts requiring tube replacement were frequent. Recognizing that vacuum-tube technology was not appropriate for computers, manufacturers quickly took advantage of the new solid-state technology (semiconductor diodes and transistors) that had just emerged in 1950. By the end of the 1950s, IBM had sold 1,800 computers for use in business and science. During the same decade, assembly language and then high-level computer languages were developed to make the programming of computers an easier task.

The 1960s saw the rapid spread of computers into business, industry, and university education. By 1970, IBM had sold 35,000 computers, three times the number sold by 1964.

Reservation clerks work at computer terminals at the American Airlines national reservation office in Fort Worth, Texas. In the 1960s, computers allowed airlines to develop an electronic reservation system, which networked workers across the nation.

With the development of integrated circuits, computer size and cost decreased while capacity increased. Computers far better than those that sold for hundreds of thousands of dollars in the 1950s could be purchased for hundreds of dollars in the 1980s.

The development of simple computer-on-a-chip machines led to the computerization of many industrial procedures such as process control in chemical plants, robot-controlled operations, computerized automobile systems, and, of course, the development of personal computers with ever-expanding memories.

Computers and Communication

Computers made it possible for businesses to establish a central processing unit (CPU) with cables and telephone lines connecting it to input-output terminals as well as databases spread across the country. Airlines developed reservation systems that enabled workers in offices across the nation to know what seats were available for every flight. A central bank could be in constant communication with branches spread over a wide area, allowing transactions made in one bank to be immediately recorded at a central office. Telephone switching came under computer control; factories, businesses, and offices were computer automated; and computers gained ever-widening use in science, education, graphics, and homes.

Word-processing programs have made writing easier, and as more schools, businesses, and homes have come online, the Internet has gained increasing use as a means of communication. E-mail and voice mail enable orders, directives, and messages generated on computers to reach receivers far faster than any form of postal service. Vast amounts of information on virtually any topic are available to students, businesses, and researchers through connections to databases and experts in the user's field. People can exchange information on an informal basis at electronic chat centers and bulletin boards, and many people now work at home because their computers allow them to perform tasks as easily at home as in an office. As a result, businesses require less space and fewer workers, eliminating costly and time-consuming commuting between home and work.

Other Impacts of Computers on Society

The Department of Defense first established the Advanced Research Projects Agency (ARPA) and ARPAnet, a network connecting the computers of various universities and companies working on research projects for the military. The idea was to allow these research groups to exchange information and remain in contact should communications be disrupted by an enemy attack. Although ARPAnet was the forerunner of the Internet, which had profound effects on civilian communication, the military has always been involved in funding computer research and advancement because computers have played an increasingly significant role in the military. Although we normally associate military use of computers with remote sensing, targeting, and guidance systems for missiles and other weapons, the military uses computers for many purposes. These include administrative functions such as accounting, management and maintenance of systems, supplies, and training operations. The military has integrated its computers into a system of command, control, communication, and intelligence known as C3I. Computers made it possible to develop weapons with greater accuracy, velocity, and range and to establish better intelligence, surveillance, and reconnaissance by combining satellites and computers.

Of course, government use of computers is not limited to the military. As early as 1951, UNIVAC was used in compiling the U.S. census. Today, government agencies at the federal, state, and local level spend billions of dollars each year on computing and telecommunication services. Taxes can be filed electronically. Vast amounts of information exist in government databases, such as that of the Social Security Administration, and various government services can be accessed through computer networks.

During the 1970s, many schools began to include computer literacy and computer programming courses as part of their curriculums. Generally, a school had several terminals connected through a telephone line to a mainframe at a major university or corporation. Later, as microelectronics led to the production of reasonably priced personal computers, microcomputers became an important educational tool in many schools. Computer-assisted instruction using software that provided demonstrations, tutorials, and drill-and-practice in various skills became widely used. In some schools where adequate funding was available, computers are used to develop word-processing skills so that students could take advantage of the technology to make writing easier and readily correctable. In addition, computers are used to access educational games and databases, make use of spreadsheets in math and science courses, develop graphics for presentations, and analyze data. Teachers and administrators use computers for record keeping, grading, developing lesson plans and work sheets, and other school-related functions. The dormitory rooms in most colleges and in many preparatory schools now contain computers connected to a network so that students can not only access various sources of information but can also send papers and reports to their teachers who, in turn, can respond via the same network.

Although computers are now evident in nearly every school in the United States, many families cannot afford a personal computer. As a result, the educational opportunities open to the haves, as compared to the have-nots, continue to expand. The plight of the educationally disadvantaged is compounded by the fact that the schools attended by less-privileged children generally lack the funds needed to purchase sufficient computers to close the gap. However, in some states attempts are being made to provide educational equality by diverting more state funding to schools that serve poorer communities.

Although it was the military that fostered computer research and development, it was the post–World War II business world that made computers a vital part of their operating procedures and a saleable machine. Large businesses pioneered the use of computers for bookkeeping and record storage and manipulation. Airlines that developed automated ticketing and seat selection in the early 1960s were soon followed by hotels, theaters, sports arenas, car rental companies, time-share resorts, and other businesses that used computer networks. With the advent of microcomputers, even small businesses became computerized. Direct user transaction systems made possible by computers in the early 1980s enabled businesses and private investors to move funds among various accounts. Similarly, credit and automatic teller machine (ATM) cards made shopping and cash withdrawals easier. By the 1990s, online services enabled people to shop, bank, invest, and purchase tickets using their home computers. Advanced decision-support processes made possible by artificial intelligence programs have helped individuals and companies make decisions about financial planning, portfolio management, loans, and stock trading. The use of computers in commerce has reduced costs, improved quality, increased both capacity and the speed of transactions, and played a major part in the development of a global economy.

Computers and telecommunications, which rely on computerized equipment, have enabled companies to establish divisions around the world while maintaining central control. The development of transnational businesses and a global economy with fewer tariff barriers has been fostered by the deregulation and privatization of transportation, communication, and health organizations. The trend has been accompanied, too, by governmental organizations such as the United Nations, UNESCO, WHO, Law of the Sea Conferences, and others that extend beyond national boundaries. At the same time, professional, labor, consumer, and women's organizations have taken on a global nature that is reflected by a plethora of international meetings held by such groups.

A growing world economy has led to increased national specialization that has caused people to lose jobs or move to other states or nations. Developed nations that were formerly industrial in nature, such as the United States and Japan, now lead the world in electronic technology and information services, while the production of conventional goods has moved to less-developed nations where labor is cheap, tax exemptions are prevalent, and cooperative governments seek foreign investments.

A computer-dependent economy has had an impact on labor, but it has not produced the widespread unemployment foreseen by Norbert Wiener. Certainly, computers have made skills such as welding, filing, and recording data redundant, if not obsolete, but they have also led to a need for new skills such as supervision and knowledge production. Nearly half the jobs in the United States are now related to information services. Office employees spend more time than in the past at computer keyboards, where they do word processing, filing, copying, and communicating. Today's secretaries are able to work more efficiently than previously, but with far less variety in the tasks they perform. Computers provide managers with easy access to data, the ability to be more productive, and telecommunications that reduce the need to travel while increasing the rate of flow of information.

The ultimate effect of computers on labor is not known. It is likely that the growing separation in salaries paid to those needed to create new knowledge and to those engaged in low-paying personal services jobs will continue. The improved efficiencies made possible by computers may lead to a society that enjoys more leisure or to longer working hours for the haves and more unemployment among the have-nots.

See also:
Analog and Digital Signals; Compact Disc; Computer; Computer Addition; Computer Programming; Diode; Electronic Mail; Internet; Microprocessor; Modem; Number; Scanner; Tape Recorder; Transistor; Videotex; Voice Mail; Wiener, Norbert.

References:
Arbib, M. A. *Brains, Machines, and Mathematics*, 2nd ed. New York: Springer-Verlag, 1987.
Augarten, Stan. *Bit by Bit: An Illustrated History of Computers and their Inventors*. New York: Houghton Mifflin, 1984.
International Encyclopedia of Communications. New York: Oxford University Press, 1989.
Wiener, Norbert. *Cybernetics: Or Control and Communication in the Animals and the Machine*, 2nd ed. Cambridge, MA: MIT Press, 1961.

Copier
See Xerography.

Cordless Telephone
See Telephone.

Counterfeiting
See Forgery.

Cryptology
Cryptology is the art and technology of secret communications. Cryptography involves writing messages in a secret form using codes and ciphers. Cryptanalysis is the solution, or translation, of secret messages so that they can be read in plaintext.

Cryptology has been used almost as long as writing. It probably has developed in every culture that uses writing as soon as writing itself becomes so widespread that it is no longer a secret form of communication. In our own culture, parents sometimes communicate by spelling words when their preschool children are present. To the children, who cannot yet read or write, the parents are using a secret language.

Codes and Ciphers
Codes are cryptographic systems in which symbols, letters, or words have arbitrary meanings established by the author(s) of the system. If a code consists of words, the words are usually pronounceable. Ciphers are cryptographic systems in which plain-text letters usually are transposed or substituted based on a predetermined key. Because the words are made by transposition or substitution of letters, they are generally unpronounceable.

One of the most common codes, the Morse code, is not secret. It consists of a series of dots and dashes used to represent letters and was originally used to transmit messages by telegraph. Stores sometimes use codes to provide sales clerks with the price the store paid for items so they will not place them at a sale price less than the cost to the store. For example, the letters in the word *surveying* could be used to represent the digits 1 to 9, while the letter O could represent zero (0).

S U R V E Y I N G
1 2 3 4 5 6 7 8 9

Thus, a sweater labeled "$24.98 (SUVG)" would indicate that the cost to the store was $12.49.

In one of his Sherlock Holmes stories, *The Adventure of the Dancing Men*, Sir Arthur Conan Doyle used a code consisting of stick figures drawn to look like dancing men. Each figure represents one letter of the alphabet.

A ciphertext message might read "PHHW PH LQ WKH FDVEDK." If this message is written in the cipher attributed to Julius Caesar, when decoded it would read "MEET ME IN THE CASBAH." In the Julius Caesar cipher, a letter represents the third letter preceding it in a circularly arranged alphabet. Thus D = A, E = B, F = C, C = Z, and so on. Another approach is to substitute numbers for letters. For example, the letters in the alphabet might be numbered from 1 through 26, substituting 1 for *a*, 2 for *b*, and 26 for *z*. Or a more complicated numbering system might be chosen, using just three numbers, where *a* = 111, *b* = 112, *c* = 113, *d* = 121, and *z* = 332. Another simple example of ciphertext is HABSAC EHT NI EM TEEM, which is simply MEET ME IN THE CASBAH written backwards.

These are very simple examples of ciphers and codes. Much more complex ones can be and have been devised.

Technology and Cryptology

Telegraphy enabled secret messages to be transmitted rapidly and stimulated the development of more complex codes and ciphers that could be easily changed. With radio, messages could be received anywhere within the broadcasting range of the transmitter. However, because radio messages can be so easily intercepted, a number of countries created intelligence forces dedicated to the tasks of cryptanalysis and to devising more difficult codes and ciphers.

In 1917, Gilbert S. Vernam, an American engineer, invented an electromechanical ciphering device that converted plaintext messages on the punched tape fed to a teletypewriter into encrypted messages. On the receiving end, a similar device could convert the encrypted message into plaintext.

The ability of computers to store and manipulate billions of bits of information has led to the development of extremely complex cryptographic systems that can be shown to be secure if properly used. One such system is used by the Central Intelligence Agency, and banks and businesses now use computerized cryptography to ensure that electronically transferred funds are secure.

While cryptographers can scramble data into digital codes so that only those with the proper keys can decipher them, law enforcement agencies and the National Security Agency continue to demand that such cryptography be so constructed that they can use their own cryptanalysis programs to access secret messages. They argue that without being able to monitor messages sent by criminals, terrorists, and other enemies, vast numbers of American citizens could be killed and the nation crippled.

To help maintain the security sought by the National Security Agency, the Federal Bureau of Investigation, and other organizations, the State and Commerce Departments seize patent applications for cryptographic inventions and restrict their export. In fact, when considered for export, such inventions are classified as munitions.

On the other hand, software companies argue that such restrictions limit their profits and hamper innovation. A 1996 report by the National Research Council maintains that "widespread commercial and private use of cryptography is inevitable in the long run and . . . its advantages . . . outweigh its disadvantages." The council found U.S. companies unable to compete with foreign producers of cryptographic software who are not subject to such restrictions. The council recommended that the government relax its restrictions on exports and permit the free export of an encryption key that will make cryptanalysis 65,000 times more difficult. While recognizing that the world's evil elements may take advantage of better cryptography, the council believed that a world with more secure information was worth the risk. The final decision will rest with the courts.

See also:
Computer; Espionage; Writing.
References:
Gardner, Robert. *Crime Lab 101*. New York: Walker, 1992.
International Encyclopedia of Communications. New York: Oxford University Press, 1989.
Levy, Steven. "Scared Bitless." *Newsweek*, 10 June 1996.
"Secret Plans." *The Economist*, 6 May 1995.
Waller, Douglas. "Spies in Cyberspace." *Time*, 20 March 1995.

Cuneiform

Cuneiform is a family of scripts that represents the earliest known system of writing. Cuneiform was used principally by the Mesopotamian peoples of the ancient Near East. The chief writing material of the ancient Near East was the clay tablet, which was exposed to the sun or baked in kilns to assure durability. Cuneiform was the result of scribes using a stylus (a hard, sharp, pointed instrument) to impress figures on the damp clay tablet. The stylus created the triangular, wedged-shaped symbols—broad at one end and pointed at the other. It is from these marks that the term *cuneiform* (from the Latin *cuneus*, for "wedge," and *formas*, meaning "shape") is derived.

No exact date for the origin of cuneiform has been established, but most historians attribute the initial development, sometime around 3000 B.C., to the Sumerian and Akkadian civilizations of southeastern Iraq. Most of the extant cuneiform texts are written in the languages of those civilizations. The earliest clay tablets were discovered at Uruk, Ur, Nippur, and other ancient cities of the region. The clay tablets are the most widely preserved form of cuneiform, but other examples have been uncovered that are carved in stone and scratched or engraved in metal.

Cuneiform evolved from a crude form of pictographic writing in which pictures are used to represent words. For example, water might be illustrated by two wavy lines. Speculation is that the initial freehand pictures were used for elemental accounting and administrative purposes. As time progressed, the Sumerians and others realized that writing could be made faster and more efficient by eliminating the drawings, which were difficult to inscribe on clay tablets. Ultimately, a type of shorthand linear representation—a combination of straight, short stroked lines—was standardized and replaced the earlier pictographic version. Some signs were as simple as one wedge; others were more intricate, involving 30 or more wedges. Convenience and speed generated other changes in the writing. For example, the direction of the writing was standardized as left to right to avoid smudging incised figures, and signs were shifted 90 degrees so they appeared horizontal rather than vertical, as in the older columnar writing.

A second progression in the development of cuneiform was writing to express abstract ideas. There were pictographic means to depict abstractions, usually by joining two signs, but these were not enough to meet the expanding demands of the language. Ancient linguists resorted to ideograms or word signs. For example, the sign for mouth might also mean speak, or the symbol for sun could signify light, brightness, or day.

The final stage in the evolution was the introduction of phonetic language, in which signs came to represent sounds. Consequently, a single cuneiform sign could signify an object, an abstract idea or concept, or a syllable. To eliminate some of the confusion, or so scribes thought, determinatives were added to words. These were unpronounced signs before or after a word that denoted the classification of a sign as a country, proper name, plural, or some other function.

Although cuneiform became the common written language of the ancient Near East, its complexity was staggering. Sumer and Babylonia used over 600 signs; the Assyrians and Hittites reduced the number to about

350, but even the simplest writing of Persia involved 39 signs. Ancient scribes had syllabaries, which were lists of signs and their meanings, to aid them. Nonetheless, surviving tablets cover a myriad of topics and testify as to how pervasive cuneiform was. Hammurabi's famous legal code was written in cuneiform, as was most of the scientific and technical knowledge of Sumer and Babylon. Affairs of state, treaties, and diplomatic correspondence were routinely recorded in cuneiform, even in Egypt. The writing also survives in the form of literature, most notably in the Babylonian epic *Gelgamesh*. The world's oldest known medical text is in cuneiform.

Scholars had a difficult time deciphering cuneiform texts not only because of the complexity of the language, with so many diverse characters serving numerous functions, but also because of regional and cultural variations. Although cuneiform has been known to scholars since the seventeenth century, the first real attention to the language came as the result of discoveries at Persepolis, the ancient capital of Persia, which provided a key to the variant cuneiform styles. G. F. Grotefend, a German, was among the first to recognize cuneiform as a type of writing and not mere decoration. Using the trilingual Persepolis tablets, his knowledge of Persian, and the repetition of certain character groups, Grotefend identified a few words in the inscriptions. He translated the word *king* and the names *Darius* and *Xerxes*.

Henry Rawlinson, an English adventurer and diplomat in Persia, made the most dramatic advances in cuneiform studies. In 1837, Rawlinson painstakingly copied and studied the cliff face inscriptions of the Behistun Rock in Iran. Similar to Grotefend's Persepolis tablets, this monument recorded the exploits of Darius I in three languages—Old Persian, Elamite, and Babylonian. Grotefend's efforts were less demanding because he was working with the later alphabetical cuneiform, in which each sign corresponded to a sound. However, Rawlinson was dealing with the more intricate earlier script. Using the comparative linguistic techniques of his predecessors, Rawlinson first translated the Old Persian inscription in 1846. He then moved on to successfully crack the more difficult Babylonian cuneiform by the late 1850s. His work established the basis for deciphering and publishing cuneiform that continues even today.

See also:
Hieroglyphics; Writing.
References:
Ceram, C. W. *Gods, Graves and Scholars: The Story of Archaeology*. New York: Bantam, 1972.
Chiera, Edward. *They Wrote on Clay*. Chicago: University of Chicago Press, 1956.
Walker, C. B. *Cuneiform*. Berkeley, CA: University of California Press, 1987.

Cybernetics

See Wiener, Norbert.

Daguerre, Louis-Jacques Mandé (1789–1851)

The French artist who invented the first practical form of photography, Louis-Jacques Mandé Daguerre gave his name to the daguerreotype. Daguerre's process eclipsed all others due to the speed of development and the unequaled clarity of the image. Until the mid–nineteenth century, Daguerre's method was the most widely used photographic procedure.

At 16, Daguerre was apprenticed to the Paris Opera as a theatrical scene painter and designer. His first notable individual achievement was the 1822 creation of the Diorama, a large panoramic painting done on both sides of semitransparent theatrical gauze. Presented in a special theater, the half-hour programs used imaginative lighting from windows and skylights to illuminate subtly realistic effects such as the movement of trees and animals. It was a very successful venture, and Daguerre and his partner also opened a Diorama in London.

Dissatisfied with mere artistic illusions, Daguerre wanted to create images of real objects. He began to experiment but made no real progress until 1829, when he formed a partnership with Joseph Nicéphore Niepce. Niepce was credited with taking the first permanent photograph, the results of a process he called heliography. The major disadvantage of the method was the developing time of 7 to 8 hours needed to produce a visible image. The two men agreed to work toward a solution of this critical problem. What was to have been a ten-year pact lasted only four years before Niepce died in 1833. Niepce's work provided background and a starting point for Daguerre, but he was never really convinced the older man's ideas would work. Discarding Niepce's concepts as impractical, Daguerre proceeded on his own to develop a completely new system.

Daguerre began experimenting with copper plates coated with silver on one side. He exposed the silver to a box of iodine. Fumes from the iodine reacted with the silver to produce a light-sensitive coating of silver iodide on the plate. When exposed to light through a camera lens, the silver iodide was reduced to silver based upon the intensity of the light. Nevertheless, when the plates were removed from the camera Daguerre was left with only a latent image invisible to the eye and, as such, worthless. How to create a positive image remained the question. Daguerre's dilemma resulted in one of the great legends of photography.

At some time in 1835—no exact date has been established—the frustrated inventor put some exposed plates in his chemical cupboard, intending to clean the plates for reuse at a later time. When Daguerre retrieved the plates, he was surprised to find a developed image. Through trial and error he learned that mercury vapor from an old spill worked the miracle. Daguerre also realized that the transformation from latent to positive image took only 20 to 30 minutes, as compared with the hours heliography required.

It took another two years to finalize the process. The last problem for Daguerre was how to make the print permanent and prevent fading. Common salt was the answer. After exposure to the mercury vapor, the plate was washed in a common salt solution, which removed the unexposed silver iodide and stabilized the picture. Washing with water and drying completed the revolutionary process. In 1837, Daguerre took the first successful daguerreotype, a still life, which is preserved in the collection of the Société Française de Photographie in Paris.

In March 1839, the Paris Diorama burned, and Daguerre was faced with mounting debts. In partnership with Niepce's son, Daguerre decided to market their new process. There was no interest. In the end, the French government, perhaps as a matter of national pride and with the idea of making the invention available to the general public, bought out the two men. Both men were given generous lifetime annuities in return for their photographic secrets. Daguerre's pension was a little larger because he also was required to reveal the intricacies that made the Diorama successful. The details of the photographic method were made public at a meeting of the French Academy of Science on 19 August 1839. Within a year daguerreotypes were being made all over the world.

By the 1850s, people began to look beyond the daguerreotype, seeking better, more convenient pictures. The daguerreotype had limitations that inspired continual experimentation. First, because the process required metal plates for each exposure, photography was expensive. Second, daguerreotypes could not be copied or reproduced, so each picture was unique. Finally, the picture was reversed as a mirror image. Daguerre took no real interest in further developing or refining his invention. He retired to his country home and died there on 10 July 1851.

See also:
Photography.
References:
Gernsheim, Helmut, and Alison Gernsheim. *The History of Photography 1685–1914*. New York: McGraw-Hill, 1969.
Gernsheim, Helmut, and Alison Gernsheim. *LJM Daguerre: The History of the Diorama and the Daguerreotype*. New York: Dover, 1968.
Newhall, Beaumont. *The History of Photography*. New York: Museum of Modern Art, 1982.

Dance

Dance is an art form that uses body movements to communicate emotion, tell a story, or carry out a ritual. Music usually accompanies dancing.

Dancing probably preceded humankind, since many animals dance to attract a mate. It has been part of human culture for a very long time. Archeologists are confident that humans have been dancing for at least 15,000 years, based on ancient cave paintings. In Egypt, tomb paintings from ca. 2000 B.C. show women moving in rhythmic patterns. Dancers are also depicted on ancient Greek vases.

Primitive people, lacking scientific knowledge, performed dances to influence the gods or spirits that they believed controlled nature. They would dance before a hunt or before spring planting, hoping that what they communicated to the gods through dance would occur in fact. When it did, they danced to give thanks to the spirits. If a good harvest or hunt was not forthcoming, they thought the spirits were angry and danced to appease them. The Pueblo Indians of North America danced dressed as eagles in hopes that the eagle spirit would bring them rain. Australian Aborigines mimic movements of kangaroos and other animals in dances to preserve their lands.

Many of the dances of long ago have become part of the cultural heritage of people and are still performed today. In many cultures, dancing was part of ceremonies marking birth, marriage, death, illness, harvesting, or hunting, or was done at any time that magic or special powers were believed to be needed. Many of the dances for these events became ritualized, meaning that the dance done at a death ceremony, for example, would be performed with the same pattern of steps each time. As the rituals in complex societies such as those in Egypt or India became more elaborate, only those trained in the steps or body patterns were able to perform the dances, and thus was born theater dance. An example of these elaborate dances is found in India. Dating to the fifth century A.D., the complex techniques and rules in the Natya Sastra of Bharata and the Abhinaya Darpana of Nandikesvara are well established and still control the classic dance of India today. These more complex ancient dances were done not only for religious purposes, but to entertain leaders as well. Such dance forms as ballet and modern dance have developed from these ancient forms of entertainment. They can tell a story, express a feeling, or just demonstrate the pure beauty and enjoyment of body movement.

Some ritualized dances became the folk dances of various cultures and are now done for pleasure. Square dances were originally performed to celebrate harvests; the Cossack sword dance from the Ukraine was done before battle to encourage warriors; the Maypole dance is an offspring of an old fertility ritual. Other folk dances were developed just for the fun of moving and socializing. The enjoyment of leaping and kicking is demonstrated in the aurresku, a Basque folk dance.

Climate, geography, and even clothing and footwear can influence the dance of different cultures. Think about dancing in clogs on hard earth as compared to dancing barefoot in sand. In a very hot climate, such as in India, dances are sometimes more centered on intricate hand movements than on total body movement. In a cold climate, such as in Russia, the dances tend to contain very vigorous and explosive motions that keep the participants warm. In spacious areas, dances can be carried out in long lines or formations.

Dance has also been used to communicate social and political views, to disclose racist attitudes, to portray the struggles of the poor and the aspirations of the common people, and to show social inequality and oppression. Dance is a very powerful medium that can convey a message through the movement of the entire body, including facial expressions and gestures.

Dance has also been used to help people express their emotions or relieve stress through exercise and movement when they are having psychological trouble. It can be used as therapy. Several years ago, a program was undertaken in which six nonverbal children who were visually and hearing impaired were involved in an intense dance program. It had been noted that these children tended to communicate through extraordinary movement, using patterns of nonverbal gestures directed toward a source of light. Dance therapy encouraged this inclination, and the children showed significantly more social interaction after the program was completed.

—Barbara Gardner Conklin

See also:
Cave Painting; Nonverbal Communication; Psychoanalysis.

References:
Anderson, Lydia. *Folk Dancing*. New York: Watts, 1981.
Bond, Karen. "Personal Style as a Mediator of Engagement in Dance: Watching Terpsichore Rise." *Dance Research Journal*, Spring 1994.
Chujoy, Anatole. *The Dance Encyclopedia*. New York: A. S. Barnes, 1949.

Darwin, Charles (1809–1882)

Charles Darwin was an English naturalist, two of whose books, *The Origin of Species* and *The Descent of Man*, changed forever humankind's view of itself and its origin. In fact, Darwin's work probably changed our view of humanity as dramatically as Newton's *Principia Mathematica* changed our view of the world and the universe. Another of Darwin's books, *The Expression of the Emotions in Man and Animals*, marked the beginning of research in nonverbal communication.

Darwin, who shared a birth date with Abraham Lincoln (12 February 1809), was the son of a wealthy physician and grandson of the poet and physician Erasmus Darwin. Despite the wishes of his father, who wanted him to study medicine or theology, Darwin showed a real interest only in his hobby—natural history—which he pursued at Cambridge.

A major turning point in Darwin's life occurred in 1831, when he accepted an unpaid position as naturalist on board HMS *Beagle* and began a five-year scientific voyage to map the coast of South America. Darwin had read some of the work of Sir Charles Lyell, a geologist who recognized that the earth's rocks revealed a long history of slow but unequivocal change. During the voyage, Darwin observed evidence of similar change among living things. He was struck by the diversity of organisms and particularly by the 14 species of finches on the Galápagos Islands, 650 miles off the coast of Ecuador. None of these species could be found on the mainland. He speculated that a seed-eating variety of finch had reached the islands thousands of years ago. During that time he believed the descendants of the ancestral finch species had evolved into the 14 species he found there in 1835. Some species had become insect eaters, some grew to feast on larger seeds, and some on harder seeds.

After his return to England in 1836, Darwin began to think about what might cause the diversity of organisms and the evolution of new species. In 1838, he read *An Essay on the Principle of Population* by Thomas Malthus, who maintained that humans reproduce faster than the food supply. As a result, Malthus maintained, population growth is eventually diminished by starvation, disease, or war. This was the key Darwin needed. He saw at once that competition for food would allow for the survival of only those organisms best adapted to the environment. Without the evolution of new species, the original finches on the Galápagos Islands would have multiplied until they exhausted the supply of seeds. But if some of the birds became adapted to eating a different kind of seed or could metabolize insects, they would have an advantage and enjoy an untapped niche of the environment.

Environmental pressure, he realized, would lead to new, better-adapted species. Nature itself would select one form of life over another and provide avenues for the emergence of those organisms that could best take advantage of the opportunities. This "natural selection" would lead to diverse species and a never-ending process in which better-adapted organisms replace those that are less well adapted. Giraffes developed longer necks over time because those born with longer necks were able to eat more leaves from trees and therefore were more likely to survive and reproduce similar long-necked giraffes. Natural variation coupled with natural selection could explain the process of evolution. However, it was not until Gregor Mendel's work on genetics was discovered by Hugo de Vries in 1900 that the cause of natural variation was identified.

Darwin began to write a book about his theory of evolution by natural selection in 1844, but 14 years later, despite constant urging to publish by Lyell, who recognized the significance of Darwin's idea, he had still not completed the work. Darwin's hesitancy in publishing was probably related to his private and perfectionist nature and his reluctance to face or argue with hostile opponents. He realized that his ideas would be attacked by other scientists as well as the clergy, who held to the notion that species were immutable. In fact, there is evidence that Darwin would have preferred to see the book published after his death provided that the priority of the theory should be his. Imagine his shock when, on 18 June 1858, he received a paper from the English naturalist Alfred Russel Wallace. Wallace had developed the same theory as Darwin. In Darwin's words, "I never saw a more striking coincidence; if Wallace had my manuscript sketch written out in 1842, he could not have made a better short abstract."

Darwin made no attempt to claim priority. Instead he collaborated with Wallace, and papers by both men were read at the July 1858 meeting of the Linnaean Society. The following year, Darwin published *The Origin of Species*. The book immediately stirred controversy, for many believed it was contrary to biblical teachings. The polemic was fueled by Lyell, whose book *The Antiquity of Man* presented evidence supporting the idea that *Homo sapiens*, too, had evolved from earlier species. In 1871, Darwin supported Lyell's position with additional evidence in *The Descent of Man*.

In *The Expression of the Emotions in Man and Animals*, Darwin anticipated ethology—the scientific study of animal behavior under natural conditions. He suggested that communication through emotional expressions evolved from past ancestral forms. Studies have shown that facial expressions of fear, anger, sadness, disgust, and happiness are indeed universal for humans regardless of their cultural background. Darwin believed, for example, that the lowering of the brow, which is associated with anger, was originally a means of shading the eyes and improving one's view of the organism responsible for the emotion. Breaking eye contact (looking away) seems to be a mollifying signal among many species. Humans also use it to display shyness.

By the time of his death in 1882, Darwin's theory had become widely accepted among scientists. The acceptance was based not only on the overwhelming evidence advanced by both Darwin and Lyell, but by the strong arguments presented by Thomas Huxley, a firm disciple of Darwin. In a famous debate between Huxley and Bishop Samuel Wilberforce, Wilberforce denounced what he called Darwin's hypothesis with brilliant wit and sarcasm, after which he turned to Huxley and asked whether Huxley claimed descent from the monkey through his grandfather or his grandmother. Huxley responded that Darwin's theory—supported by overwhelming evidence—was much more than a hypothesis, pointed out the bishop's scientific ignorance, and closed by stating that he would prefer a monkey as an ancestor rather than someone who used wit and charm to obscure the truth.

In recognition of his accomplishments, Darwin was buried in Westminster Abbey near Sir Isaac Newton and Michael Faraday, two other renowned English scientists. It was the only recognition granted him by a government that strongly opposed Darwinism.

References:

Asimov, Isaac. *Asimov's Biographical Encyclopedia of Science and Technology*. New York: Doubleday, 1964.

Bronowski, J. *The Ascent of Man*. Boston: Little, Brown, 1973.

Darwin, Charles. *On the Origin of Species by Means of Natural Selection, or the Preservation of Favoured Races in the Struggle for Life*. New York: Modern Library, 1993.

International Encyclopedia of Communications. New York: Oxford University Press, 1989.

De Forest, Lee (1873–1961)

American engineer and inventor whose invention of the triode tube established the foundation of the modern electronics industry and secured for Lee De Forest the title, "Father of Radio."

At age six, De Forest's family moved from Council Bluffs, Iowa, where he was born, to Talladega, Alabama. De Forest's father, a Congregational minister, accepted a position as president of all-black Talladega College. The resultant social pressure isolated the family from the local white community and provided a solitary childhood for their son. Nonetheless, De Forest displayed an early interest in science, invention, and machines. He constructed a rudimentary electric motor and built models of a locomotive and blast furnace. Reflecting his family's notions of the ministry, the would-be inventor enrolled at Yale University, where an ancestor had established a De Forest family scholarship.

The Yale years (1893–1899), perhaps due to limited family finances, saw the young De Forest labeled as an aloof, eccentric loner buried in studies and always tinkering with his major interest, the "wireless" (radio). De Forest completed his Ph.D. in 1899, specializing in theoretical physics and electricity. His dissertation on the reflection of Hertzian (radio) waves was one of the earliest scholarly works on the subject.

Upon graduation, De Forest joined Western Electric in Chicago. He moved to Milwaukee, but by 1900 he was back in Chicago as a teacher with the Armour Institute. He received a small stipend but, more significantly, was given the use of a laboratory in which to pursue his work. During this period De Forest, like all wireless scientists at that time, was preoccupied with the creation of a stronger, more powerful, and more sensitive radio detector. De Forest's solution was what he called a Sponder.

The Sponder was a success from the beginning, and De Forest was able to form his own company, the American De Forest Wireless Telegraphy Company, in 1902. In direct competition with the industry's recognized leader, the Marconi Company, De Forest's enterprise got a big boost in 1904, when his equipment carried the first wireless news report about the Russo-Japanese War. The company prospered by supplying wireless telegraph components to oceangoing vessels and, in particular, the U.S. Navy. De Forest

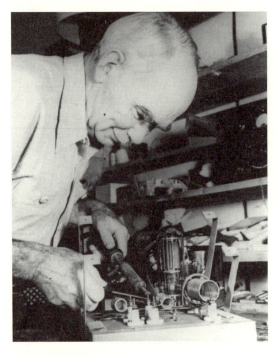

American engineer and inventor Lee De Forest.

was rapidly becoming the most recognizable American name in wireless operations when misfortune struck.

It turned out that De Forest's Sponder was strikingly similar to a device patented by another radio pioneer, Reginald Fessenden. In 1905, a court-ordered injunction prohibited further manufacturing of the Sponder due to patent infringement, and De Forest's company went bankrupt the next year. This event foreshadowed similar financial and business problems that plagued De Forest throughout his life. His next business venture failed as well and ended with an indictment for mail fraud, from which he was eventually cleared, although two of his associates went to jail. Lack of any real business sense limited the financial benefits De Forest might have enjoyed as a result of his inventive success.

Despite the business failure, 1906 was a watershed year in De Forest's career. Discouraged by the Fessenden patent fight, De Forest decided to refocus his efforts. Marconi had given the world dots and dashes, but De Forest's real interest was in transmit-

ting sound, especially voices and music. Skeptics might scoff, but he wanted a continuous broadcast of information and music. In the parlance of the day this was called wireless telephony, but increasingly people simply referred to it as radio. To finance this interest, De Forest's new company installed high-powered radio stations at naval bases, and De Forest himself developed several different antenna systems.

More significant than De Forest's change of priorities was the invention of the device most associated with his name, the revolutionary triode vacuum tube. De Forest called his tube the audion and patented it in 1907.

At first no one, not even De Forest, appreciated the importance of the triode. De Forest finally grasped the audion's potential after moving to California, where in 1912 he served as chief research engineer for the Federal Telegraph Company. There, researchers discovered that by cascading—that is, linking a chain of audions together—it was possible to amplify and repeat weak radio signals better than anything then on the market. The results had major consequences for long-range telephonic and radio communication. The triode made possible not only radio and television, but also the earliest computers. The transistors of the 1960s were smaller more efficient versions of the triode, and the microchips and integrated systems of today are technologically enhanced triodes combined with other components. As far as De Forest was concerned, however, the audion made receivers and transmitters more efficient, an advancement to be sure, but hardly revolutionary. In January 1920, De Forest showed off his new technology by broadcasting an opera from New York City, the first such broadcast of its kind.

AT&T was keenly interested in the audion, but bad luck continued to frustrate De Forest even at the moment of his greatest accomplishment. Once again, charges of patent infringement led to prolonged litigation. In 1914 the Marconi Company alleged that De Forest's triode was based upon the work done by John Ambrose Fleming, who developed the diode in 1904. The case was in court for almost 30 years before the court decided in favor of De Forest in 1943.

The lawsuit and poor business investments once again brought De Forest to the brink of bankruptcy. To forestall his creditors, De Forest arranged to sell most of his patents on tubes, circuits, components, and, of course, the audion to AT&T for a fraction of their worth. Using the triode as a line amplifier, AT&T established transcontinental telephone service in 1915. By 1923, the "Father of Radio" had left radio research for good.

De Forest moved on to other projects, most notably development of "talking pictures." By the early 1920s, he had perfected a method of recording sound optically on film, which he named Phonofilm. In April 1923, De Forest demonstrated his sound films for the first time at the Rivoli Theater in New York City. Hollywood, enjoying a prosperous period with silent films, was not interested in jeopardizing that success with experiments and ignored De Forest's innovation. Interestingly, when sound did come to the movies in 1926 and 1927, the system adopted was very similar to De Forest's. In 1934, he founded Lee De Forest Labs. There he continued to pursue his interests, which included color television and high-speed facsimile transmission. The last of his 300 patents was issued when he was 83. De Forest died in Hollywood, California, on 2 July 1961.

See also:
Diode; Radio; Transistor.

References:
Chipman, Robert A. "De Forest and the Triode Detector." *Scientific American*, March 1965.
"Lee De Forest, 87, Radio Pioneer Dies." *New York Times*, 2 July 1961.
Levine, Israel E. *Electronics Pioneer: Lee De Forest*. Milwood, NY: Associated Faculty Press, 1964.

Debate

See Forensics.

Defamation

Defamation is libel or slander. Generally, libel involves writing or pictures—something that has permanence—whereas slander involves spoken words or gestures. Both terms refer to communication that is damaging to someone's reputation and causes that person to lose prestige or standing. Any claim of defamation by a plaintiff must be directed against a living person.

Historically, punishment for slander can be traced back to ninth-century England, but legal sanctions against libel and slander were first enacted by Parliament in 1275. However, compensation for libel or slander consisted of an apology from the defendant. There was no monetary compensation.

In the United States, libel has come to mean primarily defamation through the mass media—radio, television, newspapers, magazines, etc. Slander involves defamation by speech in a face-to-face confrontation that was viewed by one or more witnesses. Proof of slander is very difficult because the plaintiff must demonstrate harm resulting from the slanderous remarks. Usually, defamation that takes place on radio or television, even though it is by spoken words, is treated as libel because these media are regarded as more powerful agents of defamation than ordinary speech.

Libel is a civil rather than a criminal offense. The plaintiff must prove that the defamatory statements were published and seen by the plaintiff, the defendant, and other people, and that the plaintiff was clearly identified as the subject of the defamation. In addition, the judge must agree that the words are truly defamatory, and the jury must decide that the words are both false and defamatory. Words that are true, even though defamatory, are not regarded as libelous. If the jury finds the defendant guilty of libel, it then decides on the severity of the damage. In some cases the jury has placed the damages at $1 because they did not find that the plaintiff had been damaged by the statements.

Public officials and public figures who bring charges of libel against someone are far less likely to receive compensation than ordinary citizens. In *New York Times v. Sullivan* (1964), the Supreme Court ruled that public officials cannot recover damages for defamation unless they can prove that the statements made by the defendant were made with actual malice. In that decision, Justice William Brennan wrote that a public official cannot recover damages for a defamatory falsehood relating to his official conduct unless he proves that the statement was made with actual malice—that is, with knowledge that it was false or with reckless disregard of whether it was false or not.

The Court held that to maintain freedom of speech and press, the risk of honest mistakes must be tolerated. The case essentially eliminated libel prosecutions against the media by public officials. In subsequent cases, the principle of actual malice was applied to public figures as well as public officials.

References:

Henderson, Bruce. *How to Bulletproof Your Manuscript*. Cincinnati: Writer's Digest Books, 1986.

Lewis, Anthony. *Make No Law: The Sullivan Case and the First Amendment*. New York: Random House, 1991.

Delphi

See Online Services.

Desktop Publishing

See Electronic Publishing.

Diary

A diary is a daily record of events, experiences, thoughts, and observations. Although diaries are primarily personal, they are often written as journals, which are frequently thought to be less personal, and are sometimes written with the understanding that others will read them. Regardless of whether the writing is viewed as diary or journal, personal or public, the record can be a source of useful information to the writer engaged in preparing an autobiography or to someone else writing a biography. Often, people in public life keep a diary or journal with the realization that their thoughts and perceptions will become public at a future date through either their own writings or those of a biographer or historian.

Diaries or journals serve as primary sources for historians, providing insight into events and the reasons for personal actions, and an understanding of the cultural or social values and standards of the time. A historian, like any of us, would not read the diary of a living person because those words may be personal and not for other eyes. The diarist's death, however, changes our perspective and that of the historian as well.

Diary writing became popular during the seventeenth century in Europe, but travel journals (logs) were common among ship captains and explorers a century earlier. Early artists and scientists, such as Leonardo da Vinci (1452–1519), who wrote his notes so that a mirror was required to read them, were in a sense diarists, too.

The Diary of Samuel Pepys is a record of events, both public and private, in Pepys's life as a public servant in London from 1660 through 1669. It contains keen observations of public events, including the Plague of 1665 and the Great Fire of London in 1666. Like da Vinci, Pepys wrote in code. His writing was first decoded early in the nineteenth century, but it was eight decades into the twentieth century before the diary was published in its entirety.

The diaries of William Byrd II, a wealthy Virginia landowner, provided a wealth of information about eighteenth-century colonists. Harold L. Ickes, an honest, dedicated, and competent administrator and curmudgeon who served as Secretary of the Interior from 1933 to 1946, kept a diary, later published, that criticized public officials and provided historical insights into the Roosevelt administration and the New Deal.

The *Diary of Anne Frank*, written in 1942 through 1944 by a young German Jewish child hiding from the Nazis and published shortly after World War II, provided a vivid account of a child's fearful life during the Hitler regime.

Diaries have also served as the format for a number of novels. Examples include Russian author Nikolai Gogal's *The Diary of a Madman*, written in 1835, and American author Saul Bellow's *Dangling Man*, published in 1944.

References:
Frank, Anne. *The Diary of Anne Frank*. New York: Doubleday, 1995.
Ickes, Harold L. *The Secret Diaries of Harold L. Ickes*. New York: Simon & Schuster, 1953.
International Encyclopedia of Communications. New York: Oxford University Press, 1989.

Diode

A diode is an electronic device that permits electric charge to flow in only one direction. Diodes can be used to rectify an electric current; that is, to change an alternating current (AC), one that moves back and forth, to a direct current (DC), which flows in only one direction. The first diodes consisted of electrodes sealed within vacuum tubes. Today, most diodes are made of solid semiconductors.

While engaged in his long quest to invent a satisfactory lightbulb, Thomas Edison discovered that when a metal (cathode) is heated inside a vacuum tube, an electric current will cross the vacuum to a positively charged plate (called the anode). However, the current will not cross the vacuum if the plate is negatively charged. This discovery, which came to be known as the Edison effect, was used by John A. Fleming (1849–1945) in developing the vacuum-tube diode, or rectifier.

After the discovery of electrons during the 1890s, it was clear that the Edison effect was a result of electrons moving across the vacuum. Heating the metal increased the energy of its electrons to the point that they could "boil" off the surface. Because electrons carry a negative charge, they are attracted to the anode only if it is positively charged. Fleming realized that since charge can flow only one way across a vacuum, he could use an evacuated tube to convert an alternating current to a direct current.

A hot, glowing coil served as the cathode, where electrons boiled off the wire much like the steam produced when water boils. The electrons streamed across the tube to the metal anode during the time that it was positively charged. When it became negatively charged, the current would cease to flow, just as water stops flowing when a faucet is turned off. (This is why these tubes were sometimes called Fleming valves.)

The diode described would produce a pulsating current. Since most AC sources have a frequency of 60 hertz, the diode would produce 60 pulses of current each second. A duo-diode with two anodes, each connected to an opposite side of the source, provided 120 pulses of direct current per second. By adding a filter to the circuit, the pulsating nature of the DC current was converted to a steady flow of charge.

Diodes are an integral component of almost every electronic device used in communications, including radios, television sets, and recorders. But today's diodes are semiconductors, which serve the same purpose as vacuum-tube diodes but are based on a different principle.

Semiconductors such as silicon and germanium exist as crystals in which the atoms have four electrons in the so-called valence band. Such a configuration of electrons allows them to form four chemical bonds with adjacent atoms. Only a small amount of energy is needed to elevate an electron to the conduction band, where it is free to move through the crystal. However, the number of electrons that have enough energy to reach the conduction band is limited at ordinary temperatures. As a result, substances such as silicon and germanium have far fewer electrons available to conduct charge than metals, which are good conductors because they have an abundance of electrons in the conduction bands. It is their limited conductivity relative to metals that led these solids to be called semiconductors.

Unlike metals, which show a decrease in conductivity with increasing temperature,

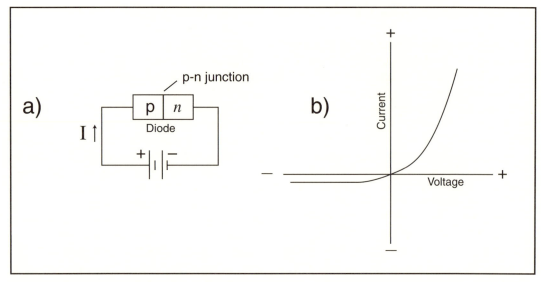

Figure 1. A current (I) will flow when the diode is connected as shown (panel a). Very little current flows when either the battery or the diode is reversed. The graph (panel b) shows how voltage across, and current through, the diode are related. The curve on the right side of the graph shows voltage and current when the diode is connected as shown in panel a. The curve on the left shows voltage and current when either the diode or battery is reversed.

semiconductors become better conductors as their temperature rises. The additional thermal energy (heat) frees more electrons to the conduction bands, where they are free to move through the crystal. When an electron moves from the valence band to the conduction band, it leaves a vacancy, or hole, that can be filled by electrons from neighboring atoms. These holes, which lack electrons, can be thought of as positive charge because they attract electrons, which are the elementary negative charge. Thus, charge can move through a semiconductor as negative electrons or as positive holes. Holes moving to the right are the equivalent of electrons moving to the left. In a semiconductor, there are always equal numbers of holes and free electrons.

We can draw an analogy between a semiconductor crystal and a parking garage. A crystal with no broken bonds (all its electrons are in the valence band, where they are held in fixed positions) is like the floor of a parking garage that is filled with cars. There is no place for a car to be moved, and so all must remain in place. However, if one car is

moved to a floor above, where it can move about freely, then the "hole" that it leaves allows a car to be moved into it, which in turn leaves a hole that can be filled by another car on the nearly filled floor.

Diodes are made from semiconductors that have been "doped" with other atoms. For example, germanium crystals can be doped by adding a small number of arsenic atoms—about one arsenic atom to every 10 billion germanium atoms. Arsenic atoms are about the same size as germanium atoms, but they have five valence electrons instead of four. When they replace a germanium atom in a crystal, they use four of their valence electrons to form bonds with neighboring germanium atoms. The fifth electron can escape to the conduction band and thus increase the conductivity of the crystal. Diodes made in this way are said to be n-type semiconductors because they conduct charge by increasing the number of negative charges (electrons) that are free to move.

Germanium crystals might also be doped with gallium. Gallium and germanium atoms are also of similar size, but gallium has only three valance electrons. In order to form four bonds with nearby germanium atoms, a gallium atom must "borrow" an electron from a germanium atom, leaving the germanium atom with a hole. The holes, like electrons, can move through the crystal and serve as charge carriers. Because holes behave as if they were positive charges, a germanium atom doped with gallium is said to be a p-type semiconductor.

Figure 1a shows a diode connected to a battery. As with all diodes, one side is a p-type semiconductor, and the other side is an n-type semiconductor. The region where they meet is called a p-n junction. The graph in Figure 1b shows that current flow increases with voltage when the circuit is arranged so that the p-type end of the diode is connected to the positive terminal of the battery and the n-type end to the negative terminal as shown in Figure 1a. The graph also reveals that when the battery or diode is reversed, very little current flows.

With the circuit connected as shown in Figure 1a, electrons would readily flow through the p-n junction from right to left because there are plenty of free electrons in the n-type semiconductor. Similarly, holes would flow through the same junction from left to right because holes abound in the p-type semiconductor. However, if the battery were reversed, the force on electrons would be from the p-type semiconductor across the junction to the n-type semiconductor. The force on the holes would be from the n-type to the p-type semiconductor at the junction. Since there are few electrons in the p-type end of the diode and few holes in the n-type end, there would be very little charge flow across the junction.

Because semiconductor diodes can be very small and are easily joined to other components on tiny silicon chips, integrated circuits containing hundreds of individual circuits are now made for various electronic devices. Computers that once filled a large room with vacuum tubes and wires can now be carried about in a small case. Semiconductors are far superior to the vacuum tubes of old. They are rugged, inexpensive, effi-cient, require no warm-up time, use little power, and seldom fail.

Light-emitting diodes (LEDs) are made by using gallium arsenide phosphide (GaAsP) as the p-n junction. As the name implies, LEDs are used to produce light. They are commonly found in the digital display of numbers on clocks, watches, and other electronic instruments. The light is emitted when the diode is given a large forward voltage, that is, when the p-type side of the diode is connected to the positive terminal of a power source and the n-type side is connected to the negative terminal of the same source. As holes are pushed across the junction into the n-region and electrons into the p-region, the electrons and holes combine with accompanying energy losses that in many cases release photons of visible light.

The opposite effect also takes place. A thin piece of silicon or germanium can act as a photodiode. If light falling on the semiconductor contains photons with energy equal to or larger than the gap between the valence and conduction bands, electrons in the valence band can absorb the photons and jump to the conduction band, thus increasing the conductivity of the semiconductor. The resulting electric current will be proportional to the intensity of the light. This photoelectric current can be used to control a circuit used in a burglar alarm, an automatic door opener, or some other photosensitive electronic device.

See also:
Computer; Microelectronics; Photoelectric Cell; Transistor.

References:
Gardner, Robert. *Communication*. New York: Twenty-First Century, 1994.
Haber-Schaim, Uri, et al. *PSSC Physics*, 7th ed. Dubuque, IA: Kendall/Hunt 1991.
Macaulay, David. *The Way Things Work*. Boston: Houghton Mifflin, 1988.
Sears, Francis W., Mark Zemansky, and Hugh D. Young: *College Physics*. Reading, MA: Addison-Wesley, 1985.

Direct Broadcasting Satellite Systems

A system that sends a television signal directly to homes from a satellite using super-high-frequency radio waves. The initial signal, which originates at a ground station, is sent to a geostationary satellite, a satellite that remains in a fixed position above the earth's surface because its period is 24 hours. The satellite is essentially a TV repeater station that beams the signal back to earth, where it is received as radiation by consumers' receivers.

Because the satellite sends a signal that is a hundred times stronger than ordinary signals from satellites, the receiving dish, called a homesat terminal, may be as small as 18 inches (0.46 meter) in diameter. It can be attached to a roof or the side of a house without dominating the building. The terminal converts the radiant signal from the satellite to one that is compatible with the consumer's television set. The size of the receiver, made possible by the stronger signal, eliminates the need for 3- to 5-meter diameter dishes that were used to receive earlier, less intense, television signals from satellites.

Direct broadcast satellites, because of the intensity of the signal they send back to earth, can provide only three high-powered channels. In order to meet the multichannel demands of most patrons, a number of satellites, each beaming three channels, are clustered in orbit to provide many channels.

See also:
Electromagnetic Waves; Satellite; Television.

Disney, Walter Elias (1901–1966)

American filmmaker, producer and businessman. As the creator of Mickey Mouse, Donald Duck, and other memorable cartoon characters, Walt Disney was one of the most popular figures in post–World War II American culture. His development of animated feature-length motion pictures and live-action family films created a "magic kingdom" that has become synonymous with family entertainment.

Disney was born in Chicago on 1 December 1901. A high school dropout, he briefly served as an ambulance driver in France during World War I and returned to his home in Kansas City in 1919. There he settled into a job as a commercial artist, making crude one- to two-minute cartoon advertising shorts. In 1922, Disney and fellow artist Ub Iwerks began their own animation studio. Iwerks, Disney's lifelong collaborator, was instrumental in the ultimate success of Disney Studios due to his artistic and technological skills. However, in 1922, the two men were starving artists nursing an ailing business. In 1923, they moved to Hollywood.

Housed in an uncle's garage, Disney Studios produced two undistinguished cartoon series, *Alice in Cartoonland* and *Oswald the Lucky Rabbit*. The studio, plagued by financial problems, limped along on the edge of bankruptcy. In 1927, Disney ceased drawing to devote his full time to marketing and securing distributors for the company's work. Mickey Mouse, the foundation of the Disney empire, was conceived on a train while Disney was returning from a disappointing financial trip to New York City. Immediately upon returning to Hollywood, Disney set the studio to work on a cartoon series with a mouse as the principal character. Drawn in simple style to aid the animation process, the new character, originally christened Mortimer, debuted in two short silent films that went unnoticed. Nonetheless, Disney was on the brink of realizing financial solvency as well as his first real professional recognition.

Mickey Mouse might well have gone the way of Disney's earlier creations given the lack of interest initially generated. Fortunately, Disney was working in an industry in transition. A technological revolution involving sound and color was just beginning to transform movies forever. Disney embraced the innovations and was one of the first to appreciate how sound could be an integral part of the moviegoing experience. In 1928, Disney Studios produced the first sound cartoon, *Steamboat Willie*. Willie, or Mickey Mouse, was drawn by Iwerk, and Disney himself provided the voice of his feature

Walt Disney poses with his most famous cartoon creation, Mickey Mouse.

character. The production was an immediate sensation, and Disney rushed to add sound to his first two shorts. He signed a 15-cartoon deal with Columbia Pictures, and Disney's days of struggle and poverty were over.

Buoyed by success, Disney sought to diversify his endeavors. In 1929, he introduced his *Silly Symphonies*, most notably "The Skeleton Dance," to the delight of audiences. These cartoons were a departure from the expected in that they did not use Disney's regular characters. The *Silly Symphonies* helped refine animation techniques, but more significantly, they continued the innovative exper-

imentation with sound and music. A second revolution in motion pictures occurred in the 1930s with the introduction of color film. Disney quickly abandoned black-and-white film in favor of the new technology and achieved international renown with his color adaptation of *The Three Little Pigs*.

During the 1930s, Disney's short films grew into a major entertainment phenomenon aided by the progressive introduction of characters. Pluto appeared in 1933, and the irascible Donald Duck debuted in 1934. In 1938, Disney was confident enough to launch a major new venture, feature-length animated films. Though by today's standards the animation of *Snow White* is crude, the film—Disney's first feature-length production—premiered to rave reviews. *Snow White*'s success committed Disney to feature-length animation, and he stayed with the proven formula of using children's stories to develop his next projects. Films like *Pinocchio* (1940), *Fantasia* (1940), *Dumbo* (1941), and *Bambi* (1942) strained the fragile resources of the studio but paid off handsomely at the box office. Not even World War II could slow the Disney machine. During the war years Disney created training films for American troops.

The postwar years, the 1950s, and 1960s were golden years for the Disney studio. Those decades established Disney's position in popular culture and made the studio a major power in filmdom. Feature-length animated classics, like *Cinderella* (1950) and *Peter Pan* (1953), remained staple Disney productions, but seeking new, more profitable challenges, the prosperous businessman altered the direction of his company. In 1950, Disney entered the live-action film field with his production of *Treasure Island*. He followed this success with similar films like *20,000 Leagues under the Sea* (1954), *Old Yeller* (1957), and *Pollyanna* (1960). A series of nature documentaries begun at about the same time added more profit and luster to the Disney studio. His culminating effort was the dazzling *Mary Poppins* (1964), which combined animation, live action, and special effects. Disney's accomplishments were recognized by his peers. He was honored with 31 Academy Awards.

In 1954, Disney invaded television with the expected glowing results. He produced memorable serialized half-hour programs like "Davy Crockett," "Zorro," and "The Swamp Fox." One of the most popular television shows of the era was Disney's "Mickey Mouse Club." In 1955, Disney once again displayed his golden touch by opening Disneyland at Anaheim, California. The park was a hit, but Disney, still not satisfied, was planning his masterpiece, Disney World, when he died on 15 December 1966.

See also:
Cartoon; Motion Pictures.

References:
Miller, Diane Disney, as told to Peter Martin. *The Story of Walt Disney*. New York: Holt, 1957.
Mosley, Leonard. *Disney's World: A Biography*. New York: Stein & Day, 1985.
Schickel, Richard. "Bring Forth the Mouse." *American Heritage*, April 1968.

Dynamo

A dynamo, or generator, is a machine that is designed to produce electrical energy from some other form of energy. Any machine used for communication that does not depend on a battery is probably powered by a dynamo.

The basic principle underlying a dynamo's capacity to produce electrical energy was discovered by Michael Faraday in 1831. If the magnetic field across a wire changes, electric charges within the wire experience a force that pushes them along the wire. Since negatively charged electrons are the only charged particles that are free to move, it is they that move along the wire. This causes one end of the wire, where the electrons accumulate, to become negative and the other end, where there is a deficiency of electrons, to become positive. As a result, the ends of the wire become oppositely charged, creating a potential difference (voltage) much like that across the poles of a battery.

To understand what happens within a dynamo, imagine a bar magnet that is plunged in and out of a coil of wire. As the magnet enters the coil, the magnetic field inside the coil increases. The induced voltage drives charge, let us say, clockwise around the coil and out into any circuit connected to the coil. When the magnet is pulled out of the coil, the magnetic field within the coil decreases and charge is driven in the opposite direction around the coil and circuit. The result is an alternating current (AC) that flows back and forth. The magnitude of the induced voltage will depend on the strength of the magnet, the speed at which the magnet moves, and the number of turns in the coil.

Thomas Edison stands by his original dynamo in the Edison Works plant in Orange, New Jersey, ca. 1906.

The circuits in your home are probably AC circuits in which the electric current alternates back and forth 60 times per second. Of course, the alternating voltage that drives the current does not come from someone pushing a bar magnet in and out of a coil of wire. At electric power plants, large coils of wire can be rotated in the strong magnetic fields of powerful electromagnets. During half of the coils' rotation, as the magnetic field through the coil grows, the induced voltage pushes electrons in one direction; during the next half-turn, as the magnetic field through the coil shrinks, electrons are pushed in the opposite direction. A graph of the induced voltage produced in a power company's generator shows a wave that rises to a peak of about +175 volts and then falls to a minimum of approximately –175 volts before rising to another +175-volt peak. The time from one positive peak to the next is 1/60 second, and the effective voltage is ±125 volts.

The law of conservation of energy tells us that because energy cannot be created, the electrical energy that is generated must come from some other energy source. That source is the work required to turn the coils, which is most likely to come from the kinetic energy of water flowing over a dam or the steam produced by burning fossil fuels or the heat released when atoms undergo fission in an atomic reactor.

Dynamos can produce direct current (DC) as well as alternating current. This is accomplished by connecting the ends of the rotating coil to a split-ring commutator. The commutator rotates so that one brush leading to the external circuit is always touching the side of the ring from which electrons are emerging from the coil and the other brush is always connected to the side of the ring to which electrons are entering. As a result of this arrangement, current always flows in the same direction in the circuit connected to the dynamo.

See also:
Battery; Faraday, Michael; Magnetic Field.
References:
Gardner, Robert. *Famous Experiments You Can Do*. New York: Watts, 1990.
Macaulay, David. *The Way Things Work*. Boston: Houghton Mifflin, 1988.

Eastman, George (1854–1932)

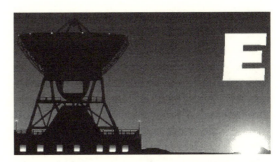

Inventor, manufacturer, and philanthropist, George Eastman developed the innovative flexible film and Kodak system that made photography accessible to the general public regardless of age, skill, or economic status.

When Eastman was 6 his father died, leaving the family nearly destitute. Forced to take in boarders, his mother struggled to hold the family together. Eastman left school at age 14 to help support his mother and two sisters. Beginning as an errand boy in an insurance agency, he ultimately became a bookkeeper in a local bank in Rochester, New York.

In 1877, Eastman planned a vacation to Santo Domingo. To record his trip, the frugal bookkeeper purchased photographic equipment and took lessons in its use. At the time, photography was an expensive and specialized undertaking. Photographers were literally walking chemistry laboratories, carrying and using noxious chemicals to develop pictures. Cameras were awkward and heavy; 70 pounds was not unusual. They required a cumbersome tripod and fragile glass plates coated with a light-sensitive film that recorded the image. The plates had to be developed immediately, before the plates dried, or the image would be lost. The vacation never happened, but Eastman discovered a hobby that became the focus of the rest of his life.

The great quest of photographers in Eastman's time was to devise a simpler picture-taking method that would eliminate the burdensome preparation and need for immediate development of the glass plates, thereby reducing some of the expense of the profession. Inspired by an article in the British *Journal of Photography*, Eastman joined the effort. He began experimenting at night in his mother's kitchen with a dry-plate process that would capture an image and hold it until the plate could be developed at a later time. Ultimately successful, Eastman patented his formula and in 1880, without quitting his day job, convinced one of his mother's boarders, Henry Strong, to become his partner. With $2,000 the men launched the Eastman Dry Plate Company. The company was an immediate success, and in January 1881 Eastman finally left banking to devote his full time to the fledgling enterprise.

Although a major improvement over the earlier processes, the dry-plate process did not eliminate the fragile, unwieldy glass plates or the complex developing procedures they required. In 1884, Eastman introduced his newest advancement, the revolutionary flexible film. By applying his dry-plate emulsion to paper, Eastman, in effect, created a series of plates that could go through a camera. The next year, Eastman and William Walker refined the idea by creating a roll holder that fit any plate-back camera and allowed the film to be advanced from within. Continued experimentation led to a celluloid-backed film that eliminated the picture distortions due to the grain of the backing paper. This celluloid film provided the foundation for a new industry and opened yet another market for Eastman products. Thomas Edison used the film, arranged in 54-foot lengths, to make his moving pictures.

Next, Eastman turned to cameras in an effort to make them "as convenient as a pencil." In September 1888, Eastman offered the public his new Kodak camera. The Kodak name had no real significance. It was the result of playing with letter combinations that included Eastman's favorite character, K. The Kodak was a camera reduced to its bare essentials. It was a wooden box, weighing 22 ounces, with a lens, shutter, and film. There was no viewfinder; the camera was aimed along sight lines inscribed on the top of the box. The Kodak was already packed with enough film for 100 exposures and included a memo book to keep track of the snapshots.

At $25 the camera was still expensive, considering that a suit sold for $15 and $50 was sufficient as a down payment for a small house.

Eastman was convinced that the most difficult aspect of photography for the amateurs was developing prints, so the Kodak system provided a remedy. After the film was completed, the camera and its enclosed film were sent to the factory at Rochester, where a technician removed the film and developed it into 2.5-inch photos. For an additional $10 the camera was reloaded with another 100 exposures and returned to the customer. Never was the Eastman slogan "You press the button, we do the rest" more appropriate.

In 1892, the firm was renamed Eastman Kodak, and the next years saw further advancements that made photography cheaper and easier. A viewfinder and adjustable focus were added to the camera. A pocket Kodak was marketed in 1895, and in 1897 a folding camera was introduced. Prints were enlarged and took on the rectangular shape familiar today. Eastman's efforts culminated in 1900 with the Brownie camera. Shrewdly directed to children, the Brownie was inexpensive at $1, and its film cost only 15 cents for a six-exposure role. By 1915, Kodak dominated the photographic supply market and manufactured 90 percent of all roll film. In 1925, at age 71 and plagued by a spinal ailment, Eastman retired from active participation in his corporation.

Eastman never married, and with few personal expenses he gave freely of his fortune. The prime beneficiary of his generosity was the University of Rochester. Lesser donations went to the Tuskegee and Hampton Institutes as well as the Massachusetts Institute of Technology. Not one to forget his loyal employees, Eastman introduced a profit-sharing program and stock option plan for them and, of course, gave generously to various community projects. Long in ill health, he took his own life at age 77. The note he left read, "My work is done. Why wait?"

In 1987, Eastman Kodak appeared to reinvent itself. The company introduced a new line of cameras designed for one-time use that came preloaded with film. When the film was finished, the camera was returned to the factory and the prints developed. In effect, Kodak cameras were back to their original design.

See also:
Camera; Photography; Photography, Amateur; Photojournalism.

References:
Brayer, Betsy. *George Eastman*. Baltimore: Johns Hopkins University Press, 1995.
Oxford, Edward. "George Eastman: The Man Who Wrought Kodak." *American History Illustrated*, September 1988.
Weisberger, Bernard A. "You Press the Button, We Do the Rest." *American Heritage*, October 1972.

Echolocation
See Sonography.

Edison, Thomas Alva (1847–1931)

American inventor, manufacturer, and businessman, Thomas Edison was one of the most prolific inventors in history. At the time of his death in 1931, Edison held over 1,000 patents. His visionary leadership successfully inaugurated the electrical age and contributed to nearly every electrical advance of his lifetime. Most closely identified with the first durable, practical, and commercially successful lightbulb, Edison also made improvements in the telegraph and telephone, and his invention of the phonograph and motion picture camera changed the world. The "Wizard of Menlo Park" is often credited with creating the business of invention as a result of the establishment of his "invention factory" at West Orange, New Jersey, which became the prototype of the modern industrial research lab.

Edison was born in Milan, Ohio, in 1847, the youngest child of his family. His genius went largely unrecognized in his early life, and his formal education ended before he completed grammar school. After Edison was labeled a slow learner and uneducable,

Thomas Edison adjusts the lens of an early motion picture projector in 1905. Projectors, such as the one pictured here, were developed from Edison's 1891 invention, the Kinetoscope, which allowed a single viewer to watch 15-second silent films.

his mother, a former schoolteacher, withdrew her son from school and undertook his education herself. The young boy became a voracious reader, and most of his knowledge was acquired through independent study. At age ten, Edison built his first laboratory in his parents' cellar and began teaching himself chemistry and electricity. His education was not without a price for his hard-pressed parents. The family barn and icehouse were casualties of young Edison's experiments.

At age 12, to finance his continuing scientific experiments, Edison began selling candy and other small items aboard the railroad between Detroit and home in Port Huron, Michigan. Inspired by his success, Edison diversified his operation by publishing the *Weekly Herald* newspaper. He also established a new lab in the corner of a freight

car. An accidental fire in the rolling lab cost Edison his job and led to an enduring legend. Supposedly, an infuriated conductor, in putting Edison off the train, boxed his ears and left the erstwhile scientist partially deaf. In reality, a childhood bout of scarlet fever left Edison hearing impaired, and degenerative deafness troubled him all his life.

The demise of his lab might have cost Edison his job, but finding another position led him to his lifelong interest, electricity. By the time he was 16, Edison had taught himself telegraphy, and he was quickly recognized for his speed and accuracy as an operator. He was even beginning to acquire a reputation as a mechanical troubleshooter who could fix most machines. In October 1868, Edison filed a patent for his first invention, the electric vote recorder, which was designed to replace the antiquated ballot system and recorded the vote by electrical means.

The financial failure of this initial effort taught Edison a valuable lesson and led him to formulate not only a career-guiding principle but also a pattern for his creativity. He resolved to determine a need for something and invent a solution, but only if the result was commercially marketable.

Edison's fiscal fortunes began to change when he moved to New York City in 1869. The 21-year-old found a position with a commodity brokerage. When the firm's telegraphic apparatus for supplying brokers with stock and transaction news broke down, Edison repaired it. Based upon this experience and further investigation, Edison created his first major invention, the stock ticker. The $40,000 he subsequently earned from the innovation allowed Edison to set himself up as an independent manufacturer and inventor in Newark, New Jersey. Between 1868 and 1875, Edison devoted his attention to telegraphic improvements. The young wonder also worked on an autotelegraph for transmitting handwritten messages, which led to what Edison called the "electric pen." This innovation created duplicate copies of printed matter from a stencil. Edison sold the discovery to A. B. Dick, who marketed the device as the mimeograph.

In 1875, Edison moved his operation to Menlo Park, New Jersey, where he established a new "invention factory." The businessman-inventor envisioned an environment in which creative collaborators could pool their ideas and fashion practical, marketable inventions. Although Edison's name eventually appeared on more than 1,000 patents, most were the result of a collective effort in his research labs. Edison estimated the prototype of the modern industrial research facility would produce a minor invention every ten days and a major breakthrough every six months or so. This was wishful speculation on Edison's part, but in just ten years the lab received 420 patents, including Edison's most famous inventions—the light bulb and the phonograph. The original lab later was purchased by Henry Ford,

a longtime friend and admirer of Edison, for permanent exhibit at Ford's Dearborn, Michigan, museum.

Edison's Menlo Park venture paid immediate dividends. The laboratory's initial success was the carbon telephone transmitter, which extended the clarity and range of Bell's new telephone. The modern telephone uses essentially the same device. Edison's favorite invention, and the only one of his efforts considered completely original, was the phonograph. The idea for what many considered the greatest invention of the age was the result of Edison's work on a repeater telegraph. Edison used a needle to record telegraph messages on a waxed paper strip. The needle made indentations in response to incoming signals. The tape was turned over, and the indentations became bumps. A needle going over the bumps made and broke a circuit, which sent a message. Legend has it that Edison heard a tape running at high speed and was reminded of a musical tone, which led to the idea of reproducing the human voice.

The first phonograph recorded sounds using a needle that registered sound vibrations and inscribed them on a tinfoil-covered cylinder, the earliest form of a sound recording. When the tinfoil was played back through a megaphone-like horn, the sounds were repeated. The term *phonograph*, meaning "sound writing," seemed a logical name for the invention. The machine was considered a mere novelty, interesting and amazing to be sure, but a curiosity. Only Edison had faith in his work. Ten years later Emile Berliner, a German immigrant, enhanced the phonograph's entertainment value by inventing the first flat-disc record player.

In 1879, Edison put the phonograph aside to begin the undertaking he is best known for today. There were a number of international competitors vying to crate a practical, marketable incandescent lightbulb. The most formidable of these men was Joseph Wilson Swan, an Englishman who had successfully developed a filament lightbulb, but the short illuminative life of Swan's invention rendered it commercially unusable. Edison was determined to solve the riddle of the long-lasting bulb. Focusing on a filament that would not burn out, the Menlo Park associates tested over 6,000 substances, from bamboo to platinum, in a yearlong quest. The electrical wizard finally settled on a carbonized thread, which burned for 40 hours. On 21 October 1879, Edison established his place as a genius in the popular imagination by successfully demonstrating his invention. In 1882, to increase popular acceptance and use of the lightbulb, Edison built the first electric generation and distribution station, on Pearl Street in New York City. Edison's electric light company eventually became the basis for the formation of the General Electric Company in 1892.

Edison's continued success and ambition prompted yet another move. In 1887, he relocated his "invention factory" to West Orange, New Jersey. Ten times the size of Menlo Park, the new facility allowed him to expand his interests and inquiries. In 1962, the laboratory and the inventor's home, Glenmont, were designated the Edison National Historical Site.

As the nineteenth century drew to a close, Edison was accorded near-mythic folk hero status and was certainly financially secure. Yet there were other projects that interested him, and chief among these was photographically reproducing motion and action—moving pictures. With the invaluable assistance of his colleague, W. K. L. Dickson, Edison developed the Kinetograph, a massive piano-sized motion picture camera patented in 1891.

George Eastman's invention of flexible celluloid film gave Dickson the opportunity to perfect "roller photography." Using 50 feet of film, purchased for $2.50, Dickson invented the first movie film. The Edison assistant perforated the film along the edges so a hand-cranked sprocket could move the film horizontally behind the lens. Each frame became a slightly different picture so that, when viewed in rapid sequence, the film gave the illusion of motion. The film was shown in a Kinetoscope, a peep show–like box, which debuted in a New York City penny arcade in 1894. Going on location to make films to meet the growing Kinetoscope demand was out of the question, given the cumbersome burden of Edison's camera. Unfazed, Edison built the first motion picture studio on his lot in 1893. The studio, known as Black Maria, was nothing more than a tar-papered shack that Edison used to film dancers, boxers, acrobats, and contemporary celebrities like Annie Oakley or Buffalo Bill.

The concept of modern projection never occurred to Edison. The French Lumière brothers patented the process in 1895. Edison resisted the innovation for a time because his Kinetoscope was so successful. He reasoned that showing his films to so many customers simultaneously would undermine the Kinetoscope market. The Lumières' success forced Edison to act, and he acquired a patent for a projector from Thomas Armat in 1895. Typically, Edison made some improvements and marketed it in 1896 as the Edison Vitascope.

Edison collapsed while working in his lab on 1 August 1931. The great inventor lingered until 18 October 1931, when he finally died at his home in West Orange. As a compliment to the man who changed the world, millions dimmed their lights on the evening of Edison's funeral.

See also:
Motion Pictures; Phonograph.
References:
Baldwin, Neil. *Edison: Inventing the Century*. New York: Hyperion Press, 1995.
Josephson, Matthew. *Edison: A Biography*. New York: McGraw-Hill, 1959.
McGinty, Brian. "The Great Invention." *American History Illustrated*, August 1979.

EDVAC
See Computer.

Electric Field
Around any charged particle, object, or plate, we can envision an electric field consisting of imaginary lines of electric force extending from the charge or charges. The direction of

the field at any point is given by the direction of the electric force on a unit positive charge placed at that point. The strength of the field is defined as the force that would be exerted on a unit positive charge placed at that point. All these points together make up the electric field, which is commonly represented by a series of lines. The concentration of the lines indicates the strength of the field; the direction of the arrowheads on the lines gives the direction of the field.

Electric fields are found in all communication devices that are powered by electricity. The electric field lines in an ordinary conducting wire are parallel to the wire and serve to drive electrons along the wire. The charges on the parallel plates of a capacitor produce an electric field that is of uniform strength between the plates and perpendicular to the plates themselves. It is the electric field in a cathode-ray tube of a television set that accelerates electrons out of the electron gun and starts them on their path toward the fluorescent screen, where the images we view are formed. Along their path to the screen, the electrons can be deflected off their straight-line path by the electric fields that exist between oppositely charged electric plates found between the electron gun and the screen.

> **See also:**
> Capacitor; Electromagnetic Waves; Magnetic Field; Television.

Electric Generator
See Dynamo.

Electrical Relay
See Relay; Telegraph.

Electrical Resistor
Most electrical instruments used for communication include circuits that contain electrical resistors. They are called resistors because they resist, or oppose, the flow of electric current. Adding a resistor to an electric circuit is similar to placing a small-diameter pipe in a piping system that delivers water. The narrow pipe reduces the flow of water; an electrical resistor impedes the flow of electric charge.

The resistance of a length of wire through which an electric current is flowing is defined as the ratio of the voltage across the ends of the wire to the current flowing through the wire. If the voltage is 10 volts and the current is 0.50 ampere, the resistance of the wire is 20 ohms. (An ohm is defined as 1 volt per ampere.) Resistors are made to have a particular resistance. For example, a 10-ohm resistor will allow a current of 1.0 ampere to flow through it when the voltage across the leads at the ends of the resistor is 10 volts. If the voltage is increased to 20 volts, 2.0 amperes will flow through the resistor. A 20-ohm resistor will allow only half as much current to flow as a 10-ohm resistor given the same voltage, while a 5-ohm resistor allows twice as much current to flow.

Resistors are made in several ways. The least precisely made resistors consist of graphite (carbon) packed in a Bakelite case. Wire-wound resistors are made by wrapping a resistant alloy wire such as nichrome around a ceramic core. Film-type resistors consist of a thin film of carbon or metal alloy spread over an insulating substrate.

Electrical resistance can be increased by wiring resistors in series, one after the other. Two 10-ohm resistors wired in series have a total resistance of 20 ohms. The same two resistors wired in parallel (side by side) would have a resistance of 5 ohms. The reason for this is that the cross-sectional area of two resistors side by side is twice that of one resistor, and resistance varies inversely with area; that is, doubling the area halves the resistance.

It is also possible to change resistance in a circuit by using a variable resistor. Such a resistor has a sliding contact and, because the resistance of a wire is proportional to its length, the resistance can be changed by moving the sliding contact so that more or less of the wire is in the circuit. Such resistors with three terminals are used in low-power circuits to control volume in radios and amplifiers and are called potentiometers.

Table 1. Resistor Color Coding

Color on first three bands	Number represented by color on band	Tolerance (4th band)
Black	0	Brown ±1%
Brown	1	Red ±2%
Red	2	Gold ±5%
Orange	3	Silver ±10%
Yellow	4	No band ±20%
Green	5	
Blue	6	
Violet	7	
Gray	8	
White	9	

The resistance (in ohms) and percentage tolerance of a resistor can be found by reading the color-coded bands that encircle it, as shown in Table 1. The first two bands represent numbers, the third band gives the number of zeros that follow the two numbers, and the fourth band indicates the resistor's tolerance. Thus, a resistor with bands that show the colors red, green, brown, gold is a 250-ohm resistor with ±5 percent tolerance.

See also:
Diode; Electric Field.

Electrode
See Battery.

Electromagnet

Electromagnets, which are an essential component in many communication devices, consist of a coil of insulated wire wound around a soft iron core. When an electric current flows through the coil, the soft iron becomes magnetized and the coil and its iron core act like a bar magnet.

In 1819, Hans Christian Oersted discovered that an electric current creates a magnetic field that encircles the current. When a magnetic compass is placed above or below a current-carrying wire, the compass needle is deflected perpendicular to the current in a direction that is predictable.

Further experiments by André Ampère revealed that if the wire is wound to form a cylindrical coil (a solenoid), the magnetic field produced when current flows in the wire will be similar to the field around a bar magnet. One end of the coil will behave like the north pole of a magnet; the other end will behave like a south pole. Such coils will, when current flows through them, attract or repel one another just as do bar magnets.

Early in the nineteenth century, the English scientist William Sturgeon found that the strength of a magnet made from a coil of wire could be increased by placing a soft iron bar in the center of the coil. The magnetic lines of force seemed to become concentrated in the iron. Sturgeon was able to lift a 9-pound weight with his electromagnet, which itself weighed only about a pound.

The American physicist Joseph Henry found that by insulating the wire he could wind many turns in cylindrical fashion about a soft iron core. The greater the number of turns, the stronger the magnet. In fact, during a demonstration of electromagnets at Yale University in 1831, Henry was able to lift more than a ton of iron with his device. Similar strong electromagnets are used to lift magnetizable metals today. The electromagnets essential in communication devices such as telephones, telegraphs, and relays are considerably weaker but extremely useful.

The advantage of an electromagnet is that it acts like a magnet only while current flows in the coiled wire. As soon as the current is turned off, the coil's magnetism is lost. Thus, an electromagnet can be used as a switch. When current flows, the electromagnet might be used to attract a piece of metal and thereby close an electric circuit. When the current is turned off, the attractive force disappears, and gravity or a spring can be used to pull the metal from the coil and break the circuit.

See also:
Henry, Joseph; Loudspeaker; Microphone; Oersted, Hans Christian.

Electromagnetic Waves

Electromagnetic waves consist of electric and magnetic fields oscillating at right angles to one another as they travel through space at the speed of light (300,000 kilometers per second). They constitute the basic means of long-range communication today.

In speech, the sounds that make up words are transported from the speaker's mouth to the listener's ears by sound waves. The sound waves are formed by the back-and-forth movement of air molecules. Unless there is a medium such as air, water, wood, metal, or other matter to carry the sound waves, there will be no oral communication.

Although sound waves are the major means of conversational communication, electromagnetic waves provide a way of communicating over long distances. Radio, television, radar, and wireless telephone and telegraphy allow us to transmit words or other information not only through air but across the vacuum of outer space as well. No material medium, such as air or water, is needed to carry electromagnetic waves.

Maxwell and the Nature of Electromagnetic Waves

The source of all electromagnetic waves is electrical. A changing electric field will cause electric charges, such as those in a metal wire, to accelerate. Whenever electric charges accelerate, an electromagnetic wave is produced. If the charges are made to oscillate in a periodic manner, as they are when they move up and down the antenna of a radio transmitter, the waves will have a frequency and a wavelength that reflects the rate at which the charges oscillate. The changing electric field, which is parallel to the accelerating charges, is accompanied by a changing magnetic field, and the two fields, oscillating at right angles to one another and to the direction in which the waves move, travel through space at a speed of 300,000 kilometers per second (186,000 miles per second).

The existence of electromagnetic waves was predicted by James Clerk Maxwell in his 1873 *Treatise on Electricity and Magnetism*, which was based on equations he had formulated nearly ten years earlier. From the experimental and theoretical work of Hans Christian Oersted, Carl Friedrich Gauss, Michael Faraday, André-Marie Ampère, and others, Maxwell knew that electric fields surround electric charges and that magnetic fields encircle these charges when they move. Based on the experimental work of his predecessors, Maxwell also knew that a magnetic field can be produced by a changing electric field as well as by moving charges and that changing magnetic fields give rise to electric fields. Building on this established knowledge and using his own magnificent mathematical talent, Maxwell developed equations that predicted the emission of electromagnetic waves whenever electric charges accelerate. His equations led him to believe that these waves would travel at the speed of light, strongly suggesting that visible light with wavelengths ranging from 390 to 750 nanometers (3.9×10^{-7} meters to 7.5×10^{-7} meters) and frequencies of 4.0×10^{14} hertz to 7.7×10^{14} hertz are one form of electromagnetic waves.

Hertz and the Discovery of Electromagnetic Waves

In 1887, Heinrich Hertz—after whom the hertz, the unit for frequency (vibrations per second), is named—was able to produce and detect the electromagnetic waves that Maxwell had predicted. Hertz also demonstrated through careful experiments that these waves had the same properties of reflection, refraction, and diffraction as did visible light. Hertz's experiments helped to confirm Maxwell's belief that light was one example of electromagnetic waves.

The radio waves used in broadcasting are produced by accelerating electric charges up and down long antennas. The wavelengths of radio waves range from about 3 to 550 meters. The speed at which any periodic wave travels is equal to the product of its wavelength and frequency. Think of a series of water waves that pass by. If 100 waves pass by in 10 seconds (a frequency of 10 hertz, or 10 waves per second) and the distance from

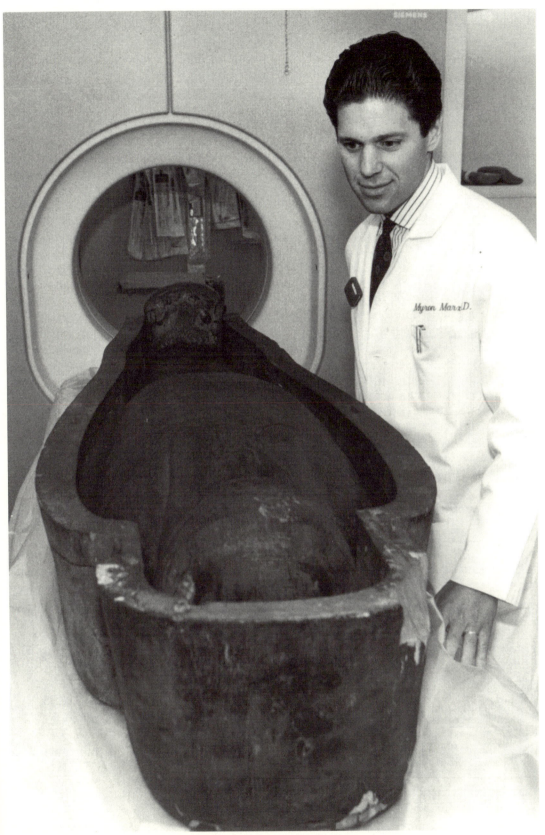

Dr. Myron Marx takes a computerized axial tomography (CAT) scan of an Egyptian mummy at Brigham and Women's Hospital in Boston. The CAT scan allows researchers to study mummies without unwrapping the shrouds or even disturbing the coffin. A CAT scan involves passing a series of X rays—very short electromagnetic waves—through thin slices of the body.

one wave crest to the next (the wavelength) is 0.3 meter, then by the time the one-hundredth wave passes, the first wave will be 30 meters beyond (100 × 0.3 meter = 30 meters). Since the wave moved that distance in 10 seconds, its speed must be 3 meters per second. The same result is obtained by multiplying the wavelength (0.3 meter) by the frequency (10 hertz).

Those who accepted Maxwell's convincing treatise believed that there must be a medium that carries electromagnetic waves. At that time all known wave phenomena required a medium to carry the waves. Water waves move along the surface of that liquid. Sound waves are carried by the molecules that make up air, water, wood, steel, and other kinds of matter. But through what medium do light and other electromagnetic waves travel?

To satisfy this perceived need for a medium, physicists invented the ether—an invisible, solid, massless, elastic material that fills all space. Despite numerous attempts, all efforts to detect the ether failed. Early in the twentieth century, Albert Einstein showed that there is no need for an ether. The oscillating electric and magnetic fields that constitute an electromagnetic wave can maintain themselves as they travel through empty space.

The Electromagnetic Spectrum

The electromagnetic spectrum extends from radio to gamma waves, from wavelengths greater than 10 kilometers to those less than 0.00001 nanometers (10^{-14} meter). Radio waves, the longest waves in the spectrum, are produced from large devices such as radio antennas, in which electric charges oscillate up and down at a frequency corresponding to that of the waves emitted. The high-frequency, short wavelengths of gamma radiation arise from the acceleration of charges within the tiny confines (10^{-14} meter) of atomic nuclei.

Near the other end of the electromagnetic spectrum, the very short wavelengths associated with X rays are invaluable in communicating information because they are ab-sorbed or reflected by dense matter such as bone or metal but readily penetrate soft tissue such as muscle and fat. They are produced when electrons moving at velocities close to one-fifth the speed of light collide with a solid metal target. The rapid deceleration of the electrons as they come to rest produces electromagnetic waves with wavelengths of approximately half an atom in size. Film sensitive to X rays can readily detect broken bones hidden by softer tissue.

Visible light, which plays such a vital role in human communication, has just the right amount of energy to initiate chemical reactions that give rise to nerve impulses in the retina of the human eye or that convert silver ions to silver metal in photographic film. It is quite likely that the sun's peak radiation, which occurs at 520 nanometers, a wavelength near the middle of the visible spectrum, played a major role in the evolution of the human eye.

See also:
Faraday, Michael; Hertz, Heinrich Rudolf; Marconi, Guglielmo; Maxwell, James Clerk; Oersted, Hans Christian; Radar; Radio; Television.

References:
How It Works: The Illustrated Encyclopedia of Science and Technology, vol. 15. New York and London: Marshall Cavendish, 1978.
Magill, Frank N., ed. *Magill's Survey of Science; Physical Science Series*, vol. 2. Pasadena, CA: Salem Press, 1992.
Science and Technology Illustrated, vol. 15. Chicago: Encyclopedia Britannica, 1984.
Wheeler, Gerald F., and Larry D. Kirkpatrick. *Physics: Building a World View*. Englewood Cliffs, NJ: Prentice-Hall, 1983.

Electronic Mail (E-mail)

Electronic mail (E-mail) is a system that allows a message generated on one computer to be sent to another computer over telephone lines. Large corporations and commercial online companies such as CompuServe, MCI Mail, and Easy Link offer E-mail service. Communication can be virtually instantaneous if the recipients are at their computers. If no one is "home," the message is stored in the receiver's "mail-box"—a file at the host system's main computer. People expecting E-mail can check their "mailbox" periodically for messages, which they can then read on screen or download or print for reading later.

E-mail is much faster and generally less expensive than paying postage for ordinary mail delivery, provided it is sent to the correct address. An address on the Internet has two parts. The part before the "at" sign (@) is the name of the user. The part after the @ is the domain—the computer to which the message will be sent. E-mail to someone named Dennis Shortelle, who accesses the Internet through America Online (AOL), might be addressed to dshortelle@aol.com. The *com* in the address indicates that AOL is a commercial enterprise. If the address is at a school, college, or university, "edu" rather than "com" would appear at the end of the address.

The recipient's E-mail program usually has an icon or an alert sound that indicates an incoming message. E-mail enthusiasts often abbreviate common phrases, including "by the way" (BTW), "real soon now" (RSN), and "thanks in advance" (TIA). Because E-mail is often written in haste, attempts at subtle sarcasm by the writer may be read as caustic remarks by the recipient.

In addition to E-mail, computers with fax modems can also be used to send and receive facsimiles (faxes). This eliminates the need for a separate fax machine.

Most businesses are now connected to the Internet through a commercial online service such as America Online, CompuServe, Prodigy, or a local Internet service provider that provides access to the Internet as well as the software needed to download information onto the business's computer. With Internet access a company can send and receive E-mail, which is becoming the accepted means of communication among businesses both large and small. Price lists, quotations, specifications, reports, and various documentation can be sent to any place in the world by E-mail almost instantaneously following a request. Many companies have es-

tablished sites on the Internet that are accessible to other businesses and potential customers. These sites provide information, including photographs and even videos, pertaining to the companies' products.

See also:
Computer; Fax Machine; Internet; Modem.
Reference:
Levine, John R., and Carol Baroudi. *The Internet for Dummies*, 2nd ed. Foster City, CA: IDG Books, 1994.

Electronic Publishing

Although the term electronic publishing is somewhat ambiguous, it generally refers to material that is published in a computer-accessible manner, usually as a CD-ROM or on the Internet. In a broader sense, electronic publishing can include paper publications from a desktop publishing computer program or any form of printing involving computers.

During the last decade of the twentieth century, an increasing number of magazines, journals, and newspapers have become available in an electronic format. Some materials is stored in database or hypertext-linked formats. Hypertext is a technique of data formatting and presentation that allows the users to interact with the text or graphics on their computer monitors. "Clicking" on a word or symbol reveals a cross-reference that may be in the form of text, graphics, or even a video. The data involved may be on different computers, possibly in different parts of the world.

The computer's ability to store written and graphical matter in digital form, combined with access through the Internet, makes individual electronic publishing possible. Researchers can gather, organize, and print materials obtained from various electronic databases. One of the persistent problems with electronic publishing is how to protect data and the associated investment of time and money on a wide-open network such as the Internet.

Some believe that within a decade all scholarly journals will be published electronically. However, paper publishing has certain advantages that cannot be discounted. Editing, reviewing, refereeing, and the addition of suitable graphics and photos can probably be done more economically for wide distribution by an established print-on-paper publishing firm.

The arguments that electronic publishing is free and that it will make publishers and libraries obsolete are myths. Electronic publishing costs are sometimes hidden because they are paid for by parent organizations such as a university or company. Although storage costs continue to decline, large databases must still be paid for, and there are the inescapable overhead costs that include staff, rent, software, hardware, maintenance, and access to the Internet. Publishers and libraries serve as intermediaries between authors and readers. Publishers increase the value of written material by reviewing and editing, and they bring efficiencies of scale to their operations. Libraries add value to written matter through sharing, collecting, evaluating, organizing, archiving, and providing access to resources.

Desktop publishing programs enable a user to produce printed matter with a variety of typefaces (fonts) in various styles and sizes, and these programs offer other typesetting capabilities such as hyphenation and margin alignment (justification). Such programs make page layouts possible and allow users to see them in a format that is often referred to as "what you see is what you get." In other words, the image on the computer monitor corresponds exactly to the appearance of the finished document, which usually is printed on a laser printer.

Adding a scanner to the computer allows the desktop publisher to incorporate visuals and text from other sources. A color laser printer can provide an attractive finished product.

See also:
Computer; Internet; Publishing.
References:
International Encyclopedia of Communications. New York: Oxford University Press, 1989.
Tenopir, Carol, and Donald W. King. "Setting the Record Straight on Journal Publishing: Myth vs. Reality." *Library Journal*, 15 March 1996.
Wood, James. *Desktop Magic.* New York: Van Nostrand Reinhold, 1994.

Endoscopy
See Fiber Optics.

Entropy
See Wiener, Norbert.

Esperanto
Esperanto was proposed as an international second language that would allow people who speak different languages to communicate. Esperanto's basic vocabulary stems from the Romance languages as well as German, English, and Latin. The language is especially noted for its logical construction and ease of acquisition. It is the most widely used international language in the world.

Physician and linguist Ludwig L. Zamenhof (1859–1917) devised Esperanto based on his own experience growing up in Bialystok, Poland. Bialystok was a multiethnic and linguistically diverse region, factors that generated tension and hostility among its residents. Zamenhof hoped his creation would promote worldwide understanding and peace as well as forge cultural and economic bonds among nations. The doctor established the basic rules of his language in his 1887 publication, *Lingvo Internacia*, which he wrote under the pseudonym of Dr. Esperanto ("one who hopes" in the new language). Two years later the first Esperanto journal, *La Esperantisto*, began publication in Nuremberg, Germany. The first Esperanto international congress was held in France in 1905, the same year that saw the organization of the American Esperanto Association in Boston.

Esperanto was specifically designed to be logical, uniform, and therefore easy to learn. The alphabet is 28 letters, a slightly modified version of the Latin alphabet. Each letter has only one sound, which is always pronounced, and there are no combinations of letters used to produce a sound. This lends itself to a simple phonetic spelling. Esperanto grammar is composed of 16 basic rules, and there are no exceptions or irregularities. Parts of speech are formed by a consistent, easily remembered set of endings. Nouns end in *o*, adjectives in *a*, adverbs in *e*, verbs in *l*, and plurals are formed by adding *f*. For example, *belo* is the root for "beauty," the adjective *bela* means "beautiful," and *bele*, the adverbial form, connotes "beautifully." Similarly, using a number of prefixes and suffixes, Esperanto reduces the number of vocabulary words to basic international root words. *Granda* means "great." *Mal* is the prefix meaning "the opposite," so *malgranda* is "small." Another example involves the suffix *ef*, meaning "place of." *Lernefo*, then, is a noun, as indicated by the ending *o*. *Lern* is the root word for "learn," and *-ef* means "in place of." Putting all this together, *lernefo* literally means "a place of learning," or a school.

Esperantists see a number of advantages to the language, aside from ease of acquisition, as a vehicle for international communication. It has been tested for 80 years and is used in some 80 countries today. Estimates of how many people are familiar with the language are uncertain, ranging from 50,000 to 2 million. There is an impressive list of Esperantist publications, including 100 current periodicals, and a literary tradition that includes translations of such major works as the Old Testament, the Koran, and selections of poetry and fiction. Regular radio and television broadcasts emanating from world capitals like Bern, Beijing, Vienna, or Prague have helped spread Esperanto usage.

Adherents proudly point to the fact that Esperanto is a second language and would not replace native vernacular. Furthermore, it is a politically unbiased and neutral language that belongs to no one country. Newer nations in Africa or Asia might be reluctant to accept English as an official language because of political overtones, as has also been the case in Quebec, but Esperanto would pose no such problem. Finally, as the concept of the global village matures in the Computer Age and the demands of increased travel and international business grow, proponents see an international language as a greater necessity.

Esperanto is not without critics. Linguists contend that the uniformity of the language is superficial. For example, the rule that all nouns must end in *o* does not take into account place names like Canada or Austria. The universal *USA* is altered to *Usono*. Furthermore, many words that end in *o* are not nouns and have become exceptions to the rule. Word formation appears to be the biggest hurdle for those disenchanted with Esperanto. In order to aid memorization, the vocabulary is simplified, and the use of prefixes and suffixes has led to some real distortions. *Lernefo* for "school" and *flegmalsanulefo* for "hospital" are but two examples of this criticism. Opponents of Esperanto contend its relative obscurity is the result of its own program of an oversimplified and distorted vocabulary as well as inconsistent rules. This makes the language much harder to learn than its adherents would have the world believe. Nonetheless, Esperanto has become synonymous in the popular mind with both artificial and international language today.

See also:
Artificial Language.
References:
Forster, Peter G. *The Esperanto Movement.* Hawthorne, NY: Mounton, 1982.
Janton, Pierre. *Esperanto: Language, Literature, and Community.* Albany, NY: SUNY Press, 1993.

Espionage

Espionage is the act of spying on another organized group (often another nation) in order to obtain secret information. It is carried out to obtain military, political, or business-related information. A foreign agent may use forgery to establish a fictitious identity and then steal secret information or obtain it from someone with access to it. Information can be intercepted in various ways: by eavesdropping, opening mail, reading telegrams, monitoring radio messages, tapping telephone wires, accessing a computer database, obtaining or buying information from someone for hire or someone sympathetic to the enemy's cause, or by any other devious means possible. Once obtained, information is transmitted to the agent's superiors—usually an organized espionage agency—by mail, telecommunications, or courier.

Methods used to prevent secret messages or data from being intercepted include everything from whispering and sealing envelopes to metal shielding to prevent electrical leaks, bug detection and passwords, and, of course, messages written in code.

Counterespionage, which involves the prevention of espionage, uses the same techniques as espionage. One method is to plant an agent in the enemy's espionage organization. For example, an American CIA agent might have become a member of the former Soviet Union's KGB.

Another approach is to catch an enemy agent and convince that person to become a "double agent"; that is, provide false information to his own organization while sending any useful data to the foreign nation's operatives. In return for such cooperation, the agent avoids prosecution and may also receive financial rewards.

History

Espionage is probably as old as human civilization. The Bible reveals that Moses used spies, one of whom was Joshua. Espionage was not uncommon in ancient China, and there are reports of wax-covered messages written on silk and carried in the rectums of couriers. Capturing the courier and recovering the message was, and still is in more subtle ways, the most direct form of counterespionage.

What might be called modern espionage had its origins in England during the reign of Elizabeth I in the sixteenth century. Thereafter, many countries used spies and counterespionage to obtain information about enemies or potential enemies. Although the American colonies during the Revolution had no formal espionage agency, amateurs such as Nathan Hale did spy on the British, and the British had plenty of help from Tories who remained loyal to the crown.

Information gleaned by espionage was originally carried by hand or by agents on horseback. Carrier pigeons were later used and continued to be used through World War II. By 1914, when World War I began, telegraphs, telephones, and wireless (radio) made rapid transmission of information possible. To prevent opposing forces from intercepting the same information, codes were developed that were far more complex than those used by courier-carried communications. After the British cut the German transatlantic cable in 1914, the Germans had to rely on wireless or cables under the control of neutral nations to convey coded messages. One such message, sent by German foreign minister Arthur Zimmermann to the German minister in Mexico, was instrumental in bringing the United States into the war. Zimmermann's message, which was decoded by British agents who had cracked the German code, suggested that if the United States entered the war against Germany, Mexico should become a German ally. In return, following a German victory, Mexico would regain the land in Texas, New Mexico, and Arizona that had originally been part of Mexico.

During World War II, Germany and Japan developed complex electromechanical machines to send coded messages. But the British, who soon broke the German code, were aware of German troop movements through most of the war. In the Pacific, U.S. forces were able to break the Japanese codes and gain an edge in that theater. In addition to such technological devices as microphotography and small radio receivers that were easily hidden, the United States made use of Navajo Code Talkers to transmit information.

During the cold war between the United States and the Soviet Union following World War II, computer programs were used to unlock codes, and spy planes and satellites took detailed photographs of naval and military movements and installations. At ground level, sophisticated listening and video devices were used to monitor known or suspected espionage or counterespionage agents.

Recent Technology, Espionage, and Economics

A computer network of 35 intelligence organizations called Intelink now provides almost instant access to any U.S. classified information. Photographs taken by Pentagon spy satellites are available online within a minute of the time they are taken. It used to require months for CIA workers to identify terrorists who might serve as double agents. With the analysis program available on Intelink, these people can be pinpointed in a matter of seconds.

Although hackers have succeeded in circumventing Internet security to obtain the confidential files of companies and colleges, CIA officials are confident that Intelink's encrypted information, protected as well by passwords, is inaccessible to unauthorized personnel. Nevertheless, computer experts are hired to find weaknesses in the system, and they periodically try to hack their way onto Intelink. To prevent internal espionage, an ever-present possibility, terminals inside CIA headquarters are routinely examined for suspicious activity.

The CIA and other intelligence organizations use the Internet as a source of valuable data in addition to the information available on their Intelink system. Combined with other knowledge, the transport of nuclear weapons can often be detected simply by watching the online bulletin boards of shipping companies. Information about crops and industrial production, once classified by the Soviet Union, is now available on the Internet. Resistance groups in many countries now publish on the Internet material that used to be found only in underground newsletters.

Sometimes a simple question on an electronic bulletin board is all that is needed to obtain vast amounts of information about semiclassified knowledge. According to Thomas V. Sobczak (as reported by Douglas Waller in *Time*), when Sobczak raised the question, "How good is aircraft stealth technology?" on a bulletin board for aerospace engineers, he received more information that he could use.

With the end of the cold war, some are questioning the wisdom of spending taxpayer dollars on the CIA, particularly since much of the espionage now being conducted is concerned with "economic intelligence"— information that will likely go to giant American corporations. While such data may be useful to these companies, its value in terms of the national interest is certainly questionable. However, America's unfavorable balance of trade has led the administration and Congress to promote exports, and one way to do that, they believe, is to provide companies with intelligence information that can give them an economic edge in competition with foreign firms.

Whether the CIA can obtain economic information that cannot be obtained by Commerce Department workers through open sources is questionable. Many believe that if there is a need for an intelligence agency, it should avoid redundancy and limit its activities to matters that truly affect national security—hostile political figures, espionage, and military matters such as terrorist groups, nuclear weapons, and other activities that could threaten the lives of American citizens.

See also:
Cryptology; Navajo Code Talkers; Satellite.
References:
International Encyclopedia of Communications. New York: Oxford University Press, 1989.
Lane, Charles. "Why Spy?" *New Republic*, 27 March 1995.
Sussman, Vic. "Lost in Kofka Territory." *U.S. News & World Report*, 3 April 1995.
Waller, Douglas. "Spies in Cyberspace." *Time*, 20 March 1995.

Extension Service

The Extension Service communicates information gathered by land-grant universities and the United States Department of Agriculture to farmers, families, and young people.

In 1862, the United States Congress passed the Morrill Act. Introduced by Vermont Senator Justin S. Morrill, the act offered each state a grant of 30,000 acres of federal land per congressman to establish a college of agriculture and mechanics. Today, many of these land-grant colleges have grown to become outstanding universities, including Cornell, Purdue, Ohio State, the University of Illinois, and the University of Connecticut.

In terms of agricultural education, these colleges have three primary functions: (1) to teach their students the principles of modern agriculture; (2) to carry on research in agriculture; and (3) to communicate knowledge about agriculture through the extension service. Many of the universities have established agricultural experiment stations to carry out research on plant physiology, agronomy, genetics, artificial insemination, and a variety of other topics. Their discoveries become known to farmers through the extension service.

The Cooperative Extension System is a partnership of federal, state, and county governments. Its purpose is to communicate information gathered by land-grant colleges and universities, their experiment stations, and the U.S. Department of Agriculture to farmers, families, and youth. This is done by county agents who, together with the volunteers they train, carry out a variety of programs, hold workshops and meetings, publish newsletters, make radio and television broadcasts, and pay personal visits.

In many counties the Extension Service includes an agent who oversees and promotes the activities of 4-H clubs. The 4-H stands for head, heart, hands, and health, and the clubs are designed to help boys and girls learn about improved methods of agriculture and home economics. Many 4-H club members go on to enroll in land-grant colleges and universities and pursue an education leading to agriculture or agricultural research.

References:

Furnas, J. C. *The Americans: A Social History of the United States 1587–1914.* New York: G. P. Putnam's Sons, 1969.

Garraty, John A. *The American Nation: A History of the United States to 1877.* New York: Harper & Row, 1971.

Extrasensory Perception (ESP)

See Telepathy.

Faraday, Michael (1791–1867)

Michael Faraday's experimental work provided the basic science for the technology that underlies most of today's communication devices. Faraday's work illustrates his belief that the practical benefits of pure open inquiry unrestricted by utilitarian demands can lead not only to the acquisition and understanding of natural laws, but to practical applications as well. Fifty years elapsed before Faraday's basic discoveries led to the dawning of the electrified world we know today.

Michael Faraday was born on the outskirts of London on 22 September 1791. His family was poor and he received only a rudimentary education, a factor that prevented him from using the mathematical techniques of most nineteenth-century physical scientists. At age 14 he was apprenticed to a bookbinder and bookseller, a job that brought him in contact with a great variety of books and led him to become an omnivorous reader. It was also a vocation in which he developed the superb manual skills that served him so well as an experimental scientist.

The Faraday family were Sandemanians, a small fundamentalist religious sect that stressed love, community, and the Bible as one's source of guidance. Ever faithful to his religious beliefs, Faraday was a kind, gentle, and unassuming man who had no interest in money or worldly goods. He regarded his work as an effort to reveal the divine truths found in nature. For religious reasons, he refused knighthood, the presidency of the Royal Society, and a number of other honors. Sarah Barnard, whom he married in 1821, shared his faith, and together, though childless, they enjoyed a happy and loving life.

Early Career

Faraday's reading whetted his enthusiasm for science, and he joined a science discussion group at age 19. Two years later, in an effort to bring new ideas to the group, he attended a series of lectures by Sir Humphrey Davy at the Royal Institution in London. He was so impressed that he sent Davy the notes and related drawings he had made during and following the lectures, along with an application to become Davy's laboratory assistant at the Royal Institution. When the position became available a few months later, Davy offered it to Faraday, who immediately accepted despite a reduction in salary.

Faraday virtually lived at and for the laboratory. His keen mind enabled him to rapidly acquire an understanding of science and experimental techniques. In 1823, while conducting some experiments for Davy, Faraday found a way to liquefy chlorine and then other gases by subjecting them to high pressure and low temperatures. Although recognizing that his protégé had more talent than he, Davy resented Faraday's failure to give him what he considered due credit in the paper Faraday published on gas liquefaction. Thereafter, their relationship was never the same. Davy cast the only dissenting vote when Faraday was elected to the Royal Society in 1824.

A year later, Faraday discovered benzene, an organic chemical widely used as a base for many synthetic compounds, and began extensive research to further Davy's work in electrochemistry. His research was interrupted during the late 1820s, when the Royal Institution took on the task of improving the optical glass used in lenses for the Board of Longitude. Faraday spent two full years overseeing the project because the Royal Institution needed the funds.

To help fund the Institution further, Faraday, following in the footsteps of his mentor Davy, began a series of lectures to explain science to the public, an audience that often included England's royal family. His success as a lecturer and demonstrator led him to initiate the Christmas Courses of Lectures for Juvenile Audiences. Two of these courses— *The Chemical History of a Candle* and *The Various Forces of Nature*—were published in book form. They remain as classics of scientific literature.

Faraday's Work in Electrochemistry

By 1832, Faraday was able to extend Davy's work with electrolysis to the point where he could quantify the process in what are now known as Faraday's laws of electrolysis. The laws state that the mass of a substance deposited or entering solution at an electrode during electrolysis is (1) proportional to the charge that has passed through the electrolytic solution; (2) proportional to the atomic weight of that substance; and (3) inversely proportional to the valence of the element deposited.

Faraday's work is easily explained using the atomic theory. An electrolyte (a solution that conducts electric charge) contains ions (atoms that carry a charge). Molten sodium chloride (table salt) consists of positive sodium ions (Na^+) and negative chloride ions (Cl^-). During electrolysis of this pure salt, sodium collects at the cathode (negative electrode) and chlorine collects at the anode (positive electrode). The sodium ions each combine with one electron to form neutral sodium atoms, while the chloride ions give up an electron each to form neutral chlorine atoms. It is clear that twice as much charge (electrons) will be needed to liberate twice as much sodium or chlorine from solution.

Heavier ions, such as those of potassium (K^+), will result in more mass being deposited for the same charge than is true of sodium. In fact, the ratio of masses deposited will be the same as the ratio of the atomic weights of potassium and sodium (39:23). However, copper ions (Cu^{++}), which carry a charge of +2, require twice as much charge to deposit an atom as do sodium or potassium ions, which carry a single positive charge.

Strangely, Faraday was never enthusiastic about the atomic theory of matter; yet, the validity of his work is revealed by the fact that the terms he used—electrodes, electrolyte, cathode, anode, anion, cation—are still widely used in science today. In recognition of his many contributions to science, the quantity of electrical charge (6.02×10^{23} electrons) required to liberate one equivalent weight of an element from solution (23 grams of sodium, 39 grams of hydrogen, 32 grams of copper) is called a faraday.

Faraday's Work in Electromagnetism

In 1821, shortly after Hans Christian Oersted had shown that a magnetic field surrounds an electric current, Richard Philips, editor of the *Annals of Philosophy*, asked Faraday to write an article about electromagnetism. In preparing the paper, Faraday duplicated Oersted's experiment and then carried out experiments of his own. He discovered that the magnetic field around an electric current will cause a magnet to rotate about the wire carrying the current. Using this principle of electromagnetic rotation, Faraday built the world's first electric motor. It was the first time that electrical energy was converted to mechanical energy. It was certainly not the last time.

If a magnetic field can be produced by an electric current, then, reasoned Faraday, it should be possible to produce an electric current from a magnetic field. But ten years passed before Faraday (and Joseph Henry in the United States) succeeded in producing an electric current from a magnetic field. From his work with electromagnets, Faraday knew that if he wrapped a coil of wire around an iron ring and connected the coil to a battery, a magnetic field would be established in the iron. What would happen, he wondered, if a second coil of wire was wrapped around the iron ring and connected to a galvanometer (a device used to detect electric current)?

The result was not what he expected. Instead of a steady current, he saw the galvanometer needle deflect briefly when the magnetic field was established. It deflected again, but the other way, when the magnetic field was removed by disconnecting the circuit connected to the battery. With his keen ability to visualize, Faraday pictured magnetic fields as lines of force permeating space. He reasoned that a current was induced (charges were made to move) when the expanding lines of force generated by the current in the coil connected to the battery spread across the wires in the coil connected to the galvanometer. When the current that produced the magnetic field was disconnected, the collapsing lines of force again cut the coil, inducing a current in the opposite direction.

Faraday demonstrated the effect in one of his many lectures to the public at the Royal Institution by moving a magnet into and out of a coil of wire connected to a galvanometer. When the magnet was thrust into the coil, the galvanometer showed a sudden burst of current. When the magnet was not moving, the galvanometer was at its zero rest position. When the magnet was pulled from the coil, the galvanometer needle again deflected, but in the opposite direction.

To produce a constant current, Faraday turned a copper disc so that its edge turned between the poles of a horseshoe magnet. The current induced in the copper could be conducted away through wires and used to turn a small electric motor. Faraday had discovered the principle that is used today in power plants that provide the electricity needed to power our modern devices of communication.

Faraday's theoretical view of magnetic and electric forces as lines of force (fields) was foreign to his fellow scientists with their Newtonian, mathematical view of the world. But James Clerk Maxwell used Faraday's lines-of-force paradigm in developing the field equations that turned Faraday's model into a set of rigorous mathematical equations that explained light as electromagnetic waves and correctly predicted its speed.

In his later years Faraday's mental powers declined, and he drifted into senility. His demise was probably the result of mercury poisoning. Nineteenth-century and early twentieth-century experimental scientists,

"mad hatters," and others who spent many hours in the presence of mercury vapors were often afflicted by mental disorders.

See also:
Battery; Computer; Dynamo; Electromagnet; Henry, Joseph; Maxwell, James Clerk; Oersted, Hans Christian; Telegraph; Telephone Switching.

References:
Gillispie, Charles Coulston, ed. *Dictionary of Scientific Biography*. New York: Scribner's, 1981.
James, Frank. "Time, Tide, and Michael Faraday." *History Today*, September 1991.
MacDonald, D. K. C. *Faraday, Maxwell, and Kelvin*. Garden City, NY: Doubleday, 1964.
Magill, Frank N., ed. *The Great Scientists*. Danbury, CT: Grolier, 1989.
Williams, L. Pearce. *Michael Faraday: A Biography*. New York: Basic Books, 1965.

Fax Machine (Facsimile)

A fax machine is a device that scans a document using light and the photoelectric effect. Scanning produces electrical signals that the machine sends via telephone to another fax machine, where the signals are used to reproduce a copy of the original document.

The transmission of words and images by facsimile, which means "to make similar," has recently become a very popular means of communication, especially in the business world. However, facsimile machines have been in use since the 1920s. Newspapers transmitted photographs by facsimile, and businesses, police departments, and the military exchanged printed data via fax. Early machines were slow, but the development of digital techniques and the establishment of standards that made it possible for different machines to respond to one another over telephone lines has made facsimile an increasingly popular means of transmitting printed matter.

To fax a document, the material to be copied is first scanned by shining a light onto the document. During the scanning process, light reflected from the paper enters a photoelectric cell, a detector that converts the reflected light to an electric current. The strength of the current depends on the intensity of the light received by the detector. The current is amplified and changed to sound before entering a telephone line.

At the receiving end of the telephone line, the sound is converted back to electrical signals. These signals are inverted so that large currents, produced where the light was intense, become small currents and vice versa. The signals travel along a stylus that makes contact with heat-sensitive paper on a drum. The stylus at the receiving end moves along the paper in the same way that the scanner moves along the original document at the sender's machine. As the stylus moves across the paper, the electric current in it heats the paper, which contains carbon. When the current is large, more carbon is "burned," making the paper darker. Smaller currents produce grayish areas. When the current is zero, the paper remains white. Since the currents have been inverted, those parts of the original document that reflected a lot of light are now white, and those parts that reflected very little light are dark because the large currents produce considerable carbon.

See also:
Analog and Digital Signals; Computer; Electronic Mail; Telephone.
Reference:
Gardner, Robert. *Communication*. New York: Twenty-First Century, 1994.

Federal Communications Commission

The Federal Communications Commission (FCC) is an independent regulatory body directly responsible to Congress. It was formed to oversee and manage interstate and foreign communication by radio, television, microwave, satellite, wire, and cable in the public interest. Preceded by the Federal Radio Commission, the FCC was established by the Communications Act of 1934. The act expanded the agency's initial mandate to cover all interstate communication, including telephone and telegraph services. Additional regulatory responsibilities were established by the Satellite Act of 1962.

The FCC is composed of five members appointed by the president of the United States with the advice and consent of the Senate. Furthermore, no three members of the commission may be of the same political party. One commissioner is designated as chairman and serves at the discretion of the president.

The commission has three main bureaus. The Mass Media Bureau regulates most radio and television broadcasts and issues construction permits and operators' licenses. The Common Carrier Bureau is most often associated with regulation of the rates and services of public utilities such as the telephone and telegraph as well as satellite communication. The Private Radio Bureau regulates all radio services other than broadcast, common carrier, or cable. These include police, taxi, and citizens band radio as well as all safety, commercial, and personal radio facilities. The FCC also plays a role in national defense by administering the Emergency Broadcast System for use in national crises.

The FCC has not been without controversy. It was FCC chairman Newton Minnow who declared television a "vast wasteland" in 1961. The FCC has been involved in the debate over the quality and propriety of children's television. In 1987, the agency abolished the Fairness Doctrine, which required television and radio to present opposing viewpoints on controversial issues. Nonetheless, the FCC remains responsible for monitoring the equal-time provision, which is intended to ensure balanced broadcast time for political candidates. Most recently a great deal of discussion has centered on the FCC's role in supervising cable television.

See also:
Radio; Radio and Society; Radio History; Sarnoff, David; Television; Television and Society.
References:
Congressional Quarterly's Federal Regulatory Directory. Washington, DC: Congressional Quarterly, 1986.
Office of the Federal Registrar, National Archives and Records Administration. *United States Government Manual*. Washington, DC: Government Printing Office, 1994.

Stern, Robert H. *The Federal Communications Commission and TV*. Salem, NH: Ayer, 1979.

Federal Express

A service offering efficient overnight delivery of packages, Federal Express was conceived by Frederick Smith, who first developed the idea while a student at Yale in the early 1960s. Smith recognized that shipment of freight by air using other companies' airlines, the normal mode in the 1960s, was inefficient and ineffective.

To provide the "absolutely, positively overnight!" deliveries that became the company's advertising slogan, Smith purchased from Pan American Airways a fleet of Falcon fan-jets that he modified to carry freight instead of passengers. At night, which Smith realized was a downtime for passenger service, these planes carried packages and letters from major cities across the United States to the company's hub in Memphis, Tennessee. From about 11:00 P.M. to 4:00 A.M., Federal Express planes would arrive, be unloaded, and have their cargo sorted and rerouted onto aircraft that would then fly back to Miami, New York, Los Angeles, or other major cities, usually arriving before dawn. At the various airports, the packages and letters would be sorted and sent by truck to distribution centers in and around the city. From there, couriers in the now-familiar FedEx vans delivered to the various businesses and homes designated by the center. Couriers usually made two trips. The first trip was to deliver priority overnight materials for customers, who paid the premium price to ensure parcels arrived by the next morning. The second was to distribute standard overnight packages and letters for which FedEx promised delivery by the next business day (not necessarily before noon) and to pick up items to be sent to Memphis that night.

The FedEx Hub in Memphis

The key to Federal Express's prompt and efficient deliveries was the Memphis hub, designed and organized by operations chief Mike Fitzgerald, a former United Parcel Service employee. The first hub was a building 1,000 feet long and 250 feet wide that contained a network of conveyor belts. Packages unloaded from the planes were placed on these belts and carried to workstations, where sorters—mostly part-time employees from local colleges—separated the packages and placed them on belts that would carry them to a second workstation. The second workstation might, for example, receive all packages destined to reach the Northeast. At this station, packages bound for Boston would be placed on one belt and packages for New York City on another. At the next station, the packages for New York would be removed and loaded onto a plane scheduled to fly to New York, or they would be loaded onto a plane headed for Boston.

By 1981, the huge Memphis hub had been enlarged to more than three times its original area. Shortly thereafter, FedEx executives realized that further increases in the size of the hub could not efficiently handle the increased volume, even with an automated system using bar codes and scanners similar to those used by the Postal Service to help in nightly sorting. Consequently, regional hubs with similar unloading, sorting, and loading centers were built.

About 1 million packages a day now pass through the Memphis hub, a far cry from the 6 packages that traveled there on FedEx's first night of operation on 12 March 1973. A month later there were still only 183 packages from 22 cities, and by the end of that month FedEx had a deficit of $4.4 million. Smith did not give up on his dream; he raised more money and continued to work around the clock to make the venture a success. By July 1975, the company was showing a small profit, and by the end of fiscal year 1976, profits were at $3.6 million. By 1991, Federal Express was the nation's most profitable airline, although it carried no passengers, with a net income of nearly $321 million.

As early as 1978, it became clear that the Falcon fan-jets were too small to carry all the Federal Express freight from major cities.

Consequently, the company began adding larger planes to its fleet—DC-10s, 727s, and 737s. At the Memphis hub, even a 727 could be unloaded by one of Mike Fitzgerald's crews in 18 minutes.

Competition

Federal Express's major competitor is United Parcel Service (UPS), the world's largest package delivery company. It employs a quarter-million people, has a gross income in excess of $15 billion, and delivers an average of 11 million parcels each working day. UPS began in 1907 when James Casey and Claude Ryan, both teenagers at the time, borrowed $100 and started operating a messenger service for companies in Seattle, Washington. Their company prospered and expanded to include package deliveries. Twelve years after its founding, the company became known as United Parcel Service. By 1950, UPS was providing delivery service for stores in more than 12 cities, and in 1952 it became a common carrier—meaning that it would deliver for and to the general public—and was subject to regulation by public authorities.

To meet the overnight delivery competition from Federal Express, UPS bought its own fleet of planes and established air service in 1982. Additional competition for domestic overnight air express, on a lesser scale, came also from Purolator Courier, the U.S. Postal Service, Airborne Freight, and Emery Air Freight.

In an effort to avoid competition from facsimiles, which provide almost instant delivery of messages, FedEx established ZapMail during the mid-1980s. ZapMail was essentially facsimile transmission from one FedEx office to another. Smith thought that by having such a service in place, businesses would use ZapMail and not purchase their own machines. But when the price of fax machines fell to $300, companies as well as individuals began faxing directly to one another. After three years of struggling to make ZapMail into a moneymaker, Smith gave up in 1989 after losing about a third of a billion dollars in the venture.

FedEx Overseas

In 1989, Federal Express, which was then making $4.6 billion per year and providing 45 percent of the domestic overnight air deliveries, bought Flying Tigers, an international heavy freight company with landing rights in many foreign countries, for $880 million. Overseas deliveries lost $75 million the first year, and the company spent $100 million to repair Flying Tiger's fleet of old 747s. In 1992, Federal Express bailed out of intra-European courier service, leaving on-ground deliveries to other companies. UPS, on the other hand, has spent $1 billion buying European delivery companies.

The growing market for air freight in Asia has attracted Federal Express as well as UPS, TNT Express (an Australian conglomerate), and DHL (a Brussels-based company). Asia is ripe for development of air freight because major cities are far apart, many are separated by ocean, and ground transportation is poorly developed. The potential in Asia is confirmed by the fact that air express on that continent has been enjoying an annual growth of nearly 50 percent.

Federal Express plans to transfer its domestic model to Asia. It built its primary hub at Subic Bay in the Philippines, where the airport is open all night. FedEx also runs direct routes between the United States and China. UPS has hubs in Hong Kong and Singapore; TNT uses Manila as its hub. DHL plans to use other airlines to ship its freight. All these companies are betting on forecasts predicting that by early in the twenty-first century, half the goods made in Asia will be bought on the same continent.

See also:
Fax Machine; Postal Service; Scanner; Universal Product Code.

References:
Greising, David. "Watch Out for Flying Packages." *Business Week*, 14 November 1994.
Kessler, Andrew J. "Price Fix." *Forbes*, 12 August 1996.
"Pass the Parcel." *The Economist*, 18 March 1995.
Sigafoos, Robert A. *Absolutely Positively Overnight!* Memphis, TN: Saint Luke's Press, 1983.

Trimble, Vance. *Overnight Success*. New York: Crown, 1993.

Feedback

See Wiener, Norbert.

Fessenden, Reginald A. (1866–1932)

Born in East Bolton, Quebec, Canada, Reginald Fessenden is second only to Thomas Edison in the number of patents obtained for a variety of inventions. As a young man Fessenden worked for Edison at Menlo Park, New Jersey, but in 1890, tired of working in the shadow of his employer, he went to work for Edison's rival, Westinghouse.

Fessenden is probably best remembered as the first person to send a continuous modulated radio wave so that speech and music could be transmitted through space and received by individual radios. By the time of his historic broadcast on Christmas Eve in 1906, Fessenden was a physics professor at the University of Pittsburgh. Using a high-frequency, oscillating-current generator that he had designed, Fessenden modulated the radio waves from his transmitter with a microphone. His Christmas greeting and music were sent from a station at Brant Rock, Massachusetts, and received by wireless operators aboard ships along the Atlantic Coast as far south as Norfolk, Virginia. The operators had been asked in advance to listen for Fessenden's message.

Before the Brant Rock broadcast, radio had consisted of bursts of radio waves in dot-dash fashion, similar to what one heard when Morse code was transmitted by telegraph over wire. Fessenden's success in sending voice and music by wireless was comparable to Bell's invention of the telephone, which allowed voice to be transmitted along wires that had previously carried only the electrical impulses used to transmit telegraph signals.

Fessenden's success led him to continue demonstrating his invention by transmitting modulated radio broadcasts between two stations during the winter of 1906–1907. AT&T sent representatives to investigate radiotelephony, but they never offered to buy Fessenden's idea. The only real interest came from amateurs who sent messages to one another, and Fessenden's company floundered. It was not until 1920 that station KDKA, regarded as the first true radio station, was established in Pittsburgh. By that time, detection and amplification of radio signals using De Forest's triode vacuum tube made headphones unnecessary, and radio stations began to spring up near every major city.

Following the failure of his modulated radio transmitting system to gain backing and widespread acceptance, Fessenden turned primarily to inventions related to naval electronics. Among his many inventions were a sonic depth finder, a radio compass, signaling devices for submarines, a turboelectric drive for battleships, and a smoke cloud used in tank warfare. By the time of his death, Fessenden held patents for more than 500 inventions, including the heterodyne circuit that he developed in 1912.

See also:
Electromagnetic Waves; Heterodyning; Modulation; Morse, Samuel F. B.; Radio; Telegraph.

References:
Asimov, Isaac. *Asimov's Biographical Encyclopedia of Science and Technology*. Garden City, NY: Doubleday, 1964.
International Encyclopedia of Communications. New York: Oxford University Press, 1989.

Fiber Optics

Fiber optics use thin glass or plastic fibers to carry light. The fibers are used to transmit audio and visual information to traditional devices such as telephones, television, and computers. They can also illuminate and transmit images of objects normally hidden from view, such as the lining of the human stomach. Fiber optics play a major role in the rapidly growing field of photonics—the transmission and processing of information using photons rather than electrons. The advantage of photons is that they have no mass or charge and, therefore, move at the speed of light and are not affected by electric or magnetic fields.

Very little of the light sent along optical fibers escapes, because the light is totally reflected within the glass or plastic. Total internal reflection occurs whenever light is enclosed in a medium with a much higher index of refraction than the medium surrounding it. (The index of refraction of a substance is a measure of its ability to bend light. A glass lens, for example, forms images because it bends the light entering it from air. The refractive index of glass is greater than that of air.) Because all the light is reflected within the fibers and none escapes, the signal maintains its intensity over long distances.

The rapid advances that have occurred in fiber optics stem in part from the fact that silica (SiO_2) is an abundant, strong, and chemically stable compound. Strands of silica 120 microns in diameter (0.12 millimeter) are very flexible, and the application of a polymer coating makes the glass resistant to damage and corrosion.

Fiber Optics and Telecommunications

Fiber-optic technology has wide application, but its greatest impact has been in telecommunications, where it offers significant advantages over electronic methods of transmitting information. The advantages include greater carrying capacity, smaller cables, lower costs, reduced loss of signal intensity, and less interference due to stray electric and magnetic fields and lightning.

In 1978, AT&T demonstrated the first communications system using fiber optics. Today, most long-distance telephone calls travel along glass rather than metal cables, and fiber optics are being installed in many local exchanges.

In fiber-optic telephone communication, voice inputs are coded and sent along glass fibers by a semiconductor laser as digital signals—light pulses representing 0s and 1s—at a rate of about 100 million bits per second. More recent systems operate at billions of bits per second, and the rate is doubling about every two years. Although no light es-

capes from the glass fibers, a tiny fraction of it is absorbed or scattered along every kilometer, so the signals have to be regenerated at about 20- to 60-mile (30- to 100-kilometer) intervals. At the receiving end of the call, the signals are decoded, converted back to audio, and amplified.

In many systems the signals are regenerated by converting the light signal to an electrical one, amplifying and shaping the pulse, and then using a semiconductor diode laser to retransmit the light signal. Regenerating the signal electronically has been the bottleneck of fiber-optic communication. However, the development of erbium-doped fiber amplifiers that can be spliced into long, glass transmission fibers provides a way around this bottleneck.

A fiber amplifier is made by doping—adding impurities to the core of a silica fiber with erbium ions as it is made. The amplifier is pumped with a semiconductor diode laser that produces infrared light with a wavelength of 1.48 or 0.98 microns. The signal, infrared light with a wavelength of approximately 1.55 microns, is amplified by a factor of about 1,000 as the excited erbium ions undergo stimulated emission. Transatlantic and transpacific fiber-optic cables (6,000 and 9,000 kilometers long, respectively) with fiber amplifiers are now in use.

The information superhighway of the future will require fiber-optic cables to transmit vast amounts of data. Eventually a single fiber-optic cable will reach every home. That cable will carry information now conveyed separately by television, telephone, and computer. However, it is likely to be several decades before optical fibers replace the last copper wire leading to separate homes and terminals. Until that happens, switching systems will convert the light signals that have traveled long distances on glass to electrical impulses that will travel along copper wire to the electronic devices in individual dwellings.

Other Uses of Fiber Optics

Rather than opening the body with large incisions, doctors can use "light pipes," called endoscopes, made of optical fibers to transmit light into and out of the body so that they can look inside various parts of their patients' bodies. Using specially designed endoscopes, physicians can look inside the bronchial tubes with the help of a bronchoscope, into the esophagus with an esophagoscope, into the stomach with a gastroscope, or into the ear with an otoscope. By adding another tube to the endoscope, surgeons can perform operations through a small incision that will admit a bundle of optical fibers and a small surgical tool.

The fibers carrying light to the inside of the body can twist and turn about one another in any haphazard fashion. However, if images of the internal tissues are to be viewed with the eye or through a television monitor, there must be a one-to-one correspondence in the positions of the approximately 750,000 individual fibers at both ends of the endoscope; otherwise, the result will be a jumbled collage of image pieces. How they lie in the middle is not important, but the positions of the fibers at both ends of the cable carrying light to a viewer must match.

Uses for endoscopes or similar flexible fiber-optic devices are not limited to medicine. They find extensive use in industry as a way to view internal parts of machinery; as sensors to measure pressure, temperature, flow rates, rotation, and other variables; as high-intensity illuminators; and as instrument illuminators. Rigid fiber optics, in which the fibers are fused into a solid block, are used for image transfer in fax machines, phototypesetting, and computer graphics.

See also:
Computer; Internet; Laser; Telephone; Television; Television and Society; Videotex.

References:
Bixby, Robert. "News News." *Compute*, June 1994.
Glass, Alastair M. "Fiber Optics." *Physics Today*, October 1993.
"The Optical Enlightenment." *The Economist*, 6 July 1991.
Williams, Trevor I. *The History of Invention: From Stone Axes to Silicon Chips*. New York: Facts on File, 1987.

Field, Cyrus West (1819–1892)

Once one of the most famous men of his era, Cyrus Field is relatively unknown today despite his ceaseless promotion and development of the transatlantic cable, one of the engineering wonders of the nineteenth century.

Field, with his brothers David, a prominent lawyer and judge; Stephen, a Supreme Court justice; Henry, a clergyman and writer; and Matthew, a civil engineer, formed one of nineteenth-century America's most prominent families. Born in Stockbridge, Massachusetts, in 1819, Field declined the educational advantages afforded his brothers and left school at age 15 to work in New York City's A. T. Steward dry-goods store. After five years, Field moved on to various other positions until 1841, when he established his own wholesale paper distribution company. In ten years, at age 34, Field retired with an estimated wealth of $250,000.

Retirement gave the ex-businessman a chance to indulge his wanderlust. Field traveled to England and throughout South America, but by 1854 he was back in New York seeking a new diversion. Through his engineer brother, Matthew, Field chanced to meet a Canadian engineer, F. N. Gisborne. Gisborne was directing a plan to lay telegraph cable in the Canadian provinces and from Newfoundland to New York City, which in conjunction with a steamer from Newfoundland to Ireland would provide the fast relay of transoceanic information. After laying only 40 miles of the line, the company was near bankruptcy and Gisborne desperately needed new investors.

Field listened intently. He immediately conceived of eliminating the steamer and establishing a transatlantic telegraph connection. Field invested his own fortune and 13 years of his time to see the project to completion.

Experiments by Samuel F. B. Morse, the distinguished inventor, and Ezra Cornell, of university fame, proved that a submarine cable could work over short distances. Mindful of the geographic and mechanical problems presented by his idea, Field promptly contracted Matthew Fontaine

Landing of the Transatlantic Cable at Trinity Bay, Newfoundland, in 1858. Cyrus Field, one of the most famous men of his era, is credited with establishing the first transatlantic cable after successfully joining Valentia, Ireland, and Trinity Bay, Newfoundland.

Maury, the nation's leading oceanographer and chief of the Naval Observatory, about the feasibility of the proposal. Maury affirmed Field's enthusiasm, reporting that recently completed naval soundings of the ocean floor from Newfoundland to Ireland revealed a plateau at an average depth of 1,500 to 2,000 fathoms. Field next sought the assistance of Morse, knowing that Morse's reputation and support would be critical in gaining investors. Morse also agreed that the project had promise.

Field began his operation in 1857, after three years of tireless promotion, with an initial investment of $1.5 million. Beset by numerous financial and mechanical difficulties, Field failed in his first two attempts to unite the continents telegraphically. On the third try, Field successfully joined Valentia, Ireland, and Trinity Bay, Newfoundland. The line was completed on 5 August 1858, and on 13 August, Queen Victoria sent the first message over the new cable, congratulating President James Buchanan on the achievement.

Field's triumph was recognized in New York with a huge parade, a banquet, and a massive fireworks display that accidentally set the cupola on City Hall ablaze. The New York press heralded him as "Cyrus the Great." The acclaim was short lived, however. On 25 September, the signal went dead after only seven weeks of operation and 400 messages. An angry and resentful public cried hoax and fraud. With his credibility close to ruin, Field suffered personal problems as well when his business was ravaged by fire. Financially troubled, the ex-hero was forced to mortgage his home. The outbreak of the Civil War further delayed Field's attempts to see his project to completion.

Nonetheless, Field persisted in his conviction and renewed his efforts in 1865, only to fail again. In 1866, on his fifth attempt, Field finally established the first permanent transatlantic telegraph link. The last years of Field's life were a constant struggle against financial ruin. His fortune was drained by friends who took advantage of him, a series of bad investments in railroads and newspapers, and his son's bankruptcy.

See also:
Transatlantic Cable.

References:
Carter, Samuel. *Cyrus Field: Man of Two Worlds*. New York: G. P. Putnam & Sons, 1968.
D'Oench, Derry. "It Took a Man from Stockbridge Three Tries to Join Two Worlds." *Berkshire Evening Eagle*, 11 May 1951.
McDonald, Philip B. *A Saga of the Seas*. New York: Wilson-Erickson, 1937.

Flag

A flag is a piece of colored cloth that can serve as a symbol, a means of identification, or a signaling device (semaphore). Ships are identified by the flags they fly; each nation is identified by a particular flag. The design of national flags, which are used to communicate a sense of loyalty and patriotism, usually reflect a symbolism of historical significance. For example, the flag of Great Britain, known as the Union Jack, combines the crosses of the patron saints of England (Saint George), Scotland (Saint Andrew), and Ireland (Saint Patrick).

Although the history of the flag of the United States is cluttered with myths, it is clear that the stars and stripes were the result of a resolution by the Continental Congress in 1777, which read, "Resolved: that the flag of the United States be 13 stripes, alternate red and white; that the union be 13 stars, white in a blue field, representing a new constellation."

As the resolution reveals, there was no indication of who designed the flag, nor were there instructions regarding the arrangement of the stars, although it is clear that each star represents one of the 13 states that made up the union. Furthermore, the flag designed by the Continental Congress played no role in the Revolution, because the war was over before the flags became available to the army. During the war a variety of state and local flags were used to rally the troops. The legend about Betsy Ross designing and sewing a flag for General George Washington, which she related to a grandchild who did not report the story until just before the nation's centennial, has never been documented by historians.

After Vermont and Kentucky joined the union in 1791 and 1792, respectively, the flag was changed to 15 stars and 15 stripes. It was this flag that Francis Scott Key described in "The Star Spangled Banner." But after the War of 1812, a decision was made to keep the original 13 stripes and add stars to represent new states added to the union. As a result, the current flag has 50 white stars on a blue background along with the original 13 red and white stripes.

Although the American flag serves to communicate a love of country, it has also been used as a symbol for protest. Opponents of national policies, such as the war in Vietnam, have burned the flag as a way of symbolizing their opposition. Although Congress passed a law protecting the flag from desecration, the Supreme Court, citing the First Amendment, ruled the law unconstitutional. The First Amendment to the United States Constitution states, "Congress shall pass no law . . . abridging the freedom of speech, or of the press; or the right of the people peaceably to assemble, and to petition the government for a redress of grievances." The Court argued that burning the flag is a form of free speech that cannot be denied.

See also:
Semaphore.

References:
Coggins, Jack. *Flashes and Flags: The Story of Signaling*. New York: Dodd, Mead, 1963.
Crampton, W. G. *Flag*. New York: Knopf, 1989.
Panati, Charles. *Extraordinary Origins of Everyday Things*. New York: Harper & Row, 1987.
Skarmeas, Mary. "Flags for Home." *Ideals*, June 1995.

Webster's Concise Encyclopedia of Flags and Coats of Arms. New York: Crescent Books, 1985.

Flare

A flare is a device designed to release an intense light, usually colored, to signal distress or provide illumination. Flares are widely used on railroads and highways, at sea, and in military operations.

The earliest flares used a mixture of sulfur, potassium nitrate (saltpeter), and arsenic trisulfide (orpiment) to produce a bluish white light. Early in the nineteenth century, after it was discovered that potassium chlorate could be used as an oxidizing agent, mixtures containing this salt and others that produced colored light at high temperatures were used to make flares for use in signaling distress.

Today, flares are standard equipment in boats, trucks, military vehicles, and many automobiles. Placed around a disabled truck, flares alert passing police cars and other truckers that a trucker is in distress and alert cars to avoid a serious collision. Recently, flares have been developed that fit onto the fenders of trucks. Should the truck develop problems, the flares can be quickly and safely ignited.

For boats there are now aerial flares. Punching a hole in the flare and pulling a chain causes the burning flare to rise as high as 500 feet, where it is visible over a radius of 28 miles. To a small boat stranded at sea with a storm approaching, such a flare can truly be a lifesaver.

References:

"Fender-Flare Installation." *Motor Trend*, April 1996.
"Word Up." *Boating*, March 1995.

FM

See Modulation.

Forensics

Forensics is communication that involves argumentation. Aristotle defined forensics as the arguments that take place in a court of law, and it is this meaning that pertains to forensic science and forensic medicine, which have to do with the collection of evidence that can help to establish the guilt or innocence of a person accused of a crime.

Debating, one aspect of forensics that is a major extracurricular activity in many universities, colleges, and high schools, began in classical Greece, where it was introduced by Protagoras. Often called "the father of debate," Protagoras required his students to argue both sides of an issue, a skill that was valuable in a society in which citizens were expected to orally defend their positions in court or in political forums. Today's academic debates are governed by rules that set time limits for constructive and rebuttal speeches and cross-examination of opponents.

In democracies, legislative debates are regarded as an essential part of reaching reasonable decisions. All legislatures have rules that govern their debates. The U.S. Senate, famous for its filibusters, has one of the least restrictive set of rules. Since the famous Lincoln-Douglas debates in the 1858 campaign for a U.S. Senate seat from Illinois, debates between candidates for political office have gained increasing acceptance at all levels. In 1960, the first debate between presidential candidates was seen on television. John F. Kennedy, the Democratic nominee who went on to win the election, debated the Republican candidate, Richard M. Nixon.

Carefully controlled debate before judges or a jury has been the basis for making decisions about justice in courts of law for centuries. However, forensic methods have also gained wide acceptance in resolving issues in such diverse disciplines as science, medicine, religion, education, and the arts.

A forensic approach to resolving questions is based on the realization that many issues are fraught with uncertainties that cannot be resolved by pure logic or empirical measurements. Debating issues such as these through free and thorough discussion by advocates and opponents provides the best way to reach a decision according to forensic philosophy, a philosophy essential to a democracy. However, although debates may lead to a consensus in small organizations, they are seldom followed by unanimous votes in legislatures, where issues are generally decided by majority rule.

See also:
Homiletics; Oratory.
References:
Frank, David A. *Creative Speaking*, 2nd ed. Lincolnwood, IL: National Textbook, 1995.
International Encyclopedia of Communications. New York: Oxford University Press, 1989.
Robinson, William C. *Oratory: A Manual for Advocates*. Littleton, CO: Rothman, 1993.

Forgery

Forgery is essentially a form of lying or deceiving. It occurs when someone makes or changes a written document or instrument with the intent to defraud. It involves the fraudulent alteration or falsification of bonds, stock certificates, deeds, mortgages, money orders, promissory notes, bills of exchange or lading, receipts, railroad or airline tickets, accounts, public records, or other instruments in order to deceive or trick another person or persons. Forgery may pertain to altering or erasing part or all of a document, printing in blank spaces over a valid signature, using a fictitious name, or doing anything to an instrument that might have an impact on the liabilities or legal rights of another citizen.

Forgery is often carried out as a way of obtaining money illegally, as when someone writes a check and signs it with another person's name. If the forger manages to cash the check at a bank, then, in some states, he or she is also guilty of another crime called uttering a forged document. In some states both crimes are regarded as forgery.

The forging of government obligations such as paper money or bonds is called counterfeiting. The Secret Service was originally formed to track down counterfeiters. It was so successful that counterfeiting was greatly reduced; however, recent advances in copying techniques have made counterfeiting an easier crime to accomplish. However, the red and blue fibers found in real bills are usually printed by counterfeiters, which is one way that banks identify counterfeit money. Bank tellers suspicious of a bill will look closely at the back of the paper because counterfeiters generally pay less attention to the backs of bills.

The Treasury Department is constantly devising methods to detect counterfeit bills and make the work of counterfeiters more difficult. A number of private and public companies are also in the business of fighting forgery. One such company recently developed an ink that can be made with an individual's DNA. The bank or other receiver of signed legal tender can easily identify a signature made with the individual's DNA-infused ink provided that it has the hand-held scanner that can read the biochemical markers.

Forgery is not limited to the business world. Scientists have been found guilty of forging experimental data in an effort to gain professional standing or provide evidence to support a particular hypothesis. And forgery in the art world is very common because, although art has aesthetic value, it also serves as an investment for art collectors. The monetary value of a piece of art, be it a painting, sculpture, or carving, depends on the artist who created it as well as the object itself. A work by Michelangelo is worth much more than one that is identical but created by a forger.

Forgery in art may consist of a replica complete with forged signature, an authentic work that has been restored, or, very commonly, a pastiche—a work that a famous artist might have done, but never did—in a style that effectively mimics the artist's other work.

To determine whether a work of art is authentic, it may be subjected to scientific or critical analysis. Science may be helpful in showing that a painting might be authentic. For example, samples of the paint may establish the era in which the painting was done, and X rays may determine what is under the paint; however, scientific analysis cannot prove authenticity and is generally of little value with recent works.

Critical analysis uses the eyes of experts familiar with artists and their work to determine if forgery has been committed. Of course, such analyses are subjective, and in cases that reach the courts, the opinions of witnesses—experts who reach opposite conclusions—are often used by both sides in a dispute.

References:
"Signing with Your Genes." *Popular Mechanics*, September 1995.
"Work and Lies in the Promised Land." *World Press Review*, June 1995.

Gallaudet, Thomas H. (1787–1851)

American educator of the hearing impaired, Thomas Gallaudet established the first public school for deaf children in the United States. Gallaudet was born in Philadelphia but moved to Hartford, Connecticut, with his family when he was 13. Two years later he enrolled at Yale, graduating in 1805 at age 17. The succeeding years found Gallaudet engaged in a number of different pursuits. He studied law for a time and attended graduate school at Yale while working as a tutor to support himself. Persistent health problems led his doctor to recommend a more active lifestyle, and Gallaudet became a traveling salesman in rural Kentucky and Ohio. In 1812, he returned to the East Coast and enrolled at Andover Theological Seminary. Plagued by recurring ill health, Gallaudet graduated but was forced to give up his ministerial ambitions, and he once again searched for a new livelihood.

During the winter following his graduation, Gallaudet befriended his neighbor Alice Cogswell, a girl who had lost her hearing as a victim of a childhood bout of spotted fever. Gallaudet tried to teach the girl but finally realized that she needed an experienced teacher of the deaf and advised her father to engage a qualified professional. The senior Cogswell decided to raise funds to send Gallaudet to Europe to study continental techniques of educating the deaf, a trip that changed his life. Although the study tour began in England, Gallaudet was disappointed by the reception he received there and pushed on to France. At the Institut Royal Sourds-Muets, one of the earliest schools for the deaf, Gallaudet found what he needed. The institute's system was based on the manual alphabet sign language, which had been perfected by the school's director, Abbe Roche Ambroise Secard. In 1816, after seven months in France, Gallaudet returned to Hartford accompanied by the brilliant teacher Laurent Clerc.

The two men raised funds to establish the country's first school for the deaf. In 1817, the Connecticut Asylum opened in Hartford with seven students. The addition of state appropriations made Gallaudet's school the first ever to receive public funds for special education. Gallaudet was principal of the school until his retirement in 1830. Today, his vision is embodied in the modern successor of his school, the American School for the Deaf, in West Hartford, Connecticut. Most gratifying to the educator-minister was the fact that several teachers at the Connecticut Asylum founded schools for the deaf elsewhere. By 1863, there were 22 such schools in the country.

In 1821, Gallaudet married Sophia Fowler, a former student. They had eight children, and two followed in their father's footsteps. Gallaudet's oldest son, Thomas Jr., became a well-known Episcopal minister to the deaf in New York City. The youngest son, Edward, founded a school for the deaf in Washington, D.C., in 1864, and in 1894 the school was renamed Gallaudet College in memory of his father. Now Gallaudet University, it remains the only liberal arts college in the world devoted exclusively to the education of the hearing impaired.

Gallaudet's retirement from his school did not end his professional career. He was offered positions at Dartmouth and the City College of New York but turned them down. Gallaudet was a pioneer in advocating higher education for women and stressed the need for qualified female teachers. He helped establish the Hartford Female Seminary in 1825. His concern for education led to the creation of public normal schools in Connecticut. Gallaudet gave the dedication address and served on the faculty at what became Central Connecticut State University. Gallaudet also busied himself writing children's books for the Foreign Missionary Society, articles on education for the hearing impaired, and even a volume of sermons. In 1837, he was appointed chaplain at the Hartford Retreat for the Insane, a position he held until his death. On 10 September 1851, Gallaudet, then almost 64 years old, died peacefully in his sleep.

See also:
American Sign Language; Communication among the Hearing Impaired; Keller, Helen Adams; Sign Language.

Gallup, George H. (1901–1984)

The American public opinion analyst who pioneered modern polling techniques to measure public opinion, George Gallup made opinion polling one of the characteristics of late-twentieth-century life. He was so successful that Gallup has become synonymous in the popular mind with opinion poll.

Born in Jefferson City, Iowa, on 18 November 1901, Gallup worked his way through Iowa State University as a scholarship student and later as an instructor in journalism. He graduated in 1923 and went on to earn an M.A. in psychology and, in 1928, a Ph.D. in journalism. His doctoral dissertation on measuring reader interests in newspapers contained the basic ideas and methods of his life work.

In the three years following his graduation, Gallup was the chairman of the journalism department at Drake University and taught journalism at Northwestern University. During that time he pursued his doctoral interests by conducting a number of reader-interest surveys for midwestern newspapers and suggesting various promotional programs based upon his results. In 1932, he left academia and began a 15-year relationship with the Young and Rubican Advertising Agency of New York City as director of research. In 1937, he was appointed vice-president of the agency, a position he held until 1947.

Gallup's duties for Young and Rubican were to assess and evaluate radio programming, reader interest in newspaper feature

George H. Gallup, famous public opinion analyst, monitors a poll return in an ABC radio station in this undated photograph.

stories, and the appeal of consumer products. Gallup devised a system of measuring the public's response to the firm's advertising by means of surveys based on interviews. His interviews represented a statistical cross section of the nation. Answers to simple questions—usually a yes, no, or no opinion—provided the statistical data Gallup required. Some surveys entailed more complete answers, but generally an analysis required two weeks.

In 1935, Gallup established the American Institute of Public Opinion (AIPO) in Princeton, New Jersey, to conduct national polls on political and social issues. Concentrating at first on current events and radio programming, the AIPO developed a reputation for reliability and efficient data analysis. Gallup's major breakthrough came in the 1936 presidential election. The *Literary Digest*, considered at that time to be the most dependable gauge of public opinion, predicted victory for Alfred M. Landon based upon returns from 2 million mailed ballots.

Using the small sampling technique he had developed, Gallup's poll correctly forecast a Roosevelt win by a comfortable margin. Although not the prime purpose of the Gallup polls, predicting the presidential sweepstakes has made the polls a highly visible part of American life. Only once, when Harry S. Truman won an upset victory in 1948, has the poll been wrong in predicting the next president.

Gallup opened the British Institute of Public Opinion in 1936. Great Britain was the first of some 30 countries to use his poll, allowing Gallup to make international comparisons of data.

At the age of 82, Gallup gave control of AIPO to his son, George Jr. A year later, the elder Gallup died of a heart attack at his summer home near Bern, Switzerland.

See also:
Public Opinion.

References:
Current Biography.New York: H. H. Wilson, 1952.
International Encyclopedia of Communications. New York: Oxford University Press, 1989.

GEnie
See Online Services.

Goebbels, Paul Joseph (1897–1945)

The Nazi German politician and administrator who controlled Third Reich communication, Goebbels believed that if you told the masses loudly enough and often enough, they would believe. He relied on the emotional appeal of propaganda through the use of slogans, rituals, pageantry, and stereotypical formulas, which were epitomized in the Nuremberg party rallies. Goebbels introduced Nazism's "Heil Hitler" greeting as well as the concept of a Fuehrer. His complete and uncritical devotion to Adolf Hitler created not only the image of a political leader but also that of a German savior. Goebbels served as Reich Minister of Propaganda and Public Enlightenment from 1933 until his suicide at the Hitler bunker in Berlin, on 1 May 1945.

Goebbels was born to devout Catholic working-class parents in Rheydt, Germany, on 29 October 1897. Ironically, he was far from the blond, blue-eyed Nazi stereotype trumpeted in his later propaganda. He was dark-haired, brown-eyed, small in stature, and appeared very frail. As a child Goebbels contracted polio, which left him with a deformed foot and permanent limp. Taunted by his peers and unable to participate in physical activity, Goebbels turned to academics for his success. He was a top scholar, and his parents hoped he would pursue a career in medicine or the church.

During World War I, Goebbels was rejected for service with the German army due to his disability. In later years he preferred to say little about his lack of military experience and allowed associates to assume that he had been an early casualty of the conflict. Dejectedly, Goebbels decided to continue his education, but his work at the University of Bonn was nearly cut short by family financial problems. His parents, laboring under the illusion of their son's religiousness, applied for aid from a local fund established to help finance the education of future priests. Goebbels took the loan, although he had no intention of entering the priesthood, and in 1931 he was embarrassed to be brought to court for his delay in repaying the loan.

Goebbels's university career reads like a travelogue of the German higher education system. Although viewed as a good student, he attended eight universities for varying lengths of time, possibly due to the special curriculum features of each school. Nonetheless, he graduated from Heidelberg with a Ph.D. in philology in 1921. As the most intellectual member of the Nazi upper echelon, he was derisively referred to as the "little doctor."

Goebbels had great literary ambitions after graduation. He wrote a novel, which remained deservedly unknown until the late 1920s, when his position as a Nazi, rather than the book's literary value, led to publication. However, even his position could not salvage two plays he wrote, and the numerous articles he submitted to newspapers also met rejection. By 1923, Goebbels was unemployed and financially desperate.

While Goebbels suffered his own personal crisis in 1923, Germany also faced postwar trials. The French, dissatisfied with Germany's default on paying the World War I indemnity, occupied the Ruhr, the country's industrial heartland. Politically, the French occupation led to a renewal of German nationalism and the rise of disparate organizations determined to recapture Germany's position in European affairs. Motivated by the injustice of the French action, patriotism, financial need, and ambition, Goebbels entered the political fray. He first heard Adolph Hitler speak in 1923 and was immediately smitten. In 1924, he became the managing editor of a right-wing nationalist newspaper, which brought him to the attention of Nazi organizers. By the spring of 1925, he was a member of the party and working for the *National Socialist Letter*, the first official voice of Nazism. For the next two decades, Goebbels dedicated himself to the proposition that Hitler was the savior of Germany from communism and Jews and that Nazi ideology was the salvation of the nation.

For Goebbels, 1926 was a critical year. Hitler took Goebbels with him as a supporting orator on a speaking tour of Bavaria, where Goebbels distinguished himself as an outstanding orator and impressed his patron and idol. Goebbels was given an opportunity to showcase his organizational skills and party loyalty when he was appointed *gauleiter* (district chief) of Berlin in November 1926. In nationalist circles the German capital was labeled "Red Berlin" due to the pervasive Communist and socialist presence in the city.

The Nazi faction in Berlin was an inconsequential, disorganized shambles struggling for an identity. Recognition and respect in the capital were essential if the Nazis were to play a policy-making role in the future Germany. Goebbels immediately signaled his primacy by expelling 400 members of the Nazi Party as unfit. Beyond establishing a responsible, dedicated cadre of party members, Goebbels sought to break down the wall of anonymity that plagued Nazi recruiting efforts. Believing that hatred was better than no recognition, Goebbels resorted to a campaign of agitation and violence that received nationwide attention. He sanctioned a crusade of street fights, barroom brawls, and police confrontations and further aggravated the volatile situation by promoting Nazi parades, complete with music, banners, and slogans, through the politically disputed sections of Berlin. Anyone killed in these efforts could be assured of a spectacular hero's funeral and enshrinement as a Nazi martyr.

Goebbels's creation in 1927 of a party newspaper, *Der Angriff (The Attack)*, served to further the civil strife. *Der Angriff*, only a thinly veiled attempt at a newspaper, was in reality one more forum that allowed Goebbels to heap abuse on the Nazi Party's enemies. Goebbels conquered Berlin for the Nazis, and the city became his base of his operations.

Goebbels's achievements in Berlin did not go unrewarded. In 1928, he was elected as one of 12 Nazi delegates in the Reichstag, the German parliament. The electoral victory, followed by a triumph in the 1930 vote, brought the Nazi Party national recognition as well as a legal podium from which to extol its dogma. Nazi successes were directly attributable to Goebbels, who in 1930 became the party's director of propaganda and as such was the main campaign architect in paving the way for Hitler's rise to ultimate power.

When Hitler became chancellor in 1933, he brought his prominent propagandist with him. At 35 years old, Goebbels joined the Reich cabinet as Minister of Propaganda and Public Enlightenment. His charge was to coordinate all national institutions for the advancement of Nazi ideology. Instrumental in these efforts was his creation of the Reich Chamber of Culture, which had direct control of mass communications, literature, music, art, and film. Goebbels controlled the cultural life of Germany, systematically purging Jews and anyone who failed to recognize the preeminence of the Third Reich, and sparked a mass migration of the country's most talented artists and scientists.

Goebbels immediately grasped the importance of the new media—radio and television, the latter in its infancy. Just 11 days after his appointment, Goebbels took over radio broadcasting, which would become the mainstay of his propaganda activities, from the German Post Office and its National Broadcast Company. He ordered manufacturers to design and produce inexpensive radios he called "people's receivers"; his opponents called them "Goebbels blasters." To assure maximum audiences, Goebbels ordered all cafes and restaurants to have radios. "Reich loudspeakers" atop columns dotted streets and squares. Broadcasts were arranged during working hours to assure maximum attention. In 1935, Goebbels began the world's first regular television service, a closed-circuit system restricted to Berlin.

With the outbreak of World War II, Goebbels's prime task shifted to maintaining German morale. Early victories made his job easy, and the propaganda ministry assured the homeland of a quick victory. Goebbels concentrated his early propaganda on creating dissension among the Allies. For example, initial German broadcasts stated that England was prepared to fight Nazism to the last Frenchman.

Goebbels encouraged the belief that there was serious domestic opposition to Allied policies regarding Germany. The British fascist William Joyce, nicknamed Lord Haw Haw in England, was used as an example of the mythical pro-Nazi sentiment in Allied countries. Goebbels used American and British broadcasters like Axis Sally to further the notion of division in Allied ranks. The British were characterized as effete snobs, the Russians as subhumans plagued by anti-Stalin uprisings, and the Americans as inefficient.

The real test for the propaganda minister came when the initial triumphs turned to defeat and Allied forces began to move against Hitler and bomb the fatherland. Goebbels had to provide a substitute for military victory to unify the masses. Considerations of world domination and the superior race gave way to a fight for the survival of Germany. Germany had to win or face the cruel retribution of the victorious Allies. Goebbels's previous lies, boasting, and promise of success exposed his office to disbelief and eventual ridicule. Goebbels carried the additional burden of a demoralized Fuehrer. Hitler appeared in public only twice after the disastrous defeat at Stalingrad in February 1943, and Goebbels stepped forward as the spokesman of the Third Reich. He spared no energy or time in visiting damaged cities and towns. He organized relief units to aid the war-ravaged populace. Goebbels initiated a 60-hour workweek and raised special battalions from the medically unfit and older population to continue the fight.

In July 1944, an attempted coup against Hitler was stopped, thanks in large part to Goebbels's quick thinking. He immediately declared martial law in Berlin and held the city for his Fuehrer. As a reward for his loyalty, Goebbels was promoted to General Plenipotentiary for Mobilization of Total War, which made him the most powerful person in the Third Reich after Hitler and Heinrich Himmler. By this time nothing could save Nazi Germany, and the "little doctor," loyal to the end, remained with Hitler to share his fate. He had his six children killed by lethal injection rather than have them grow up in a non-Nazi Germany and then ordered an officer to shoot his wife and himself.

References:

Heiber, Helmut. *Goebbels: A Biography*. New York: Da Capo, 1983.

Lochner, Louis, ed. *The Goebbels Diaries*. New York: Popular Library, 1948.

Reuth, Ralf Georg. *Goebbels*. New York: Harcourt Brace, 1993.

Wykes, Alan. *Goebbels*. New York: Ballantine Books, 1973.

Goodyear Blimp

The Goodyear Tire and Rubber Company began building lighter-than-air ships in 1919. During the 1930s a fleet of a dozen such ships toured the United States as part of Goodyear's advertising strategy. Even today, the word *blimp* brings to mind Goodyear, and vice versa.

During World War II, the government took over the Goodyear fleet, which was used by the U.S. Navy for reconnaissance duty.

Three Goodyear blimps are still flying. One—the *Spirit of Akron*—was launched in 1989. Although Goodyear no longer builds blimps, these airships remain highly visible. They frequently hover above sporting events, such as the World Series or professional football games, serving not only to advertise the Goodyear Company but to provide television audiences with a spectacular bird's-eye view of the contest.

Gramophone

See Phonograph.

Griffith, D. W. (1875–1948)

American motion picture director and one of the most influential artists to work in the movie industry, D. W. Griffith made innovative use of film technique. His two most important films, *Birth of a Nation* and *Intolerance,* secured his status as a visionary film pioneer.

Born in Oldham County, Kentucky, Griffith was one of seven children. His father, something of a local character as a veteran of the Mexican and Civil Wars, as well as the state legislature, died when the boy was ten years old. Debt forced the family to sell its farm and move to Louisville, Kentucky, where the widow operated a boardinghouse. Griffith had no formal education beyond his early high school years and took a number of jobs to supplement the family finances. His experience as a clerk in a bookstore, where he read extensively, served to counterbalance his educational deficiencies.

Griffith's ambition was to be a writer and an actor, and during the initial stages of his career he tried to combine the two roles with only limited success. After a brief stint as a newspaper reporter, he joined several different regional acting troupes and performed in local productions. A mediocre actor, he had to take other jobs to pay the bills while continuing his writing. Slightly more successful as an author, Griffith sold a story to *Cosmopolitan* and a poem to *Leslie's Weekly*, two leading magazines of the period. He was further encouraged in 1906 when his play *The Fool and the Girl* was purchased for the princely sum of $1,000. His elation was short lived, however; the play folded after only a week on stage. The would-be playwright and actor was married in the same year, and it became clear that money matters demanded a change of direction.

At the suggestion of a friend, Griffith began to peddle his scripts to the new motion picture industry. At the time, motion pictures were considered a passing fad, crass, vulgar, and the almost exclusive domain of the less-sophisticated working class and immigrants. Fearful about his reputation in the theater, Griffith reluctantly convinced himself that his inquiries were a stopgap measure until he could get steady employment on the legitimate stage and sell scripts to reputable producers. He approached the Edison studio in New Jersey with a script, which was rejected, but he did secure the lead in Edwin S. Porter's film, *Rescue from an Eagle's Nest.* When he finished the film and some other shorts, he moved to the American Biograph Studio in New York.

Biograph had limped along for most of its existence due to persistent litigation for patent infringements. The issues resolved, executive Henry Marvin looked forward to financial stability and realized the need to revitalize the studio's production and establish better marketing. In June 1908, Marvin bought six of Griffith's scripts, hired him as an actor, and offered him a trial position as director. Griffith's first production, *The Adventures of Dollie*, a standard melodrama of the day, was shot on location in Connecticut in two days. The film was a workmanlike effort and gave no hint of Griffith's future genius, but it did secure his future as a director. The independence Griffith enjoyed at Biograph allowed him to develop the two genres most associated with his work—the sentimental melodrama and the historical epic. With G. W. "Billy" Bitzer, his cameraman and collaborator, Griffith made nearly 500 one- and two-reel pictures for Biograph, at the rate of about two per week, between 1908 and 1913. Using catchy titles like *The Pirates' Gold, The Girl and the Outlaw,* or *Bandits of Waterloo,* the new director revived Biograph's fortunes.

Ironically, Griffith, the stage devotee, advanced the status of motion pictures beyond the image of a poor stepchild of the theater to entertainment respectability and acceptance. His film *Pippa Passes* (1909) was the first movie reviewed by the *New York Times.* Furthermore, Griffith proved that films could deal with serious issues (in his 1912 dramatization of Darwin's *Man's Genesis*) and with social concerns (in his 1909 adaptation of a Frank Norris novel, *The Pit*).

Beyond financial success, Griffith's tenure at Biograph was revolutionary in a technical sense. Undoubtedly, many of the innovations claimed as his own or credited to him were employed by others, but his persistent use and refinement of those techniques proved to be his lasting legacy to filmdom. In its youth, filmmaking was a haphazard process in which quality was not always a priority. Films were shot quickly, swiftly screened, and released to theaters to begin earning revenue for the studio's next project.

In contrast, Griffith was a demanding taskmaster in his creations. He required authenticity and realism. When possible, he filmed on location, outside the studio, in Connecticut, northern New Jersey, or even distant Los Angeles. He was a stickler for detail and is reputed to have established the first studio research department. Others might quickly establish a shot and shoot it, but Griffith required frequent rehearsals before filming. He rejected the stage conventions of exaggerated gestures and actions in favor of subtle expression and simple, purposeful movements typical of real people. Even Griffith's makeup department strove for the realistic look in plying their trade. Griffith encouraged his actors to study people to better understand the emotions he required. His dramatic use of lighting to convey mood and tone put his work ahead of the competition. Completion of a film did not mean immediate release to theaters. Grif-

fith is often cited as the first film editor, and his short, rapid editing methods, which added dramatic effect to the picture, became a hallmark of a Griffith enterprise.

Griffith's most revolutionary accomplishment, however, was use of camera movement. The visionary director realized that motion pictures could offer more than just a stationary camera filming a stagelike production. Used effectively, the camera could create mood and become a means of expression. The nature of the shot became as important as the scene to Griffith. He regularly moved cameras to get different angles of the same scene. Despite the initial reservations of his colleague Bitzer, Griffith used frequent close-ups. A staple of early pictures was the chase scene, and to provide realism and tension Griffith mounted his cameras on trucks. Other elements of his repertoire included fade-ins and fade-outs as well as night photography.

Griffith's expertise and control extended to his actors. He had a keen eye for talent and developed a remarkable stable of performers. Lionel Barrymore, Mary Pickford, the Gish sisters, and Mack Sennett all worked under Griffith's direction. Griffith gave some indication of the future by combining his multiple talents to produce *New York Hat* (1912), with Pickford and Barrymore, and *The Battle of Elderbush Gulch* (1913) for Biograph. By 1913, studio executives were pleased with the lucrative one-reel format and saw little reason to change their operation despite increased competition from longer European features. Griffith wanted to make longer films and grew increasingly restless at the intransigence of the financiers. He concluded his sojourn at Biograph by directing the first American four-reeler, *Judith of Bethulia* (1913). The costly biblical epic was a box office smash, but it fractured the already strained relationship, and Griffith left the studio in the same year.

Griffith, already established as a major force in the American cinema, moved to the Mutual Film Company. He was eventually joined by Bitzer and a number of his actors. He directed several longer films in 1914, but these were revenue-raising preludes to a greater conception he had nursed for some time. Griffith wanted to tell the "true story" of the Reconstruction period, and the vehicle for this was his purchase of *The Clansman*, a Thomas Dixon novel that traced the rise of the Ku Klux Klan in post–Civil War South Carolina through the overthrow of the Reconstruction government in the late 1870s. Griffith mounted a monumental effort that had Hollywood insiders questioning his sanity. *Birth of a Nation*, the 12-reel, three-hour blockbuster, cost $110,000, more than three times the cost of any previous film. Griffith not only directed but also arranged the music and even experimented with color through tinting. Even at $2 a ticket when it was released in 1915, the film was an immediate hit and went on to gross $48 million in Griffith's lifetime. It was the top money-producing film until *Gone with the Wind* was released in 1939. Griffith's personal profit from the film was in the vicinity of $1 million. His masterpiece remains one of the landmarks of American filmmaking, but it is also one of the most controversial films of the first half-century of the silver screen.

Critics raved, and the popularity of the movie vaulted motion pictures to the top of the entertainment world. Nonetheless, the African-American community was outraged at Griffith's blatant racism in the portrayal of black men and characterized the film as a call for white racial solidarity. Stung by the criticism, Griffith responded quickly. He published a pamphlet, *The Rise and Fall of Free Speech in America*, and began his second great film, *Intolerance*, which was released in 1916. Griffith tried to weave a complex story about four different historical eras—the modern United States, sixteenth-century Paris, Palestine in the time of Christ, and ancient Babylon—which only confused moviegoers. Although critically acclaimed for technical merit, *Intolerance* never approached the popularity of *Birth of a Nation*. Furthermore, production costs of $2 million, much of it used to construct the elaborate sets of the Babylonian segment, forced Griffith to the edge of bankruptcy. Griffith left the country before the film's release to do some propaganda work for the British government, which resulted in *Hearts of the World* and *The Great Love* (1918).

The 1920s were not kind to the renowned director. He bounced from studio to studio, seeking both creative freedom and funds necessary to make his movies. Griffith further complicated his accounts by building his own studio, only to close it in 1925 due to losses. Between 1917 and 1924, he made 18 pictures, about half of which were done just to raise money or fulfill contractual obligations. The remaining films, although less ambitious than his two major accomplishments, did contribute to his reputation, and critics have regarded them as generally underrated. Included in this category are *Broken Blossom* (1919), a historical drama of the French Revolution entitled *Orphans of the Storm* (1921), and Griffith's last independent project, *Isn't Life Wonderful* (1924).

By 1930, Griffith was barely a presence in Hollywood and was all but forgotten. His later, uninspired work gave no indication of his former stature, but he proved his doubters wrong when he directed his first sound picture, *Abraham Lincoln*, starring Walter Huston. Although the film had faults, it was good enough to be dubbed one of the year's ten best by the *New York Times*. Encouraged, Griffith in 1931 produced another sound film, *The Struggle*. The story of an alcoholic, with a strong temperance message, the film failed miserably. Griffith never made another film, and apparently Hollywood had no further interest in him.

The last 17 years of Griffith's life were a battle against mounting debts, alcoholism, and increased bitterness over Hollywood's collective amnesia. There were brief moments of recaptured glory, as in 1938 when Griffith donated his films and papers to the Museum of Modern Art in New York, or in 1940 when the museum ran a retrospective of his career, but there were never any calls for a job. Griffith died alone and neglected in his room at Hollywood's Knickerbocker Hotel, the victim of a stroke, on 28 July 1948.

See also:
Motion Pictures.

References:
Henderson, Robert M. *D.W. Griffith: His Life and Work*. New York: Oxford University Press, 1972.
Lindsey, David. "The Master of American Cinema: D. W. Griffith." *American History Illustrated*, December 1976.
Schickel, Richard. *D. W. Griffith: An American Life*. New York: Simon & Schuster, 1984.

Gutenberg, Johann
(ca. 1394–1468)

A German inventor, Johann Gutenberg developed a process of printing from movable type that was to become the basis of mass communication for more than 400 years. His invention revolutionized the transmission of knowledge and was a forerunner of the modern printing industry. The landmark process not only permitted publication of multiple identical copies, but also allowed a printer to produce in one day what it took a scribe one year to produce by hand. Consequently, manuscripts were reproduced more efficiently, cheaply, and accurately than was possible using scribes. The availability of printed materials opened the world of ideas and learning to a new public and accelerated Europe's move toward the Renaissance. Gutenberg, however, was not the inventor of printing. The evolution of printing was too gradual for any one person to be singled out as the inventor.

Very little is definitely known about Gutenberg's life or the intellectual origin and development of his invention. Historical deduction, based primarily on contemporary legal proceedings and documents, reveals only a skeletal framework of his life. Gutenberg was born in Mainz, Germany, but the exact date is undetermined. Sources place the date anywhere from 1394 to 1400, but no solid evidence exists to support those estimates. The inventor's full name was Johann Genfleisch. Exactly why he used Gutenberg for his last name is unknown, although it is speculated that the name was derived from his family home. The Genfleisch family was considered upper class because the father held a responsible position in the local archbishop's

mint. Apparently a number of the family were metal craftsmen, and the youngest son readily joined the trade, a decision that would serve him well in developing movable type.

In 1428, civil conflict in his native city forced the young craftsman to migrate to the Rhine River city of Strasbourg. Gutenberg supported himself by producing metal crafts, especially badges given to pilgrims to signify the conclusion of their holy travel. He also taught semiprecious stonecutting and polishing. Court records from Strasbourg shed some light on Gutenberg's work during this period, in particular a 1439 partnership dispute. In 1434, Gutenberg developed a partnership with Andreas Dritzehn and the Heilmann brothers, agreeing to instruct them and reveal some "secrets." When Dritzehn died of the plague in 1438, Gutenberg considered the relationship ended, but Dritzehn's family did not. The Dritzehns sued to retain their investment and took Gutenberg to court. Circumstantial evidence presented during the trial indicated that Gutenberg's "secret" might have been printing with movable type, although no printed evidence exists to support the claim. The case was settled in Gutenberg's favor, and he stayed in Strasbourg until 1444.

In 1448, Gutenberg returned to Mainz and secured several loans to continue his work. His patron was Johann Fust, a lawyer-businessman in the city. At first Fust was simply an investor who held Gutenberg's tools as collateral, but after making more loans he became a partner in the enterprise. Gutenberg had two advantages: He knew how to work with metal, and he had only 23 letters to use, since there was no F, V, or W. This may explain why his method was not discovered earlier among nations with more complex alphabets.

Gutenberg probably initially published small commissions, including a poem, a propaganda pamphlet on the Turkish invasion, and papal indulgences. However, his publication of the 42-line Bible that bears his name remains the outstanding example of the birth of printing in Europe. The Gutenberg edition of Saint Jerome's Latin version of the Scriptures was the first complete book printed with movable type. Today, 47 copies of the priceless book exist; 13 copies in the United States are held by such institutions as Harvard University, Yale University, the Library of Congress, and the New York Public Library. Unfortunately, the edition is unsigned and shows no date or place of publication. Historians, then, can only speculate on Gutenberg's role in its publication. A note exists from Pope Pius II stating that the printing of the Bible was well advanced in October 1454 and assuming that it would be completed by the end of 1455. Furthermore, two dates written in a Bible at the Bibliothèque Nationale in Paris indicate that the book was for sale before August 1456. Since several years must have elapsed between the printing and distributing of the tome, it seems reasonable to attribute it to Gutenberg.

Although not the inventor of printing, Gutenberg did invent a practical system of movable type that led to letterpress or relief printing. The essential component in Gutenberg's process was the casting of letters, one at a time, from reusable molds. Single letters were engraved in relief and then punched into a softer metal to make dies, or matrices. The ingenious segment of the procedure was Gutenberg's invention of a three-part mold that surrounded the matrices. The mold slid together to form a receptacle for a molten mixture of lead and antimony. Once the cast metal replica cooled, the mold could be disassembled and reused. The cast letters required very little hand-finishing and were uniform in size, which was important in making the final image on the paper. This innovation allowed printers to use the type to create any text of any length, from single words to multiple pages. Ink was applied to the raised surface of the letter and pressed on the paper. Upon completion of the project, the type could be broken down and stored for reuse.

A second achievement of Gutenberg's has received scant notice. He had to create a new ink to go with his revolutionary type. The old woodblock ink, which was water-based, would not adhere to the metal type. The new ink required a fresh chemical makeup. Gutenberg, borrowing from Flemish painters, devised a combination of boiled linseed oil and lampblack to meet his needs. Finally, Gutenberg also altered the printing press to make it more serviceable.

In 1455, Gutenberg again found himself in court. Unable to repay his partner, Gutenberg was sued by Fust, who won the claim, took over Gutenberg's shop, and with his son-in-law Peter Schoeffer established a prosperous and long-lived printing business. They produced the Latin *Psalter* (hymnal), which was the first book in Europe to show the date of publication as well as the printer's name.

Gutenberg never prospered financially from his innovations, and he was plagued by fiscal difficulties for the remainder of his life. He might have reestablished his printing shop with funds from other investors, but it is difficult to determine what, if anything, he printed. Certainly he produced smaller works, like a calendar, grammar books, and indulgences, but there is no solid evidence that he produced any further major publications. There is some conjecture that he printed the *Catholicon*, in Mainz in the 1460s, or the 36-line Bamberg Bible.

In 1465, Gutenberg finally secured some financial stability. The archbishop of Mainz gave him a pension, exempted the printer from taxation, and provided a yearly allowance of cloth and wine. Gutenberg died in 1468 and was buried in Mainz's Franciscan cemetery.

Gutenberg lived long enough to realize the significance of his achievement. Printing spread rapidly throughout Europe. At the time of his death, at least eight major cities had printing establishments, and by 1500 there were active presses in 242 cities.

See also:
Printing.

References:
Feldman, Anthony, and Peter Ford. *Scientists and Inventors*. New York: Facts on File, 1979.
Ing, Janet. *Johann Gutenberg and His Bible: A Historical Study*. Los Angeles: Dawsons, 1988.
Scholderer, Victor. *Johann Gutenberg: The Inventor of Printing*. London: Trustees of the British Museum, 1970.

HDTV
See Television.

Hearst, William Randolph (1863–1951)

An American newspaper publisher, William Randolph Hearst is considered by many to be the most famous and controversial media mogul of the modern era. He is credited with creating yellow journalism, a deliberately sensational style of reporting that placed a premium on scandal and personalities. Using his inherited wealth, Hearst built a chain of newspapers that covered the entire country. He was accused of manipulating the news to serve his own ends and especially his largely unfulfilled political aspirations.

George Hearst, William's father, was a wealthy man due to his partnership in two of the richest mines in Nevada, and he eventually was elected a senator from California. As a young man, William Hearst appeared to be interested in very little and was an uninspired student. He failed to graduate from Saint Paul's School in New Hampshire and was expelled from Harvard for his involvement in college pranks.

In 1880, George Hearst purchased the *San Francisco Examiner*. The daily was never profitable, but it did serve as a convenient platform for the senator's views and those of his political allies. Returning home from the ill-fated Harvard venture, the younger Hearst asked his father for the paper as a gift. Not surprisingly, the answer was no, and Hearst moved to New York, where he secured a reporter's job with Joseph Pulitzer's *New York World*.

Persistence eventually paid off, and George Hearst finally gave the *Examiner* to his son. The first issue by the new owner appeared on 4 March 1887. Young Hearst spent his family's money freely to turn the paper around, most notably by hiring well-paid, quality staffers and upgrading machinery. The *Examiner* courted the urban working masses, and Hearst sought to pattern his publication after the prominent Eastern dailies, like the *World*. The *Examiner*'s bold

headlines screamed about crime, disasters, and scandals, reporting each in lurid detail. Additionally, there were human-interest stories, sports and women's sections, and always plenty of pictures. News became a commodity for the masses, and the *Examiner* was an industry leader.

The senior Hearst died in 1891. Concerned about his son's spending, the senator left his considerable fortune to his wife. In time, she sold her stock in the Anaconda Company and gave the $7.5 million profit to her son. Financially confident, Hearst moved to challenge Pulitzer for media preeminence. In 1895, he purchased an undistinguished metropolitan daily, the *New York Journal*, and began a circulation war between his *Journal* and Pulitzer's *World*. The businessmen fought to outdo each other, and sensationalistic news reports dominated each paper. One particular battle over staff had far-reaching results. Hearst tried to lure Richard Outcault, creator of the popular cartoon "The Yellow Kid," to his publication. The name of the comic was derived from the yellow ink used to print the cartoon. Consequently, the term "yellow press" was coined to describe the content of the battling papers. Hearst was successful in hiring Outcault, and as a result both comic strips and color became prominent parts of American newspapers.

The competition between the *Journal* and the *World* reached a climax with the 1898 Spanish-American War. Both papers supported the Cuban rebels and called for American intervention. Hearst sent the renowned artist Frederic Remington to Cuba as a war correspondent with the admonition, "You furnish the pictures and I'll furnish the war." Although not always accurate, the

Journal was the more sensationalistic and angered a number of professionals with its bold-faced exploitation of the crisis. Nonetheless, Hearst could triumphantly point to a major circulation increase for his paper.

At about the same period, Hearst began to expand his empire. In 1900, he acquired the *Chicago American* and later purchased papers in Atlanta, Boston, and Los Angeles, as well as other smaller papers across the nation. Aside from the characteristics of "yellow journalism," which included the use of comics, bold headlines, and color, Hearst's greatest legacy may be the news services he pioneered. King Features Services and the International News Service supplied other newspapers with columns, editorials, articles, and even pictures. Magazines provided another avenue of investment and expansion. Hearst bought several periodicals, including *Good Housekeeping*, *Harpers Bazaar*, and *Cosmopolitan*. In 1935, at the height of his influence and power, Hearst owned 28 newspapers, 13 magazines, eight radio stations, two movie companies, extensive real estate holdings, including his palatial San Simeon estate, numerous art treasures, and stock in various enterprises.

Influential as he was, Hearst was consistently frustrated by his failure to realize his political ambitions. His media power allowed him to support generously the candidates he favored or to attack unrelentingly those he opposed. Nonetheless, Hearst wanted personal recognition. He served two lackluster terms in the House of Representatives and ran unsuccessfully twice for the mayor of New York. Between those campaigns he tried to get elected governor of New York, failing in the 1906 race.

By 1937, the Depression, overexpansion, and the lavish spending to simply accumulate material wealth caught up with Hearst. He stopped construction on the fabled San Simeon estate, took a pay cut from $500,000 to $100,000, and was forced to liquidate some of his holdings. Nonetheless, only drastic action in 1941 restored his financial solvency and allowed a resumption of his accustomed lifestyle. Hearst owned the largest private collection of art in the world. It was so vast that he did not realize what he had, and a significant part of it was just warehoused. In 1941, with the aid of Gimbel's Department Store in New York City, Hearst literally held a warehouse sale. Dubbed "the sale of the century" by the press, the clearance was a resounding success and netted Hearst about $50 million. Infuriatingly, just blocks away, Orson Welles's film *Citizen Kane*, a thinly disguised version of Hearst's life, depicting a crude, greedy newspaper magnate, opened.

Hearst died on 14 August 1951. At the time of his death he still owned the largest newspaper empire in the nation and left an estate valued at $60 million.

See also:
Newspaper; Photography; Photojournalism; Printing.

References:
Carlisle, Rodney P. *Hearst and the New Deal: The Progressive as Reactionary*. New York: Garland, 1979.
Hoopes, Roy. "The 40-Year Run." *American Heritage*, November 1992.
Swanberg, W. A. *Citizen Hearst: A Biography of William Randolph Hearst*. New York: Scribner's, 1961.

Henry, Joseph (1797–1878)

Born in Albany, New York, Joseph Henry became America's foremost scientist during the nineteenth century and was the first director of the Smithsonian Institution.

Henry's family was poor and, to make matters worse, his father died when Joseph was six. He was sent to live with his grandmother while his mother struggled to support herself and Joseph's younger brother. He attended school but did not do well, so his grandmother found him a job in a general store when he was ten. He was not a very effective worker, but he was an attractive, tall, blond, blue-eyed boy who appealed to people who traded at the store.

When a pet rabbit escaped from its pen, Henry followed it under a church. After capturing his pet, Henry was attracted by a beam of light falling through an opening in the floor to a room above. There he discovered a number of books, and although he read poorly, he became so interested in *A Fool of Quality* by Sir Philip Brooks that he read it several times and became an avid reader.

A year later, Henry returned to live with his mother and was apprenticed to a watchmaker at the age of 13. Although Henry disliked the work, he acquired the mechanical skills that would later serve him well in assembling equipment for his various experiments. At the age of 16, inspired by a book entitled *Lectures on Experimental Philosophy*, Henry realized the importance of education and returned to school at Albany Academy, paying his tuition by teaching in a country school for $15 a month. After graduating, he continued to teach and tutor for nine years. Among those he tutored were the children of Stephen Van Rensselaer and Henry James, who was to become a well-known clergyman and father of William and Henry James.

After studying medicine for a brief time, Henry seemed to be in the early stages of a nervous breakdown. Van Rensselaer, who had grown to appreciate Henry's ability when the young man tutored his children, persuaded a judge to appoint Henry as surveyor for a state road that was to cross New York from Kingston on the Hudson River west to Lake Erie. A winter in the open air working as a surveyor enabled the young man to regain his health.

In 1826, Henry returned to Albany Academy as a teacher of science and mathematics. While there, he married his first cousin, Harriet Alexander, in 1830. She was nearly 15 years younger than he, but the marriage apparently was a happy one.

Research with Electromagnets

Fascinated by Oersted's discovery of the connection between electricity and magnetism and by Sturgeon's application of that discovery in constructing an electromagnet, Henry set out to build an electromagnet stronger than Sturgeon's. He soon discovered that the strength of the device depended on the number of windings in the coil. However, if the coils were wrapped too

closely, they touched one another, creating a short circuit. To overcome this difficulty, Henry wrapped insulation around the wire instead of the iron core. In that way, he could wind many turns of wire on top of one another. Since insulation for wiring was not available in this preelectric age, Henry tore strips from one of his wife's old silk petticoats and wrapped them around the wire, a boring task that took hours of his time, but his patience paid off. By winding hundreds of turns of insulated wire around an iron core, Henry was able to make electromagnets that would lift more than a ton of iron.

Henry's investigation of electromagnets was not limited to demonstrating the great lifting potential of Sturgeon's original invention. He was also interested in the use of much smaller versions that could be used in electric circuits. Henry found, as had Georg Ohm several years earlier, that electrical resistance increases with the length of the wire through which a current flows. Consequently, there was a limit to the distance that an electromagnet could be separated from the battery that supplied the current needed to activate it. To circumvent this difficulty, Henry invented the relay in 1835. His relay consisted of a small iron key that could be lifted by a very small current in an electromagnet. When the key was raised, it closed another circuit connected to a battery. The second circuit could then activate another relay, and the process could be repeated as often as needed. Using relays, Henry was able to ring a bell with an electromagnet that responded to an electrical signal sent from more than a mile away. With relays, the telegraph, which he had in effect invented, became a valuable means of long-distance communication. Without relays, the telegraph would have been an interesting but insignificant toy.

Henry's work provided the basic principle needed to build the telegraph, the world's first practical means of communicating over long distances. Samuel F. B. Morse, however, patented the device and is usually credited with its invention. Despite his dependence on Henry's basic research into electromagnets and relays and the skill of his mechanic, Alfred Vail, Morse was reluctant to share the credit for the invention. Without these two men, Morse would have floundered, for he lacked both mechanical skill and a firm grasp of fundamental scientific principles. Later, after many scientists credited Henry with inventing the telegraph and people sued Morse, claiming that the machine belonged in the public domain because Henry never asked for a patent, Morse wrote a 90-page pamphlet on the history of the telegraph in which he claimed to be the sole inventor. The pamphlet barely mentioned Henry, widely regarded as the true inventor of the telegraph.

Rather than become engaged in a personal controversy with Morse, Henry asked the Smithsonian Board of Regents to establish a special committee to investigate Morse's assertions. The committee concluded that Morse's claims were not truthful.

Henry never tried to patent any of his inventions because he believed that scientific knowledge should be shared openly with everyone. It was this philosophy that led him to offer ideas and suggestions to Morse and also to William Cooke and Charles Wheatstone, whom he visited while in England. Shortly after Henry's trip abroad, Cooke and Wheatstone, in 1837, invented their own version of the telegraph using relays remarkably similar to those Henry had described to them.

Henry, Faraday, and Electromagnetic Induction

In August 1830, Henry discovered the principle of electromagnetic induction when he found that a changing magnetic field in one coil would cause a voltage and current to develop in a completely separate coil. Because of his teaching duties at Albany Academy, Henry put off publishing his discovery until the following August. Before that, however, he read Faraday's account of a similar experiment revealing induction. When Henry did publish his results, nearly a year after his discovery, he gave Faraday full credit for publishing first, but his paper was the first to announce the discovery of self-inductance. Henry was able to demonstrate that a current and voltage could be induced not only in a second coil, as Faraday had discovered, but was always present in the initial coil as well. The self-induced voltage opposed the voltage driving current through the initial coil because it arose from what later came to be known as a back EMF or a back voltage. As a result, there is a time delay during which a current in a coil rises to its maximum value. Shortly after Henry's paper appeared, Faraday confirmed the principle of self-inductance and gave Henry full credit for the discovery.

A year later, Henry published a paper describing the electric motors he had first built in 1829. The commutator, which he invented, made electric motors possible because it allowed the current to reverse direction and thus keep the motor's armature and shaft turning in the same direction. At that time, electric motors were regarded as toys, but today we realize the significance of Henry's motor. Electric motors can be made in any size and put to many uses. We see them everywhere, in computers, vacuum cleaners, automobiles, refrigerators, shavers, pencil sharpeners, pumps, and hundreds of other devices and appliances.

Henry also discovered the principle underlying present-day transformers. Transformers allow high-voltage electricity to be converted to a safer low-voltage form that enters homes and businesses. Transformers also allow the voltage from power plants to be stepped up to a higher voltage for transmission over long distances.

Henry as an Administrator

In addition to being an outstanding scientist, Henry was an accomplished administrator. In 1832, as a result his research successes, he was offered the Chair of Natural Philosophy (physics) at the College of New Jersey (which later became Princeton University), a position he held for the next 14 years. There Henry was able to continue his research while teaching physics and sometimes chemistry as well. In his teaching, Henry tried to communicate to students the nature of scientific inquiry by having them gather facts through experimentation and then try to establish a general principle by induction rather than by simply presenting principles and showing how to reason deductively from established general laws and theories.

In 1846, Congress established the Smithsonian Institution in Washington, D.C. The will of James Smithson, a British chemist and mineralogist who had died in 1829, included a bequest of £100,000 (approximately $500,000) to the United States to be used "for the increase and diffusion of knowledge among men." The money didn't reach the U.S. government until 1838, and it was another nine years before the Smithsonian Board of Regents, established by Congress, asked Henry to study Smithson's will and establish a plan to utilize the bequest. Henry concluded that the money should be used to advance science and benefit all mankind through research and publication.

Congress received Henry's plan with thanks and then proceeded to add buildings, a museum, a library, and an art gallery in order to showcase the institution. To Henry, the buildings were all unnecessary window dressing to the cause that he believed Smithson had sought. Nevertheless, the Board of Regents elected Henry as the first secretary and director of the Smithsonian Institution, a post that he held for 32 years. While there, he carried out extensive research in meteorology and discovered that sunspots radiate considerably less heat than the rest of the sun's surface. He used his administrative position to encourage the development of science and mathematics in the United States and the worldwide exchange of scientific information. The Smithsonian became the world's principal agent of scientific communication. It collected and published technical papers and statistics and sent them to interested people and organizations throughout the world. It examined America's archeological treasures, began a study of Native Americans, and provided assistance to young scientists. Henry put the telegraph to scientific use by collecting weather reports from volunteer observers in various parts of the country who reported their findings to the Smithsonian—a program that later served as a basis for the establishment of the U.S. Weather Bureau.

During the Civil War Henry advised Lincoln on science-related issues and screened hundreds of inventors whose work occasionally proved to be of value to the war effort. During the war Lincoln asked Henry about the validity of spiritualism, to which Mrs. Lincoln had turned following the death of their son Willie. Henry, who held spiritualists in disdain, explained to the president how these people communicated their spiritual "messages," usually in the form of knocks (one for yes, two for no), to their gullible patrons. Their techniques included "popping" their knuckles or, in daylight, using their biceps to activate clicking telegraphic devices attached to their arms.

Henry became widely known and respected for his work, his honesty, and his patience among scientists, inventors, and government officials. He was widely regarded as the country's outstanding physicist. In recognition of his unselfish contributions to science, the International Electrical Congress in 1893 established the henry as the unit for electrical inductance.

See also:
Electromagnet; Field, Cyrus West; Morse, Samuel F. B.; Telegraph.

References:
Asimov, Isaac. *Asimov's Biographical Encyclopedia of Science and Technology*. Garden City, NY: Doubleday, 1964.
Jahns, Patricia. *Joseph Henry, Father of American Electronics*. Englewood Cliffs, NJ: Prentice-Hall, 1971.
Jahns, Patricia. *Matthew Fontaine Maury and Joseph Henry, Scientists of the Civil War*. New York: Hastings House, 1961.

Hertz, Heinrich Rudolf (1857–1894)

Heinrich Hertz was an outstanding nineteenth-century German physicist who confirmed Maxwell's theory of electromagnetic radiation by demonstrating the existence of electromagnetic waves. During his research, Hertz also discovered the photoelectric effect and showed that electromagnetic waves, initially referred to as Hertzian waves, have the same properties as light waves. Hertz, who is best known for his experimental work, was also a very capable theoretical physicist.

Hertz was born in Hamburg, Germany, on 22 February 1857. His father, a successful attorney and judge, was of Jewish ancestry, although his family had converted to Lutheranism. His mother, Ann Elisabeth Pfefferkorn, was a beautiful woman who encouraged Heinrich and his three brothers and sister to develop their individual talents and interests. Heinrich was said to have received his kind and friendly nature from his mother and his strong sense of duty from his father.

At age six, Hertz was enrolled in a private elementary school, where he remained for nine years. In 1872, he began two years of tutoring to prepare for Johanneum Gymnasium. Hertz was artistic, loved poetry, and seemed genuinely interested in all his subjects, which included Latin, Greek, Arabic, and even Sanskrit, but it was clear that he was truly gifted in mathematics and science. During his teens he also attended courses at an industrial school, where he learned carpentry and metalworking—skills that proved beneficial to an experimental scientist, for he was capable of making much of the equipment he needed.

Because Hertz had decided on a career in engineering, he spent a year after passing his *Abitur* (an examination that qualified him for any German university) as an intern to a master builder in the Public Works Department in Frankfurt in order to fulfill a requirement for his license as a structural engineer. However, after a year of engineering studies and another year in the military, which was required of all German youths, Hertz decided to switch to the natural sciences. In 1878, he began a program leading to a doctorate in physics at the Friedrich-Wilhelm University in Berlin, where he studied under Hermann Helmholtz and Gustav Kirchhoff, two of Germany's greatest scientists.

By the spring of 1880, Hertz had obtained his doctorate magna cum laude, an unusual accomplishment given the tough standards established by Helmholtz and Kirchhoff. Shortly thereafter, Helmholtz offered Hertz an assistantship at the Physics Institute. Despite a heavy instructional load, Hertz was able to publish 14 papers in three years before leaving to take a teaching position in Kiel.

Hertz's two years in Kiel were disappointing and depressing. He was frustrated by the lack of equipment and research facilities, and his moods were as dark as the long winter nights at 54.5 degrees latitude. Fortunately, an early Christmas present arrived on 20 December 1884, in the form of an offer to chair the physics department at Technische Hochschule in Karlsruhe. Not only did the facilities allow for solid research, but while there he met Elisabeth Doll, whom he married on 31 July 1886.

In the autumn following his marriage, Hertz began the investigations for which he is best remembered. Working with spark micrometers, he discovered quite by accident that sparks generated between two metal spheres connected to a primary coil produced smaller sparks across a gap in a secondary coil some distance away. As so often happens in science, Hertz's alert mind recognized the importance of what had been an accidental observation. He quickly determined that the effect could not be due to direct induction. Because he was familiar with Maxwell's theory of electromagnetic radiation, Hertz realized that what he had observed was probably the result of electromagnetic waves that traveled through the space between the two coils.

James Clerk Maxwell had predicted the existence of electromagnetic waves as early as 1856. According to Maxwell's theory, accelerating electric charges give rise to electric and magnetic fields that travel through space as transverse waves. According to Maxwell's calculations, these waves would travel at the speed of light because light was one form of such radiation.

Hertz knew that the sparks produced by

his primary coil would result in an oscillating electric current. As early as 1842, Joseph Henry had postulated that a spark across a Leyden jar capacitor would result in an oscillating current for a brief period. Later, Henry's prediction had been confirmed. Since an oscillating current would mean that charges had to change direction (and, therefore, velocity), Hertz realized that electromagnetic waves should be produced if Maxwell's theory was valid. He knew, too, that he could change the rate at which the charges jumped across the gap by changing the width of the spark gap. Changing the gap could therefore change the rate of oscillation and, thereby, the wavelength of the electromagnetic waves.

To detect the oscillating electric field that should accompany the electromagnetic waves, Hertz placed a loop of wire with a single spark gap a few feet away from his transmitter. He reasoned that when the field reached the loop, it would push charges within the wire back and forth. By adjusting the distance between the spheres in his transmitter, he was able to match the rate of oscillation of the charges in his receiver with those in his transmitter. When sparks began jumping back and forth across the gap in the receiver, he knew the rates matched. Later, Hertz was able to detect these same waves at distances of several hundred feet.

By generating 66-centimeter waves at a frequency estimated to be 450 megacycles, Hertz showed that within experimental error the waves predicted by Maxwell were moving at the speed of light, 300,000 kilometers per second. After placing his spark gap at the focal point of a parabolic, Hertz was able to produce a beam of radiation and show that the waves had the same properties as light; that is, they could be reflected, refracted, and polarized. Furthermore, the energy in the waves could be absorbed, just as light is absorbed, by letting them pass through metal. This effect can be noticed when the radio signal diminishes or disappears in a car traveling across a bridge made of metal girders.

During his investigation of electromagnetic waves, Hertz noticed that light shining on the poles of his secondary spark gap increased the sparking rate. By a series of careful experiments he was able to demonstrate that it was ultraviolet light that was responsible for the increased rate of discharge. Hertz had discovered the photoelectric effect. A year later, Wilhelm Hallwachs showed that it was negative charge that was rapidly driven away by the ultraviolet light.

Within a decade after Hertz published his 1888 paper, "The Forces of Electric Oscillations, Treated According to Maxwell's Theory," Marconi and others recognized the significance of his discovery as a means of long-distance communication. Their investigations led to wireless telegraphy and eventually to radio, television, and microwave signals.

On 10 December 1888, Hertz accepted the physics chair at Bonn with the understanding that his teaching load would be minimal so that he could devote most of his time to the research he so enjoyed. Unfortunately, shortly after his arrival in Bonn, Hertz began to be plagued by a variety of illnesses. As a result, he turned increasingly to writing. His clearly written explanations of Maxwell's theory, coupled with his experimental work at Karlsruhe, convinced most physicists that Maxwell was right. In recognition of his outstanding accomplishments, Hertz was awarded the Rumford medal by the Royal Society in 1890.

Following prolonged ill health, Hertz died of septicemia on 1 January 1894, leaving his wife and two young daughters. He was only 36 years old. *The Principles of Mechanics Presented in a New Form*, which he had written during the last two years of his life, was published after his death. In it, Hertz attempted to provide a basis for understanding the ether—the medium believed necessary for transmitting electromagnetic waves.

In October 1933, the International Electrotechnical Commission honored Hertz by establishing the hertz as the unit of frequency. It is appropriate that radio and television stations express their broadcast frequencies in terms of kilohertz or megahertz, because their origin can be traced to Hertz's discovery of a means of producing and detecting electromagnetic waves.

See also:
Electromagnetic Waves; Maxwell, James Clerk.

References:
Asimov, Isaac. *Asimov's Biographical Encyclopedia of Science and Technology*. Garden City, NY: Doubleday, 1964.
Gardner, Robert. *Communication*. New York: Twenty-First Century, 1994.
Mulligan, Joseph F., ed. *Heinrich Rudolf Hertz (1857–1894): A Collection of Articles and Addresses*. New York: Garland, 1994.

Heterodyning

The heterodyne circuit, which increases the strength of a received radio signal, was invented by Reginald Fessenden in 1901. However, the superheterodyne circuit developed by Edwin Armstrong in 1918 made the tuning of a radio receiver a simple one-control-knob procedure. The superheterodyne circuit allows all stages of amplification after mixing to operate at a frequency of 455 kilohertz for all amplitude modulation (AM) radios. Before Armstrong's invention, the tuned radio frequency (TRF) receiver required separate tuning for each stage of the amplification process.

Each radio station transmits electromagnetic waves with a particular frequency—a frequency assigned by the Federal Communications Commission. A dial set to receive signals from a station that broadcasts at 700 kilohertz, for example, is tuned to 700. The local oscillator inside the receiver is automatically tuned to 455 kilohertz above the frequency on the dial; in this case it is tuned to 1,155 kilohertz. As a result, two signals are sent to the mixer. One will be the 700-kilohertz signal from the station that was received by the antenna, and the other will be the 1,155-kilohertz signal from the local oscillator. The frequencies of the mixer output will be 1,855 kilohertz (1,155 + 700) and 455 kilohertz (1,155 – 700). Both frequencies contain the same information, but only the lower frequency, which is always 455 kilohertz, is selected. Consequently, all stages of amplification after mixing will be for a single fixed frequency.

Heterodyning is also used in frequency modulation (FM) radio, where the fixed frequency is 10.7 kilohertz, and in television, where it is 4.5 megahertz.

See also:
Amplifier; Electromagnetic Waves; Modulation; Oscillator; Radio.

Reference:
Gosling, William, ed. *The Radio Receivers*. Piscataway, NJ: Institute of Electrical Engineers, 1986.

Hieroglyphics

Hieroglyphics is the pictorial system of writing used in ancient Egypt. The term derives from the Greek *hieros,* meaning "holy," and *glyphein,* meaning "to engrave." Developed at about the same time that cuneiform was evolving in Mesopotamia, hieroglyphics also served a decorative role on monuments, temples, tombs, and coffins. Although hieroglyphics is one of the most important writing systems of the ancient world, little is known about its origin. Reasonable estimates have established the introduction of hieroglyphics at 3200 B.C., although a simpler form may have existed earlier. The system remained essentially unchanged, except for the addition of signs, through the early Christian era. The last known datable hieroglyphics were inscribed at Philae in A.D. 394.

Authorities calculate that there were about 700 signs in classical Egyptian hieroglyphics, and over time this number increased to 5,000 or 6,000 during the Ptolemaic period. Characters were written in continuous horizontal or vertical lines with no punctuation or breaks to indicate where words and sentences began and ended. Hieroglyphics were normally read from right to left, but some were written from bottom to top or in alternating directions. Signs representing people or animals gave a clue to reading hieroglyphics, since they usually faced the beginning of the inscription. The complete hieroglyphic system was complicated by the multiple functions of the signs.

Signs could be read in three ways—as a picture, sound, or classifier.

Nowhere is the example of hieroglyphics as a combination of art and writing more evident than in the early stages of its development. Pictograms or ideograms were stylized drawings. They usually emphasized the familiar characteristics of everyday objects and were meant to depict the object or something that had a close connection to it. For example, the hieroglyph for "sun" could also signify "day" or "light." This alternate, synonymous usage could confuse readers, and to overcome bewilderment the system was refined by shifting to phonetic writing. Symbols were employed as phonograms; that is, syllables and sounds used in spelling. Not intended to convey meaning, phonograms indicated a sound that, combined with other sounds, created a word different in meaning from the pictogram. Phonograms were always consonants. Since vowels were not written in hieroglyphics, but assumed by the reader, Egyptologists have to speculate about the missing vowels to create words. Finally, there were determinatives. These signs were placed before or after a word but had no phonetic value. They were used to clarify the meaning of the preceding sign(s) by indicating the category, type, or general class of a word. Hieroglyphic words and sentences seldom used signs with one function but were a mixture of phonometric signs and pictograms. The Egyptians never adapted the more convenient alphabetical system used today.

The intricate hieroglyphic system was considered too cumbersome for daily use or for tasks that required speedy notation. Consequently, scribes developed a more usable, less formal script. Hieratic writing, which developed parallel to the more formal hieroglyphics, was a cursive system that represented signs in rounder and simpler form. Hieroglyphics might be compared to today's printing, whereas hieratic writing was similar to handwriting and lacked the pictorial quality of hieroglyphics.

In or around the seventh century B.C., a third system, demotic writing, appeared. The most widespread and popular form of hieroglyphics, demotic writing was a more cursive version of hieratic writing and could be compared to shorthand. It bears little resemblance to the classical hieroglyphic characters, although the signs served the same functions.

Real advances were not made in breaking the hieroglyphic riddle until the beginning of the nineteenth century. In 1799, Napoleon's soldiers, while digging trenches during his Egyptian campaign, unearthed the tabletop-sized Rosetta stone. Later captured by the British and now in the British Museum, the stone was a trilingual decree of Ptolemy V dated ca. 196 B.C. The use of three scripts assured that the whole nation would understand the king's intentions. Greek was the language of government, demotic writing was understood by most literate Egyptians, and hieroglyphics served religious purposes and informed posterity. The Greek provided a key to the other languages.

In 1822, Jean-François Champollion (1790–1832), a French Egyptologist, began the decoding process, building on the work of other scholars as well as his knowledge of the Coptic language. Champollion used the Rosetta stone to identify the names of Cleopatra and Ptolemy inside cartouches in the inscriptions. Cartouches were ovals, used in most Egyptian inscriptions, which usually enclosed the names of kings and queens. Champollion used the Greek letters to enlarge his hieroglyphic vocabulary and completed the translation by 1828. Egyptologists have succeeded in demystifying hieroglyphics, but some aspects still baffle the experts. For example, it is still not known how the language was spoken and how words were pronounced. Not all words can be transcribed due to the lack of vowels.

See also:
Cuneiform; Writing.

References:
Ceram, C. W. *Gods, Graves and Scholars: The Story of Archeology.* New York: Bantam Books, 1972.
Gean, Georges. *Writing: The Story of Alphabets and Scripts.* New York: Harry C. Abrams, 1992.

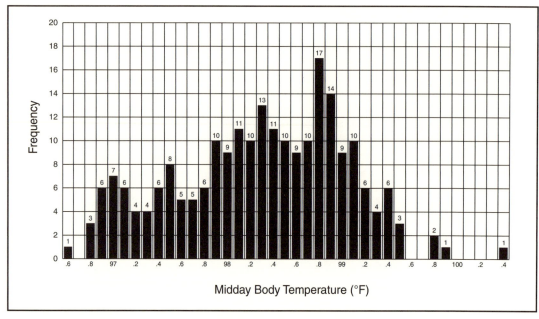

Figure 1. A typical histogram, in this case showing midday body temperatures of 227 subjects in 0.1-degree Fahrenheit increments.

Histogram

A histogram, also known as a bar graph, is a graphical device designed to show the distribution of a continuous variable. It provides a visual means of representing a frequency distribution. The frequency of a value is shown on the vertical (y) axis. The horizontal (x) axis is divided into equal intervals. The number of intervals along the horizontal axis is chosen for convenience. Each interval represents a discrete range of the value being measured or observed. The larger the data sample, the narrower the intervals that may be chosen. With small data samples there may be gaps between the intervals because some intervals will have a frequency of 0.

Suppose a medical researcher collects data on normal, healthy, human midday body temperatures. The researcher decides to show the frequency of people with different body temperatures at intervals of 0.1 degree Fahrenheit. Such a histogram involving 227 subjects is shown in Figure 1.

Frequencies may be either absolute or relative. For small samples, the frequency is usually given in absolute (actual) numbers. For large samples, relative frequencies are often used. A sample of a million marriages classified according to the age of the bride would probably be given as a relative frequency. If 30 percent of the women were married between the ages of 23.5 and 25.5 years, the vertical bar extending from 23.5 to 25.5 on the horizontal axis would rise to the 30 or 0.30 level on the vertical axis.

If a careful choice of interval and relative frequency is made, the entire area of the histogram can be made to equal 1.0. The area of each rectangular vertical bar will then be the relative frequency based on a total frequency of 1.0. For example, if an interval of 0.01 is chosen and there are 100 samples, the total area will be 1.0 (100 × 0.01). A bar representing a frequency of 18 would have an area of 0.18 (18 × 0.01), or 18 percent of the total area.

Reference:
Gardner, Robert, and Edward Shore. *Math & Society: Reading Life in Numbers.* New York: Watts, 1995.

Holography

Holography is a photographic technique used to produce three-dimensional images.

The method was first developed and described by Dennis Gabor in 1947. Gabor's first holograms, however, lacked depth because he did not have a coherent light beam—something that became available following the invention of the laser by Theo Maiman in 1960.

To make a hologram, a laser beam is diverged and split into two parts. Light from one of the beams (the object beam) is reflected from the object to a photographic plate. Light from the second beam (the reference beam) shines on the plate. Light from two beams, which are in phase, produces an interference pattern that is recorded in the silver emulsion as a negative of a conventional photograph.

After the film is developed, it constitutes the hologram. When the film is illuminated by coherent light of the same frequency as that used to make it, light passing through the small openings in the film is diffracted, creating a three-dimensional real image behind the hologram. The image has not only depth but shows parallax as well; that is, its perspective changes when viewed from different positions.

With a very complicated process, it is also possible to make holograms using ordinary light. By sacrificing depth along one dimension, reasonably clear, brightly colored holograms known as rainbow holograms can be produced. Such holograms are used in making passports and credit cards. The use of holography makes duplication of such cards difficult.

In the future, holography may lead to the use of light patterns as a means of providing computer memory. It may also be used to generate three-dimensional movies and television, and it is already giving rise to new art forms. Furthermore, acoustic holography using ultrasound is being utilized in underwater experiments, and microwave holograms provide useful maps of terrain.

See also:
Laser; Photography.
References:
Macaulay, David. *The Way Things Work.* Boston: Houghton Mifflin, 1988.
Sears, Francis W., Mark W. Zemansky, and Hugh D. Young. *College Physics.* Reading, MA: Addison-Wesley, 1985.
Wheeler, Gerald F., and Larry D. Kirkpatrick. *Physics: Building a World View.* Englewood Cliffs, NJ: Prentice-Hall, 1983.

Homeostasis
See Wiener, Norbert.

Homiletics
Homiletics is the art of preaching, and homilies are sermons designed to educate a congregation about some practical matter. Homiletics, derived from the Greek *homiletikos* ("of conversation") and *homilia* ("dealings with another"), prescribes the best techniques for effective preaching.

Many religions believe that God communicates to humans through the homilist, and because homiletic preaching is an act of worship, it requires authorization. Consequently, many denominations demand that homilists be ordained and demonstrate a personal morality that makes them worthy of bringing God's word to a congregation.

Christian homilies began with Jesus. According to the Gospel of Luke, Jesus' career began with a homily on the Book of Isaiah at a synagogue in Nazareth. The Koran, which means "recital," is believed to be a direct personal address by God through the voice of Muhammad that provides an authoritative interpretation of scripture. The Koran, therefore, can be viewed as a long homily from God. As a result, those who accept the Koran as the word of God believe it needs no interpretation. Christians and Hebrews, on the other hand, have found it necessary to interpret the scriptures to meet the needs of changing times.

Because homilies are an interpretation of text, homilists had to be literate. This was not a problem in the early days of Christianity because of the high degree of literacy in Hellenistic culture. But with the decline of education and the erosion of Greek and Latin during the early Middle Ages, there was a concomitant decline in the quality and quantity of homilies. By the twelfth and thirteenth centuries, conditions changed and noted homilists gave rise to the Franciscan and Dominican orders, whose friars spread the word of God and the church far and wide. As the power of the church grew, homilies began to take on secular as well as religious meaning. The church-fostered crusades—repeated efforts to regain the Holy Land from Islam—were led by laymen with worldly as well as religious goals.

By the sixteenth century, papal interpretation of the scripture and abuses within the church gave rise to the Reformation. The rise of Protestantism, fostered in part by the printing press, restored the Bible, rather than the church, as the main contact with God. But the divine purpose of homiletics would remain tainted by politics and nationalism. Preaching led to the Crusades, but the colonization of America, the westward expansion of the United States with its cry of Manifest Destiny, and the formation of Israel are a few of the many illustrations of the secularization of homiletics.

Today, homilies are often regarded as stories with a moral, but not necessarily of a religious nature.

See also:
Forensics; Oratory.
References:
Brinkley, David. *David Brinkley's Homilies*. New York: Knopf, 1996.
International Encyclopedia of Communications. New York: Oxford University Press, 1989.

Hubble Space Telescope
See Satellite.

Icon

An icon is a pictorial representation or likeness of a person, object, or concept. The word is derived from the Greek *eikenai*, meaning "to resemble," and is often associated with small painted wooden panels found in Eastern Christian churches.

Use of icons can be traced to the beginnings of human civilization. Icons played an important role in religion by conveying meanings that word symbols could not before the general public became literate. Archeologists have discovered small statuettes of heavy-breasted, heavy-thighed women that were carved by members of ancient polytheistic religions and are believed to be icons symbolizing fertility. Egyptian icons often combined a human body and an animal's head. Ptah (the creator) was represented by a bull's head on a human body, Hathor (the mother goddess) had a cow's head, and the body of Re (the sun god) had the head of a hawk.

Icons were not part of early Christianity. Because of their Judaic origins, early Christians viewed icons as graven images, which were forbidden in Judaism. Although representations of Christ were not carved or painted before the fifth century, icons of lambs and fish were used as symbols of Christ.

Most of the religious icons used to represent God, Christ, or various saints were stylized and painted or carved in accordance with rules established by the church. For example, two keys came to represent Saint Peter in early Christianity.

More recently, icons have taken on a new meaning in connection with computer software. The term *icon* now refers to small pictures that appear on a computer screen to represent discs, file folders, programs, and documents. A user clicks on an icon with the mouse to open the disc, folder, document, or program represented by that icon. To avoid confusion, many of the icons found in computer software also carry identifying titles.

See also:
Artifact; Computers and Society.

Ideogram

See Cuneiform; Hieroglyphics.

Inductor

An inductor is a device that introduces inductance into an electric circuit. When a switch is thrown to close an electric circuit, a current begins to flow. However, the current grows from zero to a maximum during a finite period; it does not reach its maximum instantaneously. The reason for this delay is that once charge begins to move, a magnetic field is established around the flowing charge. The growing magnetic field produces an electric field that opposes the current, in accordance with Lenz's Law. Once the current reaches its maximum value, the magnetic field becomes constant and the opposing electric field disappears because the electric field forms only when the magnetic field is changing. Similarly, when a switch opens a circuit, the magnetic field shrinks to zero. While the field is shrinking, a current is induced that tends to keep the charges flowing in the same direction. This property of a conductor to produce a so-called back electromotive force (EMF)—a voltage that opposes any change in voltage or current—is called inductance. It is measured in a unit known as the henry in honor of Joseph Henry, who first discovered inductance.

The inductance, L, in a circuit is determined by the equation

$$L = \frac{V}{\Delta I / \Delta t} = \frac{\text{Back EMF}}{\Delta I / \Delta t}$$

where V is the back voltage that opposes the voltage driving the current and $\Delta I / \Delta t$ is the time rate of change in the back current. One henry is equal to 1 volt per ampere per second. The inductance is small for an ordinary conducting wire; consequently, the time required for a current to reach its maximum is less than a millionth of a second. Winding the wire into a coil will cause the magnetic field to become larger, the back EMF and back current to increase, and the time needed to reach maximum current to grow longer. Still greater magnetic fields and correspondingly greater inductance can be obtained by placing a soft iron core within the coil. Inductance coils, together with capacitors, play a major role in building the resonance circuits used to tune radios and produce oscillatory circuits.

See also:
Capacitor; Electrical Resistor; Henry, Joseph; Magnetic Field; Oscillator; Radio.

Information Superhighway

The information superhighway is often regarded as synonymous with the Internet. However, it is viewed here as a union of television and computers that will provide rapid access to, and the exchange of, vast amounts of information, much of which will allow for interaction between sender and receiver.

The Internet is a computer network. The information superhighway lies in the future. It will be built when fiber-optic cables carrying digital signals allow thousands of times more data to be transmitted per second than is possible now. With a user-friendly computer, television, telephone, and printer all interconnected as one machine, it will be possible to shop at home by browsing through on-screen catalogs or stores, place orders by typing on a keyboard, and pay by entering a credit card in a slot beside the television screen.

In addition to shopping, users will be able to send E-mail, order current movies on a pay-for-viewing basis, select any past or present TV program to watch at any time, bank and pay bills, obtain information about the stock market, play video games, talk on videophones, participate in interactive quiz or talk shows, buy electronic "tickets" for concerts or sports events, obtain travel information, and place reservations for hotels and airline tickets. Instead of commuting by car, train, or bus, employees will be able to telecommute because it will be possible for most people to work at home. Face-to-face interaction with colleagues or clients will be possible through video conferences. Want a second medical opinion? Send tests, X rays, MRIs, and other data electronically to a second doctor, who will be able to make a diagnosis and respond via the information superhighway. A pocket communicator smaller than a cellular phone that transmits and receives radio waves will allow users to stay in touch with their home terminal as well as people trying to reach them. Access to reading material will expand; books and magazines will be viewed by pressing a few keys and calling up the desired pages, graphics and all, which can then be perused on-screen or downloaded or printed for later reading. Schools will share outstanding teachers whose presentations will be stored electronically so they may be accessed at any time.

Of course, the information superhighway will make some current technologies obsolete. Pocket-size communicators will negate the need for pagers. Videocassette recorders, cassette players, and video stores will no longer be needed. Mail-order catalogs will no longer be burdens for the few remaining postal carriers; telephone books will be obsolete because the entire nation's telephone numbers can already be stored on CD-ROMs. Textbook publishers may provide materials electronically, but teachers will be able to select the printed or visual matter they want to use for in-class and homework assignments on terminals in classrooms.

See also:
Computer; Electronic Mail; Fiber Optics; Internet; Telephone; Television.
References:
Gardner, Robert. *Communication*. New York: Twenty-First Century, 1994.
Gardner, Robert, and Dennis Shortelle. *The Future and the Past*. New York: Messner, 1989.

Intelsat
See Satellite.

Intercommunicating System (Intercom)

An intercommunicating system, or intercom, allows business or personal communication to take place between two or more parties. Usually the system is within the same building or building complex, ship, aircraft, or spaceship. It may also provide music while waiting, push-to-talk buttons, station bridging, and exclusion.

The intercom may consist of a telephone system that allows direct communication between two or more stations on the same premises. Or it may be a two-way communication system with microphone and loudspeaker at each station that allows people to talk to one another within a limited area. There are also one-way intercoms that allow one to receive but not transmit sounds. Such systems could be as widely divergent as one that enables a parent to hear a baby crying in a nursery or another that allows a spy to listen to conversations between foreign officials.

> **See also:**
> Loudspeaker; Microphone; Telephone.

Internet

The Internet is a distributed network consisting of many millions of computers storing text, graphics, video, and audio files that are all linked together via telephone and other types of high-speed data lines.

History

The Internet had its beginnings in the mid-1960s as a Defense Department initiative. The premise behind a distributed system of information was that even if one part of the network was malfunctioning, important information could be sent along an alternate route or routes and still arrive at its intended destination. Information sent over the Internet is sent via small parcels of information called "packets." Using an established set of more than 100 rules collectively called Trans-mission Control Protocol/Internet Protocol (TCP/IP) to which all software must adhere, the transmitted information is coded, broken into packets, routed through various methods over many different data lines, and reassembled in a usable manner at the receiving computer.

The TCP/IP protocols ensured that there were standards for exchanging information among different networks and types of computers. As these protocols grew to be accepted, the Internet began to expand into the academic arena. To support this effort, a backbone of Internet supercomputers called NSFnet was established by the National Science Foundation (NSF) in the late 1980s. These supercomputers allowed for faster data transmission, and a number of Internet tools were developed to take advantage of this fast new network.

As more consumers learned about this fabulous network called the Internet, local access providers began to rent space on the NSFnet backbone to provide service to their customers. As the privatization of the Internet grew, the NSF bowed out and commercial telecommunications companies took over maintenance of the large Internet backbone of supercomputers and data lines. This commercialization has allowed for astounding growth of the Internet and Internet access. Only about a third of the Internet remains devoted to research and educational networking; the major Internet traffic now involves commercial communication.

Computers utilizing the Internet are identified by a domain name system (DNS) address. This address is broken into four parts, each separated by a period. From right to left, this address moves from the very general to the very specific. To make these cryptic numbers easier to remember, text is often assigned to the specific DNS to facilitate the process for the end user. For example, it may be possible to reach a local newspaper whose DNS is 205.214.22.2 by typing www.herald.com.

Access to the Internet

Access to the Internet is commonly done in one of three ways—via terminal access, dial-up access, or a dedicated connection. Whichever way the connection occurs, the computer used to access the Internet is called a host.

With a terminal account, the user has only text-based access to the Internet. It may involve dialing in via a modem from the local computer to the host computer to connect. The information is stored on the host computer, and the local machine is used primarily to input text and display output. Through a two-step process, information can be downloaded from the host computer to the local computer.

Dial-up access is the most common method of connecting to the Internet. With this type of access, the user, through a modem, dials into the host computer to establish a temporary, direct connection to the Internet. The host computer is permanently connected to the Internet at all times. When this temporary connection is made, the user becomes a host and can then run the programs located on his local hard drive in order to access the different areas of the Internet. The rate at which information can flow via a standard telephone line is rated in kilobytes per second. The current standard is 28.8 kilobytes per second.

With a dedicated connection, the local computer becomes a host computer and is connected to the Internet at all times. There is a dedicated phone link over a leased line to create this high-speed connection. The speed of these types of connections, often referred to as 56K, T1, and T3, involve special wiring that allow data to be transmitted thousands of times faster than along ordinary phone lines.

Pieces of the Internet

The Internet is made up of many different methods of accessing and presenting information. The much discussed World Wide Web (WWW) provides what appears to be universal access to many facets of the Internet. Most Internet tools work via the client/server model. This means that the server computers supply the information when requested by the client computer's software. These two computers are connected via a network of some type for the time needed to complete this process.

Every place on the Internet has an address, which is called a uniform resource locator (URL). This address designates what protocol is being accessed (mail, gopher, file transfer protocol, or World Wide Web) and what computer the information resides on, and it provides a standard way for the user to access much of the information on the Internet via the Web browser. Because of this seamless access to all of the protocols, the Web browser is fast becoming the standard access software for Internet use.

The World Wide Web: The introduction of the World Wide Web created a huge growth of interest in the Internet. With the World Wide Web, users can hear sounds and see color pictures and videos. The World Wide Web also introduced a new concept called hypertext, thus the protocol for utilizing the Web is called hypertext transfer protocol (HTTP). Hypertext is the ability to click on a highlighted word (called a hyperlink) and go directly to that information. This makes the Web a nonsequential learning experience and allows users to learn in their own way and at their own pace. This method of access is called "browsing," and the piece of software used to access the WWW is called a "browser." Because the Web allows viewers to see and hear items other than text, the term "hypertext" has been expanded to "hypermedia."

Electronic Mail: One of the most common uses of the Internet is electronic mail, or E-mail. This protocol allows users on the Internet to send messages over the network to other users or groups of users. These messages are stored on servers or mail hosts until the recipient logs on to retrieve them. The set of rules for electronic mail, which is shared by all computers on the Internet, is called simple mail transport protocol (SMTP). To send a piece of E-mail, the user identifies the recipient, the subject of the message, and the sender, types the document, and sends the E-mail message. Every user of an Internet service is given an E-mail address. It is very important to type this address exactly as it is given . Each E-mail address has two parts: user ID and domain name. These two parts are separated by the "@" symbol. A typical E-mail address might be jsmith@compnet.com.

File Transfer Protocol: The set of rules and the procedure for transferring data and text files between computers on the Internet is called file transfer protocol (FTP). With FTP, users log on to a computer archive of files at a remote site, find the files they want, and transfer those files to their local computer. Hundreds of programs that are available as "try before you buy" shareware may be downloaded via FTP.

Gopher: This information is found on computers called "gopher servers." Gopher information is arranged in menus and allows linear access to large amounts of very useful information. The user chooses menu items and works downward or upward to the information being sought. A keyword search tool, called Veronica, indexes this information and makes it easier for the user to access the large number of data and text files contained on gopher servers.

Telnet: Telnet is the protocol used to directly connect to another computer with which the user has an account or is allowed public access. This type of access is only text-based, but since it produces little strain on the host computer, it is commonly used for large databases of text such as library card catalogs and magazine indices.

The Future of the Internet

The growth and development of the Internet is dependent upon bandwidth. Bandwidth is the amount of information that can flow over data lines at one time and at what speed. Think of it as a plumbing system in which the backbone contains tunnels 6 feet in diameter. The host narrows this down to a 2-foot pipe, and the information flows from the host to the local computer via a 1-inch pipe. Until the problem of bandwidth expansion to the local computer is solved, the amount and type of information that can flow will be limited.

As fiber-optic cables, satellite technologies, and TV-cable modems are investigated, prospects are sure to brighten soon. With increased bandwidth, full-motion video and compact disc–quality audio will become commonplace. The Internet is still in its infancy. Look for exciting developments in the upcoming years.

—Kathleen Schrock

See also:
Computer; Electronic Mail; Fiber Optics; Modem; Online Services; Videotex.
References:
Gorman, Christine. "AT&T Rewires the Net." *Time*, 11 March 1996.
Pfaffenberger, Bryan. *The World Wide Web Bible*, 2nd ed. New York: MIS Press, 1996.
"Welcome to Cyberspace." *Time*, Spring 1995 special issue.

ITU
See Satellite.

Keller, Helen Adams (1880–1968)

Helen Keller was born on 27 June 1880. A first child, she was adored by her parents and was a bright and lively infant. However, in February 1882, she became very ill. Modern doctors believe she probably had scarlet fever, but the doctors of her time called her sickness "acute congestion of the stomach and brain." In a few weeks, Keller was completely deaf and blind.

Keller, in a world of silent darkness, lost what speech she had acquired before her sickness but developed simple signs to communicate her wants and needs to others. As she grew older, her frustration and loneliness increased. "The desire to express myself grew," Keller recalled. "The few signs I used became less and less adequate, and my failures to make myself understood were invariably followed by outbursts of passion."

During the nineteenth century, many people believed that blind and deaf individuals were also simpleminded. People close to the Kellers suggested that their daughter be committed to an institution. The Kellers refused and searched for other ways to help their daughter. An eye doctor in Baltimore suggested that Keller's parents take her to Washington, D.C., to see Alexander Graham Bell, who was involved with the education of the deaf. His invention of the telephone was a result of his effort to help deaf children learn to speak. Bell recommended that the Kellers contact Michael Anagnos, director of the Perkins Institution for the Blind in Boston.

Anagnos was the son-in-law of Samuel Howe, who had gained recognition for himself and the Perkins Institution by teaching a young deaf and blind girl, Laura Bridgman, to communicate with others by using a manual alphabet. A manual alphabet consists of letters traced on a person's palm. Anagnos recommended that Anne Sullivan serve as Helen's teacher. Sullivan had been a student at Perkins Institution, to which she had come as a young adolescent in 1880, illiterate and almost blind, from the poorhouse in Tewksbury, Massachusetts. She underwent many eye operations and received intense instruction while at Perkins.

On 5 April 1887, Keller "discovered" language. "Someone was drawing water, and my teacher placed my hand under the spout. As the cold stream gushed over one hand, she spelled into the other the word water, first slowly, then rapidly. I stood still, my whole attention fixed upon the motions of her fingers. Suddenly I felt a misty consciousness as of something forgotten—a thrill of returning thought; and somehow the mystery of language was revealed to me. I knew then that 'w-a-t-e-r' meant the wonderful, cool something that was flowing over my hand. That living word awakened my soul, gave it light, hope, joy, set it free!"

Within three months, Keller had acquired a vocabulary of 300 words and was composing simple sentences by spelling into her teacher's hand. The next step in Keller's education was to teach her to read. To do this Sullivan began by first forming a letter in Keller's hand and then placing her fingers on a piece of cardboard on which the letters had been embossed. Keller learned the entire raised alphabet in one day and was able to read all the words she already knew. Keller's education continued at a fast pace. She learned to read and write in Braille, a system of writing for the blind developed by Louis Braille in 1826. It consists of raised dots representing letters and combinations of letters. The reader interprets the dots by touch.

In the fall of 1889, a teacher at Perkins returned from a trip to Norway, where she had seen a deaf and blind woman who was learning to speak. Helen immediately wanted to learn to speak also. After six weeks of instruction at the Horace Mann

School for the Deaf, Keller could speak, but her speech was thick and monotonic. Dr. Bell believed firmly that deaf people should be taught to speak. He encouraged Keller's parents to send her to the Wright-Humanson School in New York City, which specialized in teaching the deaf to talk. However, Helen's voice remained toneless and difficult to understand despite special training.

In the fall of 1900, Keller entered Radcliffe College after passing the very difficult entrance exams. During her college years, Keller was asked to write a magazine article about her life. Her article, "The Story of My Life," was published in 1902 and was later expanded into a book that was published in 1903. Keller graduated cum laude from Radcliffe in 1904. She had accomplished a fantastic feat. Blind and deaf, she had succeeded at one of the most prestigious colleges in America.

By age 24 Keller was world famous because of her incredible accomplishments. Now she needed to decide what she wanted to do with her education. She had already gained success as a writer, and it seemed logical to pursue that as a career. Once Keller decided to write, her typewriter was never silent. Helen wrote one magazine article after another. Her second book, published in 1908 and titled *The World I Live In*, was a collection of essays explaining how she used her senses of touch, taste, and smell to know the world.

Keller grew tired of writing about herself and began to write about controversial subjects such as women's rights, the conditions of the working class, and economic reform. By 1912, editors lost interest in her articles because of her unpopular beliefs, so she and Anne Sullivan began a lecture tour. At each appearance, Sullivan would speak about her methods of teaching Keller, then the two would demonstrate how Keller read Sullivan's lips with her fingertips. Finally, Keller would speak directly to the audience, and Sullivan would repeat her words. Although her audiences could understand little of what she said, Keller was one of America's best-loved public speakers.

Keller also worked for the American Foundation for the Blind, helping to raise over $1 million—an amazing sum in the 1920s—and she worked for the blind in other ways. She was upset by the confusion of having five different reading systems for the blind. Her work for standardization was rewarded in 1932 with international acceptance of Braille's original finger-read alphabet.

Despite the lack of enthusiasm for her political writings, Helen continued to enjoy success when she wrote about herself. The second volume of her autobiography, *Midstream*, was published in 1929.

Anne Sullivan died in October 1936. She had been Keller's teacher, friend, and companion for almost 50 years. Keller was devastated, but she continued her worldwide work for the blind and deaf. In 1955, after the nearly completed manuscript had been destroyed in a fire, Keller's *Teacher: Anne Sullivan Macy* was published. It was her memorial to her devoted friend and teacher.

In 1943, Keller began to tour military hospitals. She comforted and encouraged men and women who had been blinded or deafened in the war. She felt it was one of the most rewarding experiences of her life. Between 1946 and 1957, Keller visited hospitals and schools in 35 countries on five continents, helping to organize and support programs for the handicapped. As Keller grew older, nations around the world showed their appreciation for her accomplishments. In 1964, President Lyndon Johnson presented Keller with the nation's highest civilian award, the Presidential Medal of Freedom.

Helen Keller died on 1 June 1968, a few weeks before her eighty-eighth birthday. Her writings and public appearances had changed the way the world treated and educated the handicapped. Through her own example, by facing challenges and overcoming her handicaps, Helen Keller gave hope to millions of others.

—*Barbara Gardner Conklin*

See also:
Bell, Alexander Graham; Communication

among the Hearing Impaired; Communication among the Visually Impaired; Telephone.

References:

Keller, Helen. *The Story of My Life*. Boston: Houghton Mifflin, 1904.

Markham, Lois. *Helen Keller*. New York: Watts, 1993.

Wepman, Dennis. *Helen Keller*. New York: Chelsea House, 1987.

Land, Edwin H. (1909–1991)

American inventor and self-taught physicist, Edwin Land held over 500 patents. His most notable success was the instant one-step Polaroid photographic process. Most of Land's inventions derived from his work with polarized light, which he began as a student at Harvard University. The Bridgeport, Connecticut, native left Harvard before his graduation to devote his full time to his scientific interests.

In the early 1930s, Land perfected what became known as the Polaroid J Sheet—the first synthetic light-polarizing (glare-reducing) material. In 1932, Land joined Harvard physics instructor George Wheelwright III to form Land-Wheelwright Labs. The firm, which at first specialized in chemical and optical research, developed Land's polarization materials for commercial use and built its success on that device. Eastman Kodak used polarized filters in their cameras in 1935, and American Optical marketed polarized sunglasses in 1936.

In 1937, the 28-year-old Land established the Polaroid Corporation in Cambridge, Massachusetts, and continued his success during World War II by supplying optical elements for periscopes, goggles, and night-vision instruments. His polarized filters found use in aerial cameras and bombsights. Unlike many companies then dependent on military contracts, Polaroid prospered in the post–World War II years. Turning profits back into the company, Polaroid Labs developed three-dimensional movies and movie projectors in the 1940s and the ultraviolet microscope in the 1950s.

Land's most memorable invention combined his childhood interest in photography and his technical wizardry. On a 1943 vacation to Santa Fe, New Mexico, Land's three-year-old daughter asked why she could not immediately see the pictures Land had just taken. His interest aroused, Land took a one-hour walk around town and conceived the basis for his brilliant one-step photographic process.

Although the Polaroid Land Camera, as it came to be called, has undergone numerous refinements, Land's initial conception has remained essentially unchanged. After snapping a picture, the photographer pulled photographic paper through two steel rollers, which ruptured a pod of developing reagent. The reagent, a jellied compound, was spread evenly across the surface of the paper, developing and fixing a sepia-toned image. In early models, the process took one minute, but later improvements lowered the time to a few seconds.

Polaroid introduced the camera in time for Christmas, 1948. Public acceptance was immediate and overwhelming, and the company sold 5 million cameras in the first year. Professional photographers might have dismissed the innovation as a fad or gimmick, but the camera found numerous applications in industry, medicine, and the military. Black-and-white film replaced sepia in 1950, and by 1963 Land had succeeded in developing a system that provided "instant" color photographs.

In the 1960s, Polaroid continued to attract a large share of the photographic market through continued innovation and improvement. The 1965 Swinger camera, priced at a reasonable $20, produced black-and-white photos and competed with Kodak's Instamatic. The 1969 Colorpack II, an inexpensive color camera, also sold well. In late 1972, Polaroid introduced its best-selling S 70 model, which produced nearly instantaneous prints through a very sophisticated process involving 17 chemicals built into the photographic paper. As a further convenience, the battery that powered the camera was built into the film pack rather than the camera.

Polaroid's success record was blemished in 1977 with the introduction of Polarvision,

155

an instant movie camera system. A high price, no sound-recording capability, and competition from video cameras doomed Polarvision from the start, and in 1979 Polaroid ceased production after suffering major losses. In 1980, Land, who had retired as president of the company in 1975, resigned as chief executive officer to become more involved in research and to serve as a consultant.

See also:
Camera; Photography; Photography, Amateur.

References:
Cobb, Emma. "Instant History." *American Heritage Invention and Technology*, Fall 1987. *International Encyclopedia of Communications.* New York: Oxford University Press, 1989. Olshakers, Mark. *The Instant Image: Edwin Land and the Polaroid Experience.* New York: Stein & Day, 1978.

Language

Language is the complex system of communication using symbols—spoken and sometimes written—that characterizes the species *Homo sapiens.* Other animals are able to communicate information, even about things not immediate or present—honeybees, for example, can indicate the location of rich sources of nectar and pollen by a characteristic "dance"—but they cannot do so voluntarily. There is evidence that the higher primates, such as chimpanzees, can communicate with symbols if carefully taught, but they have no extensive symbolic language of their own.

With language, which we use voluntarily based on tacitly agreed-upon rules, we can communicate virtually infinite numbers of messages about things, people, and ideas, immediate or not, present or not. Time is not a barrier to communication through language; we can recount the past, discuss the present, or anticipate the future. Language is our tool for developing and exploring our imaginations or creating abstract ideas.

Many cultures have no written language, but speech is common to all. Speech appears to be an inherent aspect of being human. We learn to speak without being taught; we learn by listening, imitating, and exercising our vocal apparatus. We babble and gurgle as we develop a repertoire of sounds and learn to discriminate among them by some process not fully understood. On the other hand, we must be taught to read and write; these skills are not innate qualities of being human. The language we first speak is the one we hear as infants, the language of the people who rear us—usually our parents. If we hear more than one language as infants, as may be the case for children raised by bilingual parents, we will speak two languages as naturally as most people speak one. We can, of course, learn other languages, but it is seldom as easy as the one(s) we learn first. In fact, there is evidence that if a language is not learned by adolescence, the capacity to learn one may be lost.

Our first words refer to objects immediately present—mama, dada, ball, dog, cat. Later, we realize that words can be used as symbols for things not present and learn to formulate ideas that have nothing to do with physical objects. Somehow, we learn the grammar of our spoken language. We learn that people will understand, "I can run fast," but will not comprehend, "Fast can run I."

A language is produced by a speaking community of humans who agree among themselves that the sounds we call words have a certain meaning and can be strung together in certain ways by a system called semantics. The English-speaking community agrees that the word "dog" means a certain kind of readily recognized animal and includes a number of different breeds. The French-speaking community has agreed to refer to the same animals by the word *chien*, and the German-speaking community by the word *hund*, a term so like our English word *hound* that it suggests a common origin for our European languages.

Although different languages use different sounds to represent the same object or idea, there are great similarities among languages. All use grammatical patterns to convey meaning through words (speech sounds) that constitute what we would call sentences; all have words we would classify as nouns and verbs; and all have a means of distinguishing statements from questions and questions from commands.

The Origin of Language

The origin of speech, which undoubtedly preceded writing, is unknown. Some believe it evolved at the same time as the emergence of *Homo sapiens,* which probably occurred approximately 100,000 years ago. However, there is fossil evidence to show that a large brain, which many associate with speech and language, was characteristic of *Homo habilis,* a species similar to humans that lived about 2 million years ago. There is also evidence that *Homo habilis* used tools, and many argue that language, perhaps in the form of grunts, gestures, and signs, evolved at the same time that an erect, large-brained species with opposable thumbs began to use tools.

The emergence of speech might have been unique, or it might have occurred in several different places. Whatever its origin, speech has diversified into at least 4,000 different spoken languages among the world's present 6 billion people. Only approximately 300 of these languages are written, and fewer than 100 have a significant body of literature, but all share in that unique human quality called speech.

Changes in Language

In 1755, Samuel Johnson's *Dictionary of the English Language* was published. Johnson's masterpiece attempted to establish an authoritative standard for the English language by registering the meaning of words as they had been used by authors during the previous two centuries. Less than a century later, Noah Webster's *American Dictionary of the English Language* (1828) reflected spoken rather than written language and recorded English words and language as they existed, not as an elite segment of society might like them to be. Webster's work, which took 20 years to complete, established those parts of English that were truly American, and although Webster recognized that the English language had changed in America, he sought to eliminate differences in the pronunciation of words and to establish his own authoritative spelling of them.

Conservative linguists, like Johnson, strive to maintain the purity of a language. Liberal linguists accept the inevitable fact that languages change and are disposed to explain how a language works, not how it *should* work according to long-established rules of usage. Some change is unavoidable; technological and social changes demand it. Someone had to invent a word—software— for the code that makes computers do the things they do. A term had to be invented for a program—Head Start—that seeks to better prepare students for kindergarten. But whether necessary or not, new words evolve and the meanings of old words change.

Dialects, or variations of the same language, reflect regional, cultural, or class differences. We immediately recognize that someone who says, "Pahk the cah in the yahd," is from the Boston area. Grammar changes, too. The proper use of "who" and "whom" seems less important to English teachers than it used to; we hear educated people say they "feel badly" about something, although language purists know they should "feel bad."

Within a culture, a certain variety of speech is often associated with high socioeconomic standing. Those lacking such a mode of speech are often subject to discrimination, either consciously or unconsciously, when seeking employment or admission to other programs that would allow them to attain higher economic, social, or professional standing. And members of professional groups, be they doctors, lawyers, teachers, engineers, computer programmers, or those in other vocational niches, have their own peculiar vocabularies and modes of expression that seem foreign to the layman's ear.

See also:
Esperanto; Nonverbal Communication; Reading; Speech; Webster, Noah; Writing.
References:
Aitchison, Jean. *Language Change: Progress or Decay?* New York: Cambridge University Press, 1991.

Caird, Rod. *Ape Man: The Story of Human Evolution*. New York: Macmillan, 1994.

"Can You Say What You Want?" *The Economist*, 11 May 1996.

Davis, Joel. *Mother Tongue: How Humans Create Language*. New York: Birch Lane Press, 1994.

International Encyclopedia of Communications. New York: Oxford University Press, 1989.

Laser

Laser is an acronym for light amplification by stimulated emission of radiation. Lasers are widely used in communications, particularly in connection with optical discs and fiber optics. Because light waves have a much higher frequency than radio or television waves, they are capable of carrying a correspondingly greater quantity of information. The laser has been known since 1960, when Theo Maiman discovered a way to produce a coherent beam of visible light using a ruby crystal.

A laser is a tube that contains a crystalline rod or a smaller tube filled with a fluid (gas or liquid). At one end of the laser is a mirror; at the other end is a partially silvered mirror through which the light beam emerges. The laser is activated by adding energy, a process called pumping the laser. In a ruby laser, atoms in the ruby rod are illuminated by photons from a green light source. Some of the atoms absorb this energy, and electrons within these excited atoms jump to an orbital farther from the atom's nucleus. These electrons quickly fall to an intermediate orbital and then, more slowly, to their original orbital. The drop from the intermediate to the original level is accompanied by the release of red light of a specific wavelength. When a photon of this red light passes by another excited atom at an intermediate state, it stimulates that atom to lose its energy and release its own red light. These two photons stimulate two more excited atoms, and the process continues until a large number of photons with identical energy are moving along the ruby rod's axis. Some light passes through the sides of the crystal and is lost, but light moving along the axis continues to stimulate the emission of more light as it is reflected back and forth by the mirrors at the ends of the laser. Since the front mirror is only partially silvered, it reflects much of the light back into the laser. Reflected photons stimulate more excited atoms to release light. The unreflected photons pass through the front mirror, producing the laser beam.

A laser produces a very narrow, intense light beam that remains parallel over long distances because the light is coherent. This means that the light is monochromatic (one wavelength) and in phase (the wave crests and troughs are side by side). The laser is based on the principle that atoms absorb and release only discrete quantities of energy. By absorbing just the right amount of energy, an electron in an atom can jump from one orbital to another one farther from the nucleus. These orbitals constitute the different possible energy levels in an atom. They may be thought of as unevenly spaced rungs on a cylindrical ladder in which the upper rungs represent higher energy states. An atom that has absorbed energy will soon lose its energy as the electron falls back to lower orbits until the atom reaches its normal or ground-state level. As an electron falls from one energy level to a lower one, the energy is released as light of a particular wavelength and, therefore, a very definite color, which might or might not be visible to the human eye.

A laser's narrow coherent beam makes it ideal for surveying or measuring large distances. By timing a laser pulse from earth to moon and back, the moon's distance can be measured to within centimeters. Lasers are also used extensively in medicine; in the precise drilling, cutting, melting, and welding of metals; in holography; in spectrography and the separation of isotopes; and in the fusion of compressed microscopic pellets of hydrogen into helium, a process that takes place in stars and hydrogen bombs, causing the release of vast amounts of energy. Ultimately, if this process can be made both sustainable and controllable, it may replace fossil fuels as our major source of electric power.

A great variety of lasers now exists. These include the helium-neon lasers found in many school laboratories, solid-state lasers that can be incorporated into microchips, and even electron lasers that emit light when electrons are made to vibrate in a magnetic field. Laser light need not be visible. There are lasers that produce photons found in infrared, ultraviolet, and even the X-ray regions of the electromagnetic spectrum.

See also:
Compact Disc; Electromagnetic Waves; Fiber Optics; Microelectronics; Universal Product Code.

References:
Bromberg, Joan Lisa. "Amazing Light." *American Heritage Invention & Technology,* Spring 1992.
Macaulay, David. *The Way Things Work.* Boston: Houghton Mifflin, 1988.
Williams, Trevor I. *The History of Invention: From Stone Axes to Silicon Chips.* New York: Facts on File, 1987.

Libel
See Defamation.

Library

A library is a place in which a collection of books and other materials has been assembled and organized to accommodate patrons. For more than 2,500 years the three main functions of libraries have been to collect, preserve, and make available sources of knowledge preserved on materials ranging from clay tablets to electronic databases.

History

The earliest library is believed to have been one established in Nineveh around 650 B.C. It consisted of clay tablets and was used to maintain records needed in the administration of the Assyrian Empire.

Although it is likely that there were libraries during the time of Plato and Aristotle in Greece, there are no records of such facilities. However, following the death of Alexander the Great in 323 B.C., a museum with a library was established in Alexandria, Egypt. There the texts of the classic Greek writers were collected, copied, and preserved for several hundred years. There, too, about a half-million books on papyrus scrolls were stored and used by scholars.

Libraries existed throughout the Roman Empire, but the most extensive collections were in private libraries such as those of Cicero and Pliny the Younger. Although the libraries at Alexandria and Pergamum (now Bergama, Turkey) were destroyed, the classical literature of Greece and Rome was preserved by libraries in Constantinople (now Istanbul) for more than a thousand years.

In Europe following the collapse of the Roman Empire and throughout much of the Middle Ages, books were to be found primarily in private libraries, monasteries, and cathedrals. Monks copied many manuscripts onto pages made of parchment, which were then assembled as codices (books) with wooden covers. The growth of universities beginning in the eleventh century was accompanied by collections of books in their colleges where scholars came together. The advent of printing in the fifteenth century accelerated the growth of libraries as books became less expensive and more widely available. In America, libraries were established shortly after the first settlements in each of the colonies. John Harvard established the first academic library at Harvard College in 1638, and 93 years later, under Benjamin Franklin's leadership, the first subscription library in America was established in Philadelphia. Members of the library paid dues that were used to buy books, which were then shared through lending. Extensive growth of libraries awaited the nineteenth-century spread of literacy.

Types of Libraries

In addition to extensive private libraries owned by a number of wealthy individuals, there are several types of libraries today in which books and other materials are shared. Most countries have a national library; in the United States the national library is the Library of Congress. The Harvard Library was the nation's first college library, but today nearly every university, college, and school has a room, if not a building, to house its library. There are also special libraries that contain materials for a restricted readership. These include medical, law, and government agency libraries, as well as a number of others, most of them established after World War I, that provide information for businesses, various professional groups, trade associations, and other organizations. Most special libraries carry a large number of journals because their readers generally require up-to-date information.

Public libraries are the most familiar type. The first public library opened in the United States in 1803 at Salisbury, Connecticut, following a gift of 150 books from a local citizen, but it was another half-century before libraries supported by local taxes and administered by a staff hired by an elected board of trustees became widespread. This growth was due in part to the increased literacy among the general public. For Andrew Carnegie and others, public libraries became a favorite form of philanthropy.

Unlike school and special libraries, public libraries generally provide works of fiction and other materials, such as videos and puzzles, that are used for leisure and recreation as well as educational and cultural materials related to learning and research. In many public libraries the circulation centers on fiction.

The Library of Congress

The Library of Congress, established in 1800, is the national library of the United States. Originally part of the Capitol, its contents were largely destroyed when it was shelled by the British during the War of 1812. The library was revitalized in 1815 when Congress appropriated money to buy Thomas Jefferson's 6,000-volume collection. Since 1870, it has also administered the copyright system, under which it receives a copy of every book copyrighted in the United States. As a result the library houses more than 15 million books and more than 40 million manuscripts. The library also has developed a widely used system of cataloging by subject classification, publishes the National Union Catalog, prints and distributes data used by

libraries in cataloging their books, and actively supports research, collecting, and preservation of American folklore, arts, and crafts.

Modern Libraries

The twentieth century has seen dramatic changes in libraries. Through computer networks and interlibrary loans, patrons have access not only to the shelves of their local libraries but to the contents of libraries throughout the world. Microfilm, microfiche, videotapes, CD-ROMs, and electronic databases have increased storage capacity immensely, while computers have facilitated cataloging, record keeping, circulation, and the time-consuming filing and sorting of cards that used to consume a librarian's time. Bar codes and laser scanners have eliminated stamped cards; due dates and fines are now stored in databases, not file drawers. Cataloging is done at a central location, eliminating the need for each library to enter bibliographic information and subject descriptions for every new book added to the shelves. International Standard Book Description (ISBD) numbers (ISBNs), found in every new book published, provide a unique means of identifying any book regardless of the system (usually Dewey decimal or Library of Congress) used to catalog it. Card catalogs are part of history because libraries are now equipped with computerized catalogs and electronic links to a vast network of libraries that greatly enhance the availability of information and provide ready access to diverse points of view on any controversial subject.

Libraries and the Future

The time-saving technologies that are now part of nearly every library are an essential tool of librarians preparing to meet the challenges of the twenty-first century. With reduced funding and increased demands for services, many public librarians are finding their vocation a stressful one. To meet public needs, libraries are offering additional services such as homework centers, information centers for health care (particularly for the elderly), access to the Internet and other databases, and places for groups to meet. At a time when many argue that computer networks and the Internet make libraries obsolete, libraries are forced to educate the public about their role as the keepers and preservers of knowledge, whether historical, cultural, political, or scientific.

With access to information becoming so dependent on expensive tools such as computers, libraries and their staffs have the difficult task of trying to provide equal access to information for all citizens. Those who cannot afford computers can use those at libraries. Librarians are asked to offer their expertise in making the Telecommunications Act of 1996, which seeks to make electronic access to information available to all, a reality rather than a dream.

As James Billington reminded us in the June/July 1996 issue of *American Libraries*, information is not knowledge. The beauty of books and journals, available to all in libraries, is that they have passed through the hands of publishers and librarians. Publishers add value through reviews, checks of accuracy, and editing. Librarians add value by evaluating, collecting, archiving, organizing, and making materials readily available in a communal place where people from all walks of life, regardless of their religious or political beliefs, can sit side by side in a room where books and journals with very different points of view on many controversial subjects rest together on the same shelves. It should not surprise us to learn that immigrants from countries governed by authoritarian rule marvel at American libraries where access to knowledge is free and open to all.

See also:
Book; Internet; Publishing; Reading; Writing.
References:
Billington, James. "A Technological Flood Requires Human Navigators." *American Libraries*, June/July 1996.
Holt, Glen. "Life on 'The Edge of Chaos.'" *Library Journal*, 1 March 1996.
International Encyclopedia of Communications. New York: Oxford University Press, 1989.
St. Lifer, Evan. "Libraries' Crucial Role in the 1996 Telecomm Act." *Library Journal*, 15 March 1996.
Tenopir, Carol, and Donald W. King. "Setting the Record Straight on Journal Publishing: Myth vs. Reality." *Library Journal*, 15 March 1996.

Library of Congress
See Library.

Lie Detector
Lie detectors, or polygraphs, are used to measure changes in the body's autonomic responses; that is, responses controlled by the autonomic nervous system, which controls involuntary, unconscious actions of smooth muscle and glands. Polygraphs can simultaneously record changes in pulse, breathing rate, blood pressure, blood flow, brain waves, and the galvanic skin response, which is a measurement of the skin's electrical resistance.

Most polygraphs measure just three indicators while a subject is asked a series of questions. Rate and depth of respiration is measured by means of straps that wrap around the chest and abdomen. Blood pressure is detected by an inflatable cuff around the upper arm, and the electrical resistance of the skin is measured with electrodes that touch the fingertips. If the person's perspiration rate increases, the electrical resistance of the skin decreases and more current flows between the electrodes. Leads from these instruments are connected to inked styluses that record the data on a roll of moving paper. Because several sets of data are recorded graphically at the same time, the lie detector was called a polygraph shortly after it was developed in 1921 by John A. Larson, a medical student at the University of California.

The idea behind the polygraph is that questions about a crime or inappropriate behavior will cause emotions that in turn will produce physiological responses, such as increased perspiration, that can be detected by the instruments. A control question (one unrelated to the crime of which the subject is

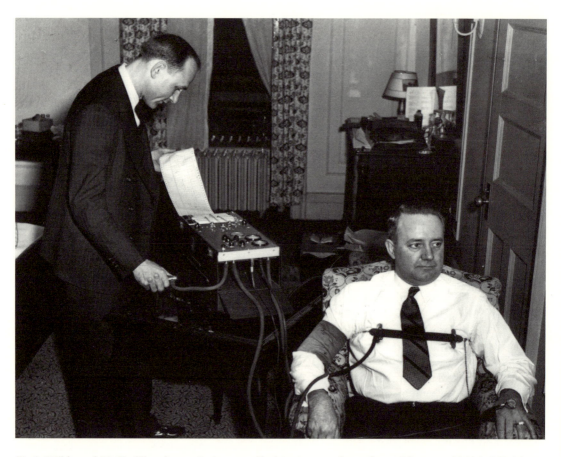

E. A. Wildy and M. R. Allen demonstrate a new lie detector, or polygraph, on 8 January 1941 in Washington, D.C. Polygraphs measure three indicators (rate and depth of respiration, blood pressure, and perspiration rate) while a subject is asked a series of questions.

suspected) designed to elicit a lie might be, "Have you ever taken something that didn't belong to you?"

In response to such a question, the surprised or embarrassed subject might respond, "No!" At the same time, the polygraph record will reveal a physiological response brought on by the question. When asked the pertinent question, "Did you shoot (the victim of the crime) on December 24?," the same subject, if innocent, may respond in the negative and show no significant physiological response. On the other hand, if the subject is guilty, the question is likely to evoke a greater response than did the control question. Over a one- or two-hour period, a pattern emerges. An innocent person will show greater physiological response to control questions designed to elicit a response than to pertinent questions related to the crime, whereas a guilty subject will react more to pertinent questions related to the crime and less to control questions.

As many psychologists and physiologists have argued, there are other factors, such as reaction to the examiner, the phrasing of questions, the rate at which questions are posed, and the order in which the questions are presented, that can elicit similar responses. On the other hand, sociopaths, or people who have superb control of their emotions, might be able to lie without being detected. For example, Aldrich Ames, a CIA agent convicted of spying for Russia, was able to beat polygraph tests in 1986 and again in 1991.

Because data provided by lie detectors are not always reliable, polygraph tests are not acceptable evidence in the courts of some states. In other states, both the defense and the prosecution must agree to a lie detector test before it is administered or admitted as evidence.

Other ways to detect deception include behavioral clues and systematic questioning. Facial expressions, sweating, squirming, failure to maintain eye contact, and other body language often indicate that a subject is lying.

Following passage of the Employee Polygraph Protections Act by Congress in 1988, companies have turned to "honesty tests" for preemployment screening. In addition to direct questions about honesty, these tests include more subtle questions designed to provide information about the subject's work ethic and personal habits.

As occurs with many types of testing, those writing the questions and evaluating the answers may have a different frame of reference and distinctly different values than those responding to the questions. Consequently, honesty tests may discriminate against individuals because of their culture rather than their honesty. The same is true of oral questions designed to elicit behavioral clues. A question regarded as neutral by the examiner may evoke an emotional response from an examinee for reasons unbeknownst to the person who phrased the question. By the same token, a key question designed to produce telltale body language by a guilty party may elicit no response in a subject because of his or her cultural background.

References:
International Encyclopedia of Communications. New York: Oxford University Press, 1989.
Science and Technology Illustrated, vol. 15. Chicago: Encyclopedia Britannica, 1984.
"Searching for Another Mole." *Newsweek*, 28 March 1994.
Zonderman, Jon. *Beyond the Crime Lab: The New Science of Investigation*. New York: Wiley, 1990.

Linotype
See Mergenthaler, Ottmar.

Lithography
See Printing.

Loudspeaker

A loudspeaker (often called simply a speaker) changes electrical energy to sound. Before 1925, most sounds were reproduced mechanically. For example, a phonograph record was made by a stylus vibrating in response to sound waves. As the stylus vibrated, it cut a groove in a master disc or cylinder that rotated beneath it. Copies of the master were then pressed in a hard resin or other medium. The recorded sounds were reproduced by the vibrations of another stylus moving along the irregular groove in the record and amplified mechanically by a flared horn that acted much like a megaphone.

Beyond Horns to Loudspeakers

Later, wire coils and a small permanent magnet were attached to the vibrating stylus. When a coil of wire moves in a magnetic field, a voltage develops that will produce a current in the wires. Consequently, the small coils oscillating in the vicinity of a permanent magnet caused an electric current to flow in the coils. The strength and direction of the current depend on the rate and direction of motion of the coils. Thus, the electric current can reproduce the intensity and frequency of the sound waves.

Although patents for primitive loudspeakers were filed in Germany by Werner von Siemens and in England by Oliver Lodge during the late nineteenth century, the first speakers to effectively convert electrical signals from a stylus to sound waves were primarily the work of Chester W. Rice and Edward W. Kellogg at General Electric in 1924. They realized that with triode vacuum tubes, it was possible to amplify electric currents to a point where they would cause a membrane to vibrate audibly. Their research, published in 1925 in a paper entitled "Notes on the Development of a New Type of Horn-less Loudspeaker," is still regarded as a classic, and present-day speakers are very similar to the one they developed.

The Dynamic Loudspeaker

A loudspeaker is a transducer because it converts one form of energy (electricity) to another (sound). The source of the electrical energy can vary. Its origin might be found in the coils attached to a stylus vibrating in a magnetic field, sound waves converted to electric currents by a microphone, radio or television waves received by an antenna, or radioactive particles striking the detector of a Geiger counter. Regardless of the source, the ever-changing electric current in a typical loudspeaker flows through a coil of wire, called the voice coil. (See Figure 1.) This coil and the iron core it encircles constitutes an electromagnet. When electric current flows through the wire, a magnetic field is produced. The iron core serves to concentrate the lines of magnetic force that make up the magnetic field. Like a bar magnet, the electromagnet has a north and a south pole. The strength of the magnetic field depends on the current in the coil. If the current is large, the field is strong; if the current is small, the field is weak.

The voice coil is located within the magnetic field of a permanent magnet, which is one of the most expensive parts of a good speaker. Like any two magnets, the permanent magnet and the electromagnet may attract or repel one another. The direction of the force (attraction or repulsion) on the voice coil, which can move back and forth, depends on the direction of the current in the coil; the strength of the force depends on the magnitude of the current.

The outer circumference of the large end of the cone found at the front of the speaker is attached to a metal frame by a springy material. The smaller, inner, rear circumference of the cone is connected to the voice coil. When the voice coil moves, the cone moves. If the current in the coil is large because it was produced at the source by a loud sound, then the coil moves through a large distance.

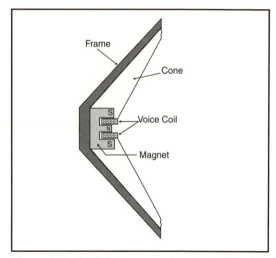

Figure 1. A simplified cross section of a loudspeaker.

If the current is small because it was produced by a whisper, the coil and its attached cone move only a small distance. If the current oscillates at a rapid rate because it was produced by a high-pitched sound, the coil and cone vibrate at the same high frequency. A current that arises because of a lower-pitched sound will oscillate at a lower rate, and so will the coil and the cone.

As the cone (which is often made of molded paper fibers) vibrates, it pushes against the air, putting it into motion. When the cone moves outward, it pushes the air together, creating concentrated regions of air molecules, called compressions, where the air pressure is greater than the pressure of the surrounding air. When the cone moves inward, it reduces the concentration of air molecules, creating a region, called a rarefaction, where the pressure is lower than that of the surrounding air. The compressions and rarefactions move outward and away from the speaker as sound waves. The distance from one compression (or rarefaction) to the next is the wavelength of the sound wave.

The Electrostatic Speaker

The speaker described above is called a dynamic speaker. If it is well made, the sounds coming from it will be nearly identical to the sounds that gave rise to the electric currents that were amplified and then sent to the voice coil. A less common loudspeaker is the electrostatic speaker. It consists of a thin, taut, metal diaphragm or a plastic diaphragm coated with a conducting material. The diaphragm is tightly suspended between two perforated metal plates or a series of closely spaced parallel wires. A DC voltage of 1,000 volts or more is maintained across the two plates. The diaphragm between the plates carries a charge and moves in response to changes in the electric field between the plates. The field between the plates changes because sound waves converted to electrical signals are superimposed on the voltage supplied to the plates. As the voltage fluctuates in response to these signals, the charged diaphragm responds by moving back and forth. Its motion produces sound waves in the same way as the moving cone in the dynamic speaker.

Woofers and Tweeters

It is difficult to obtain good response to the entire range of sound frequencies with a single speaker. For that reason, many speakers contain a large unit (woofer) for low-frequency sounds and a smaller unit (tweeter) for high-frequency sounds. Some modern high-quality speakers contain three units. A bass speaker approximately 10 inches in diameter is used for low-frequency sounds of 30 to 500 hertz with wavelengths of 2.2 to 38 feet; a middle range speaker about 6 inches across is used for frequencies from 500 to 4,000 hertz with wavelengths of 3.4 inches to 2.2 feet; and a small tweeter provides sounds ranging from 4,000 to 16,000 hertz that have wavelengths of 0.8 to 3.4 inches.

Price

The basic configuration of dynamic speakers has not changed in decades. Nevertheless, approximately 4.5 million speakers are sold each year under 300 different brand names. The price of speakers, which can range from as little as $50 to as much as $10,000, is primarily related to their capacity to supply deep bass frequencies.

Miniature battery-driven "powered" speakers with built-in amplifiers sell for $30 to $300. These speakers, together with microelectronics, have been instrumental in the development of portable tape or CD players.

See also:
Microelectronics; Microphone; Oersted, Hans Christian; Transistor.

References:
Gardner, Robert. *Communication*. New York: Twenty-First Century, 1994.
How It Works: The Illustrated Encyclopedia of Science and Technology, vol. 15. New York and London: Marshall Cavendish, 1978.
Macaulay, David. *The Way Things Work*. Boston: Houghton Mifflin, 1988.
Science and Technology Illustrated, vol. 15. Chicago: Encyclopedia Britannica, 1984.

Luce, Henry R. (1898–1967)

Editor, publisher, and creator of the modern news magazine, Henry R. Luce was the founder and principal architect of the publishing empire known as Time, Inc. As such, he was considered one of the most influential journalists of the first half of the twentieth century. He served as editor in chief, publisher, and owner of *Time, Fortune, Life,* and *Sports Illustrated* as well as other media-related enterprises involving his corporation.

Luce was the oldest child of Presbyterian missionaries. Born in China on 3 April 1898, he spent his early years in that country, a fact that contributed to his lifelong interest in Asian affairs. At age 15 he enrolled at the Hotchkiss School in Connecticut where, as a scholarship student, he waited on tables and swept classrooms to help pay tuition. While at Hotchkiss, Luce was editor of the school newspaper and met his best friend and later business partner, Briton Hadden. The two were inseparable and enrolled together at Yale University in 1916. Both worked for the *Yale Daily News*, where Luce served as managing editor. The idea of a news magazine to better inform the public about world events appears to have originated during Luce's Yale years, but graduation split the two friends before the notion ever evolved beyond discussion. After a year at Oxford, Luce found work with the *Chicago Daily News*, and in 1922 the two prep-school friends were reunited at the *Baltimore News*. Conversations about the magazine that would give the most significant weekly news in a concise, analytical style resurfaced in Baltimore, and Luce and Hadden quit the *News* to begin their new periodical.

Using their Yale contacts, family, and friends, the aspiring entrepreneurs raised $86,000 of the estimated $100,000 start-up costs. The first issue of *Time* debuted on 3 March 1923, with Hadden as editor and Luce as business manager. The 25-year-olds paid themselves weekly salaries of $30 and employed a staff of three writers. The initial circulation was about 12,000, a number that doubled within a year. In 1927, *Time* showed a small profit; by 1938, it was the nation's leading weekly publication.

Buoyed by the success of his initial venture, Luce founded a second magazine, *Fortune*, in February 1930. A deluxe magazine selling for the unheard of price of $1, *Fortune* was aimed at the business community to "give business literature" and report on prominent personalities. Before the first issue hit the newsstand, Briton Hadden died of septicemia in 1929. A saddened and shaken Luce took up the burden of editor in chief of both magazines, a position he held for all Time, Inc., publications until 1964. *Fortune* was an instant success, and Luce was celebrated for his golden touch in the face of the financial devastation of the Great Depression.

During the 1930s, Luce carried *Time*'s success beyond the print media to radio with "The March of Time," an accomplishment that he extended to a newsreel format.

In 1935, Luce married Clare Booth Brokaw. At the time of the marriage, Brokaw was successful in her own right as an editor and prominent playwright. Later, she served as congresswoman from Connecticut as well as ambassador to Italy. Although she held no official position in her husband's company, it has been suggested that she inspired Luce to pioneer yet another innovative magazine. In 1936, he launched *Life Magazine*, a new venture in photojournalism. With the biggest first issue printing in magazine history, *Life* was an instant success. Within one month, circulation passed a half million, and by the end of a year it skyrocketed to 2 million. *Life*'s coverage of World War II, both overseas and on the home front, made it extremely popular in the 1940s. In 1954, still pursuing the photojournalism theme, Luce broke his first printing record and continued his good fortune in establishing *Sports Illustrated*.

In 1961, near the end of Luce's tenure at Time, Inc., the company established a book publishing division. Time-Life books are characterized by well-written text and are heavily illustrated. In April 1964, Luce resigned as editor in chief of Time, Inc., but he continued until his death in 1967 to be involved with the company he established.

See also:

Photojournalism.

References:

Baughman, James L. *Henry R. Luce and the Rise of the American News Media*. Boston: Twayne Publishers, 1987.
Herzstein, Robert Edwin. *Henry R. Luce: A Political Portrait of the Man Who Created the American Century*. New York: Scribner's, 1994.
Martin, Ralph G. *Henry and Clare: An Intimate Portrait of the Luces*. New York: Putnam, 1991.
Swanberg, W. A. *Luce and His Empire*. New York: Scribner's, 1972.

Lucent Technologies

See American Telephone & Telegraph Company.

Magnetic Field

Around any moving or spinning electrical charge or charges can be envisioned a magnetic field consisting of imaginary lines of magnetic force. The direction of the field at any point is given by the direction that the north-seeking pole of a bar magnet would assume if placed at that point. Tiny compass needles, which are bar magnets, can be used to map magnetic field lines. The concentration of the lines indicates the strength of the field. Magnetic fields are found in all electrically powered communication devices, and in many of them, such as telephones, telegraphs, radios, televisions, and tape recorders, the fields play a vital role.

When an electric current (a flow of charge) in a wire or a coil of wire has a component perpendicular to a magnetic field, there will be a force on the wire or coil that is perpendicular to both the current and the magnetic field. The force exerted by a magnetic field on moving charges in a wire is the fundamental principle behind electric motors and meters.

The same principle applies to a beam of charged particles. The electron beam that strikes a television screen is swept across the screen by a magnetic field perpendicular to the path of the moving charges. As the strength of the field is increased by a growing current in the coils that produce it, the force on the charges increases, pushing the beam farther off its straight-line path.

Michael Faraday was the first to show that changing the magnetic field through a coil of wire will exert a force on charges within the wire and induce a voltage. This principle, too, has had wide application in communications. It is the principle that underlies the electric generator, which provides the electric power required by all electrical devices that are not battery driven.

See also:
Electromagnet; Electromagnetic Waves; Faraday, Michael; Henry, Joseph; Phonograph; Radio; Relay; Tape Recorder; Telegraph; Telephone; Television.
References:
Haber-Schaim, Uri, et al. *PSSC Physics*, 7th ed. Dubuque, IA: Kendall/Hunt, 1991.

Macaulay, David. *The Way Things Work.* Boston: Houghton Mifflin, 1988.

Magnetic Resonance Imaging (MRI)

See Scanner.

Magnetron

A magnetron is an oscillator that produces the microwaves used in radar and microwave ovens. It consists of a hollow metallic cylinder that surrounds a narrow cathode along its axis. Like a diode vacuum tube, the cathode emits electrons when it is heated. The electrons stream toward the wall of the outer cylinder, which is positively charged so that it serves as the anode. A strong magnetic field parallel to the axis of the cylinder forces the electrons into a curved path as they move toward the anode.

A force is required to make particles move along a curved path. To make a ball on a string move in a circle, for example, an inward pull must be exerted on the string. When a force acts on an object, the object accelerates (changes its velocity). The inward force on a ball circling at the end of a string causes the ball to change its direction as it moves along a circular path. Since the direction of the ball changes, its velocity changes because velocity is defined as the magnitude and direction of an object's speed. Consequently, any object moving in a circle is accelerating. When charged particles such as electrons accelerate, electromagnetic waves are released.

The electromagnetic waves produced by the accelerating electrons in a magnetron are reflected along a waveguide to a ceramic

167

window that is transparent to microwaves just as glass is transparent to visible light. The emerging beam constitutes the radar beam that is sent into the atmosphere or the radiation that enters a microwave oven.

See also:
Electromagnetic Waves; Radar.

Marconi, Guglielmo (1874–1937)

Guglielmo Marconi, an inventor and businessman, took the theoretical work of James Clerk Maxwell and the experimental work of Heinrich Hertz related to electromagnetic waves and made practical use of them. He was largely responsible for the development of wireless telegraphy, which in turn led to the development of radio and eventually to virtually instantaneous worldwide communication.

Marconi was the youngest son of Giuseppe Marconi, a successful Italian businessman, and Annie Jameson Marconi, Giuseppe's Irish wife. Born on 25 April 1874, Guglielmo later became known as the "Wizard of Wireless." He was educated by tutors, and although he never attended formal classes at a university, he did receive extended tutorial instruction from capable teachers, including Augusto Righi, a physicist at the University of Bologna.

In 1894, at age 20, Marconi read detailed accounts of the experiments performed seven years earlier by Heinrich Hertz confirming James Clerk Maxwell's prediction that accelerated charges would release electromagnetic waves. Because of his interest in and enthusiasm for electronics, Marconi immediately realized the practical implications of Hertz's discovery for communication. Within a year, by grounding both transmitter and detector and increasing the power of the transmitter, Marconi was able to send and detect hertzian waves over a distance greater than 1 mile. He was also able to pulse the waves so that a signal could be sent in Morse code. By using a coherer, Marconi was able to convert radio waves in a receiver to electric currents.

Unable to convince Italian authorities of the commercial potential of wireless communication, Marconi traveled to England with his mother in 1896. His facility with the English language, which he learned from her, enabled him to gain the support of William Preece, a Post Office official, and George Kemp, an electrical engineer. In England, he obtained the first patent for his grounded transmitter and receiver. There, too, he made his first major breakthrough when he was invited to provide firsthand reports of the Kingstown Yacht regatta—an event of great interest to then-reigning Queen Victoria. By placing a transmitter on a ship offshore and a receiver at a lighthouse, Marconi was able to relay information about the race, as it took place, to people onshore.

Marconi's success was well received by the British aristocracy and the media. The publicity helped him to obtain support for further development of his wireless telegraphy. In 1897, he formed a company that in 1900 became the Marconi Wireless Telegraph Company. On 27 March 1899, he was successful in transmitting signals across the English Channel. Thirty-two days later, wireless equipment on board the *East Goodwind Sands* lightship enabled the crew to send a distress call that led to their rescue.

In the autumn of 1899, at the invitation of the *New York Herald*, Marconi used his wireless to report the America's Cup race. From a ship following the racing vessels, Marconi transmitted the progress of the race to *Herald* reporters on land. The publicity surrounding Marconi's ability to provide instantaneous commentary on the event as it progressed led to receptions in his honor, speaking engagements, and the generation of much public enthusiasm. More importantly, the U.S. Navy carried out ship-to-ship tests of Marconi's wireless to communicate between the carrier *New York* and the battleship *Massachusetts*. The tests were successful at distances as great as 36 miles.

On 26 April 1900, Marconi was granted British patent number 7,777 for his tuned aerial. With patent in hand, he turned to the business aspects of his inventions by build-

Inventor and businessman Guglielmo Marconi, 1922.

ing a broadcasting station at Poldhu on the English coast. After demonstrating that his station could transmit signals over distances as great as 150 miles, Marconi increased the power of the transmitter a hundredfold and began his quest to send messages across the Atlantic Ocean—a feat that Thomas Edison had proclaimed to be impossible. Edison argued that because electromagnetic waves move in straight paths, the earth's curvature would make it impossible for these waves to be transmitted over great distances.

In 1901, at a site in Wellfleet, Massachusetts, on the outer dunes of Cape Cod, Marconi built 20 masts 200 feet in height and set in circular fashion 165 feet from the edge of a cliff overlooking the Atlantic. (The remains of that site can be seen there today.) As many Cape Cod residents predicted, the towers were blown down by the high winds of a northeasterly storm on 25 November 1901, before any signals could be sent. The disaster did not surprise Marconi, because comparable towers at Poldhu, England, had met a similar fate two months earlier.

The Poldhu towers were replaced by an antenna suspended from two 150-foot wooden masts. The Cape Cod towers were later replaced by four 210-foot wooden towers, but not before a signal was transmitted across the ocean. On 12 December 1901, at a site near Saint John's, Newfoundland, the first transatlantic wireless signals were detected. The Poldhu station, broadcasting the letter *S* (3 dots in Morse code) was detected on an aerial suspended from a kite by Marconi and his assistant, G. S. Kemp.

As Marconi prepared to build a permanent tower in Newfoundland, the project was brought to a halt by threats of legal action from the Anglo-American Telegraph Company, which claimed exclusive communication rights in Newfoundland. Recognizing the importance of Marconi's work, the Canadian government offered him a site near Glace Bay, Nova Scotia. At that site, on 17 December 1902, the first messages were transmitted and received between Glace Bay and Poldhu.

A month later, on 18 January 1903, a message was transmitted from the station on Cape Cod to Poldhu, a distance exceeding 3,000 miles. Marconi had anticipated sending the message to Glace Bay where it would be received and retransmitted to England; however, acknowledgment was received, albeit unexpectedly, from Poldhu. The message sent by Marconi read as follows:

His Majesty, Edward VII
London, Eng.

In taking advantage of the wonderful triumph of scientific research and ingenuity which has been achieved in perfecting a system of wireless telegraphy, I extend on behalf of the American people most cordial greetings and good wishes to you and all people of the British Empire.
Theodore Roosevelt
Wellfleet, Mass., Jan. 19, 1903

The date on the message, 19 January, was a day later than the day the message was sent because it was transmitted late in the evening from Wellfleet at a clock time that was five hours earlier than the time in England, which was then past midnight. A reply from the king to President Roosevelt was received by wireless on the following day.

A year earlier, following his successful wireless transmission between England and Newfoundland, Marconi was honored in New York City for his accomplishments by the American Institute of Electrical Engineers. At about the same time, Thomas Edison, who was "eating some crow," said, "I would like to meet that young man who had the monumental audacity to attempt and to succeed in jumping an electrical wave across the Atlantic."

Despite Edison's earlier remark that long-distance transmission of wireless signals was impossible because electromagnetic waves travel in straight lines, Marconi was convinced by his experimental results that radio waves are reflected by the atmosphere. His success in sending transatlantic signals convinced even Edison, and in 1924 the discovery of a region of ions and electrons in the at-

mosphere at an altitude above 50 miles, known now as the ionosphere, provided an explanation for the reflection of these waves. In fact, before communications satellites were placed in orbits about the earth, bouncing radio waves off the ionosphere was the primary means of long-range radio communication. Furthermore, because sunlight reduces the concentration of the charged particles in the upper atmosphere, Marconi could at last explain why he found the hours on either side of midnight most conducive to long-range transmission of wireless signals.

In the years that followed Marconi's successful transmission and reception of radio waves to and from stations an ocean apart, he continued to invent and to expand his business interests. Stations owned by Marconi's company, the Marconi Wireless Telegraph Company, sent wireless news broadcasts each evening that were received by luxury liners at sea such as the *Lusitania* and *Campania*. "Marconi-grams" could be sent for 50 cents to people on board these ships or to friends in foreign lands across the Atlantic.

Ships began to routinely use wireless to communicate weather information and to seek help through SOS signals in emergencies. On 15 April 1912, a large passenger ship, the *Titanic*, struck an iceberg in the North Atlantic and sank. An SOS sent by the sinking ship and received by the *Carpathia* resulted in the saving of 712 lives. Unfortunately, nearly twice as many lives were lost because a ship closer to the scene had turned off its wireless only minutes before the *Titanic* began signaling for help.

After World War I, technological improvements led most stations to abandon the spark-gap method of generating signals in favor of oscillating currents from electrical generators. As early as 1906, Reginald A. Fessenden was successful in modulating a radio wave so that it could carry an audio signal. He broadcast music from an experimental station at Brant Rock, Massachusetts. The signal was received and the music heard by several U.S. Navy ships in nearby waters. Marconi was aware of, and involved in, the development of technology leading to improved radio transmission. By 1920, he was broadcasting the news on a regular basis from his transmitter at Chelmsford, England.

In 1909, Marconi was awarded the Nobel Prize for his work in developing the wireless telegraph. It might have been the greatest honor of his life, but glory followed him even in death, which overtook him on 20 July 1937. The next day radio stations around the world recognized his great accomplishments with two minutes of silence.

See also:
Coherer; Electromagnetic Waves; Fessenden, Reginald A.; Hertz, Heinrich Rudolf; Radio.

References:
Asimov, Isaac. *Asimov's Biographical Encyclopedia of Science and Technology.* Garden City, NY: Doubleday, 1964.
Canby, Edward Tatnall. "More Marconi." *Audio,* August 1995.
Dunlap, Orrin Elmer. *Marconi: The Man and His Wireless.* New Stratford, NH: Arno Press, 1971.
Gumston, David. *Marconi, Father of Radio.* New York: Crowell-Collier Press, 1967.
Jensen, Peter R. *In Marconi's Footsteps: Early Radio.* Cincinnati: Kangaroo Press, 1994.
Whatley, Michael E. *Marconi Wireless on Cape Cod: South Wellfleet, Massachusetts 1901–1917.* N. Eastham, MA: Nauset Marsh, 1987.

Mathematics and Communication

Although those who suffer from math anxiety may be reluctant to believe it, mathematics is indispensable to communication. Numbers convey everything from the number of cows in a herd to the magnitude of the national debt.

Computers, which certainly play a significant role in communication, operate on the basis of the binary number system, which contains only two numbers, 0 and 1. In the computer, a 0 can be represented by a switch that is off and a 1 by a switch that is on. The binary system can be used to represent any number in any other base. For example, the number 7 in base 10 (0, 1, 2, 3, 4, 5, 6, 7, 8, 9), the base we most commonly use, is written as 111 in the binary system because $7 = 1 \times 2^2 + 1 \times 2^1 + 1 \times 2^0$. The number 12 in base 10 would be 1100 in binary because $12 = 1 \times 2^3 + 1 \times 2^2 + 0 \times 2^1 + 0 \times 2^0$.

Of course, a person using a computer does not have to be familiar with base-2 mathematics in order to operate the machine any more than the driver of an automobile has to understand machinery. As a result, the significance of mathematics in communication is sometimes hidden. However, there are plenty of examples where the role of mathematics is clearly evident. Almost any newspaper, magazine, or financial report contains graphs and charts. Graphs are not limited to scientific papers or books. They are also employed to reveal population growth, sales, earnings, unemployment, consumer confidence, temperature, and a variety of other variables as a function of time, place, or some other quantity. Number-filled charts are used to compare the gross national product, population, energy consumption, life expectancy, grain or oil production, and a host of other quantities for different countries, and every newspaper's sports section contains league standings in terms of games won and lost, winning percentages, batting averages, yards gained passing or running, and so on. Clearly, mathematics plays a major role in communicating information.

See also:
Computer Addition.

References:
Gardner, Robert, and Edward Shore. *Math and Society: Reading Life in Numbers.* New York: Watts, 1995.
Gardner, Robert, and Edward Shore. *Math in Science and Nature: Finding Patterns in the World Around Us.* New York: Watts, 1994.
Gardner, Robert, and Edward Shore. *Math You Really Need.* Portland, ME: Walch, 1996.

Maxwell, James Clerk (1831–1878)

James Clerk Maxwell unified the work of earlier scientists on electricity and magnetism into a comprehensive theory that predicted the existence of electromagnetic waves that move at the speed of light.

Maxwell was born in Edinburgh, Scotland, in 1831. As a boy he was fascinated by science and the questions that it raised. In attempting to unite the experimental evidence about electricity and magnetism into a comprehensive theory, he developed four mathematical equations that came to be known as Maxwell's equations. The mathematics involved is difficult, but the first equation codifies the relationship between electrical charges, electric fields, and distance. The second equation recognizes the impossibility of isolating magnetic poles, and the third and fourth equations show how changing magnetic fields induce electric fields and how changing electric fields induce magnetic fields.

In examining the consequences of his equations, Maxwell discovered that it should be possible to generate oscillating electric and magnetic fields that would travel through space in wavelike fashion at the speed of light (300,000 kilometers per second). This discovery convinced him that visible light was an electromagnetic phenomenon that traveled through space with frequencies ranging from 4.3 to 7.5×10^{14} hertz.

Because he lived in a mechanical age, Maxwell sensed the need to explain the medium on which such waves might travel. To do so, he conceived the ether—an invisible, solid, massless, elastic material that filled all space. Early in the twentieth century, Albert Einstein showed that there is no need for an ether. The oscillating electric and magnetic fields that constitute an electromagnetic wave can maintain themselves as they travel through empty space.

References:

Asimov, Isaac. *Asimov's Biographical Encyclopedia of Science and Technology*, Garden City, NY: Doubleday, 1964.
Sagan, Carl. "Where Did TV Come From?" *Parade*, 17 September 1995.

MCI

See American Telephone & Telegraph Company.

Mergenthaler, Ottmar (1854–1899)

The post–Civil War era transformed American journalism. American urban society demanded increasingly more information and easier accessibility. Between 1870 and 1910, the circulation of newspapers increased ninefold. The number of books published between 1880 and 1917 quadrupled, and mass-circulation magazines became fixtures on newsstands. Although many reasons may be cited for the expansion of publishing, one man and his invention stand out—Ottmar Mergenthaler and his Linotype machine. Thomas Edison called the first automatic typesetting machine the "eighth wonder of the world," and it radically changed the entire publishing industry.

Despite innovations in the printing process over the course of the nineteenth century, production speed and volume remained shackled by the tedious and arduous task of hand composition and the subsequent redistribution of the individual pieces of type. The mechanical demands of creating an efficient yet affordable device were overwhelming. The ideal machine had to first assemble letters into lines of type. Next, it had to "justify" the margins (put the type into column width), with the words equally spaced on the line. Finally, and most importantly, it had to redistribute the individual pieces of type so they could be reused.

Others had realized the limitation involved in hand setting the printed page. The most spectacular effort to develop mechanized typesetting might have been the work of James W. Paige of Hartford, Connecticut. For 20 years and at a cost of $2 million, Paige labored to produce a 3-ton mechanical monster. The contrivance had 1,800 parts and was so complex that only the inventor could repair it in the event of a breakdown. Only two of these machines were ever built, and Paige went to the poorhouse. Another American, Timothy Alden, suffered a breakdown after a futile 17-year effort. Paulovich Knaghininsky died an alcoholic after making similar efforts. An 1840 French attempt required seven men to work the apparatus.

It was left to a German immigrant, Ottmar Mergenthaler, to solve the riddle of the automated typesetter. Mergenthaler was born in Hatchel, Germany, in 1854. Although Mergenthaler was recognized as mechanically gifted, family finances did not allow him to attend school regularly, so he attended night classes while serving an apprenticeship to a local watchmaker. In 1872, the young mechanic emigrated to the United States and took a position working for a relative in a Washington, D.C., machine shop that eventually moved to Baltimore. The business produced scientific instruments for the U.S. Signal Corps and built models to accompany U.S. patent requests.

While working in the shop, Mergenthaler became interested in the engineering and design problems posed by a power-driven typesetter. After abortive attempts in 1877 and 1878, he began to make some headway. Mergenthaler's ultimate design had an operator working a typewriter-like keyboard. The keyboard selected copper type letters that fell from a magazine of channel-like compartments, which held 20 identical characters, and mechanically fit them in line. The words were automatically spaced or "justified" to column width by a system of wedge-shaped bars. This line of type served as a mold, and when molten lead was pumped into it, an entire line of type, or slug, was produced with the printing surface on one face. These slugs were then assembled in trays, called galleys, for the presses. Meanwhile, and most importantly, the machine automatically returned the copper type to the magazine at the top of the machine. After the lead slugs were used, they could be stored or melted down for reuse.

Mergenthaler successfully piloted the first public appearance of his device in July 1886 at the *New York Tribune*. Whitelaw Reid, an editor at the paper, suggested the name *Lin-O-Type*, and it stuck. The impact of the machine was immediate. Using traditional hand-composition methods, it was possible to set between 1,500 and 2,000 letters an hour. Mergenthaler's "hot metal" technique countered with between 5,000 and 6,000

characters an hour. Mergenthaler continued to make improvements on his invention, but he eventually contracted tuberculosis and died on 28 October 1899 at age 45.

The Linotype, which some have called the greatest single improvement in printing since the press itself, is dwarfed by modern technology. Computers can compose more than 3 million characters an hour. Mergenthaler's machine, once an essential part of any newspaper, is now relegated to small-town or regional publications and is often viewed as a cumbersome antique for specialty printing. Soon the craft of "hot metal" typesetting will go the way of hand composition.

See also:
Printing; Publishing.

References:
DeCamp, L. Sprague. *The Heroic Age of American Invention.* Garden City, NY: Doubleday, 1961.
Feldman, Anthony, and Peter Ford. *Scientists And Inventors.* New York: Facts on File, 1979.
Gustaitis, Joseph. "Ottmar Mergenthaler's Wonderful Machine." *American History Illustrated*, June 1986.

Microchip
See Microelectronics.

Microelectronics
As the word implies, microelectronics has to do with the miniature devices used in electronics. Electrons, which are the negative particles found in the atoms of matter, are normally paired with positive protons. The electrons in the outer regions of metallic atoms are free to move from atom to atom, producing an electric current. Electrons are also able to move across a vacuum and through substances known as semiconductors. The term *electronic* refers to devices that control electrons as they move. These devices include resistors, which restrict the flow of electrons; capacitors, which store electrons on parallel plates; and vacuum tubes and semiconductors, which can convert alternating current to direct current or amplify or turn off currents.

Vacuum tubes were essential to electronics through most of the first half of the twentieth century, but semiconductors have dominated electronics during the second half of the century. The invention of the semiconductor diode and transistor and manufacturing techniques involving integrated circuits have miniaturized electronics, giving rise to microelectronics.

The connection between communication and electricity was first realized by Michael Faraday and Joseph Henry, who discovered that a changing current in one coil of wire can induce a current in another totally separate coil. Before Marconi made use of Faraday's and Henry's discovery in developing wireless telegraphy, which in turn led to the development of radio, the telegraph and the telephone made long-distance communication possible by using electric currents and electromagnets.

An effort to improve wireless telegraphy led John Fleming and Lee De Forest to develop the vacuum-tube diode and triode, respectively. Vacuum tubes gave rise to an electronics industry that has always been closely connected with communication, especially radio and television. To reduce operating costs and size while improving efficiency, vacuum tubes became smaller and more rugged and were made to last longer. However, there was a limit to the miniaturization of these tubes that prevented the devices from ever achieving the portable dimensions that would make them satisfactory for mobile use.

During World War II, the development of radar, which required high-frequency wave generators and receivers, taxed the limits of vacuum-tube technology and forced researchers to return to the crystal detectors used in the early days of radio. Shortly after the war, the development of programmable computers led, in 1946, to the 30-ton ENIAC, a monstrous computer built at the University of Pennsylvania. The circuits of this machine contained 18,000 vacuum tubes and drew 140 kilowatts of power, a far cry from today's desktop or laptop microcomputers.

In 1948, William Shockley, John Bardeen,

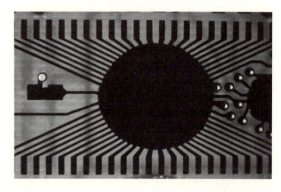

Microprocessors, like the one pictured here, are only several millimeters in width and contain millions of components. Beginning in the 1970s, these miniature devices made it possible to design not only smaller radios and pocket calculators, but also computers that could fit on a desktop.

and Walter Brattain, working at Bell Laboratories, reported the invention of the transistor, an outcome of their research into semiconductor crystals. By adding impurities such as arsenic or antimony to germanium or silicon, a process known as doping, they were able to make n-type semiconductors. Doping silicon with atoms of aluminum, boron, or gallium led to p-type semiconductors. The designation p or n refers to the way charge is transmitted in the crystal. In an n-type crystal, charge is carried by electrons; in a p-type crystal, charge is carried by "holes"—the absence of electrons, which is the equivalent of positive charge. Eight years later, these scientists were awarded the Nobel Prize in physics.

The discovery at Bell Labs was followed by rapid progress in the manufacturing of transistors. As the price of these tiny electronic devices fell, solid-state technology replaced vacuum tubes. Because transistors are very small, they marked a major breakthrough in making small, lightweight, portable electronic gadgets of all kinds. People began to buy transistor radios that required no warm-up time and could be carried in a pocket. Computers of reasonable size and weight could be built with solid-state components. Soon the demand for computers by the business community encouraged the electronics industry to search for more efficient ways to manufacture their electronic circuits. It was found that successive layers of material could be built on a single tiny silicon chip. The silicon is first coated with silicon dioxide, which is an insulator. Patterns are made on the chip using photolithographic techniques that involve etching, exposure to ultraviolet light, dissolving, masking, and doping. The end result is an integrated circuit that has millions of components on a chip several millimeters wide.

By 1970, programmable chips were being produced. Known as microprocessors, these chips form the core of a computer. Microprocessors made it possible to design not only pocket calculators, but computers that could fit on a desktop. The personal computer was born.

The miniaturization of electronics and the success of microprocessors has led, in turn, to the growth of digital signals. These digital signals, based on the binary codes used in computers, are replacing the analog transmission of data and sound in all phases of communication.

See also:
Computer; Diode; Transistor.

References:
International Encyclopedia of Communications. New York: Oxford University Press, 1989. Macaulay, David. *The Way Things Work.* Boston: Houghton Mifflin, 1988. Sears, Francis W., Mark W. Zemansky, and Hugh D. Young. *College Physics.* Reading, MA: Addison-Wesley, 1985.

Microphone

A microphone changes sound waves to electrical impulses. Because a microphone converts one form of energy to another, it is a transducer.

It is possible to make a very simple, but inefficient, mechanical microphone that relies solely on vibrations created by sound waves. Such a microphone can be made from a pair of tin cans, each open at one end, connected through their intact ends by a long, taut string. The words of a person speaking into one of the cans can be heard by a second person whose ear is against the open end of the other container. A person speaks into one can, and the sound waves cause the bottom of the can to vibrate. The vibrations are carried by the taut string to the bottom of the other can, which vibrates in response to the pulses carried along the connecting string. The listener can hear words spoken into the other can. Unfortunately, this inexpensive system does not work beyond 20 to 30 feet because so much energy is lost to the vibrating materials.

Types of Microphones

Carbon Microphone: The carbon microphone is the oldest of several types of commercial microphones. It is rugged and inexpensive but produces sound of rather poor quality. The carbon microphone consists of a thin metal diaphragm that fits against one side of a container, which holds loosely packed carbon granules. The changing pressure of sound waves causes the diaphragm to move back and forth. When the diaphragm moves inward under the impact of a compressed portion of a wave, it increases the pressure on the carbon granules, causing them to pack together more tightly. The electrical resistance of the carbon decreases as the pressure on the particles increases. The result is an increase in the electric current flowing in the circuit. This increased current is amplified before it reaches a loudspeaker or telephone receiver.

The louder the sound, the greater the pressure applied to the diaphragm and the greater the increase in pressure on the carbon. Consequently, because the current flowing from the microphone is inversely related to the resistance of the carbon, the current is greater when the sound is louder. A greater current from the microphone means a greater current flowing to the loudspeaker or receiver, where a louder sound will be produced.

If the pitch of the sound is high, more sound waves will reach the microphone each second, and there will be an equally greater number of changes in current in the same period. A lower pitch produces fewer waves per unit time and, concurrently, fewer current changes. The number of current pulses reaching the speaker each second, which is the same as the number of sound waves striking the microphone's diaphragm in the same period, determines the pitch of the sound produced by the loudspeaker. Since the two frequencies are the same, the pitch of the sound received at the microphone is the same as the pitch emitted at the speaker.

Dynamic Microphone: The dynamic microphone is essentially a dynamic loudspeaker in reverse. It contains a coil of wire (the voice coil) that is attached to a diaphragm. When the diaphragm moves under the impact of sound waves, the coil moves with it. Since the coil is in the magnetic field of a permanent magnet, the changing magnetic field through the moving coil induces a varying and alternating voltage that drives a corresponding current through an amplifier connected to a loudspeaker.

Because the current changes at the same rate as the sound waves that produce it, the amplified current will drive the loudspeaker at the same rate as the sound striking the microphone's diaphragm, thus duplicating the pitch of the sound entering the microphone. The louder the sound, the greater the motion of the voice coil attached to the diaphragm. The larger the movement of the coil, the greater the induced voltage and the greater the current; the larger the current, the greater the amplitude of vibration of the speaker cone.

Crystal Microphone: The crystal microphone is based on the piezoelectric effect. The effect is evident with certain crystals, such as quartz and Rochelle salt (sodium potassium tartrate). When one of these crystals is squeezed, a potential difference (voltage) develops between opposite faces of the crystal. When sound waves strike such a crystal, the alternating pressure caused by the compressions and rarefactions produce a varying voltage across the crystal. The changing electric potential can be used to drive a current from microphone to speaker through an amplifier.

Crystal microphones are inexpensive, and they produce high-quality sound and a high-output voltage. However, they are sensitive to heat and humidity, and as might be expected, they are easily damaged by shock.

Ribbon Microphone: Ribbon microphones can reproduce high-quality sound, and they are sometimes used in commercial recording and broadcasting. The name comes from the structure of the microphone, which consists of a thin, corrugated metallic ribbon that is suspended between the north and south poles of a permanent magnet. The ribbon vibrates in response to sound waves striking it. As it does so, the ribbon moves across lines of magnetic force, giving rise to a small alternating voltage. The small voltage requires significant amplification of the tiny electric currents that are produced before they are fed to a loudspeaker or recorder.

Capacitor Microphone: The capacitor or condenser microphone is widely used in broadcasting and recording. Its name comes from the fact that its metal diaphragm is one plate of a capacitor, which is also known as a condenser. The other plate, separated from the diaphragm by a small distance, is firmly fixed in place. When a capacitor is charged, as it is when the microphone is connected to a battery or a power source, positive charge collects on one plate and negative charge on the other plate. When the compression region of a sound wave strikes the diaphragm, it moves closer to the fixed plate. Since capacitance is inversely proportional to the distance between the plates of a capacitor, the capacitance increases when the diaphragm moves closer to the fixed plate. The increase in capacitance means that more charge can move onto the plates. This is reasonable because if the plates move closer together, the charges on the two plates will exert larger attracting forces on the opposite charges across the small gap in space that separates them.

When a rarefaction region of a sound wave strikes the diaphragm, the diaphragm moves out, the plates are farther apart, and less charge accumulates on the plates. The charges moving on and off the plates as the vibrating diaphragm causes changes in capacitance are accompanied by moving charge along wires in other parts of the circuit that lead to a battery or power source and an amplifier. Since the oscillating charge flow is synchronized with the sound waves, the electrical signals can be used to activate a speaker, recorder, mixer, or synthesizer.

See also:
Amplifier; Faraday, Michael; Loudspeaker; Oersted, Hans Christian; Tape Recorder.

References:
Asimov, Isaac. *Asimov's New Guide to Science.* New York: Basic Books, 1984.
Gardner, Robert. *Communication.* New York: Twenty-First Century, 1994.
How It Works: The Illustrated Encyclopedia of Science and Technology, vol. 16. New York and London: Marshall Cavendish, 1978.
Macaulay, David. *The Way Things Work.* Boston: Houghton Mifflin, 1988.
Science and Technology Illustrated, vol. 15. Chicago: Encyclopedia Britannica, 1984.

Microprocessor

Microprocessors are tiny silicon wafers, or chips, that hold a computer's central processing unit (CPU) as well as some or all of a computer's random-access memory (RAM) and read-only memory (ROM). Microprocessors are the major components in personal computers and computer-controlled appliances and devices in homes and cars. The first chips developed in the late 1960s could store about 1,000 bytes (characters) of information. (A byte contains 8 bits—0s and 1s.) By 1979, 64-kilobyte chips had been developed, and these were soon followed by 256-kilobyte chips. Today, chips can store millions or billions of characters.

Each chip is a tiny wafer of silicon that contains thousands of transistors, resistors, and capacitors in circuits that act as memory cells, registers, adders, and other devices needed to store and process information. The circuits on these chips are called integrated circuits (ICs) because their components are created simultaneously on a single chip. Before the introduction of integrated circuits, circuit components were manufactured separately and connected by soldered wires. Integrated cir-

cuits have reduced both manufacturing costs and the incidence of circuit failure.

In making a microprocessor, the silicon is coated with silicon dioxide, an insulating material. Patterns are then made on the chip using photolithographic techniques that involve etching, exposure to ultraviolet light, dissolving, masking, and doping. The result is integrated circuits with millions of components on a chip several millimeters wide.

Microprocessors made it possible to produce not only the pocket calculators that led to the demise of slide rules, but computers that could fit on a desktop as well. These personal computers and the expanded Internet that now links many of them have changed society in ways that we still do not fully understand.

The development and increasing use of microprocessors has led, in turn, to the replacement of analog signals by digital signals—signals based on the binary code that is used in computers. Digital signals are rapidly replacing the analog transmission of information in all phases of communication.

See also:
Analog and Digital Signals; Capacitor; Computer; Microelectronics; Transistor.

Modem

A modem is a device that can be connected to a computer for the purpose of transferring information over telephone lines. The term modem is an acronym for modulator-demodulator.

In order to transmit computer data over most telephone lines, the computer's digital data must be modulated (converted to analog signals). This can be done by converting the bits (0s and 1s) of digital data from the computer into two different frequencies, such as 1,200 hertz or 2,200 hertz. At the other end of the line, the data must be demodulated (changed back to digital data) so that the receiving computer can accept them. Modems connected to the sending and receiving computers carry out the digital-analog-digital conversions that allow the two computers to communicate.

The major problem with modems is that the transmission of data over wire cables is much slower than the rate at which computers can send or receive information. Furthermore, noisy lines can garble the signals so that they are meaningless to the receiving computer. Although computers have built-in devices coded to detect garbled data and require the sender to retransmit the message, the result can be repeated sendings and considerable lost time.

Most modems today have a baud rate (the rate at which data is transmitted) of 28,800 or 33,600 bits per second. Many older modems were much slower, with baud rates in the hundreds of bits per second. Data transmission is much faster over fiber-optic cables, on which information can be transmitted digitally. Using fiber optics, data can be sent at billions of bits per second. At such rates, an entire encyclopedia can be transmitted in less than a second rather than the hours or days that would be required using modems.

See also:
Computer; Fiber Optics.

Modulation

Modulation is the periodic variation of one or more properties of a signal. For example, the waves of air entering a telephone microphone have been modulated in amplitude and frequency by the voice mechanism of the person who is speaking. In the telephone's microphone, the modulated waves are changed to electrical signals that closely correspond to the sound waves that created them. The electrical signals are carried by wires to a receiver where they are demodulated; that is, converted back to sound waves that closely resemble those produced by the speaker.

More commonly, modulation is associated with amplitude modulation (AM) and frequency modulation (FM). In AM radio, the amplitude of the radio wave—the so-called carrier wave—is changed by sound waves, which have a much lower frequency than radio waves. As shown in Figure 1a, the sound waves are superimposed on the carrier

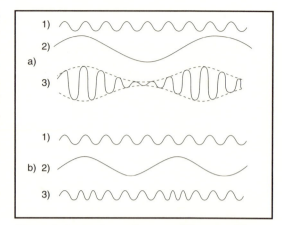

Figure 1. In panel a, radio waves (1) are used to carry sound waves (2) by amplitude modulation, or AM (3). In panel b, radio waves (1) are used to carry sound waves (2) by frequency modulation, or FM (3). The ratio of radio waves to sound waves is much greater than is shown here.

radio wave. Federal Communications Commission (FCC) regulations set the maximum modulating frequency of AM radio at 5,000 hertz. This is less than 1 percent of the frequency of even the longest AM radio waves, which range from 535 to 1,605 kilohertz.

In FM radio, the frequency rather than the amplitude of the radio waves is modulated with sound waves as shown in Figure 1b. The variation in frequency is proportional to the amplitude of the sound; the rate at which this variation takes place depends on the frequency of the sound. The advantage of FM is that the signals are not affected by interference from electrical phenomena such as lightning, transformers, and electric motors, which can produce static in AM receivers. These all produce a change in the amplitude of an electromagnetic wave, but unlike AM, the amplitude of an FM wave carries no information.

With the advent of digital signals, pulse code modulation is being used to convert an audio or other signal into a series of binary pulses (0s and 1s) that can be sent along cables and later demodulated—changed back into the original signals.

See also:
Analog and Digital Signals; Electromagnetic Waves; Radio.

References:

Coates, R. F. *Modern Communication Systems,* 2nd ed. Atlantic Highlands, NJ: Macmillan UK, 1983.

Macaulay, David. *The Way Things Work.* Boston: Houghton Mifflin, 1988.

Morse Code

See Telegraph.

Morse, Samuel F. B. (1791–1892)

One of the most versatile and controversial Americans of the nineteenth century, Samuel F. B. Morse was an artist, politician, and businessman, but he is most widely recognized as the inventor of the telegraph. In its day, the telegraph, the first modern form of communication, was just as awe inspiring as today's high-speed computers. For the first time, messages could travel great distances faster than man.

Born in Charlestown, Massachusetts, the son of a prominent Congregational minister, Morse attended Philips Andover Academy and joined his two brothers at Yale when he was 16. At the university Morse was exposed to some of the brightest scientific minds of his era, attending lectures and demonstrations by Jeremiah Day and Benjamin Silliman. Morse graduated in 1810, but nothing in his education or interests remotely suggested his future acclaim as an inventor or scientist. Due to his skill in drawing, Morse believed that his future lay in the art world. In 1811, he went to England to study and pursue his calling. Morse's first major project, "The Dying Hercules," was honored with a gold medal, and a painting based on the composition received recognition at a Royal Academy exhibit. However, Morse won more praise than commissions, and he returned to the United States in 1815.

The homecoming did little to relieve Morse's financial distress. Morse was the stereotypical "starving artist," although with a workmanlike reputation. From 1816 to 1818, Morse was an itinerant portraitist traveling throughout Vermont, New Hampshire, and eventually the South, picking up commissions where he could. Although his work was praiseworthy, it failed to gain Morse any financial security. To supplement his meager income from art, Morse took up tinkering and invention. Just as he had been as an artist, Morse was creatively successful as an inventor, designing an improved fire engine pump and a marble-carving machine, but both machines were financially disappointing. The 1820s were nothing short of disastrous for the aspiring artist. Morse's wife died in 1825, followed in rapid succession by his father and mother. In 1829, the disillusioned 29-year-old returned to England not only for solace, but also to revive his flagging career.

In Europe Morse managed to support himself by selling reproductions of the European masters to wealthy Americans back home. By 1832, the expatriate began preparations to return to New York City. On the eve of his departure, Morse saw the French semaphore system and noted its inefficiency and slowness.

The trip to America changed Morse's life. On board ship he fell into a conversation with Dr. Charles T. Jackson about the still-experimental use of electricity in communication. Morse was intrigued and immediately retreated to his cabin and drew up some rudimentary sketches of a device to send messages by means of an electrical circuit with an electromagnet as the prime component. Morse's enthusiasm was the exuberance of a nonscientist with limited experience who little realized the challenge of finalizing his vision. Experiments with a magnetic telegraph were not new. William F. Cooke and Charles Wheatstone, two groundbreaking English researchers, were well on their way to developing a working mechanism. However, Morse knew nothing of these efforts. To him a successful undertaking just might provide the independence that would allow him to continue his painting unburdened by financial concerns. To Morse, science was merely a promising diversion, an adjunct to his real love—art.

Shortly after his arrival in New York, Morse accepted an unsalaried position as the first professor of art at an American college. Working at what is today New York University, Morse had to rely on student fees from his teaching to meet his expenses and support his children, who lived with relatives. Nonetheless, obtaining the position was a fortunate turn for the artist. Morse had scientific colleagues who could augment his lack of applied knowledge and experience. Laboratories were available for his experimental needs, and most significantly, the appointment ultimately led to the financial assistance Morse needed to succeed. In 1835, working part-time from his earlier sketches, Morse concocted a complex prototype using found materials like an old picture frame and the wheels of an old clock. Morse's full attention was diverted from his crude apparatus when he became involved in the anti-Catholic, antiforeign Nativist movement. In 1836, he ran for mayor of New York on the Native American ticket, garnering fewer than 2,000 votes. Undaunted, he made a second bid for the office in 1841, failing even more miserably.

Events in 1836 and 1837 abruptly jolted Morse to reality. First, news from overseas heralded advances in the European version of the telegraph, and Morse realized that his work would be wasted if he did not move ahead. Morse's reluctance to plunge into refining his device was the result of his preoccupation with his artistic dreams and his unwillingness to admit that he could not make a living as an artist. In one final attempt to realize his ambition, Morse applied for the commission to paint a mural on the rotunda of the Capitol. His rejection was the final blow, and after spending half his life as an artist, Morse surrendered.

In September 1837, Morse showed his invention to Leonard Gale, a university colleague and professor of chemistry. Morse was frustrated by the principal problem faced by all his predecessors in electronic communication—how to send a current over a long distance without weakening the power of the signal. In late 1837, Morse transmitted a current over 1,700 feet of wire strung around a classroom, but was stymied at greater distances. Gale's familiarity with Joseph Henry's electromagnetic induction experiments led to suggestions on an improved battery and electromagnet. However, it was Henry himself who suggested using periodic relays to sustain and strengthen the electrical signal and in so doing saved the telegraph from obscurity. In January 1838, the improved telegraph sent a signal over a 10-mile circuit in Gale's classroom, firmly establishing the feasibility of long-distance electrical communication.

A close observer of the Morse investigations was a recent graduate of the school, Albert Vail. Vail's father was the prosperous owner of the Speedwell Iron Works in Morristown, New Jersey. The younger Vail saw the potential of the new communication medium and offered his mechanical expertise and financial support to improve the invention in return for a partnership. Vail finally constructed a stronger and sturdier telegraph that could be used in public demonstrations to investors. Gale and Vail were made partners, and Morse set out on a round of demonstrations in Morristown, Philadelphia, New York, and in February 1838, Washington, D.C.

The telegraphy demonstration before the House Commerce Committee, which had been charged with developing a modern, rapid communication system for the nation, was impressive, but the government failed to appropriate any funds. One convert was the committee chairman, Frances "Fog" Smith of Maine, who offered his legal services and access to Washington contacts in exchange for a partnership. Morse accepted, and Smith underwrote a trip to Europe to stimulate interest and secure preliminary contracts and patents. However, the Europeans, especially the English, were working on their own form of telegraph. They received Morse and his invention unenthusiastically, and no money was forthcoming. The one positive result of the voyage was Morse's new interest in the photographic concepts and techniques of Louis Daguerre. When Morse returned to

New York in 1839, he opened a studio specializing in daguerreotypes and became one of America's preeminent early photographers. Unsatisfied with that recognition, Morse wanted to return to his portraiture. Daguerre himself warned Morse that photographic portraits were impossible due to the length of time a subject would have to sit motionless to record a good image. Morse, in collaboration with professor John W. Draper, developed faster processing chemicals and better lenses that enabled him to earn a living for three years until he returned to Congress to renew his request for money.

December 1842 found Morse once again before Congress, pitching the efficacy of his invention. This time he was successful. A curious Congress appropriated $30,000 to build an experimental line from Baltimore to Washington, over 40 miles. The Baltimore & Ohio Railroad (B&O) allowed the use of their right-of-way as long as the roadbed was not injured and the company not embarrassed.

Morse's enthusiasm must have been short lived due to the realization that he knew nothing about actually building a telegraph line. His experience was strictly confined to a laboratory environment. The initial attempt to lay insulated wire in a protective pipe proved a failure. Ezra Cornell created a plow that could open a trench, lay the pipe, and close the ditch in one operation. Cornell ultimately made a fortune in the telegraph industry, which later enabled him to endow the university that bears his name. The undertaking was very expensive, and the system shorted out with only a mile of line laid. With most of the money already spent and seemingly no prospect for success, Morse's assistants quit. Smith, seeking to salvage his reputation, openly attacked Morse. Charles Grafton Page of the Patent Office provided the suggestion that saved the project. Page proposed using the English method of stringing wires on poles and using the earth as a ground. On 24 May 1844, Cornell completed the project, connecting the B & O Railroad depot in Baltimore with the Supreme Court Chambers in Washington, where the telegraph was set up for the official demonstration. It took Morse one minute to send the famous first message, "What hath God wrought," to Vail in Baltimore, thus establishing the telegraph as the communication media of the future.

Although Morse became famous, the business aspect of the enterprise was a real struggle. Morse hoped the federal government would take over the enterprise, and he and his partners offered to sell their interests for $100,000. The government rejected the offer, and Morse and associates formed their own company in 1845. Other investors were not as reluctant as the government. There was major competition for the country's communication dollars, and hundreds of companies began their own lines. This competition culminated in 1856 with merger of about 100 small companies to form Western Union. At best Morse earned approximately $80,000 from his invention, which enabled him to live comfortably, but not before he fought the requisite patent battles. One biographer claimed the assaults on Morse's patent rights showed the darkest side of his personality. Morse steadfastly refused to acknowledge any of the assistance he received in developing the telegraph. This was particularly the case with Joseph Henry, who had always been Morse's supporter. Morse insisted that the telegraph was his invention and his alone. The Supreme Court agreed, upholding his patent rights in 1854.

See also:
Cryptology; Henry, Joseph; Telegraph.

References:
Davidson, Marshall B. "What Samuel Wrought." *American Heritage*, April 1961.
Klein, Maury. "What Hath God Wrought." *American Heritage Invention and Technology*, Spring 1993.
Mabee, Carleton. *The American Leonardo: A Life of Samuel F. B. Morse.* New York: Octagon Books, 1969.

Motion Photography

Photography has led to a better understanding of motion. Sequential details of a motion can be analyzed through a series of photographs of a moving object.

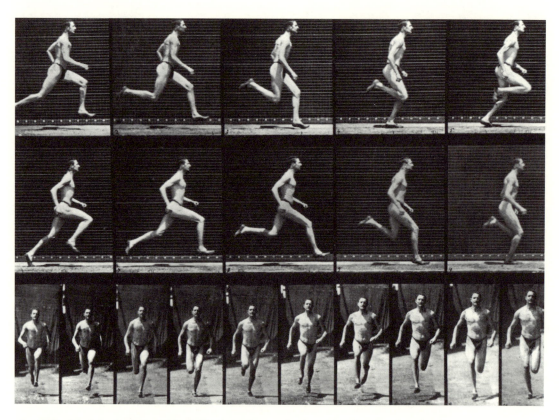

An 1887 plate from Eadweard Muybridge's motion study shows 20 photographs taken in a rapid sequence. Muybridge's study demonstrated the value of photography in analyzing human and animal locomotion and anticipated the invention of the motion picture.

In the early days of photography, the exposure times required to produce a clear image were so long that any movement resulted in a blurring of the image. By 1860, smaller cameras, faster lenses, and a shutter system enabled photographers to "freeze" motion that took place in bright light.

In 1872, Leland Stanford, a horse breeder and the wealthy governor of California, hired the distinguished English photographer Eadweard Muybridge to investigate the various gaits of horses. For years, people had disagreed as to whether or not all four feet of a galloping horse were ever off the ground at the same time. The motions occur so rapidly that the human eye cannot detect the details. By 1878, Muybridge had succeeded in taking rapid sequential photographs of horses in various gaits by using a large number of cameras. The shutters of successive cameras were tripped at equal distances along a

horse's path by an electrical system devised by John Isaacs, an engineer who had helped build the American Central Pacific Railroad that had been financed by Stanford. The exposure times were on the order of 1/1000 second. Since the fastest race horses run at a speed of about 1 kilometer per minute, the distance traveled by such a horse in 1/1000 second was only about 1.5 centimeters. Consequently, the motion could be analyzed in great detail. The photographs clearly revealed that a galloping horse does indeed have all four feet off the ground at one point in its rapid sequence of repeated movements.

In 1873, Muybridge developed what became known as the zoopraxiscope, a device that projected painted images of his photographs of animals. When the images were projected in rapid succession, the persistence of vision gave the illusion of motion.

At the invitation of the University of Pennsylvania, Muybridge expanded his study of motion, and in 1887 his monumental work *Animal Locomotion* was published in 11 volumes. It contained 782 plates each with 12 to 36 images taken in sequence to reveal the details of the animal's gait.

After seeing Muybridge's photographs in 1878, Étienne-Jules Marey, a brilliant French physiologist, recognized the value of photographs in analyzing animal locomotion. To avoid the need for a large number of cameras, Marey used a stroboscope in front of a camera with an open shutter. The stroboscope consisted of a slotted disc that rotated in front of the camera's lens. Each time an open slot moved in front of the lens, it produced an image of the moving organism that was superimposed on the previous image. To avoid confusion among images where the motion was slow, Marey used white paper and reflective buttons and stripes on darkened bodies to produce a more graphical photograph that made analysis easier. Marey's technique came to be known as chronophotography.

In 1892, Marey's assistant, Georges Demeny, developed the photophone. It used a series of images projected in slow motion to show the movement of human lips. It proved to be a valuable tool for helping deaf-mutes learn to speak or read lips.

Additional work using chronophotography and flash photography was used to scientifically analyze workers' motions and to study ballistics. Further advances in high-speed shutter systems and short-time flash photography, fathered by Harold E. Edgerton, led to microsecond analysis of motion and the ability to photograph a bullet moving at 1,000 meters per second so that it appears to be at rest, with no blurring, since the bullet moves only 1 millimeter during the microsecond exposure.

See also:
Motion Pictures, Photography.
References:
Edgerton, Harold E. "Making a Splash." *National Geographic*, February 1996.
Edgerton, Harold E., and James R. Killian. *Moments of Vision: The Stroboscopic Revolution in Photography*. Cambridge, MA: MIT Press, 1979.
Haber-Schaim, Uri, et al. *PSSC Physics*, 7th ed. Dubuque, IA: Kendall/Hunt, 1991.
International Encyclopedia of Communications. New York: Oxford University Press, 1989.
Williams, Trevor I. *The History of Invention: From Stone Axes to Silicon Chips*. New York: Facts on File, 1987.

Motion Pictures (Movies)

A series of successive still pictures taken of a moving object, when projected onto a screen at a rate of 20 or more images per second, produces the illusion of smooth motion. Objects in the photographs are seen as moving smoothly when the pictures are projected in rapid succession because of persistence of vision. The images that form on the retina of the eye persist for about one-tenth of a second. If a second image forms in the eye in less than that time, it blends with the first image. As a result, the image appears to change smoothly rather than in the jerky fashion that would result if the images were projected, for example, at five images per second.

Motion pictures (movies), as we know them, were preceded by a number of devices based on the persistence of vision. Eadweard Muybridge's zoopraxiscope and Étienne-Jules Marey's chronophotography technique both evolved from experiments in which motion photography was used to analyze the details of animal locomotion. By 1890, Marey was recording successive photographs on roll film, which could then be projected onto a screen at the same rate they were taken or at a slower rate to produce slow motion. Marey had developed all the mechanisms needed for making movies, but he used the technique to study animal locomotion. He was not interested in applying his invention to entertainment.

Muybridge, on the other hand, suggested combining his zoopraxiscope with Edison's phonograph to add sound to the projected images. After initially dismissing the idea as a toy, Edison in 1891 invented the Kinetoscope, which gave a single viewer 15 seconds of action by projecting images on successive film frames at 15 frames per second. Five years later Edison added music and voice to the Kinetoscope, and Kinetoscope parlors sprang into existence. For a small fee, viewers could watch a number of different scenes coupled with narration.

Because Edison never obtained a patent for his Kinetoscope, Louis and Auguste Lumière were able to adapt the device for projecting images on a screen for viewing by a large audience. The brothers called their ingenious invention the cinematograph. It combined a portable camera with a machine for printing the film and a system that allowed the film's developed frames to be projected in rapid succession. The first audience to pay to see a movie on the Lumières' cinematograph entered the Grand Café at 14 Boulevard des Capucines in Paris on 28 December 1895. A new industry was born, one that would grow rapidly to giant proportions.

Films initially were used largely by magicians as part of their acts. To a person who had never seen a motion picture, a well-known figure walking across a screen was surely magic. For the first few years movies were generally less than a minute long, and the subjects were news events, interesting locales, and famous performers. By 1908, films as long as 15 minutes were being made throughout the Western world and included comedy, narratives, documentaries, fantasies, and melodramas. Most filming took place in bright sunlight, on outdoor stages, or in brightly lit rooms.

By 1915, the motion picture industry was centered in Hollywood, California. This was partly due to a decline in European films during World War I, which began in 1914. By the end of the war, Hollywood studios were producing several hundred movies a year for a worldwide market. Hollywood films gave rise to typecasting—the practice of choosing roles for actors that fit their natural personalities and then repeatedly casting them in similar roles. Movie stars such as Rudolph Valentino, Lon Chaney, Buster Keaton, and Greta Garbo became widely known and recognized, as did movie directors such as Cecil B. DeMille and Eric von Stroheim.

Movies with Sound and Color

From the beginning, movie producers recognized that sound was an important part of a film. Early silent films were often accompanied by a pianist who played music appropriate for the mood of the film as it progressed. Later, attempts were made to put sounds and voices on phonograph records that were played as the film was shown. However, it was very difficult to synchronize sound and pictures.

In the early 1920s, Lee De Forest invented the Phonofilm system, which allowed a sound track to be recorded along one side of the film. The Radio Corporation of America used De Forest's invention, but different studios used competing sound-on-film systems, all of which were incompatible with one another.

The transition from silent to sound films was rapid. By 1930, practically all films for wide audience viewing were "talkies." Although the union of sound and moving film was popular, it created new problems for directors. The microphones picked up not only voices but other sounds as well, including the running camera and the carbon-arc lamps. To prevent such background noise, incandescent lamps with tungsten filaments were introduced, and cameras and their operators were placed in soundproof rooms. With actors who could not move far from their microphones and cameras with an angle of rotation limited to about 30 degrees fixed in soundproof booths, motion went out of movies until "mufflers" were made for movie cameras. As a result, many of the initial sound movies were adaptations of stage plays with ample dialogue but little action.

To avoid sound distortion the successive frames of a film had to move at a steady rate through the camera. This was accomplished by using cameras with electric motors to move film instead of the hand-cranked cameras that had been used to make silent films. The motors moved film at a steady 24 frames per second.

The advent of sound films led to the demise of many silent film stars who lacked the well-modulated voices required for talkies. Furthermore, the stars of the silent era had never had to memorize a script, and many were unable to do so effectively. It was this change in filming that attracted many actors from Broadway to Hollywood.

The next breakthrough were movies filmed in color. The first full-length color film, *Becky Sharp*, appeared in 1935. Thereafter, an increasing number of movies were produced in color, and Hollywood attempted to meet the competition from television following World War II by producing most films in color. At that time, all television broadcasts were seen in black and white. The movie industry probably survived because in the 1950s they began making films for television, and television networks began purchasing and showing old movies to avoid the excessive costs of fully live TV.

Movie Cameras and Projectors

The film used to make movies consists of frames that come in five standard widths—70, 35, 16, and 8 millimeter, and super-8. A strip of film has sprocket holes on each side. These holes fit into the teeth on the sprocket wheel much like the chain on a bicycle fits onto the sprocket that is driven by the pedals. An electric motor turns the sprocket wheel at a steady rate, moving the film from one spool to another.

In a movie camera, a lens focuses light and images through a small gate with an opening that matches the size of each frame on the film. As the film is moved through the gate by the sprocket wheel, a claw connected to a crank momentarily stops the film at the same time that a spinning shutter exposes the film to the light. When the shutter covers the gate opening, the claw releases and the film sprocket wheel pulls the film through the gate to the next frame. The shutter also reflects light through a prism to a viewfinder so that the photographer can see exactly what is being filmed.

Normally the camera exposes 24 frames each second. To produce slow-motion films, the number of frames exposed per second is increased. For example, to halve the speed at which the motion appears to take place, the film is moved through the gate at 48 frames per second. When the film is projected at 24 frames per second, the motion is slowed by a factor of two.

If sound is to accompany the movie, a sound track is produced along one side of the film. Electrical impulses from the microphone activate a light source. The light beam, the intensity of which varies with the voltage from the microphone, is projected through the narrow strip of film that constitutes the sound track. The amount that the film develops depends on the intensity of the light.

A movie projector is similar to a movie camera working in reverse. Light from a bright bulb is concentrated on the film by a condensing lens. Like the movie camera, a claw moves the film one frame at a time through the gate. When the film is stopped momentarily, the light passes through the film and then through a lens that focuses the image on a screen. While the claw is pulling one frame past the gate and bringing the next frame into it, a rotating shutter blocks the light. Consequently, only nonmoving images are projected onto the screen. The illusion of motion results because the image persists on the retina until the next one appears, so that the images appear to move smoothly from one position to another relative to a fixed background. Although the projector moves the film at 24 frames per second, each frame is projected twice so that 48 views are shown each second to reduce flickering.

If there is a sound track, a light beam shines through it onto a photocell that converts the light to an electrical signal, which ideally is identical to the one that was received from the microphone when the movie was made. These electrical signals are then amplified and used to drive a loudspeaker. Because the sound track and images are made simultaneously, the sound and images are synchronized.

See also:
Amplifier; De Forest, Lee; Loudspeaker; Microphone; Motion Photography; Photoelectric

Cell; Television; Television and Society.

References:
International Encyclopedia of Communications.
New York: Oxford University Press, 1989.
Macaulay, David. *The Way Things Work.*
Boston: Houghton Mifflin, 1988.
Williams, Trevor I. *The History of Invention:
From Stone Axes to Silicon Chips.* New York:
Facts on File, 1987.

Multiplexing

Multiplexing allows separate signals, such as different telephone conversations, to be sent along the same wire or cable simultaneously.

In time-division multiplexing, signals that share the same line are sampled rapidly one after the other in cyclical fashion and the samples, together with routing signals, are sent in digital form in the order they were taken along the common wire or cable. At the other end of the line the signals are decoded, converted back into their original form, and routed to the correct receiver. Because the sampling is done so rapidly in comparison to the rate at which the original signals (such as the sound of a human voice) are generated, the gaps between samples taken go unnoticed.

In frequency-division multiplexing, each message is identified by a separate subcarrier frequency, then all the subcarriers are combined to modulate a fixed carrier frequency. In the case of transmission by wire, modulated subcarrier frequencies may be transmitted without the need for a common carrier. At the receiver, subcarriers are separated by frequency selection, and the message is recovered and sent to the proper receiver.

Muybridge, Eadweard

See Motion Photography.

Navajo Code Talkers

Navajo Code Talkers was a special program of the Marine Corps in World War II, when Navajos were used to develop and implement one of the few unbroken codes in history. There was some historical precedent for the use of Native Americans speaking their language as a code in modern combat. Both the Canadian and U.S. armies had limited success with such efforts in World War I, most notably the U.S. experiment with the Choctaws of Company D, 141st Infantry. One dilemma was that Native American languages lacked combat-specific words such as machine gun or grenade.

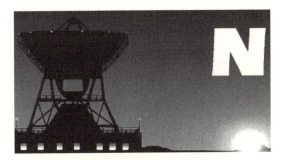

Philip Johnston, the son of missionaries, grew up speaking Navajo and conceived an unbreakable military code based upon it. Due to the tonal nature of Navajo speech, words changed meaning based upon pitch and inflection. The language was largely unwritten and not a subject of linguistic study. Johnston, a civil engineer in Los Angeles, approached Major General Clayton B. Vogel of the Marine Corps with his idea and arranged a demonstration. Impressed, Vogel requested authorization to recruit 200 Navajos for code duty. Washington granted permission for 30 men to begin a pilot program.

In April 1942, the new 382 Platoon began regular basic training at Camp Elliot, California. Their training differed in one respect from that of other marines. They had to create a new military code. This was complicated by the fact that any code had to account for the different dialects on the Navajo reservation. Furthermore, the code had to be memorized, since nothing could be written down for fear of capture. Using the familiar, the Navajos based the code on nature as a reference. Birds indicated planes, a buzzard was a bomber, and fish denoted types of ships. Descriptive words particular to Navajo life described other military details. The commanding officer became war chief, and a fortification was a cliff dwelling. Countries and leaders were christened by physical characteristics. Africa was "Blackie," the United States was "Our Mother," Hitler became "Mustache Smeller," and Mussolini

was "Big Gourd Chin." The originators also made up their own expressions and played word games. "District" became "deer," "ice" meant "strict," and "potato" indicated "grenades." If the enemy ever did begin to decipher the code, the Navajos could switch to an alphabetic cipher. In this case, the first letter of the English translation of a Navajo word corresponded to a letter. To add further confusion, any of three words, or later eight, could be used for each letter. For example, *A* could be represented by the Navajo words for ant, apple, or ax. Far from static, the code was reviewed before invasions and could be modified as necessary.

When the code was completed, Naval Intelligence spent three weeks trying to break it and failed to decipher a single message. White recruits familiar with Navajo could not deal with everyday conversational Navajo, and even untrained Navajos, although they might pick up words, could not break the code. Code Talkers worked with all six Marine divisions in the Pacific and served with distinction on Iwo Jima, Saipan, and Guadalcanal. The code was finally declassified in 1968, and President Reagan declared 14 August 1982 National Code Talkers Day to recognize the service of the 420 Code Talkers.

See also:
Cryptology.
References:
Boxler, Margaret T. *Winds of Freedom*. Darien, CT: Two Bytes Publishing Co., 1992.
Escue, Lynn. "Coded Contributions: Navajo Talkers and the Pacific War." *History Today*, July 1991.
Sullivan, Freyda. "The Navajo Code Talkers of World War II." *The Tombstone Epitaph*, December 1996.

Watson, Bruce. "Navajo Code Talkers: A Few Good Men." *Smithsonian*, August 1993.
Wilson, William R. "Code Talkers." *American History*, February 1997.

NAVSTAR

NAVSTAR is a system of 24 satellites in orbits around the earth's poles at altitudes of approximately 10,000 miles (16,000 kilometers). They were placed there by the U.S. Defense Department at a cost of $10 billion and constitute a global positioning system (GPS) that allows military navigators to determine longitude and latitude to within a meter.

The satellites carry atomic clocks that transmit radio signals at very precise moments. Radio receivers are connected to computers that automatically compare the time the signal was sent with the time it is received. Using this information and the fact that radio signals travel at the speed of light (186,000 miles, or 300,000 kilometers, per second), the distance of the receiver from the satellite can be determined. One such signal indicates how far the receiver is from one satellite. A second, third, and fourth signal from three other NAVSTAR satellites provide the data needed to establish a single position, because these four signals can intersect at only one point on the earth's spherical surface. That point is the position of the receiver.

GPS played a significant part in bringing the Gulf War to a speedy conclusion in 1991. Because the military still controls NAVSTAR, the satellites transmit two types of signals. One, received by military personnel, is coded and highly precise; the other is degraded for civilian use and can establish position to within about 100 feet (30 meters). Although the civilian signal is less accurate than the military signal, it is still an amazing feat on a globe 25,000 miles (40,000 kilometers) in circumference. To someone lost in the wilderness, knowing their position on a map to within 100 feet (one-third the length of a football field, or about 1.0 second of longitude or latitude) would be far more accuracy than is needed for that person to decide that he or she is no longer lost.

With GPS, pilots can stay within 10 feet (3 meters) of the glide slope during landings, and airports can operate under all weather conditions. Some cars now equipped with GPS have a map on the dashboard that allows the driver to read the vehicle's location. Handheld GPS receivers the size of a small telephone can be purchased for about $200. These small computerized receivers, which show longitude and latitude on a small screen, can also store in their memories the positions of various landmarks, providing a record for an easy-to-follow return path for long-distance hikers or wilderness explorers.

See also:
Computer; Radio; Satellite.
References:
"Finding the Future." *The Economist*, 6 November 1993.
Gardner, Robert. *Where on Earth Am I?* New York: Watts, 1996.
Mitani, Sam. "GPS and the No-Longer Lost Generation." *Road and Track*, July 1994.
Morrison, Philip, and Phylis Morrison. *The Ring of Truth: An Inquiry into How We Know What We Know*. New York: Random House, 1987.

Newsletter

The newsletter is a specialized publication that is usually dedicated to one subject or organization. The origin of newsletters is unknown, but they flourished in England during the seventeenth century. At a time when the British government controlled printing, newsletters provided a means of circumventing censorship.

Although newsletters declined with the growth of newspapers and magazines during the eighteenth and nineteenth centuries, they became popular again during the twentieth century as a means by which groups and organizations such as libraries, associations, families, alumni organizations, special interest groups, investment companies, retirement plans, travel and health organizations, and others keep members informed of meetings, activities, and changes. Such newsletters are generally free. Master copies are often prepared on a word processor, and

An Air Force Delta II launch vehicle carries the nineteenth NAVSTAR Global Positioning System satellite into orbit on 29 March 1993 at Kennedy Space Center in Florida.

inexpensive copies are made using xerography. The proliferation of microcomputers during the 1980s and 1990s has led to an increased number of newsletters, many of which are available online.

Commercially published newsletters, such as the *Kiplinger Washington Letter*, require a paid subscription and are less numerous than those published by nonprofit organizations whose publishing costs are covered by dues or donations. Most commercial newsletters, a number of which are targeted for the business world, have a smaller circulation than the Kiplinger newsletter and carry a higher subscription price.

See also:
Computer; Publishing; Xerography.

References:
Burns, Robert E. "Homilist: Don't Let Your Golden Chances Pass You By." *U.S. Catholic*, February 1995.
International Encyclopedia of Communications. New York: Oxford University Press, 1989.
Krech, Bob. "Improve Parent Communication with a Newsletter." *Instructor*, September 1995.
Mutter, John. "Del Rey Creates 'Cybercommunity.'" *Publishers Weekly*, 19 December 1994.

Newspaper

A newspaper is an unbound publication, issued daily or at regular intervals, that provides current information printed on large, inexpensive sheets of paper. Depending on the newspaper, that information may include national, international, and local news, as well as information about art, books, computers, finance, home improvements, entertainment, science and technology, sports, and ways to deal with personal problems.

There are approximately 1,800 daily newspapers in the United States, with a total circulation of more than 65 million. Roughly 750 of these dailies publish larger Sunday editions that include an abundance of special news stories, features, and advertising. These papers reach 90 percent of those citizens who can read. In addition, approximately 7,500 newspapers, mostly of a local

nature, are published weekly, semiweekly, or monthly, and an additional 600 free newspapers print news relevant to a particular audience or group of buyers.

The *New York Times, Washington Post,* and *Los Angeles Times* are among the dailies that are generally regarded as being of highest quality. They provide comprehensive and well-written national and international news as well as sound analysis and interpretation of all facets of newsworthy subjects by capable columnists and editors.

In addition to newspapers published in English, approximately 1,000 foreign-language newspapers published in 40 languages are circulated to 9 million readers in the United States. Papers such as the *Chicago Daily Defender, Amsterdam News, Pittsburgh News Courier,* and *Baltimore Afro-American* are published for predominantly African-American readers. A great many school newspapers are also published, and approximately 100 of the nation's 2,000 college papers are published as dailies.

Newspapers are both private, in the sense that they are profit-making businesses, and public because they provide vast quantities of information that the public relies upon. Because of their public nature, newspapers enjoy protection under the First Amendment, as well as lower mail rates. Because of the private nature of the newspaper business, most newspapers depend on advertising to make a profit. Paid subscriptions do not cover the cost of publishing most newspapers.

History

Although newspapers are associated with print, the first documents that provided what is normally regarded as news were handwritten newsletters that contained information about events in Rome and were circulated throughout the rest of the empire. The first printed news, reproduced from wooden type, appeared in China during the seventh century. In Europe members of the Fugger family—German merchants and bankers—circulated a newsletter to literate members of their various holdings during the fifteenth and sixteenth centuries. In London the *Corante* reported news from the European continent on a weekly basis beginning in 1621.

Benjamin Harris published the first newspaper in the American colonies, *Publick Occurrences*, in 1690. Unfortunately, the paper's criticism of government officials was not well received, and Harris's unlicensed paper was shut down immediately after its inaugural edition. A more successful paper was launched in 1704, when John Campbell began publishing the *Boston News-Letter*. Similar newsletters soon evolved into what we regard as newspapers.

Early in the nineteenth century, Friedrich Koenig developed a flatbed cylinder press that used a rotating cylinder instead of a platen (a flat plate) to press sheets of paper against type set in a flatbed. By 1844 Richard Hoe had invented a rotary press in which type was attached to the surface of a rotating cylinder rather than a flatbed. Shortly after Hoe's invention, the *Philadelphia Ledger* was printing at a rate of 8,000 sheets per hour. Hoe's rotary press—together with the web press, which keeps a continuous roll of paper moving through the printing process—led to wide acceptance of the steam-powered automatic rotary cylinder press during the last quarter of the nineteenth century.

While these changes in the printing process were taking place, the price of paper was declining as wood pulp replaced rags as the primary source of paper. These factors, together with the rise of universal education and increased public literacy, led to the rapid growth of newspapers.

In general, late-nineteenth-century newspapers were operated by hard-nosed editors and powerful publishers who maintained personal but independent viewpoints and whose papers were supported by paying subscribers. Dramatic changes took place around the end of the nineteenth century, when papers like Joseph Pulitzer's *New York World* and William Randolph Hearst's *New York Journal* began publishing sensational news, stories, and reports and conducting editorial crusades against certain political and business interests. It was the *World* that introduced the first comic, *The Yellow Kid*, and their lead was soon followed by most newspapers.

Competition for subscribers, particularly in large cities such as New York, led to circulation wars among newspapers and the realization that advertising could provide additional income. By 1900, advertising was a newspaper's primary source of income. This led to further competition among newspapers for advertising, which, in turn, led to more circulation wars because circulation figures were closely watched by advertisers.

Newspapers remained predominantly local until the late twentieth century, when facsimile machines, satellite communication, and fiber-optic cable made possible virtually simultaneous publishing in different parts of the country. Today, the *Wall Street Journal*, *Christian Science Monitor*, *USA Today*, and *New York Times* are truly national newspapers. At the same time, conglomerates have replaced individuals as the owners of newspapers. Today, most local papers are owned by giant corporations that control a large number of newspapers.

Freedom of the Press

Throughout most of its history, the American press has enjoyed a degree of freedom seldom found in other parts of the world where governments frequently own or control news sources. Freedom of the press was regarded as an essential right even before the First Amendment became part of the Constitution in 1791. As early as 1725, Benjamin Edes and John Gill, owners of the *Boston Gazette*, defied authorities and led the revolt against the British Crown. In New York in 1735, Peter Zenger, regarded as the "father of the free press" and the official owner of the *New York Weekly*, was tried for libel under charges brought by the colony's governor. His defender, attorney Andrew Hamilton, argued that true statements published by Zenger could not be regarded as libel, and although truth as a defense against libel did not become part of New York's legal code until 1804, the jury found Zenger innocent of charges brought by an unpopular governor.

Shortly after the government of the United States was initiated in 1789, the freedom of the press was clearly evident as the two opposing political parties—the Democratic Republicans and the Federalists—hurled vitriolic reports at one another. It was nearly another half-century before any newspapers could be regarded as sources of impartial news.

Newspaper Advantages: Convenience and Coverage

A newspaper employs a variety of people: at least one manager, who may also be the owner and publisher of the paper; journalists; editors; reporters, who gather the news; photographers; cartoonists; artists; an advertising department, which designs, sells, and writes the advertising material that sustains the paper; and a printing staff, although printing often is handled by a subcontractor. Together these people can produce a good newspaper—one that is a convenient source of information because it is inexpensive; offers clear presentation of data relevant to the reader in a format that can be reviewed, saved, and copied; provides thorough news coverage on a regular basis; can be read at a time that is convenient to the reader; and provides advertising that is relevant and useful to the price-conscious local reader. A newspaper can also be a place where conflicting political and other ideas can be presented for consideration by an undecided public. At the same time, such a paper, through good reporting, can expose officials who abuse their power.

Newspapers face serious challenges despite the convenience and extensive coverage they offer. Most of today's citizens obtain their news from television viewing, which requires less time and considerably less effort than reading a newspaper. At the same time, there is a growing trend toward obtaining news through the Internet. Nevertheless, newspapers continue to offer thorough and comprehensive information on a wide variety of subjects.

See also:
Censorship; Defamation; Hearst, William

Randolph; Newsletter; Printing; Publishing; Scripps, Edward Wyllis; Zenger Trial.
References:
International Encyclopedia of Communications. New York: Oxford University Press, 1989.
Stauffer, Dennis. *Mediasmart: How to Handle a Reporter, by a Reporter*. Minneapolis: Minne-Apple Press, 1994.
Stephens, Mitchell. *Writing and Reporting the News*. New York: Rinehart & Winston, 1986.
Walter, F. Virginia. *Great Newspaper Crafts*. New York: Sterling, 1991.

Nonverbal Communication

Technically, nonverbal communication—sometimes called body language—involves any communication that does not use words. However, the term usually refers to any means of expression other than voice—body movements, gestures, facial expressions, separation distance, clothing, touch, smell, etc.—that exist when two or more people communicate in each other's presence. Nonverbal communication, accompanied perhaps by grunts, quite possibly was the first means of interpersonal communication among humans or prehumans. We certainly see nonverbal communication among animals and between animals and humans. We respond quite differently, and rightly so, to a growling dog whose ears are laid back than to a silent dog with erect ears and a wagging tail.

Facial expressions are probably the easiest body language to understand. Someone's fear, sadness, anger, disgust, joy, surprise, or sulking is readily communicated by that person's facial expression. Other forms of nonverbal communication, such as posture or positions of arms, legs, feet, shoulders, and hands, unless overt, are more difficult to detect. However, the body language may be there; many people simply do not sense it because they are verbally oriented. This is borne out by the fact that people who are hearing impaired seem to be more capable of interpreting body language than those with a normal sense of hearing.

Nonverbal communication may be unintentional and is often an expression of emotion or attitude. The dilation of the pupil when viewing something pleasant or interesting is a reflex action and a giveaway in a poker game to an opponent who is familiar with this aspect of body language. Body language often modifies a sender's spoken words and may reveal discrepancies between what is said and what is felt. What a person does is often as important as what that person says. A clenched fist in front of a scowling face conveys a very different message than an extended hand and a smile. We all understand the meaning of a thumbs-up sign, a knowing wink, a raised eyebrow, a thumb and index finger joined to form a circle, and the all-too-often clenched fist with raised middle finger. Specific acts often have specific meanings, but nonverbal cues are not always easy to interpret.

See also:
Clothes; Darwin, Charles; Language.

References:
"Body Language." *American Salesman*, September 1996.
Fast, Julius. *Body Language*. New York: Pocket Books, 1970.
Feeney, Sheila. "What I Got When I Acted like a Guy." *Redbook*, April 1995.
McDonald, Kim A. "The Body Language of Leadership." *Chronicle of Higher Education*, 5 January 1996.
Quilliam, Susan. *Body Language*. New York: Crescent Books, 1995.

Number

A number is one of a series of symbols that has a unique meaning in a fixed order. Cardinal numbers, such as 7, 23, or 96, indicate quantity but not order. Ordinal numbers, such as first, second, or third, indicate position in a series or order.

One of the major advances in the history of communication was the development of numbers. It occurred many times in many places and evolved from the simple process of counting, which was used to measure and compare the quantity of objects such as sheep or the passage of time (days, moons, and years).

Although the concept of number devel-

Figure 1. Arabic numerals (a) *compared to our own symbols designating the same numbers* (b).

oped differently in different cultures, there are common elements to be found in all cultures. The Arabic numerals shown in Figure 1 are quite different from our own 1, 2, 3, 4, 5, 6, 7, 8, 9, and 0, but both sets of numerals are abstract symbols with the same meaning. They represent numbers that are distinct from concrete objects. The symbol 8 can represent eight of anything—days, dogs, sticks, or the result of multiplying 4 by 2 or dividing 16 by 2. Although numbers were initially used in physical situations, they can be considered in a purely abstract sense quite apart from actual objects. Mathematically, 2×1 is the same as 4×0.5; however, while you might be content with four half-loaves of bread in place of two whole loaves, you would surely balk at accepting four teacups cut in half as replacements for two intact cups.

Mathematicians tend to use numbers as abstractions; scientists often attach units to numbers to identify what the numbers represent. For example, attaching the unit miles per hour to 50 tells us immediately that we are dealing with a speed—the distance traveled per unit of time. If we multiply speed by time, we can obtain the distance traveled. A speed of 50 miles per hour multiplied by 2 hours gives us a distance of 100 miles. If the same speed is divided by the same time, we obtain 25 miles per hour per hour, or 25 miles/hour^2, which is an acceleration or the rate at which speed increases. If the time were divided by the speed, we would have 0.04 hours^2 per mile, which has no physical significance but is a perfectly valid mathematical operation.

In most cultures, probably because all people normally have ten fingers on which to count, the number base is 10. To indicate anything less than 10, we use the numerals 1 to 9. When we reach 10 we write 10 to show that we have one ten and no numbers less than 10. The number 123 indicates that we have 1 hundred (10 tens), 2 tens (20), and 3 ones. Some cultures developed numbers using a base of 20 (Mayan) and even 60 (Babylonian). It has been suggested that base 12 would be easier to use than base 10 for a number of reasons. The number 10 is divisible by only 1, 2, and 5, but 12 is divisible by 1, 2, 3, 4, and 6. When one-third of 10 is expressed as a decimal, we obtain the never-ending 0.333 . . . , but one-third of 12 would be 4/12, which as a decimal in base 12 would be written 0.4. Of course, a base-12 system would require two more symbols for numbers, so the units might be written 1, 2, 3, 4, 5, 6, 7, 8, 9, _, and Ò. The number that we write as 12 in base 10 would be 10 in base 12, indicating that we have 1 twelve and no ones. Similarly, the number 15 in base 10 would be 13 in base 12 to show 1 twelve and 3 ones. The number 2 _ would indicate 2 twelves and _ (10) ones.

Although the early history of some number systems lacked positional notation, all systems eventually incorporated it. Thus, the position of the numbers and meaning of 345 is very different from 453, 435, 534, 543, or 354. Early Egyptian numerals simply listed the symbols for units, tens, hundreds, and so on. To find the number indicated, they had to add the numbers represented by all the symbols.

Although we accept the symbol zero without a second thought today, its invention was a breakthrough in communication. Many people confuse zero with nothing. But zero is something; it is a number. If a person never opens a bank account at a certain bank, the balance at that bank is nothing; there is no balance, because there is no account there. However, if that person has an account with the bank and writes checks that transfer all the money in that account to others, then the balance is zero.

Zero is a number and is treated as a number. For example, the sum of $5 + 0 = 5$, just as $5 + 1 = 6$ and $5 \times 0 = 0$. The reason that $5 \times 0 =$ 0 is that zero added to itself 5 times (which is what 5×0 means) is 0 ($0 + 0 + 0 + 0 + 0 = 0$). For the same reason, the product of any number multiplied by zero is zero. Zero, however, has some unique qualities. Any number divided by zero, such as $5/0$, is undefined. We know that $6/3 = 2$ because $3 \times 2 = 6$; the divisor times the quotient always equals the dividend. But consider $5/0 = n$, where n is a number. In this case, $n \times 0 \neq 5$; $n \times 0 = 0$. There is no value of n for which $5/0 = n$; division by zero is meaningless.

The invention of zero is the basis for our present system of writing numbers. It is zero that allows us to distinguish 44 from 404 and 440. The zero is a place holder. The number 404 shows us that we have 4 hundreds, 0 tens, and 4 ones. Another way to say the same thing is $4 \times 100 + 0 \times 10 + 4 \times 1$, or $4 \times 10^2 + 0 \times 10^1 + 4 \times 10^0$. In our number system, the numbers to the left of the decimal indicate the number we have used to multiply successive powers of ten (the base of our most common number system). The number 2,345, for example, can be seen to be $2 \times 10^3 + 3 \times 10^2 + 4 \times 10^1 + 5 \times 10^0$. Regardless of the number base used, n^0, where n is any number, is defined as 1. Thus, $1^0 = 1$, $2^0 = 1$, $3^0 = 1$, $4^0 = 1$, ...

As mentioned earlier, a system using base 12 would in many ways be more useful than base 10, which is solely anatomical rather than logical in origin. Computer technology is built on a base-2 number system and has only two numbers, 0 and 1. The number that in base 10 has a value of 44 would be written 101100 in base 2 because

$$101100 = 1 \times 2^5 + 0 \times 2^4 + 1 \times 2^3 + 1 \times 2^2 + 0 \times 2^1 + 0 \times 2^0.$$

Thus, $2^5 + 2^3 + 2^2 = 32 + 8 + 4 = 44$ in base 10.

Base 2 is ideal for computer technology. In computers a series of switches carries out various operations. A 1 can be used to turn a switch on and a 0 to turn it off. Thus, the internal control of computer switches can be built on a binary number system consisting of 1s and 0s.

See also:
Computer; Computer Addition; Mathematics and Communication.
References:
International Encyclopedia of Communications.
New York: Oxford University Press, 1989.
Kline, Morris. *Mathematics and the Physical World*. New York: Crowell, 1959.
Newman, James R., ed. *The World of Mathematics*. New York: Simon & Schuster, 1956.

Oersted, Hans Christian (1777–1851)

Born in Rudkøbing, Langeland, Hans Christian Oersted was the son of a Danish apothecary. Oersted spent part of his childhood teaching himself arithmetic, and when he was 12 he began working in his father's shop. There he developed an interest in chemistry that led him to apply for admission to the University of Copenhagen when he was 17. Six years later, Oersted had his doctorate in medicine. In 1806, at age 29, Oersted returned to his alma mater as professor of physics and chemistry, and in 1829 he was appointed director of the Polytechnic Institute in Copenhagen.

In 1819, reportedly while performing a demonstration to illustrate a point in one of his popular lectures on the independence of electrical and magnetic forces, Oersted made the momentous discovery that made him famous. His discovery, known today as the Oersted effect, revealed a connection between electricity and magnetism, exactly the opposite of what his demonstration was designed to show. He accidentally brought a magnetic compass near a wire that was carrying an electric current. Suddenly the compass needle turned and aligned itself perpendicular to the wire's axis, something that was not supposed to happen according to the belief at that time that electricity and magnetism were completely independent phenomena.

Oersted's discovery that moving electric charges (an electric current) produce a magnetic field that surrounds the current marked the beginning of the study of electromagnetism, and applications of electromagnetism constitute the basic principle underlying many communication devices such as the telegraph, telephone, radio, and television. The announcement of Oersted's discovery in 1820 served to stimulate a flourish of research among such notable scientists as Francois Arago and André-Marie Ampère. Later, Joseph Henry and Michael Faraday showed that just as moving electric charge was always accompanied by an electric current, so could an electric current be induced by a changing magnetic field.

Although Oersted's greatest contribution to science was his discovery of a connection between electricity and magnetism, he was also a very capable chemist. He was the first to isolate the element aluminum by reacting aluminum chloride with sodium.

See also:
Electromagnet; Faraday, Michael; Henry, Joseph; Maxwell, James Clerk; Telegraph; Telephone.

References:
Asimov, Isaac. *Asimov's Biographical Encyclopedia of Science and Technology*. Garden City, NY: Doubleday, 1964.
Gardner, Robert. *Famous Experiments You Can Do*. New York: Watts, 1990.
Holton, Gerald, and Duane H. D. Roller. *Foundations of Modern Physical Science*. Reading, MA: Addison-Wesley, 1958.

Olfactory Communication

Olfactory communication involves the sense of smell. Olfaction is generally recognized as a common means of communication in animals other than humans. Dogs and a number of other animals mark their territory with urine. The urine's odor identifies the boundaries of the animal's territory. The distinct odor of a female mammal in heat will attract males of the same species. Pheromones released by ants upon finding a good source of food leave a scent as the insects return to the anthill. Other ants are attracted by the odor and follow it to the food source. Pheromones released by a female moth can be detected a mile away by males of the same species. Recent research reveals that when male lobsters fight they squeeze the fluid from a previously unrecognized gland into their urine, which is released during the fight. The fluid

197

has a distinct odor that the loser will remember and avoid for a week following the fight.

Olfaction occurs in humans, too, but often goes unrecognized because we rely so heavily on sight and sound for communicating. To see how much can be communicated by the nose, arrange to be guided, blindfolded and with ears plugged, down a city street and into some stores. Smell the freshly baked bread or pies cooking in a bakery; hydrocarbon vapors reveal the proximity of a gasoline station; the distinct odor of chocolate is a clear indicator of a candy store; the odor of oranges and apples reveals a nearby fruit stand; and the aromas from a perfumery are unmistakable. If a similar experiment were conducted in a rural area, the smoke from burning leaves or a wood fire would be recognizable, and the odor of damp pine needles would reveal the presence of that species of tree. The scent of roses early in June would be readily identified, and every country boy or girl would recognize the presence of new-mown hay or a freshly cut lawn.

The sense of smell is initiated by airborne chemicals that stimulate receptors in the olfactory epithelium, a patch of tissue located near the top of the nasal cavity. Impulses set up in these receptors at the end of the olfactory nerves travel to a center in the brain. From there, nerve fibers connect with other parts of the brain that produce arousal, emotions, and cognition. The sense of smell, combined with sense of taste—sweet, sour, salty, and bitter—gives rise to our perception of flavors.

All senses—sight, sound, touch, taste, and smell—can produce vivid memories. But smell is particularly effective in evoking memories, probably because the olfactory nerves connect directly to the parts of the brain where memories are stored. The French novelist Marcel Proust was keenly aware of the childhood memories initiated by tastes and smells, and he recorded many of them.

Social and personal behavior is sometimes determined by olfactory communication. A person with offensive body odor or bad breath is likely to be remembered as someone to avoid. On the other hand, mothers and babies can often identify one another by odor alone. The T-shirts of siblings and offspring can usually be identified by smell. In experiments in which young women were exposed to the pheromone androstenol, the subjects reported increased irritability during menstruation and tended to view their moods as submissive rather than aggressive. Other experiments have shown that exposure to musklike odors or to secretions from human armpits can change the timing of menstrual periods.

Research in olfactory communication is in its infancy. However, if olfaction effects identified in social animals can be identified in humans, the findings could have a profound effect on our understanding of human conduct and communication.

References:

Budiansky, Stephen. "What Animals Say." *U.S. News & World Report*, 5 June 1995.
International Encyclopedia of Communications. New York: Oxford University Press, 1989.
Restak, Richard. *The Brain.* New York: Bantam Books, 1984.

Online Services

Online services are accessed by a computer connected to a phone line through a modem. In addition to providing E-mail service that allows users to send messages through phone lines to other computers, commercial online services provide access to information-rich databases on virtually every major subject area, provide up-to-date world and national news, connect computers to national networks, open bulletin boards where ideas are shared about special interests, enable users to shop online for a great variety of items, help students with their homework or offer them a variety of games, provide up-to-the-minute stock quotes and other financial data, and allow access to a vast number of free files and software.

America Online (AOL) is the largest of the commercial online services. Choosing the Internet connection on AOL's opening screen will lead the user to a menu that provides easy access to all facets of the Internet. CompuServe, the oldest online service, provides services similar to AOL, as do Prodigy, Delphi, eWorld, GEnie, and other commercial online servers.

In 1996, these commercial online services charged approximately $10 per month for four to five hours of access, and additional access was available at an hourly fee of $3 to $5 per hour. To meet competition, AOL in the fall of 1996 offered unlimited access for $19.95 per month. The result was a dramatic increase in subscribers, many of whom maintained their connections around the clock. The increased use made access difficult for many customers, and threats of a class-action suit were discussed.

To combat the accessibility of pornography and other material deemed inappropriate for children, CompuServe in 1996 introduced Wow, which is designed for families and offers distinctly different versions for adults and children. It provides a master account for an adult and five subaccounts for other family members. If any subaccount is designated as a child's account, a special children's version will appear when the child logs on. The children's version offers no chat rooms and limits users' access to preapproved Web sites. It is also possible for parents to screen all E-mail before it reaches their children's mailboxes.

Users who log onto the Internet for a significant number of hours can face connection charges amounting to hundreds of dollars each month. For these users, access can also be obtained through local and national Internet service providers such as NetCom, Performance Systems International (PSInet), and UUnet at a flat fee of $20 to $30 per month without time limits. However, because of the growing number of Net surfers, patrons are often frustrated by busy phone lines.

In March 1996, AT&T offered its 80 million customers five hours of free Internet access per month or unlimited access for $20 per month on its new Worldnet. For many AT&T customers, and others who switched

to AT&T, this low cost paved the pathway to the Internet.

See also:
American Telephone & Telegraph Company; Computer; Internet; Modem.

References:
Ayre, Rick. "New Paths to the Net." *PC Magazine*, 10 October 1995.
Gorman, Christine. "AT&T Rewires the Net." *Time*, 11 March 1996.
Levine, John R., and Carol Baroudi. *The Internet for Dummies*, 2nd ed. Foster City, CA: IDG Books, 1994.

Oratory
Oratory is the art of using effective speech in front of an audience so that it accepts the orator's point of view. Oratory is usually, but not necessarily, associated with political or legal settings.

Unlike the ordinary speech used in conversation, oratory is more formal and makes greater use of parallelism, aphorisms, metaphors, and similes. Many orators also use humor to gain an audience's attention, initiate a more relaxed atmosphere, or make those present aware that the speaker has a sense of humor, which is regarded as an admirable quality by today's society.

In addition to language skills, successful oratory involves tempo, voice volume and quality, gestures, expressions, and knowing when to pause. People do not appreciate monotony, whining, stiff posture, or rapid-fire speech. With the rise of television and the capacity of its zoom lens–equipped cameras to cover a TV screen with an orator's face alone, expression and good looks have become increasingly important in oratory.

The oldest existing text on oratory is Aristotle's *Rhetoric* (ca. 330 B.C.), in which he describes three kinds of oratory—forensic, deliberative, and ceremonial. Forensic oratory, which is used in courts, is designed to prove innocence or guilt. Deliberative oratory seeks, by using reason, emotion, the orator's charisma, or all three, to convince an audience that a particular idea or action is appropriate or inappropriate. Ceremonial oratory, which is delivered at funerals, inaugurations, dedications, and various opening ceremonies, usually involves praise and sentiment.

See also:
Forensics; Homiletics.
References:
International Encyclopedia of Communications. New York: Oxford University Press, 1989.
"'Iron Curtain' Speech Recalled." *American History*, March/April 1996.
Lind, Michael. "Jordan's Rules." *New Republic*, 12 February 1996.
Robinson, William C. *Oratory: A Manual for Advocates.* Littleton, CO: Rothman, 1993.
Rosenblatt, Roger. "Mr. Speaker." *New Republic*, 26 December 1994.

Oscillator

An oscillator is a device that produces a periodic change in the direction of flow of electrical charges. Charges will flow, usually for a short period, in one direction and then flow in the opposite direction. The simplest oscillator consists of a capacitor and inductor. The periodic oscillation of charge is analogous to the up-and-down motion of a mass attached to the end of a suspended spring. The mathematical equations that describe the two types of oscillation are very similar.

The changing direction of charge flow produced by an oscillator is accompanied by the generation of electromagnetic waves. Thus, oscillators lie at the very heart of transmitters used to send the electromagnetic waves used by such communication devices as radio, radio telephony, television, and radar, as well as sound and signal generators and other electronic instruments.

The earliest oscillator used by Hertz to generate electromagnetic waves was an inductance-capacitor circuit that, when connected to a spark gap, produced an oscillating flow of charge accompanied by sparks. The electrical energy surged back and forth until it was dissipated as radiation and heat in the circuit. In other words, the oscillations were damped. Later oscillators used triode vacuum tubes (and more recently, transistors) to take some of the output energy, amplify it, and feed it back into the circuit to maintain a signal of constant strength.

Where an extremely stable frequency is required, crystal oscillators are used. These oscillators can produce a signal frequency that is constant to within 1 part in 20 million. The frequency of the waves generated at a radio station may be controlled by a quartz crystal vibrating at its natural frequency, a frequency that depends on the size of the crystal.

The principle underlying crystal oscillators is the piezoelectric effect. When pressure is applied to certain crystals, such as quartz, a voltage develops across the crystal as positive charges are forced one way and negative charges are forced in the opposite direction. In effect, squeezing the crystal turns it into a battery that can drive charge around a circuit. The reverse holds true as well. When a potential difference is applied to a quartz crystal, it vibrates, producing a voltage that oscillates at the same frequency as the crystal. The steady oscillating voltage from the crystal can be used to drive charges up and down an antenna, which results in the formation of electromagnetic waves. In the case of radio transmission, these carrier waves are modulated and amplified before they reach the antenna.

See also:
Hertz, Heinrich Rudolf; Maxwell, James Clerk; Modulation; Radar; Radio; Television.

Pager

A pager is a device used to alert users that they are being paged and should respond by making a telephone call. The pager is essentially a radio receiver that produces a distinct tone or buzz when activated by a signal. The pager has its own telephone number. When that number is dialed by a caller, the signal goes to a special network, where a transmitter sends a radio wave frequency to which the pager is pretuned.

With some pagers, the telephone number of the caller is indicated on the device itself. In less sophisticated models, the person receiving the signal is expected to call a base number where the base telephone is located. This might be an office, hospital, or police, fire, or emergency station.

See also:
Electromagnetic Waves; Radio; Telephone.

Pen

A pen is an implement used for writing or drawing with ink or a similar fluid. The word *pen* comes from the Latin word *penna,* meaning "feather."

Before there were pens, the conventional instrument for writing was the stylus, a bone, reed, or wooden twig used to make impressions on wet clay tablets that were hardened in ovens. The stylus is identified primarily with the ancient Middle Eastern civilizations of Sumer, Babylon, and Assyria. The Greeks and Romans also employed styli of iron, silver, bronze, or other hard substances to write on wooden boards coated with wax. One end of the stylus was sharp and did the etching; the rounded opposite end was used to smooth out mistakes. The Chinese used brushes of camel or rat hair for writing.

The earliest direct ancestor of the modern pen may well be the reed pens of ancient Egypt. The availability of papyrus sheets required a more delicate tool than the stylus, and the plentiful Nile reeds fulfilled the need. In about 3000 to 2800 B.C., the Egyptians began using reeds, rushes, or pieces of bamboo that were frayed or curved to a

point to apply ink to papyrus. The tubular implements supported a narrow column of fluid, similar to a straw in a drink, which was slowly released by skilled scribes to produce written work. The reed pen was used extensively throughout the Mediterranean basin and western Asia during the Greek and Roman era and until the Middle Ages.

Reeds may have been the first pens, but experimentation continued in the quest to acquire more efficient writing tools. As writing spread throughout Europe, reeds were not always available, and alternative means of writing became necessary. The quill pen reigned as the standard writing implement from its introduction in about the sixth century B.C. until the mid–nineteenth century. It is uncertain when and where pens of bird feathers were first introduced, but the work of Saint Isidore of Seville (ca. A.D. 560–636) contained an early reference to quills, and it seems reasonable to assume that the pen was used earlier. Operating on a principle similar to the reed pen, the tubelike quill offered more control in writing and neater, finer results. Its flexible tip made it more durable. Quills were made from the flight feathers of large birds, usually swans, geese, or turkeys. Left wing feathers were considered the best because their curvature was better suited to right-handed writers, and goose quills were preferred because of their strength. The nib (the point of the pen) had to be constantly resharpened with a small knife fittingly called a penknife, a form of which survives today as the pocketknife.

The quill pen had two obvious disadvantages. First, it only held enough ink to write a few words, and consequently the ink supply had to be constantly replenished by dipping.

Second, it had a very short life span because of wear from resharpening and the aging process. Attempts to solve the writing tip problem saw the marketing, with little success, of nibs made from animal horn, tortoise shell, or costly gold. The pioneering work in the 1780s of John Mitchell, a native of Birmingham, England, led to the mass production of inexpensive, longer-lasting steel-tipped pens after 1830. Although steel pens were hailed as a modern breakthrough at the time, archeologists at Pompeii and sites in England and Germany later discovered that ancient Romans also had metal pens, although they do not appear to have been widely used. By the middle of the nineteenth century, the quill pen followed its predecessor, the reed pen, into obscurity.

The steel-tipped pen had a hairline split that divided the nib into two parts. Just above the split, the two halves formed a reservoir that filled as the pen was dipped in ink. Gravity and capillary action conducted the ink from the reservoir down the split in the nib to the paper. Writing implements had improved significantly since the time of Sumer, but eliminating the inconvenience of continually dipping the pen remained a problem.

Fountain pens, initially called reservoir pens because they held their own ink supply, appeared very early in England. Samuel Pepys, the diarist, recorded that he had one in 1663, and in 1738 Ephrain Chamber's *Cyclopedia* described the implement. Early designs by two Englishmen, Joseph Bramah (1809) and John Joseph Parker (1832), assured an even flow of ink to the tip, but the prototypes were plagued by leaking and clotting. It was left to an American inventor, L. E. Waterman, to devise the first practical fountain pen in 1884.

The initial Waterman model, although it eliminated dipping, had to be carefully filled with an eyedropper, a time-consuming process. In 1908, his company perfected a self-filling pen that used a lever on the exterior of the pen, which was pulled up to expel air from a flexible reservoir sac in the barrel of the pen. When the lever was released, a vacuum was created, and ink from a container flowed into the reservoir sac. Gravity and the capillary action then caused the highly fluid ink to flow to the steel tip. Pressure on the flexible nib began the process of drawing ink to the writing point. Waterman's product was so successful that his name became synonymous with the fountain pen. His pens came to symbolize status and prestige and were often selected as gifts for special occasions like birthdays or graduations.

The most recent innovation in fountain pen design was the introduction of the cartridge pen. In this fountain pen, an ink-filled cartridge is placed in a chamber in the barrel. As the most prevalent and best-selling fountain pen, it has eliminated the mess of filling the reservoir.

The successor to the fountain pen, the ballpoint pen, appeared during World War II. This was not the first incarnation of today's most popular pen, however. The earliest patent on a crude conception of the ballpoint belongs to John Loud. Loud's revolutionary 1888 proposal called for replacing the nib with a small ball housed in a socket that had tiny grooves in it to lubricate and distribute ink around the ball.

Loud's device never made a ripple in the writing market, and it was not until 50 years later that Lazlo and George Biro finally developed a workable, marketable ballpoint pen. The two Hungarian brothers—Lazlo, a printer's proofreader, and George, a chemist—experimented throughout the 1930s and finally produced a ballpoint pen in 1938. With the advent of World War II, the brothers migrated to Argentina and continued work on the project. By taking advantage of wartime technological improvements in precision-ground ball bearings, they were able to begin small-scale production. Balls of steel, brass, or tungsten were bathed in ink from a reservoir on top of the tip. Relying on gravity, ink from the tube entered improved feed channels and fed the ball, which rotated and transferred ink to the surface. The dependency on a gravity feed explains why pens do not function well, even today, when the point is higher than the end of the pen. When the pen was not in use, the ball sealed the end of the reservoir and prevented the ink from drying out. In 1943, a British financier, Henry Martin, established a factory in England, and the durable, dependable "writing stick" became standard issue for Royal Air Force pilots in the closing days of World War II. Martin's firm was eventually bought out by the French company BIC, which went on to develop the inexpensive disposable pens that are familiar today.

Americans were not far behind the Europeans in grasping the potential of the Biros's innovation. In 1945, Milton Reynolds, a Chicago businessman on a trip to Argentina, was intrigued by the Biros's nibless pens and bought some as he returned to the United States. Upon his return he discovered the Loud patent, but he was resourceful enough to modify the Biro pen without infringing on the patent. In October 1945, a New York department store offered the new device for a "modest" $12.50. Long lines of customers scooped up the new pens, and the store sold 25,000 in a week. The commercial success of the ballpoint did not end developmental problems, however. The steel balls often stuck, causing messy blots. The supposedly leakproof pens leaked, the ink had a tendency to smudge, and the pens skipped. Modifications, such as quick-drying ink developed by American chemist Francis Set in 1949 and microscopic scuffing of the smooth stainless steel ball, eventually led the ballpoint to replace the fountain pen as the writing implement of choice.

Since the early 1960s, two new writing instruments have reached the marketplace— soft-tip and roller-ball pens. Soft-tip pens, sometimes referred to as felt tips, are named for the writing point of the pen, which is usually a porous material of hard felt or fiber bundles with a sponge-like reservoir. One or more narrow channels feed the tip through capillary action as soon as the pen begins to write. Roller-ball pens combine features of ballpoint and fountain pens. As in the ballpoint, there is a ball that rotates in a socket at the tip, but the ink is the more fluid type used in fountain pens. Roller balls can have either a capillary reservoir, like the soft-tip pens, or a reservoir like the ballpoint.

Specialty pens are designed for a specific purpose. For example, a lettering pen used to create calligraphy may have a number of interchangeable points designed to create different types of characters. Other examples are pens used in drafting or mechanical drawing.

See also:
Pencil; Writing.

References:
Grigson, Geoffrey, and Charles Harvard Gibbs-Smith, eds. *Things*. New York: Hawthorn Books, 1957.
Panati, Charles. *Browser's Book of Beginnings*. Boston: Houghton Mifflin, 1984.

Pencil

The pencil is the most common and widely used implement for writing, marking, or drawing. A pencil consists of a solid core of marking material wrapped in a holder of wood, plastic, or metal. Roughly 10 billion pencils are produced worldwide annually, with the United States accounting for 2 billion of the total, or almost ten pencils for every American. Mislabeled as the "lead pencil," the pencil contains no lead and never has. The core of a pencil is a mixture of graphite and clay, which serves as the marking substance.

The use of a solid marking material to draw or write is as old as man's earliest efforts to communicate. In prehistoric times, soft rocks or charred wood were used to draw on hard rock surfaces. The ancient Romans and Greeks used lead or silver to write, and their choice of material extended to the Middle Ages. The earliest direct ancestor of the modern pencil stems from the discovery in 1564 of a large and unusually pure deposit of graphite near Borrowdale, England. Incorrectly believed to be a form of lead, and called black lead or plumbago, graphite was cut into small square sticks and used for writing. A major difficulty was that graphite often left as much residue on the users' hands as it did on paper. To remedy this, string or twine was wrapped around the stick. The string could be unwound to expose more writing material, and the innovation was referred to as a "lead pen." In 1565, Conrad Gesner, a German naturalist, made the earliest known reference to a pencil when he described putting graphite into a wooden holder to record his notes and make sketches. In 1779, Carl Wilhelm Scheele, a Swedish chemist, realized that the writing substance was a form of carbon, and in 1789 the new element was christened graphite from the Greek *graphen*, "to write." Germans were the earliest producers of cased pencils, graphite sealed in a wooden sheath. The Faber family of Nuremberg was especially prominent in manufacturing pencils. In 1861, Eberhard Faber, grandson of the founder of the Faber company in Germany, established the first full-scale pencil factory in the United States. It was not until the start of the nineteenth century that pencils were widely used, and even then they posed no real threat to the quill pen as the preeminent writing instrument.

The Borrowdale mine produced natural graphite for more than 200 years, but by the 1700s the mine was depleted, and pencil usage declined despite the discovery of other graphite deposits. The turnaround for the pencil came in 1795, when Nicholas Jacques Conte, a Frenchman, invented the process that is still fundamentally the way pencils are produced today. Conte devised a blend of powdered graphite and clay. His mixture was as smooth as graphite but more durable, which made pencils more reliable. The two ingredients were mixed with water, and the pasty result was put into long, thin molds. The mixture was then dried and fired in a kiln, creating sticks of graphite. Conte also realized that varying the ratio of clay to graphite would create a harder or softer writing core. Less clay and more graphite created a softer core, which made dark, heavy lines. More clay and less graphite made a harder core, which produced a finer, lighter line. Today, hardness is designated by numbers from 1 (the softest) to 4 (the hardest). Number 2 is the most commonly used pencil today. In 1896, Edward G. Ackeson, an American inventor, developed a process to make synthetic graphite from coke, and today all pencils in the United States use manufactured graphite rather than the natural form.

There are three main types of pencils: colored, cased, and mechanical. Colored pencils became widespread after 1850, when the invention of aniline dyes made colored cores possible. The combination of pigments and dyes is created in the same manner as the core of a standard pencil, but it is not kiln dried.

Cased pencils outsell all other writing instruments and are the most commonly used pencils today. They consist of a wooden case and a black writing core. Cedar is the wood of choice for the casing because it is straight grained, easily cut, and does not splinter or warp. Cedar logs are sawed into narrow strips, called slats, which are dried, stained, and waxed before shipment to the factory. In the early 1800s, William Moore and James Dixon, two American investors working separately, contributed to perfecting a machine to cut and groove the slats. A grooved half-slat is coated with glue, the core is added, and a similarly grooved half-slat is pressed on top. Pencils are manufactured primarily in round and hexagonal forms. Hexagonal is preferred because the flat sides prevent the pencil from rolling off flat surfaces, and the hexagonal shape produces more pencils per slat than the round. In 1858, Hyman Lipman, a Philadelphia inventor, added the final touch to the modern pencil. His addition at the upper end of the pencil was a small metal band, called a ferrule, which held an eraser. Lipman sold his pencil-with-eraser patent in 1872 to Joseph Rechendorfer of New York for $100,000.

The inconvenience and mess of sharpening pencils was eliminated by the mechanical pencil. First marketed in 1822, the mechanical pencil was the creation of S. Morden and J. I. Hawkins, two British inventors. The metal or plastic case uses the same core material as the older wooden pencil, but with a continuous mechanical feed of the lead to the tip.

See also:
Pen; Writing.
Reference:
Petroski, Henry. *The Pencil: A History of Design and Circumstance*. New York: Knopf, 1992.

Phonograph

The first device used to play back recorded sound, the phonograph was invented by Thomas Edison in 1877. To record sound, Edison used a thin metal diaphragm that vibrated in response to sound waves. A metal stylus attached to the diaphragm transferred the vibrations to a sheet of waxed paper or tinfoil fixed to a cylinder that rotated beneath the stylus. The stylus vibrated up and down with the same frequency as the sound waves that struck the attached diaphragm, at an amplitude corresponding to the loudness of the sound. Initially the cylinder was rotated by hand; later, spring-driven and electric motors were developed. By mounting the cylinder on a long horizontal screw, Edison was able to make the cylinder move sideways beneath the stylus as it rotated. As a result of these two simultaneous motions, the stylus recorded sound as continuous undulating spiral track in the wax or metal.

To play back the recording, Edison simply reversed the procedure. As the stylus retraced the spiral track, its vibrations were passed back to the diaphragm and from there were amplified mechanically by a megaphone-like horn. This principle can be demonstrated by sticking a common pin through the narrow end of a simple megaphone made from a sheet of rolled paper. With the pin resting gently in the groove of an old record placed on a turntable, sound will be heard coming from the wide end of the megaphone as the record rotates.

Edison's invention enhanced his fame but not his fortune. Although people were intrigued by a device that could record sound, few enjoyed listening to the recordings. The sound that came from the primitive phonograph was quite different from the sound that went into the recording. Furthermore, there was no way to make a copy of a recording. A second record could be made only by having the performer repeat the performance, and recordings would wear out after a few playings. In 1886, Chichester Bell found a way to improve Edison's phonograph. He coated the cylinder with a harder wax, which greatly improved the life span of a recording.

Two years later Emile Berliner invented the disc record. The disc was placed horizontally on a machine he called the Gramophone. As the record turned, a stylus connected to a horn vibrated back and forth rather than up and down, as Edison's had. Disc records eventually proved to be more popular than Edison's cylinders and produced a larger volume of sound. Furthermore, Berliner's invention greatly improved the market for sound recordings because it was possible to make copies of a disc record. The original recording could be electroplated, and the resulting copper plate could serve as a master disc for pressing large numbers of copies on hard, shellac resin discs. Using Berliner's recording method, a band had to play but once in order for thousands of people to hear the same sounds on phonographs in homes around the world. By the early 1900s, Enrico Caruso and other celebrities were recording regularly.

During the 1920s, some manufacturers began to use electric rather than windup spring motors to rotate the turntables on which the records were played. Even so, they continued to make spring-driven phonographs because many homes did not have electricity.

By the late 1920s, electricity was used to record and play sound as well as turn the discs. The output from a microphone, which converts sound waves into electrical pulses analogous to the sounds, can be amplified and used to drive the stylus, which cuts a groove in the wax or lacquer coating on a master disc. A precise screw moves the cutting head across the disc as it rotates, producing a single spiral groove in the disc.

A family listens to a coin-operated phonograph on a street corner in Salina, Kansas, ca. 1890s. Lloyd C. Mitchell, the only man in the photograph and owner of the machine pictured here, kept his phonograph at street corners to attract potential customers.

Similarly, when a record copied from the master disc is played, wire coils attached to a vibrating stylus passing along the recorded groove move in the field of a permanent magnet and set up electric currents. These electrical pulses are amplified and sent to a loudspeaker that produces the same sounds used to make the recording.

During the 1940s, plastics began to replace shellac resin in making records. The use of plastic led to long-playing (LP) records because with plastic it was possible to use a narrower and more closely packed groove. Stereophonic sound recordings appeared during the 1950s. Two widely separated microphones are used in making stereo records, and the signals from each microphone are used to cut two separate tracks, one on either wall of a single groove. When such a record is played, each track is amplified by a separate channel in the stereo amplifier and fed to a separate loudspeaker. Using two loudspeakers, the listener hears the slight differences in sound picked up by the two microphones, just as each ear picks up slightly different sounds. The brain senses the slight differences, producing a three-dimensional quality that gives the listener a sense of "being there."

See also:
Compact Disc; Microphone; Tape Recorder.
References:
How It Works: The Illustrated Encyclopedia of Science and Technology, vol. 15. New York and London: Marshall Cavendish, 1978.
Macaulay, David. *The Way Things Work.*

Boston: Houghton Mifflin, 1988.
The New Book of Popular Science. Danbury, CT: Grolier, 1992.
Science and Technology Illustrated, vol. 15. Chicago: Encyclopedia Britannica, 1984.Williams, Trevor I. *The History of Invention: From Stone Axes to Silicon Chips.* New York: Facts on File, 1987.

Photocell
See Diode; Photoelectric Cell.

Photoelectric Cell

A photoelectric cell is a device that converts light energy to electrical energy. Photoelectric cells are used extensively in a variety of communication technologies, including burglar alarms, motion picture sound tracks, light meters, and supermarket scanners.

The photoelectric effect—the release of electrons when certain surfaces are illuminated—was discovered by Heinrich Hertz in the late nineteenth century and explained a few years later by Albert Einstein. If we consider light to be made up of photons whose energy is proportional to the light's wavelength (light appears to be both wave and particle in nature), we find that the energy of the photons is proportional to the frequency of the light or inversely proportional to its wavelength. When these photons are absorbed by atoms in a photoelectric surface, electrons will escape provided the energy of the photons exceeds the energy binding the electrons to the atoms. Thus, there is a threshold frequency for a photoelectric surface. For example, if electrons begin to be emitted when yellow light strikes a certain photoelectric surface, there will be no emission if red light is used, because it has a lower frequency and less energy than yellow light. On the other hand, blue light, which has a greater frequency, will emit electrons with considerably more energy. The emitted electrons can be collected to produce an electric current. The energy of the photoelectrons can be measured by applying a retarding voltage to the cell. The energy per electron will equal the retarding voltage (1 volt = 1.6×10^{-19} joules/electron) at the point that the current is reduced to zero.

Modern photoelectric cells are generally made with semiconducting materials such as silicon. If light falling on the semiconductor contains photons with energy equal to or larger than the gap between the valence and conduction bands, electrons in the valence band can absorb the photons and jump to the conduction band, increasing the conductivity of the semiconductor. The resulting electric current will be proportional to the intensity of the light. This photoelectric current can be amplified and used as an electrical signal or to control other circuits.

See also:
Burglar Alarm; Compact Disc; Diode; Motion Pictures; Smoke Detector; Universal Product Code.

Photography

Photography is a process by which two-dimensional images are produced on sensitized surfaces by means of light. The term photography means "writing with light."

Most communicators would agree that "a photograph is worth a thousand words," whether spoken or written. Rather than try to explain the appearance of a new baby in a lengthy letter, the parents send a photograph. Instead of describing what the bride wore, her mother sends a photograph of the wedding. Photographs enable humans to tie together and remember moments in their lives. Family picnics, babies, graduations, religious ceremonies, team and class pictures, and views seen on trips to foreign lands can all be seen again in photographs.

However, photographs play an important role in communication beyond family records of life's moments. Photographs are widely used in entertainment, including motion pictures; in advertising, where seeing a photograph of the object communicates much more than a lengthy description; as a source of legal evidence in courts and in forensic science; in medicine, where X rays, CAT scans, and MRIs have become routine diagnostic tools; and in identifying chemical components through spectroscopy. In many other ways photography provides a way to communicate useful information or set a mood. Microelectronics is possible only through the optical reduction of circuits that can then be photographically etched onto the tiny silicon chips so critical in the development of current information technology.

History of Photography

Some sixteenth-century Italian artists made use of the camera obscura—a small windowless room with a tiny pinhole on one side through which light can enter. When light from a natural scene passes through a pinhole, it creates an inverted image of the scene outside on a paper or canvas within the camera obscura. The artist can then paint the perfectly scaled scene using colors that match those of nature as closely as possible.

To make a simple pinhole image of the sun, use a pin to punch a small hole in the center of a file card. Turn the file card toward the sun and hold a second card beneath the pinhole. The sun's image will appear on the lower card. If the distance between the cards is increased, the sun's image will grow larger.

A century later, a lens was often used in place of the pinhole to form an image in the camera obscura. Many people recognized the similarity between a lens-based camera obscura and the human eye. Experiments with dissected animal eyes revealed that inverted images do form on the retinas of eyes, and the human eye has been likened to a camera ever since. Of course, the images formed by a camera obscura could not be moved and were not permanent. The images faded with darkness or as thick clouds covered the sun.

In 1725, Johann Heinrich Schulze at the University of Alfdorf discovered that chalk moistened with silver nitrate and nitric acid would darken when exposed to light. It was another century, however, before anyone combined this knowledge with the camera obscura to form images that could be preserved. By the late 1700s, new elements were being discovered and chemistry was growing at an accelerated pace. The develop-

An 1889 Kodak ad reads "You press the button, we do the rest." Eastman's $25 Kodak camera allowed anyone—regardless of film processing and developing knowledge—to take pictures.

ments in chemistry, coupled with a knowledge of how to form images using pinholes, lenses, and concave mirrors, led to optimism about the possibility of making images that could be preserved.

In the 1790s, Humphry Davy and Thomas Wedgewood discovered a way to make photograms. They pressed leaves, lace, and other finely structured objects against pieces of leather that had been soaked in a solution of silver nitrate and then exposed the combination to sunlight. Clear images of the objects appeared on the leather after a few hours, but the images faded with time as the silver nitrate darkened.

In 1824, Claude and Joseph Nicéphore Niepce developed a system they called heliography. They coated a lithographic stone with a bituminous lacquer, placed it in a camera, and exposed the stone to images made by bright reflected sunlight for eight hours or more. A distinct image could be seen on the stone.

Five years later, Joseph Nicéphore Niepce and Louis Daguerre joined forces to improve and commercialize heliography; however, through persistence and luck, Daguerre, a Parisian painter with no background in science, discovered a much better means of obtaining and preserving images. His process, which became known as the daguerreotype, was purchased by the French government in 1839 and was never patented.

Daguerreotypes were made by coating a copper plate with silver iodide. The plate was then placed in a camera, exposed for approximately 30 minutes in bright light, and then developed by exposing it to mercury vapors. The images were quite clear, and the process was relatively inexpensive. Within a short time improvements in the chemistry of the daguerreotype reduced exposure time to a minute or less and made it possible to take studio portraits—the first commercial use of photography. A commercial use for daguerreotypes gave rise to an industry that supplied materials to professional photographers.

While the daguerreotype made commercial photography possible, its end product was a single photograph. For patrons wanting copies of their portraits, a second sitting was necessary. However, at the same time that the daguerreotype was being developed in France, W. H. F. Talbot, an Englishman, was developing the first system to use negatives from which positive copies could be made. Talbot impregnated paper with silver salts. Exposure to light produced negative images on the paper, which he then washed with a solution that "fixed" them. From the negatives, positive prints could be made in abundance.

By 1841, Talbot had patented the calotype process, by which negatives could be produced with exposure times as short as one second. The major fault with the process was that the fibrous paper negatives provided prints that lacked fine detail.

In 1851, another Englishman, Frederick Scott Archer, invented the wet-plate process, which provided very satisfactory images. In wet-plate photography, a glass plate was dipped into a solution of silver nitrate immediately before it was exposed in a camera. The exposure time could be as short as a half-second in very bright light, but the plate had to be developed immediately. Once developed, the plate could be used to make high-quality prints at low cost. Although a wet-plate photographer had to carry a heavy load of equipment to take photographs outside a studio, Archer's invention led to a rapid expansion of commercial photography. Soon books and newspapers were being printed with photographs to accompany stories, articles, or explanations.

The Rise of Modern Photography

Until 1874, photographers had to make their own plates and paper for prints, but in that year George Eastman, using the results of extensive research by many, developed a method for placing emulsions of silver salts in gelatin on long strips of paper, and later celluloid, that could be rolled on a spool and stored for months. Eastman's work was not only a boon for professional photographers; it opened the way for amateur photographers as well. By 1888, Eastman was promoting his Kodak camera with the words, "You press the button—we do the rest!" Just as a person with no knowledge of mechanics can drive an automobile, so the amateur armed with a Kodak could, with reasonable care, take high-quality photographs without knowing anything about the science or technology associated with cameras, lenses, film, or film processing and developing. The first Kodak camera, which held enough film for 100 negatives, had to be returned for development and reloading, but the camera was soon changed so that rolls of film could be removed and replaced easily by the owner. In recent years, single-use cameras, similar to the original preloaded Kodaks, have become increasingly popular. Of approximately 70 million cameras sold annually in the United States, 75 percent are the single-use variety. They appeal to amateurs because the most frequent cause of failure—improper loading—is avoided.

Significant improvements have been made in photographic products since Eastman's Kodak camera and roll film first became available, but Eastman established the basic model for photography for the next century. Today, we have cameras with wide-aperture lenses, much faster exposure times for film that is more sensitive and less grainy, and electric lights that negate the need for sunlight. We have orthochromatic and panchromatic films that are sensitive to all wavelengths of visible light, an improvement over Eastman's early film, which responded primarily to the shorter wavelengths—the violet and blue end of the visible spectrum. We also have cameras with miniature electronics that automatically focus and adjust exposure time on the basis of available light. However, the two major developments in photography during the twentieth century were the development of color film for popular use and Edwin Land's Polaroid camera.

Film used to produce colored transparencies (slides) was available in the 1930s, but widespread use of film from which colored prints could be developed did not occur until the 1950s. Land's Polaroid camera, in which development of the film took place within the camera, allowing almost instant availability of prints, was introduced in 1946. By 1963, Polaroid cameras that could produce colored prints were available.

Film and Darkrooms

When black-and-white film in a camera is exposed to light, photons striking the crystals of silver salts in the emulsion coating the plastic film begin to change the silver ions in the salts to metallic silver. Fine particles of silver are black, and it is these particles that ultimately give rise to an image. Before it is processed, film that has been rewound in a cartridge within a camera must be wound onto a reel in a darkroom to avoid further exposure. The film is then immersed in a developing solution that increases the concentration of silver in those portions of the film that were exposed to light. A second solution—a stop bath—is then used to stop the action of the developer. Next, the film is placed in a fixing solution to remove silver salts that may remain. Once the film is fixed, the image is permanent and the film insensitive to light. Finally, the film is washed and dried.

At this point, the frames of film consist of negatives; that is, the regions of the image where light was intense are black, and areas that were not exposed are white because no silver was deposited. An image of a black square on a white background will appear as a white square on a black background on the negative. Enlarged images formed by shining light through a negative and a lens can be imposed on light-sensitive paper to produce a positive image. The images will be positive (similar to the original image in the camera) because, using the example cited, little light will pass through the dark background in the negative, and much light will pass through the white square. The paper is then developed into prints in a manner similar to the way film is developed to form negatives.

Coming Innovations

In 1996, Eastman Kodak, together with Fuji, Nikon, Canon, and Minolta, introduced the Advanced Photo System (APS). APS is designed to make film loading foolproof. A plastic film canister, about the size of an AA battery, is simply dropped into a small, thin APS camera, where it is automatically wound. The frames of the film are only two-thirds as long as those on the now-popular 35-millimeter film. However, Eastman Kodak maintains that prints made from these smaller frames cannot be distinguished from those obtained with today's standard film. Even though APS film is made of a new thinner material, the chemical process involved in developing it is unchanged. After it is developed, the film can be rewound into the same cartridge that was dropped into the camera, which reduces the chance of damaging or losing negatives.

The so-called smart film has magnetic strips on which data can be recorded. The camera is equipped with sensors that allow it to transmit information onto the film. As the film is used, information about date, time, exposure speed and number, and format are recorded on the film. The data is then read by newly designed photofinishing machines that respond to the data and print pertinent information on the back of each print. It is also possible to change the length-to-width ratio of pictures as they are taken. The companies believe that the new system will increase sales of cameras, film, prints, and enlargements by as much as a third and expand the market among the 3 billion people who have yet to buy a camera. However, critics are skeptical because so many people feel comfortable using the cameras they already own.

Another more distant innovation is the possibility of producing reusable film. Chemists at the University of Osaka in Japan have developed polyalnilin, a polymer on which images can be made and erased. However, additional testing is required to determine how long images made on the film will last.

In contrast to these developments, digital photography does not use film. Instead, the camera processes images as digital files and stores them on a built-in miniature disc drive. The images can then be downloaded to a desktop computer or converted to CD-ROM files. Readily available software allows digital images to be edited and retouched; inserted into desktop-published documents, including Web pages; or output as conventional paper prints or film transparencies. Digital photography has gained increasing acceptance in the publishing and graphics industries since the early 1990s, and it has begun to make inroads into the consumer market as the equipment becomes more affordable.

See also:
Camera; Eastman, George; Microelectronics; Motion Pictures; Photography, Amateur; Photography, Color; Photojournalism.

References:
"A Camera-Ready Revolution?" *Consumers' Research Magazine*, October 1994.
International Encyclopedia of Communications. New York: Oxford University Press, 1989.
Macaulay, David. *The Way Things Work.* Boston: Houghton Mifflin, 1988.
"Negative Vibes." *The Economist*, 26 August 1995.
Noldechen, Arno. "Brief Exposures." *World Press Review*, November 1993.
Williams, Trevor I. *The History of Invention: From Stone Axes to Silicon Chips.* New York: Facts on File, 1987.

Photography, Amateur

There are two kinds of amateur photographers. The greatest number by far are those who take snapshots, send the film off to be developed, and then enjoy putting the prints into albums or sending them to friends or relatives as a form of visual communication. But there are also amateurs who develop their own film, make their own prints, and experiment with various techniques and special effects. These people are amateurs only because photography is their hobby; they do not work as professional photographers, although some of them could.

Before the 1890s, there were few, if any, amateur photographers. The cost of cameras, plates, chemicals, and processing equipment made photography too expensive for all but professionals. In addition, photography was viewed initially as a means of producing accurate images of objects and people or accurately documenting a story or event. The idea of using a camera for entertainment or art developed later.

Between 1871 and 1888, George Eastman (who was a bank employee experimenting with photography in his free time) and a number of colleagues developed the materials that made amateur photography possible. In 1874, Eastman found a way to place emulsions of silver salts in gelatin on long strips of paper, and later on celluloid, that could be rolled on a spool and stored for months. Eastman's work opened the way for amateur photographers in the following decade.

In 1888, Eastman introduced a camera that could be mass-produced. He called it the Kodak camera. The origin of the name Kodak seems to have been Eastman's preference for the letter *K*. The first Kodak was a box camera 3.25 inches x 3.75 inches x 6.5 inches that had a lens with a 57-millimeter (2.25-inch) fixed-focus lens set at $f/9$ and a fixed shutter speed. The camera came loaded with a roll of film that allowed the buyer to take 100 pictures. After 100 exposures the camera was returned to the factory, where the film was developed and the camera reloaded. The camera and prints were then returned to the amateur photographer.

By 1891, Eastman had marketed a daylight-loading camera and film with a leader so that users could load their own cameras.

After the film had been exposed, it could be rewound into its canister within the camera and taken to a photography shop for processing. By 1898, 1.5 million cameras had been sold and Eastman had developed a mass market.

To extend the market to children and others who still could not afford his $25 Kodak, Eastman introduced the Brownie camera in 1902. In its first year 100,000 Brownies were sold for $1 each. The camera, with minor changes, remained popular until the 1950s. The Brownie made it possible for almost everyone to become an amateur photographer.

Within a decade after World War II, somewhat more sophisticated cameras were made available to amateurs. These cameras, often miniaturized, had automatic exposure and flash mechanisms and could be used with color film. Polaroid cameras, introduced in 1947, developed film within the camera immediately after exposure, and after some further development were able to produce finished prints within a few seconds. Polaroid cameras made amateur photography a social event. People would gather around to look at pictures of themselves that had been taken only minutes earlier.

Eastman's success came from separating camera use from film processing. Taking photographs was easy with a Kodak, but developing film was more difficult and willingly left to professionals by most amateurs. Land's success was based on automatically developing a print within the camera immediately after exposure. Between 1947 and 1952, a half-million Polaroid cameras were sold for slightly less than $100 each. During the same period, 200 million Polaroid pictures were taken.

Many families had an ordinary camera and a Polaroid, especially after the price of Polaroid cameras was reduced to less than $20 and Polaroid color film became available. But Polaroids were not limited to amateurs. Professional photographers used Polaroids, particularly before taking still photos, to be sure that they had correct lighting and exposure time. They would then shoot the scene on regular film.

During the twentieth century, snapshots and photo albums containing these pictures became one of a family's most valued possessions. Most families have photographs of children and adults at various stages of their lives. Amateur photography has, for most people, replaced diaries and scrapbooks as a way to record one's life history and communicate that information to others. Weddings, birthdays, athletic teams, class pictures, and trips to various places in the world can all be preserved and used to refresh our memories or communicate information to others.

See also:
Camera; Eastman, George; Land, Edwin; Motion Pictures; Photography; Photography, Color; Photojournalism.

References:
International Encyclopedia of Communications. New York: Oxford University Press, 1989.
Macaulay, David. *The Way Things Work.* Boston: Houghton Mifflin, 1988.
Williams, Trevor I. *The History of Invention: From Stone Axes to Silicon Chips.* New York: Facts on File, 1987.

Photography, Color

Color brings an added dimension to photographs, movies, and television screens; it enhances communication. Film that made color photography possible became available in 1907, but the developing process was so difficult and costly that popular use was delayed for nearly 50 years.

Film and Color

Just as white light can be separated into its component colors by a prism, so the colors that make up white light can be combined to make other colors, including white. Shining blue and red light onto a white screen produces magenta, a pinkish purple color. Cyan is the color seen when blue and green light combine, and yellow is seen when red and green light unite. When red, green, and blue light—the primary colors of light—are combined, the result is white light.

Color photographs are made by combining the three primary colors of light, but first the light entering a camera is separated into colors by layers within the film. It is then recombined to produce the colors that were present in the original image.

The film used to take color photographs consists of three separate, thin transparent layers that respond to different colors. Silver is deposited in those layers that receive the colored light to which they are sensitive. For example, if blue light is present, silver will be deposited in the top (blue-sensitive) layer in those regions through which blue light passes. Green light will produce silver in the middle layer, and red light will cause silver to be formed in the third (bottom) layer of the film. Of course, white light will generate silver in all three layers.

During development of the film, silver salts in these three layers of film couple with specific dyes. A yellow dye couples with the silver in the blue-sensitive layer; a magenta dye joins with silver in the green-sensitive layer; and a cyan dye couples with silver in the red-sensitive layer. A fixing solution is then used to wash away the black silver, leaving the colored dyes layered in the negative's emulsion.

If the negative is then illuminated with white light, the region where blue light struck the film now contains a yellow dye in the upper blue-sensitive layer and will, therefore, transmit red and green light and absorb blue. Similarly, the magenta dye that formed in the middle layer regions where green light struck the film will allow red and blue to pass while absorbing green. In those regions of the image that were red, the cyan dye in the lower red-sensitive layer of film will transmit blue and green light while absorbing red. Where white light fell on the film, all three layers will contain dyes and no light will pass through the very dark negative. Of course, colors such as cyan, magenta, and yellow will stimulate dye formation in two of the three layers. Cyan, for example, will stimulate dyes to form in both the green- and blue-sensitive layers.

If the light coming through the negative falls on photographic paper used to make color prints, which has its own three color-sensitive layers, effects similar to those that took place in the film will occur in the paper. The red and green light coming through the regions of the negative where the blue-sensitive layer formed yellow dyes will deposit silver in the lower two layers of the paper, where cyan and magenta dyes couple with it. Red and blue light coming through the green-sensitive layer of the negative where magenta dyes were deposited will produce silver, and the cyan and yellow dyes that couple with it in the bottom and top layers of the photographic paper. Blue and green light passing through the regions of film where only the red-sensitive layer was affected will form silver and the coupled yellow and magenta dyes in the upper two layers of the paper. Of course, no light will pass through those parts of the negative where all three layers deposited dyes; and all colors will pass through white regions of the negative and stimulate dye formation in all three layers of the paper.

After the paper is developed, the print will show the original colors that fell on the film. In those regions of the print where no light came through the negative and no dyes were deposited in any of the layers, the paper will reflect all colors and the print will be white. Where all the light came through the negative, all the dyes were deposited in the paper. This part of the print will be dark because together the three dyes will absorb all the primary colors. The regions of the print where red and green light came through the yellow dye in the blue-sensitive layer of the negative will reflect blue light because the magenta dye in the red-sensitive layer of the paper will absorb green light and the cyan dye in the red-sensitive layer of the print will absorb red light leaving only blue light to be reflected. Similarly, the regions of the print where blue and red light came through the magenta dye in the green-sensitive layer of the negative will appear green, and the regions where blue and green light came through the cyan dye of the red-sensitive layer will be red.

See also:
Camera; Motion Pictures; Photography; Photography, Amateur; Photojournalism.

References:
Gardner, Robert. *Optics*. New York: Twenty-First Century, 1994.
International Encyclopedia of Communications. New York: Oxford University Press, 1989.
Macaulay, David. *The Way Things Work*. Boston: Houghton Mifflin, 1988.
"Negative Vibes." *The Economist*, 26 August 1995.
Williams, Trevor I. *The History of Invention: From Stone Axes to Silicon Chips*. New York: Facts on File, 1987.

Photojournalism

Photojournalism uses photographs to tell a story, describe an event, or establish a mood. Today, readers expect to see photographs in newspapers and magazines, but this expectation did not exist a century ago.

History of Photojournalism

Probably the earliest use of pictures in news reporting appeared in *The Illustrated London News* on 4 June 1842. An artist had sketched the attempted assassination of Queen Victoria by a man with a pistol. The sketch was converted to a woodcut and printed on the front page beside a written account of the incident.

Illustrated news did not gain immediate or rapid popularity. William Wordsworth (1770–1850), the poet laureate of England, vehemently opposed the idea. In a sonnet entitled *Illustrated Books and Newspapers*, he wrote:

Avaunt this vile abuse of pictured
    page!
Must eyes be all in all, the tongue and
    ear
Nothing? Heaven keep us from a
    lower stage!

Despite an intellectual opposition to illustrations and a sense that photographs were artistically inferior to the work of artists and engravers, *The Illustrated London News* did appeal to many readers. In the United States, *Harper's Weekly* and *Frank Leslie's Illustrated Newspaper* brought home the reality of war by publishing engraved copies of some of the 7,000 wet-plate photographs taken by Mathew Brady and his photographic team who covered the Civil War. Publishers found that pictures of crime, natural disasters, floods, fires, and earthquakes, as well as war, boosted circulation and profits. Photographs of exotic places, foreign cultures, and famous people also attracted readers.

Illustrations in newspapers from 1850 until near the end of the nineteenth century were made by having an artist sketch the scene to be printed. Dark areas in the sketch would appear as many small dark pen strokes. The drawing was copied onto a smooth block of wood, and an engraver would then cut away all the wood on the block's surface except for the lines drawn by the artist. When the block was pressed against clay, it made an impression from which a cast was made by pouring molten lead onto the clay. The lead hardened as it cooled, forming a cast that could be placed on a printing press.

When publishers began using photographs, the photographs simply replaced the artist's sketch. An engraver still cut the woodblock to make a cast that could be used for printing. There was no way to copy the photograph directly.

The first use of a halftone, which made the printing of photographs possible, appeared in the New York *Daily Graphic* in 1880. Stephen H. Horgan produced the halftone using a photograph called "Shantytown"—a picture of a squatters' camp taken by H. J. Newton. However, the illustrated press was made truly popular by Joseph Pulitzer. In 1883, Pulitzer bought the faltering *New York World* and turned it into the nation's most profitable newspaper. The paper sold because it featured blood and crime along with photos of animals, celebrities, and pretty women.

In 1890, Jacob Riis, a reporter for the *New York Tribune*, published an illustrated book, *How the Other Half Lives*, depicting life in a New York ghetto. Riis's book, the first to reveal in detail the darker side of American society through photography, made it evident

Joseph Pulitzer made the World *the nation's most profitable newspaper when he purchased the illustrated paper in 1883. The paper featured photographs of celebrities, animals, and pretty women.*

that pictures could bring to readers a reality that could not be equaled by words. In 1903, *National Geographic*'s publication of a halftone photograph of Philippine women working in rice fields brought such a response that the magazine began sending photographers to take pictures of exotic people and places throughout the world, a practice that continues to this day.

The 1890s saw the development of better cameras, roll film, and a flash mechanism made from magnesium powder, potassium chlorate, and antimony sulfide that made night photography possible. During this decade, too, use of halftone photography began to spread. On 21 January 1897, the *New York Tribune* became the first mass-circulation daily newspaper to publish a halftone photograph. The photograph was a rather unexciting picture of Thomas C. Platt, who was then New York's newest U.S. senator. Soon after, the *Tribune* began publishing a series of photo-illustrated stories showing conditions in New York's ghettos.

Although the *New York Tribune* had shown that halftone photographs could be printed on a massive and daily basis, there was not a rapid shift to halftone printing by newspapers. Publishers had a significant investment in artists and engravers. It was 1910 before halftone printing of photographs had engravers looking for another profession.

In 1919, the *Illustrated Daily News*, which later became the *Daily News*, made its debut in New York. By 1924, this picture-laden, sensationalistic newspaper featuring crime, sex, and marital problems had the largest circulation of any newspaper in the United States. Photo-illustrated newspapers had clearly gained popularity.

By the 1930s, new cameras with faster lenses, such as the Ermanox and 35-millimeter Leica, made it possible to capture human motion on film. This development led many sportswriters to place action photographs of athletes beside their columns or to produce photo-essays about athletes and athletics.

The heyday for photojournalism came with the introduction in 1936 of *Life* as a weekly magazine by Henry Luce's Time, Inc. *Life* was followed shortly thereafter by *Look*, a Cowles Publications' photographic magazine. *Life* hired such outstanding photographers as Margaret Bourke-White and Alfred Eisenstaedt, both of whom generated a great number of notable photo news essays often based on the personal history and lives of ordinary people. The Depression of the 1930s was also covered by Walker Evans and Dorothea Lange, two photographers commissioned by the Farm Security Administration to document the devastating effects of a prolonged drought as well as economic pressures facing farm families in America.

During World War II, *Life* employed 6,700 people in 360 offices around the world. Because of its popularity, *Life* dominated magazine advertising and was a very profitable enterprise. However, by the late 1960s, advertisers were turning to television. The combination of competition from television and higher postal rates led Time, Inc., to cease publishing *Life* in 1972. Six years later, *Life* resumed as a monthly magazine, but it never regained its former circulation and it employed no staff photographers. All its pictures were provided by freelance photographers.

Although photographers continued to provide action photos and associated stories during the Korean and Vietnam wars, television news coverage became dominant during the 1960s. Photojournalists turned increasingly to social issues or stories that could be covered from a personal and more intimate perspective.

Most photojournalists now work through agencies that sell to magazines, newspapers, book publishers, and authors. Such agencies as Magnum, Black Star, Gamma, Sygma, Contact, and others have more than a million photographs in their files.

Photojournalism and Privacy

Because strife and scandals supported by photographic evidence make headline news, agencies will pay thousands of dollars for photographs of celebrities in embarrassing situations. As a result, photojournalists eager to achieve financial rewards are often rightly regarded as ruthless mercenaries.

As early as 1890, Samuel D. Warren and Louis D. Brandeis (who later became a Supreme Court justice) raised the issue of privacy and journalism in the *Harvard Law Review*. They foresaw the problems that might confront an individual's right to privacy when pursued by an overzealous press armed with cameras.

Generally, public figures as well as criminals and those accused of crimes have been regarded as fair game by the press and the courts. A person seeking publicity, as most public figures do, cannot suddenly cry for their privacy when caught in a situation that could be a source of embarrassment. The courts have agreed with the press that the public has a right to be informed. On the other hand, persons who are not public figures have the right to be free from unwanted publicity if it is not of public concern.

For years courts resisted the news media's request to allow photographers or television cameras in courtrooms. However, in *Chandler v. Florida* (1981), the U.S. Supreme Court held that states may allow camera coverage of trials, and most states have responded by allowing at least some photographic coverage at trials. The issue received considerable publicity during the murder trial of O. J. Simpson in California during 1995 when Judge Ito threatened to remove TV cameras from the courtroom.

Examples of Photojournalistic Excesses

In an effort to sell papers, photojournalists have often carried their work to extremes in pursuing public figures or in attempting to sway public opinion. The outbreak of the Spanish-American War can be attributed to the journalistic excesses of Pulitzer's *World* and William Randolph Hearst's *New York Journal*. In an effort to force the government to declare war at a time when Spain had virtually agreed to all U.S. demands regarding Cuba, these papers published false and faked photographs of the battleship *Maine*, which sunk in Havana harbor for reasons that were never fully known. The results of the papers' inaccurate and inflammatory accounts and photographs, which came to be known as "yellow journalism," so inflamed the citizens and the Congress that President McKinley felt compelled to ask for a declaration of war.

On 13 January 1928, the giant headline on the first page of the New York *Daily News* read "DEAD!" Below the headline was a photograph of Ruth Snyder, who had been convicted of murdering her husband, being executed in the electric chair at Sing Sing prison. Although photographs of executions were not illegal, both custom and the warden at Sing Sing opposed photographs of executions. Determined to obtain a picture of Snyder's execution, the *Daily News* hired Tom Howard, a photographer with the *Chicago Tribune*, who was unfamiliar to the security guards at the prison. With a small prefocused camera taped to his lower leg and a cable release wire running up his leg to his pocket, Howard attended the execution and took the picture that appeared the next day. Actually, Howard made three exposures to capture Mrs. Snyder's position when the deadly electric current was on, off, and on again. The result was a photograph of a body that appeared to be vibrating.

Other photojournalists have risked life and limb to photograph Elizabeth Taylor dining "alone" with former husband Eddie Fisher, or Brigitte Bardot bathing in the nude. Charles Lindbergh and his wife fled the country to keep their surviving son from publicity after the kidnapping and murder of their infant son. Jacqueline Onassis brought lawsuits against pursuing photographer Ron Galella, and various celebrities have hired body guards to shield them from unwanted cameras. At least one photojournalist became famous for being inventive, or for what might be called "doing his thinking ahead of time." As reported by veteran press photographer Louis Liotta, Arthur Fellig (also known as Weegee, and Liotta's mentor) was a genius. Weegee, knowing that summer heat would soon envelop the city, would ask a woman and her children to pretend to be sleeping in their underwear on a fire escape. He would take the picture, and when the weather turned hot the picture would be ready for the printer. To obtain a famous picture known as "The Critic," in which two well-dressed socialites arriving at the opera are seen walking past a glaring and shabbily dressed bystander, Weegee, according to Liotta, paid a homeless woman to move in beside the two wealthy women on cue.

A century ago pictures were just beginning to play a role in communication. Today, in a world dominated by television, pictures seem to have replaced the written word as the primary form of mass communication.

See also:
Photography; Photography, Amateur; Printing.

References:
Editors of Time-Life Books. *Life Library of Photography: Photojournalism.* Alexandria, VA: Time-Life Books, 1971.
International Encyclopedia of Communications. New York: Oxford University Press, 1989.
Rogers, Madeline. "The Picture Snatchers." *American Heritage*, October 1994.

Picture Telephone
See Telephone.

Polygraph
See Lie Detector.

Pony Express
The Pony Express was a short-lived and financially disastrous venture that provided mail service between Saint Joseph, Missouri, and Sacramento, California. The brainchild of William Hepburn Russell, of the stage and freight firm Russell, Majors & Waddell, the Pony Express operated for only 19 months, from April 1860 to October 1861, before it was put out of business by the transcontinental railroad and telegraph systems.

Russell and his financially strapped company were seeking to wrest the lucrative government mail contract from their main competitor, the Butterfield Overland Company. Butterfield used the southern route from Saint Louis via Memphis, Tennessee, and El Paso, Texas, to Los Angeles. Russell was convinced that the shorter, though more hazardous and seldom-used central route through the nation's heartland was more efficient. He envisioned a system of expert horsemen riding in relays to deliver weekly mail in eight to ten days, as opposed to the three weeks it took Butterfield. Saint Joseph was selected as the eastern terminus because it represented the westernmost point of railroad and telegraph expansion. Russell's proposal was aided by governmental concern that the imminent Civil War would interrupt important West Coast mail service via the southern route.

Although his partners remained skeptical, Russell forged ahead. The basis of the Central Overland Pony Express route was easily established since Russell, Majors & Waddell had a stage line to Salt Lake City. Russell extended the route to Sacramento, establishing 165 relay stations to supply fresh mounts and riders. Home stations, about 40 to 50 miles apart and the larger of the stops, provided food and sleeping quarters and often served as stage stops. Relay stations, 10 to 15 miles apart, were generally one-man operations that provided fresh horses. Asked to ride from 75 to 100 miles per turn and allowed only two minutes for each change of horses, Pony Expressmen had to average 10 miles an hour to meet the schedule. To aid in quickly transferring the mail, the company developed the mochila, a leather apron with two slits to fit over the saddle. Two rectangular pouches behind and in front of each leg, on both sides, carried the mail. The weight of the rider held the mochila in place, and it could be removed and transferred to the next horse with one quick motion as the riders dismounted. Twenty pounds of mail was considered the optimum carrying weight, though in actuality most deliveries were below the maximum. Initially, the charge was $5 per half-ounce, plus the regular 10-cent U.S. mail stamp. However, as financial problems increased, the company dropped prices to as low as $1 per half-ounce and instituted biweekly deliveries. Today, an envelope with a Pony Express stamp affixed may bring $8,000 to $10,000 at auctions.

Convinced that a lighter load made a faster pony, the company recruited jockey-like riders of no more than 130 pounds. It further required a pledge forswearing profane language, drinking, gambling, or abuse of the horses. The salary was fixed at $125 per month plus room and board. The most famous of the 80 to 100 or so riders was 15-year-old William Cody. The young horseman once rode 322 miles in one effort when no relief riders were available. Although impressive, this feat was considerably short of "Pony Bob" Haslam's record of 380 miles in about 36 hours. Later known as "Buffalo Bill," Cody immortalized the Pony Express era by making it a staple part of his world-famous *Wild West Show*.

The Pony Express, although an efficient delivery system, was ultimately a victim of technology and continuous financial problems. Two months after the start of the company, Congress authorized funds to build a transcontinental telegraph line. Following the route of the Pony Express, the system was completed in October 1861. Two days later, the Pony Express suspended operation, and in the following year Russell, Majors & Waddell declared bankruptcy.

References:

Brown, Dee. "The Pony Express." *American History Illustrated*, November 1976.
Rowe, Findley. "The Pony Express: Grit and Glory." *National Geographic*, July 1980.
Settle, Raymond, and Mary Settle. *Saddle and Spurs: The Pony Express Saga*. Lincoln: University of Nebraska Press, 1972.

Pornography

Pornography consists of any kind of communication—written material, films, photographs, devices, etc.—that is considered obscene. The term is derived from the Greek word *pornographos*, which means "writing about prostitutes."

Although there are strong views on pornography, there is little agreement on its definition. This situation stems in part from the fact that views of what is indecent change with time and place. James Joyce's *Ulysses*, written in 1922, was regarded as pornography and banned in the United States until 1933. Today, it is regarded by many as a great piece of literature. What people in the United States might consider obscene is seen quite differently in Denmark, where no attempt is made to control pornography.

Legally, pornography is referred to as obscenity and can be seen as having a certain structure. It presents sexual activity in a form that the general public regards as unacceptable, even though some of the acts might be regarded as acceptable if performed in private. Because the sexual actions are presented in a form intended to make them appear to be normal, they may produce shock or embarrassment among those who view, read, or hear them. The characters found in pornographic material are strictly sexual beings. They are unreal because they have no morals and no fear that their actions could result in pregnancy or venereal disease. Finally, pornography sometimes depicts bondage and pain in which one participant may suffer because of another's actions.

A more liberal view of pornography comes from a psychoanalytic frame of reference in which the material is seen as wish-fulfilling fantasies resulting from sexual sublimation. Those who support such a hypothesis see pornography as harmless or even helpful in reducing psychological tension. A somewhat less liberal theory sees pornography as the equivalent of prostitution—a way in which monogamous individuals can release their sexual frustrations without carrying out illegal or health-endangering behavior. From a conservative point of view, pornography is seen as evidence of a declining civilization or a reflection of a sick or dying society. Some feminists see pornography as the extension of a male-dominated, misogynistic society that will disappear as sexual equality becomes a reality.

Studies on pornography appear to be inconclusive. Research in 1970 by the National Commission on Obscenity and Pornography found no evidence that pornography leads to antisocial behavior. Other studies, which found that pornographic materials were being used by people of both sexes and from all socioeconomic levels, have drawn similar conclusions. On the other hand, some recent research seems to indicate that the violence toward women found in some pornography can affect the attitude of male viewers and possibly lead to rape and sexual abuse.

See also:
Censorship; Psychoanalysis.

References:
Huber, Peter. "Electronic Smut." *Forbes,* 13 July 1995.

International Encyclopedia of Communications. New York: Oxford University Press, 1989.

Itzin, Catherine, ed. *Pornography: Women, Violence, and Civil Liberties.* New York: Oxford University Press, 1992.

Orr, Lisa, ed. *Censorship: Opposing Viewpoints.* San Diego, CA: Greenhaven Press, 1990.

Positron Emission Tomography (PET)
See Scanner.

Postal Service

A postal service collects, sorts, and delivers mail. In most countries postal service is a government function.

The familiar postman's motto, "Neither snow, nor rain, nor gloom of night stays these couriers from the swift completion of their appointed rounds," was written by Herodotus, a Greek historian, in the fifth century B.C. It was a salute to the Persian postal system, which extended across Persia with stations 14 miles apart and mounted couriers to carry royal messages across the land.

Although the Persian postal system was perhaps the best in ancient times, it was not the first or only one. Oral messages were carried by couriers long before writing was invented. Egyptian riders relayed written messages on horseback as early as 2000 B.C., and there was an extensive courier system in China by the time of the Chan dynasty (1027–256 B.C.).

The Roman emperor Augustus (27–14 B.C.) established *cursus pulicus,* a postal system, as a way of holding the vast empire together. Paved Roman roads enabled couriers in chariots or on horseback to carry correspondence outward from Rome to places as distant as northern Europe, Carthage, Asia, Macedonia, and Spain.

The decline of the Roman Empire in the fifth century A.D. virtually eliminated postal service in the Western world. Monasteries used private couriers to maintain communication within their orders, and later a few universities provided courier service between students and their families, but it was 1477 before Louis XI established a postal service throughout France. England, Italy, and the German city-states soon followed suit.

In North America during colonial times, residents of coastal cities could send letters abroad with sea captains who would deliver the letters to taverns and coffeehouses, where recipients could pick them up and send their own letters westward with the same ships to taverns in America. Similarly, government mail was carried abroad or between eastern ports on naval vessels. Any mail between inland cities was carried by

Airmail service in Philadelphia, Pennsylvania, begins as mailbags are transferred from a U.S. mail wagon to an airplane in May 1918.

private couriers, but in 1672 New York governor Francis Lovelace established the first overland postal route in North America. It followed Indian paths between Boston and New York that came to be known as the Boston Post Road, and later as Route 1. Postal service between Portsmouth, New Hampshire, and Philadelphia became available in 1693 and was extended to Annapolis, Maryland, in 1727, to Williamsburg, Virginia, in 1732, and to Montreal and Quebec in 1763.

Benjamin Franklin, who became the postmaster in Philadelphia in 1737, was largely responsible for improved mail service between the colonies after being appointed deputy postmaster general for America in 1753. He served until 1774, when he was dismissed because of his sympathy for independence from England. A year later he was appointed to the same position by the Continental Congress, a post he held until November 1776, when he was sent to France to seek their help in fighting the Revolution.

In the eighteenth century, postal service was widely regarded as a function of government, and Article 1, Section 8 of the U.S. Constitution states that Congress shall have the power to establish post offices and post roads. When George Washington appointed Samuel Osgood as the first postmaster general in 1789, there were 75 post offices in the 13 states and 2,400 miles of post roads. A decade later both the miles of road and the number of post offices had increased by a factor of five.

Postal Systems in the Nineteenth and Twentieth Centuries

In 1837, Rowland Hill published the results of his study of postal systems, which revealed that the major cost in providing mail service was the time spent by clerks in determining postage based on distance, keeping accurate accounts and reports, and collecting money from people receiving mail. He recommended establishing a uniform fee based on weight, not distance, that would be paid by the sender using stamps that could be purchased in advance of sending. Congress authorized stamps in 1847, and in 1863 they established a uniform rate of 3 cents for a letter weighing half an ounce or less. The lower cost eliminated competition from most private carriers.

Another major change was the development and growth of railroads. Completion of the transcontinental railroad in 1869 reduced delivery time between New York and San Francisco from three weeks (by coach) to one week. Efficiency was further enhanced by the Railway Mail Service. A network of postal cars moved the mail from city to city while clerks in those cars sorted mail en route, reducing the need to sort mail in local city post offices.

The Montgolfier brothers initiated the first transport of mail through the air with the successful flight of their hot-air balloon in 1783. The 1920s and 1930s saw a brief but rapid growth in mail carried around the world by dirigibles. Lighter-than-air mail service ended following the *Hindenburg* disaster in 1937, when the ship's hydrogen, the gas used for its buoyancy, caught fire at Lakehurst, New Jersey. A few private citizens have used carrier pigeons for light deliveries, but in the long run it was the Wright brothers' success with heavier-than-air ships that led to a manyfold increase in the speed of regular mail delivery.

The first scheduled airmail delivery took place in 1911, and by 1918 regular airmail service existed between New York and Washington, D.C. Gradually airplanes replaced the railroads as the principal mail carrier, a trend that accelerated after World War II. Practically all long-distance mail now moves by air, and sorting tasks have returned to the post offices. Trucks, automobiles, and pedestrians carry mail to nearby cities and deliver local mail from post offices.

The U.S. Postal Service

Under the Postal Reorganization Act of 1970, the U.S. Postal Service was created as a nonprofit organization under the executive branch of government. The Postal Service, which replaced the old Post Office Department, is governed by an 11-member board of governors, nine of whom are appointed to nine-year terms by the president with Senate approval. These nine choose a postmaster general, and those ten then choose the eleventh member, who serves as deputy postmaster general. An independent five-member Postal Rate Commission, appointed by the president, rules on postal rate changes proposed by the board of governors.

The 1970 act removed the postal service from political control, which had existed since the President Andrew Jackson introduced postmasterships as a means of patronage. However, despite increased rates designed to reduce tax burdens and make the service self-sufficient, the postal service often operates at a loss as it strives to meet competition from private carriers, such as Federal Express and United Parcel Service, and other means of communication such as E-mail, telephone, and facsimiles.

In 1995, the U.S. Postal Service employed 740,000 people in 28,322 post offices that handled 177 billion pieces of mail, or nearly 240,000 pieces of mail per employee and about 6 million pieces per post office. To sort such vast amounts of mail, the Postal Service is becoming increasingly automated. Since 1963, each post office has been identified by a five-digit ZIP code, and senders are asked to include the ZIP code as part of the mailing address on all items mailed. The first two numbers of the ZIP code for all post offices in Massachusetts, for example, are 01 or 02. The distribution center that sorts the mail destined for the Cape Cod post offices in Massachusetts is identified by the first three numbers of the ZIP code—026—the numbers that indicate a post office on Cape Cod. The last two numbers of the ZIP identify the particular post office. For example, 02653 indicates the Orleans post office.

Typically, mail at a processing center is placed on a moving belt that sorts the envelopes by size while clerks remove irregularly shaped items that the system cannot sort. The envelopes are then sent through a machine that can sense the stamp by means of the code printed on the stamp. The machine turns the envelopes so that the stamped upper-right-hand corners are all turned the same way. It then cancels the stamp using a marker that gives the date, time, and location of the distribution center. A letter-sorting machine carries the envelopes on a belt past an optical character reader that scans the ZIP code on each item for a computer that controls the spraying of the proper bar code on the envelope. The bar code is read by another scanner, and each envelope is sent to a bin that corresponds to a distribution center based on the first three numbers of the ZIP code. When the letters reach the distribution center, they are placed on another moving belt, where the bar code is read for the last two numbers of the ZIP code and separated into bins that will be taken to the proper post office for delivery.

Since 1983, there has been a ZIP-plus-four code to enhance the ease of distribution at local post offices. For example, 02651-0256 indicates post office box 256 at the North Eastham, Massachusetts, post office. The last four numbers may also be used to indicate a postal route, an office building, or a particular part of a city. To further reduce the burden of sorting, bulk mailers are now required to affix their own bar codes so that about 40 percent of the mail can be sent directly to a scanner that reads bar codes for sorting.

The Future of "Snail Mail"

Postal service is often referred to as "snail mail" because it moves so slowly relative to electronic communication. Fax machines, E-mail, and electronic fund transfers decreased business mail volume by one-third between 1988 and 1995. Nevertheless, the volume of postal service mail increased by 5 percent largely due to business-to-home communication—catalogs, bills, payments, and advertisements. But with the construction of the information superhighway, can the postal service survive?

Postal officials argue that their system provides universal service. Neither a computer nor even electricity is required for mail delivery. However, the postal service is changing in an effort to meet, accept, and respond to the competition. To prevent forgery, the post office offers certified E-mail similar to certified and registered mail. Plans are also under way to install public computer stations at post offices, where anyone can gain access to free government information and send E-mail through the postal service to those who aren't connected to the Internet.

See also:
Computer; Electronic Mail; Fax Machine; Information Superhighway; Internet; Pony Express; Telephone; Universal Product Code.

References:
Browne, Christopher. *Getting the Message: The Story of the Post Office*. Dover, NH: A. Sutton, 1993.
Graham, Richard B. *U.S. Postal History*. Sidney, OH: Linn's Stamp News, 1990
International Encyclopedia of Communications. New York: Oxford University Press, 1989.
"The Snail's Revenge." *The Economist*, 5 August 1995.

Power Plant

Electric power plants convert other forms of energy to electrical energy. Most power plants produce enough electricity to meet the needs of one or more cities or towns. Since most communication devices such as radios, television sets, computers, and telephones are driven by electrical energy, electric power plants are the energy source for much communication.

In most power plants, fossil fuel is burned to produce the heat needed to generate steam. The steam, under pressure, is used to turn a turbine, which rotates an electric generator that produces electrical energy. In the United States, most of our electricity comes from the burning of fossil fuels. Approximately 56 percent of the electrical energy generated in the United States comes from burning coal; about 10 percent is generated by the heat supplied by burning natural gas; and about 3 percent is generated by burning oil. Approximately 20 percent of the electricity is generated by nuclear energy (the fission of uranium or plutonium), and nearly 10 percent is obtained from hydroelectric power plants, where the kinetic energy of falling water flowing through dams is used to turn turbines.

Within electric generators, changing magnetic fields produced by rotating giant magnets induce voltage in large coils of wire. The generated voltage, usually at approximately 2,200 volts, is increased by a factor of 100 or more by means of step-up transformers. The energy travels along low-resistance wires to substations, where step-down transformers reduce the voltage before it travels shorter distances to consumers. Before the electricity enters homes and businesses, additional transformers reduce the voltage once more to 110 or 220 volts.

Today, nearly all power plants generate alternating current (AC), but the first power plant, built in New York City in 1882 under the direction of Thomas Edison, provided direct current (DC). Edison's competitor, George Westinghouse, founder of the company that bears his name, realized that it would be difficult to transmit DC electricity over great distances because so much of the energy would be lost as heat. By using AC, transformers could be used to raise the voltage from a power plant to thousands of volts. By doing so, the electric current could be made very small, greatly reducing the electric energy converted to heat in the transmission wires. Only AC could be used to transmit electrical energy over large distances. Edison's approach would have required local power plants, an economically infeasible approach for rural areas.

The predominance of power plants that burn fossil fuels poses problems for the future. There is a limited supply of fossil fuels, and plants that burn them pollute the air. This is particularly true of coal, the fuel most commonly used in power plants. However, all fossil fuels produce carbon dioxide as a by-product of burning. During the past century the concentration of carbon dioxide in the atmosphere has increased by nearly 20 percent, giving rise to what many call the greenhouse effect—an effect that many scientists believe is causing the earth's average temperature to rise.

Short of eliminating electricity as a source of power, other ways must be found to generate electrical energy. In California many acres are covered by wind turbines whose spinning blades are used to generate electricity. In France an experimental plant uses scores of mirrors to reflect sunlight onto a giant curved mirror that focuses the light onto a boiler in which steam is generated and used to turn a turbine. In a few places, geothermal energy can provide the necessary steam. In some coastal areas, the energy found in the daily tides can be used to power electric generators.

Although approximately 16 percent of the world's electricity is generated in nuclear power plants, fear of nuclear disaster and radioactive waste disposal problems make the public reluctant to expand such a source. Nevertheless, nuclear power plants do not produce carbon dioxide.

The future source of electric power remains uncertain. In the more distant future, plants using atomic fusion—the energy that fuels the sun—may provide us with electric power. Vast arrays of photovoltaic cells in orbit about the earth may generate and focus powerful microwave beams onto generating stations around the earth that will convert the radiant energy to electricity. Perhaps all of the methods above will be used, or perhaps an unforeseen source will be developed. What is certain is that communication depends on a good source of electricity.

See also:
Dynamo; Electric Field; Faraday, Michael; Henry, Joseph; Magnetic Field; Transformer.

Printing

Printing generally involves the use of ink and a printing press or some similar device to transfer characters and images from an original to multiple copies so that the copies can be widely disseminated to readers. The development of effective ways to copy original documents in quantity made it possible to communicate ideas widely and rapidly.

History of Printing

Writing preceded printing, and initially copying was done by rewriting the words. The first process for making multiple copies of a document that avoided the tedious task of rewriting each word appears to have been developed in Asia. (The first datable text, the *Dharani Sutra,* was published in Korea sometime between 704 and 751, and the first book to be printed is believed to be the *Diamond Sutra,* in 868.)

The first "printing press" involved chiseling characters into a smooth stone slab. The slab was then covered with moist paper that was pressed into the incised characters. After drying, the raised portions of the paper were wiped with an ink-soaked cloth. A dry sheet of blank paper was then pressed against the inked paper. Since the characters were depressed and, therefore, not inked, the copy appeared as a negative—that is, white characters on an inked background. The process was slow, but other than copying by hand or using a seal, it was probably the first method used to make multiple copies of a document.

Later, a process for printing positive copies was invented. A carver cut away the wood to form raised characters on a large wooden block. After the characters were covered with ink, sheets of paper were pressed against them repeatedly to make as many copies as were needed.

In China, too, movable type was first used during the eleventh century. Clay was shaped into characters and then heated to make it hard. Later, metal was used to make type. Before inking, the characters were placed and held in position by a soft mixture of wax, resin, and ash that covered a shallow tray.

Movable type was probably reinvented in Western culture before Johann Gutenberg invented the printing press in Mainz, Germany, around 1450. Gutenberg made two significant improvements over the printing methods developed in Asia. First, Gutenberg made metal dies of letters, which were then used to make molds for letters. With the molds, he could cast as many copies of a character as he needed to set type. The cast letters fit together and aligned perfectly. The lead alloy letters were set in a chase (a flat frame) and held in place with wedges. The assembled characters were arranged in lines as the mirror image of the way they would appear on a printed page. A sheet of paper, large enough to print eight pages at a time, was attached to a tympan (another frame) that was connected to the chase by hinges. A platen (flat plate) controlled by a large screw and attached lever was then used to press the paper against the print. Second, Gutenberg's press could print on both sides of the paper and produced copies with much clearer print than had been possible with block printing.

Once initiated, printing developed much more rapidly in Europe than in China because in Europe, where the alphabet was used, a printer needed only about 50 different characters. A Chinese printer had to use thousands of different characters to set print.

Early in the nineteenth century, Friedrich Koenig developed a flatbed cylinder press that used a rotating cylinder instead of a platen to press sheets of paper against type in a flatbed. By 1844, Richard Hoe had invented the rotary press, in which the type was attached to the surface of a rotating cylinder. Several smaller rollers provided the pressure needed to keep the paper against the type. Hoe's rotary press, together with the web press, which kept a continuous roll of paper moving through the printing process, led to widespread acceptance of the steam-powered automatic rotary cylinder press during the last quarter of the nineteenth century.

Type continued to be set by hand, much as it was by Gutenberg, until the middle of the nineteenth century. It was not until 1886 that Ottmar Mergenthaler introduced the Linotype, which used a keyboard to set type.

Following World War II, photocomposition began to replace metal typesetting. Initially, photographic images were formed on lithographic plates, but today photocomposition involves scanning, computers, and laser beams. The end product of all methods of photocomposition is the exposure of char-

Johann Gutenburg checks the first proof from his invention, the printing press, ca. 1450.

acters on film or photosensitive paper that is then used to make a printing plate.

A laser typesetter is used in composing most books today. Signals are sent to a typesetter by a keyboard. A computer-controlled laser beam is turned on and off as it sweeps across film. The developed film reveals the text and pictures created by laser light. Images in the film can be projected onto plates coated with light-sensitive chemicals. Further treatment of the plates will depend on the method of printing used.

Methods of Printing

The three most common methods of printing are letterpress; gravure, or intaglio; and lithography, or offset.

Letterpress printing uses raised characters, and ink that is applied to the characters is transferred to paper pressed against them. Once the type is set, three kinds of presses may be used to print copies—platen, flatbed cylinder, or rotary. To mass-produce newspapers and books, a rotary press is used. It consists of two cylinders, one of which carries the type. The second cylinder, which is blank, presses the paper against the type as it is drawn between the cylinders. A series of such cylinders are used to print long rolls of paper that move continuously through the presses. The output is continuously cut into sections and assembled into the final newspapers or books.

Gravure, or intaglio, printing is similar to letterpress in reverse; that is, the characters are not raised but appear as depressions in the plate. Before the paper is pressed against the inked plate, a "doctor blade" sweeps across the plate's surface, clearing away any ink between the depressions. Gravure typesetting is often done photographically. The set type is photographed onto a thin metal plate coated with a photosensitive substance. The plate is then placed in an acid bath in which the acid attacks (etches) only those parts of the plate where the images fell. As a result, the type appears as shallow depressions in the plate. The plate is then attached to a rotary press for printing. A similar process can now be done by using a computer-controlled laser to make the plate. Some magazines, color sections of newspapers, and packaging are printed on rotogravure presses.

Lithography (literally "stone writing"), or offset printing, involves no raised or impressed characters. Instead it makes use of a principle first developed on stone. If one writes on a smooth stone surface with a grease pencil, wipes the dampened stone with ink, and then washes the surface with water, the ink will stick to the greasy letters but be washed away from other areas by the water. Stones are no longer used in lithography. Instead light is projected through a photographic negative of the original page onto a thin, light-sensitive sheet of zinc or aluminum coated with a special photosensitive chemical. The plate is then treated with a lacquer that sticks to the images. Next, a wet roller moves over the plate. The dark lacquered parts of the plate repel water, but the water remains on the lighter parts of the image on the plate. When ink is added to the plate, it sticks to the dark lacquered areas but not the lighter wet regions. Paper pressed against the plate picks up the ink, forming letters and images and providing a copy of the original page. A more recent system uses a laser to scan digitally stored type and transfer it to the photographic plate. In offset lithographic printing, the most commonly used method, the inked image is first transferred to a rubber-coated cylinder, which then transfers the ink to the paper that it rolls over.

Halftone Printing

Halftone printing allows the various shades of gray, as well as black and white, to appear on paper. Development of halftone techniques enabled photographs to be printed in newspapers and books. Before 1880, there was no way to print the various shades of gray in a black-and-white photograph. When publishers first began using photographs, the photographs simply replaced an artist's line drawing. An engraver used the photograph as a model but still had to cut a woodblock to make a plate that could be inked and then used for printing. There was no way to copy the photograph directly.

A printing press can print only black; it cannot print the continuous tones in a black-and-white photograph. How, then, is it possible to print the black-and white photographs that we see daily in newspapers and books? These pictures are certainly perceived as having a variety of shades from black to white. Viewed through a strong magnifying glass, a photograph in a book or newspaper will be seen to be made up of many tiny black dots. Where the picture appears to be dark, the dots are close together. Where the picture is light, the dots are far apart. The spacing of the dots determines the shade of gray that is seen in the printed photograph.

To break a photograph into tiny dots so that it can be printed on a printing press, a photograph of the photographic print is taken through a halftone screen, a piece of clear plastic with many closely spaced parallel lines placed at right angles to one another so that they form tiny squares. When the film is developed, it will consist of many tiny dots. This film is placed on a metal sheet that is coated with a photosensitive material. When a bright light illuminates the film, the light passes through the light spots on the film, but not the dark ones. Where the light passes through, it hardens the coating on the metal plate.

The plate is then washed to remove the unhardened parts of the coating that were not exposed to the bright light. When the plate is placed in an acid bath, the acid dissolves (etches) the uncoated bare regions of the metal, leaving tiny round plateaus of coated metal with valleys in between. The result is a halftone plate.

During the printing process, a roller spreads ink over the plate. The ink reaches the tiny raised plateaus, but it does not penetrate the valleys that have been etched away. When paper is pressed against the plate during printing, a pattern of tiny black dots is transferred to the paper. Depending on the density of the dots, the print will appear to range from black, where the dots are densely packed, to light gray, where the dots are widely spaced.

Color photographs that appear in print consist of tiny dots that are yellow, cyan, and magenta as well as black. The reason is that color plates are printed from four separate halftone plates.

Color Printing

To print in color requires four inks—black, cyan (bluish green), yellow, and magenta (purplish pink). Separate plates must be prepared for each ink. The original is scanned for black plus each of the three colors, and a separate image is made of each one by a computer that uses the light signals from the scanner to produce dots of different sizes for each of the four images.

During the printing process, the sheets pass through four separate inked plates, one for each color, made from the four images. The four inks are applied separately as tiny dots, based on information transferred to the computer when the original material was scanned. For example, the red portion of a printed page will be speckled with closely placed dots of magenta and yellow inks because the human eye sees the combination of these two pigments as red. When viewed with a magnifying glass, a colored picture in a book or magazine will be seen to be made up of many tiny colored dots.

Nonimpact Printing

The methods of printing described thus far depend upon pressing a paper surface against print. However, there are methods of printing that do not involve pressure. These include xerography, photography, and screen printing. The same is true of the laser and inkjet printers commonly used to print documents composed on desktop computers.

See also:
Mergenthaler, Ottmar; Photography; Photojournalism; Xerography.
References:
Aylesworth, Thomas G., ed. *It Works like This: A Collection of Machines from Nature and Science Magazine.* Garden City, NY: Natural History Press, 1968.
International Encyclopedia of Communications. New York: Oxford University Press, 1989.
Macaulay, David. *The Way Things Work.* Boston: Houghton Mifflin, 1988.
Ultimate Visual Dictionary. New York and London: Dorling Kindersley, 1994.
Williams, Trevor I. *The History of Invention: From Stone Axes to Silicon Chips.* New York: Facts on File, 1987.

Prodigy
See Online Services.

Propaganda
See Goebbels, Paul Joseph.

Psychoanalysis

Psychoanalysis is a system of communication between a patient and a doctor (a psychiatrist) that is used to treat mental disorders. The system was first developed by Sigmund Freud, a Viennese physician, during the last decade of the nineteenth century. In his book *The Interpretation of Dreams* (1899), Freud argued that dreams provide a physician with a way of reading the patient's unconscious mind where, he believed, dreams are formulated and serve as a bridge between the conscious and unconscious mind. For Freud, dreams were the model for communicating with the unconscious mind in psychoanalytic theory. But he believed that the unconscious sometimes reveals itself in the conscious mind through slips of the tongue, jokes, facial tics, compulsive behavior, and in other ways.

In traditional psychiatry the patient lies on a couch and through free association tells the analyst, who is out of sight, of his thoughts, wishes, fantasies, dreams, and innermost feelings. The patient is encouraged to talk about everything that comes to mind; nothing is to be repressed. With time, as the patient relaxes and feels more at ease with the analyst, events and painful remembrances from childhood emerge. A competent analyst may be able to interpret the patient's current anxieties, fears, or compulsions in light of the repressed conflicts and traumas of the past. With the doctor's help, the patient connects past with present and finds the reasons for current difficulties. Finally, the analyst helps the patient resolve those problems by developing new patterns of behavior based on the insights that have been achieved by probing the past.

Since Freud began applying his theories, many other methods and theories of psychoanalysis have been developed. For example, interpersonal therapy is used to help people see how behavioral patterns, relationships, and conflicts can create problems. Early psychologists such as Ivan Pavlov and B. F. Skinner provided the basis for behavioral therapy, which can lead to behavioral modification, a technique that is widely used to treat smoking, gluttony, alcoholism, drugs, and some forms of mental illness. Various approaches are used. In aversion therapy, undesirable behavior leads to punishment or the withholding of rewards. Desensitization involves the gradual increase in exposure to an object or situation that produces fear or anxiety. With biofeedback, patients receive information about their heart rate, blood pressure, and other measurable factors that help them to control these involuntary responses to anxiety. Relaxation therapy uses meditation techniques to achieve a more tranquil response to stress. Cognitive therapists believe that some thought patterns are harmful to a patient's mental well-being by causing them to respond in inappropriate ways to certain stimuli. To eliminate such responses, therapists try to reshape a person's thought patterns to change their responses. In operant conditioning, desirable behavior is rewarded and undesirable behavior is punished or brings no reward.

Many therapists now use a pragmatic approach and apply whatever method seems most appropriate for the individual in question. It is generally recognized today that some serious mental illnesses, such as schizophrenia, manic depression, and psychoses, cannot be cured by psychoanalysis. However, many patients with these disorders have been able to lead reasonably normal lives by taking chemicals such as tranquilizers, antidepressants, sedatives, and other controlled substances.

References:
Brill, A. A., ed. *The Basic Writings of Sigmund Freud*. New York: Random House, 1938.
Freud, Sigmund. *On Dreams*. New York: Norton, 1952.
Kramer, Peter D. *Listening to Prozac*. New York: Viking, 1993.
Mondimore, Francis, and M. D. Mark. *Depression: The Mood Disease*. Baltimore: Johns Hopkins University Press, 1990.

Psychokinesis
See Telepathy.

Psychotherapy
See Psychoanalysis.

Public Opinion

Public opinion is generally regarded as an opinion about an issue that is shared by a number of people. Sometimes the public is quite unified on an opinion; at other times there may be two or more very different opinions dividing the public about an issue.

In authoritarian countries, public opinion is controlled by the use of propaganda and censorship. In democratic societies, public opinion is often divided and can change dramatically with time and events. Public opinion is gauged by conducting polls in which a sample of the public is asked questions to determine how they feel or think about specific issues. On an issue such as gun control, for example, a segment of the population feels strongly that guns should be subject to intense government control; an opposing segment believes that anyone has the right to own a gun; and another group, often a majority, is indifferent.

The founding fathers believed that the people would elect to positions of leadership individuals whose sentiments regarding political issues were viewed as acceptable by the majority. These leaders would then act wisely in governing and enacting legislation. Because of the vast improvements in communication and transportation that have taken place, today's political leaders are more aware of public opinion, particularly the opinion of special-interest groups that spend millions of dollars to sway public opinion and public officials. As a result, the opinions of a small but intense minority often have a greater effect on public policy than the less potent majority. Furthermore, elected public officials now conduct their own public opinion polls in an effort to find the position of their voting constituency with regard to issues on which they must vote or take a stand. This raises the question of whether political leaders are leading or following the public.

Generally, people's opinions of long-term positions, such as affiliation with a political party or church, reflect the influence of those close to them—family members, friends, teachers, union leaders, supervisors, etc. On current issues, people are strongly influenced by the media—newspapers, magazines, television, and radio. Although the media may not be successful in telling the public *how* to think about an issue, it is able to set the agenda in terms of *what* issues the public thinks about. It is the media that often decides which issues are important, and the issues brought to the public's attention frequently have a sensational flair. In a newspaper, matters of policy are often shunted to the inside pages to make room on the front page for histrionic stories about some aspect of a politician's personal life. As a result, the public may have a strong opinion about the politician and how they will vote but have no opinion about a serious matter of public policy.

Changing the prevailing public opinion or attitude is not easy. Most social movements, such as woman suffrage, begin as a strong belief held by a significant number of highly motivated individuals who try to influence others by speaking out, distributing literature, and gaining media support. If the issue receives increasing support from the public, more proponents feel confident about speaking out in its favor. As opponents see their position weakening, they are more likely to remain quiet until finally the proponent's position becomes the public's opinion on the issue. In the case of woman suffrage, the change in public opinion culminated in 1920 with the passage of the Nineteenth Amendment.

See also:
Gallup, George H.; Roper, Elmo Burns, Jr.
References:
Budiansky, Stephen. "Consulting the Oracle." *U.S. News & World Report*, 4 December 1995. Fineman, Howard. "The Power of Talk." *Newsweek*, 8 February 1993. *International Encyclopedia of Communications.* New York: Oxford University Press, 1989.

Publishing

In its broadest sense, publishing means to make publicly known. Its general meaning is the preparation and dissemination of written material for public consumption. The materials include books, such as textbooks, fiction, nonfiction, drama, and poetry, as well as magazines and newspapers. However, the advent of electronics, microelectronics, and microcomputers has expanded publishing to include audio and videotapes, computer software, and CD-ROMs as part of the publishing industry.

Practically every contract between a publisher and an author now includes clauses regarding subsidiary rights from the sale of the book for use as software, as part of an electronic database, and for audio and videotapes as well as the usual rights pertaining to periodicals, films, foreign sales, microfilm, and book clubs. A number of authors have refused to sign such contracts, for if the content of their manuscript is suitable for CD-ROMs, they might find it more rewarding financially to deal with a software company such as Microsoft.

Of course, anyone can publish their own writings on the Internet. In a sense, it's a return to the days before printing presses, when authors had to make handwritten copies of their manuscripts if they sought to distribute their work. The Internet makes copying and distribution much easier, but an author who publishes gratis on the Internet needs another occupation to make a living.

The Beginning of Publishing

The introduction of Gutenberg's printing press around 1450 marked the beginning of modern publishing. Before that time, self-publishing was the rule. Authors simply distributed handwritten copies of their manuscripts.

In the United States, publishers such as J. B. Lippincott, John Wiley, G. P. Putnam's Sons, Charles Scribner's Sons, Harper, and others first appeared in the late eighteenth and early nineteenth centuries. They were regarded as both publishers and booksellers. The distinction among publishers, printers, and booksellers still remains blurred for many companies today, but a publisher is generally viewed as a company that arranges the production of books that bear their imprint, which they then distribute. The publishing industry consists of a network of organizations that cooperate in selecting, producing, and distributing information, including printed matter such as books, magazines, and newspapers.

During the nineteenth century, characteristics of today's publishing industry began to take shape. An editor at a publishing company would obtain a manuscript from an author and work with that person to produce a book. The author would receive a certain portion of monies earned from sales of the book as periodically paid royalties. A production division would design the book and oversee its printing and binding. A group dedicated to marketing and sales would see that publicity and advertising reached book-

stores and various other booksellers. By the beginning of the twentieth century, with a growing literate population in the United States, mail-order publishing became increasingly popular. During the last half of the twentieth century, publishers frequently sold the subsidiary rights for paperback reprints, movies, television, software, CD-ROMs, and other electronic media.

Although censorship of books and articles has been prevalent in other countries, there has never been formal censorship in the United States. In fact, the First Amendment of the U.S. Constitution guarantees freedom of the press as well as freedom of speech.

Following World War I, a thriving U.S. economy coupled with a literate public led to a growth in publishing and the appearance of new publishers such as Random House (1924) and Simon & Schuster (1925). This same decade saw the rise of book clubs that provided books through the mail at reduced prices.

Changes in Publishing

The 1930s marked the beginning of a publishing revolution—the appearance of paperbacks. It began at Penguin Press in England in 1936 and was soon prevalent in the United States. By the 1950s, classics and nonfiction as well as fiction were being published as paperback books. Today, we find paperbacks being sold in places where only magazines and newspapers were sold before—drugstores, discount stores, supermarkets, and newsstands. It is this wide access that has made it possible to publish paperbacks at such low prices.

Because of the vast sales potential of paperbacks, the paperback rights for a bestseller may be worth millions of dollars. Many such books are advertised in conjunction with a film version of the book. As a result, some publishers have changed from quiet, scholarly family firms to become a part of corporate show business.

The likelihood of large profits for a relatively small investment has attracted big business to publishing. During the past three decades, publishing, with the exception of a few independent publishers, has changed from a traditional family enterprise to a corporate industry. Giant corporations such as Gulf and Western, Time, Inc., CBS, and others have purchased smaller publishing houses and are engaged in a wide variety of media involving both print and nonprint.

Critics argue that publishing conglomerates stifle creativity with their emphasis on the bottom line and best-sellers. They claim that the works of less well known, though talented, authors go unpublished, resulting in a lack of diversity. They also maintain that printed matter has become subordinate to other media forms because a book is viewed as part of a total investment package that will generate monies from subsidiary rights purchased by film, television, magazine, newspaper, video, electronic, and other media companies. However, both fiction and nonfiction books of undisputed quality are being written, and the number of bookstores continues to grow.

The use of computers and other electronic technology by publishers has made it possible to provide the public with books on current topics or events shortly after they appear on the evening news. This technology has also opened new markets—audiotapes of books, encyclopedias on a single CD-ROM disk, and a seemingly infinite variety of information through the Internet. The use of computers in all phases of publishing has also produced closer ties between the editorial and printing phases of publishing because computers have made it so easy to reshape text and graphics.

The growth during the 1980s of personal computers—made possible by microelectronics, sophisticated but easy-to-use word processing, drawing and painting software, the laser printer, and scanners—has made desktop publishing a reality. An individual can provide high-quality page layouts with graphics, photographs, and art that can be transferred to a printer.

Publishers and Patrons

What a publisher publishes depends on its tradition, its top management's awareness of who buys its books, and, most importantly, the major patrons who purchase its books. Many publishers have traditionally had a special niche in the industry. It might be textbooks, references, religious writings, children's books, or some other special subject area.

The patrons of most publishers are organizations that provide most of the cash that keeps the publisher in business. For newspapers and magazines, the primary patrons are advertisers. For book publishers it is bookstores, book jobbers, school boards or state boards of education, and universities and their bookstores who are the major patrons.

To provide the material they publish, book and magazine publishers rely primarily on freelance writers, some of whom use literary agents to make contacts with publishers. Newspapers, on the other hand, tend to hire reporters as salaried personnel because they must have stories and articles on a daily basis. Book and magazine editors will sometimes ask an author to write a book or article on a particular topic that their market research indicates has a potential for large sales. They may also specify length, nature of illustrations, and whether to use color, depending on sales forecasts, competition, cost, and aesthetics.

See also:
Computer; Electronic Publishing; Internet; Microelectronics; Newspaper; Photojournalism; Printing; Writing.

References:
International Encyclopedia of Communications. New York: Oxford University Press, 1989.
"Who Owns the Word?" *Newsweek,* 14 August 1995.

Radar

Radar is an acronym for radio detection and ranging. It is a device that uses electromagnetic waves for detecting and locating objects that reflect the radiation. By measuring the time delay between transmitted pulses and the reception of their echoes, the distance to the object that reflected the waves can be determined. Changes in the frequency of transmitted pulses and their echoes can be used to determine the velocity of moving objects. Present-day transportation, astronomy, and weather forecasting would be impossible without the information provided by radar.

The wavelength of the radiation beamed by radar transmitters generally is between 2 meters and 1 centimeter (150 megahertz and 30 gigahertz). The longer wavelengths characteristic of most radio stations would simply bend (diffract) around most of the objects that radar is used to detect. In water, waves pass around objects that are small relative to the distance between the crests of the waves. Objects comparable to or larger than the wavelength will reflect the waves. The same is true of radar.

Since electromagnetic waves travel at a velocity of 300,000 kilometers per second (km/s), the distance to an object can be determined by measuring the time delay between the transmission of a wave pulse and the reception of its echo. If that time delay is a millisecond (0.001 second), then the pulse traveled 300,000 km/s × 0.001 s = 300 km. Since the pulse's echo traveled to and from the object, the distance to the object is 300 km/2 = 150 km.

History

Before 1890, Heinrich Hertz demonstrated that radio waves can be reflected, and by 1904 Christian Hülsmeyer patented the use of electromagnetic radiation for range finding. Guglielmo Marconi carried out experiments using radiolocation on the ocean during the 1920s. During the same decade, experiments at the U.S. Naval Research Laboratory used radio pulses and their echoes to detect the ionosphere and its height. During their investigation, the researchers detected signal interference when a boat passed between their transmitter and receiver. Later, they noted a similar effect when airplanes passed through their beams.

In February 1935, Robert Watson-Watt responded to the British Air Ministry, which had inquired whether it was possible to build a "death ray" machine. In his memorandum, Watson-Watt explained that death ray machines were in the realm of science fiction. However, he also described the basic principles involved in developing a radiolocation device and suggested that one could be built. Within two months research on radar began, and when World War II broke out, a chain of radar stations had been built along the coast of Great Britain. Radar enabled the British to establish a warning system that alerted fighter pilots and English citizens of impending German attacks 20 minutes before the enemy planes reached the west side of the English Channel.

The invention of the magnetron in 1942 provided a small, light source of high-frequency radio waves. Magnetrons no larger than a fist, together with a small concave antenna, could be mounted within an aircraft, giving it the ability to detect enemy planes or bombing targets. Without doubt, radar was instrumental in the success of Allied forces during World War II.

Magnetrons were found to have a domestic use after the war. They are the source of the radiation in microwave ovens. When centimeter-length electromagnetic waves are absorbed by the molecules in food, they cause the molecules to vibrate in the same way they do when heated in a more conventional oven. However, the microwave energy can reach the molecules deep within the food immediately. The energy does not have to be conducted inward from the surface, as is the case in older modes of cooking.

Pulsed and Continuous-Wave Radar

Radar signals may be transmitted as short bursts (pulses) of radiation or as a continuous beam of waves. Pulsed radar is the more commonly used of the two, but in either case the radiation is directed along a beam, and the reflected beam is received and analyzed to detect the location and/or speed of objects within the range of the device.

A radar station, which may be stationary or mobile, consists of a transmitter, a receiver, and an indicator. The transmitter uses an oscillator and rotating antenna to send out a beam of high-frequency radio waves that can detect objects in all directions. The small portion of the waves that are reflected back to the station are picked up by the antenna of a receiver and amplified before being sent to an indicator where they are displayed, usually on some kind of screen where the object or objects that reflect the waves appear as phosphorescent "blips." A scale on the screen, which is based on the time delay between pulse and echo, reveals the distance to the reflector and its direction.

How Radar Is Used

The uses of radar range from outer space exploration to microwave ovens. Space probes equipped with radar have been used to map the surface of other planets in our solar system. Microwave ovens in modern kitchens generate waves that are absorbed by food and converted to heat.

Radar makes it possible for air-traffic controllers to locate each airplane in the high-density air traffic around major airports. In addition to the primary radar used to locate airplanes, secondary radar is used to activate transponders on the aircraft, which send information about the plane's altitude, identity, and destination to the control center. Radar systems known as ground-control approach (GCA) at the ends of airport and air-

craft carrier runways provide automatic guidance so that airplanes can land even when visibility is limited.

Radar transmitters and receivers on airplanes make it possible for pilots to determine their altitude above ground level. Ordinary altimeters, which are based on air-pressure measurements, indicate height above sea level. However, planes flying over high terrain need to know more than their altitude relative to the sea. A radar altimeter communicates the distance between the plane and the ground below.

Radar is used to maintain safety on the water as well as in the air. Marine radar, found on all major ships, is used to detect nearby vessels, shorelines, and buoys. Onshore radar in harbors is used to guide ships in and out of port. Only with radar can ships move safely through fog-covered seas and harbors.

Radar plays an important role in weather forecasting and warnings. Radar waves on the order of a centimeter can detect rain, hurricanes, tornadoes, and weather fronts, map their paths, and determine their rate of approach long before they reach the weather center. Radar, together with weather satellites, enables meteorologists to make forecasts that are much more accurate than was possible with older methods.

Giant, concave dish-shaped radio telescopes also send and receive radar signals as well as other radio waves. By studying the received echoes, astronomers can learn much about the objects that reflect those waves. For instance, radar waves picked up by such telescopes provided evidence supporting the big bang theory of the universe.

Scientists used radar to study the surface of the moon long before humans walked on it, and they have used radar to penetrate the cloud-covered surface of Venus and map its terrain. They have also used radar echoes to make accurate measurements of the distances to the moon and nearby planets. A meteorite streaking through the atmosphere leaves a trail of ions that can be detected and analyzed by radar to determine its speed, size, and direction. The National Aeronautics and Space Administration uses radar extensively in tracking and guiding its rockets and space vehicles.

Radar is widely used in the military to search for airplanes, ships, and missiles as well as to direct air traffic. Radar, together with computers, is also used by the military to direct missiles at enemy targets and to intercept and guide antiballistic projectiles. Radar on board bombers can map the terrain leading to a target.

Many drivers guilty of speeding are familiar with the use of radar by the police, who use it extensively to determine the velocity of automobiles on highways. Similar handheld radar devices are seen at baseball parks, where they are used to measure the velocity of a pitcher's fast ball. The transmitters and receivers on police cars use continuous-wave radar of a fixed frequency. The reflected beam coming back from a car has a slightly different frequency than the transmitted beam because of the Doppler effect. The Doppler effect with sound waves is commonly experienced when the pitch of a train whistle or a car horn is higher as it approaches than when it moves away. When the train or car is approaching, the emitted sound waves are squeezed closer together and so have a higher frequency than would be true if the source of the sound were stationary. As the whistle or horn moves away, the waves are stretched out, and the frequency of the sound is diminished because fewer waves reach the ear every second. Radar guns can detect the difference between the frequency of the signals sent and received. If the reflected signal is from an approaching vehicle, it will reflect signals more frequently than if the vehicle were standing still. Therefore, the returning signals will have a shorter wavelength and a higher frequency than the transmitted waves. If a car is moving away from the signal, it will reflect pulses less frequently. Consequently, the returning pulses will have a longer wavelength and a lower frequency than those being sent. Whether the car is coming or going, the frequency difference is quickly interpreted by a computer and displayed as a speed.

See also:
Electromagnetic Waves; Hertz, Heinrich Rudolf; Magnetron; Microelectronics; Radio; Sonography.
References:
Buderi, Robert. *The Invention That Changed the World*. New York: Simon & Schuster, 1996.
Macaulay, David. *The Way Things Work*. Boston: Houghton Mifflin, 1988.
The New Book of Popular Science. Danbury, CT: Grolier, 1992.
Williams, Trevor I. *The History of Invention: From Stone Axes to Silicon Chips*. New York: Facts on File, 1987.

Radio

Radio is a communication medium that transmits and receives sound by means of electromagnetic waves. During the second quarter of the twentieth century, radio was the predominant form of mass communication.

The Development of Radio Technology

During the early nineteenth century, both Michael Faraday and Joseph Henry discovered that an electric current in one wire can induce a current in another wire without any direct contact. Building on this initial discovery and the other experimental work on magnetism and electricity carried out by these two scientific giants, James Clerk Maxwell developed the mathematics needed to unify, expand, and codify their work into a complete theory that would lead to a revolution in communication. Maxwell's equations suggested that accelerating electric charges would be accompanied by the release of electromagnetic waves that would travel at the speed of light (300,000 kilometers per second). Visible light constituted but one small segment of the electromagnetic spectrum, and Maxwell's work indicated that a wide range of wavelengths was possible.

In 1888, 21 years after Maxwell predicted the existence of electromagnetic waves, Heinrich Hertz in Germany discovered a way to generate and receive such waves. Seven years later, Guglielmo Marconi found a practical application for the waves when he developed the wireless telegraph, which was the forerunner of radio.

Marconi's transmitters were activated by a key so that the waves could be sent as long and short pulses and received as dots and dashes similar to the Morse code heard on a telegraph receiver. The difference was that the messages were sent without wires. They traveled through space as electromagnetic waves, not as electrical pulses moving within a metallic conductor.

The continuous electromagnetic waves generated by today's radio stations make it possible to receive words and music rather than dots and dashes. In order to allow messages from different senders to be broadcast, radio stations are assigned a wave with particular frequency on which they transmit information. AM radio stations communicate with listeners by generating wavelengths that range from 187 to 560 meters with a frequency of 535 to 1,605 kilohertz. FM stations use waves with a frequency of 88 to 108 megahertz that have wavelengths of 2.8 to 3.4 meters. Shortwave radio, which is used by hobbyists (sometimes called "ham" operators) and national world news services, uses frequencies that lie for the most part between those used by AM and FM stations. Because each station is assigned a particular broadcast frequency, listeners can tune their dials to the station they choose.

The frequency of the waves generated at a radio station may be controlled by a quartz crystal that vibrates at a natural frequency. The frequency of vibration depends on the size of the crystal. Using the piezoelectric effect, the vibration can be changed to a voltage that oscillates at the same frequency as the crystal.

The electrical signals from the crystal give rise to the carrier waves, which are modified by pulses from a microphone. These pulses arise from sound waves containing the information the station wishes to transmit to listeners. The sound waves are added to the carrier wave by a process known as modulation. The modulated signal is amplified and sent to an antenna, where it forces electrons to oscillate up and down a long vertical antenna. The acceleration of electrons results in the formation of electromagnetic waves that radiate through space at the speed of light and with a frequency that corresponds to the rate at which the electrons oscillate. Incidentally, the product of the wavelength and frequency of an electromagnetic wave always equals the speed of light. Consequently, as wavelength increases, frequency decreases; thus, doubling the frequency of the radiation halves the wavelength.

When the radio waves reach a receiving antenna, they cause electrons in the antenna to oscillate weakly at the same frequency as the waves. Of course, waves from other stations also reach the antenna, but a process known as heterodyning allows single-dial tuning so that the radio responds to the frequency of the station the listener wants to hear. For example, if a pure radio wave of 1,000 kilohertz reaches a radio antenna, the listener will hear nothing, because the carrier wave alone provides no information. The signal used to modulate the carrier wave holds the information to be communicated. The received signal is amplified and filtered to remove the carrier wave so that only the sound signal remains to drive the loudspeaker within the radio.

Radio Circuits

A resonant or tuned circuit is one of the most important circuits in communication. It is used to select the station. The simplest resonant circuit consists of a capacitor and an inductor (Figure 1a). If the capacitor is charged and the circuit is then closed so that the capacitor begins to discharge as electrons flow around the circuit from the negative to the positive plate, the discharge will not be instantaneous; instead, it will require a finite period of time. Current flowing through the inductor produces a magnetic field that will oppose the flow of charge. The capacitor's rate of discharge will depend on the capacitance and the inductance, but when the electric field between the plates becomes zero, the current will be zero, and the magnetic field will be decreasing within the inductor.

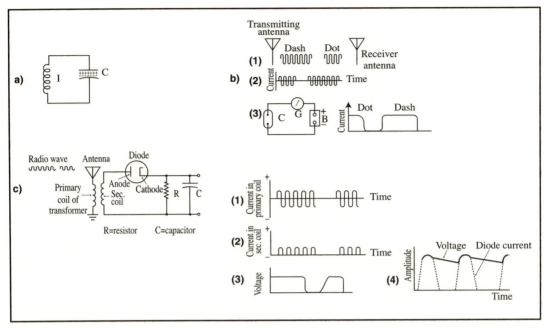

Figure 1. a, I = inductor and C = capacitor. b1, Radio waves reaching receiving antenna; b2, current in receiving antenna; b3, left, coherer circuit, in which C = coherer, G = galvanometer, B = battery; b3, right, current detected by galvanometer. c, Diode rectifier; c1, current versus time in primary coil; c2, current versus time in secondary coil that is in series with a diode; c3, voltage across capacitor (C) and resistor (R); c4, charge on capacitor versus time (solid line) and current through diode (dotted line).

The changing magnetic field, this time changing in the opposite direction, will cause the current to continue to flow in the same direction as before until the plates are again charged, but with charges of opposite sign from before. The positive plate will now be negatively charged, and vice versa. The electrons then begin to flow in the opposite direction around the circuit, and similar but oppositely directed magnetic fields grow and shrink, producing a charge flow that returns the circuit to very nearly its original state. This back-and-forth flow of charge, much like the oscillation of a swing or pendulum, has a frequency that is given by one over two pi times the square root of the product of the inductance and capacitance, or

$$f = \frac{1}{2\pi} \sqrt{LC}$$

where L is the inductance and C the capacitance. The frequency at which the charge oscillates depends on the inductance and ca-

pacitance. If the inductance is a thousandth of a henry (10^{-3} h) and the capacitance is a millionth of a farad (10^{-6} f, or 1 μf), then the frequency will be 5,000 hertz. With a receiver's variable capacitor, the tuning circuit can be adjusted to match the frequency of the carrier wave that the listener wishes to receive.

The frequency of radio waves is much too large to be detected by a speaker or a galvanometer. In the early days of wireless, when messages were sent by Morse code, a coherer could respond to the signals satisfactorily because the coherer conducted throughout the time that the electromagnetic field oscillated through it. The pulses of electromagnetic radiation through the coherer tube were enough to move a galvanometer needle (Figure 1*b*).

With John Fleming's invention of the diode, a much more sensitive means of detecting radio waves became available. In the diagram shown in Figure 1*c*, the same dot-

237

dash wave code is used for clarity. However, we could be considering a modulated wave, which would have a frequency of hundreds or thousands that could be detected.

The radio wave entering the antenna produces an oscillating current in the antenna and primary coil of the transformer that matches that of the radio wave; that is, the current flows both ways through the wire (Figure 1c, panel 1). However, the current in the secondary coil is in series with the diode. Since current will flow through the diode only when its anode is positive, the current in the secondary coil of the transformer will also flow in only one direction (DC). The current in the circuit containing the diode will show only the positive portions of the current produced by the oscillating electric field in the antenna (Figure 1c, panel 2). The voltage across the resistor (R) and capacitor (C) is shown in Figure 1c, panel 3. The capacitor in parallel with the resistor serves to smooth the output voltage to match the signal. The first current pulse charges the capacitor; then, before it can discharge significantly, a second pulse recharges it (Figure 1c, panel 4).

The diode served to detect radio waves, but the signal was often not strong enough to drive a speaker. However, two years after Fleming developed the diode vacuum tube, Lee De Forest invented the triode, a device that could amplify the signal from the diode and made radio as we know it possible. De Forest added a grid—a cylinder of thin wires that surrounded the cathode. A small change in the voltage on the grid can produce a large change in the current flowing from cathode to anode.

The circuit shown in Figure 2 contains a triode. The grid (dotted line) is between the cathode and the anode. The triode is used to amplify an antenna signal that has been rectified by a diode. It is in series with a bias (in this case negative) voltage applied to the grid circuit, so the grid voltage is the sum of the bias voltage and the signal voltage. Normally, the grid carries a negative charge and repels some of the electrons that boil off the cathode. By making the grid less negative, more electrons will reach the anode. The cur-

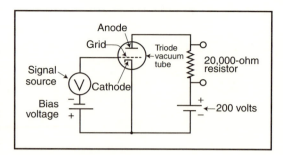

Figure 2. A radio circuit.

rent through the triode is driven by a 200-volt battery, and the triode is in series with a 20,000-ohm resistor or load, which serves as the voltage source for another part of the circuit that leads, perhaps, to a speaker.

If the grid voltage is –3 volts and the current flow through the triode is a milliampere (10^{-3} A), then the voltage across the load will be the current times the resistance, or 20 volts, because

$$20,000 \text{ ohms} \times 1.0 \times 10^{-3} \text{ A} = 20 \text{ volts.}$$

With the grid at –2 volts, the current through the triode might be 2 milliamps. Then, the voltage across the resistor would double to 40 volts because

$$20,000 \text{ ohms} \times 2.0 \times 10^{-3} \text{ A} = 40 \text{ volts.}$$

A change of 1 volt at the grid results in a change of 20 volts (40 – 20) at the load, which is an amplification of 20.

Today, most diode and triode vacuum tubes have been replaced by solid-state diodes and transistors. The emitter, base, and collector of a transistor are analogous to the cathode, grid, and anode of a triode vacuum tube. Just as a small grid voltage can control a larger output voltage, so a small signal to the base of a transistor can control a large current between the emitter and collector.

Citizens Band Radio

Citizens band (CB) radio, which was introduced in 1947, allows its users to communicate with others within a region of 5 to 20 miles depending on conditions and the power of the transmitter. It is particularly popular with truckers, who use CB radios to exchange information about weather, road conditions, emergencies, and speed traps.

CB transmitters and receivers operate at 4 watts of power on the 27 megahertz band using AM signals. There are 40 separate channels between 26.965 and 27.405 megahertz. Channel 19 serves as a party line for the exchange of local information; channel 9 is reserved for sending information about emergencies. Base stations are connected to 120-volt AC lines. The mobile rigs found in trucks and cars and small handheld walkie-talkies are powered by batteries.

CB communication has developed its own colorful jargon. "Superslabs" are interstate highways, reckless drivers are referred to as "kamikazes," speeders are called "high rollers," people who talk too long are called "ratchet jaws," and the police are known as "smoky."

See also:
Battery; Capacitor; Coherer; Diode; Electromagnetic Waves; Inductor; Loudspeaker; Marconi, Guglielmo; Microphone; Modulation; Radio and Society; Radio History; Sarnoff, David; Television; Television and Society; Transistor.

References:
Gardner, Robert. *Communication*. New York: Twenty-First Century, 1994.
International Encyclopedia of Communications. New York: Oxford University Press, 1989.
Jensen, Peter R. *In Marconi's Footsteps: Early Radio*. Cincinnati: Kangaroo Press, 1994.
Macaulay, David. *The Way Things Work*. Boston: Houghton Mifflin, 1988.
Newman, James R., ed. *The World of Mathematics*. New York: Simon & Schuster, 1956.
Wheeler, Gerald F., and Larry D. Kirkpatrick. *Physics: Building a World View*. Englewood Cliffs, NJ: Prentice-Hall, 1983.

Radio and Society

Radio's major impact on society occurred during the 1930s. With a depressed economy that prevented families from spending money on entertainment and travel, they could find enjoyment in their own living rooms by listening to the radio. People began to listen faithfully to their favorite programs, many of which contained a story line. As the threat of war grew in Europe and in the Pacific, adult listeners relied heavily on radio news programs for up-to-date information. After the war began, nightly radio news broadcasts featuring correspondents close to the action kept the civilian population informed, while recorded programs boosted the morale of American troops, who could continue to listen to their favorite programs.

Radio required more imagination than television, just as a book requires more imagination than a movie. Although sound effects, such as a creaking door, were often used to create fear or interest, listeners could not see the actors or setting of a radio drama, the players in a sports broadcast, or the musicians playing at a symphony. They had to imagine the faces, the action, and the setting. As a result, the social and psychological impact of radio was often more pronounced than is true of television. On Halloween in 1938, the Mercury Theater of the Air, under the direction and narration of Orson Welles, presented "The War of the Worlds," based on an H. G. Wells novel about an invasion of earth by Martians. The program, which included simulated eyewitness reports and news flashes, was so well done that thousands of listeners fled their homes or called police stations to ask what they should do.

Post–World War II Radio

After World War II, television antennas began to appear on rooftops, and by 1960 television had replaced radio as America's primary source of entertainment. Nevertheless, radio remains an important part of our culture. As television took over the national networks, radio stations took on a local character supported by local sponsors, and their number grew. During the 40 years following World War II, licensed radio stations increased by a factor of ten. Today, we still find radios in most homes as well as in automobiles, trucks, and offices. Radio is used as a source of quick news, traffic reports, background music, and as an alarm clock. How-

Radio building was a popular trend in the 1920s. Here, a Brooklyn radio store owner instructs a young teen in the art of making his own wireless set. By the 1930s, the radio boom had hit as the number of homes with radios increased from one-third in 1930 to two-thirds in 1935.

ever, many local radio stations, in order to compete with television, have had to court a particular audience. This becomes evident by turning the radio dial. There are rock stations; stations that play only classical, pop, western, or country music; and stations that specialize in news, religion, or talk shows. Some stations encourage listeners to call in and contribute to the conversational theme of the day.

By using transistors and batteries, radios can be made so small that they can easily be carried from place to place in a pocket. Joggers and walkers use special earphones that allow them to listen to their pocket radios even while they exercise. They are probably tuned to their own favorite local station.

However, national radio might make a comeback. In May 1996, the Associated Press reported that the Federal Communications Commission is considering a plan to license radio stations that could be heard throughout the country, primarily in automobiles and trucks. Using satellites and digital technology, these stations would provide a service known as digital audio radio. After buying a special digital radio and paying a fee, users would receive a tiny disc-shaped antenna that could be attached to a vehicle. They would then have access to a package of channels broadcasting at a frequency of 25 megahertz that would provide sports, news, and weather information as well as economic reports and various kinds of music.

See also:
Federal Communications Commission; Radio History; Sarnoff, David; Television; Television and Society.

References:
International Encyclopedia of Communications.
New York: Oxford University Press, 1989.
Macaulay, David. *The Way Things Work.*
Boston: Houghton Mifflin, 1988.
Williams, Trevor I. *The History of Invention: From Stone Axes to Silicon Chips.* New York: Facts on File, 1987.

Radio History

The first continuous radio waves to carry uncoded messages were sent on Christmas Day 1906 by Reginald Fessenden, a Canadian electrical engineer who demonstrated that continuous electromagnetic waves could be used to carry sound. From his transmitter at Brant Rock, Massachusetts, he sent words and music to ships off the Atlantic coast.

Following Fessenden's demonstration, there was extensive experimentation by amateur radio operators, electrical engineers, researchers, inventors, the military, and companies interested in communication. It was soon discovered that vacuum tubes—both diodes and triodes, which were invented by Sir John Fleming and by Lee De Forest, respectively, in 1904 and 1906—vastly improved the clarity of the information carried by continuous radio waves, and the electronics industry was born.

During World War I, radio was restricted to military use. After the war, however, companies such as General Electric, Westinghouse, and Western Electric that had supplied the armed forces with radio equipment turned their attention to the civilian market. In an effort to increase public awareness of the marvels of radio and to develop a market for its products, Westinghouse established the first radio station—KDKA—in Pittsburgh just in time to broadcast the returns of the 1920 election.

The Westinghouse experiment worked. Radios sold as fast as they could be manufactured, and new stations were established across the country. To avoid signal interference, the Department of Commerce required stations to be licensed and assigned different carrier wave broadcast frequencies to stations in the same region of the country.

Westinghouse, together with General Electric, AT&T, and United Fruit, bought American Marconi from the British parent company and formed the Radio Corporation of America (RCA). Other groups, such as churches, hotels, newspapers, and universities, also became interested in establishing radio stations. To meet operating costs, stations began as early as 1922 to seek sponsors who provided funds in return for advertising. The commercialization of radio led to national networks such as the National Broadcasting Company (NBC), a subsidiary of RCA, which was formed in 1926. Two years later, the Columbia Broadcasting System (CBS) was founded under the auspices of William Paley, a cigar company magnate who wanted to promote sales on a nationwide basis.

Sponsors hired advertising agencies to produce the programs and commercials for the networks. The agencies tried to attract listeners with a variety of programs, including soap operas, drama, comedy, name bands, and symphonies, but the bottom line was sales. If the program and the commercials increased sales, they stayed on the airwaves. If they did not, the sponsor looked for a new program or a new medium.

In Europe, radio, which was generally under government control, sought to enlighten rather than sell. The British Broadcasting System (BBC) decided what it thought the public should hear. As a result, radio programs in Great Britain were more informative and serious than those in the United States.

The rapid growth of broadcasting stations during the 1920s led some stations to ignore the Department of Commerce and shift their broadcast frequency. When the courts ruled that the Commerce Department had no right to license stations, Congress passed the Radio Act of 1927, which established the five-member Federal Radio Commission (FRC) to regulate the industry and set standards. Seven years later, as part of President Roosevelt's New Deal, a similar act established the Federal Communications Commission (FCC) to permanently oversee and regulate radio.

Radio flourished during the 1930s. The number of homes with radios increased from one-third in 1930 to two-thirds in 1935. People began to listen faithfully to their favorite programs and news broadcasts. As the war in Europe became imminent, networks sent commentators abroad, and the radio became a source of world news featuring people who were on the scene.

During World War II, the U.S. War Department made sure that broadcasting stations followed the troops and that recordings of major programs were sent to these stations. Being able to hear their favorite programs was a morale booster for soldiers and sailors far from home. Attempts by Axis powers to discourage U.S. servicemen with propaganda broadcasts by Tokyo Rose and Axis Sally backfired as soldiers found their comments amusing because they were so unfounded. Back in the states, civilians were able to learn about the war in detail by listening to radio correspondents who followed the troops in Europe and the Pacific.

After World War II, many thought that the rise of television would mark the demise of radio. However, radio has survived and remains an important part of our culture.

See also:
Fessenden, Reginald A.; Radio; Radio and Society; Sarnoff, David; Television; Television and Society.

References:
International Encyclopedia of Communications. New York: Oxford University Press, 1989. Macaulay, David. *The Way Things Work.* Boston: Houghton Mifflin, 1988. Williams, Trevor I. *The History of Invention: From Stone Axes to Silicon Chips.* New York: Facts on File, 1987.

Radio Telescope
See Radar.

Radioactive Dating
See Carbon Dating.

Radiotelegraphy (Wireless Telegraphy)

Radiotelegraphy is the transmission of coded messages by radio waves rather by the wires used in ordinary telegraphy. It was developed by Guglielmo Marconi who, after reading accounts of the experiments performed by Heinrich Hertz confirming James Clerk Maxwell's prediction that accelerated charges produce electromagnetic waves, recognized the practical implications for communication.

Marconi quickly set to work building a transmitter and detector that could send and detect Hertzian waves over a distance greater than 1 mile. Marconi's transmitter was activated by a key so that the radio waves could be sent as long and short pulses and received as dots and dashes similar to the Morse code heard on a telegraph receiver. Using a coherer, Marconi's receiver converted the radio waves to electric currents.

Later, Marconi successfully used his wireless telegraph to transmit radio waves across the Atlantic Ocean. This feat amazed and confused inventor Thomas Edison, who had maintained that long-distance transmission of wireless signals was impossible because electromagnetic waves travel in straight lines.

Marconi's success in long-distance transmission convinced him that radio waves are reflected back. We now know that the reflection is caused by the ionosphere, which extends upward from an altitude of about 50 miles (80 kilometers) to outer space. Within the ionosphere is a vast number of positively charged ions and free electrons. It is these charged particles that reflect radio waves back to the earth's surface and thus enable radio waves, which travel in straight lines, to be transmitted along the earth's curved surface for great distances. Because solar energy reduces the concentration of charges in the upper atmosphere, transmission of radio waves over long distances is generally better at night than during the day.

See also:
Electromagnetic Waves; Marconi, Guglielmo; Radio; Telegraph.

Reading

Reading is the ability to interpret and find meaning in the symbols that constitute a written language. The ability to read provides an individual with the fundamental skill needed to obtain meaning from the study of such academic disciplines as literature, history, science, and mathematics.

A person who can read is said to be literate, and literate members of a culture can share in a vast amount of common knowledge. They can learn the history of their society, its major literary works, and the civics needed to understand and possibly engage in its government.

Historically, literacy within a society has been of two types: high-level literacy for a privileged few and low-level literacy for the masses. To fully appreciate the complexities of today's technological world and to act and vote wisely in a democracy require a high level of literacy for all. A number of studies have shown that reading and writing involve higher mental processes than speech and that literacy brings with it an increased capacity for abstract thought and reasoning.

Research reveals that learning to read begins not in first grade, but during infancy. Children who are held, cuddled, and talked and read to, and who engage in a rich variety of experiential and language activities during infancy and early childhood, learn to read much more readily than children who lack such a background. The prereading skills that emerge from such nurturing—familiarity with one's native language, an awareness of the distinct sounds in words, and an ability to recognize letters and numbers—are essential to learning to read. James Trelease, a lecturer and reading expert, recommends that parents continue to read to their children throughout their school years. Because listening vocabulary and comprehension exceed reading vocabulary and comprehension, children benefit by listening to a reader through whom they become familiar with words they will later read.

Learning to read involves first mastering a code that allows one to translate written words to their oral equivalents. After that, practice provides fluency and automatic recognition of printed words. How the code that enables one to read is mastered is a matter of contention. The whole-language approach places the emphasis on the meaning of whole words, which the student learns by a "see and say" method. The phonics approach to reading involves recognizing symbols that represent sounds. The emphasis here is on breaking a word into recognizable syllables. With phonics, a child can use word-attack skills to decipher unfamiliar words.

Most people agree that children probably best learn to read if some combination of the two approaches is used. Phonics alone can be boring, but when combined with reading whole words it allows children to engage in the thrill of reading words they recognize while learning how to decode words they don't know.

A number of people, including Jeanne S. Chall, believe that people reach different levels of reading ability in the course of their education. Chall suggests six stages of reading. The first stage is really prereading, in which children recognize letters, can tell a story based on the pictures in a book, and enjoy being read to by someone older. The sixth stage is the most advanced. It is the reading ability expected of college and graduate students, who must comprehend difficult material and integrate it with their own knowledge and experience to create new ideas. Although most early-twentieth-century Americans probably read at the third stage, a level that allows one to read familiar stories and materials fluently, many believe that today's society requires at least a fifth-stage ability. This is the reading level expected of high school graduates, who should be able to read and understand a wide range of complex, unfamiliar materials from textbooks as well as high-quality literature, newspapers, and magazines.

The ever-changing nature of today's technologically oriented society makes the learning of new skills and new ideas a lifelong process. Consequently, the expectation that citizens read at a level commensurate with a

243

sound high school education seems not only reasonable but essential.

See also:
Communication among the Hearing Impaired; Communication among the Visually Impaired; Language; Speech; Writing.

References:
Anderson, Richard C., et al. *Becoming a Nation of Readers. The Report of the Commission on Reading.* Pittsburgh: National Academy of Education, 1985.

Chall, Jeanne S. *Stages of Reading Development.* New York: McGraw-Hill, 1983.

"Here Are Some of the Best Resources for Teaching Reading." *Learning,* May/June 1996.

International Encyclopedia of Communications. New York: Oxford University Press, 1989.

Nash, Madeleine J. "Fertile Minds." *Time,* 3 February 1997.

Relay

A relay is an electrically controlled switch used to open and close electric circuits. The most common relay consists of an electromagnet and a movable metallic armature, often attached to a spring, that is attracted by the electromagnet's core when a current flows in the electromagnet. The change in the armature's position is used to open or close a circuit.

Although several watts of power are required to operate an electromechanical relay such as the one described above, the development of transistors, which operate at very low power, made it possible and necessary for microelectronics to develop low-power relays. These transistor-suitable relays are made by enclosing two thin, springlike magnetic strips (reeds) within a small glass nitrogen-filled tube that is surrounded by a coil of wire. The nitrogen provides an inert environment that prevents the reeds from corroding as they would if oxygen were present. When current flows through the coil, a magnetic field is produced. The field causes the reeds, which are only 0.004 inch (100 microns) apart, to attract one another, thus closing a circuit. When current stops flowing through the coil, the magnetic field vanishes, the reeds separate, and the circuit is broken. Such transistorized relays are a basic compo-

nent of telephone switching and other computerized systems.

See also:
Burglar Alarm; Electromagnet; Henry, Joseph; Microelectronics; Telegraph; Telephone; Telephone Switching.

References:
How It Works: The Illustrated Encyclopedia of Science and Technology. New York and London: Marshall Cavendish, 1978.

Jahns, Patricia. *Joseph Henry, Father of American Electronics.* Englewood Cliffs, NJ: Prentice-Hall, 1971.

Jahns, Patricia. *Matthew Fontaine Maury and Joseph Henry, Scientists of the Civil War.* New York: Hastings House, 1961.

Rhetoric
See Oratory.

Road Signs
See Signage.

Robot

Robots are machines that carry out human tasks, and robotics is the development of the hardware and software used to make and operate robots. Robots are used primarily to perform repetitive assembly-line jobs that require great precision, and work that would be hazardous to humans. Computers are programmed to communicate the instructions needed for robots to carry out their work.

The origin of the word *robot,* which was first applied to machines in the 1920s, is to be found in a play entitled *R. U. R.* (for Rossum's Universal Robots) by the Czech author Karel Capek. *Robot* is a Czech word meaning "forced labor." In Capek's play, robots were human-shaped machines used to perform slave labor. The robots revolted and took over the world.

Electronic robots are a twentieth-century phenomenon, but the first machines "programmed" to move themselves go back much farther in time. Geared machines that incorporated a clock drive to produce re-

A student at DeVry Institute of Technology studies a large metal robotic arm.

peated complex movement were not uncommon in the 1700s, but they were toys designed to amuse the wealthy by writing messages or playing simple tunes on a piano.

Most robots have a "hand" that allows them to perform manipulative tasks. The hand, which is usually attached to a "wrist" built to carry out human movements related to pitch, yaw, and roll—as well as spin, which is not possible with a human wrist—can be fitted with a variety of tools and measuring devices that allow it to move materials or do jobs formerly performed by tools under human control. Using computer control it is possible to reprogram as well as program robots. Consequently, a robot programmed to carry out a particular task can be reprogrammed to do a very different job. Generally, robots are powered by electric motors, but pneumatic controls are sometimes used.

A robot can be "taught" to carry out a certain maneuver by having someone guide the robot's arm, wrist, and hand through the required motions. A series of angular sensors measure the angles in each joint as the motion takes place. These sensors are equipped with optical decoders, similar to bar-code readers, that send binary signals to a computer connected to the robot. The computer stores the angles in its memory as codes that can later be retrieved and used to move the robot through the same motion repeatedly. For more precise movements, such as those used in robotic surgery, the computer can be programmed to make movements more intricate than any that can be performed by the steadiest human hand.

Unlike humans, robots do not breathe or become bored or tired. They are ideal for doing tasks regarded by humans as repetitive, dangerous, or unpleasant. Furthermore, they can work where air is unavailable, such as underwater and in outer space, in the presence of toxic fumes or radiation, and in temperatures that would burn or freeze human flesh. In the automobile industry, where only approximately half the assembly process is carried out by humans, robots perform most of the welding, inspecting, die

casting, and spray painting. More delicately designed robots have been used to paint not automobile bodies but the canvases normally regarded as the domain of human artists. Such robots can be programmed to mass-produce scenes from nature, portraits, or abstract paintings. Can this be art?

It is easy to see how controlled repetitive-motion exercise used in the rehabilitation of joints following such surgery as hip and knee replacements could be assigned to robots that, unlike a physical therapist, would never tire. More difficult to comprehend is the experimental work now in progress in which robotic devices are used in surgery, including brain surgery. The computerized instructions fed to the robot enable it to perform motions so precise that surgeons seem increasingly inclined to place their patients in the hands of their robotic assistants when delicate and difficult techniques are required.

Although present-day robots lack sensors that can match human eyes and fingers, one goal of researchers is to develop computer-integrated manufacturing using robots with sight and touch sensors comparable to humans. These robots would not only carry out tasks that now require human sensitivity; they would also be able to share data, which is to say, communicate with one another. Such robots would be able to teach other robots. Some people question whether robotics can ever reach such a goal; others believe it is only a matter of time.

As robots take over more jobs, what happens to the humans displaced from their work? Will the increased production made possible by robotics create jobs requiring greater skill, or will robots give rise to ever-increasing unemployment?

See also:

Computer; Wiener, Norbert.

References:

Considine, Douglas M., ed. *Van Nostrand's Scientific Encyclopedia*, 8th ed. New York: Van Nostrand, 1995.
Macaulay, David. *The Way Things Work.* Boston: Houghton Mifflin, 1988.
Tanaka, Jennifer, et al. "Vincent Van Robo." *Newsweek*, 8 May 1995.

Taylor, Rupert. "The End of Work." *Canada & the World*, November 1993.

Role Playing

Shakespeare's words—"All the world's a stage, and all the men and women merely players"—ring as true today as when he wrote them 400 years ago. Everyone has a status in work and society, and for each status there is a role—a set of expectations for behavior. In a corporation there is a social structure that can often be summarized by means of a chart showing who is subordinate to whom and how different divisions are related to one another. For each position on the chart, there is a job description specifying the behavior expected for that particular role.

In role playing, a person is asked to assume a role other than the one that person normally has for the purpose of making that person (and those who watch the drama unfold) aware of the circumstances that guide the individual who normally lives that particular role. At a job interview for a position as manager of a store, a candidate might be asked to assume that role while the interviewer takes on the part of a dissatisfied customer. In school, a student in a civics class might play the role of the city's mayor while other students assume roles as city councilors or heads of various departments. Students might also assume roles in a history class so that they and those watching the "play" can see both sides of a current issue under debate in Congress or the positions taken by Union president Abraham Lincoln and Confederate president Jefferson Davis at the beginning of the Civil War. The chief executive officer (CEO) of a business might ask an employee to assume the role of CEO in order to convey to this and other employees watching the play why the company is not making as much money as its employees might think it should be. Through role playing, the CEO can reveal the many costs involved in running a business, such as advertising, health insurance, rent, taxes, materials, and maintenance.

By role playing, a person or persons can better understand the reasons and forces that cause another person or group to behave as they do. Role playing, therefore, can be valuable in many ways. It can communicate to employees why management acts as it does, and vice versa. It can help students to understand that issues can be viewed from different perspectives or demonstrate why a teacher or administrator behaved in a certain way or made a particular decision. It can be used in marriage or other counseling to help people understand why other people respond or behave as they do. In general, role-playing helps people to see the world from a different perspective than their own and to be more understanding and tolerant of other people and other points of view.

References:
Cage, Mary Crystal. "Mixing the Outrageous with the Educational." *Chronicle of Higher Education*, 24 March 1995.
Dobrzynski, Judith H. "Executive Tests Now Plumb New Depths of Job Seeker." *New York Times*, 2 September 1996.
Matimore, Bryan W. "Eureka." *Futurist*, March/April 1995.
"On-the-Spot Screen Test." *Inc.*, December 1994.
"Open-Book Management 101." *Inc.*, August 1996.

Roper, Elmo Burns, Jr. (1900–1971)

Elmo Roper, a public opinion analyst, was the first to develop a scientific poll to make political forecasts. Roper was born on 31 July 1900 in Hebron, Nebraska, where he attended public schools. Although he attended the University of Minnesota and the University of Edinburgh, he never received a degree. In 1921, he opened a jewelry store in Creston, Iowa. A year later he married Dorothy C. Shaw, and they had two children.

In 1928, Roper became a clock salesman, a career that he pursued with different companies for five years. During this period he developed an interest in consumer preferences and sales management that led him in 1933 to join with Paul T. Cherington and Richardson

Wood to form the marketing research firm of Cherington, Roper & Wood. The firm designed and used questionnaires to interview people who represented a cross section of American society. Based on their subjects' responses, they were able to forecast sales figures for various products. Because the nation was in a devastating depression during the 1930s, companies were willing to pay a relatively small sum to Cherington, Roper & Wood to find out if a product would sell before investing large amounts of money in it.

Roper developed a design for opinion polls that allowed him to make accurate predictions using relatively small samples. His success led Henry Luce to hire Cherington, Roper & Wood in 1935 to conduct surveys of public opinion. He also hired Roper to write a regular column, which continued for 15 years, for *Fortune* magazine. In 1938, Roper established his own firm, Roper Research Associates.

Roper had gained prominence in 1936 when he predicted, to within 1 percent of the actual count, a landslide victory for Franklin D. Roosevelt. In 1940 and 1944, his predictions were within half a percentage point of the popular vote. In 1948, like all the other pollsters, Roper predicted incorrectly that Thomas Dewey would win the election, and he failed to conduct last-minute surveys that, if accurate, would have shown incumbent Harry Truman to be the winning candidate. Although Roper incorrectly predicted Nixon over Kennedy in the very close election of 1960, his sampling techniques became widely used by other pollsters and political campaign strategists.

Roper's firm did not limit itself to public opinion surveys on political, economic, and social issues for *Fortune*. It also carried out marketing research for life insurance, meat, oil, power, tobacco, and broadcasting companies, among others. During World War II, Roper served as deputy director of the Office of Strategic Services, and for one year he taught journalism at Columbia University. Roper also worked as a broadcaster for CBS and an editor-at-large for the *Saturday Review*, and he performed analyses for various magazines and radio stations.

After the war Roper became associated with a number of liberal causes and organizations while continuing to work with the firm he had founded. He wrote *You and Your Leaders*, which was published in 1957, and in 1959 he received, and certainly merited, the Julian Woodward Award of the American Association for Public Opinion Research.

Roper retired in 1966 to his home in Redding, Connecticut, where he served on various town boards. He continued to work to conserve the local environment and also owned an experimental farm in Nebraska, where he investigated soil conservation. During his later years, he came to the conclusion that predicting elections was a useless task and that the true purpose of polling should be to identify the need for information that could be used to surmount public ignorance. He had great faith that the people would make judicious decisions if they had thorough and objective information.

Roper died on 30 April 1971 in the Norwalk (Connecticut) Hospital at the age of 70.

See also:
Gallup, George H.; Luce, Henry R.; Public Opinion.

Reference:
International Encyclopedia of Communications. New York: Oxford University Press, 1989.

Sarnoff, David (1891–1971)

A communications executive who was a pioneer in the development of radio and television in the United States, David Sarnoff led a life that was a classic American success story. A Russian immigrant who began in the electronics industry as a wireless operator, Sarnoff's drive and dedication led him to the position of chairman of the board and chief executive officer of the Radio Corporation of America (RCA). Sarnoff's six decades of leadership established a giant in the electronics field that dominated radio production and broadcasting and eventually evolved into the most significant business in American television.

Sarnoff was born in Uzhan, Russia, on 27 February 1891, the oldest of five children. The family emigrated to New York City's Lower East Side when Sarnoff was nine years old. Sarnoff attended school through the eighth grade, but his house-painter father's illness forced David, the oldest son, to help support his immigrant family. As a newsboy, Sarnoff contributed financially to the family while making some educational progress through the Educational Alliance, an East Side settlement house.

The year 1906 was a momentous one for Sarnoff. He took a job at the Commercial Cable Company as a messenger boy for $5 dollars a week. In his spare moments, Sarnoff taught himself Morse code and became a very accomplished telegraph operator. Years later, as president of RCA, he had a telegraph key built into his desk drawer and never tired of displaying his skill as an operator to anyone who entered his office. Unfortunately, the aspiring telegrapher was fired from his position when he had the temerity to complain about being required to work on the Jewish holy days. In a stroke of monumental good luck, a friend told him about an opening at the Marconi Wireless Telegraph Company of America. Sarnoff did get a job, not as an operator, but as an office boy with a 50-cent raise over his previous position. Acting in a way that was to become typical of his later business life, Sarnoff attacked the small technical library at Marconi and

scoured the New York Public Library for material on Marconi and the wireless. Sarnoff met his idol on one of Marconi's frequent trips to New York and became his personal messenger. The Italian inventor took a personal interest in his young employee and became his mentor. One year later, shortly after his seventeenth birthday, Sarnoff was promoted to junior operator and finally gave up his paper routes to devote all his energies to his new occupation.

Marconi's support promised quick advancement for the young novice, who proved himself a worthy protégé. In 1908, Sarnoff readily accepted a hardship position at Marconi's station on Nantucket Island. The job not only provided more money but also allowed Sarnoff time to continue studying. By 1909, Sarnoff had been promoted to manager of the Sea Gate station in Brooklyn, where he supervised operators older than himself. A series of other positions followed in rapid succession. In 1912 he took over as manager of the station atop the Wanamaker Department Store in New York City. The station was primarily a publicity gimmick for the Marconi and Wanamaker businesses, which planned to lure curious consumers to the store and after shopping encourage them to see the wireless equipment. The Marconi staff were essentially guides who explained the equipment and answered questions. Sarnoff did not seem to mind, since he kept store hours that allowed him to take night classes in electrical engineering at Pratt Institute.

Sarnoff developed an outstanding knowledge of the wireless industry and had an impressive résumé with the field's most recognized company, but it was the *Titanic* disaster that vaulted the wireless, its potential, and

Sarnoff to national prominence. The Sarnoff legend, already off to a creditable start due to his rapid advancement in the company, was considerably enhanced by the 1912 tragedy. On 14 April 1912, the *Titanic* struck an iceberg and sank on her maiden voyage, taking many of her crew and passengers with her. Sarnoff, manning the Wanamaker station, allegedly heard the first reports of the catastrophe and stayed at his post for hours relaying information from the rescue ships as he received it. Without doubt, Sarnoff played a part in reporting the accident, but the apocryphal story conveniently neglects the fact that the store was closed at the time of the disaster. Over the years, Sarnoff's role was magnified and became part of radio folklore, and Sarnoff did little to correct the record. Nonetheless, the accident demonstrated the practical importance of the new medium and led Congress to mandate that ships install wireless equipment and maintain operators to ensure safety at sea.

Promotions continued on a regular basis for Sarnoff, and the Marconi Company prospered. However, by 1915, Sarnoff, whose variety of experience in the field made him invaluable, was convinced that the company was losing its technical edge. On 30 September, he wrote a prophetic memorandum outlining a new vision for Marconi. He suggested the development of radio as a "household utility," like a piano or phonograph. The "radio music box," as he termed it, would broadcast programs into homes over several wavelengths that could be changed upon request. There was no response from the company. Not only would Sarnoff's project require a reorientation of the company, which was secure in its leadership role and unconcerned with voice communication, but Marconi himself felt that radio was a figment of the writer's imagination. Furthermore, the company could not expend energy and resources in a new venture. Competition from the government and AT&T was increasing, World War I had begun, and radio was relegated to a secondary consideration. Sarnoff reached a crossroad in his career. As an engineer with no college degree,

his prospect for further advancement was limited. He decided that management was a more practical alternative.

The conclusion of World War I brought new pressures for the Marconi Company. The U.S. government and navy, convinced of the importance of wireless communication and determined not to allow the British to control the new system, as they did the transoceanic cable, urged Marconi to sell his interests in the American subsidiary to an American company. In 1919, General Electric (GE), with ultimate financial support from Westinghouse, AT&T, and United Fruit, bought American Marconi and established the Radio Corporation of America (RCA). The Marconi staff, including their commercial manager, Sarnoff, were absorbed into the new company. RCA sold radios manufactured by GE and Westinghouse, as well as radio tubes and components. As part of the restructuring, Chairman Owen D. Young called on the most experienced, knowledgeable, and competent man in the business for his assessment of radio and its future. In January 1920, Sarnoff responded with a comprehensive 28-page report reiterating his earlier proposal that broadcasting was the future of radio. Moderately interested, Young directed that $25,000 be spent to develop the simple "music box" described in Sarnoff's memorandum.

The less-than-enthusiastic development pace at RCA disheartened Sarnoff, and he was devastated when Westinghouse began its own broadcast system with KDKA in Pittsburgh. Westinghouse's success in broadcasting the 1920 election returns sparked the development of several new stations before RCA awoke from its stupor. In danger of being defeated by a rival's implementation of his idea, Sarnoff reacted quickly. On 21 July 1921, RCA regained at least part of its acclaim as the industry leader with the successful broadcast of the heavyweight championship prize fight from Jersey City, New Jersey. His efforts finally recognized, Sarnoff was appointed vice-president of RCA in 1922.

The 1920s were a period of unbridled success for RCA and Sarnoff. In 1926, Sarnoff established the National Broadcasting Corporation (NBC) to provide high-quality programming to the nation. RCA's wide diversification began in 1928 as Sarnoff and Joseph P. Kennedy combined to create the RKO motion picture company using RCA sound equipment.

Sarnoff took over the Victor Talking Machine Company in 1929. For several years RCA had built components for the Victor radio-phonograph, and now the communications giant owned not only Victor's production facilities but also their lucrative phonograph record operation. Sarnoff's role in RCA's prosperity was rewarded with his appointment as president in 1930 at the age of 39.

The Great Depression of the 1930s might have crushed a lesser company, but to Sarnoff it was a test. From its inception, RCA was besieged by monopoly charges, and the corporation's success in the 1920s did little to diminish those accusations. In 1932, under government pressure, GE and Westinghouse severed their ties with RCA. The newfound independence allowed Sarnoff to begin the pursuit of another new technology. As early as 1923, Sarnoff had written a memo to the RCA board extolling the promise of a new product—television. Not even the Depression cut RCA's research budget as television became Sarnoff's new fascination. Sarnoff's ambition was fueled by meeting, and ultimately hiring as head of RCA's research bureau, Vladimir Zworykin. Zworykin was the foremost proponent of an all-electric television system and was the new medium's lead inventor. In 1939, television was introduced at the New York World's Fair, but it was not mass-marketed until after World War II.

Television, which developed rapidly during the post–World War II period, is without a doubt the major medium for mass communication today. But many do not realize that it could have become popular before the war had a feud not developed between Sarnoff and inventor Edwin Armstrong, the man who devised the heterodyne system that made radio tuning a simple task.

Sarnoff had suggested that Armstrong find a way to eliminate the static that is often associated with AM radio, which was the only radio at that time. In 1933, Armstrong invited Sarnoff to look at his solution. It consisted of a room full of equipment used for an entirely new means of broadcasting, namely frequency modulated (FM) radio. Sarnoff was not interested because he was planning to use RCA's financial resources to develop television, not a more sophisticated form of radio. Armstrong, who believed that FM radio was his major accomplishment as an inventor, discovered that Sarnoff was seeking to prevent the development of FM in order to promote television.

Sarnoff and Armstrong battled in courts, patent offices, and Federal Communications Commission (FCC) hearings for years. As a result, the development of both television and FM radio was delayed until after World War II. However, as the battles raged, Armstrong, using his own resources, built an FM station in New Jersey to demonstrate its superiority to AM radio. General Electric recognized the potential of Armstrong's invention and began to consider it seriously as war broke out in Europe. The FCC, also recognizing the significance of Armstrong's work, decided in 1940 that the sound system used by future television broadcasters in the United States should use FM. Armstrong eventually won all the court cases against Sarnoff and RCA. Unfortunately, the decisions went to him posthumously. In 1954, virtually bankrupt and physically spent, Armstrong committed suicide.

Nicknamed "The General" for his service in World War II, Sarnoff spent many of his later years overseeing the development of color television. RCA spent millions of dollars in research and development and in return received industrywide ridicule. The joke was that an engineer was needed to adjust the color with as many as five knobs, but Sarnoff was obsessed with the project. However, it was not until the early 1960s that RCA began to recoup its considerable investment. Sarnoff's greatest victory before his skeptical peers not only confirmed his insight but made RCA the industry leader again.

In 1965, Sarnoff turned over operations of RCA to his son, Robert, though he remained chairman of the board. A debilitating disease struck him in 1968 and ended his voice in the company. After a three-year struggle, the man who shaped an industry died in his sleep on 12 December 1971.

Without the Sarnoff touch, RCA declined. Forsaking its original field of electronics, the corporation began to diversify. Poor investments eroded the financial resources accumulated by the success of color television. In 1986, RCA came full circle when it was taken over and dismantled by its original parent, General Electric.

See also:
Television; Television and Society; Zworykin, Vladimir Kosma.

References:
Barnouw, Erik. *A Tower of Babel: A History of Broadcasting in the United States to 1933.* New York: Oxford University Press, 1966.
Lewis, Tom. *Empire of the Air: The Men Who Made Radio.* New York: HarperCollins, 1991.
Sarnoff, Lizette. "My Life with a Genius." *Good Housekeeping,* June 1955.

Satellite

Natural satellites are objects that orbit a planet. The earth's only natural satellite is our moon. However, we have known since Sir Isaac Newton published his *Principia* in 1686 that artificial satellites are possible. Newton showed that at altitudes close to the earth's surface, all that is needed is to provide the potential satellite with a horizontal velocity of 17,500 miles (28,500 kilometers) per hour. At such a speed, the earth will curve away from the satellite at the same rate that gravity pulls it earthward. The only problem was finding a way to achieve such high speeds. Nearly 300 years later, rocket technology provided the force that was needed, and the Soviet Union launched *Sputnik* on 4 October 1957. The United States soon followed with *Explorer 1* on 31 January 1958.

Today, there are thousands of artificial satellites in a variety of orbits about the earth. Before 1982, all artificial satellites were launched on the backs of rockets that propelled them into space. Since that time, some satellites have been carried into orbit aboard

one of the National Aeronautics and Space Administration (NASA) space shuttles.

Many satellites are designed to improve communication and to provide information that cannot be obtained on earth's surface. Once in orbit, most satellites use sunlight as their energy source. While the satellites are in darkness, storage batteries provide electricity, but the batteries are recharged on the other side of the earth by solar energy. These satellites require electricity in order to power attitude-control units, receivers, transmitters, antennas, sensors, and other equipment.

The period of different satellites—the time it takes a satellite to make one trip around the earth—depends on the satellite's orbit. Artificial satellites in orbits close to the earth, such as the space shuttle, have periods of about 80 to 90 minutes and velocities close to 18,000 miles (29,000 kilometers) per hour. The moon, with an orbit approximately 60 times the radius of the earth, or about 240,000 miles (380,000 kilometers), has a period of nearly a month and moves around the earth with a velocity of about 2,250 miles (3,600 kilometers) per hour. In between, at a distance of 6.63 earth radii from the earth's center, satellites have a period of 24 hours and speeds of about 6,900 miles (11,100 kilometers) per hour. The periods of these satellites match the earth's rotation. Consequently, they will stay in one place above the earth. To us, they appear to be motionless. These syncom (synchronous communications) or geostationary satellites, which have circular orbits above the earth's equator, are used to relay radio, telephone, and television signals around the world.

Communications Satellites

In terms of communication, satellites serve two distinct functions. One is to transmit information from one place on earth to another. A second is to make observations from space and collect, process, and transmit data about the earth and its environment to ground stations.

Satellites that are used to transmit information from one place on earth to another are referred to as *communications satellites*, although observational satellites certainly pro-

The Advanced Communications Technology Satellite (ACTS) begins orbiting the earth following its release from the space shuttle Discovery *on 12 September 1993.*

vide us with vast amounts of information, which is certainly a form of communication.

The first communications satellite was *Echo 1*, launched on 12 August 1960. It was nothing more than a huge plastic balloon 100 feet (30 meters) in diameter. It was followed by *Echo 2* and several other passive satellites —passive because they simply reflected signals back to earth. *Telstar 1*, launched by AT&T in 1962, was the first active communications satellite. It was capable of amplifying

and retransmitting 60 simultaneous telephone calls. Since then numerous communications satellites have been placed in orbit by national governments as well as private companies specializing in communication. A number of these satellites are in synchronous orbits.

Communications satellites are designed primarily to provide point-to-point linking of long-distance telephone calls, relay television signals (both transoceanic and within national boundaries), and transmit data between telecommunication networks. International services are provided by the International Telecommunications Satellite Consortium (Intelsat), which includes 114 nations with 800 ground stations. Most members of Intelsat are national governments, but the United States established the Communications Satellite Corporation (Comsat) as a government-sponsored corporation with ownership split between private companies and the government to oversee communications satellites. Comsat pays Intelsat for the use of satellites that it does not own and sells services to communications companies such as AT&T. There are a number of other international satellite consortiums, including Intersputnik (Russia and a number of Eastern European nations), Arabsat (20 Arabian countries), Eutelsat (26 European nations), and Immarsat, which was established to provide international communication for ships at sea.

The International Telecommunication Union (ITU), a United Nations agency, is responsible for the regulation and management of international communication through satellites. ITU assigns frequencies for ground stations, which send messages at one frequency and receive signals at a different frequency. One of the major problems with satellite communications is that most available frequencies are already in use. This problem is being surmounted, in part, by a gradual conversion to digital processing.

Satellites as Observational Platforms

Since the launch of *Tiros 1* in 1960, satellites have been used to provide meteorologists with weather data that include not only the position of cloud cover, which can be seen every day on television, but information about jet streams, sea ice, snow cover, fronts, and hurricanes as well. By 1966, a system of weather satellites provided worldwide coverage. Today, synchronous meteorological satellites (SMS), first launched in 1974, provide a complete view of each hemisphere from their positions fixed 5.63 earth radii above points on opposite sides of the equator.

In addition to weather satellites, there are satellites that measure or monitor reflected sunlight, radiation, the earth's magnetic and gravitational fields, ocean currents, ice cover, vegetation, soils, marine life, and land formations. By using satellite photographs, cartographers have been able to map the earth's total surface. Before the Space Age, only about a third of the earth had been accurately mapped using aerial photography. Navigation satellites, including the NAVSTAR satellites of the Global Positioning System, enable earthbound ships, planes, and even cars and hikers to determine their position to within a few meters.

Remote sensing data supplied by the U.S. Landsat series and the Soviet Union's *Soyuz 5* and *Soyuz 6* have been used to estimate world wheat production as well as provide vast amounts of information used in forestry, range management, hydrology, evaluating energy resources, providing warnings of floods and other disasters, and in monitoring the environment. *Seasat*, launched in 1978, used radar to measure altitudes of mountains and other land formations, wave heights, tides, and ocean currents. Other instruments on board were used to measure winds, rain, humidity, temperatures, changes in sea ice, and to collect other useful scientific data.

Military reconnaissance satellites have been used extensively by the United States and the Soviet Union (and presently by Russia) to observe missile sites, weapons deployment, wars, and war games. The televised photographs supplied by *Tiros 1,* although adequate for meteorologists, were not sufficiently clear for military surveillance. Consequently, *Corona/Discover 14* was launched on 18 August 1960. This satellite used cameras and film to photograph military targets. The encapsulated film was then ejected downward from the satellite and recovered in the atmosphere by military aircraft.

Since 1976, the U.S. military has used KH-11 satellites for surveillance activities. Equipped with telescopes, video cameras, and digital systems, they are said to be capable of resolving images of objects on earth to within centimeters, making it possible to read ordinary signs and even identify people.

The Hubble Space Telescope

The Hubble Space Telescope, which was placed in orbit in 1990 and repaired because of a faulty mirror in 1993, has provided astronomers with clear views of galaxies believed to be billions of light-years away. The information it has sent back to earth has already raised serious questions about current theories regarding the age and origin of the universe, while providing evidence of stars other than our sun that have planets in orbit about them.

Astronomers looked forward to placing a telescope in space for many years. Because light does not have to pass through earth's atmosphere before reaching the Hubble Telescope, the images are much clearer. The atmosphere absorbs some light before it reaches earth-based telescopes, and it is opaque to wavelengths shorter than 290 nanometers (2.9×10^{-7} meters). During daylight hours, so much light is scattered by the air that only the sun, the moon, and Venus are visible through a telescope. Furthermore, moonlight and airglow due to charged particles from the sun limit the exposure time of telescopic photographs, thus also limiting the magnitude of stars that can be captured on film. Finally, the repeated bending of light due to temperature differences in the atmosphere makes it difficult to obtain clear, undistorted images even through a cloudless sky.

See also:
American Telephone & Telegraph Company; Cartography; Fiber Optics; NAVSTAR; Telephone; Television.

References:
International Encyclopedia of Communications. New York: Oxford University Press, 1989.
Macaulay, David. *The Way Things Work.* Boston: Houghton Mifflin, 1988.

Scanner

A scanner is a device that collects information by repeatedly sweeping an area or region systematically, point by point. A radar beam, for example, sweeps a circular region looking for aircraft, rain, snow, or other objects that will reflect the beam back to a receiver. Scanners are also used to create or reproduce images. An image is produced on a television screen when an electron beam sweeps repeatedly and rapidly across the screen. Other types of scanners are widely used in business, printing, science, and medicine.

If a scanner is attached to a computer, visuals and text scanned from other sources may be incorporated into the document being prepared on the computer. During the scanning process, light is reflected from the paper and enters a photoelectric cell (the detector), where the light energy is converted to an electric current. The strength of the current depends on the intensity of the light received by the detector. The current is then converted to a digital signal that the computer can interpret. To copy colored images, the original is scanned in turn through red, green, and blue filters and again converted to digital signals that the computer can communicate to a color printer. Fax machines operate in a similar manner, except that the signal is transferred to a telephone line rather than a computer. The use of scanners in printing, sonography, fax machines, and thermography is discussed in other entries. This article focuses on the use of several scanning devices that have made dramatic changes in the practice of medicine and the ability of physicians to obtain information about internal organs and tissues.

Computerized axial tomography is a method of passing X rays through a particular plane section of a solid object, usually the human body. Computerized axial tomography was developed in 1972 and has been used extensively ever since because it can communicate valuable information, albeit at a high price, about unseen parts of the human body that cannot be reached even by endoscopy. A doughnut-shaped machine, the CAT scanner encircles the patient to be examined. An X-ray source produces a narrow, fanlike beam that passes through a thin cross-sectional slice of the patient's body.

Sensors on the opposite side of the doughnut respond quantitatively to the radiation that reaches them. The sensors, which can detect density differences as small as 1 percent, are connected to a computer that stores the information. The X-ray source is moved a few degrees, and then another X-ray beam passes through the body at a slightly different angle. This process continues until a series of shots of the same slice have been taken all around the body. The computer can then put the separate scans together to produce a single image of the cross section of the body that was examined.

A series of scans can be made at different levels to provide a three-dimensional image of an organ. Small tumors and other anomalies far too small to be seen by older methods are readily discovered in CAT scans. Using a more recent technique known as dynamic spatial reconstruction (DSR), a series of scans can be made very quickly, providing a three-dimensional image of the organ or region under examination. Such analyses can show the heart as it beats, the stomach as it moves, and blood as it flows through vessels.

Bone scans are also made using an X-ray source. A scanner detects the amount of radiation that is absorbed. Because the mineral in bone absorbs X rays, bone scans can be used to detect the early stages of osteoporosis, a condition in which the mineral content of bones diminishes, making them more brittle and less resistant to fractures as well as less capable of absorbing high-energy photons.

Magnetic resonance imaging (MRI), developed in the early 1980s, is based on the response of hydrogen or other atoms to a strong magnetic field. A patient is placed in a tunnel with walls that are filled with electromagnets. When the electromagnets are turned on, they produce a strong magnetic field. Hydrogen atoms, which constitute two-thirds of the atoms in every molecule of water—the most abundant compound in living tissue—are themselves tiny magnets. In response to the strong field, the hydrogen atoms all become aligned in the same direction, parallel to the magnetic field, in a manner similar to the way iron filings line up

when placed near a magnet. The atoms are then bombarded by a pulse from a powerful radio wave source. The wavelength of the pulse is one that causes the atoms to move out of their previous alignment. But after a few milliseconds the atoms each lose a quantum of energy and realign as before. The energy is released as faint radio waves that the MRI scanner can detect, and a computer processes the signals and produces an image of the region scanned. These images can be stored so that a physician can later examine a cross section or sections of the patient, as with CAT scans. The advantage of an MRI is that it requires no damaging radiation and provides better images of soft tissue because the water content of different types of tissue varies enough to alter the magnitude of the detector's response. Consequently, MRI can form images that reveal cartilage, ligaments, muscles, blood vessels, spinal fluid, and herniated discs, as well as hard-to-find tumors. Because of the intense magnetic field used in MRI, it cannot be used safely with patients whose bodies contain such metallic materials as pacemakers or joint pins.

Positron emission tomography (PET) works on the principle that some radioactive elements release positrons when they undergo natural decay. For example, the nuclei of one unstable isotope of sodium have 11 protons and 11 neutrons. (Stable sodium atoms have 11 protons and 12 neutrons.) The unstable sodium nuclei decay by releasing a positron from their nuclei, thereby giving rise to nuclei of the element neon with 10 protons and 12 neutrons. The positrons released combine almost immediately with electrons, and both are annihilated with the accompanying release of gamma rays that can be detected.

A patient is given an injection of sugar or protein or inhales a gas containing a radioactive element that releases positrons. The chemical is taken up by cells in the tissue being investigated. The patient is then placed in a machine similar to one used with computerized tomography. A PET scanner with a detector that responds to gamma rays sends data to a computer, where they are analyzed and used to produce an image of area scanned.

See also:

Computer; Fax Machine; Fiber Optics; Printing; Radar; Sonography; Television; Thermography.

Scripps, Edward Wyllis (1854–1926)

Edward Scripps, an American newspaper publisher, established the first successful chain of daily newspapers in the United States. Anchored in the Midwest and along the West Coast, the Scripps chain at various times encompassed more than 30 newspapers in 15 states. Scripps later founded the United Press Association, which became United Press International (UPI) in 1958.

Scripps, the youngest in a family of 13 children, was born in Rushville, Illinois, on 18 June 1854. He worked on the family farm until he was 18 and then moved to Detroit, where his half brother James served as business manager and editor of the *Detroit Tribune*. In 1872, James Scripps established his own paper, the *Detroit Evening News*, and Edward worked for him for four years.

In 1874, with the financial support of his family, Edward Scripps launched his own career by acquiring the *Cleveland Penny Press*, which he later renamed the *Press*. It became the flagship enterprise of the family's publishing empire. With James supplying the capital, the family purchased other inexpensive evening dailies in Saint Louis, Cincinnati, and Buffalo, thus securing their place in newspaper history as developers of the first successful newspaper chain.

Scripps, the self-styled "damned old crank," had a falling out with his mentor brother in 1889 over financial and editorial policies. Edward Scripps was a liberal Democrat, and James was a conservative Republican. The two went their separate ways, but the younger Scripps retained control of the *Cincinnati Post*, which became the linchpin of a new newspaper chain. In 1895, Scripps, joined by his half brother George, formed a partnership with Milton McRae

and created the Scripps-McRae Newspaper League. McRae headed the organization, and the millionaire Scripps set policy and went into semiretirement on his San Diego farm. In a flurry of activity between 1897 and 1911, the partnership acquired newspapers in Akron and Toledo, Ohio; Oklahoma City, Oklahoma; and Houston, Texas. Although some were eventually sold as unprofitable, most were still under Scripps's control when he died in 1926.

Semiretirement must not have agreed with the tycoon. Scripps began to put together another chain of papers on the West Coast in the 1890s. The *San Francisco News* was his strongest investment, but at least ten other papers displayed the Scripps masthead in coastal cities, including Tacoma and Seattle, Washington; Portland, Oregon; and Los Angeles and Oakland, California. The Scripps Coast League of Newspapers operated independently of the Scripps-McRae partnership. In 1911, Scripps experimented with an "adless" newspaper called the *Day Book* in Chicago. Poet Carl Sandburg was the lead reporter, and the paper steadily increased circulation until 1917, when World War I drove up the price of newsprint and Scripps's ill health forced him to abandon the venture.

Scripps's formula for success was simple. He focused on the smaller, but growing, industrial cities of the country that had uninspired newspapers. He proudly pointed out that his papers were written for "the 95 percent"—the ordinary people—whereas his competition was editorially anti–working class or overly intellectual. The inexpensive and well-written Scripps-group papers enjoyed the reputation of being politically independent and relished defying the status quo. For example, Scripps supported Theodore Roosevelt and his third party in 1912. Reformer Woodrow Wilson was a favorite, and the chain waged an unrelenting war against political corruption whenever it was found.

The Scripps method of operation was just as uncomplicated. Scripps sent in young, ambitious editors and business managers to jump-start a paper. If they were successful,

Scripps made 49 percent of the stock available to the employees. Failure meant replacement. If there was no profit in ten years, the paper was discarded as unsalvageable.

Scripps not only printed and distributed the news; he also organized and sold it to other papers, revolutionizing journalism. He created two regional, cooperative news services from his own papers to supply news and columns about events from their individual circulation areas. In 1902, he expanded his regional idea and formed the first newspaper syndicate, the Newspaper Enterprise Association, which sold illustrations, cartoons, columns, and feature articles on a contract basis. More specialized agencies, like the Science Service and Acme News Pictures, followed in later years. Scripps's greatest coup was in 1904, when he took over the rival Publisher's Press Agency. In 1907, Scripps-McRae Publisher's Press was renamed the United Press Association, which became UPI in 1958.

In 1914, Scripps and McRae split, and Edward's son, James George Scripps, took control of his father's holdings. In 1920, father and son fought, and the elder Scripps finally retired, giving the family empire to his second son, Robert Paine Scripps. In 1922, Roy W. Howard became a partner, and the Scripps-Howard chain began a new era.

Edward Scripps died on 3 March 1926 of a stroke on board his yacht in Monrovia Bay, Liberia. He was buried at sea.

See also:
Newspaper.
References:
Emery, Edwin. *The Press and America: An Interpretative History of the Mass Media*. Englewood Cliffs, NJ: Prentice-Hall, 1972.
Preece, Charles O. *Edward Wyllis and Ellen Browning Scripps: An Unmatched Pair*. San Diego, CA: Charles O. Preece, 1990.
Trimble, Vance. *The Astonishing Mr. Scripps: The Turbulent Life of America's Penny Press Lord*. Ames: Iowa State University Press, 1992.

Seismograph

A seismograph, or seismometer, is a device used to communicate information about the origin and strength of earthquakes, explosions, and other earthshaking events. A seismograph is made up of a large mass that, due to its inertia, remains at rest relative to the seismic waves that sweep across the earth's surface. Most present-day seismographs consist of a heavy coil of wire suspended in a magnetic field. When the source of the magnetic field, which is firmly fixed to the earth, moves in response to an earthquake or explosion, the inertia of the heavy coil causes it to lag behind the motion of the ground. As a result, the magnetic field through the coil changes, giving rise to induced voltages in the coil that are recorded.

Seismographs that are fixed in place usually measure vibrations along both axes of a plane as well as vertical wave motion. Smaller, portable seismographs are used by geologists and engineers to detect seismic waves produced by small explosions, collisions of falling weights with the ground, and the impact of high-pressure air on water. From the pattern of reflected waves produced on the seismographs, scientists can draw maps of the region beneath the earth's surface and determine whether certain sites are safe for building foundations or judge the likelihood of finding oil, gas, or minerals.

Locating Earthquakes

Each year there are about a million earthquakes intense enough to be recorded on seismographs. About 1 percent of these are strong enough to be felt. The region of the earth's crust where large amounts of energy is suddenly released is called the focus of an earthquake. It may be located anywhere from 0 to 450 miles below the surface but usually is within the first 60 miles. The point on the earth's surface directly above the focus is called the epicenter. The release of the strain gives rise to seismic waves that move through the earth, much as waves move outward when a pebble is dropped into water or as sound waves move through air. These seismic waves consist of primary (P) waves followed by secondary (S) waves and long (L) waves. The P waves are longitudinal waves in which particles are forced to

Three geologists use Geotek seismographs to measure the aftershock effects from an earthquake.

move back and forth like the molecules of air in a sound wave. P waves can travel through the earth's molten core and move at a high speed (6.7 miles per second), reaching the opposite side of the earth in 20 minutes. S waves are transverse waves because the up-and-down and/or to-and-fro motion of the matter through which the wave travels is perpendicular to the movement of the wave. The waves generated by snapping a rope, for example, are transverse waves. These S waves travel more slowly than P waves and, because they cannot travel through liquid, they do not penetrate the earth's molten center. L waves, which are both transverse and longitudinal, move along the earth's surface and cause much of an earthquake's structural damage.

The time of arrival of P and S waves at three different seismograph locations can be used to pinpoint the epicenter. From the arrival time and the velocity of the waves, the distance of the epicenter from each seismograph can be determined, but the direction remains unknown. On a map, a circle can be drawn about the location of each seismograph. The radius of each circle is made equal to the distance of the seismograph from the point where the energy was released. The single point where the three circles intersect on the map can be used to determine the epicenter.

The magnitude of an earthquake, as determined by the amplitude of the waves at a distance of 100 miles from the epicenter, is measured on the Richter scale, a scale of 1 to 9 developed by Charles Richter in 1935. Because the scale is logarithmic, each successive number represents a ten-fold increase in energy. An earthquake with a magnitude of 7, for example, is ten times as great as one with a magnitude of 6 and one-tenth as great as one with a magnitude of 8.

Before 1935, the more subjective Mercalli or modified Mercalli scale was used to measure earthquake intensity. It has 12 levels. A level I earthquake cannot be felt and is detectable only by seismographs. Level VI earthquakes, on the other hand, can be felt by everyone in the vicinity; heavy furniture moves, books fall from shelves, and trees shake. A level XII earthquake results in nearly total destruction. Large masses of rocks are moved, and objects are thrown violently into the air.

More than half of all earthquakes occur at the intersections of the tectonic plates that make up the earth's crust. When these giant plates under stress slip past or against one another, the resulting earthquake is called an interplate earthquake. The Kuril Island earthquake on 4 October 1994 surprised most seismologists. These islands lie west of an undersea trench where the Pacific plate is sliding under the Asian plate. According to seismic gap theory, an earthquake is least likely to occur along segments of a plate boundary that has had a recent earthquake, because time is required for new strains to build and reach a breaking point. Since there had been a major earthquake near the Kurils in 1969, it was not believed that another would occur there in this century. However, the 1994 earthquake turned out to be an intraplate earthquake caused by a fracture within the Pacific plate.

There are so many undetected intraplate faults (lines of weakness) within plates that many seismologists believe accurate predictions of when earthquakes will occur are not possible with our present models. Nevertheless, earthquakes are often preceded by ominous signals. Small tremors called foreshocks frequently, but not always, precede an earthquake. Growing strains in the earth's crust are often, but again not always, accompanied by a gradual long-term vertical motion of the land in the region where an earthquake will later occur. Russian seismologists have had some success in predicting earthquakes by watching for changes in the ratio of the velocities of P and S waves. They have found, too, that a sudden drop in the radon content of ground water is a good indicator. Others have detected changes in the earth's magnetic field and the conductivity of rocks in the earth's crust as well as noticeable changes in the water levels in wells prior to an earthquake.

There is some evidence that animals can detect an impending quake. Those that live underground, like snakes and mice, are said to leave their burrows; bottom-dwelling fish move to the surface, while dogs, horses, and pheasants become noisy and exhibit nervous behavior. Whether such signs are a valid means of predicting earthquakes is questioned by many seismologists.

See also:
Electromagnetic Waves; Loudspeaker.

References:
Bolt, Bruce A. *Earthquakes and Geological Discovery*. New York: Scientific American Library, 1993.

Tributsch, Helmut. *When Snakes Awake: Animals and Earthquake Prediction*. Cambridge, MA: MIT Press, 1982.

Wakefield, Julie, and Daniel Pendick. "Earthquake Reality Check." *Earth*, August 1995.

Semaphore

Semaphore is a visual signaling method, usually by means of flags, lights, or movable arms, to represent letters, numbers, and other information. The Greeks and Romans communicated over short distances by means of torches and flags. King James II of England devised an early set of ship-to-ship naval signals when he was lord high admiral of the navy.

The invention of the telescope around 1600 considerably enhanced the efficiency and desirability of visual signals. Claude Chappe, a French engineer, developed and popularized a functional system of semaphore communication in 1794. Chappe erected a series of towers, 5 to 10 miles apart, between Paris and Lille, a distance of 144 miles. The key to the system was a wooden post in each tower with a set of pivoting arms attached. Chappe devised a code in which the positions of the arms could be read as different letters or words. Staffed by men with telescopes, the towers relayed the messages along the route. It took two minutes to complete the delivery, a speed no system then in existence could match. Eventually Chappe's brainchild extended over 3,000 miles from Paris to Brest and Strasbourg. So impressed were the British, then at war with France, that the admiralty adopted a similar system from London to the naval ports of Deal and Portsmouth.

While the semaphore system enjoyed some success, it was labor intensive and, more importantly, subject to climatic conditions. Even before the telegraph made semaphore obsolete, it fell into disuse. Nonetheless, the procedure was preserved by an English telegraphic engineer, Hutton Gregory, who modified Chappe's plan and created a mechanical semaphore system for railroads that is still in use today. Metal arms or rows of lights mounted on posts beside railroad tracks are used to indicate how switches on the tracks are set.

Another method derived from Chappe's original version is used by the U.S. Navy for short-range ship-to-ship communication. The messenger holds a half-red and half-yellow flag in each hand and moves his arms to different angles, indicating letters of the alphabet or words. A similar method was used the Boy Scouts of America. Although convenient for emergency communication because the equipment is simple and inexpensive, the procedure can be used only in good visibility.

Semiconductor
See Diode.

Sequoyah (ca. 1770–1843)

Sequoyah, a Native American artisan and teacher, is the only person known to have developed a syllabary—a set of written characters, each of which represents a syllable—for a living language. Sequoyah's syllabary represented all the sounds of the spoken Cherokee language, which when combined could produce a written language.

Very little is known about Sequoyah's early life. He was probably born in the lower Appalachian region at Taskigi, in the North Carolina colony, ca. 1770. Sequoyah was raised by his Native American mother after his father Nathaniel Gist, a Virginia trader and explorer, abandoned the family before

Sequoyah was born. Later in life Sequoyah adapted the name George to use with his father's last name, which was frequently misspelled Guess. There is no record that Sequoyah ever attended school or that he spoke or understood English. This lack of education or linguistic background makes Sequoyah's creation of the syllabary all the more remarkable.

A debilitating accident left Sequoyah with a permanent limp. Some accounts attributed the injury to a hunting accident, others to a war injury, and the *Cherokee Advocate* attributed his disability to an arthritic knee. Whatever the cause, Sequoyah turned to a more sedentary lifestyle as a self-taught silversmith and blacksmith. Apparently Sequoyah was quite prosperous, but no example of his artistry survives today. Legend maintains that Sequoyah kept his accounts by drawing pictures of the customers and using symbolic codes for labor and prices. Another scholar states that the artist asked a white man to write his name so that he could learn it to sign his jewelry. On his 1828 visit to Washington, D.C., Sequoyah, when asked why he invented the syllabary, allegedly stated it was because what men knew was often lost, and yet whites did not forget things. Clearly, Sequoyah was intrigued with the white man's "talking leaves" and the ability to convey messages.

In 1809, Sequoyah began a 12-year quest to develop a written language for his people. The would-be inventor, struggling with his near-obsession, was ridiculed by his family and tribe and accused of witchcraft, and at one point his cabin was burned. In 1818, in the midst of his efforts, Sequoyah was among the first group of Cherokees to relocate to the west under the American government's Indian Removal Policy. Sequoyah settled near present-day Russellville, Arkansas, where he operated a salt works, blacksmith shop, and trading post as he continued his main work on the syllabary.

Borrowing symbols from English, Greek, and the *McGuffy Reader*, simply because they were convenient, Sequoyah assigned each Cherokee word a symbol. This system proved impractical because of the amount of memorization required to associate each word with a sign. Eventually Sequoyah realized that Cherokee was a language of recurring sounds and that capturing these might be the key to a written language. In 1821, Sequoyah finally presented his syllabary to the Cherokee nation.

Stories abound about how Sequoyah presented his innovation to a skeptical people and overcame their reluctance to even try the system. The most common legend involves Sequoyah's daughter, Ahyoha, who was the first pupil to study the syllabary, or *A-ga-yuh*. Skeptics were converted when Sequoyah demonstrated how he and his daughter could communicate, even when widely separated, by reading messages written with the syllabary. The system was so logical and simple that it took no more than a week to master, although three to four days appeared to be the norm. Within months a Native American population, reviled as savages by their enemies, became literate.

Praise for Sequoyah's work was not universal. White missionaries were critical because the syllabary was unlike any other alphabet. They argued further that the use of the syllabary would intellectually isolate the tribe. Nonetheless, the acceptance of the system was so widespread that by 1824 part of the Bible and the laws of the Cherokee nation were available in translation. In 1828, the *Cherokee Phoenix*, a weekly newspaper, began publication. The most complete file of the *Phoenix* is in the British Museum, and the Smithsonian has some of the paper's type.

Sequoyah's triumph as the inventor of the written Cherokee language brought him fame and respect. In 1824, the Cherokee legislature, in appreciation of his accomplishment, bestowed on him a specially minted silver medal. Sequoyah returned the honor by devoting himself to the needs of his people. In 1828, he was selected as part of a delegation of the Arkansas Cherokee and sent to Washington, D.C., to discuss unresolved treaty difficulties. During the visit, Charles Bird King painted the only known portrait of Sequoyah, holding his syllabary and with his silver medal clearly visible. The subsequent treaty continued the American removal policy by trading territory farther west, in Oklahoma, for the land in Arkansas. The following year Sequoyah and his family moved to the Oklahoma Indian Territory, settling near present-day Sallisaw, Oklahoma, where his farmstead is now a state historic site. Sequoyah was also instrumental in aiding his nation in perhaps its time of greatest need. In 1838, the Eastern Cherokees were forcibly evacuated from their homeland and marched west on the horrific "Trail of Tears." About one-quarter of the population perished on the journey. It was Sequoyah who eased the newcomers' transition and helped integrate them with the "old settlers." In 1841, Sequoyah was granted a lifetime pension, which was eventually extended to his wife. Many consider this the first literary pension in U.S. history. Certainly it was the first such allotment given by a Native American tribe.

Unwilling to rest as he grew older, Sequoyah embarked on his final mission in 1842. According to tribal folklore, a band of Cherokees migrated across the Mississippi River at about the time Sequoyah was born. Sequoyah hoped to find the band, teach them the written language, and reunite the nation. Beset by difficulties from the start of the expedition, the feeble Sequoyah was not up to the hardships. He died near San Fernando, Mexico, in August 1843 and was buried in an unmarked grave. Oklahoma later recognized Sequoyah's contributions to the state, as well as his distinguished services and historical import, when he was selected as one of Oklahoma's two representatives in National Statuary Hall in the Capitol at Washington, D.C.

References:

Davis, John B. "The Life and Work of Sequoyah." *The Chronicles of Oklahoma*, June 1930.

Foreman, Grant. *Sequoyah*. Norman: University of Oklahoma Press, 1959.

Hoig, Stan. *Sequoyah: The Cherokee Genius*. Oklahoma City: Oklahoma Historical Society, 1995.

Sermon

See Homiletics.

SETI

See Communication with Extraterrestrial Intelligence.

Sholes, Christopher Latham (1819–1890)

Although relatively unknown today, Christopher Sholes had a tremendous impact on modern society. Sholes developed the first practical and commercially marketable typewriter. His device not only revolutionized American business but ultimately offered women better-paying employment as a result of the demand for skilled clerical workers created by his innovation.

Born in 1819, the son of a Pennsylvania cabinetmaker, Sholes sought his fortune in the upper Midwest after an apprenticeship in printing. He held several editorial positions in Wisconsin, was a postmaster, and even served in the state legislature.

The idea of a typewriter as a speedy alternative to handwriting fascinated inventors as early as 1713, when Queen Anne of Great Britain issued a royal patent for a typewriter-like device. Despite this interest and numerous attempts, no reliable, compact, affordable option with the speed necessary to compete with pen and paper was available by the mid–nineteenth century. In 1864, Sholes and his friend Samuel Soule patented a machine that numbered book pages consecutively. Later inspired by an 1867 *Scientific American* article about Englishman John Pratt's attempts to produce a typewriter, and encouraged by inventor friends Soule and Carlos Glidden, Sholes began his work. Utilizing ideas from his page-numbering machine, Sholes patented the first working model in 1867. However, it was not until July 1868 that Sholes achieved real success in being able to type faster than a human could write. Sholes's crude machine lacked a keyboard layout, a shift key for upper-case and lower-

Christopher Latham Sholes poses with his patented typewriter in this undated photo.

case letters, and the familiar typewriter carriage. Soule and Glidden soon abandoned the project, but Sholes continued to refine his machine. Over the next five years he produced 50 variations of the original model and even manufactured some of the 1870 version, but with no notable acclaim.

By 1873, lacking the financial resources to mass-produce and market the instrument, Sholes sought some sort of financial return for his lengthy effort. With the aid of newspaper acquaintance and promoter James Densmore, Sholes sold his patents to Philo Remington of E. Remington & Sons for $12,000. Sholes's remark about the sale—"All my life I have been trying to escape being a millionaire and now I think I have succeeded"—proved prophetic.

See also:
Typewriter.
References:
Feldman, Anthony, and Peter Ford. *Scientists and Inventors*. New York: Facts on File, 1979.
Flatow, Ira. *They All Laughed*. New York: HarperCollins, 1992.
Hylander, C. J. *American Inventors*. New York:

Macmillan, 1955.
Polley, Jane, ed. *Stories behind Everyday Things*. Pleasantville, NY: Readers Digest, 1980.
Robbins, Peggy. "Tale of the Typewriter." *American History Illustrated*, February 1981: 4.

Shorthand

Shorthand is a system of writing that uses symbols and characters to make it possible for someone using the system to record information quickly and even verbatim. It is used most commonly in taking dictation or notes during a lecture.

The first known system of shorthand was developed by Cicero's secretary, Marcus Tullius Tiro, in 63 B.C. The system, which came to be known as Tironian notes, was used by Julius Caesar and was exported to Egypt in A.D. 155. Roman reporters, known as *notarii*, used the system and incorporated shorthand techniques that remain as a part of our written language. For example, *notarii* would often use just the initial letters of names as they recorded information. The use of *A.D.* for *anno Domini*, *P.S.* for *postscriptum*, and *n.b.* for *nota bene* are examples, but we have expanded this form of shorthand to include many more—*B.C.* for before Christ, *I.Q.* for intelligence quotient, *B.A.* for bachelor of arts, and hundreds more.

Tironian notes and other shorthand systems were used in ancient times to record oratory, recited poems, and details of meetings. However, these systems were lost during the Dark Ages, along with Latin (for which Tironian notes had been developed) and the ability of most people to read or write.

In 1588, Timothy Bright, known as "the father of modern shorthand," developed a system that he dedicated to Queen Elizabeth, who then granted him a patent for a "shorte and new kynde of writing by character to the furtherance of good language." Bright's and others' systems were often used as a form of secret writing that could not be read by others. Samuel Pepy's diary, in which he recorded much about life in seventeenth-century London, including eyewitness accounts of the Great Plague and the Great Fire, were written in shorthand. Two centuries later they were discovered and transcribed.

Modern Systems of Shorthand

The first system to use symbols to represent sounds was developed by Sir Isaac Pitman in 1837. Light (unvoiced) sounds were represented by light strokes and heavy (voiced) sounds by heavy strokes. He represented 12 vowel symbols by means of light and heavy dots and dashes; consonants were represented by a series of hooks, circles, hoops, and lines. Pitman's system, in modified form, remains the most widely used shorthand outside the United States.

The system most commonly used in the United States was developed by John Robert Gregg in 1888. He used lines of different length, shape, and orientation to represent voiced and unvoiced sounds, with circles and hooks to represent vowel sounds. His system, which was simple and easy to learn, used phonetic signs to represent signs without being so finely discriminating as to cause confusion. Unlike Pitman's complex system—which used light and heavy strokes along with hooks, circles, and loops combined with different slopes and positions on a line—Gregg's shorthand was all written on a line with the hand in one position, as in ordinary writing. Vowels and consonants merged, and the writing, which could be done quickly and legibly, was easy to learn.

Lacking success in England, where Pitman's method was well established, Gregg moved to the United States. Although initial attempts to publish and sell his system failed in Boston, he was much more successful in Chicago and throughout the western United States, where businesses were growing and high schools were introducing business courses to train young women to become secretaries.

Other Shorthand Methods

In court trials, legislative sessions, hearings, and investigations, a typewriter-like machine known as a stenograph or stenotype is used to record information verbatim. The machine, which is light, compact, portable, and quiet, has a keyboard with 17 symbols that allows the recorder to enter shorthand quickly (up to 320 words per minute) and more accurately than a tape recorder, which can't ask a witness to speak up, by simultaneously striking keys that produce words.

Other systems, called speed writing, consist only of longhand letters or longhand letters and symbols. Although these systems do not allow information to be recorded as rapidly as shorthand, they are easy to learn by simply adapting longhand writing. In speed writing, consonants are used to form the framework of the writing. Only important vowels are written; the rest are omitted.

References:
Burke, James. "Connections." *Scientific American*, May 1996.
"For the Record." *Life*, February 1995.
Simpson, Marge. "Untitled." *Seventeen*, May 1996.

Shortwave Radio
See Radio.

Sign Language

Languages do not have to use sound. People can communicate using their hands, facial expressions, and body movements. We use our hands to communicate in many ways, such as waving, pointing, touching, and shaking hands. Drivers use hand signals to show other drivers what they intend to do. Sports referees, traffic police, baseball players, animal trainers, and others use hand signs to communicate.

Some scholars believe that the first language used in prehistoric times by human ancestors consisted of signs and gestures. Early man could have used sign language in many ways. During a hunt, for example, hunters could signal when sneaking up on their prey, planning a hunt, or describing something out of sight.

Native Americans definitely communicated hunting messages through signs. The Plains Indians—Sioux, Cheyenne, Blackfoot, and Kiowa—all used sign language; it was the key to intertribal relations. Different tribes who did not speak the same language could communicate through signs. At the campsite, older people used sign language when their hearing became poor. When the first Europeans came to America, they communicated with the natives through sign language. Sign language was used by North American tribes in negotiating a treaty with William Penn. Sign language is still used today at intertribal powwows and ceremonial celebrations.

The primary types of sign languages are those developed and used by the hearing impaired. Throughout history, wherever people have had hearing impairments, signed languages have developed to aid communication. Because the hearing impaired cannot communicate by sounds, they use a visual-gestural language that is better suited to their needs. Just as spoken language is more than a collection of sounds, so sign language is much more than a collection of gestures. Every sign has a distinctive hand shape, movement, and meaning. What a person's face and body are doing while that person is signing is just as important as what the hands are "saying."

In the United States, the sign language that is used most often among hearing-impaired people is American Sign Language (ASL). ASL is a separate language, and it should not be confused with several other sign systems used in the United States that have been developed to communicate the spoken language through manual gestures. Unlike ASL, which has its own set of rules, these sign systems follow the semantic rules of the English language. Therefore, they are called systems of manually coded English (MCE), or signing English.

Fingerspelling is the representation of letters of the alphabet by finger positions. It is used in ASL or MCE to spell out words such as names and other proper nouns. People have used fingerspelling for a very long time. In Bibles from the beginning of the first century are pages that show alphabet hand shapes. Monks in the Middle Ages, sworn to

silence, used fingerspelling to communicate. People skilled in fingerspelling can communicate a message very quickly.

There is no true universal sign language, but many different sign languages, such as American, British, French, German, Dutch, and Norwegian. It is interesting to note that hearing-impaired people from different countries are able to communicate with one another quite well in spite of using different sign languages. They are skilled in picking up visual and gestural cues that enable them to communicate across language barriers that frustrate people who rely on speech.

—*Barbara Gardner Conklin*

See also:
American Sign Language; Communication among the Hearing Impaired; Communication among the Visually Impaired; Keller, Helen Adams.

References:
Baker, Charlotte, and Carol Padden. *American Sign Language: A Look at Its History, Structure, and Community.* Silver Spring. MD: T. J. Publishers, 1979.
Fant, Louie J. *Sign Language.* Acton, CA: Joyce Media, 1977.

Signage

Signage consists of signs—not necessarily with words—that are designed to guide, inform, or influence those who read or observe them. Signs are essential in everyday life. Without signage, one would have difficulty locating an office in a skyscraper or a book in a library.

Signs vary greatly in length and complexity. Many signs consist of only one or two words or symbols. Some familiar signs have no words at all but are symbols readily recognized by a passing public—a striped barber pole, a cigar-store Indian, or a giant tooth or pair of eyeglasses, for example. In contrast, signs in parks or historic sites can be rather lengthy and provide large amounts of information. Generally, small signs are associated with high-class businesses and establishments. Large flashing signs usually are not found above a store that sells expensive clothes or merchandise.

Traffic Signs

Today's roads and highways are accompanied by far too many signs, but some of them are valuable. Local residents may find that an elevated sign advertising fuel detracts from the environment, but it is certainly helpful to a driver whose fuel gauge indicates zero.

As those who have prepared for a driver's license test know, the shape of traffic signs has as much significance as the words printed on the sign. For example, the shape of a stop sign is octagonal throughout the United States. Similarly, yield signs are triangles with the base at the top of the sign and the apex at the bottom; signs indicating railroad crossings are circular; warning signs are diamond-shaped; rectangles in which the long side is vertical are regulatory signs; rectangles in which the long side is horizontal provide guidance information; pennant-shaped signs (triangles with vertical bases) indicate that no passing is allowed; pentagonal signs are used to make drivers aware of a school; and isosceles trapezoids indicate recreational areas or parks.

There is also a color code for traffic signs and lights. Red indicates stop, or something a driver or pedestrian is forbidden from doing. Yellow signs or lights are warnings or suggest that drivers use caution. Green lights or signs indicate that traffic may move, or they may provide directional guidance. Black-and-white signs show speed limits or directions. Blue signs contain information about services for motorists such as lodging, food, fuel, or rest areas. Orange signs are used to warn drivers about construction or maintenance operations on the highway, and signs showing public recreational areas and scenic places have a brown background.

International Signage

Today, people frequently travel to countries where they cannot speak or read the language, but this does not usually prevent them from driving automobiles even though they cannot read the traffic signs. To reduce accidents caused by an inability to read signs, the United States and other countries are moving toward an international system of traffic signs in which sign shapes and symbols, rather than words, are emphasized.

As European countries adopt the octagonal stop sign, the United States is converting to international traffic standards, such as red-and-white "Yield" and "Do Not Enter" signs, as well as using the red circle with a diagonal slash to show things that are not allowed. For example, a black, inverted U-shaped arrow inside a red circle with a red slash across it indicates "No U-Turn." A black outline of a human form walking inside a red circle with a red slash across it indicates "No Pedestrians Allowed." When these international traffic signs are in use throughout the world, driving in foreign lands will be less dangerous for visitors and natives alike.

See also:
Icon.

References:
Brancatelli, Joe. "European Sign Language." *Travel Holiday*, May 1995.
Brown, Ann. "Sign Language." *Black Enterprise*, September 1996.
Burgi, Michael. "Signs of the Times." *Mediaweek*, 4 March 1996.
Hollingsworth, Caroline. "Traffic-ometry: The New Shape of Mathematics." *Teaching PreK-8*, January 1995.
International Encyclopedia of Communications. New York: Oxford University Press, 1989.
"Signs of Life." *Car and Driver*, November 1995.

Silicon Chip
See Microelectronics.

Slander
See Defamation.

Smoke Detector

A smoke detector or smoke alarm is designed to emit a warning signal in response to smoke.

Because smoke detectors can be purchased for a few dollars, all buildings where people sleep or work should be equipped with these devices so that any danger due to smoke or fire can be communicated to occupants.

Because warm, smoky air is less dense than ordinary air, smoke detectors should be located high on walls or on ceilings. To ensure that they awaken anyone who is sleeping, they should be located near bedroom doors.

Many new homes and offices have smoke alarms that are connected directly to a household circuit. For older homes, battery-powered smoke alarms are available.

There are two kinds of smoke detectors. One operates by means of a photoelectric current; the other is based on a flow of ions between two electrodes. In the photoelectric device, a light beam in a photocell is used to maintain a small, steady current across the detector. When smoke particles enter the detector, they scatter the light in the beam and reduce the photoelectric current to the point where a relay turns on a circuit that activates a bell, buzzer, or some similar auditory signal.

In a detector that uses an ionic beam, radiation from a radioactive source placed in the detector ionizes air molecules between the electrodes. The attraction between these ions and the oppositely charged electrodes establishes a small current within the detector. Any smoke particles that enter the detector are attracted to the ions and become attached to them. The increased mass of the smoke-laden ions reduces their velocity and, thereby, the rate of ion flow between the electrodes. The decrease in current is detected by a microchip, which then activates an auditory alarm.

See also:
Diode; Photoelectric Cell; Relay.

Smoke Signals and Native American Communication

Native Americans, although usually lacking a written language, were able to communicate at a distance through smoke signals, blanket waving, flashes of reflected sunlight, movements of lances or arms, or maneuvers while on horseback. Some of these methods have been or continue to be used by other cultures.

By building a smoky fire and alternately covering and uncovering the fire with a blanket, an Indian could release puffs of smoke that could be seen up to 60 miles away across the open plains. A chief stationed on a hilltop could flash instructions to a band of warriors on the plains below. By waving his lance or his arms in different ways, a scout at a good position to observe buffalo or an approaching enemy could send information and instructions to others some distance away. Dr. Albert Myer, an army surgeon, developed a code using flags after watching Comanche warriors communicate by waving their lances. His code was later adopted by the army signal corps. All these methods of communication required a code known to both sender and receiver. The Native Americans regarded their codes as sacred and never to be conveyed to those outside their cultures.

Of course, in forested areas visual signals were of little value. Tribes in those regions used vocal signals, such as the sounds of animals—owls, wolves, ravens, songbirds, and foxes—to convey information to others within hearing range.

Telephones and radios came too late to be used by Native Americans of the Old West in their fight to maintain their way of life. However, they did make good use of these methods of communication as members of the armed forces of the United States during World Wars I and II. In 1918, during the Meuse-Argonne campaign, the army used Choctaws to send information over telephone lines. Germans who tapped the Allied phone lines were completely confounded by the sounds they heard. During World War II, voice signals were often sent by telephone and radio. Japanese soldiers eavesdropping on these telephone and radio messages were as confused as the Germans had been in World War I because the voices were those of Navajo Code Talkers speaking their native tongue.

See also:
Navajo Code Talkers; Talking Drums.

References:
Editors of Time-Life Books. *The Way of the Warrior*. Alexandria, VA: Time-Life Books, 1993.

International Encyclopedia of Communications. New York: Oxford University Press, 1989.

Sonography

Sonography is the use of ultrasound (high-frequency sound waves) to obtain information. All sounds with a frequency beyond the range of human hearing—20,000 vibrations per second—are said to be ultrasonic.

One important form of sonography is *sonar*, an acronym for sound navigation ranging, which transmits and receives ultrasonic waves. Because the speed of sound in water is known, the time delay between the sending of an ultrasounding pulse toward the sea bottom and its returning echo can readily determine the water's depth. By measuring the depth at closely spaced points, the contour of the ocean's bottom can be mapped very accurately. With higher-frequency waves, sonar can be used to detect schools of fish and shipwrecks. During World War II, sonar was used to detect enemy submarines.

Sonar is often confused with radar because both sonar and radar transmit waves and receive their echoes. Unlike radar, however, sonar works by emitting ultrasonic pulses of sound that are reflected and then detected by receivers. Like radar, sonar determines the distance to a reflector by measuring the time between the transmission of a pulse and the reception of its echo.

Sonar is usually used in water, where sound waves travel at about 4,690 feet (1,430 meters) per second, or 3,200 miles per hour. In air, sound travels at about 1,115 feet (340 meters) per second, or 760 miles per hour. This is much slower than radar pulses, which travel at the speed of light, or 186,000 miles (300,000 kilometers) per second. Sonar is useless in detecting airplanes because jet-powered planes travel at speeds close to the speed of sound. Supersonic airplanes travel faster than sound.

Ultrasound systems using the principle of sonar are used extensively in medicine. The instrument consists of a computer, a scanning probe, and a monitor. The probe both transmits the sound waves produced by a transducer and receives ultrasound waves after they have been reflected by internal tissue. The echoes are received by the probe and sent to the computer as electrical impulses that are analyzed and projected as closely spaced points of light on a monitor. Like all information obtained using reflected waves, those of high frequency provide a more detailed view than do those of low frequency because there is more reflection and less diffraction as wavelength decreases. Ultrasound echoes processed by computers can create images of internal organs and of a fetus within a pregnant woman's uterus. Such images can be used to examine hearts or to check the health of unborn babies.

Sonography is also used to examine hearts and heart valves as well as blood flow. In color Doppler flow imaging, the reflected waves can provide colored images that allow doctors to detect blood clots and narrowing of blood vessels. When projected as a narrow beam, ultrasound can be used in place of a scalpel. At the focal point of a refracted beam of high-frequency sound waves, the resulting heat and vibrations can be used to destroy tissue. Consequently, ultrasound is often used to break up gall stones and kidney stones too large to pass through the urinary tract. It is also used in brain surgery and in dentistry where it can be used to remove plaque and in place of a mechanical drill.

Of course, nature "discovered" sonar long before humans. Bats, dolphins, and many whales use a system of echolocation to detect objects. They send out ultrasonic pulses and listen for the echoes. Because bats can hear sounds of 1,000 to 120,000 vibrations per second, they can detect the contours of the external world by listening to the reflected sound waves they emit. Bats are as aware of their surroundings in darkness as they are in daylight. Experiments have shown that even in total darkness bats can detect and avoid wires 1 millimeter in diameter. With such a discriminating system of sonar, it is not surprising that they can find and feast on small flying insects while maneuvering through the darkest of nights.

Dolphins, who can hear sounds of 150 to 150,000 vibrations per second, turn their heads as they emit a beam of ultrasonic sound waves. Their ears and brains are so sensitive to the echoes returning from their scanning beams that they can distinguish copper from aluminum and plastic from glass. Their sonar can differentiate a ball with a 2.5-inch diameter from one that is 2.25 inches across. There is some evidence that dolphins and whales use their high-pitched "voices" to communicate among themselves as well as to search for food.

See also:
Radar; Scanner; Transducer.
References:
Gardner, Robert. *The Whale Watchers' Guide.* New York: Messner, 1984.
Griffin, Donald R. "More about Bat 'Radar.'" *Scientific American*, July 1958.
Macaulay, David. *The Way Things Work.* Boston: Houghton Mifflin, 1988.
The New Book of Popular Science. Danbury, CT: Grolier, 1992.
Williams, Trevor I. *The History of Invention: From Stone Axes to Silicon Chips.* New York: Facts on File, 1987.

Sound Recording

See Compact Disc; Edison, Thomas Alva; Motion Pictures; Phonograph; Tape Recorder.

Special Effects

Special effects are photographic, mechanical, and computer techniques used to produce images that would be too difficult, dangerous, expensive, time consuming, or even impossible to obtain by conventional methods of moviemaking. Some techniques have been used throughout the history of cinema. Others, involving computerized images, are quite recent.

A few special effects found in the theater are also used in films. Low-lying fog is made by pumping steam into a trough containing dry ice (solid carbon dioxide). Smoke can be made by heating mineral oil and then forcing out the vapor with carbon dioxide under pressure. Snowflakes are actually fireproof pieces of white plastic dropped from a platform above the actors.

Special Optical Effects

Early cinematographers knew that by cranking their cameras at 48 or 12 frames per second and then projecting the film at 24 frames per second, they could make the people or objects seen on-screen appear to move twice or half as fast as normal. By using a small lens aperture, both near and distant objects form sharp images on film; thus, a miniature model of a dinosaur placed near the camera may appear much larger than a man some distance away. An actor could be made to disappear by simply stopping the camera, having the actor walk offstage, and then resuming the filming. Ghosts appear when the mirror image of an actor offstage is formed by reflecting light using a large sheet of glass at an angle of 45 degrees to the audience.

One money-saving technique that was discovered quite early by cinematographers is the glass shot. A plate of glass with a painting of a background is held in front of the camera so that it blends in with the actors in the foreground.

In a matte shot, only part of the film in a frame is exposed; the rest is covered by a card (matte) cut to the desired shape. After shooting the exposed parts of the frames, the film is rewound, the exposed parts of the film are covered with a counter-matte, and the previously matted portions of the film are exposed. In a scene taken through a train window, a traveling matte might be used. The matte is changed from frame to frame to provide a background that appears to be

A special effects technician makes adjustments to the Millennium Falcon *spaceship model that appeared in the 1977 feature* Star Wars. *The illusion of giant spaceships amid the stars and galaxies was created by filming model spaceships against a background of black velvet laced with small lights.*

moving. These techniques are now generally done with an optical printer that allows the filmmaker to blend images from two strips of film. Such a printer allows rain, lightning, thunder, and other such elements to be added after the human action has been shot.

In an effect known as rear projection, the actors perform in front of a translucent screen onto which a previously filmed background scene is projected from behind the screen. The background projector and the camera used to film the actors must be synchronized so that the shutters in front of both lenses are open at the same time. Otherwise, the background would appear dark. In front projection, the background is projected onto the screen from the same line of sight as the camera. This is accomplished by placing a lightly silvered mirror at an angle of 45 degrees in front of the camera's lens. The mirror is then used to reflect the images from the projector onto the screen along exactly the same sight line as that seen through the camera that will photograph the actors. As a re-

sult, any shadows cast by the actors onto the screen where the background appears are not seen by the camera because they are covered by the actors' bodies.

Despite the low intensity of the light reflected by the lightly silvered mirror, the background appears bright because the screen is made of tiny glass beads that are excellent reflectors. At the same time, the actors' bodies are poor reflectors, so the dim background images that fall on their bodies are not visible on the final film.

Special Mechanical Effects

One of the great special effects in early sound movies was the giant ape who appeared in the 1933 film *King Kong*. The filming was done using an 18-inch model ape and model buildings so that the animal appeared to be 50 feet tall. The ape's actions were shot frame by frame, as in animation. Between frames, the positions of King Kong's body parts were changed ever so slightly so that the frames, when projected at normal speed, gave the illusion of smooth motion. In the 1977 feature *Star Wars,* model spaceships were photographed against a background of black velvet laced with tiny lights. The audiences saw giant spaceships against a background of stars and galaxies. Miniature models of the real objects are commonly used to show buildings or entire cities on fire, earthquakes, ships in raging typhoons, and the ever-popular World War I and II dogfights between planes. In the 1996 film *Independence Day,* in which the United States is attacked by aliens, a 4-yard-long white plaster model of the White House was built. Included within the structure were miniature models of the furniture so that when the aliens bombed the building, pieces of chairs and tables flying through the air would make the explosion look authentic.

The bullet hits so common in today's all-too-violent films are made by placing a small amount of explosive and a red fluid in a plastic bag that is hidden by the victim's clothing. When the small charge is detonated by the actor or by a remote radio signal, the explosive tears open the bag, blows a hole in the clothing, and exposes a red fluid that appears to be blood. Stabbings are done using a resin knife blade covered with metallic paint. Tiny openings in the blade release a red fluid when the attacker squeezes the knife handle. A human seen immersed in flames is usually an actor's double covered with asbestos and carrying an air supply. Less intense burnings are accomplished by coating clothing with alcohol. The alcohol burns, but not the clothes.

In westerns, air guns are used to fire arrows that find their way to the blue-coated soldiers by following very fine wires attached to cork-covered metal plates hidden beneath the soldiers' clothing.

Computerized Special Effects

Analog video images can be changed to digital code and transferred to a computer screen for viewing. There they can be manipulated electronically to generate weird or physically impossible images. Using computer graphics software, it is also possible to create and manipulate synthetic images such as the dinosaurs seen in Stephen Spielberg's *Jurassic Park* (1993) or to mix real and synthetic images to create the impossible, head-on-backwards look of Meryl Streep in *Death Becomes Her* (1992).

George Lucas, who made *Star Wars,* owns Industrial Light & Magic (ILM), the company responsible for many of Hollywood's most noted special effects. ILM was responsible for the 25 minutes of storm scenes in the 1996 film *Twister.* The computer graphics used in *Twister* are not to be found on an ordinary computer. The computer memory for the scenes in *Twister* required 17 trillion bytes. Storing that much information would require more than 10 million floppy disks.

See also:
Animation; Motion Photography; Motion Pictures.

References:
Bailey, Adrian. *Walt Disney's World of Fantasy.* New York: Gallery Books, 1987.
Finch, Christopher. *Special Effects: Creating Movie Magic.* New York: Abbeville Press, 1984.
Guttman, Monika. "Hollywood Falls in Love with Technology." *U.S. News & World Report,* 19 February 1996.
Kaplan, David A. "Grand Illusions." *Newsweek,* 13 May 1996.
Schecter, Harold. *Film Tricks: Special Effects in the Movies.* New York: H. Quist, 1980.
Solomon, Charles. *The History of Animation: Enchanted Drawings.* Avenal, NJ: Random House Value, 1994.

Speech

Speech, the most common form of communication among humans, is also perhaps a unique characteristic of our species. Speech consists of vocal sounds that are combined to express a speaker's emotions, feelings, thoughts, and opinions.

Speech is an aspect of language that involves encoding messages so that they can be understood by other humans who share the same rules for encoding. Although speech is the most widely used form of language among humans, many people communicate by writing and in nonverbal ways as well. Communication by speech makes use of inflection and body language, such as facial expressions and gestures, in an effort to add meaning and interest to the words. As a result, spoken language is generally not as lengthy as written language, which must compensate for its lack of the nonverbal aids.

Normally speech is thought of as a method of communication among people who are in close proximity to one another. However, since the invention of the telephone, radio, and television, voice communication can take place over vast distances.

The sound waves that are produced by speech can generate electrical impulses that can be recorded. Such recordings are called voice prints. Voice-print patterns are unique for each individual; that is, an individual's voice print when speaking a given word is different from the voice print seen when someone else speaks the same word. Each voice, therefore, is as unique as a fingerprint. Consequently, voice prints are sometimes useful to law enforcement agencies.

Making Sounds

Humans make vocal sounds by exhaling air through the larynx, where the vocal folds are located. Normally, these folds are relatively far apart and not under tension. However, when a person speaks, muscles controlled by nerve impulses from the brain bring the folds closer together under varying amounts of tension. The greater the tension, the higher the frequency of the sound produced. Air passing through the larynx causes the vocal folds to vibrate, producing sound waves that resonate as they travel through the oral and nasal cavities before leaving through the mouth. The sounds that emerge are modified by the size and shape of the oral and nasal cavities and the positions of the tongue and lips.

The movements made in speaking produce a sequence of specific sounds called phonemes, which are the smallest units of the sounds that constitute speech. For example, the "b" sound in "bet" is a phoneme and

is different than the "p" sound (another phoneme) in "pet." Every spoken language has a unique way of joining phonemes to form syllables and words, but no major languages have a phoneme that is unique. The International Phonetic Alphabet consists of letters and symbols that allow one to write the speech sounds of all languages.

The nerve impulses that govern the muscular movements used in speaking come from a speech center just below the left temple (in most people) in the brain's cerebral cortex known as Broca's area. Recognition of speech sounds is located in another region of the cortex just behind the left ear in most people. It is known as Wernicke's area and receives sensory nerve impulses that originate in the ear.

The Origin of Speech

Marty Sereno, a neurobiologist at the University of California at San Diego, agrees that Broca's and Wernicke's areas are involved in speech because damage to these areas affects a person's ability to speak or understand what is said. However, Sereno believes that speech and speech comprehension are not limited to these parts of the cerebrum but are spread all over the brain. Speech began, he believes, not as a divine gift or the development of a new region of the brain, but by minor "rewiring" of the complex visual areas of the cerebrum.

Attaining experimental evidence for his theory, which Sereno admits is very complex, has not been easy. But recently, by using functional magnetic resonance imaging (fMRI) together with a computer program developed by Anders Dale that displays the three-dimensional cortex on a two-dimensional screen, Sereno and his colleagues can see localized brain activity. A subject engaged in a linguistic task, particularly an interesting one, shows high-level activity in visual areas of the brain. Furthermore, other researchers have found that stimulating those visual areas with electrodes during brain surgery produces the same kind of speech inhibition that occurs when Broca's area is stimulated.

Sereno agrees that the old theory makes sense. There should be a place in the brain where impulses come together and the mind operates on them to produce meaningful responses; however, his research leads him to believe that the brain isn't wired that way. But if specific regions devoted to speech did not emerge by evolution, how did speech begin? The answer, according to Sereno, is related to birds and their vocal abilities, not to nonhuman primates who lack an ability to learn verbally. Apes make many sounds, but they have no syntax. Ape calls can be arranged in any order without any effect on the ape receiving the sounds. Furthermore, unlike humans, a monkey deaf from birth can make the same sounds as a normal monkey; a songbird, if deafened as a chick, will never sing.

Songbirds learn to sing much as humans learn to speak. Chicks listen before they begin to make sounds, and their initial attempts to imitate their parents' songs are like a baby's babbling and gurgling. Later, they produce song fragments, similar to a baby's first words. Only after much practice do they sing the complex songs of their adult songbird species. Birds have all that's needed for a spoken language—an anatomical source of sounds, distinct sounds, and the ability to put sounds together in a specific order. The only drawback is they don't have anything to say except "Stay out of my territory!" or "Come mate with me!"

Sereno argues that the capacity to make different noises evolved in early humans or prehumans, and they could have used it to attract mates. But making speech has anatomical complications as well as mental demands. In nonhuman primates the larynx is located high in the throat so the base of the tongue covers it during eating and drinking. Humans are born with a similarly placed larynx, which prevents babies from choking, but by the time they start to talk, the larynx has descended so that the tongue can now move to allow the formation of vowel sounds without blocking the flow of air from the larynx. Our ability to speak a symbolic language, the unique quality that sets us apart from other animals, has a price. It is accompanied by the risk of choking whenever we eat or drink.

Why, in the course of evolution, would natural selection have placed humans at an increased risk for choking? Perhaps because sexual selection, not communication, was the cause of the modification in vocal anatomy. Then the minor rewiring of the visual areas of the brain, as suggested by Sereno, enabled the already existing vocal machinery to make language possible. Of course, we will probably never know for certain how human speech originated, but theories such as Sereno's will lead us to a greater understanding of how our present brains enable us to speak.

See also:
Artificial Language; Esperanto; Language; Nonverbal Communication; Writing.

References:
Caird, Rod. *Ape Man: The Story of Human Evolution.* New York: Macmillan, 1994.
Gardner, Robert. *Crime Lab 101.* New York: Walker, 1992.
Gutin, Jo Ann C. "A Brain That Talks." *Discover,* June 1996.
International Encyclopedia of Communications. New York: Oxford University Press, 1989.
Science and Technology Illustrated, vols. 7 and 24. Chicago: Encyclopedia Britannica, 1984.

Talking Drums

Lacking literacy and technology, some cultures have made limited use of drums as a means of communication over distances. The talking drums of west-central Africa are probably the best known, but they are not the only ones. Since the maximum range of talking drums, which require skilled drummers, is about 5 miles, messages have to be relayed from drummer to drummer to cover significant distances. Consequently, drums are used only to transmit important events.

Although the drum messages are sent as a code, the code is not anything like the familiar Morse code because even if the drummers are literate, their cultures have no alphabet. Instead, the drummers represent words by imitating their rhythm and tone using their drums. The tone can be altered by changing the tension in the drum's membrane. Talking drums are appropriate for African languages, which are based more on rhythm and tone than those of European origin. Nevertheless, the number of distinct words that can be transmitted using drums is probably not more than 500.

See also:
Smoke Signals and Native American Communication.
References:
International Encyclopedia of Communications.
New York: Oxford University Press, 1989.

Tape Recorder

A tape recorder is a device that will record and play back audio and visual information. To record sound on tape, electric currents produced by sound waves entering a microphone travel through the coils of an electromagnet (the recording head). The changing electric current in the coils is accompanied by corresponding changes in the magnetic field between the poles of the electromagnet. As the chemically coated tape moves at a steady rate through the changing magnetic field just below the magnetic poles in the recording head, a magnetic pattern is established in the tiny crystals of iron or chromium oxide embedded in the tape. The

magnetic pattern is determined by the signal, which may provide information about images, sounds, or digital data.

When the tape on which information has been magnetically recorded is passed through another head (playback head), it produces weak electric currents in the coils of small electromagnets within the head. In the case of sound recordings, these signals are amplified before they are sent to a loudspeaker, where they can reproduce quite accurately the sound that originally entered the microphone. Signals that originated from visual images are sent to a television monitor, and digital signals are fed into a digital decoder.

During a recording, the tape passes through another head, known as the erase head, before it enters the recording head. The erase head provides a strong magnetic field that removes any magnetic pattern that might have been placed on the tape during an earlier recording. Audio tape recorders, which are used to record and play back sound, divide the tape into four tracks—two on each side. The two parallel tracks on one side allow the two stereo signals to be recorded or played simultaneously.

By 1985, research scientists and engineers had become so successful in recording sound on thin plastic tapes coated with iron oxide, chromium dioxide, or metal that audiotapes were outselling plastic phonograph records.

Fixed-Head and Rotary-Head Recorders

Video and digital audiotape machines are sometimes called rotary-head recorders because the heads rotate as tape moves by them. Analog audio recorders are called fixed-head recorders because the heads remain in one position. A video or digital recording must include more information than an analog audio recording. Video recording, for example, must include information about color, brightness, and synchronization as well as sound. To allow all the necessary information to be recorded on tape, the recording head of a video recorder, really two heads at opposite sides of a cylinder, rotates rapidly as recording tape passes by the head at an angle. The tape is held against the rotating cylinder by capstans so that half the cylinder, and thus one of the heads, is always close to the tape. The result is a series of diagonal magnetic patterns or tracks that lie across the tape. Placed end to end the diagonal tracks are much longer than the tape itself. In this way, the rotating-head recorder uses its tape more efficiently than a fixed-head recorder that places parallel patterns along the entire tape.

The audio signal that accompanies a video recording may be recorded separately as a track parallel to the tape along one edge or as a part of the video signal. The latter, which provides a better quality of sound, can be recorded as a stereophonic signal and is referred to as a HiFi video recording.

Videotape Recorders and Camcorders

During the 1970s, Sony introduced Betamax, a cassette that enclosed a half-inch tape for use in a videocassette recorder (VCR) that could be connected to a home television set. At about the same time, Japan Victor Company (JVC) produced a similar cassette and recorder called a Video Home System (VHS). The two systems were incompatible, and over the years since they were introduced, VHS has become the predominant home video system.

Super VHS (S-VHS) provides somewhat sharper images and uses sturdier tape, which is helpful for users who make multiple tape-to-tape copies. The S-VHS system can tape and play in VHS mode as well as S-VHS; however, the S-VHS tapes cannot be used in VHS machines.

Smaller 8-millimeter (0.25-inch) videotape

cassettes used in camcorders may someday replace VHS. Their size permits them to be used with miniature TV sets that have built-in VCRs that will play 8-millimeter videotapes.

The combination of a small battery-powered VCR with a color video camera gave rise to the camera-recorder combination widely known as the camcorder. The light and sound signals from the camera and stereo microphones are recorded on videotape. The recording can be played on a compatible VCR and viewed on a television screen. The ability to produce home "movies" using light, portable camcorders has made them very popular.

The most recent 8-millimeter camcorders sell well because they are compact, light, and easy to carry. Their cassettes, which hold tape sufficient for two hours of recording, can be played on an 8-millimeter VCR, a TV through a cable connection, or an ordinary VCR with an adapter. The VHS-C camcorders produced by JVC contain cassettes that will hold 40 minutes of recorded tape at high speed or two hours at slow speed. These cassettes can be played in a VHS VCR using a battery-powered adapter. The original standard full-sized camcorders, which are heavier and bulkier, are becoming less popular. However, they can serve as a VCR for playing movies recorded on VCR cassettes, which hold two hours of recorded material.

Price

The price of a VCR ranges from $200 to $2,000. Expect to pay an additional $50 for models with high-fidelity sound. The small, light, highly portable 8-millimeter camcorders sell for $450 to $1,500 or more. The cassettes used with these machines sell for about $5. The JVC VHS-C camcorders start at about $500, but S-VHS-C models will sell for $1,200 or more. Tapes cost about $6, more for S-VHS tapes. The standard full-size camcorders cost anywhere from $500 to $1,100, but their tapes cost only about $3.

See also:
Analog and Digital Signals; Computer; Electromagnet.

References:
"*Consumer Reports* 1995 Buying Guide." *Consumer Reports*, 15 December 1994.
Macaulay, David. *The Way Things Work.* Boston: Houghton Mifflin, 1988.
The New Book of Popular Science. Danbury, CT: Grolier, 1992.

Teaching

Teaching is the planned, purposeful attempt to help others learn. Learning—the process of changing because of experience—can occur through both cognitive and affective avenues. For example, a student can, with help from a teacher, develop the thought processes required to solve theorems in geometry. By so doing, the student gains confidence in his ability to think for himself and may change his attitude toward education. A student who examines the history of, and evidence related to, racial issues may overcome deep-seated prejudice. In short, learning leads to the acquisition of knowledge, skills, beliefs, and understandings. These attainments can provide an individual with a new mental outlook that leads him or her to change behavior and achieve new and different meaning from experiences past, present, and future.

The best teachers provide their students with the tools to learn *how* to learn so that they can continue to grow intellectually and personally throughout their lives. Change is ever present in today's complex society, and to cope with it one must know how to learn new skills, develop or adapt to new ideas, and think both objectively and creatively.

Teachers, in addition to being experts in the field they teach, whether it be preschool education or graduate-level courses in nuclear energy, must also be skilled communicators. Teaching demands sound skills of communication, communication that extends beyond the walls of their classrooms to the parents of those they teach, the administrators for whom they work, and their peers with whom they work.

Preparation of Teachers

People interested in becoming teachers at the elementary or secondary level pursue an undergraduate program consisting of liberal arts, professional, and subject matter courses in the area that they plan to teach. The professional courses will include teaching skills, learning theory, methods of assessment, educational history, philosophy, pedagogy, and practice teaching.

For secondary teachers, approximately one-fifth of the curriculum is devoted to professional courses; the remaining course load is approximately equally divided among liberal arts and specific subject matter courses such as biology, history, English, foreign language, chemistry, etc., with emphasis on the discipline the student plans to teach. For those preparing to teach at the elementary level, professional and liberal arts courses each constitute approximately half the prescribed curriculum. Future requirements may include a fifth year or a master's degree before being certified to teach.

Teaching Methods

Traditionally, teachers have used lectures as the primary means of transmitting knowledge. Although this method is still the predominant form of teaching college courses with large enrollments, other approaches are becoming widely used. Discussion or seminar classes are used extensively at the secondary level and in college courses, particularly in advanced courses where enrollments are small. At the elementary level, there is a good deal of small group work in which the teacher interacts with a small number of students from a larger class, while others in the class work on assignments or with teacher aides. The groups are generally made up of students of comparable ability. However, there is also a growing trend toward cooperative learning in which students of different abilities are grouped together and asked to tackle various assignments. The strategy is for the ablest students to help (tutor) the less able, while all contribute something to the small-group division of tasks and discussions that focus on an overall assignment.

Recently, particularly where specific skills are being developed, simulations have played a large role in the teaching process. In teacher training courses a student will be asked to teach a specific lesson to the rest of the class. Pilots use flight simulators to learn to fly, and driver education courses use computer programs that simulate driving conditions. Although simulations have not been used in a large number of classrooms, science teachers sometimes used course content to illustrate the scientific method, that is, to examine data, formulate hypotheses, test them experimentally, and then reject, modify, or tentatively accept the hypotheses. Simulations have also been used in other disciplines such as history classes where "senators" debate historical and current issues. At the elementary level, simulations are used in various ways. Students, for example, may set up and run "stores" using play money.

Except for science and home economics courses, where lab and practical work played an important role, technology was not used extensively in classrooms before the 1990s. Computers have become an important teaching component in today's schools. In many schools there is a computer in every classroom as well as a computer lab where each member of an entire class can work at a terminal. Computer-assisted instruction (CIA) uses specially designed software to provide drill and practice exercises or introduce games that require the use of reading, writing, grammar, math, and other skills. Tutorial programs help students learn or improve various skills such as typing. Word-processing programs have made writing and rewriting tasks far less onerous. In addition, teachers are using computers to keep records, enter and calculate grades, and write reports and lesson plans.

In addition to computers, many schools use films, overhead projectors, educational television, and videos. At the college level, live television is being used to make it possible for students on different campuses to take the same course. Images are carried by dedicated telephone lines from one classroom to another classroom some distance away, where students can not only sit in on the distant class but interact with the teacher

and students through another camera that sends images in the other direction.

Despite the increasing use of technology in education, it is not likely that the learning that results from personal interactions between students and thoughtful, dedicated teachers can ever be replaced by machines of any kind.

See also:
Computer; Computers and Society; Reading; Writing.

References:
Crow, Gary A. *Children at Risk*. New York: Schocken Books, 1978.
Kohl, Herbert R. *On Teaching*. New York: Schocken Books, 1976.
Meier, Deborah. *The Power of Their Ideas: Lessons for America from a Small School in Harlem*. Boston: Beacon Press, 1995.

Telecommunications

Telecommunications is the communication of signals over a long distance. Given that definition, early means of communication such as smoke signals, talking drums, flags, lamps, and mirrors to reflect pulses of light are forms of telecommunication. However, over the last 150 years, telecommunications has come to mean long-distance communication by electrical means, beginning with the telegraph in 1837. Nearly 40 years later the telephone made it possible to communicate by voice over a relatively long distance. Shortly after the beginning of the twentieth century, wireless telegraphy made transoceanic communication a reality. Two decades later radio stations were sending signals through the atmosphere. After World War II, television became widespread, and the emergence of space-age technology gave rise to communications satellites that made it possible to transmit television, telephone, and telegraph signals around the world almost instantaneously.

Every telecommunications system has a terminal such as a telephone, fax, computer, or radio transmitter. In some cases, as with the telephone, the interaction is two-way. In others, such as radio and television, the communication is one-way, from sender to receiver. However, talk radio often encourages the audience to participate, and television is becoming increasingly two-way as viewers respond to polls and order goods from home-shopping channels. At the terminal, a signal is produced that allows a message to be transmitted by wire or electromagnetic waves to a receiver, where the signal is converted to a form that listeners or viewers can understand, such as sound from a telephone receiver, print from a fax machine, or images and sound from a television monitor.

Telecommunications is made possible by networks with switching systems, relay stations, and satellites that carry personal telephone calls around the globe. Similarly, television networks can bring a program originating in Atlanta, Georgia, where the 1996 Summer Olympics were held, to cities throughout the United States and, via satellite, to viewers on the other side of the earth.

While satellites have extended the range of signals, fiber optics, which use light signals transmitted along glass fibers rather than electrical pulses along wires, offer a vast increase in the volume of signals that can be transmitted per second. A single glass fiber can replace more than 10,000 copper telephone wires. Eventually, light may become the only signals used in telecommunications networks.

During the mid-1960s, the Department of Defense established a network of computers that grew into what is known today as the Internet. Through the Internet it is possible to exchange messages using electronic mail, post notices on computer community bulletin boards, access databases, and exchange computer programs with millions of other users who are connected to the network.

The signals used in the earliest forms of telecommunication—telegraph and telephone—were carried by wire. Marconi introduced signals carried by electromagnetic waves with his wireless telegraphy just before the beginning of the twentieth century. Later, radio and television signals were sent by generating modulated electromagnetic waves. All these transmitters used analog

signals. The great expansion of communication in the late twentieth century was made possible by the digital signals used in computers. With digital coding there is less distortion. Much more information can be sent per unit time, and data from voice, image, and graphics are easily integrated.

With high-definition television, which uses digital signals, television can be readily coupled with computers. The union of television and computers, together with fiber optics, will vastly enhance telecommunications and make it possible for television to become a truly interactive form of communication leading to the information superhighway.

See also:
Analog and Digital Signals; Electromagnetic Waves; Fax Machine; Fiber Optics; Information Superhighway; Internet; Marconi, Guglielmo; Radio; Telegraph; Telephone; Television; Television Network.

Telegraph

The literal meaning of the word *telegraph* is "writing at a distance." In that sense, talking drums, church bells, semaphore, and smoke signals are forms of telegraphy. The more common meaning of telegraph is a device for sending unmodulated electrical signals, usually by wire.

Early Telegraphy

One of the earliest suggestions for such an instrument was a 26-wire device with one wire for each letter. The idea was to apply static electricity to the transmitting end of the wire. The charge would be carried along the wire to a pith ball at the receiving end. There, the pith ball would be attracted and then repelled as it received charge from the wire. Each pith ball would carry a letter so that the person receiving the message would record the letters as the pith balls were repelled from their individual wires. After each letter was sent as a static electric charge signal on a wire, the sender would ground the wire and it would be ready for recharging.

In 1804, Francisco Salvá built a device similar to the one described above. It used tiny electrolytic cells to indicate letters. The ends of two wires from opposite poles of a battery were submerged in small lettered vials of acid. Activation of the circuit by pressing a switch caused tiny bubbles of hydrogen to form in the acid. Salvá's device was shown to work over distances as great as a half-mile.

By 1830, all the ingredients required for a practical commercial telegraph were in place. Alessandro Volta had invented the battery. Hans Christian Oersted had shown in 1819 that every electric current was encircled by a magnetic field and that the direction of the field depended on the direction of the current, which was assumed to be the direction of positive charge flow, that is, from the positive pole of a battery to the negative pole. In 1823, William Sturgeon built an electromagnet that provided a magnetic field stronger than any previously produced by winding wire into a coil so that it produced a field similar to that of a bar magnet. Sturgeon's coil was wound on a core of iron that served to concentrate the magnetic lines of force inside the coil. People also had learned how to make copper wire, a metal nearly six times more effective as a conductor than iron, which was the more commonly used wire before that time.

In 1837, following a visit by the American scientist Joseph Henry, William Cooke and Charles Wheatstone in England devised and patented a telegraph that used five switches to activate five wires at a sender that led to five magnetic needles at a receiver. Two of the needles on a diamond grid would turn in response to a letter entered when the sender pressed a lettered key. The two needles, responding to the strength and direction of electric current in a wire beneath them, would turn until they pointed to a particular letter on the grid. Of course, it was difficult to adjust the sender and receiver so that the needles turned just the right amount. Because electrical resistance is proportional to the length of the wire through which electric charge travels, the strength of the current reaching the receiver depended on the distance between sender and receiver. Nevertheless, Cooke and Wheatstone were able to send messages that could be sensibly translated at a receiver. By 1842, they had developed a more satisfactory two-needle telegraph that used a code involving the number and direction of needle deflections to indicate characters.

A somewhat different system of telegraphy was developed in the United States by Samuel Finley Breese Morse with the help of physicist Joseph Henry and mechanic Alfred Vail. In 1835, they used an electromagnet to move a pendulum to which they attached a magnetized pen. Pulsing currents in the electromagnet would deflect the pen and leave marks on a paper strip that moved beneath the tip of the pen.

Morse Code

To develop an efficient code for sending signals, Vail visited a printing shop where he learned that the most commonly used character in the English language was the letter *E*. The printer had 12,000 *E*s, 9,000 *T*s (the next most commonly used letter), 8,000 *A*s, and so on down to 200 *Z*s, the least commonly used letter in the alphabet. The code that they developed, a system of dots and dashes, which can be made by turning on a current for two different lengths of time, is shown in Figure 1. The code made use of Vail's research by using the simplest signals to send the most commonly used letters. The more complicated series of dots and dashes

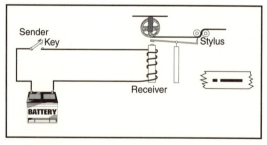

Figure 1. When the telegraph key at the sender is depressed, closing the circuit, the receiver's electromagnet attracts the metallic stylus arm, causing the stylus to mark a dot or dash on the paper strip that runs above it. A pattern showing the letter A *in Morse code (• –, or dot-dash) marked on the paper strip is shown at the right.*

Table 1. Morse Code			
A • –	B – • • •	C – • – •	D – • •
E •	F • • – •	G – – •	H • • • •
I • •	J • – – –	K – • –	L • – • •
M – –	N – •	O – – –	P • – – •
Q – – • –	R • – •	S • • •	T –
U • • –	V • • • –	W • – –	X – • • –
Y – • – –	Z – – • •		
1 • – – – –	2 • • – – –	3 • • • – –	4 • • • • –
5 • • • • •	6 – • • • •	7 – – • • •	8 – – – • •
9 – – – – •	0 – – – – –		
, (comma) – • • – –		. (period) • – • – • –	
? (question) • • – – • •		; (semicolon) – • – • – •	
: (colon) – – – • • •		/ (slash) – • • – •	
- (hyphen) – • • • • –		' (apostrophe) • – – – – •	
( ) (parenthesis) – • – – • –		— (underline) • • – – • –	

were reserved for the less commonly used letters, such as *X* and *Z*.

The Morse code, which was used in telegraphy, can also be used for signaling visually with flashes of light or waves of a flag. The code allows a sender to transmit numbers and punctuation as well as letters (see Table 1). What Morse had not anticipated was that skilled operators could record a received message by simply listening to the sounds of the clicking electromagnets. They did not need to see the dots and dashes left on paper by his recording pen. This meant the telegraph could be reduced to a sending key (switch) to make or break a circuit, a battery to provide a current, a line of insulated copper wire to connect sender and receiver, and a sounder at the receiving end of the line. The sounder was nothing more than an iron armature that made a clicking sound when it was attracted to and struck the stop at one end of an activated electromagnet.

Practical Telegraphy

The first practical telegraph line was built for Cooke and Wheatstone's invention in 1838. It connected Paddington Station with West Drayton Station, 13 miles away. In 1844, Morse sent the first long-distance message—"What hath God wrought?"—over a 37-mile telegraph line between Baltimore and Washington, D.C. By 1861, the first transcontinental telegraph line had been built, and a telegraph network connected distant U.S. cities.

After several unsuccessful attempts beginning in 1857, an 1,850-mile transatlantic cable was laid along the ocean floor by a huge former passenger ship, the *Great Eastern*. The cable allowed messages to be transmitted across the Atlantic Ocean, making possible almost instant communication between the United States and Europe.

The major problem in sending telegraph messages along wires was that the signal faded with distance because of electrical resistance. Joseph Henry inadvertently solved the problem of sending long-distance messages by telegraph during his investigation of electromagnets, and he gladly shared his knowledge with Morse, who is usually credited with inventing the telegraph. To activate even large electromagnets over large distances, Henry invented the electrical relay in 1835. His relay was basically a small iron key that could be raised by even a weak current in an electromagnet. Once the key was raised, it could be used to close another circuit connected to a battery. The second circuit could then activate another relay. In this way, relays could maintain the strength of a current over large distances.

As telegraphy grew, a number of small companies were formed in anticipation of the profits to be made in this new mode of communication that sent messages practically instantaneously over long distances. In 1856, Hiram Sibley consolidated a number of these small companies to form the Western Union Telegraph Company. The size of this new company gave Sibley the capital necessary to engage in major projects such as the development of a transcontinental telegraph line. The line, completed in 1861, caused the demise of the Pony Express, which had been the fastest means of communication between Saint Joseph, Missouri, and Sacramento, California, at that time. In the ten years following Sibley's formation of Western Union, the number of telegraph offices grew from 132 to 4,000. By 1866, the 4,000 offices connected more than 75,000 miles of telegraph lines crisscrossing the United States.

Improved Telegraphy

During the years following the establishment of telegraphy as the world's fastest means of communication, a number of improvements were made. Wheatstone invented a way to prepare a punched paper tape so that a message could be stored as holes in the paper and then be transmitted at a higher speed (up to 400 words per minute) than any operator could send by tapping a key. At the receiving end, an electromagnet moved an inked roller against paper to form dots and dashes. In 1855, David Hughes devised a receiver that would print the message, and in 1870 the French inventor Émile Baudot invented multiplexing, a system that allowed several messages to be sent simultaneously along the same wire.

By 1915, a keyboard had been developed that allowed a sender to type the message by perforating a tape that moved past the keyboard. At the receiver, a reperforator punched a new tape. That tape, in turn, could be used to activate a printer, which printed the message on paper tape with a gummed backing. The tape with the message could then be stuck to a common Western Union form and be ready for delivery.

By 1930, Teletype was quite prevalent. A sender would type a message, and the same message would be typed out on a receiver almost simultaneously. Today, these messages are carried from station to station by microwave signals with relay towers at approximately 30-mile intervals. International Teletype signals can be relayed across oceans by using geosynchronous satellites in orbits 22,300 miles above the earth.

Before the beginning of World War II, most of the old telegraphy technology was replaced by teleprinter equipment. However, radio telegraphy using Morse code continues to this day.

See also:
Electromagnet; Fax Machine; Field, Cyrus West; Henry, Joseph; Morse, Samuel F. B.; Multiplexing; Oersted, Hans Christian; Pony Express; Radio; Relay; Telephone; Teleprinter.

References:
Asimov, Isaac. *Asimov's Biographical Encyclopedia of Science and Technology*. Garden City, NY: Doubleday, 1964.
Asimov, Isaac. *Asimov's New Guide to Science*. New York: Basic Books, 1984.
Davidson, Marshall B. "What Samuel Wrought." *American Heritage*, April 1961.
Gardner, Robert. *Communication*. New York: Twenty-First Century, 1994.
Gardner, Robert. *Space: Frontier of the Future*. Garden City, NY: Doubleday, 1980.
How It Works: The Illustrated Encyclopedia of Science and Technology. New York and London: Marshall Cavendish, 1978.
Sassaman, Richard. "What Hath Morse Wrought." *American History Illustrated*, April 1988.
Williams, Trevor I. *The History of Invention: From Stone Axes to Silicon Chips*. New York: Facts on File, 1987.

Telepathy

The literal meaning of the word *telepathy* is "to feel at a distance," from the Greek *tele* (at a distance) and *patheia* (feeling). Despite the literal meaning, telepathy is often regarded as the ability to communicate thoughts or images between two minds without benefit of speech or any of the five senses.

Many people think they have experienced telepathy, but telepathy is usually experienced by someone who has lived with another person for a long time. Because of their long, close association, they may have similar thoughts simultaneously. Being so aware of one another's feelings, modes of thought, associations, and styles, one may often anticipate what the other is about to say. This is not telepathy, and it is not unusual; it is simply the result of empathy, intelligence, sensitivity, and knowing another person very well.

Most scientists doubt the existence of telepathy, extrasensory perception (ESP), and psychokinesis. ESP is the ability to obtain information through means other than the five senses. Psychokinesis is the ability to change matter by thought alone. Magicians and mind readers perform feats on stage that appear to involve ESP, telepathy, or psychokinesis, but most of them will admit that the feats all involve trickery. Many of those who claim to be authentic have been exposed as frauds by James "The Amazing" Randi, a conjurer himself, who has demonstrated the deceit practiced by "telepaths," faith healers, and others who con the public and some prominent scientists as well.

On the other hand, there are a number of people who think that it might be possible to communicate in ways that we do not understand. Some police departments use psychics—people who claim they can perceive things beyond the range of the senses—to try to locate missing persons or provide a vision of a crime scene. Some scientists are trying to determine whether parapsychology has any validity. One approach is to have an experimenter draw a card from a shuffled deck. The cards might have five different symbols, such as a star, circle, square, X, or triangle. The card is placed face down on a table, and the procedure is repeated at one-minute intervals. Meanwhile, a subject in another room with a synchronized clock tries to "see" through thought transfer the kind of card that has just been drawn by the experimenter and records his or her guess.

Some of these researchers claim that a few subjects produce results that are well above what would be expected from probability alone. There is also evidence from experiments conducted by Charles Honorton and Daryl Bem that those studying music and drama seem to have better telepathic powers than other students. However, these experiments have been criticized by skeptics, who claim the results are marred by accidental errors in which the experimenter prompted the subjects. Furthermore, these experiments have not been replicated by others, and in general the failure of promising results in telepathic research to be repeated in other laboratories—the benchmark of scientific validity—is the reason that telepathy, ESP, psychokinesis, and the entire field of parapsychology has not been taken seriously by most of the scientific community.

References:

Begley, Sharon. "Is There Anything to It? Evidence Please." *Newsweek*, 8 July 1996.

Harvey, Lorrin. "Mental Telepathy in the Lab: Tests Show Psychic Abilities among Actors and Musicians." *Omni*, November 1994.

Sagan, Carl. *The Demon-Haunted World*. New York: Random House, 1995.

Telephone

The telephone, which converts sound energy to electrical energy and then back to sound, is the world's most widely used means of communication. Inventor Alexander Graham Bell's first telephone message, "Mr. Watson, come here, I want you," was transmitted from one room to another in 1876. Today, millions of much lengthier telephone conversations take place on a network that stretches around the world.

Bell realized that sound waves lose their intensity rapidly as they spread out through space. In fact, the intensity is quartered every time the distance from the source of the sound doubles. As a result, speech cannot be heard by someone several miles away, even if shouted loudly. Electric currents, however, will follow the path of a wire and lose their intensity much less rapidly. Furthermore, it is possible to use relays or amplifiers to maintain the signal over even very great distances.

Inside the telephone mouthpiece is a small carbon microphone through which a tiny electric current flows. Sound waves strike a thin diaphragm that moves in and out with the same frequency as the sound waves that strike it. The inward-moving diaphragm increases the pressure on the carbon granules that lie behind it. When the diaphragm moves outward, the pressure decreases. Increased pressure squeezes the carbon granules together and reduces their electrical resistance. The decrease in resistance allows more electric current to flow through the microphone. On the other hand, a decrease in pressure increases the resistance of the carbon and reduces the current. The current through the microphone, therefore, varies directly with the pressure of the sound waves, and these electrical signals pulsate with the same frequency as the sound waves. As a result, sound is converted to a series of electrical pulses that reflect the intensity and frequency of the sound.

When these electrical pulses reach the earpiece of the person receiving the call, they flow through the coil of an electromagnet. A growing current in the coil creates a magnetic field that attracts a thin metal diaphragm in the ear piece. As the current subsides, the diaphragm moves back again. The movement of the diaphragm, therefore, reflects the intensity and frequency of the current in the coil. Consequently, the vibration of the diaphragm in the receiver duplicates that in the microphone. As a result, the sound waves produced by the moving diaphragm in the earpiece are nearly the same as those striking the microphone that were generated by the caller.

Initially all telephone signals were transmitted as electrical pulses. Today, however, telephone networks may convert electrical signals to light pulses that move along optical fibers, or to radio or microwave signals that are transmitted through space as electromagnetic waves. In order to provide clearer sound signals and meet the demands of millions of users with as few lines as possible, speech sounds are converted to digital signals and multiplexing is used so that many telephone conversations can be sent along the same line.

Cordless Phones

Cordless phones don't restrict the user to the length of a telephone cord during a telephone call, and they negate the need to move to the location of a telephone in order to answer a call. A cordless phone is actually a small, short-range radio linked by weak radio waves to its nearby base receiver-transmitter. The phone has an antenna that allows it to be separated and carried for limited distances from its base.

The Telephone and Society

Although the telegraph made it possible to transmit messages over long distances by going to a local telegraph station, the telephone made it possible to engage in person-to-person conversations from the users' own homes. The telephone has had a tremendous impact on our culture. Together with the elevator, it made skyscrapers and the modern city possible. Even though education, eco-

nomic opportunities, and the regionalization of many industries has led to the separation of family members and the breakup of multigenerational homes, the telephone has made it possible for people to maintain close family ties.

The telephone has certainly saved lives in situations where rapid transmission of information about illness, injury, or threats of either has provided a quick response. The growing use of 911 calls in emergencies results in almost immediate action by fire, police, and rescue squads. Although the telephone has diminished the art and frequency of letter writing, its speed and ease of transferring information has accelerated the exchange of scientific and technological information while making the experience of living alone bearable for even those with strong social tendencies. It is also likely that the hot line between Washington, D.C., and Moscow may have prevented World War III and the use of atomic weapons.

The telephone can also affect us psychologically. A phone call in the middle of the night can cause hearts to pound while generating fear, anxiety, or hope. It also exposes us to threatening or obscene calls and the risk of being "hung up on," as well as annoying "wrong number" calls.

Some of the anxiety associated with telephone calls has been eliminated by modern technology. It is now possible to block calls from designated numbers. Caller ID service allows screening of incoming calls and displays the number of the calling party; the user can then decide whether to answer. Customers may also arrange to have all incoming calls automatically forwarded to another number or arrange for conference calls. Call waiting service allows the user to put one caller on hold while answering a signal from another caller.

It is possible to install videophones. These telephones have a built-in television camera and screen that allow callers to see as well as talk to one another. It is questionable whether videophones will ever become popular. Many people would prefer to be heard and not seen, and the purpose of most telephone calls is to convey a message; visual images are not essential to the process.

See also:
American Telephone & Telegraph Company; Amplifier; Analog and Digital Signals; Bell, Alexander Graham; Electromagnet; Electromagnetic Waves; Fiber Optics; Henry, Joseph; Loudspeaker; Microphone; Multiplexing.
References:
Baida, Peter. "Breaking the Connection." *American Heritage,* June/July 1985.
Gardner, Robert. *Communication.* New York: Twenty-First Century, 1994.
Gardner, Robert. *This Is the Way It Works: A Collection of Machines.* Garden City, NY: Doubleday, 1980.
How It Works: The Illustrated Encyclopedia of Science and Technology. New York and London: Marshall Cavendish, 1978.
Macaulay, David. *The Way Things Work.* Boston: Houghton Mifflin, 1988.
Science and Technology Illustrated, vol. 15. Chicago: Encyclopedia Britannica, 1984.

Telephone Companies

See American Telephone & Telegraph Company.

Telephone Switching

Telephone switching allows one telephone to be connected to another so that a person-to-person conversation may take place.

Initially, connections between telephones were made by stringing a wire from one phone to another. In 1878 the first telephone switchboard was installed in New Haven, Connecticut. It enabled an operator sitting at such a board to manually connect the lines from the 21 telephones that led to the switchboard. During the next decade, more complex switchboards capable of handling thousands of calls by telephone patrons were developed. Connecting cables, called trunk lines, were established between local switchboards so that callers could make long-distance calls.

In those days callers would lift a receiver, activating a line connecting them with a local exchange. The operator would say "number please," and the caller would then state the number being called, such as "two five ring three." The operator would then connect the caller's line to the line of the person being called and activate a circuit that would ring the phones on the receiving line. Because most telephones were on party lines, several families shared a line to the exchange. For the number two five ring three (25-3), the phone was connected to line 25, and the party answered only when the phone rang three times in rapid succession. A private phone line connecting a single phone to the exchange was more expensive.

Although long-distance calls were possible in the late nineteenth century, they were limited to separations of about 1,000 miles. Over greater distances the signals became very weak and higher voice frequencies were lost, leaving sounds that could not be recognized. By 1920, these problems were solved. Inductance coils placed at intervals along a line reduced frequency distortion, and triode vacuum tubes, invented by Lee De Forest in 1906, provided a means of amplifying the signals.

In 1921, the first automated dialing system was installed in Omaha, Nebraska. Turning the dial set up electrical impulses that traveled to a switching center, where connections were made on the basis of the impulses received. These switching systems, which used electrical signals to mechanically open and close relays, were not fast enough to meet the needs of a fast-growing communications system. Today's push-button phones produce tones that serve as signals to activate semiconductor-based switches. The diodes and transistors in today's electronic switching circuitry operate thousands of times faster than the older mechanical systems.

Since the late 1930s, it has been possible to use microwaves to relay telephone as well as telegraph and television signals. Beginning in 1947, microwave relay systems were set up to transmit long-distance calls and replace the old trunk lines. Originally, relay stations, where signals are received, amplified, and sent to the next station, were placed at about 30-mile intervals, and the waves followed straight (line-of-sight) paths. A decade

Two switchboard operators, seated at the right, manually connect telephone lines from a Hamburg, New York, office in 1908.

later AT&T began using tropospheric scatter propagation to relay microwaves. This system relies on the reflection of a small fraction of the waves by the atmosphere, thus negating the need for line-of-sight relay stations.

The beginning of the Space Age in the 1960s led to the use of microwaves for global communication. Satellites revolving at 24-hour periods provide fixed positions for relaying microwaves that carry telephone, radio, television, and computer signals around the globe.

Today, there are more than 400 million telephones worldwide. Of those, nearly 40 percent are in the United States, where more than 800 million calls are made daily. Such volume is made possible by fiber-optic cables and a computer-controlled switching system based on microelectronics.

Cellular Phones

Since 1983, it has been possible for users to carry their telephones. The combination of telephone, radio, and computer technology has given the world cellular telephones. There are three parts to cellular phones: the phone itself, a network of radio antennas called base stations, and switching centers. The cellular phone is basically a radio transmitter. The radio waves generated by the phone are received at a base station antenna near the center of a geographical area called a cell, thus, cellular telephone. Signals from the base station reach a switching office, where they are sent to a local or long-distance telephone company that transfers the signals to the number dialed. If the caller moves beyond the range of one cell, the signals are automatically transferred to the base station of another cell within range.

There are three types of cellular phones: mobile, transportable, and portable. Mobile phones are permanently mounted in a vehicle, such as an automobile, and are powered by energy from the vehicle's engine. Transportable phones are carried in a case and are powered by batteries. Portable phones are battery powered and small enough to be carried by hand.

See also:
Analog and Digital Signals, Diode; Fiber Optics; Microelectronics; Multiplexing; Telephone; Transistor.

References:
Macaulay, David. *The Way Things Work.* Boston: Houghton Mifflin, 1988.
The New Book of Popular Science. Danbury, CT: Grolier, 1992.
Williams, Trevor I. *The History of Invention: From Stone Axes to Silicon Chips.* New York: Facts on File, 1987.

Teleprinter (Teletypewriter)

A teleprinter is an electromechanical device that either transmits or receives messages carried by telegraph or telephone wires. With the first teletypewriters, an operator punched Morse code into a paper tape that was then loaded into a transmitter that could read and send up to 400 words per minute. At the receiver, a paper tape perforator produced a second tape that was decoded by one or more operators.

The decoding process at the receiving end was the obvious bottleneck in the operation. The problem was solved by using a code developed by Donald Murray, a British inventor. Murray's five-unit code, which is partially shown in Table 1, provided five units for each character.

The teletypewriter developed in the 1920s used Murray's code. When a key on the teletypewriter keyboard was pressed, five long bars were released. Depending on the key pressed, one or more of the bars would extend farther than the others according to the code shown in Table 1. The extended bars would make electrical contact with a rotating cam that made and broke an electric circuit, sending current pulses along a wire to a receiver. At the receiver, the pulses of current caused electromagnets to attract the same combination of bars, causing the same character that was typed to fall into place on a rotating type head. When the letter was in place, the type head hit a sheet of paper, causing the same message that was typed on a distant teletypewriter to appear on the teleprinter where the message was received.

By 1930, teletypewriters and teleprinters were quite prevalent. Before the beginning of World War II, most of the old telegraphy technology was replaced by teleprinter equipment. Today, these messages are carried from station to station by microwave signals with relay towers at approximately

Table 1. Part of the Murray Code
The dots indicate which of the five bars connected to the key indicated in the left-hand column are activated when that key is pressed.

Character	1	2	3	4	5	Character	1	2	3	4	5
A		•	•			Q	•	•	•		•
B	•			•	•	R		•		•	
C		•	•	•		S	•		•		
D	•			•		T					•
E	•					U	•	•	•		
F	•		•	•		V		•	•	•	•
G		•		•	•	W	•	•			•
H			•		•	X	•		•	•	•
I		•	•			Y	•		•		•
J	•	•		•		Z	•				•
L		•			•	carriage return				•	
M			•	•	•	line feed		•			
N			•	•		shift	•	•	•	•	•
O				•	•	space			•		
P		•	•		•						

30-mile intervals, and the five-unit Murray code has been replaced by the eight-unit American Standard Code for Information Interchange (ASCII) code. Each keystroke produces a start pulse, an information pulse, and a stop pulse. The pulses are sent as on-off (0s and 1s) based on ASCII code. International Teletype signals can be relayed across oceans by using geosynchronous satellites in orbits 22,300 miles above the earth.

Telex is a trademark of Western Union. Telex I uses a five-unit code that transmits at 66 words per minute. Telex II uses eight-unit ASCII code. Both systems require a teletypewriter, but transmission may be by wire, microwave, satellites, or optical fiber.

Transmission of words and images by facsimile or photo telegraphy is widely used for sending messages along telephone lines today, but the technology has existed since the 1920s. Newspapers were the earliest beneficiaries of photo telegraphy because it enabled reporters to sent photographs as well as printed messages.

See also:
Analog and Digital Signals; Telegraph.
References:
Asimov, Isaac. *Asimov's Biographical Encyclopedia of Science and Technology*. Garden City, NY: Doubleday, 1964.
Asimov, Isaac. *Asimov's New Guide to Science*. New York: Basic Books, 1984.
Science and Technology Illustrated, vol. 25. Chicago: Encyclopedia Britannica, 1984.
Williams, Trevor I. *The History of Invention: From Stone Axes to Silicon Chips*. New York: Facts on File, 1987.

Teletext
See Videotex.

Teletypewriter
See Teleprinter.

Television
Television is a communication medium that transmits and receives sounds and images, including moving images, by means of electromagnetic waves or electrical signals transmitted by cable. During the second half of the twentieth century, it has been the predominant form of mass communication in the United States.

The Nipkow Disk and Early Television
In 1883, Paul Nipkow devised a disk with a spiral arrangement of small holes that came to be known as the Nipkow disk. When the disk rotated in front of a light beam, it produced pinpoints of light that moved in scanning fashion across a screen, much as the eye moves while reading a page. Nipkow's disk, which was regarded as the key to transmitting images by wire, served as the basic principle underlying television research efforts for decades.

The word *television* was first used in the *Scientific American* magazine in 1907, and it soon became a popular term. Before that time, television had been referred to as the telephonoscope, visual radio, and a variety of other terms.

The Nipkow disk was used by the Scottish inventor John Logie Baird in developing his mechanical television set. Baird, who had worked alone with minimal funding during the 1920s, joined with the British Broadcasting Corporation (BBC) in 1929 to produce and sell a number of "televisors." At the same time, General Electric in the United States was experimenting with its own version of television. Both efforts were dropped as a worldwide depression deepened and it became evident that a market for sets that produced rather poor images did not exist among citizens sufficiently pleased with the miracle of radio.

Despite the Depression, David Sarnoff, who became president of the Radio Corporation of America (RCA) in 1930, recognized the future potential of television and hired Vladimir Zworykin, a Russian inventor who had pioneered in developing television, to spearhead the program at RCA. Successful tests led Sarnoff to display RCA television at the New York World's Fair in 1939. President Franklin Roosevelt opened the exhibit on

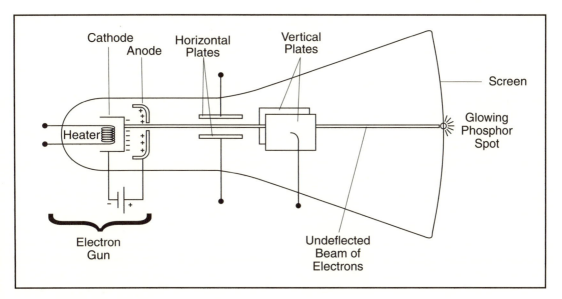

Figure 1. A cathode-ray tube.

30 April 1939 and became the first U.S. chief executive to appear on television.

What Sarnoff had not anticipated were challenges from Philo Farnsworth, who patented his own television tube in 1930, and Edwin H. Armstrong who at about the same time developed frequency-modulation (FM) radio, which Sarnoff considered a threat to television. Lawsuits brought by Armstrong and royalties demanded by Farnsworth delayed Sarnoff's efforts to market RCA sets and establish a chain of broadcasting stations. When war broke out in Europe during the New York World's Fair, people who were knowledgeable about television were soon drafted by the government to help in the development of radar for wartime use, and Sarnoff's dream had to be postponed again.

The Origins of Television Technology

The modern television set is based on discoveries made around 1900. Before that time, great strides had been achieved in the technology of making vacuum tubes and producing high-voltage electricity, which can provide electric charges with significant kinetic energy. It was found that when high voltage is applied across a vacuum tube, a greenish glow appears at the end of the tube opposite the negative electrode (cathode). When a metal plate was supported in the middle of the beam, it cast a shadow on the anode, indicating that the rays came from the cathode, hence, the term cathode rays. Experiments revealed, too, that a magnetic field deflected cathode rays and negatively charged particles in the same way.

To confirm that cathode rays were negatively charged particles, the British physicist Joseph John Thomson (1856–1940) built a vacuum tube enclosing parallel metal plates. He connected one plate to the positive terminal of a strong battery and the other plate to the negative terminal of the same battery. When a beam of cathode rays passed between the plates, their curved path revealed that they were repelled by the negative plate and attracted by the positive plate, providing confirming evidence that they were negatively charged particles. Thomson went on to show that the particles, which came to be known as electrons, were the fundamental units of negative charge found in the atoms of all matter.

The combined work of Thomson, John Fleming, and Lee De Forest led to the development of the cathode-ray tube shown in

Figure 1. The electron gun at the rear of the tube generates a beam of electrons. Electrons "boiled" off the cathode are accelerated by an electrical force that drives them toward the positively charged anode. After passing through a hole in the anode, the beam of electrons moves along a straight path until it strikes a phosphorescent screen, producing a visible dot of light. By charging the horizontal plates between the anode and the screen, the electron beam can be bent up or down. A similar pair of vertical plates can be used to bend the electron beam to the right or left.

By rapidly changing the charge on the vertical plates, the electron beam can be swept quickly across the screen. A variable voltage applied to the horizontal plates can be used to move the beam up or down as it sweeps across the screen.

How Television Works

Television signals travel through space in the same way that radio signals do. Each station uses special frequencies, called channels, to transmit its signal through the atmosphere. Very high frequencies (VHF), from 30 to 220 megahertz (MHz), and ultrahigh frequencies (UHF), from 450 to 900 MHz, are used to transmit television to homes. Channels 2 through 4 are assigned 54 to 72 MHz, channels 5 and 6 broadcast at 76 to 88 MHz, and channels 7 through 13 use 174 to 216 MHz. Channels 14 through 83 use 470 to 890 MHz. The bandwidth of each channel is 6 MHz.

The fundamental difference between radio and television is that light, usually coded in three colors, as well as sound is used to modulate the carrier waves. Although initially television signals were sent primarily by radio waves and received by antennas placed as high as possible, most sets today receive their signals via cable, and a significant number use parabolic dishes (antennas) pointed at satellites that deliver superhigh-frequency signals of 4.0 to 8.5 gigahertz (wavelengths of 3.5 to 7.5 centimeters).

Community antenna television (CATV) is a means of sharing a central antenna located at a high point where reception is optimum for the region. The signals received are amplified and sent by cable to individual homes, where the owners pay a monthly fee to a private corporation that is granted an exclusive franchise by the local government. Often, the cable company will agree not to duplicate the broadcasts of any local station and will provide free programs for schools. Initially, CATV was limited to rural areas far from any television station, but today the majority of television sets are connected to a cable.

A number of cable and online service companies are working on the technology required to connect computers to TV cables rather than to telephone lines. When that technology is in place, computers will be able to download information approximately 1,000 times faster than they can using modems connected to telephone lines.

Television Images

The home television set is very similar to the cathode-ray tube described above. However, the electrons used to create TV images are deflected not by charged plates but by magnetic fields produced by electric currents in coils of wire. The magnetic fields act on the electrons much as an ordinary magnet does when it pulls a rolling steel ball off its straight-line path.

To make a picture on a television screen, the electron beam is swept across the screen's 525 lines in one-thirtieth of a second. During each sweep, the beam may strike some 460 tiny phosphor spots. When struck by electrons the spots emit light. Together these nearly 250,000 spots create an image. A black-and-white TV image is produced by having the electron beam strike the phosphor spots in some areas of the screen and not in others. Information about brightness is determined when the carrier wave is demodulated (changed from an electromagnetic wave back to electrical impulses). Demodulating the luminance signal on the carrier wave provides the information needed to turn the electron beam on (for brightness) and off (for darkness). Since the phosphors emit light for only a short time, the images, like those in a motion picture, change so fast that the eye can't detect individual images. To the viewer, quickly changing positions of images appear as motion. Demodulation also provides an FM sound signal, which is amplified and sent to the loudspeaker, and a synchronization signal that keeps the electron beam sweeping across the picture tube face in step with the scanning beam used in the TV camera.

In color sets, demodulation provides a chrominance (color) signal as well as a luminance signal. The chrominance signal gives information about the amount of each primary color in each region of the image and is used to activate one, two, or all three of the electron guns found in a color TV. Each gun is used to beam electrons onto one of the three types of phosphors found on the screen. You can see these tiny phosphor bars that produce colored images by examining the screen with a strong magnifying glass. One kind of phosphor emits red light when struck by electrons, another produces green light, and a third releases blue light. These three primary colors of light can create all the colors in the spectrum when combined. Equal intensities of all three in the same area will be seen as white light.

Creating Television Images

The images seen on a television screen are first seen through the lens of a TV camera. Light passing through the camera's lens strikes a photosensitive surface, causing the release of electrons. Where the light is intense, many electrons are released; dim light produces fewer electrons. The electrons provide an electrically charged pattern that is scanned and used to modulate the carrier wave.

In color television, the image is separated into three colored images (red, green, and blue) by semitransparent mirrors that selectively reflect different colors. Such mirrors are only partially silvered so that only a portion of the light is reflected; the rest is transmitted. Additional filters in front of three scanning tubes allow separate electrical signals to be created for red, green, and blue light.

Because the transmitted signals are re-

ceived by both color and black-and-white sets, both a brightness and a chrominance signal must be used to modulate the carrier wave. The signals from the three color tubes are mixed to produce a brightness signal for each part of the image. These same three signals are also combined in a color encoder that allows the amounts of color in each part of the image to be modulated separately. Finally, a sound signal is added to the carrier wave before transmission. At the receiving end, a black-and-white set will respond to the brightness but not to the color signal.

High-Definition Television

High-definition television (HDTV), which uses a digital format rather than analog, will become more common in the United States during the next decade. In April 1997, the Federal Communications Commission (FCC) agreed to give TV broadcasters free channels on which to send digital signals of their programming. Transmission of digital television signals is expected to begin by 1999, but because most TV sets are designed to receive an analog signal, broadcasters will be required to transmit both types of signals until 2006, when the FCC will permit stations to discontinue their analog broadcasting. It is the cost of transmitting two types of signals for the eight-year period that led the FCC to provide free access to these airways.

High-definition television is superior to earlier TV for many reasons. It is less susceptible to interference and is more efficient. Four or five digital channels can be packed into the cable space required to carry one analog channel. Because it has twice as many lines and uses smaller phosphor spots on the monitor, the images it produces are much sharper than most viewers are used to. They are almost three-dimensional in appearance and can be viewed from positions closer to the screen. The new roomier channels will allow broadcasters to provide Internet access as well as pay-for-view movies, home shopping, and other features leading to the information superhighway.

Presently, neither cable nor direct-broadcast satellite (DBS) television have digital capability. As a result, only the approximately one-third of households that receive TV signals in wave form will be able to access the superior technology of HDTV. However, television's future lies in digital transmission, so cable and DBS will undoubtedly make adjustments to provide this service as demand for it increases.

Price

The cost of a new television set depends on its size, which is expressed as the diagonal length of the screen, and special features such as a comb filter to increase resolution, multichannel TV stereo (MTS), audio and video jacks so that the set can be connected to a VCR, a laser disc player, or a camcorder.

Generally, 13-inch sets come without many special features because they are usually used as a "second" set in most homes. They sell for about $200 to $300. The popular 20-inch sets can be purchased for about $200 to $500, depending on what features are included. Large-screen (25- to 27-inch) sets can be bought for as little as $300 or as much as $1,500. Sets with 31-inch or slightly larger screens cost between $1,000 and $2,500. Rear-projection sets with 40- to 70-inch screens, which have less clarity than smaller screens and require a large room for good viewing, cost between $1,500 and $5,500.

All new TV sets with screens larger than 13 inches must have the capacity to display the captions required for viewers who are hearing impaired. Captions are also being widely used in restaurants and bars frequented by sports enthusiasts. It reduces the noise level while providing useful information for observers.

Color sets with tiny (4-inch) screens can be purchased for $100 to $600. These sets use a liquid crystal display (LCD) and must be viewed from directly in front in rather dim light.

HDTV comes with a high price tag. Initially, these sets are expected to cost anywhere from $1,000 to $2,000 more than conventional large-screen sets. However, prices will fall as sales increase in anticipation of 2006, when television viewers will be forced to buy either a TV that can receive digital signals or a device that will convert the transmitted digital signal to analog.

See also:
Analog and Digital Signals; Antenna; Electromagnetic Waves; Modem; Modulation; Radio; Sarnoff, David; Zworykin, Vladimir Kosma.

References:
Gardner, Robert. *Communication*. New York: Twenty-First Century, 1994.
International Encyclopedia of Communications. New York: Oxford University Press, 1989.
Krantz, Michael. "A Tube for Tomorrow." *Time*, 14 April 1997.
Macaulay, David. *The Way Things Work*. Boston: Houghton Mifflin, 1988.
Williams, Trevor I. *The History of Invention: From Stone Axes to Silicon Chips*. New York: Facts on File, 1987.

Television and Society

Late-nineteenth-century futurists, after witnessing the marvels of the telephone, asked, "If sound can be transmitted by wire, why not light?" In 1879, George DuMaurier, in an article published in the British magazine *Punch*, pictured a couple watching a tennis match on a screen above their fireplace—a rather prophetic vision of the future.

In 1946, soon after World War II, the Radio Corporation of America (RCA) began selling television sets and striving to make the public aware of television's potential as a communication medium. Sports events were available to viewers, and zoom lenses made it possible to provide close-up looks at individual players and key plays. The opening of Congress was televised in 1947, and both the Republican and Democratic National Conventions were observed through the lenses of TV cameras during the summer of 1948. Harry Truman became the first president to see himself nominated on television. But in 1948, the Federal Communications Commission (FCC), after about 100 TV stations had been established, decided to stop issuing licenses for new stations and established a freeze on the manufacture of television sets while it reviewed its policies.

NBC's morning "Today" show set in 1961. Television news programs, such as the "Today" show, which featured both news briefs and magazine variety-interview segments, focused on events that could be dramatized and personalized.

The Effects of Television on Society

Because some cities had television stations and some did not, the FCC freeze (which along with the Korean War lasted into 1952) provided an opportunity to see some of the effects of television on society. In cities where television stations had been established before the freeze, there was a dramatic drop in attendance at movies, circulation of books at libraries decreased, ticket sales at sports events dropped to the point where team owners demanded local blackouts of games that were not sellouts, and restaurants complained that Sid Caesar's "Your Show of Shows" had reduced the number of patrons who traditionally dined out on Saturday evenings. Once a family owned a television set, they stayed home and enjoyed entertainment they could view at no cost.

As the new medium emerged, Hollywood pretended that television didn't exist. Television sets and the word *television* itself were never seen or mentioned in films. But in 1954, Jack Warner agreed to produce a filmed series for ABC television. The program, "Cheyenne," was so successful that soon other Hollywood studios and television networks were working together on filmed series. Some of the most successful of these—"Gunsmoke," "Perry Mason," and "Father Knows Best"—were instrumental in uniting the television and film industries.

A year after the initial Warner-ABC agreement, RKO agreed to sell 740 old movies to television stations for $25 million. RKO's deal led other studios to follow suit when they realized that there was money to be made from old films gathering dust in warehouses. Filmed series and old movies changed television from a medium in which three-quarters of its programs involved live entertainment to one in which three-quarters of its broadcast time was on film.

Film was instrumental in making the United States the world's major exporter of television programming. In authoritarian countries, television was used for propaganda as well as entertainment, but the entertainment was often American in origin. In many countries, commercial and public television have coexisted. Even Great Britain has seen the development of commercial television despite successful and judicious programming under the control of the British Broadcasting Corporation (BBC). In the United States, the Public Broadcasting System (PBS) was not established until the mid-1960s, when a number of ETV (Educational Television) stations joined to form a national network that has been financed by both private and public funds.

Television News

The change in the nature of television programming was accompanied by a change in the way television presented the news. Initially, television news consisted of an announcer reading bulletins while seated at a desk in front of a camera—essentially, visual radio. Stations soon realized that a visual medium required the expertise of those who made the short newsreels that accompanied feature movies in the days before television. The result was a move toward news programs consisting of stories that carried an emotional and visual impact rather than a careful and thoughtful analysis of an issue. National networks hired charismatic men or women who served as so-called anchors to comment on stories and events.

To a large extent, television news programs focus on events that can be dramatized and personalized. The emphasis is on emotion rather than analysis, and even though many reporters claim to be unbiased, the news is unavoidably shaped by those who report it.

Sending camera crews and reporters across the country and even to other countries made news programs expensive. Rather than having each network send crews around the world, television networks came to rely on the Associated Press (AP), United Press International (UPI), London-based Reuters, and Agence France-Presse (AFP) for much of their international news. AP and UPI are usually the source of the first images of hot news such as floods, air crashes, and sudden disasters. Networks will travel to major stories only if they appear to have some lasting appeal, as was the case with the Gulf War. But Cable News Network (CNN), with two all-news channels, makes it clear that people do rely on television for news.

Television: Its Impact and Its Future

For a quarter of a century, radio brought the words and voices of world leaders, dramatic actors, comedians, and commentators into the homes of millions of Americans, but television, which has dominated mass communication for the last half-century, provides more than words. It allows us to not only hear the words but to see the speaker including his or her body language—the gestures, winks, smiles, raised eyebrows, and frowns—whether from downtown, from the other side of the globe, or from outer space.

Through television, we can enjoy a diversity of entertainment—comedy, drama, music, sports, news, commentaries, and more. A short walk to our TV set puts us in touch with happenings that are taking place many time zones away. Satellites relay events as they happen from Olympic stadiums in Norway, Japan, France, or anywhere else in the world. A world once viewed as vast has been made smaller by television. TV cameras have enabled us to observe the moon from its surface and the earth from space as if we were the astronaut behind the lens.

Through television, viewers can travel continents away to sites where events, decisions, and conversations that may change the world are taking place. Viewing the sights, sounds, and devastation of war on television make it more realistic and far less glorious than we might have thought by reading or listening to the words of observers. Although televised scenes of crime, pestilence, and famine have had little effect in reducing the frequency of these disasters, they may have made us more sympathetic to their victims.

The potential of television has not been fully tapped. The world's greatest scientists, actors, writers, and teachers could be a visible and audible presence in classrooms around the globe. Viewers may recognize world leaders as easily as they do their neighbors, and are every bit as aware of their activities, but we seldom have an opportunity to see them discuss in detail the issues that confront them and why or how they make the decisions they do.

The ultimate union of telephone, computer, and television will provide a vast reservoir of information and entertainment and, perhaps, allow us to make better use of television. With more than 500 TV channels, the choice of movie entertainment will be limited only by the number of films that exist. It will be possible to play video games with friends in other countries, and shop at favorite stores from the comfort of the living room. Online videos will provide previews of houses for sale or rent and potential vacation sites. It will be possible to purchase airline or cruise tickets while awaiting game time for a favorite football team—a game the viewer will observe from "seats" on the 50-yard line, the end zone, and in the blimp above the stadium.

In the event of a serious illness, a doctor may arrange for a patient to be examined by one of the world's most highly regarded specialists on a different continent, an examination that will take place via television. Business problems that require the coordination of two offices a continent apart and demand immediate attention can be accomplished in a similar manner. Television, as widespread as it may be, is still in its infancy when its vast potential on the information superhighway of the future is considered.

See also:
Internet; Modulation; Radio; Radio and Society; Radio History.

References:
Gardner, Robert. *Communication*. New York: Twenty-First Century, 1994.
International Encyclopedia of Communications. New York: Oxford University Press, 1989.
Macaulay, David. *The Way Things Work*. Boston: Houghton Mifflin, 1988.
Williams, Trevor I. *The History of Invention: From Stone Axes to Silicon Chips*. New York: Facts on File, 1987.

Television Network

A television network is an arrangement of communication channels that allows programs being broadcast in one location to reach other broadcasting stations so that those programs can reach a much wider audience simultaneously.

In the United States, network services are provided by telephone companies. Intercity channels connect long-distance telephone offices in different regions so that a program originating in New York can reach Chicago, Denver, Miami, or other locations. From these central sites, local channels carry the signals, usually by cable, to broadcast studios. The long-distance and local channels are connected by a television operating center (TOC) in these telephone offices. The principal users are broadcast companies, which contract with a telephone company to bring signals from their origin to the broadcasting stations around the country that make up its network.

Intercity video channels are carried along the TD-2 radio relay routes used for long-distance telephone circuits. TD-2 is a frequency-modulated (FM) microwave radio system with relay stations spaced 25 to 30 miles (40 to 48 kilometers) apart that can carry 12 wide-band channels. Its frequency range is from 3,700 to 4,200 megahertz, and each channel can carry one video or 1,200 voice signals. Local channels, which are usually cable facilities, carry the signals from the telephone office to the broadcast studios.

Signals may also be transmitted by satellites, which now carry commercial television over the Atlantic and Pacific oceans. The network signals to satellites for overseas television originate at TOCs in New York and San Francisco.

In closed-circuit television, sports contests and other special events are carried to major cities, where they are routed via cable to theaters, hotels, stadiums, industrial conferences, and other sites where patrons have paid admission to see the event on a large television screen.

Colleges and schools as well as corporations also make extensive use of small-scale closed-circuit television for educational and training purposes. In some cases, two-way audio combined with one-way video makes it possible for those receiving the video signal to ask questions of others at the place where the audio and video signals originate. It is also possible to send two-way audio and video signals so that groups in one geographic location can exchange both audio and visual information.

In a sense, community antenna television is closed-circuit television. A cable company provides access to channels received on its centrally located antennas for a specific group of people who pay a fee for the service. The fee depends on which channels the subscriber chooses. Access to some sports channels and movie channels, such as HBO, usually requires a higher monthly fee.

See also:
Radio; Satellite; Television.

Telex
See Teleprinter.

Thermography

The word thermography literally means "heat writing." In terms of real-world application, thermography involves the conversion of infrared radiation to heat for photocopying, printing, measuring, and recording temperature; and infrared photography, which is widely used in medicine, geology, and environmental studies.

In photocopying by thermographic means, an original and a sheet of copy paper are placed together and passed through a beam of infrared radiation. The ink in the original absorbs the radiation and converts it to thermal energy. The copy paper contains heat-sensitive chemicals that change color when heated by the hot ink in the adjacent original. The resulting images that form on the copy paper lack the sharpness of other methods of copying, but they are satisfactory for rough work and are very inexpensive.

Thermographic printing involves dusting a freshly printed sheet of paper with a resinous powder that sticks only to the wet print. The rest is blown off and collected for reuse. When the dusted sheet is exposed to heat, the powder melts. It soon cools and hardens to form solid letters that rise above the paper's surface. This raised print, which can be black or colored (silver and gold are commonly used), is frequently found on commercial stationery, various social announcements, greeting cards, and some artwork.

Both contact and projection thermography are used to measure temperature. In contact thermography, a thin layer of heat-sensitive material is spread on the surface where temperature is to be measured. Exposure to ultraviolet light produces variations in brightness and color that are temperature-related. In projection thermography, infrared light from the surface whose temperature is being measured is focused by a lens onto heat-sensitive film. The patterns of color, which correspond to temperatures on the surface under examination, may be displayed on film or a screen.

A thermograph is a solid-state device that detects infrared radiation and converts it to an electrical signal that can produce an image (thermogram) on a cathode-ray oscilloscope. The image on the screen can be easily photographed. The color on the various parts of the image are related to the temperatures of the surfaces emitting the radiation.

Thermograms are widely used in industry to detect where heat is being lost from a building, a furnace, or an electrical system. Thermography is also used in medicine to detect cold spots that indicate poor circulation or hot spots that may be caused by tumors. The same technology is used in environmental and geological studies to find topographical temperatures, volcanic action, forest fires, water temperatures that reveal ocean currents, fresh/saltwater boundaries, and similar features. Many of these environmental and geological experiments are made from satellites far above the earth's surface.

See also:

Photography; Printing; Satellite; Scanner.

References:

Science and Technology Illustrated, vol. 26. Chicago: Encyclopedia Britannica, 1984.
Weaver, Kenneth F. "America's Thirst for Imported Oil, Our Energy Predicament." *National Geographic,* February 1981.

Touch

Touch, the first sense to develop, often serves as a means of nonverbal communication. Even eight-week-old human embryos respond to touch, and among infants several innate touch reflexes, such as sucking, are present at birth.

There is ample evidence that touching produces bonding between mother and child and probably between all mammalian offspring and their mothers. Young children are soothed and placated by touching and cuddling and will seek such contact if frightened, tired, upset, or in pain. Furthermore, if infants and young children are not touched, caressed, and fondled, their physical and emotional development is retarded, and they are likely to develop social and psychological problems. Indeed, there is evidence that repeated touching during infancy and early life is essential to the normal development of all primates.

Although touch is vital to young children, the amount of touching between children and parents gradually decreases as children grow older and more independent. By adolescence, it has often reached the formal or ritualistic form of handshakes that is found among adults. While handshakes are the usual form of greeting between males or unfamiliar members of both sexes, brief hugs and kisses on the cheek are not uncommon between female friends or relatives or family members of the opposite sex.

Handshakes are not limited to greetings; they are also used to congratulate or thank someone, to seal a deal or a bet, or even to indicate brotherhood among members of a fraternity who recognize a distinct and secret form of handshake. Similarly, a pat on the back, a touch of the shoulder, or even a gentle punch can serve as a friendly gesture or a means of offering congratulations.

Although holding and touching is not generally an accepted mode of behavior between unfamiliar members of the opposite sex, it is accepted when two people, even if strangers, are dancing. Generally, adolescent or adult males do not kiss, hug, or pat each other in public. However, such forms of touching are regarded as normal among male teammates during sports contests, and especially following a victory.

After adolescence, touching in various forms, such as hand-holding, is a way of expressing affection between two sexually mature individuals when done with mutual acceptance. More intimate touching is accepted by two individuals who are lovers or mates.

Touching between adults that would not be socially condoned is permitted when it is essential to a task. For example, society sees nothing wrong with a barber or a hair dresser touching a customer's ears, face, head, back, and hair. In primitive cultures medicine men or women often practice the laying-on of hands to soothe, drive away evil spirits, or bring healing spirits to a patient. And, of course, the appropriate touching of any part of the body by a medical practitioner is accepted in Western culture. Medical research indicates that the gentle touching of patients by doctors and nurses often has a positive effect in reducing recovery time, lowering blood pressure, and reducing anxiety. This suggests that the laying-on of hands, whether performed by a primitive tribe's medicine man or a trained medical doctor, is beneficial and that touch may be comforting to adults as well as to infants and small children.

See also:
Communication among the Hearing Impaired; Language; Speech.
References:
Heward, William L. *Exceptional Children*. Engelwood Cliffs, NJ: Prentice-Hall, 1995.
International Encyclopedia of Communications. New York: Oxford University Press, 1989.
Nash, Madeleine J. "Fertile Minds." *Time*, 3 February 1997.

Transatlantic Cable

The story of the transatlantic cable is one of persistence. Cyrus West Field's conviction that such a project was possible, as well as the commitment by the governments of England and the United States, saw a nearly impossible project to completion. Field did not originate the idea of submarine telegraphy, but he envisioned a transatlantic system and took the first practical steps to complete the momentous endeavor.

Samuel F. B. Morse, inventor of the telegraph, experimented with underwater telegraphy as early as 1842. He laid a cable under New York harbor, but the experiment failed when the line was severed by a passing vessel. Later, Morse completed a successful 12-mile line from Fort Lee, New Jersey, to New York City. In August 1850, an Englishman, John Brett, laid a cable between England and France. Rough seas snapped the cable and ended this initial attempt at long-distance underwater telegraphy. In the following year a line was successfully completed between Dover and Calais. Its success prompted a number of imitators throughout Europe.

The real pioneer of long-distance submarine cable on this side of the Atlantic was F. N. Gisborne, a Canadian engineer. His ambitious plan called for a telegraphic link between Saint John's, Newfoundland, the American system in Maine, and ultimately New York City. From Saint John's a fleet of steamers would deliver messages to Ireland, and from there they could be distributed throughout Europe. Financial reverses hampered the implementation of the plan, and Gisborne went to New York in 1854 seeking new investors.

In New York Gisborne found more than a mere investor in Cyrus Field. A wealthy, retired businessman, Field was fascinated by the idea of going beyond Gisborne's vision and creating a transatlantic telegraph system. Such a scheme was not inconceivable. Though uncomplicated by the depths of the Atlantic Ocean, the successful European lines connecting England and Holland and Ireland and Scotland provided models. After consultations with Morse and Matthew Fontaine Maury, chief of the Naval Observatory in Washington, D.C., Field was convinced of the project's promise. Armed with his conviction and reinforced by the financial support of friends like Peter Cooper, the prosperous iron maker and founder of Cooper Union, Field began his 13-year odyssey to realize the transatlantic cable.

In April 1854, the investors in the New York, Newfoundland, and London Telegraph Company agreed to take over Gisborne's stalled Canadian operation. Field went to Newfoundland with $1.5 million, negotiated a 50-year lease for the right-of-way, and assumed the $50,000 debt of the failing Canadian company. Matthew Field supervised the construction of the line from Saint John's. The project was very costly and took two and one-half years to complete due to difficulties with terrain and weather.

July 1856 found Field and Morse in England. Field was promoting his enterprise and in search of English investors. Meanwhile, Morse, whose support lent credibility to the undertaking, continued experiments with long-distance submarine telegraphy. Through John Brett, the man responsible for the successful English Channel lines laid five years earlier, Field met Charles T. Bright. The young engineer was England's major telegraphic expert as a result of laying most of the country's underground cable as well as his own long-distance experiments.

The three men formed the Atlantic Telegraph Company to build the Newfoundland-to-Ireland segment of the line. Based upon Field's presentation, the English government agreed to subscribe to 4 percent of the costs and promised to supply ships to lay cable in return for priority in sending messages.

Encouraged by the sale of stock in England, Field returned to the United States and approached his government for aid. Senator William Seward of New York introduced a bill in Congress calling for an investment similar to England's, including ships for the project. The bill ran into opposition on two counts. First was the financial concern about a yearly subsidy and second was the longstanding anxiety about involvement in "entangling alliances" with other countries. Field himself lobbied Congress and was rewarded with victory. President Franklin Pierce signed the bill on his last day in office in 1857.

Leaving theory and experimentation behind and bolstered by financial security, Field and his associates finally began the practical work of developing the cable. Time was important since Field had pledged an operating system by 1857. The production of the cable was nothing short of miraculous. In six months, 2,500 miles of cable were produced. The cable was constructed of seven strands of copper wire twisted together and insulated by three layers of gutta-percha, a nonconducting, water-resistant tree sap that molded to the wire. A thin sheet of copper covered the gutta-percha to deter boring by marine life. A third element wrapped around the wire was tarred hemp. Eighteen strands of twisted wire provided the final protective casing. The wire was five-eighths of an inch thick and weighed 1 ton per mile.

By July 1857, the telegraph fleet was ready for sea. The major ships of the flotilla were the *Niagara*, the fastest steam frigate in the world, provided by the United States, and England's *Agamemnon*, which would complete the voyage to Newfoundland. Only 5 miles out, the first of numerous problems that plagued the project until its completion occurred. The cable broke. The line was retrieved and spliced, and the effort began again. Two days later, the cable inexplicably went dead. Just as curiously, two hours later, the signal returned. No satisfactory explanation was ever advanced to account for the interruption. Disaster struck the next day when the ships attempted to adjust the speed of the cable as it was laying out. The brake on the laying-out mechanism applied too much tension to the cable, and it snapped and dropped some 2,000 fathoms in the sea. Unpredictable weather patterns, lack of spare cable, and financial anxieties precluded continuing the crossing, and the fleet retired.

Although costly, the failure was not a complete loss. The fact that ships were in constant communication with the land base until the cable snapped proved that the transatlantic idea had merit and was possible. Field immediately began a new round of fund-raising in England and the United States. Despite the Depression of 1857, Field was successful in soliciting friends to underwrite a new expedition. The interim between voyages allowed for mechanical improvements in the laying-out mechanism. To prevent a replay of the previous disaster, a new brake was developed that released automatically if tension on the cable was too great.

In the spring of 1858, the new campaign began. The plan that year was for the ships to meet in midocean, splice their cables, and lay wire in opposite directions while maintaining constant telegraphic contact. After a storm, which threatened to destroy the *Agamemnon* due to the weight she carried, and three abortive attempts to complete the endeavor, the fleet dejectedly returned to Ireland. Even the most ardent supporters of the enterprise began to waiver, but Field held firm and persuaded the investors to try again. On 28 July 1858, the fourth attempt of that year, the fleet spliced the cable together and set out. There were moments of concern. A whale almost severed the *Agamemnon*'s cable and communication, and as in 1857, communication was broken only to unexpectedly resume. On 5 August, the *Niagara* steamed into Trinity Bay, Newfoundland. A short while later, the *Agamemnon* arrived at Valentia Bay, Ireland, and the submarine cable was completed. The *New York Times* trumpeted, "The Atlantic Cable has half undone the Declaration of 1775 [*sic*], and has gone far to make us one again, in spite of ourselves."

On 13 August 1857, the first official message was transmitted over the new cable. Queen Victoria congratulated President James Buchanan on the successful completion of the line. Field was the guest of honor at New York City's Cable Carnival. Tiffany's bought the unused cable and sold segments as souvenirs. Despite public confidence, the cable was experiencing problems, and on 25 September, after only seven weeks of operation, the signal went dead. Attempts to explain the malfunction centered on faulty insulation, damaged cable as a result of the *Agamemnon's* bout with the storm, and the possibility that excessive electric current was used in cable experiments. A disappointed public was in no mood for excuses. Field was accused of fraud in attempting to increase the value of his stock to ensure a profitable resale. The whole scheme was labeled a hoax, and the English government began a full investigation.

A stunned and shaken Field hoped to renew the project and his reputation. However, personal financial reverses and the Civil War intervened causing delays. During those years Field did what he could to promote his vision and busied himself raising funds on both sides of the Atlantic. The conclusion of the British investigation that the endeavor was feasible helped his efforts. Furthermore, the cable itself was improved, making it stronger, better insulated, and better protected. Before the Civil War was over, Field contracted with owners of the *Great Eastern* to lay the new cable.

The *Great Eastern* was a maritime monster more than five times larger than any vessel afloat. Launched in 1858, the ship had five funnels and six masts. Powered by steam-driven paddle wheels and a propeller, the ship was reliable and maneuverable. Her cargo capacity meant that the *Great Eastern* alone could lay the cable, and risky splicing could be reduced to a minimum. The hull was reinforced to carry the 7,000 tons of cable, and three large storage tanks were installed to hold the cable en route. Although the *Great Eastern* was never a commercial success, it was the ideal cable ship.

By July 1865, Field and his associates were ready for another attempt. Although they were better prepared, the combination of mechanical problems and bad luck still dogged the venture. Eight miles from shore the signal died. Slowly the cable was hauled in, revealing that an iron sliver had pierced the protective casing and caused a short circuit. The defective segment was replaced, and the process began over again. The same problem occurred later in the voyage, causing a 19-hour delay and raising the specter of sabotage. A special team of inspectors was formed to watch over the cable. Ultimately, it was determined that the weight of the coil in storage fractured the protective casing, causing iron splinters to flake off, and one of these stuck in the cable stored below.

Three-quarters of the way to Newfoundland, disaster ended the attempt. A crewman yelled a warning that a defective section of cable went overboard. The cable was still functional, but no one wanted a repeat of 1858, when the cable was operational for only a short time. Once again the cable was hauled back, but in the process an ocean swell lifted the ship, snapping the cable. Field tried to retrieve the wire by crisscrossing the ship's path. It seemed futile to try to find a 1-inch cable lost 2 miles beneath the surface with grappling hooks and rope, but they succeeded, only to have the equipment malfunction and drop the cable again. 1865 was just another year of failure.

Field was not one to give up, especially since the 1865 venture was nearly successful. As Field and his new company, the Anglo-American Telegraph Company, prepared for the 1866 attempt, there was an increased sense of urgency. A new line was being developed up through Alaska to connect with the Russian telegraph system. Field had to succeed this time. On Friday, 13 July 1866, the *Great Eastern* set to sea for the fifth attempt to complete a transatlantic cable. The route was south of the 1865 course for fear of fouling the new cable. The old cable was still operational, and Field hoped to recover it for use at a later date. The major problem for this expedition was the depths the fleet would encounter, some equal to the heights of Europe's greatest peak, Mt. Blanc. This time there were no significant problems, and on 26 July 1866 the cable was finally completed. Field retreated to his cabin, closed the door, and wept.

Yet there was still more to be done. Upon arrival in Newfoundland, Field discovered that the ten-year-old cable between Newfoundland and Cape Breton had broken the previous year. Characteristically, Field quickly chartered a ship and repaired the line in two days. Even as congratulations poured in, Field still was not satisfied. Five days later he loaded the *Great Eastern* with 700 miles of cable and returned to sea. He was after the 1865 cable. After numerous attempts with grappling hooks and rope, the cable was reclaimed and repaired, and a second transatlantic cable was brought to Newfoundland.

References:
Carter, Samuel. *Cyrus Field: Man of Two Worlds.* New York: G. P. Putnam's Sons, 1968.
Clarke, Arthur C. "I'll Put a Girdle around the Earth in Forty Minutes." *American Heritage*, October 1958.
Cowbura, Philip. "The Atlantic Cable." *History Today*, August 1966.
Cowbura, Philip. *Great Events/Four: As Reported in the New York Times.* Sand, NC: Microfilming Corporation of America, 1982.
Lindsey, David. "The First Atlantic Cable." *American History Illustrated*, January 1973.
Lindsey, David. "Lightning through Deep Water." *American History Illustrated*, February 1973.

Transducer

A transducer is a device that converts energy from one form to another. Practically every instrument used in communication is a transducer. A photoelectric cell is a trans-

ducer; it converts light to electricity. A lightbulb is a transducer; it changes electrical energy into heat and light. Telephones change sound energy to electrical pulses and then back to sound. Microphones convert sounds to electrical pulses, and loudspeakers convert the electrical energy back to sound. Radio transmitters change electrical energy to electromagnetic waves that travel through space (including the space above our atmosphere) to radio receivers, where the electromagnetic radiation is changed back to electrical energy and then to sound.

In all these changes from one form of energy to another, energy is never lost or gained. Millions of experiments have shown that energy is conserved; that is, energy is never created or destroyed. However, one form of energy is rarely changed completely to another form. If a ball is dropped onto a floor, it never rebounds to the same height from which it fell. At least a small portion of the energy is given off as heat. The bouncing ball and the floor it struck are a bit warmer than they were before the ball fell. The wires and coils used to operate a loudspeaker become warmer when the device is used, because some of the electrical energy is changed to heat rather than to sound.

The challenge in building transducers is to lose as little energy as possible to heat. However, the second law of thermodynamics states that in any energy transfer some of the energy will appear as heat.

See also:
Loudspeaker; Microphone; Radio; Telephone; Television.

Transformer

Transformers are devices used to increase or decrease alternating-current (AC) voltage. Transformers are essential to any communication device powered by alternating current.

A typical transformer consists of two coils wound around opposite sides of a common iron core. One coil, the primary, is connected to the source of electrical power. The metal core serves to contain the changing magnetic fields generated by the alternating current and voltage in the primary coil. As the current and voltage in the primary coil change, so does the magnetic field it produces. This changing field within the core is "felt" in the secondary coil, where it induces another alternating voltage and current.

The ratio of the induced voltage in the secondary to the voltage in the primary is the same as the ratio of the number of turns in the secondary coil to the number in the primary. Thus, the number of turns in the primary and secondary coils enable transformers to step up or step down the voltage. Since very little energy is lost in a transformer, the electric power—the product of current and voltage—is very nearly the same in both primary and secondary circuits.

A power plant may generate electricity at 2,200 volts. If the energy were sent over power lines at that voltage, most of it would be lost as heat. Since the power losses are equal to the resistance of the transmission lines times the square of the current, it makes sense to reduce the current. This can be done with a step-up transformer that raises the voltage to 220,000 volts by means of a transformer in which the secondary coil has 100 times as many turns as the primary. Since the current on the secondary side of the transformer will be reduced to 1/100 its value in the primary, the power losses are reduced to the square of 1/100, or 1/10,000. This ability to change AC voltages with a transformer led to the wide acceptance of AC electrical power in preference to DC.

Most electrical appliances in the home, such as radios, television sets, CD players, and personal computers, operate on 120-volt AC circuits. However, the power lines leading to homes from substations may be at 2,200 volts. Step-down transformers are used to reduce the voltage to the safer levels found in home circuits.

References:
Macaulay, David. *The Way Things Work.* Boston: Houghton Mifflin, 1988.
Sears, Francis W., Mark W. Zemansky, and Hugh D. Young. *College Physics,* 6th ed. Reading, MA: Addison-Wesley, 1985.

Transistor

A transistor is a three-terminal semiconductor that is used for amplification, switching, and detecting. The current flowing between two of the terminals can be controlled by the voltage applied to the third. The current between two pairs of terminals (the input terminals) is used to control the current through another pair (the output terminals). However, there are only three terminals; one terminal is common to both the input and output circuits. A transistor contains p- and n-type semiconductors arranged sandwich-like in a n-p-n or p-n-p manner, as shown in Figure 1.

Triode: Predecessor of the Transistor

Transistors have replaced the triode vacuum tubes used in earlier electronic devices such as radios and television. The triode, or audion, tube developed by Lee De Forest was a modification of Sir John Fleming's diode. De Forest placed a third component (thus, triode) called the grid between the cathode and anode of a diode vacuum tube. The grid was made of wires that could be charged, but the wires were so thin that they did not interfere with electrons passing through the grid to the anode.

The triode or audion, which was designed to amplify the signals from radio waves, can

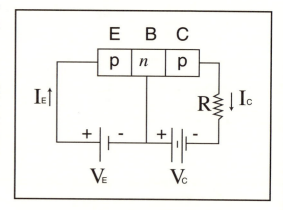

Figure 1. A transistor like the p-n-p example diagrammed here has three terminals that extend from a p-type emitter (E), an n-type base (B), and a p-type collector (C).

be used to amplify any electrical signal. If the varying current from the antenna of a radio receiver is connected to the grid of a triode, current through the grid will vary with the current coming from the antenna. By adjusting the negative charge on the grid, the current coming through the grid can be increased (amplified), thus enhancing the current pulses reaching the anode without changing their frequency. The amplified current can be sent to a loudspeaker that will respond by producing sounds of greater intensity that have the same frequency.

Vacuum-tube diodes and triodes, and even tetrodes and pentodes, were used to improve radio signals. Later, the tubes were used in televisions and computers. Such tubes required a lot of power, got hot, and eventually failed.

The Development of the Transistor

Following World War II, William Shockley, John Bardeen, and Walter Brattain, working at Bell Laboratories, found that vacuum tubes could be replaced by semiconductor crystals. By adding impurities such as arsenic or antimony to germanium or silicon— a process known as doping—they were able to make what are called n-type semiconductors. Doping silicon with atoms of aluminum, boron, or gallium led to p-type semiconductors. The designation *p* or *n* refers to the way in which charge is transmitted in the crystal. In an n-type crystal, charge is carried by electrons; in a p-type crystal, charge is carried by what are called holes—the absence of electrons, which is the equivalent of positive charge.

Today, solid p- and n-type semiconductors have replaced vacuum tubes in electronic devices. Figure 1 shows a p-n-p transistor. It has two p-n junctions where the p- and n-type semiconductor surfaces are fused. In the circuit shown, the n-type semiconductor is the common base, B, for both circuits, the one driven by battery V_E that leads to the p-type emitter, E, and battery V_C that leads to the p-type collector, C. If the current I_E through the emitter is zero, the cur-

rent I_C through the collector will be very small because the polarity of the battery would tend to push electrons through the right-hand p-n junction from right to left, and there are very few free electrons in a p-type semiconductor. At the same time, it would tend to push holes, or positive charge, through the junction from left to right, and there are few holes in the n-type semiconductor.

On the other hand, when battery V_E is connected, a current I_E will flow across the left-hand junction of the transistor from emitter to base because there are numerous holes in the p-type emitter and plenty of free electrons in the n-type base. The holes traveling from emitter to base can also travel to the base-collector n-p junction, where they come under the influence of battery V_C and are pushed across the junction, increasing current I_C. Thus, I_C can be controlled by I_E.

If the voltage of battery V_C is much greater than that of V_E, then the power, in watts, which is the product of the voltage and the current, across the load (R), can be amplified. The same circuit may also be used to amplify voltage, but a somewhat different circuit is required to amplify current.

The transistor described above is called bipolar because both electrons (negative charge) and holes (positive charge) are essential to its behavior. In field-effect transistors (FETs), the controlling charge is placed on a gate or control electrode, which is separated by a thin layer of nonconducting material (usually silicon oxide) from the silicon surface. One type of FET, called a MOSFET because of its metal-oxide-semiconductor structure, has a p-type substrate with two separate n-type regions or electrodes. One of the n-type electrodes is called the source; the other is called the drain. The gate is located between the source and the drain. When the gate is at zero voltage, no current flows through the transistor because at least one of the p-n junctions (where the n-type electrodes meet the p-type substrate) will resist charge flow, like any diode with a reverse bias. However, when the gate is connected to a positive voltage, residual electrons in the substrate are attached to the gate and provide a conducting pathway between source and drain. The magnitude of the current can be controlled by adjusting the voltage applied to the gate. The higher the positive voltage on the gate, the greater the current. Removing the voltage from the gate will break the current. Thus, a MOSFET can be used as a switch. In fact, such transistors are widely used in digital computers, where 0s (or offs) and 1s (or ons) provide the hardware for the on-off binary system circuitry.

In addition to being able to amplify currents, voltage, and power, and serve as switches, transistors can also be used as detectors, demodulators, and oscillators. They can do virtually anything that vacuum tubes can do. Semiconducting transistors and diodes have replaced vacuum tubes in most electronic devices because they are inexpensive, rugged, efficient, and long-lasting, whereas vacuum tubes are expensive, bulky, fragile, and power-demanding.

Integrated Circuits

Because transistors and diodes are so small, they can be easily joined on tiny silicon chips. Integrated circuits containing hundreds or even thousands of individual circuits are now made for various electronic devices. Computers, which once filled large rooms with vacuum tubes and wires and were capable of holding information equivalent to the words in a small book, can now be carried about in a box smaller than a briefcase and have memory equal to the words stored in 150,000 books. Furthermore, semiconductors require no warm-up time, use little power, and seldom fail. Their light weight and small size have enabled manufacturers to produce miniaturized versions of almost everything—TV cameras and receivers, radios, watches, calculators, computers, and more.

See also:
Amplifier; Computer; Computer Addition; Diode; Microelectronics.
References:
Gardner, Robert. *Communication*. New York: Twenty-First Century, 1994.
Haber-Schaim, Uri, et al. *PSSC Physics*, 7th

ed. Dubuque, IA: Kendall/Hunt, 1991.
Macaulay, David. *The Way Things Work*. Boston: Houghton Mifflin, 1988.
Sears, Francis W., Mark W. Zemansky, and Hugh D. Young. *College Physics*. Reading, MA: Addison-Wesley, 1985.

Triode
See Diode; Transistor.

Typewriter
The typewriter is a writing machine that enables the operator to produce print resembling that of a press at a greater speed than handwriting. The first recorded attempt to develop a mechanical writing device was a 1714 patent awarded to Henry Mill by Queen Anne of England. There is no record that Mill ever built his machine, nor are there any surviving drawings of his proposal. The first U.S. patent was awarded to William Austin Burt of Detroit, Michigan, in 1830 for his Typographer. Unfortunately, this model was destroyed in an 1836 fire at the Washington, D.C., patent office. Charles Thurber of Worcester, Massachusetts, patented a "mechanical choreographer" in 1843. Neither Burt's nor Thurber's invention, both of which mechanically resembled a child's toy typewriter of today, received much notoriety. Generally these and other contrivances, although capable of producing reasonable print, were slow, often times very large, and unable to compete with a clerk's longhand efforts in terms of speed and economy.

In 1873, Christopher L. Sholes and his associates developed the first practical and marketable typewriter. In that same year, Sholes sold his patents to firearms manufacturer E. Remington & Sons of Ilion, New York. After the Civil War, Remington sought to diversify. The company was already involved in the production of sewing machines, and Sholes's new invention appeared to have promise. Consequently, the first typewriters were labeled Remington, named not for the inventor but for the manufacturer.

The first Remington typewriters, sold in

An early typewriter model, ca. 1876.

1874, were priced at $125 and shared many characteristics with future models. Sholes's arrangement of characters on the keyboard, known as QUERTY after the first six letters on the keyboard, is relatively unchanged and still standard on today's computer keyboards. The keys worked a series of type bars or levers, and letters were printed by striking metal characters against an inked ribbon at a common center. A platen, or cylinder, was used to hold the paper in position, and the machine was capable of consistent letter and line spacing.

Nonetheless, there were noticeable design differences between the first Remington typewriters and later models. First, and not surprisingly, the typewriter looked like a descendant of the sewing machine. Black and stenciled with flowered designs, it had a foot treadle for a carriage return. Interestingly, the keys struck on the underside of the platen/cylinder, so it was possible to see the printing only by raising the carriage. Most significantly, there was no shift key, so the typewriter printed only capital letters.

The Remington company flirted with bankruptcy during the early years of typewriter production. So desperate were they that some machines were given away, primarily to court reporters, just to encourage endorsements. Mark Twain is credited as the first author to submit a typed manuscript to a publisher, but even this did nothing to produce sales. The typewriter was a marvel at the 1876 Centennial Exposition, where, for 25 cents, a few typed lines were given away as souvenirs. A demonstration in New York City produced awe and admiration, but still the business struggled. Not until the 1880s—perhaps due to the increasing size of corporations and their attendant record keeping, general business prosperity, or the mechanical improvements in the basic typewriter—did sales begin to skyrocket.

The Remington Model 2 debuted in 1878 and was the first typewriter equipped with a shift key that allowed printing both upper- and lower-case letters. An alternative, pioneered by Sholes and others, was a double keyboard. This keyboard had twice the number of characters, one for each upper- and lower-case figure. Touch typing, widely accepted after 1900, ultimately ended the competition between the two keyboards since the smaller, more compact Remington Model 2 keyboard was more efficient.

In the same year that the Remington Model 2 was introduced, experiments began with "visible writing," in which the line being printed could be seen without raising the carriage. John H. Williams finalized the evolution of the manual typewriter that is so familiar to generations of secretaries. Williams moved the "basket" of type bars to the front of the machine in 1890, completing the visible writing option first made available to the public in 1883. Other enhancements were the automatic reversing ribbon and an attached carriage return. By the end of the nineteenth century, the typewriter had moved from an item of curiosity to one of the most important inventions of the era and an indispensable part of the business office. Portable typewriters, more compact but less sturdy than office machines, were introduced by Frank S. Rose in 1909.

The electric typewriter was the next significant advance. Both Sholes and Thomas Edison experimented with a power-driven version of the typewriter, but with no success. In 1920, Joseph Smathers finally succeeded in devising an electric typewriter suitable for office use. Electric portables were first offered to the public in 1956. The type ball, a golf ball–like printing element with raised characters, was introduced as an alternative to the traditional type bars in 1961. This device moved much faster than type bars, required a lighter touch than manual typewriters, and offered improved legibility. When the standard type ball was removed and replaced with alternate type balls, the typewriter could produce different fonts as well as symbols needed for foreign languages.

See also:
Sholes, Christopher Latham.

References:
Feldman, Anthony, and Peter Ford. *Scientists and Inventors*. New York: Facts on File, 1979.
Flatow, Ira. *They All Laughed*. New York: HarperCollins, 1992.
Hylander, C. J. *American Inventors*. New York: Macmillan, 1955.
Polley, Jane, ed. *Stories behind Everyday Things*. Pleasantville, NY: Readers Digest, 1980.
Robbins, Peggy. "Tale of the Typewriter." *American History Illustrated*, February 1981: 4.

Universal Product Code

The Universal Product Code (UPC) consists of sets of closely spaced parallel rectangular black-and-white lines. The familiar patterns are often called bar codes and are widely used by stores, libraries, and postal and delivery services. When printed on consumer products, UPCs allow stores that use laser scanners to automatically determine prices at their checkout counters.

The parallel black-and-white lines of differing widths are a graphical representation of a code number used to identify a product. They indicate binary numbers (0s or 1s) that can be read by a computer. The binary numbers are coded to represent ordinary numbers from 0 to 9. The series of numbers that appear below the bars are the numbers represented by the code, which can be read by eye if necessary. The initial and final sets of bars are used to indicate when the scanner should start and stop responding to the coded data. For items found in a store, the first five numbers usually indicate the company that makes the product, and the second five numbers identify the particular product. Library books are often bar coded. The first set of numbers identify the library, and the second set identifies the book.

When a cashier or a librarian passes the bar code over a scanner or moves a penlike scanner over the code, a thin beam of red light from a helium-neon laser illuminates the code. Some of the light is reflected back to the scanning machine, where it is filtered before entering a photoelectric cell. When the light strikes the sensitive surface of the photoelectric cell, electrons are emitted. The light energy is changed to electrical energy. The flow of electrons from the cell constitutes an electric current. Because the intensity of the light entering the photocell varies depending on whether it was reflected by a white bar or a black bar in the code, the electric current coming from the photoelectric cell also changes in magnitude; the current comes as a series of electrical pulses that the computer reads as binary numbers.

When the electrical pulses are decoded in the scanner, they provide the numbers found in the bar code. The number is sent to a computer that matches the bar-code number with a UPC numbered file in its memory. In a supermarket, that file provides the price, a description of the item, and any additional pertinent information, such as a tax that may have to be paid or a price reduction due to a sale or coupons. That information is then sent to a terminal and a printer, where it is displayed and a printout provided for the customer almost immediately after the last item has been passed by the scanner window.

In a library, the bar code is read, and a computer terminal indicates the library to which the book belongs, whether the book is overdue and if so what charges are owed, whether the book has been requested by another patron, and other information.

In addition to reducing tedious hand labor and providing information accurately and rapidly, the UPC allows a computer to keep an inventory of a store's stock and to automatically send out orders when the stock of a particular item reaches a certain level. UPCs coupled with computers can provide useful information about what particular brands of certain items are preferred by the store's customers. In libraries, UPCs and computers can be used to determine the popularity of certain titles and topics of local patron interest, and to indicate whether or not additional titles or more copies of a particular book should be ordered.

See also:
Computer; Number; Scanner.

References:
How It Works: The Illustrated Encyclopedia of Science and Technology. New York and London: Marshall Cavendish, 1978.

Macaulay, David. *The Way Things Work.* Boston: Houghton Mifflin, 1988.

Science and Technology Illustrated, vol. 15. Chicago: Encyclopedia Britannica, 1984.

Seideman, Tony. "Bar Codes Sweep the World." In *American Inventions: A Chronicle of Achievements That Changed the World.* New York: Barnes & Noble, 1995.

V-Chip

The V-chip is a computer chip that can be installed in television sets to receive encoded information preceding each show. With the V-chip in place, parents can program their TV sets to block out shows coded to indicate high levels of violence or sex. Addition of the chip is expected to increase the cost of a television set by $5 to $30.

In July 1995, President Clinton endorsed the V-chip as a way for parents to reduce the violence their children see on television, and in February 1996 Congress passed legislation that drastically changed the rules governing telecommunications. Included in that legislation, which the president signed, was a requirement that within two years all new TV sets must contain a V-chip. Since the law will not take effect until 1998 and since TV sets have long lives, it probably will be years before the law has any major impact on what children can see on television.

In January 1994, in an effort to placate the government, which had been threatening stronger control over TV programming, the four major television networks agreed to an independent monitoring system that would evaluate programs, even though they feared it would lead to a loss of advertising. In the wake of political protests about TV violence, the networks made an effort to reduce the quantity of violence seen on television and added labels warning parents of programs that contained material deemed inappropriate for children. Nevertheless, a 1995 study by four universities showed that more than half of all TV shows contained at least some violence. The Telecommunications Bill of 1996 encouraged the television networks to devise their own rating system. Early in 1996, under pressure from Congress and the president, top executives in the TV industry agreed to devise a rating system for TV programs that would provide parents with the information needed to shield their children from sex, profanity, and violence on television. Following the meeting of these executives at a White House summit, a task force led by Jack Valenti, president of the Motion Picture Association of America, began working on a rating system.

In December 1996, the task force announced its plan for rating TV programs—one that is very similar to the G, PG, PG-13, R, and NC-17 ratings used for rating movies. The plan consisted of six categories: TV-Y (children's programs suitable for all ages), TV-7 (children's programs not appropriate for anyone under 7 years of age), TV-G (programs suitable for a general audience of all ages), TV-PG (programs where parental guidance is recommended), TV-14 (programs unsuitable for children under 14), and TV-M (programs for mature audiences only).

The ratings, which appear in newspapers and TV guides, are the responsibility of those who produce and distribute the programs. Parents can then program their V-chips to cut out shows beyond a certain rating. After the children are in bed, the chip could be reprogrammed to filter at a different level.

President Clinton, who believes the TV industry rather than the government should establish ratings, urged that the rating system proposed by the task force be tried to see if it works. TV executives and others who favor the task force's plan maintain it will work because it is simple, readable, and can be easily incorporated in the program listings published in newspapers.

On the other hand, a number of child advocacy groups oppose the plan. They believe the ratings are too vague and would like to see a system that includes a sliding-scale rating for violence, sex, and language for each program. For example, a program might be rated as V-0 S-3 L-5 where V, S, and L stand for violence, sex, and language, respectively,

309

while the numbers 0 to 5 indicate the scale level for the factor, with 0 meaning none and 5 meaning excessive.

Any government-mandated ratings system immediately leads broadcasters to raise the question of free speech as guaranteed by the First Amendment, which prohibits Congress from passing laws abridging freedom of speech. Valenti, in response to criticism about the task force's rating system, responded that any attempt to impose government-based ratings would be immediately followed by a lawsuit. Proponents of the V-chip counter that parents have the right to decide what their children shall be allowed to see and hear.

A bottom-line concern of TV networks is the effect that V-chips might have on the number of viewers watching a particular program, since a reduced audience translates to a reduction in advertising revenue. A TV-M rating (which indicates an adult-level program), if it reduces the enthusiasm of sponsors, could mark the end of provocative shows that feature controversial but substantive social issues.

See also:
Censorship; Television; Television and Society.

References:
Antonoff, Michael. "Essential Technology Guide." *Popular Science*, November 1995.
"Chipping Away at TV Violence." *U.S. News & World Report*, 24 July 1995.
Coorsh, Richard. "Dateline Washington." *Consumers' Research Magazine*, March 1994.
Zoglin, Richard. "Chips Ahoy." *Time*, 19 February 1996.
———. "Rating Wars." *Time*, 23 December 1996.

Video Disc
See Compact Disc.

Videocassette Recorder (VCR)
See Tape Recorder.

Videophone
See Telephone.

Videotex

Videotex is a signal that can be shown on a television screen. A numeric keypad resembling a pocket calculator is used to control the decoder. There is a distinct difference between videotex and teletext. Teletext is a one-way broadcast service consisting of preprogrammed pages of data that can be displayed on a TV screen. The user cannot interact with the database that provides the information. In contrast, videotex is a two-way interactive service that allows the user to select and interact with information from a menu that may include games, educational instruction, E-mail, and teleshopping, as well as financial and other services. An alphanumeric keyboard is used to interact with the decoder.

Teletext is broadcast along with regular television programs on a normal channel by using the unused lines of the standard TV signal. It is transmitted as electromagnetic waves or via cable and is essentially an electronic newspaper providing up-to-the-minute news stories as well as weather, traffic, sports, and financial information. The decoder, which may be located within the set or connected to it by a cable, collects the data page by page and stores it until a signal from the controlling keypad transfers it to the television screen as text. There is usually an index showing what is found on different numbered pages. Viewers use the keypad to select the pages they want to read. In addition to full-screen display of the teletext pages, teletext can be programmed to show printed news continuously at the bottom of the screen, to interrupt regular TV programs with special bulletins that appear at the same place, or to provide up-to-date information in a small box in one corner of the screen. The last two options are commonly used by television networks and local TV stations, the first to display important news bulletins or storm warnings and the second to show relevant information, such as the score or other pertinent data at a sports contest.

Videotex uses telephone lines or cable to transmit data to users. A computer system and software are required at the data source to provide rapid access to information requested by users and to record subscriber use time for billing purposes.

Teletext systems developed and spread quite rapidly across Europe during the late 1970s and the 1980s but were never widely accepted in the United States. Videotex never caught on in the United States either, although information services very similar to videotex, called online or interactive services, are now available through the Internet and are accessed by millions of computers in homes and businesses. Host computers at local access providers or large consumer-oriented information services such as America Online, CompuServe, GEnie, and Prodigy will connect local computers to their databases and to other computers on the Internet for a monthly fee that may be fixed or based on use time.

See also:
Computer; Computers and Society; Fiber Optics; Information Superhighway; Internet.
References:
International Encyclopedia of Communications. New York: Oxford University Press, 1989.
Science and Technology Illustrated, vol. 25. Chicago: Encyclopedia Britannica, 1984.

Virtual Reality

Virtual reality is designed to produce the illusion of being in a real place where there is motion and a changing view of a three-dimensional world with which one can interact. To reach virtual reality requires special headgear connected to a computer. It may also involve electronic gloves that act as sensory extensions or "data suits" that can translate the wearer's movements into motion on a computer screen viewed through the headgear. The computer, electronic techniques, and associated gear change the two-dimensional input of pictures into the three-dimensional output seen by the participant. By entering the world of virtual reality the user can dance, fight, or interact in a variety of ways with the computerized figures found there.

Another form of virtual reality is the cab simulator environment. Here no equipment is worn. The participant enters an enclosure that serves as a virtual world made possible by three-dimensional graphics that are computer controlled. One example is the flight simulator used to train pilots. Trainees, by using the cockpit controls, experience through virtual reality the effects of their actions, which may involve anything from a perfectly smooth landing to a crash.

Both the U.S. military and National Aeronautics and Space Administration (NASA) are conducting research on virtual reality. NASA hopes to one day use such a technique to repair satellites without having to send astronauts on space walks. A robot with television lenses for "eyes" and specially wired gloves will send visual images and touch sensations to an astronaut inside a spaceship. The astronaut, equipped with wired gloves and a helmet containing a screen on which three-dimensional images are projected by a computer, will be able to receive sensory data through the robot's eyes and gloves. By moving his own head, fingers, and hands, the astronaut will control the movements of the robot's head and hands. The result will be a virtual reality setting in which astronauts, within the safer confines of the ship, will control the movements of the robot in space, although the astronauts will feel as if they are actually in space doing the work.

See also:
Computer; Robot.
References:
Larijani, L. Casey. *The Virtual Reality Primer.* New York: McGraw-Hill, 1994.
Pimentel, Ken, and Kevin Teixeira. *Virtual Reality: Through the New Looking Glass.* New York: McGraw-Hill, 1992.

Voice Mail

Voice mail is a method for storing oral messages and providing an electronic means for delivering them to, or having them retrieved by, the intended receiver.

In a business that has voice mail, an automated attendant may answer with such words as, "Thank you for calling XYZ. If you

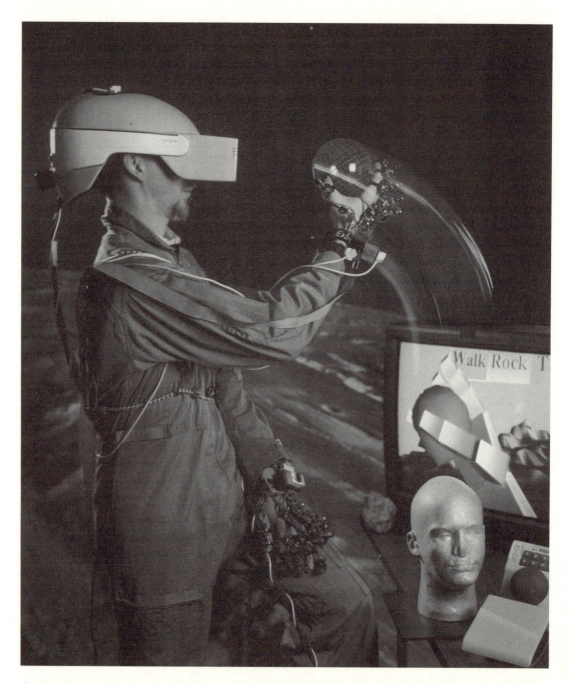

Equipped with a video helmet and virtual reality gloves, Bill Briggs lifts a virtual rock on the virtual surface of Mars at the NASA Ames Research Center at Moffett Field, California, 1994.

would like X, press 1 now. If you would like Y, press 2 now. If you would like Z, press 3 now. If you have another reason for calling, press 4."

By pressing 4, the caller may reach a living person who will direct the call to Mr. A. If Mr. A is not in, his electronic voice mail attendant directs the caller to leave a detailed message and promises that Mr. A will return the call. An hour later, Mr. A calls. He has called his voice mailbox from his cellular phone while driving to a meeting and listened to the caller's message. Because the caller gave details about his reason for calling, Mr. A is able to respond and provide the information needed.

Without voice mail, the caller probably would have left his name and number with a receptionist who, in turn, would write the name and number on a pink slip and later leave it on Mr. A's desk. When Mr. A returned—perhaps the next day, but possibly next week—he would return the call. The caller would explain what information was needed, and Mr. A. would reply, "Okay, I'll get back to you." Mr. A. would then find the information and call back.

Despite widespread resentment about talking to a machine, voice mail, as the illustration above demonstrates, is far more efficient than getting a busy signal or leaving a message with a receptionist.

Voice mail systems are sold and installed by telecommunications consultants, telephone systems companies, manufacturers of voice-processing equipment, subsidiaries of the Regional Bell Operating Companies, and others. Generally, the systems are custom designed to meet the needs of the company or organization buying the system. In 1996, the price of a voice mail system was as low as $2,500 or as high as $1 million, depending on the size and complexity of the system.

Several new models of personal computers are now equipped to provide voice mail functions. A chip developed by Rockwell International and AT&T makes it possible to add voice mail to data-and-fax modems.

Initially, voice mail was an electronic message recorder, but voice messaging (an extension of voice mail) makes more extensive communication possible. Voice messaging allows someone with a voice mailbox to send, receive, redirect, and reply to messages or send them to other people on the network. A chief executive officer can mass-mail voice messages to divisions, sales personnel, branch managers, and others spread across the country by simply pushing a few buttons on a phone pad. By pressing the *A* key on their telephones, those receiving the message can respond. A messaging provider's file server controls a special digitized telephone network designed to meet a company's needs. Those with voice mailboxes can access their calls by touch-tone phones through a local number. Once the mailbox is reached, the caller can call anyone else on the network, regardless of their location, without paying long-distance fees.

See also:
Computer; Electronic Mail; Fax Machine; Internet; Modem; Telephone.

References:
Brown, Carolyn M. "Electronic Messaging." *Black Enterprise*, November 1992.
Reed, Sandy. "Letting Your PC Pick Up the Phone." *Popular Science*, March 1994.
"Voice Mail versus Voice Messaging—Here's the Difference." *Inc.*, August 1994.

Voice Messaging
See Voice Mail.

Walkie-Talkies

Walkie-talkies are two-way radios consisting of a small portable transceiver with a range of 0.5 to 2.7 miles (0.8 to 4.5 kilometers). Walkie-talkies were developed during World War II to provide communication between advanced combat units and bases close behind them.

Modern walkie-talkies are light, portable, sturdy, and very compact—about the size of a telephone. Weight is kept to a minimum by using transistors and printed circuits enclosed in plastic cases, which also makes them strong and durable as well as light. The devices—portable because they are battery powered—contain a combined FM transmitter and receiver, both of which are pretuned to a particular frequency and operate in the VHF (30 to 220 megahertz) or UHF (450 to 900 megahertz) range.

The transmitter or receiver is activated by pressing different buttons. Because walkie-talkie broadcast frequencies overlap those used for some television channels, walkie-talkies may cause interference on nearby television sets.

Although walkie-talkies were developed for military use and still serve that purpose, they find wide civilian use as well. Police departments find them helpful in communicating traffic information, in stakeouts, and in raids. Firemen use walkie-talkies to maintain contact while in different parts of a burning building, and they are used by emergency medical technicians and by coaches at athletic contests.

In 1996, a waterproof walkie-talkie was developed for scuba divers. A headset allows the user to hear transmissions from others without affecting vital air flow. A face mask holds a small voice-activated microphone near the diver's mouth so that the diver can transmit information and breathe at the same time.

See also:
Radio; Television.
Reference:
Csatari, Jeffrey. "New Products." *Men's Health*, June 1996.

Webster, Noah (1758–1843)

Noah Webster, a lexicographer and educator, composed the first complete dictionary of English as spoken in the United States. Only the Bible has enjoyed a wider circulation than Webster's dictionary. He was a major force in standardizing spelling and pronunciation throughout the nation. For Webster, a cultural nationalist, a national language was "a brand of national union."

Webster was born and raised in West Hartford, Connecticut, one of five children. His father mortgaged and nearly lost his farm to send his son to Yale. The 16-year-old enrolled at Yale in 1774 and graduated in 1778. After graduating, Webster studied law and taught school to support himself. As a teacher Webster was frustrated by the use of English texts in American classrooms. He was convinced that just as the country had gained political independence, so too must it strive for intellectual freedom from Europe. Webster created his own texts, which emphasized American patriotic sentiments. In 1783, Webster published the first volume of his planned trilogy called the *Grammatical Institute of the English Language*. That volume, the "Blue-Backed Speller," was an immediate success and in various revisions sold over 100 million copies well into the twentieth century.

In the eighteenth century, there was little consensus in spelling even the most common words. Webster simplified much of the spelling and spelled words as he thought best. For example, he eliminated the English *-our* ending in favor of the simpler *-or*. *Labour* became *labor* and *honour* became *honor* in the new speller. By further simplifying British spelling—changing *plough* to *plow* and dropping the *k* from words like *music* or *public*, for example—Webster made American English distinctively different but also more consistent. Finally, Webster added a number of American words that were unknown to English scholars, like *skunk*, *hickory*, and *chowder*, to the speller. Webster completed his trilogy in 1784 and 1785 with a grammar book and a reader, respectively. In keeping with his nationalist philosophy, he included passages from American writers and patriots in each publication. The success of his works earned Webster the sobriquet, "Schoolmaster of America."

Although Webster was admitted to the bar in 1812, he practiced his craft for only a short time. He was absorbed in other diverse projects that have been overshadowed by his lexicographic work. He wrote treatises on various subjects, including diseases, insurance, banks, the rights of neutral nations in wartime, and the need for a strong central government. Webster worked as an editor for a number of newspapers, including New York City's first daily, *The American Minerva*. Always interested in history, Webster wrote an American history textbook and even published a translation of the Bible. Webster was also concerned about the theft of his written work. He campaigned aggressively for copyright laws, visiting each of the 13 colonies to personally advocate passage of state copyright legislation. He was also a founder of Amherst College.

Webster never forgot his goal of American cultural independence, and in 1803 he began work on his *Compendious Dictionary of the English Language*. Three years later he emerged with the first American dictionary, consisting of 5,000 entries. Webster considered this work as preliminary to a far larger compendium. For the next two decades he worked on his masterpiece, the *American Dictionary of the English Language*. Handwritten, the two-volume, 1,000-page dictionary had 70,000 entries. It was a staggering accomplishment that required research trips to Europe and compelled the 70-year-old author to be familiar with 26 languages in order to determine word origins. Although Webster's was not the first dictionary, its emphasis on concise definitions, simplified spelling, and etymological analysis placed it among the best of its kind. Nonetheless, the 1828 edition was derided as "Noah's Ark" and cost an astounding $20. It took 13 years to sell out the first printing. The 1841 edition, priced at $15, fared no better. It was not until 1847 that the dictionary, priced at a more reasonable $8, began to pay for itself. In 1850, New York and Massachusetts ordered copies for their schools, and Webster's place was secured as the preeminent wordsmith in U.S. history.

After Webster's death in 1843, at age 85, George and Charles Merriam bought the rights to his dictionary for $3,000. The success of the 1847 edition led them to purchase the copyright for the then unheard-of sum of $250,000. The Merriam-Webster dictionary remains a trusted authority on the English language today.

See also:
Language.

References:
Morgan, John S. *Noah Webster*. New York: Mason Charter, 1975.
Sargent, David C. *Noah Webster*. West Hartford, CT: The Noah Webster Foundation and Historical Society of West Hartford, 1976.

Welles, Orson (1915–1985)

American actor, director, producer, and writer for stage, screen, and radio, Orson Welles was considered a genius and one of the most radical filmmakers in Hollywood history. Welles's fame rests primarily on two projects completed before he was 30 years old. The first was a radio adaptation of H. G. Wells's *War of the Worlds*. The second—perhaps his most famous accomplishment—was his first and best-known film, *Citizen Kane*. Welles cowrote, directed, and starred in this thinly veiled biography of William Randolph Hearst. The film is considered one of the most influential motion pictures of the sound era and firmly established Welles as the "boy wonder" of Hollywood.

Orson Welles, guiding genius of the "Mercury Theatre of the Air," directs a radio play rehearsal in New York, 31 October 1938.

Born in Kenosha, Wisconsin, on 6 May 1915, Welles was considered a child prodigy by many, including his parents who died when he was young. Welles attended the progressive Todd School for Boys in Woodstock, Illinois. Though an indifferent student at best, he was encouraged in his main interest, drama, by headmaster Roger Hill.

After graduating at age 15, Welles briefly attended the Art Institute of Chicago before traveling to Ireland for a painting tour in 1931. At age 16 Welles found himself in Dublin, where he made his debut as an actor at the Gate Theatre on 13 October 1931. After unsuccessful auditions for parts in London and New York, he returned to the Todd School where, working with Hill, he wrote a series of illustrated acting editions of Shakespeare.

Following a tour with Katherine Cornell's national troupe in productions of Shaw and Shakespeare, Welles became involved in radio as well as theater projects. Because of his unique and distinctive voice, Welles prospered in radio and soon became narrator of the *March of Times* news programs. However, he was best known to mystery fans as the voice of The Shadow on the series of the same name. More significantly, Welles accepted a position as actor and director of the Negro Theatre Group, part of a New Deal effort to reduce unemployment among actors during the Great Depression of the 1930s. Collaborating with John Houseman, the group produced an all-black *Macbeth*. The setting was relocated in Haiti, and voodoo priestesses replaced the traditional witches.

Sparked by their success, Welles and Houseman established the Mercury Theatre in 1937. The ensemble quickly became known for innovative dramas produced on paltry budgets. Their first play, a modern-dress *Julius Caesar*, featured Shakespeare's Caesar and his Roman followers dressed in fascist-type uniforms. A year later, Welles convinced the Columbia Broadcasting System (CBS) to broadcast the Mercury Theatre on radio.

The basic idea of the "Mercury Theatre of the Air" was to present a series of dramatizations adapted from great literature. Nothing Welles did was as spectacularly memorable as his 1938 production of *War of the Worlds*, which has become part of the Welles legend. Welles directed and narrated what he considered to be a Halloween spoof. It consisted of a series of news flashes, complete with eyewitness accounts, about a Martian invasion of New Jersey. The spoof, mistaken as real news by thousands of listeners accustomed to program interruptions with news bulletins from European nations in the months preceding World War II, set off a nationwide panic. By today's standards the program was laughable, but the public response it produced was considered a prime example of the power of the medium.

The *War of the Worlds* broadcast brought Welles an offer from Hollywood. At age 23, with no film experience, Welles was offered a contract by RKO that gave him artistic license to do whatever he wanted. Welles arrived in Hollywood tagged as a boy wonder but viewed by insiders as a spoiled brat.

Welles's first year in Hollywood was unproductive, but his work during the next two years astonished the movie capital. Welles, in collaboration with New York drama critic Herman Mankiewicz, began his *Citizen Kane* masterpiece. *Citizen Kane* (1941) might have been Welles's most memorable work, but it was also his curse. The 25-year-old first-time producer and director also starred in and cowrote the film, which was renowned for its technical achievements and controversial story line. Technically, the film showcased the use of a wide-angle lens, a mobile camera, bizarre sets, realistic sound effects, and imaginative lighting and editing. In 1962 and 1972, *Citizen Kane* was voted the best film in motion picture history by international film critics. Nonetheless, its only Academy Award was for best screen play. The film, although a critical success, was a commercial disappointment and never captured the moviegoing public's imagination. *Citizen Kane* was the zenith of Welles's mercurial career. Everything else he attempted paled in comparison.

Welles's style might have contributed to the financial failure of *Citizen Kane*, but William Randolph Hearst, the millionaire newspaper magnate, contributed as well. *Citizen Kane* was so similar to Hearst's life that the newspaper giant exerted pressure to limit the release and showing of the film. The film's weak reception led RKO to restrict Welles's creative autonomy, and frustration followed.

Welles's second venture as director fared no better. *The Magnificent Ambersons*, which traced the decline of a mid-nineteenth-century family, failed to gain public acceptance and left critics unimpressed. Once again, fate played a role in subverting Welles's vision. Upon completing the picture, Welles traveled to South America to begin a new project. In his absence, RKO ran a test showing of the film and, based on the results, decided that major editing was required to salvage their investment. The studio felt a happier ending would be more appealing. Welles returned to Hollywood to find that he and his friends were fired and his movie destroyed. He moved to studios at Columbia and Republic Pictures but never attained the artistic level of his RKO productions.

By 1949, Welles was viewed throughout the movie industry as extravagant, unreliable, arrogant, and difficult to work with. He left Hollywood and began a 30-year exile in Europe. Turning to his own significant acting ability, Welles began to work in other people's films in order to finance his own projects. Most of his efforts were forgettable, but there were some distinguished performances, such as the sleazy Harry Lime in

Third Man (1944) and Rochester in *Jane Eyre* (1944). In 1952, the old genius resurfaced in his production of *Othello*, which won the Grand Prix at the Cannes Film Festival. Other screen credits included work in *Moby Dick* (1956), *The Long Hot Summer* (1958), and *A Man for All Seasons* (1966). Welles also produced commercials for British and French television before returning to the United States as spokesperson for a wine company.

Ironically, in his final years Welles received a number of awards recognizing his contributions to motion pictures. In 1975, he received the American Film Institute's Life Achievement Award, and in 1984 the Directors Guild of America presented him the D. W. Griffith Award.

See also:
Hearst, William Randolph; Motion Pictures; Radio and Society; Radio History.

References:
Brady, Frank. *Citizen Welles: A Biography of Orson Welles*. New York: Scribner's, 1989.
Callow, Simon. *Orson Welles: The Road to Xanadu*. New York: Viking, 1996.
Higham, Charles. *Orson Welles: The Rise and Fall of an American Genius*. New York: St. Martin's Press, 1985.
Kael, Pauline. *The Citizen Kane Book*. Boston: Little, Brown, 1971.

Wiener, Norbert (1894–1964)

Norbert Wiener is remembered primarily for his work on cybernetics, a subject that he named and formulated, and one that he defined as the study of control and communication in both animals and machines.

Wiener was a child prodigy who entered Tufts University at age 11 and received his doctorate in mathematical logic and philosophy from Harvard when he was 18. Wiener then traveled to England, where he did his postgraduate work at Cambridge under Bertrand Russell, the well-known mathematician and philosopher. After brief stints as an instructor at Harvard and the University of Maine, as a writer for the *Boston Herald* and the *Encyclopedia Americana*, and as a researcher at the Aberdeen Proving Grounds during World War I, Wiener joined the Massachusetts Institute of Technology (MIT) faculty in 1919 and remained there for 41 years.

During World War II, Wiener found a way to separate useful information transmitted by radio from undesirable disturbances. With Julian Bigelow, Wiener also worked on antiaircraft gunfire control. Bigelow and Wiener were trying to develop automatic aiming devices for antiaircraft guns. Wiener realized that aiming the gun so its shell would hit an enemy aircraft required information about the plane's speed, direction, and altitude as well as the gun's muzzle velocity, wind speed and direction, and a number of other factors. He soon realized that the device would have to send out and receive signals to detect and analyze the aircraft's motion and simultaneously aim the gun while taking into consideration the gun's parameters as well. Because the plane could change its course and speed at any time, the system would have to be capable of rapidly adjusting its calculations and redirecting the gun. Wiener recognized that the analog computers developed by Vannevar Bush at MIT could not respond fast enough to automatically aim the guns even if radar signals could accurately determine the plane's position and velocity in space.

Wiener's work, however, did lead him to realize that a group of phenomena from very different disciplines, previously regarded as unrelated, shared common principles that might fruitfully be united for purposes of investigation. The word he coined to describe this community of ideas was *cybernetics*, from the Greek word *kybernetes*, which means "steersman."

Wiener noted common factors of control and communication in automated machines, living organisms, and organizations such as businesses and manufacturing firms. There are clear similarities between the human nervous system and an automatic machine. Both use information gathered from the outside to control or modify its own actions. Consider a thermostat, perhaps the simplest automated device. A bimetallic strip bends in response to room temperature. When the temperature drops to a certain point that can be set by a homeowner, the strip is bent enough to close a switch that ignites a furnace. The furnace produces heat until the temperature of the room rises sufficiently to bend the bimetallic strip enough to open the circuit and turn off the furnace. The thermostat gathered information (temperature) from the room. It responded by closing a switch that caused a heat source to raise the temperature. Once the desired temperature was achieved, it opened the switch, and heat was no longer produced.

Now consider a very simple analogous human activity in which a person tries to bring together the tips of the two index fingers. As the two fingers approach one another, nerve impulses from the eyes are sent to the brain. There, motor impulses are generated that cause muscles in the person's arms to contract, more or less moving the two fingertips together. To demonstrate that information gathered from outside the brain by the eyes plays a role in this process, try bringing your fingertips together with your eyes closed.

Both processes described above—one performed by a human and one by a machine—involve feedback. That is, sensors or detectors (eyes or a bimetallic strip) measure performance and feed the data back to control the output. The output, in turn, affects the performance, which is measured by sensors or detectors, and so the process is repeated in an endless loop that keeps the machine, organism, business, or other entity within initially set parameters.

An airplane's automatic pilot is a good example of a more complicated system related to cybernetics. The device is programmed to maintain a certain velocity, altitude, and attitude. From a variety of instruments (sensors and detectors) the system receives data pertaining to wind speed and direction, air pressure, altitude, position, and other variables. The system uses the data it gathers to send signals to the plane's controls and engines that keep the aircraft within the parameters initially set. In a similar way, a manufacturing company adjusts its internal operations in response to data it gathers about economic and market conditions. On Wall Street, many investment companies have programmed computers to indicate that certain stocks should be sold when data fed into the machine produce a certain set of numbers. Some believe that computers will eventually be able to think, that is, to process information gathered from the outside and make a decision, response, or choice in a manner similar to the still-unexplained complicated reactions that go on in the human brain. However, continued research on computers and the human nervous system suggest that the two are very different and are not at all similar in the way they operate.

Cybernetics encompasses a great many disciplines, including homeostasis. Homeostasis is a system's ability to maintain an equilibrium. For example, many animals, including humans, maintain a constant body temperature. This is accomplished by the hypothalamus at the base of the brain, which acts in a sense like the body's thermostat. It detects the body's temperature and responds to changes in that temperature by sending impulses that either increase or decrease heat loss and heat production.

Included, too, is entropy—the tendency of systems to run down or become less ordered. As an example of entropy, consider two gases, one colored and one colorless, separated by an impermeable barrier. If the barrier is removed, the gases will mix. The orderly separation is lost. The gases become mixed, chaos reigns over order, and the two gases will never again become separated unless energy is expended. Living organisms are constantly overcoming nature's tendency to become more disordered. Growth, metabolism, reproduction, and nest building are just a few of the examples in which living organisms expend energy to counteract entropy.

Cybernetics is also concerned with bionics, servomechanisms, perception, learning, attempts to develop artificial intelligence, all automated devices, information theory, and virtually any form of communication involving an exchange of messages.

Wiener's book, *Cybernetics: Or Control and Communication in the Animals and the Machine*, first published in 1948, provided a detailed, technical view of cybernetics. His second book, *The Human Use of Human Beings*, published two years later, provided a less technical account and addressed the application of cybernetics to social issues. Wiener maintained that to understand society we must understand the various means that it uses to communicate.

Because Wiener pointed repeatedly to the great similarities between human, animal, and machine communication, many accused him of being antivitalist. However, he was careful to point out that there is a distinction between humans and animals. Only among humans, he noted, is "this desire—or rather necessity—for communication . . . the guiding motive of their whole life."

Shortly after World War II, Wiener refused to make any further contribution to military research. Although often referred to as the "father of automation," Wiener repeatedly expressed concern about the possible enslavement of human brains by machines that could learn and reproduce. These concerns, expressed in his last book, *God and Golem, Inc.*, which was published after his death, led to a National Book Award in science, philosophy, and religion.

In January 1964, shortly before Wiener died, President Johnson awarded him the National Medal of Science for his contributions to engineering, mathematics, and theories of logic. All these contributions have had a profound effect on communication and communication theory.

See also:
Computer.

References:
Arbib, M. A. *Brains, Machines, and Mathematics*, 2nd ed. New York: Springer-Verlag, 1987.
Asimov, Isaac. *Asimov's Biographical Encyclopedia of Science and Technology*. Garden City, NY: Doubleday, 1964.
Wiener, Norbert. *Cybernetics: Or Control and Communication in the Animals and the Machine*, 2nd ed. Cambridge, MA: MIT Press, 1961.

Wireless Telegraphy
See Radiotelegraphy.

Writing

Writing is the inscription of letters, symbols, or pictures that convey to readers the same meaning as the spoken words they represent. Writing is usually done on a smooth surface using an instrument such as a pen or pencil that produces marks on the surface. Today's electronic method of writing is based on lasers, computers, and the engineering and the science of electricity that led to electronics. This book was written on a computer, a tool that has been as big a boon to writing as the pencil. However, the technology of printing written words was established through the work of craftsmen and was not based on scientific principles. The growth of science itself, however—because it is so dependent on the repetition of experiments by critics—could never have blossomed without printing, books, and journals.

Writing enables humans to communicate thoughts, feelings, and ideas without being present. It extends communication to people far away, provided that written words can be transported over such distances. Through writing, ideas can be transmitted from generation to generation without distortion, as so often happens with spoken language. It was through written records that Western civilization became aware of the magnificent culture of ancient Greece. Writing may have its greatest impact in commerce and government. Written records of business transactions, laws, and regulations reduce debate over what was actually said and meant when an agreement was signed or a law enacted. Experience shows how difficult it is for people to agree on what was actually said a week or even a day ago.

Writing presupposes speech. There are cultures that have no written language, but speech is common to all societies and appears to be an inherent aspect of being human. Children do not have to be taught to speak. They learn speech by listening, imitating, and exercising their vocal apparatus. Writing and reading, on the other hand, must be taught; they are not innate abilities.

History

Like children, our ancestors learned to communicate by drawing and painting before they learned to write. Cave paintings and drawings related to hunting instructions and, perhaps, to legends, myths, and religious meanings are at least 30,000 years old. Clay tokens, fashioned by hand into a variety of shapes and then inscribed with symbols made by a pointed stick and baked, were made about 10,000 years ago. Here, symbols began to represent more complete images and, later, ideas. For example, a circle became a symbol for the sun. Later, the circle was used to indicate heat or light. Eventually a phonetic alphabet, invented by the Semitic people and greatly enhanced by the Greeks, who added vowels, linked writing directly to oral communication. Letters, or combinations of letters, were used to represent the sounds of spoken words, thus eliminating the need for a separate symbol for every meaning. In our alphabet, 26 letters can be combined to produce any word in the English language and, consequently, can represent any oral communication.

Early records and writings were done on clay tablets in Mesopotamia about 5,000 years ago. The tablets varied in size, shape, and color. After being formed, and while still soft, the tablets were inscribed using a stylus of reed, wood, bone, or, later, iron. The tablets were then dried or baked. Some writing, generally reserved for buildings and other materials on general display, was chiseled into stone, a substance that is still used and is the primary writing surface in cemeteries.

In 1846, excavations by A. H. Layard began at Nineveh, capital of the early Assyrian empire. Layard's work, and that of others who followed him, revealed a library of approximately 25,000 clay tablets that had been assembled by Ashurbanipal during his 40-year reign in the seventh century B.C.

Five millennia ago Egyptians were writing on papyrus, a paperlike material made from the stems of the aquatic sedge *Cyperus papyrus*. By 2000 B.C., they were writing on parchment (dried sheep or goat skin) as well as other materials. There were no pencils or pens. Marks were made with a brush that was made by crushing or chewing one end of a length of rush stem. During the third century B.C., the split-reed pen replaced the brush. Although artists used a variety of pigments, Egyptian scribes used only two inks: a black ink made from soot and a red ink made from iron oxide.

A material known as parchment—the partially tanned skins of sheep, goats, or pigs—was known as early as 2500 B.C., but it was not widely used as a substitute for papyrus until the second century B.C., when a method for making true parchment was perfected in the city of Pergamum in Asia Minor. The method consisted of removing the hair from an animal skin, which was then scraped and polished before it was stretched and rubbed with chalk and pumice to make it very smooth. Vellum, a finer-grained parchment, was made from the skin of calves and kids. Parchment, which became the most commonly used writing surface in Europe, maintained its dominance until after the invention of the printing press.

As the smoother parchment replaced the coarser papyrus, the quill pen, made from a bird's feather, gradually replaced the split-reed pen. The quill pen, dipped in carbon-based ink, was the preferred writing instrument in Europe from the sixth century A.D. until the nineteenth century, when the steel pen, invented in 1800, gradually replaced it. The use of graphite for making marks became widespread only after the invention of the pencil in the late eighteenth century. Ballpoint pens did not become popular until after World War II.

Paper

In the first century A.D., the Chinese were making paper to replace silk, bamboo, and wooden tablets as writing surfaces. To produce paper, they made a paste by mixing and boiling macerated rags, wood ashes, and chopped fibrous hemp and ramie plants. The liquid pulp was then poured on porous screens, where it dried to form sheets. Marks were made on the paper with a camel's-hair brush dipped in a carbon-based ink.

Papermaking spread slowly, and paper gradually replaced parchment as the preferred writing surface. It was the seventh century before paper was made in Japan, and the spread westward was still slower. The first European paper mill was built in Spain in about 1150. From there, papermaking spread to Italy (1276), France (1348), Germany (1390), and England (1494). By the sixteenth century, paper was being used throughout Europe, but only after the invention of the printing press did paper become the predominant writing surface.

In European paper mills, linen rags, sometimes mixed with cotton and straw, were used to make pulp. By the sixteenth century, Europeans were adding fillers to hold the fibers together (sizing) in the dried, very absorbent paper sheets to reduce smudging. Although bark was used in some parts of the world for making paper, it was not until the middle of the nineteenth century that wood pulp was widely used in making paper.

See also:
Cave Painting; Cuneiform; Hieroglyphics; Language; Pen; Pencil; Printing; Signage.

References:
Curtis, Gregory. "A Terrible Beauty." *Texas Monthly*, October 1995.
Grolier Multimedia Encyclopedia. CD-ROM edition. Danbury, CT: Grolier, 1995.
International Encyclopedia of Communications. New York: Oxford University Press, 1989.
Rigaud, Jean-Philippe. "Art Treasures from the Ice Age: Lascaux Cave." *National Geographic*, October 1988.
Schneider, David. "Pot Luck." *Scientific American*, July 1996.
Williams, Trevor I. *The History of Invention: From Stone Axes to Silicon Chips*. New York: Facts on File, 1987.

Xerography

Xerography, which means "dry writing," uses static electricity to make copies of printed documents. The xerographic copier, invented by Chester F. Carlson in 1938, used the first copying process not to require wet chemicals and stencils. Carlson, who worked in the patents department of an electronics corporation, was motivated to find a quick method of making copies because of his continual need to make copies of patents and blueprints. After four years, he succeeded in making a machine that used selenium, a semiconductor that conducts in light but not darkness, to transfer images from an original document to a blank sheet of paper.

It was nearly a decade before Carlson was able to obtain financial backing for his invention. Finally, the Haloid Company, a small New York company, agreed to manufacture and sell Carlson's photocopier. From this small beginning there emerged the giant Xerox Corporation, from which Carlson received royalties and dividends that made him a wealthy man.

Today, photocopiers are standard equipment in businesses, schools, banks, libraries, and even home offices. Some machines will copy both sides of a document's pages and then separate and collate the sheets for easy distribution. Xerox and other companies provide machines that are capable not only of making clear copies but of providing enlargements or reductions as well. More expensive machines can provide colored images of photographic quality.

To make a xerographic copy of print on a sheet of paper, positive charge is applied to a selenium-coated drum. Lenses and mirrors are used to focus an image of the print onto the drum. Since selenium will conduct charge in the presence of light, the charge on the drum is carried away in the bright regions of the image, leaving charge on only the dark parts of the plate. A dark toner powder, which has been negatively charged, is then sprayed onto the plate. The positive charges on the dark parts of the image attract the toner. When paper is pressed against the plate, the powder is transferred to the paper. The paper now carries the dark parts of the image that were originally on the plate. Heat is then used to seal the toner powder to the paper, and a copy of the original image comes out of the photocopier.

To make copies of colored images, the original is scanned, in turn, through red, green, and blue filters. The toner is then transferred to the paper in three layers—cyan, magenta, and yellow. These three layers overlap to provide a full-color copy of the original.

See also:
Carlson, Chester F.; Photography; Photography, Color; Printing.

References:
Gardner, Robert. *Electricity and Magnetism.* New York: Twenty-First Century, 1994.
Macaulay, David. *The Way Things Work.* Boston: Houghton Mifflin, 1988.
Williams, Trevor I. *The History of Invention: From Stone Axes to Silicon Chips.* New York: Facts on File, 1987.

Zenger Trial

The 1735 trial of John Peter Zenger, a German immigrant printer, is considered a landmark decision concerning freedom of the press in the United States. The trial established that true statements cannot be defined as libelous and that citizens can criticize the government.

Zenger's family migrated to the American colonies from the Rhenish Palatinate. At age 13 Zenger was apprenticed to William Bradford, the most prominent printer in New York. After 1718, when his apprenticeship ended, Zenger traveled and was married, but he returned to New York City and became a partner with his old master, Bradford, in establishing the city's first newspaper, the *Gazette.* The partnership lasted only one year, and in 1726 Zenger went into business for himself.

In 1732, a new governor of New York, William S. Cosby, was appointed. Only recently removed from his post as governor in Minorca due to complaints about his administration, Cosby dallied in England for a year before taking his post. The greedy and aristocratic Cosby told the New York assembly that the delay was necessary since he was working on colonial concerns. Consequently, he bullied the legislature into granting him a £1,000 "gift" as recognition of his efforts. Determined to recoup the financial losses he incurred as a result of his dismissal in Minorca, Cosby ran roughshod over the assembly, doing as he pleased, selling offices, ignoring instructions from London, and eventually tampering with the colonial court system.

In 1733 Cosby dismissed Lewis Morris, chief justice of the colonial court, who had served on the bench since 1715. Cosby cited bias, inefficiency, and unreliability as his rationale to London, but all of political New York knew it was the justice's very public opposition to the governor in a salary dispute that led to the ouster. Cosby's effrontery led to an all-out effort to replace him. The growing anti-Cosby faction needed some way to present their case to the general public, but Bradford's *Gazette,* the official voice of the government and dependent on Cosby's patronage, was not an option. Morris, William Smith, and James Alexander financed and established the *New York Weekly Journal* and hired Zenger as publisher. Zenger's command of written English was weak at best, but this made little difference because Zenger's benefactors supplied all the material he could publish. For political reasons they remained behind the scenes and never signed their articles. The only name connected with the paper was Zenger's.

Using letters to the editor, satire, and editorial comment, the authors characterized Cosby as "Nero," a "rogue governor," or "our affliction from London." Cosby was accused of crimes against the people, deceitfulness, and other misdemeanors. The first issue of the *Weekly Journal,* 5 November 1733, was an exposé devoted to Cosby's electoral irregularities in trying to keep opposition candidates, especially Morris, from election to the assembly.

Deeming the paper a threat to public security and an attack on the credibility of colonial government, Cosby petitioned the assembly and a grand jury to take action on behalf of the colony. Both declined. Reduced to his own efforts, Cosby planned a public demonstration against the offensive weekly at which several copies of the *Journal* were to be burned. No one bothered to attend. A humiliated governor had Zenger, as publisher and the only legal and accountable person he could attack, arrested on 17 November 1734. The charge was libel—"begetting ill opinions of the government and its officers." Zenger refused to name his associates, and, unable to post the excessively high bail, he was held in jail for months, where he became a symbol of the governmental tyranny he opposed. The *Journal*, maintaining its anti-Cosby policy, continued to publish through the efforts of Zenger's wife and son.

The opening phase of the trial did little to alter the growing public sympathy for the defendant. Almost immediately, Zenger's lawyers, along with his patrons William Smith and James Alexander, were dismissed from the case for questioning the impartiality of the judges. When the trial resumed in August 1735, Andrew Hamilton was at the defense table.

Hamilton, recognized as the most notable colonial lawyer of the day, was the former attorney general of Pennsylvania, speaker of the Pennsylvania assembly, and an architect of some note. His reputation and experience assured that he would not be arbitrarily removed by the judges.

According to the libel law, the prosecution merely had to prove Zenger was the publisher of the material in question to establish his guilt. The prosecution never mounted its case; Hamilton readily acknowledged that the defendant was responsible for the alleged libel. However, Hamilton went beyond the strict interpretation of the law in his defense to assert that libel meant false and scandalous charges, which the public knew the *Journal* articles were not. Zenger was simply exercising his right to expose and criticize a corrupt administration. At one time, heretics were executed for unorthodox religious views, yet in 1735 men could criticize the church. Why, then, should the civil government be exempt from review? Hamilton continued that the case went far beyond one man and, in fact, dealt with freedom of speech and the right of men to deal with the abuse of power.

Despite the judicial admonition to ignore the truthfulness of Zenger's charges and to bring a decision concerning the publisher's responsibility for libel, the jury took less than ten minutes to reach a verdict of not guilty. Officially unaffected by the decision, Cosby remained governor until his death in 1736. Within a few years, Zenger became the official government printer for New York and New Jersey. He continued to publish the *Journal* until his death in 1746. The paper ceased publication with the death of Zenger's son in 1751.

See also:
Defamation; Newspaper.
References:
Barnett, Lincoln. "The Case of Peter Zenger." *America Heritage*, December 1971.
Robbins, Peggy. "The Trial of Peter Zenger." *American History Illustrated*, December 1976.

Zero
See Number.

ZIP Code
See Postal Service.

Zworykin, Vladimir Kosma (1889–1982)
An American physicist, electrical engineer, and inventor, Vladimir Zworykin is considered the "father of television." Zworykin's two most significant inventions—the iconoscope, a rudimentary television camera, and the kinescope, the basis of the modern picture tube—led to the development of all-electric television systems. Electrical systems replaced the earlier mechanical system, which traced its roots to the work of Paul Nipkow in Germany and John Baird in England. Working for the Radio Corporation of America (RCA), Zworykin played a major role in the development of all facets of modern television.

Born in Russia, Zworykin completed his studies at the Saint Petersburg Institute of Technology. Boris Rosig, who was pursuing experiments in transmitting pictures by wire, was Zworykin's mentor. Rosig's novel mechanical television system produced flickering images of poor definition and resolution. Consequently, the innovation was more of a curiosity with limited practical appeal. Rosig proposed using an electromagnetic scanning device and a cathode-ray tube in an effort to improve the quality of the images, but he never finished his work. He was arrested during the Russian Revolution and subsequently died in exile. Nonetheless, Rosig's work inspired Zworykin and provided the foundation of his contributions to television.

After graduation, Zworykin went to Paris, where he improved his understanding of theoretical physics and experimented with X rays. The outbreak of World War I brought Zworykin back to Russia. There his expertise in radio transmitting quickly advanced him to an officer's position in the Russian Signal Corp. Convinced that the chaos of the Russian Revolution would disrupt his studies, Zworykin emigrated to the United States in 1919. He worked as a bookkeeper while he improved his language skills, and in 1920 he joined the Westinghouse Corporation, which at that time was the recognized leader of the broadcast industry and the most important radio manufacturer.

Zworykin spent the 1920s at Westinghouse working on a number of projects, including radio reception tubes and mercury rectifiers, but television remained his primary interest. In 1923 he constructed the iconoscope (from the Greek *eikon*, meaning "image," and *skopan*, "to watch"), the first practical television camera. The iconoscope used photoelectric cells as a basis for scanning and converting images to electrical current. Although the iconoscope was considered a significant breakthrough, it produced images that were dim and shadowy. Unimpressed by the device, Westinghouse executives encouraged Zworykin to make better use of his time. Outside the laboratory Zworykin was busy as well. He became a U.S. citizen in 1924 and earned a Ph.D. in physics from the University of Pittsburgh in 1926.

Zworykin continued to improve and refine his ideas despite his frustration with the lack of corporate interest. In 1929, at a convention of radio engineers in Rochester, New York, Zworykin unveiled his kinescope (from the Greek *kine*, meaning "motion") as a companion to his iconoscope. The kinescope was a cathode-ray tube with the features of a modern television picture tube. To-

gether, the two inventions provided the first practical exhibition of an electrical television system. His electrical system provided a much better-defined picture than any mechanical system. Westinghouse was still unimpressed, but the demonstration captured the imagination of David Sarnoff, who was soon to be appointed president of RCA. The visionary Sarnoff was convinced that television was the next logical venture for RCA. He persuaded Westinghouse, the major stockholder in RCA, to move Zworykin's enterprise to RCA's research facilities in Camden, New Jersey. Zworykin was named director of electronic research, and he remained with the company until he retired in 1954 with the title of honorary vice president and consultant.

By 1938, RCA was ready to begin production of its new system, but government approval was delayed until 1941. The United States' entry into World War II and the country's wartime demands on the electronic industry further postponed public marketing of the new marvel. Nonetheless, government research funds allowed Zworykin to dramatically improve the picture quality with his new invention, the image orthicon.

In his capacity as a scientific advisor to the government, Zworykin did not ignore the war effort. In 1940, he was instrumental in producing the electron microscope with James Hillier. His most noteworthy contribution to the military was the sniper scope, which allowed a rifleman to locate his target in the dark.

After the war, RCA finally began commercial sales of television. In 1946, a table model with a 10-inch screen sold for $375. Meanwhile, Zworykin turned his attention to color TV, refining his 1929 kinescope patent, which had established the basis for modern television.

When he retired in 1954, Zworykin became director of medical electronics at the Rockefeller Institute for Medical Research. He received numerous awards, and in 1967 the National Academy of Science awarded him the National Medal of Science, the nation's highest recognition.

Zworykin, Vladimir Kosma

See also:
Baird, John Logie; Sarnoff, David; Television; Television and Society.

References:
Breeden, Robert L. *Those Inventive Americans.* Washington, DC: National Geographic Society, 1971.

Lear, John. "Merchant of Vision." *Saturday Review*, 1 June 1957.

Udelson, Joseph H. *The Great Television Race: A History of the American Television Industry, 1925–1941.* Tuscaloosa, AL: University of Alabama Press, 1982.

Aitchison, Jean. *Language Change: Progress or Decay?* New York: Cambridge University Press, 1991.

"Alarm Systems for Home Security." *Consumers' Research Magazine,* October 1994.

Alger, Alexandra. "Bringing an Ancestor to Life." *Forbes,* 9 September 1996.

BIBLIOGRAPHY

American Telephone & Telegraph Company. *AT&T: The World's Networking Leader.* Shareowners report for the quarter ended 30 September 1995.

Anderson, Lydia. *Folk Dancing.* New York: Watts, 1981.

Anderson, Margo J. *The American Census: A Social History.* New Haven, CT: Yale University Press, 1988.

Anderson, Richard C., et al. *Becoming a Nation of Readers. The Report of the Commission on Reading.* Pittsburgh: National Academy of Education, 1985.

Antonoff, Michael. "Essential Technology Guide." *Popular Science,* November 1995.

Applebaum, Stanley, ed. *Simplicissimus.* New York: Dover, 1975.

Arbib, M. A. *Brains, Machines, and Mathematics,* 2nd ed. New York: Springer-Verlag, 1987.

"Art and Artifacts." *American History,* May/June 1996.

Asimov, Isaac. *Asimov's Biographical Encyclopedia of Science and Technology.* Garden City, NY: Doubleday, 1964.

———. *Asimov's Encyclopedia of Science and Technology.* Garden City, NY: Doubleday, 1964.

———. *Asimov's New Guide to Science.* New York: Basic Books, 1984.

Augarten, Stan. *Bit by Bit: An Illustrated History of Computers and their Inventors.* New York: Ticknor & Fields, 1984.

Aylesworth, Thomas G., ed. *It Works like This: A Collection of Machines from Nature and Science Magazine.* Garden City, NY: Natural History Press, 1968.

Ayre, Rick. "New Paths to the Net." *PC Magazine,* 10 October 1995.

"Bagging the Little Green Man." *Natural History,* February 1994: 60.

Baida, Peter. "Breaking the Connection." *American Heritage,* June/July 1985.

Bailey, Adrian. *Walt Disney's World of Fantasy.* New York: Gallery Books, 1987.

Baker, Charlotte, and Dennis Cokely. *American Sign Language: A Teacher's Resource Text on Grammar and Culture.* Silver Spring, MD: T. J. Publishers, 1980.

Baker, Charlotte, and Carol Padden. *American Sign Language: A Look at Its History, Structure, and Community.* Silver Spring, MD: T. J. Publishers, 1979.

Baldwin, Neil. *Edison: Inventing the Century.* New York: Hyperion Press, 1995.

Barnett, Lincoln. "The Case of Peter Zenger." *America Heritage,* December 1971.

———. "The Voice Heard Round the World." *American Heritage,* April 1965.

Barnouw, Erik. *A Tower of Babel: A History of Broadcasting in the United States to 1933.* New York: Oxford University Press, 1966.

Baughman, James L. *Henry R. Luce and the Rise of the American News Media.* Boston: Twayne Publishers, 1987.

Begley, Sharon. "Is There Anything to It? Evidence Please." *Newsweek,* 8 July 1996.

Billington, James. "A Technological Flood Requires Human Navigators." *American Libraries*, June/July 1996.

Bixby, Robert. "News News." *Compute*, June 1994.

Blair, Gwenda. "Dress Smart for Your Job." *Mademoiselle*, October 1995.

"Body Language." *American Salesman*, September 1996.

Bolt, Bruce A. *Earthquakes and Geological Discovery*. New York: Scientific American Library, 1993.

Bond, Karen. "Personal Style as a Mediator of Engagement in Dance: Watching Terpsichore Rise." *Dance Research Journal*, Spring 1994.

Boxler, Margaret T. *Winds of Freedom*. Darien, CT: Two Bytes Publishing Co., 1992.

Brady, Frank. *Citizen Welles: A Biography of Orson Welles*. New York: Scribner's, 1989.

Brancatelli, Joe. "European Sign Language." *Travel Holiday*, May 1995.

Brayer, Betsy. *George Eastman*. Baltimore: Johns Hopkins University Press, 1995.

Brill, A. A., ed. *The Basic Writings of Sigmund Freud*. New York: Random House, 1938.

Brinkley, David. *David Brinkley's Homilies*. New York: Knopf, 1996.

Bromberg, Joan Lisa. "Amazing Light." *American Heritage Invention & Technology*, Spring 1992.

Bronowski, J. *The Ascent of Man*. Boston: Little, Brown, 1973.

Brooks, John. *Telephone: The First Hundred Years*. New York: Harper, 1976.

Brown, Ann. "Sign Language." *Black Enterprise*, September 1996.

Brown, Carolyn M. "Electronic Messaging." *Black Enterprise*, November 1992.

Brown, Dee. "The Pony Express." *American History Illustrated*, November 1976.

Browne, Christopher. *Getting the Message: The Story of the Post Office*. Dover, NH: A. Sutton, 1993.

Bruce, Robert. *Alexander G. Bell and the Conquest of Solitude*. Boston: Little, Brown, 1973.

———. "A Conquest of Solitude." *American Heritage*, April 1973.

Buderi, Robert. *The Invention That Changed the World*. New York: Simon & Schuster, 1996.

Budiansky, Stephen. "Consulting the Oracle." *U.S. News & World Report*, 4 December 1995.

———. "What Animals Say." *U.S. News & World Report*, 5 June 1995.

Burgi, Michael. "Signs of the Times." *Mediaweek*, 4 March 1996.

Burke, James. "Connections." *Scientific American*, May 1996.

Burns, Robert E. "Homilist: Don't Let Your Golden Chances Pass You By." *U.S. Catholic*, February 1995.

Cage, Mary Crystal. "Mixing the Outrageous with the Educational." *Chronicle of Higher Education*, 24 March 1995.

Caird, Rod. *Ape Man: The Story of Human Evolution*. New York: Macmillan, 1994.

Callow, Simon. *Orson Welles: The Road to Xanadu*. New York: Viking, 1996.

"A Camera-Ready Revolution?" *Consumers' Research Magazine*, October 1994.

"Can You Say What You Want?" *The Economist*, 11 May 1996.

Canby, Edward Tatnall. "More Marconi." *Audio*, August 1995.

Caragata, Warren. "Crime in Cybercity." *Maclean's*, 22 May 1995.

Carlisle, Rodney P. *Hearst and the New Deal: The Progressive as Reactionary*. New York: Garland, 1979.

Carson, Gerald L. "The Great Enumeration." *American Heritage*, December 1979.

Carter, Samuel. *Cyrus Field: Man of Two Worlds*. New York: G. P. Putnam's Sons, 1968.

Ceram, C. W. *Gods, Graves and Scholars: The Story of Archaeology*. New York: Bantam Books, 1972.

Chall, Jeanne S. *Stages of Reading Development*. New York: McGraw-Hill, 1983.

"Chester F. Carlson Dead at 62; Invented Xerography Process." *New York Times*, 20 September 1968.

Chiera, Edward. *They Wrote on Clay*. Chicago: University of Chicago Press, 1956.

Ching, Francis D. K. *Architecture: Form, Space, and Order*. New York: Van Nostrand, 1979.

Chipman, Robert A. "De Forest and the Triode Detector." *Scientific American*, March 1965.

"Chipping Away at TV Violence." *U.S. News & World Report*, 24 July 1995.

Chujoy, Anatole. *The Dance Encyclopedia*. New York: A. S. Barnes, 1949.

Church, George J. "Just Three Easy Pieces." *Time*, 2 October 1995.

Clarke, Arthur C. "I'll Put a Girdle around the Earth in Forty Minutes." *American Heritage*, October 1958.

Clottes, Jean. "Rhinos and Lions and Bears (Oh My!)." *Natural History*, May 1995.

Coates, R. F. *Modern Communication Systems*, 2nd ed. Atlantic Highlands, NJ: Macmillan UK, 1983.

Cobb, Emma. "Instant History." *American Heritage Invention and Technology*, Fall 1987.

Cockburn, Alexander. "'New Lacaux' a Forgery?" *The Nation*, 20 February 1995.

Coggins, Jack. *Flashes and Flags: The Story of Signaling*. New York: Dodd, Mead, 1963.

Cohen, Sarah. "AT&T in Lucent Technologies Moves." *Electronic News*, 7 October 1996.

Congressional Quarterly's Federal Regulatory Directory. Washington, DC: Congressional Quarterly, 1986.

Considine, Douglas M., ed. *Van Nostrand's Scientific Encyclopedia*, 8th ed. New York: Van Nostrand, 1995.

"Consumer Reports 1995 Buying Guide." *Consumer Reports*, 15 December 1994.

Cooke, James. "Loglan." *Scientific American*, June 1960.

Coorsh, Richard. "Dateline Washington." *Consumers' Research Magazine*, March 1994.

Cowbura, Philip. "The Atlantic Cable." *History Today*, August 1966.

———. *Great Events/Four: As Reported in the New York Times*. Sand, NC: Microfilming Corporation of America, 1982.

Crampton, W. G. *Flag*. New York: Knopf, 1989.

Crawford, Michael. "The Language of Prom Dresses." *New Yorker*, 12 June 1995.

Crow, Gary A. *Children at Risk*. New York: Schocken Books, 1978.

Crumpley, Elsa. *It's about Time: All You Need to Know about the Origin of Time and Calendars*. Saratoga, CA: R & E Publishers, 1992.

Csatari, Jeffrey. "New Products." *Men's Health*, June 1996.

Current Biography. New York: H. H. Wilson, 1952.

Curtis, Gregory. "A Terrible Beauty." *Texas Monthly*, October 1995.

Dale, Rodney. *Timekeeping*. New York: Oxford University Press, 1992.

Darwin, Charles. *On the Origin of Species by Means of Natural Selection, or the Preservation of Favoured Races in the Struggle for Life*. New York: Modern Library, 1993.

Davidovits, Paul. *Communication*. New York: Holt, 1972.

Davidson, Marshall B. "What Samuel Wrought." *American Heritage*, April 1961.

Davis, Joel. *Mother Tongue: How Humans Create Language*. New York: Birch Lane Press, 1994.

Davis, John B. "The Life and Work of Sequoyah." *The Chronicles of Oklahoma*, June 1930.

DeCamp, L. Sprague. *The Heroic Age of American Invention*. Garden City, NY: Doubleday, 1961.

Dibbell, Julian (reported by John F. Dickerson). "Muzzling the Internet." *Time*, 18 December 1995.

Dobrzynski, Judith H. "Executive Tests Now Plumb New Depths of Job Seeker." *New York Times*, 2 September 1996.

Dodge, Robert. "Access to Popular Culture: Early American Almanacs." *Kentucky Folklore Record*, January/June 1979.

D'Oench, Derry. "It Took a Man from Stockbridge Three Tries to Join Two Worlds." *Berkshire Evening Eagle*, 11 May 1951.

Dunlap, Orrin Elmer. *Marconi: The Man and His Wireless*. New Stratford, NH: Arno Press, 1971.

Eastman, John. "Who Really Invented the Telephone?" in *People's Almanac #2*. New York: Bantam Books, 1978.

Edgerton, Harold E. "Making a Splash." *National Geographic*, February 1996.

Edgerton, Harold E., and James R. Killian. *Moments of Vision: The Stroboscopic Revolution in Photography*. Cambridge, MA: MIT Press, 1979.

Editors of Time-Life Books. *Life Library of Photography: Photojournalism*. Alexandria, VA: Time-Life Books, 1971.

———. *The Way of the Warrior*. Alexandria, VA: Time-Life Books, 1993.

Emery, Edwin. *The Press and America: An Interpretative History of the Mass Media*. Englewood Cliffs, NJ: Prentice-Hall, 1972.

Escue, Lynn. "Coded Contributions: Navajo Talkers and the Pacific War." *History Today*, July 1991.

Fant, Louie J. *Sign Language*. Acton, CA: Joyce Media, 1977.

Fast, Julius. *Body Language*. New York: Pocket Books, 1970.

Feeney, Sheila. "What I Got When I Acted like a Guy." *Redbook*, April 1995.

Feldman, Anthony, and Peter Ford. *Scientists and Inventors*. New York: Facts on File, 1979.

"Fender-Flare Installation." *Motor Trend*, April 1996.

Finch, Christopher. *Special Effects: Creating Movie Magic*. New York: Abbeville Press, 1984.

"Finding the Future." *The Economist*, 6 November 1993.

Fineman, Howard. "The Power of Talk." *Newsweek*, 8 February 1993.

Flatow, Ira. *They All Laughed*. New York: HarperCollins, 1992.

"For the Record." *Life*, February 1995.

Foreman, Grant. *Sequoyah*. Norman: University of Oklahoma Press, 1959.

Forster, Peter G. *The Esperanto Movement*. Hawthorne, NY: Mounton, 1982.

Frank, Anne. *The Diary of Anne Frank*. New York: Doubleday, 1995.

Frank, David A. *Creative Speaking*, 2nd ed. Lincolnwood, IL: National Textbook, 1995.

Freud, Sigmund. *On Dreams*. New York: Norton, 1952.

Furnas, J. C. *The Americans: A Social History of the United States 1587–1914*. New York: G. P. Putnam's Sons, 1969.

Gardner, Robert. *Communication*. New York: Twenty-First Century, 1994.

———. *Crime Lab 101*. New York: Walker, 1992.

———. *Electricity and Magnetism*. New York: Twenty-First Century, 1994.

———. *Experimenting with Time*. New York: Watts, 1995.

———. *Famous Experiments You Can Do*. New York: Watts, 1990.

———. *Optics*. New York: Twenty-First Century, 1994.

———. *Space: Frontier of the Future*. Garden City, NY: Doubleday, 1980.

———. *This Is the Way It Works: A Collection of Machines*. Garden City, NY: Doubleday, 1980.

———. *The Whale Watchers' Guide*. New York: Messner, 1984.

———. *Where on Earth Am I?* New York: Watts, 1996.

Gardner, Robert, and Edward Shore. *Math and Society: Reading Life in Numbers*. New York: Watts, 1995.

———. *Math in Science and Nature: Finding Patterns in the World Around Us*. New York: Watts, 1994.

———. *Math You Really Need*. Portland, ME: Walch, 1996.

Gardner, Robert, and Dennis Shortelle. *The Future and the Past*. New York: Messner, 1989.

Garraty, John A. *The American Nation: A History of the United States to 1877*. New York: Harper & Row, 1971.

Gean, Georges. *Writing: The Story of Alphabets and Scripts*. New York: Harry C. Abrams, 1992.

Geeta, Arand. "Library Internet Censoring Planned." *Boston Globe*, 13 February 1997.

Gernsheim, Helmut, and Alison Gernsheim. *The History of Photography 1685–1914*. New York: McGraw-Hill, 1969.

———. *LJM Daguerre: The History of the Diorama and the Daguerreotype*. New York: Dover, 1968.

Giangreco, C. Joseph, and Marianne Ranson Giangreco. *The Education of the Haering Impaired*. Springfield, IL: C. C. Thomas, 1970.

Gillispie, Charles Coulston, ed. *Dictionary of Scientific Biography*. New York: Scribner's, 1981.

Glass, Alastair M. "Fiber Optics." *Physics Today*, October 1993.

Goldstine, Herman H. *The Computer from Pascal to von Neumann*. Princeton, NJ: Princeton University Press, 1972.

Gorman, Christine. "AT&T Rewires the Net." *Time*, 11 March 1996.

Gosling, William, ed. *The Radio Receivers*. Piscataway, NJ: Institute of Electrical Engineers, 1986.

Graham, Richard B. *U.S. Postal History*. Sidney, OH: Linn's Stamp News, 1990.

Greising, David. "Watch Out for Flying Packages." *Business Week*, 14 November 1994.

Griffin, Donald R. "More about Bat 'Radar.'" *Scientific American*, July 1958.

Grigson, Geoffrey, and Charles Harvard Gibbs-Smith, eds. *Things*. New York: Hawthorn Books, 1957.

Grolier Multimedia Encyclopedia. CD-ROM edition. Danbury, CT: Grolier, 1995.

Gumston, David. *Marconi, Father of Radio*. New York: Crowell-Collier Press, 1967.

Gustaitis, Joseph. "Ottmar Mergenthaler's Wonderful Machine." *American History Illustrated*, June 1986.

Gutin, Jo Ann C. "A Brain That Talks." *Discover*, June 1996.

Guttman, Monika. "Hollywood Falls in Love with Technology." *U.S. News & World Report*, 19 February 1996.

Haber, Carol. "Two Legends Cross Paths and Part." *Electronic News*, 6 January 1997.

Haber-Schaim, Uri, et al. *PSSC Physics*, 7th ed. Dubuque, IA: Kendall/Hunt, 1991.

Hallahan, Daniel P., and James M. Kauffman. *Exceptional Children*. Boston: Allyn & Bacon, 1994.

Harley, J. B., and David Woodward, eds. *The History of Cartography*, vol. I. Chicago: University of Chicago Press, 1987.

———. *The History of Cartography*, vol. II. Chicago: University of Chicago Press, 1993.

Harvey, Lorrin. "Mental Telepathy in the Lab: Tests Show Psychic Abilities among Actors and Musicians." *Omni*, November 1994.

Heiber, Helmut. *Goebbels: A Biography*. New York: Da Capo, 1983.

Henderson, Bruce. *How to Bulletproof Your Manuscript*. Cincinnati: Writer's Digest Books, 1986.

Henderson, Robert M. *D. W. Griffith: His Life and Work*. New York: Oxford University Press, 1972.

"Here Are Some of the Best Resources for Teaching Reading." *Learning*, May/June 1996.

Herzstein, Robert Edwin. *Henry R. Luce: A Political Portrait of the Man Who Created the American Century*. New York: Scribner's, 1994.

Heward, William L. *Exceptional Children*. Engelwood Cliffs, NJ: Prentice-Hall, 1995.

Higham, Charles. *Orson Welles: The Rise and Fall of an American Genius*. New York: St. Martin's Press, 1985.

Hoig, Stan. *Sequoyah: The Cherokee Genius*. Oklahoma City: Oklahoma Historical Society, 1995.

Hollingsworth, Caroline. "Traffic-ometry: The New Shape of Mathematics." *Teaching PreK-8*, January 1995.

Holt, Glen. "Life on 'The Edge of Chaos.'" *Library Journal*, 1 March 1996.

Holton, Gerald, and Duane H. D. Roller. *Foundations of Modern Physical Science*. Reading, MA: Addison-Wesley, 1958.

Hoopes, Roy. "The 40-Year Run." *American Heritage*, November 1992.

Horn, Maurice, ed. *The World Encyclopedia of Cartoons*. New York: Chelsea House, 1980.

How It Works: The Illustrated Encyclopedia of Science and Technology. New York and London: Marshall Cavendish, 1978.

Huber, Peter. "Electronic Smut." *Forbes*, 13 July 1995.

Hylander, C. J. *American Inventors*. New York: Macmillan, 1955.

Hyman, Anthony. *Charles Babbage: Pioneer of the Modern Computer*. Princeton, NJ: Princeton University Press, 1982.

Ickes, Harold L. *The Secret Diaries of Harold L. Ickes*. New York: Simon & Schuster, 1953.

Ing, Janet. *Johann Gutenberg and His Bible: A Historical Study*. Los Angeles: Dawsons, 1988.

International Encyclopedia of Communications. New York: Oxford University Press, 1989.

"'Iron Curtain' Speech Recalled." *American History*, March/April 1996.

Itzin, Catherine, ed. *Pornography: Women, Violence, and Civil Liberties*. New York: Oxford University Press, 1992.

Jahns, Patricia. *Joseph Henry, Father of American Electronics*. Englewood Cliffs, NJ: Prentice-Hall, 1971.

———. *Matthew Fontaine Maury and Joseph Henry, Scientists of the Civil War*. New York: Hastings House, 1961.

James, Frank. "Time, Tide, and Michael Faraday." *History Today*, September 1991.

Janton, Pierre. *Esperanto: Language, Literature, and Community*. Albany, NY: SUNY Press, 1993.

Jenner, George. "Building a Babel Machine." *New Scientist*, 8 June 1996.

Jensen, Peter R. *In Marconi's Footsteps: Early Radio*. Cincinnati: Kangaroo Press, 1994.

Johanson, Donald, Lenora Johanson, and Blake Edgar. *Ancestors: In Search of Human Origins*. New York: Villard, 1994.

Jones, Roger S. *Physics for the Rest of Us*. Chicago: Contemporary Books, 1992.

Josephson, Matthew. *Edison: A Biography*. New York: McGraw-Hill, 1959.

Kael, Pauline. *The Citizen Kane Book*. Boston: Little-Brown, 1971.

Kaplan, David A. "Grand Illusions." *Newsweek*, 13 May 1996.

Kaufmann, William J., III. *Universe*. New York: Freeman, 1985.

Keller, Helen. *The Story of My Life*. Boston: Houghton Mifflin, 1904.

Kessler, Andrew J. "Price Fix." *Forbes*, 12 August 1996.

Kittredge, George L. *The Old Farmers and His Almanack*. Ganesevoort, NY: Corner House, 1974.

Klein, Maury. "What Hath God Wrought." *American Heritage Invention and Technology*, Spring 1993.

Kline, Morris. *Mathematics and the Physical World*. New York: Crowell, 1959.

Kohl, Herbert R. *On Teaching*. New York: Schocken Books, 1976.

Kramer, Peter D. *Listening to Prozac*. New York: Viking, 1993.

Krantz, Michael. "A Tube for Tomorrow." *Time*, 14 April 1997.

Krech, Bob. "Improve Parent Communication with a Newsletter." *Instructor*, September 1995.

Kupfer, Andrew. "AT&T: Ready to Run, Nowhere to Hide." *Fortune*, 29 April 1996.

Landler, Mark. "AT&T to Split into Three Companies." *New York Times*, reprinted in *Cape Cod Times*, 21 September 1995.

Lane, Charles. "Why Spy?" *New Republic*, 27 March 1995.

Large, Andrew. *The Artificial Language Movement*. Cambridge, MA: Basil Blackwell, 1985.

Larijani, L. Casey. *The Virtual Reality Primer*. New York: McGraw-Hill, 1994.

"Lee De Forest, 87, Radio Pioneer Dies." *New York Times*, 2 July 1961.

Lemonick, Michael D. "Searching for Other Worlds." *Time*, 5 February 1996.

Levine, Israel E. *Electronics Pioneer: Lee De Forest*. Milwood, NY: Associated Faculty Press, 1964.

Levine, John R., and Carol Baroudi. *The Internet for Dummies*, 2nd ed. Foster City, CA: IDG Books, 1994.

Levy, Steven. "Scared Bitless." *Newsweek*, 10 June 1996.

Lewis, Anthony. *Make No Law: The Sullivan Case and the First Amendment*. New York: Random House, 1991.

Lewis, Tom. *Empire of the Air: The Men Who Made Radio*. New York: HarperCollins, 1991.

Lind, Michael. "Jordan's Rules." *New Republic*, 12 February 1996.

Lindsey, David. "The First Atlantic Cable." *American History Illustrated*, January 1973.

————. "Lightning through Deep Water." *American History Illustrated*, February 1973.

————. "The Master of American Cinema: D. W. Griffith." *American History Illustrated*, December 1976.

Lochner, Louis, ed. *The Goebbels Diaries*. New York: Popular Library, 1948.

Mabee, Carleton. *The American Leonardo: A Life of Samuel F. B. Morse*. New York: Octagon Books, 1969.

Bibliography

Macaulay, David. *The Way Things Work.* Boston: Houghton Mifflin, 1988.

MacDonald, D. K. C. *Faraday, Maxwell, and Kelvin.* Garden City, NY: Doubleday, 1964.

Magill, Frank N., ed. *The Great Scientists.* Danbury, CT: Grolier, 1989.

———. *Magill's Survey of Science; Physical Science Series,* vol. 2. Pasadena, CA: Salem Press, 1992.

Markham, Lois. *Helen Keller.* New York: Watts, 1993.

Martin, Ralph G. *Henry and Clare: An Intimate Portrait of the Luces.* New York: Putnam, 1991.

Matimore, Bryan W. "Eureka." *Futurist,* March/April 1995.

McDonald, Kim A. "The Body Language of Leadership." *Chronicle of Higher Education,* 5 January 1996.

McDonald, Philip B. *A Saga of the Seas.* New York: Wilson-Erickson, 1937.

McGinty, Brian. "The Great Invention." *American History Illustrated,* August 1979.

Meier, Deborah. *The Power of Their Ideas: Lessons for America from a Small School in Harlem.* Boston: Beacon Press, 1995.

Miller, Diane Disney, as told to Peter Martin. *The Story of Walt Disney.* New York: Holt, 1957.

Mitani, Sam. "GPS and the No-Longer Lost Generation." *Road and Track,* July 1994.

Mondimore, Francis, and M. D. Mark. *Depression: The Mood Disease.* Baltimore: Johns Hopkins University Press, 1990.

Morell, Virginia. "The Earliest Art Becomes Older—and More Common." *Science,* 31 March 1995.

———. "Stone Age Menagerie." *Audubon,* May/June 1995.

Morgan, John S. *Noah Webster.* New York: Mason Charter, 1975.

Morrison, Philip, and Phylis Morrison. *The Ring of Truth: An Inquiry into How We Know What We Know.* New York: Random House, 1987.

Moseley, Maboth. *Irascible Genius: A Life of Charles Babbage, Inventor.* London: Hutchinson, 1964.

Mosley, Leonard. *Disney's World: A Biography.* New York: Stein & Day, 1985.

Mulligan, Joseph F., ed. *Heinrich Rudolf Hertz (1857–1894): A Collection of Articles and Addresses.* New York: Garland, 1994.

Mutter, John. "Del Rey Creates 'Cyber-community.'" *Publishers Weekly,* 19 December 1994.

"Mysteries of the Bible." *U.S. News & World Report,* 17 April 1995.

Nash, Madeleine J. "Fertile Minds." *Time,* 3 February 1997.

"National Treasure for Sale." *World Press Review,* February 1996.

"Negative Vibes." *The Economist,* 26 August 1995.

The New Book of Popular Science. Danbury, CT: Grolier, 1992.

Newhall, Beaumont. *The History of Photography.* New York: Museum of Modern Art, 1982.

Newman, James R., ed. *The World of Mathematics.* New York: Simon & Schuster, 1956.

Noldechen, Arno. "Brief Exposures." *World Press Review,* November 1993.

"NYPL Exhibit Draws Link between Cave Paintings and the Web." *School Library Journal,* May 1996.

Office of the Federal Registrar, National Archives and Records Administration. *United States Government Manual.* Washington, DC: Government Printing Office, 1994.

Olshakers, Mark. *The Instant Image: Edwin*

Land and the Polaroid Experience. New York: Stein & Day, 1978.

"On-the-Spot Screen Test." *Inc.,* December 1994.

"Only Disconnect." *The Economist,* 1 July 1995.

"Open-Book Management 101." *Inc.,* August 1996.

"The Optical Enlightenment." *The Economist,* 6 July 1991.

Orr, Lisa, ed. *Censorship: Opposing Viewpoints.* San Diego, CA: Greenhaven Press, 1990.

Oxford, Edward. "George Eastman: The Man Who Wrought Kodak." *American History Illustrated,* September 1988.

Panati, Charles. *Browser's Book of Beginnings.* Boston: Houghton Mifflin, 1984.

———. *Extraordinary Origins of Everyday Things.* New York: Harper & Row, 1987.

Panofsky, Erwin. *The Life and Art of Albrecht Durer.* Princeton, NJ: Princeton University Press, 1971.

"Pass the Parcel." *The Economist,* 18 March 1995.

Peel, Lucy, Polly Powell, and Alexander Garrett. *An Introduction to Twentieth Century Architecture.* Secaucus, NJ: Chartwell Books, 1989.

Petroski, Henry. *The Pencil: A History of Design and Circumstance.* New York: Knopf, 1992.

Pfaffenberger, Bryan. *The World Wide Web Bible,* 2nd ed. New York: MIS Press, 1996.

Pimentel, Ken, and Kevin Teixeira: *Virtual Reality: Through the New Looking Glass.* New York: McGraw-Hill, 1992.

Polley, Jane, ed. *Stories Behind Everyday Things.* Pleasantville, NY: Readers Digest, 1980.

Pornography: Women, Violence, and Civil Liberties. New York: Oxford University Press, 1992.

Preece, Charles O. *Edward Wyllis and Ellen Browning Scripps: An Unmatched Pair.* San Diego, CA: Charles O. Preece, 1990.

Putman, John J. "The Search for Modern Humans." *National Geographic,* October 1988.

Quilliam, Susan. *Body Language.* New York: Crescent Books, 1995.

Quittner, Joshua, Viveca Novak, et al. "Free Speech for the Net." *Time,* 24 June 1996.

Reed, Sandy. "Letting Your PC Pick Up the Phone." *Popular Science,* March 1994.

Restak, Richard. *The Brain.* New York: Bantam Books, 1984.

Reuth, Ralf Georg. *Goebbels.* New York: Harcourt Brace, 1993.

Rigaud, Jean-Philippe. "Art Treasures from the Ice Age: Lascaux Cave." *National Geographic,* October 1988.

Robbins, Peggy. "Tale of the Typewriter." *American History Illustrated,* February 1981: 4.

———. "The Trial of Peter Zenger." *American History Illustrated,* December 1976.

Robinson, William C. *Oratory: A Manual for Advocates.* Littleton, CO: Rothman, 1993.

Rogers, Madeline. "The Picture Snatchers." *American Heritage,* October 1994.

Rosenblatt, Roger. "Mr. Speaker." *New Republic,* 26 December 1994.

Roth, Leland M. *A Concise History of American Architecture.* New York: Harper & Row, 1979.

Rowe, Findley. "The Pony Express: Grit and Glory." *National Geographic,* July 1980.

Sagan, Carl. *The Demon-Haunted World.* New York: Random House, 1995.

———. "Where Did TV Come From?" *Parade,* 17 September 1995.

Sargent, David C. *Noah Webster.* West Hartford, CT: The Noah Webster Foundation and Historical Society of West Hartford, 1976.

Sarnoff, Lizette. "My Life with a Genius." *Good Housekeeping,* June 1955.

Sassaman, Richard. "What Hath Morse Wrought." *American History Illustrated,* April 1988.

Schecter, Harold. *Film Tricks: Special Effects in the Movies.* New York: H. Quist, 1980.

Schickel, Richard. "Bring Forth the Mouse." *American Heritage,* April 1968.

———. *D. W. Griffith: An American Life.* New York: Simon & Schuster, 1984.

Schneider, David. "Pot Luck." *Scientific American,* July 1996.

Scholderer, Victor. *Johann Gutenberg: The Inventor of Printing.* London: Trustees of the British Museum, 1970.

Science and Technology Illustrated. Chicago: Encyclopedia Britannica, 1984.

"Searching for Another Mole." *Newsweek,* 28 March 1994.

Sears, Francis W., Mark W. Zemansky, and Hugh D. Young. *College Physics.* Reading, MA: Addison-Wesley, 1985.

"Secret Plans." *The Economist,* 6 May 1995.

Seideman, Tony. "Bar Codes Sweep the World." In *American Inventions: A Chronicle of Achievements That Changed the World.* New York: Barnes & Noble, 1995.

Settle, Raymond, and Mary Settle. *Saddle and Spurs: The Pony Express Saga.* Lincoln: University of Nebraska Press, 1972.

Sigafoos, Robert A. *Absolutely Positively Overnight!* Memphis, TN: Saint Luke's Press, 1983.

"Signing with Your Genes." *Popular Mechanics,* September 1995.

"Signs of Life." *Car and Driver,* November 1995.

Simpson, Marge. "Untitled." *Seventeen,* May 1996.

Sisco, Peter. "Power Translator Professional Speaks Your Language." *PC World,* March 1995.

Skarmeas, Mary. "Flags for Home." *Ideals,* June 1995.

Sloane, Alan. "The Howling Wolves: Wall Street Has AT&T on the Run." *Newsweek,* 7 October 1996.

"The Snail's Revenge." *The Economist,* 5 August 1995.

Solomon, Charles. *The History of Animation: Enchanted Drawings.* Avenal, NJ: Random House Value, 1994.

St. Hell, Thomas Nast. "The Life and Death of Thomas Nast." *American Heritage,* October 1971.

St. Lifer, Evan. "Libraries' Crucial Role in the 1996 Telecomm Act." *Library Journal,* 15 March 1996.

Stauffer, Dennis. *Mediasmart: How to Handle a Reporter, by a Reporter.* Minneapolis: MinneApple Press, 1994.

Stephens, Mitchell. *Writing and Reporting the News.* New York: Rinehart & Winston, 1986.

Stern, Robert H. *The Federal Communications Commission and TV.* Salem, NH: Ayer, 1979.

Sullivan, Freyda. "The Navajo Code Talkers of World War II." *The Tombstone Epitaph,* December 1996.

Sussman, Vic. "Lost in Kofka Territory." *U.S. News & World Report,* 3 April 1995.

Swanberg, W. A. *Citizen Hearst: A Biography of William Randolph Hearst.* New York: Scribner's, 1961.

———. *Luce and His Empire.* New York: Scribner's, 1972.

Taeuber, Conrad. "Census." In *International*

Encyclopedia of Social Sciences. New York: Macmillan and the Free Press, 1968.

Tanaka, Jennifer, et al. "Vincent Van Robo." *Newsweek,* 8 May 1995.

Taylor, Rupert. "The End of Work." *Canada & the World,* November 1993.

Tenopir, Carol, and Donald W. King. "Setting the Record Straight on Journal Publishing: Myth vs. Reality." *Library Journal,* 15 March 1996.

"Translations: Computer Getting Better." *Business Week,* 11 December 1995.

Tributsch, Helmut. *When Snakes Awake: Animals and Earthquake Prediction.* Cambridge, MA: MIT Press, 1982.

Trimble, Vance. *The Astonishing Mr. Scripps: The Turbulent Life of America's Penny Press Lord.* Ames: Iowa State University Press, 1992.

———. *Overnight Success.* New York: Crown, 1993.

Ultimate Visual Dictionary. New York and London: Dorling Kindersley, 1994.

Verity, John. "Is NCR Ready to Ring Up Some Cash?" *Business Week,* 14 October 1996.

"Voice Mail versus Voice Messaging—Here's the Difference." *Inc.,* August 1994.

Wakefield, Julie, and Daniel Pendick. "Earthquake Reality Check." *Earth,* August 1995.

Walker, C. B. *Cuneiform.* Berkeley, CA: University of California Press, 1987.

Wallechinsky, David, and Irving Wallace. *The People's Almanac.* Garden City, NY: Doubleday, 1975.

Waller, Douglas. "Spies in Cyberspace." *Time,* 20 March 1995.

Walter, F. Virginia. *Great Newspaper Crafts.* New York: Sterling, 1991.

Watson, Bruce. "Navajo Code Talkers: A Few Good Men." *Smithsonian,* August 1993.

Watson, Thomas J. *The Education of Hearing Impaired Children.* Springfield, IL: C. C. Thomas, 1967.

Weaver, Kenneth F. "America's Thirst for Imported Oil, Our Energy Predicament." *National Geographic,* February 1981.

Webster's Concise Encyclopedia of Flags and Coats of Arms. New York: Crescent Books, 1985.

Weisberger, Bernard A. "You Press the Button, We Do the Rest." *American Heritage,* October 1972.

"Welcome to Cyberspace." *Time,* Spring 1995 special issue.

Wepman, Dennis. *Helen Keller.* New York: Chelsea House, 1987.

Whatley, Michael E. *Marconi Wireless on Cape Cod: South Wellfleet, Massachusetts 1901–1917.* N. Eastham, MA: Nauset Marsh, 1987.

Wheeler, Gerald F., and Larry D. Kirkpatrick. *Physics: Building a World View.* Englewood Cliffs, NJ: Prentice-Hall, 1983.

White, David Manning, and Robert Abel. *The Funnies: An American Idiom.* New York: Free Press, 1963.

"Who Owns the Word?" *Newsweek,* 14 August 1995.

Wiener, Norbert. *Cybernetics: Or Control and Communication in the Animals and the Machine,* 2nd ed. Cambridge, MA: MIT Press, 1961.

Williams, L. Pearce. *Michael Faraday: A Biography.* New York: Basic Books, 1965.

Williams, Trevor I. *The History of Invention: From Stone Axes to Silicon Chips.* New York: Facts on File, 1987.

Wilson, William R. "Code Talkers." *American History,* January/February 1997.

Wood, James. *Desktop Magic*. New York: Van Nostrand Reinhold, 1994.

"Word Up." *Boating,* March 1995.

"Work and Lies in the Promised Land." *World Press Review,* June 1995.

Wykes, Alan. *Goebbels*. New York: Ballantine Books, 1973.

Zoglin, Richard. "Chips Ahoy." *Time,* 19 February 1996.

———. "Rating Wars." *Time,* 23 December 1996.

Zonderman, Jon. *Beyond the Crime Lab: The New Science of Investigation*. New York: Wiley, 1990.

ILLUSTRATION CREDITS

INDEX